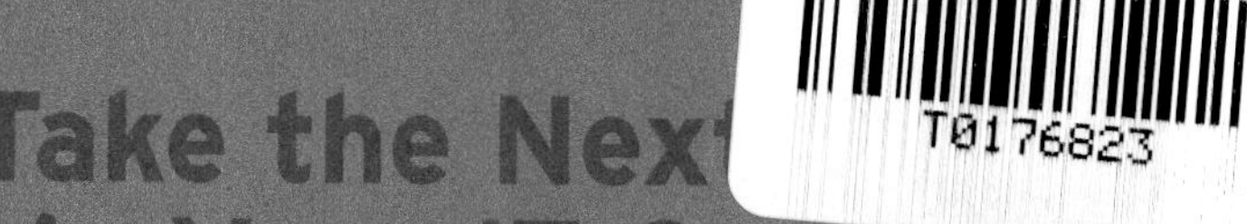
T0176823

SYBEX

CompTIA®

Cybersecurity Analyst (CySA+) Study Guide

Exam CS0-002

Second Edition

Mike Chapple

David Seidl

Published simultaneously in Canada and the United Kingdom

ISBN: 978-1-119-68405-3
ISBN: 978-1-119-68408-4 (ebk.)
ISBN: 978-1-119-68411-4 (ebk.)

For general information on our other products and services or to obtain technical support, please contact our Customer Care Department within the U.S. at (877) 762-2974, outside the U.S. at (317) 572-3993 or fax (317) 572-4002.

Wiley publishes in a variety of print and electronic formats and by print-on-demand. Some material included with standard print versions of this book may not be included in e-books or in print-on-demand. If this book refers to media such as a CD or DVD that is not included in the version you purchased, you may download this material at `http://booksupport.wiley.com`. For more information about Wiley products, visit `www.wiley.com`.

Library of Congress Control Number: 2020937966

SKY10045504_041123

I dedicate this book to my father, who was a role model of the value of hard work, commitment to family, and the importance of doing the right thing. Rest in peace, Dad.

—Mike Chapple

This book is dedicated to Ric Williams, my friend, mentor, and partner in crime through my first forays into the commercial IT world. Thanks for making my job as a "network janitor" one of the best experiences of my life.

—David Seidl

Acknowledgments

Books like this involve work from many people, and as authors, we truly appreciate the hard work and dedication that the team at Wiley shows. We would especially like to thank senior acquisitions editor Kenyon Brown. We have worked with Ken on multiple projects and consistently enjoy our work with him.

We also greatly appreciated the editing and production team for the book, including Kezia Endsley, our project editor, who brought years of experience and great talent to the project, Chris Crayton, our technical editor, who provided insightful advice and gave wonderful feedback throughout the book, Saravanan Dakshinamurthy, our production editor, who guided us through layouts, formatting, and final cleanup to produce a great book, and Liz Welch, our copy editor, who helped the text flow well. Thanks also to Runzhi "Tom" Song, Mike's research assistant at Notre Dame who helped fact-check our work. We would also like to thank the many behind-the-scenes contributors, including the graphics, production, and technical teams who make the book and companion materials into a finished product.

Our agent, Carole Jelen of Waterside Productions, continues to provide us with wonderful opportunities, advice, and assistance throughout our writing careers.

Finally, we would like to thank our families and significant others who support us through the late evenings, busy weekends, and long hours that a book like this requires to write, edit, and get to press.

About the Authors

Mike Chapple, Ph.D., CySA+, is author of the best-selling *CISSP (ISC)² Certified Information Systems Security Professional Official Study Guide* (Sybex, 2018) and the *CISSP (ISC)² Official Practice Tests* (Sybex, 2018). He is an information security professional with two decades of experience in higher education, the private sector, and government.

Mike currently serves as Teaching Professor in the IT, Analytics, and Operations department at the University of Notre Dame's Mendoza College of Business, where he teaches undergraduate and graduate courses on cybersecurity, data management, and business analytics.

Before returning to Notre Dame, Mike served as executive vice president and chief information officer of the Brand Institute, a Miami-based marketing consultancy. Mike also spent four years in the information security research group at the National Security Agency and served as an active duty intelligence officer in the U.S. Air Force.

Mike is technical editor for *Information Security Magazine* and has written more than 25 books. He earned both his B.S. and Ph.D. degrees from Notre Dame in computer science and engineering. Mike also holds an M.S. in computer science from the University of Idaho and an MBA from Auburn University. Mike holds certifications in Cybersecurity Analyst+ (CySA+), Security+, Certified Information Security Manager (CISM), Certified Cloud Security Professional (CCSP), and Certified Information Systems Security Professional (CISSP).

David Seidl is Vice President for Information Technology and CIO at Miami University. During his IT career, he has served in a variety of technical and information security roles, including serving as the Senior Director for Campus Technology Services at the University of Notre Dame where he co-led Notre Dame's move to the cloud and oversaw cloud operations, ERP, databases, identity management, and a broad range of other technologies and service. He also served as Notre Dame's Director of Information Security and led Notre Dame's information security program. He has taught information security and networking undergraduate courses as an instructor for Notre Dame's Mendoza College of Business, and he has written books on security certification and cyberwarfare, including co-authoring *CISSP (ISC)² Official Practice Tests* (Sybex, 2018) as well as the previous editions of both this book and the companion *CompTIA CySA+ Practice Tests: Exam CS0-001*.

David holds a bachelor's degree in communication technology and a master's degree in information security from Eastern Michigan University, as well as certifications in CISSP, CySA+, Pentest+, GPEN, and GCIH.

About the Authors

About the Technical Editor

Chris Crayton, MCSE, CISSP, CASP, CySA+, A+, N+, S+, is a technical consultant, trainer, author, and industry-leading technical editor. He has worked as a computer technology and networking instructor, information security director, network administrator, network engineer, and PC specialist. Chris has served as technical editor and content contributor on numerous technical titles for several of the leading publishing companies. He has also been recognized with many professional and teaching awards.

Contents at a Glance

Contents

Introduction

CompTIA Cybersecurity Analyst (CySA+) Study Guide, Second Edition, provides accessible explanations and real-world knowledge about the exam objectives that make up the Cybersecurity Analyst+ certification. This book will help you to assess your knowledge before taking the exam, as well as provide a stepping-stone to further learning in areas where you may want to expand your skillset or expertise.

Before you tackle the CySA+, you should already be a security practitioner. CompTIA suggests that test takers have about four years of existing hands-on information security experience. You should also be familiar with at least some of the tools and techniques described in this book. You don't need to know every tool, but understanding how to approach a new scenario, tool, or technology that you may not know using existing experience is critical to passing the CySA+ exam.

For up-to-the-minute updates covering additions or modifications to the CompTIA certification exams, as well as additional study tools, videos, practice questions, and bonus material, be sure to visit the Sybex website and forum at `www.sybex.com`.

CompTIA

CompTIA is a nonprofit trade organization that offers certification in a variety of IT areas, ranging from the skills that a PC support technician needs, which are covered in the A+ exam, to advanced certifications like the CompTIA Advanced Security Practitioner (CASP) certification.

CompTIA recommends that practitioners follow a cybersecurity career path as shown here:

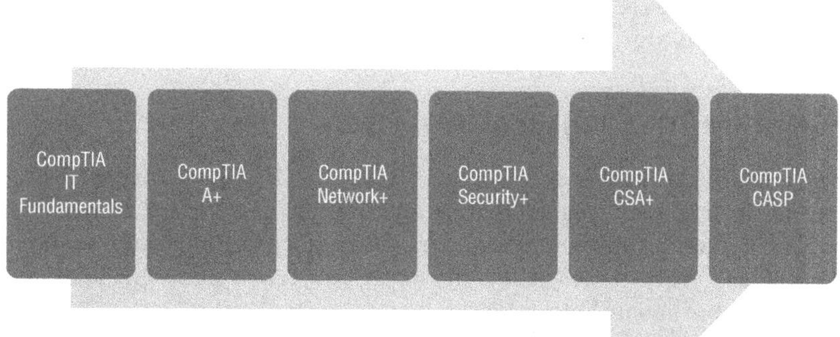

The Cybersecurity Analyst+ exam is a more advanced exam, intended for professionals with hands-on experience and who possess the knowledge covered by the prior exams.

CompTIA certifications are ISO and ANSI accredited, and they are used throughout multiple industries as a measure of technical skill and knowledge. In addition, CompTIA certifications, including the CySA+, the Security+, and the CASP certifications, have been approved by the U.S. government as Information Assurance baseline certifications and are included in the State Department's Skills Incentive Program.

The Cybersecurity Analyst+ Exam

The Cybersecurity Analyst+ exam, which CompTIA refers to as CySA+, is designed to be a vendor-neutral certification for cybersecurity, threat, and vulnerability analysts. The CySA+ certification is designed for security analysts and engineers as well as security operations center (SOC) staff, vulnerability analysts, and threat intelligence analysts. It focuses on security analytics and practical use of security tools in real-world scenarios. It covers five major domains: Threat and Vulnerability Management, Software and Systems Security, Security Operations and Monitoring, Incident Response, and Compliance and Assessment. These five areas include a range of topics, from reconnaissance to incident response and forensics, while focusing heavily on scenario-based learning.

The CySA+ exam fits between the entry-level Security+ exam and the CompTIA Advanced Security Practitioner (CASP) certification, providing a mid-career certification for those who are seeking the next step in their certification and career path.

The CySA+ exam is conducted in a format that CompTIA calls "performance-based assessment." This means that the exam uses hands-on simulations using actual security tools and scenarios to perform tasks that match those found in the daily work of a security practitioner. Exam questions may include multiple types of questions such as multiple-choice, fill-in-the-blank, multiple-response, drag-and-drop, and image-based problems.

CompTIA recommends that test takers have four years of information security–related experience before taking this exam. The exam costs $359 in the United States, with roughly equivalent prices in other locations around the globe. More details about the CySA+ exam and how to take it can be found at `certification.comptia.org/certifications/cybersecurity-analyst`.

Study and Exam Preparation Tips

A test preparation book like this cannot teach you every possible security software package, scenario, or specific technology that may appear on the exam. Instead, you should focus on whether you are familiar with the type or category of technology, tool, process, or scenario as you read the book. If you identify a gap, you may want to find additional tools to help you learn more about those topics.

CompTIA recommends the use of NetWars-style simulations, penetration testing and defensive cybersecurity simulations, and incident response training to prepare for the CySA+.

Additional resources for hands-on exercises include the following:

- Exploit-Exercises.com provides virtual machines, documentation, and challenges covering a wide range of security issues at `exploit-exercises.lains.space`.
- Hacking-Lab provides capture the flag (CTF) exercises in a variety of fields at `www.hacking-lab.com/index.html`.
- PentesterLab provides a subscription-based access to penetration testing exercises at `www.pentesterlab.com/exercises/`.
- The InfoSec Institute provides online CTF activities with bounties for written explanations of successful hacks at `ctf.infosecinstitute.com`.

Since the exam uses scenario-based learning, expect the questions to involve analysis and thought, rather than relying on simple memorization. As you might expect, it is impossible to replicate that experience in a book, so the questions here are intended to help you be confident that you know the topic well enough to think through hands-on exercises.

Taking the Exam

Once you are fully prepared to take the exam, you can visit the CompTIA website to purchase your exam voucher:

`www.comptiastore.com/Articles.asp?ID=265&category=vouchers`

CompTIA partners with Pearson VUE's testing centers, so your next step will be to locate a testing center near you. In the United States, you can do this based on your address or your ZIP code, while non-U.S. test takers may find it easier to enter their city and country. You can search for a test center near you at the Pearson Vue website, where you will need to navigate to "Find a test center."

`www.pearsonvue.com/comptia/`

Now that you know where you'd like to take the exam, simply set up a Pearson VUE testing account and schedule an exam:

`https://www.comptia.org/testing/testing-options/take-in-person-exam`

On the day of the test, take two forms of identification, and make sure to show up with plenty of time before the exam starts. Remember that you will not be able to take your notes, electronic devices (including smartphones and watches), or other materials in with you.

After the Cybersecurity Analyst+ Exam

Once you have taken the exam, you will be notified of your score immediately, so you'll know if you passed the test right away. You should keep track of your score report with your exam registration records and the email address you used to register for the exam.

Maintaining Your Certification

CompTIA certifications must be renewed on a periodic basis. To renew your certification, you can either pass the most current version of the exam, earn a qualifying higher-level CompTIA or industry certification, or complete sufficient continuing education activities to earn enough continuing education units (CEUs) to renew it.

CompTIA provides information on renewals via their website at

`www.comptia.org/continuing-education`

When you sign up to renew your certification, you will be asked to agree to the CE program's Code of Ethics, pay a renewal fee, and submit the materials required for your chosen renewal method.

A full list of the industry certifications you can use to acquire CEUs toward renewing the CySA+ can be found at

`www.comptia.org/continuing-education/choose/renew-with-a-single-activity/earn-a-higher-level-comptia-certification`

What Does This Book Cover?

This book is designed to cover the five domains included in the CySA+.

Chapter 1: Today's Cybersecurity Analyst The book starts by teaching you how to assess cybersecurity threats, as well as how to evaluate and select controls to keep your networks and systems secure.

Chapter 2: Using Threat Intelligence Security professionals need to fully understand threats in order to prevent them or to limit their impact. In this chapter, you will learn about the many types of threat intelligence, including sources and means of assessing the relevance and accuracy of a given threat intelligence source. You'll also discover how to use threat intelligence in your organization.

Chapter 3: Reconnaissance and Intelligence Gathering Gathering information about an organization and its systems is one of the things that both attackers and defenders do. In this chapter, you will learn how to acquire intelligence about an organization using popular tools and techniques. You will also learn how to limit the impact of intelligence gathering performed against your own organization.

Chapter 4: Designing a Vulnerability Management Program Managing vulnerabilities helps to keep your systems secure. In this chapter, you will learn how to identify, prioritize, and remediate vulnerabilities using a well-defined workflow and continuous assessment methodologies.

Chapter 5: Analyzing Vulnerability Scans Vulnerability reports can contain huge amounts of data about potential problems with systems. In this chapter, you will learn how to read and analyze a vulnerability scan report, what CVSS scoring is and what it means, as well as how to choose the appropriate actions to remediate the issues you have found. Along the way, you will explore common types of vulnerabilities and their impact on systems and networks.

Chapter 6: Cloud Security The widespread adoption of cloud computing dramatically impacts the work of cybersecurity analysts who must now understand how to gather, correlate, and interpret information coming from many different cloud sources. In this chapter, you'll learn about how cloud computing impacts businesses and how you can perform threat management in the cloud.

Chapter 7: Infrastructure Security and Controls A strong security architecture requires layered security procedures, technology, and processes to provide defense in depth, ensuring that a single failure won't lead to a failure. In this chapter, you will learn how to design a layered security architecture and how to analyze security designs for flaws, including single points of failure and gaps.

Chapter 8: Identity and Access Management Security The identities that we rely on to authenticate and authorize users, services, and systems are a critical layer in a defense-in-depth architecture. This chapter explains identity, authentication, and authorization concepts and systems. You will learn about the major threats to identity and identity systems as well as how to use identity as a defensive layer.

Chapter 9: Software and Hardware Development Security Creating, testing, and maintaining secure software, from simple scripts to complex applications, is critical for security analysts. In this chapter, you will learn about the software development life cycle, including different methodologies, testing and review techniques, and how secure software is created. In addition, you will learn about industry standards for secure software to provide you with the foundation you need to help keep applications and services secure. You'll also learn about tools and techniques you can use to protect hardware in your organization, including hardware assurance best practices.

Chapter 10: Security Operations and Monitoring Monitoring systems, devices, and events throughout an organization can be a monumental task. Security logs can be an invaluable resource for security analysts, allowing detection of misuse and compromise, but they can also bury important information in mountains of operational data. In this chapter, you'll learn how to analyze data from many diverse sources. You'll learn about techniques including email header analysis, rule writing for event management systems, and basic scripting and query writing.

Chapter 11: Building an Incident Response Program This chapter focuses on building a formal incident response handling program and team. You will learn the details of each stage of incident handling from preparation, to detection and analysis, to containment, eradication, and recovery, to the final postincident recovery, as well as how to classify incidents and communicate about them.

Chapter 12: Analyzing Indicators of Compromise Responding appropriately to an incident requires understanding how incidents occur and what symptoms may indicate that an event has occurred. To do that, you also need the right tools and techniques. In this chapter, you will learn about three major categories of symptoms. First, you will learn about network events, including malware beaconing, unexpected traffic, and link failures, as well as network attacks. Next, you will explore host issues, ranging from system resource consumption issues to malware defense and unauthorized changes. Finally, you will learn about service- and application-related problems.

Chapter 13: Performing Forensic Analysis and Techniques Understanding what occurred on a system, device, or network, either as part of an incident or for other purposes, frequently involves forensic analysis. In this chapter, you will learn how to build a forensic capability and how the key tools in a forensic toolkit are used.

Chapter 14: Containment, Eradication, and Recovery Once an incident has occurred and the initial phases of incident response have taken place, you will need to work on recovering from it. That process involves containing the incident to ensure that no further issues occur and then working on eradicating malware, rootkits, and other elements of a compromise. Once the incident has been cleaned up, the recovery stage can start, including reporting and preparation for future issues.

Chapter 15: Risk Management In this chapter, we look at the big picture of cybersecurity in a large organization. How do we evaluate and manage risks to ensure that we're spending our limited time and money on the controls that will have the greatest effect? That's where risk management comes into play.

Chapter 16: Policy and Compliance Policy provides the foundation of any cybersecurity program, and building an effective set of policies is critical to a successful program. In this chapter, you will acquire the tools to build a standards-based set of security policies, standards, and procedures. You will also learn how to leverage industry best practices by using guidelines and benchmarks from industry experts.

Appendix A: Practice Exam Once you have completed your studies, the practice exam will provide you with a chance to test your knowledge. Use this exam to find places where you may need to study more or to verify that you are ready to tackle the exam. We'll be rooting for you!

Appendix B: Answers to Review Questions and Practice Exam The appendix has answers to the review questions you will find at the end of each chapter and answers to the practice exam in Appendix A.

Appendix C: Answers to Lab Exercises This appendix has answers to the lab exercises you will find at the end of each chapter.

Study Guide Elements

This study guide uses a number of common elements to help you prepare. These include the following:

Summaries The summary section of each chapter briefly explains the chapter, allowing you to easily understand what it covers.

Exam Essentials The exam essentials focus on major exam topics and critical knowledge that you should take into the test. The exam essentials focus on the exam objectives provided by CompTIA.

Review Questions A set of questions at the end of each chapter will help you assess your knowledge and if you are ready to take the exam based on your knowledge of that chapter's topics.

Lab Exercises The written labs provide more in-depth practice opportunities to expand your skills and to better prepare for performance-based testing on the Cybersecurity Analyst+ exam.

Exam Note

These special notes call out issues that are found on the exam and relate directly to CySA+ exam objectives. They help you prepare for the why and how.

Additional Study Tools

This book comes with a number of additional study tools to help you prepare for the exam. They include the following.

Go to `www.wiley.com/go/Sybextestprep` to register and gain access to this interactive online learning environment and test bank with study tools.

Sybex Test Preparation Software

Sybex's test preparation software lets you prepare with electronic test versions of the review questions from each chapter, the practice exam, and the bonus exam that are included in this book. You can build and take tests on specific domains, by chapter, or cover the entire set of Cybersecurity Analyst+ exam objectives using randomized tests.

Electronic Flashcards

Our electronic flashcards are designed to help you prepare for the exam. Over 100 flashcards will ensure that you know critical terms and concepts.

Glossary of Terms

Sybex provides a full glossary of terms in PDF format, allowing quick searches and easy reference to materials in this book.

Bonus Practice Exam

In addition to the practice questions for each chapter, this book includes a full 85-question practice exam, found in Appendix A. We recommend that you use it to test your preparedness for the certification exam.

Objectives Map for CompTIA Cybersecurity Analyst (CySA+) Exam CS0-002

The following objective map for the CompTIA Cybersecurity Analyst (CySA+) certification exam will enable you to find the chapter in this book, which covers each objective for the exam.

Objectives Map

Objective	Chapter(s)
1.0 Threat and Vulnerability Management	
1.1 Explain the importance of threat data and intelligence.	Chapter 2
1.2 Given a scenario, utilize threat intelligence to support organizational security.	Chapter 2
1.3 Given a scenario, perform vulnerability management activities.	Chapters 4, 5
1.4 Given a scenario, analyze the output from common vulnerability assessment tools.	Chapters 3, 5, 6, 9
1.5 Explain the threats and vulnerabilities associated with specialized technology.	Chapter 5

Objective	Chapter(s)
1.6 Explain the threats and vulnerabilities associated with operating in the cloud.	Chapter 6
1.7 Given a scenario, implement controls to mitigate attacks and software vulnerabilities.	Chapters 5, 9
2.0 Software and Systems Security	
2.1 Given a scenario, apply security solutions for infrastructure management.	Chapters 6, 7, 8
2.2 Explain software assurance best practices.	Chapter 9
2.3 Explain hardware assurance best practices.	Chapter 9
3.0 Security Operations and Monitoring	
3.1 Given a scenario, analyze data as part of security monitoring activities.	Chapters 3, 10
3.2 Given a scenario, implement configuration changes to existing controls to improve security.	Chapter 7
3.3 Explain the importance of proactive threat hunting.	Chapter 2
3.4 Compare and contrast automation concepts and technologies.	Chapters 1, 2, 4, 7, 9, 10
4.0 Incident Response	
4.1 Explain the importance of the incident response process.	Chapter 11
4.2 Given a scenario, apply the appropriate incident response procedure.	Chapters 11, 14
4.3 Given an incident, analyze potential indicators of compromise.	Chapter 12
4.4 Given a scenario, utilize basic digital forensic techniques.	Chapter 13
5.0 Compliance and Assessment	
5.1 Understand the importance of data privacy and protection.	Chapters 1, 15
5.2 Given a scenario, apply security concepts in support of organizational risk mitigation.	Chapter 15
5.3 Explain the importance of frameworks, policies, procedures, and controls.	Chapter 16

Setting Up a Kali and Metasploitable Learning Environment

You can practice many of the techniques found in this book using open source and free tools. This section provides a brief "how to" guide to set up a Kali Linux, a Linux distribution built as a broad security toolkit, and Metasploitable, an intentionally vulnerable Linux virtual machine.

What You Need

To build a basic virtual security lab environment to run scenarios and to learn applications and tools used in this book, you will need a virtualization program and virtual machines. There are many excellent security-oriented distributions and tools beyond those in this example, and you may want to explore tools like Security Onion, the SANS SIFT forensic distribution, and CAINE as you gain experience.

Running virtual machines can require a reasonably capable PC. We like to recommend an i5 or i7 (or equivalent) CPU, at least 8 GB of RAM, and 20 GB of open space on your hard drive. If you have an SSD instead of a hard drive, you'll be much happier with the performance of your VMs.

VirtualBox

VirtualBox is a virtualization software package for x86 computers, and is available for Windows, MacOS, and Linux. You can download VirtualBox at `www.virtualbox.org/wiki/VirtualBox`.

If you are more familiar with another virtualization tool like VMWare or HyperV, you can also use those tools; however, you may have to adapt or modify these instructions to handle differences in how your preferred virtualization environment works.

> **Making It Portable**
>
> You can also build your lab so you can take it on the road by using a portable version of VirtualBox from `www.vbox.me`. Just follow the instructions on the site and put your virtual machines on an external drive of your choice. Note that this is typically a bit slower unless you have a fast USB drive.

Kali Linux

Multiple versions of Kali Linux are available at `www.kali.org/downloads/` and prebuilt Kali Linux virtual machines can be downloaded at `www.offensive-security.com/`

`kali-linux-vmware-virtualbox-image-download/`. We suggest downloading the most recent version of the Kali Linux 64-bit VBox virtual machine.

Metasploitable

You can download the Metasploitable virtual machine at `sourceforge.net/projects/metasploitable/`.

> **Usernames and Passwords**
>
> Kali's default username is `root` with the `toor` password.
>
> The Metasploitable virtual machine uses the username `msfadmin` and the `msfadmin` password.
>
> If you will ever expose either system to a live network, or you aren't sure if you will, you should change the passwords immediately after booting the virtual machines the first time!

Setting Up Your Environment

Setting up VirtualBox is quite simple. First, install the VirtualBox application. Once it is installed and you select your language, you should see a VirtualBox window like the one in Figure I.1.

To add the Kali Linux virtual machine, choose File, then Import Appliance. Navigate to the directory where you downloaded the Kali VM and import the virtual machine. Follow the wizard as it guides you through the import process, and when it is complete, you can continue with these instructions.

The Metasploitable virtual machine comes as a zip file, so you'll need to extract it first. Inside, you'll see a VMDK instead of the OVA file that VirtualBox uses for its native virtual machines. This means you have to do a little more work.

1. Click New in the VirtualBox main window.
2. Click Expert Mode and name your system; then select Linux for the type. You can leave the default alone for Version, and you can leave the memory default alone as well. See Figure I.2.
3. Select Use An Existing Virtual Hard Disk File and navigate to the location where you unzipped the `Metasploitable.vmdk` file to and select it. Then click Create.

FIGURE I.1 VirtualBox main screen

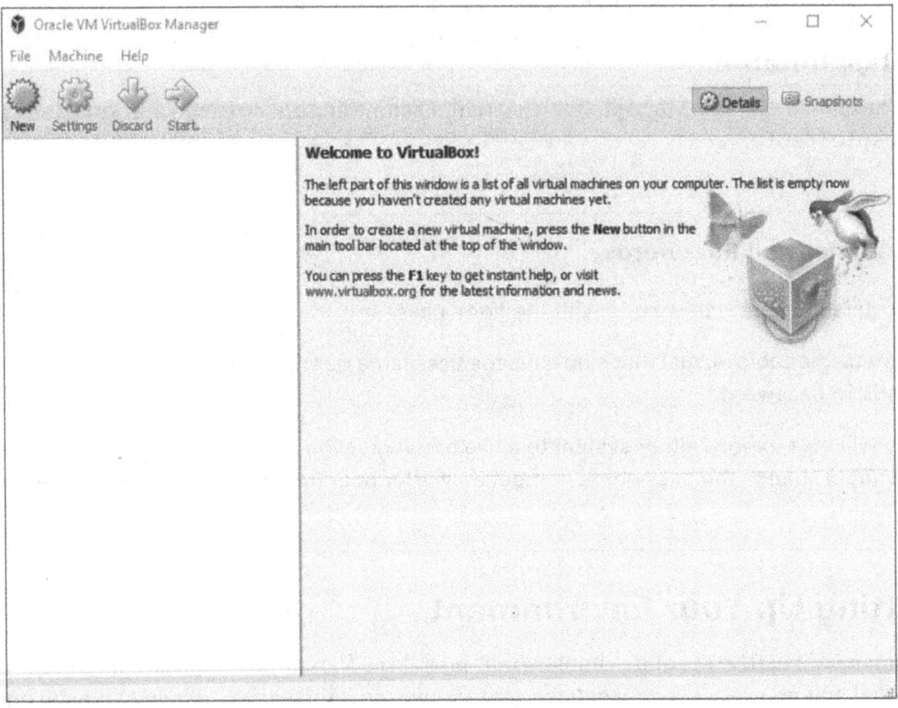

FIGURE I.2 Adding the Metasploitable VM

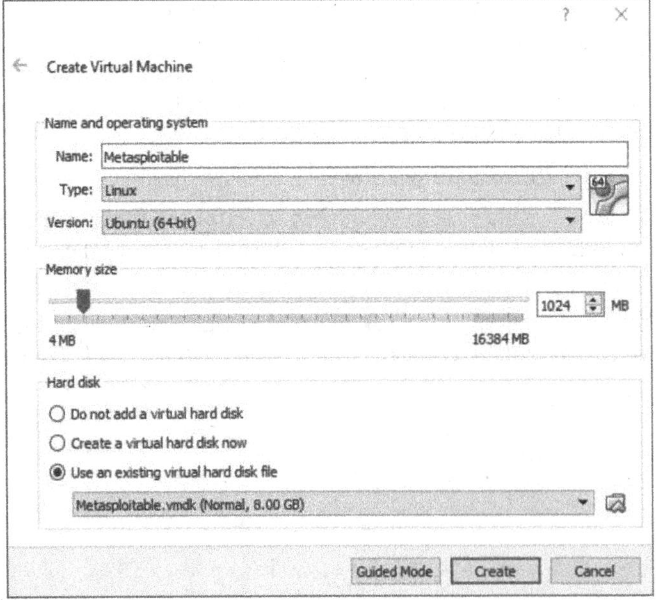

4. Now that you have both virtual machines set up, you should verify their network settings. VirtualBox allows multiple types of networks. Table I.1 shows the critical types of network connections you are likely to want to use with this environment.

   You may want to have Internet connectivity for some exercises, or to update software packages. If you are reasonably certain you know what you are doing, using a NAT Network can be very helpful. To do so, you will need to click the File ➢ Preferences menu of VirtualBox; then select Network and set up a NAT network, as shown in Figure I.3, by clicking the network card with a + icon.

TABLE I.1 Virtual machine network options

Network Name	Description
NAT	Connect the VM to your real network, through a protected NAT
NAT Network	Connect the VM and other VMs together on a protected network segment, which is also NAT'ed out to your real network
Bridged	Directly connect your VM to your actual network (possibly allowing it to get a DHCP address, be scanned, or for you to connect to it remotely)
Internal	Connect the VM to a network that exists only for virtual machines
Host Only	Connect the VM to a network that only allows it to see the VM host

FIGURE I.3 Adding a NAT network

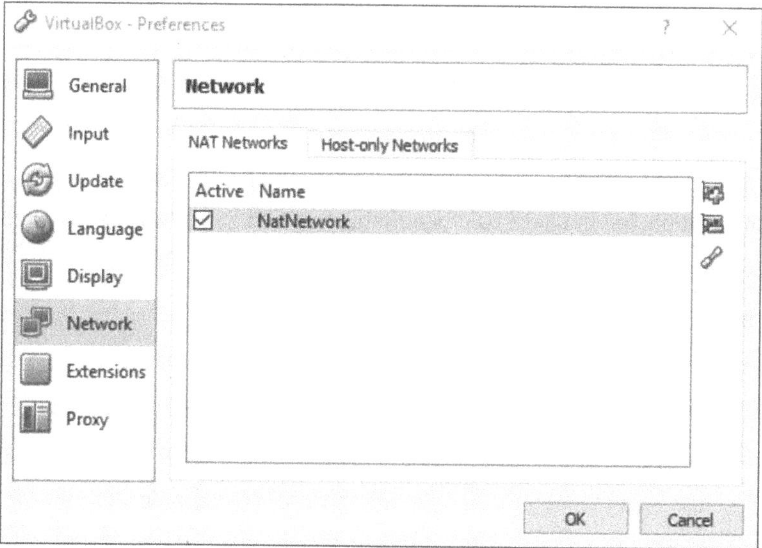

Warning: Dangerous Traffic!

If you are not comfortable with your virtual machines having outbound network access, think you may do something dangerous with them, or want to avoid any other potential issues, you should set up both virtual machines to use Internal Network instead.

5. Once your NAT network exists, you can set both machines to use it by clicking on them, then clicking the Settings gear icon in the VirtualBox interface. From there, click Network, and set the network adapter to be attached to the NAT network you just set up. See Figure I.4.

FIGURE I.4 Configuring VMs for the NAT network

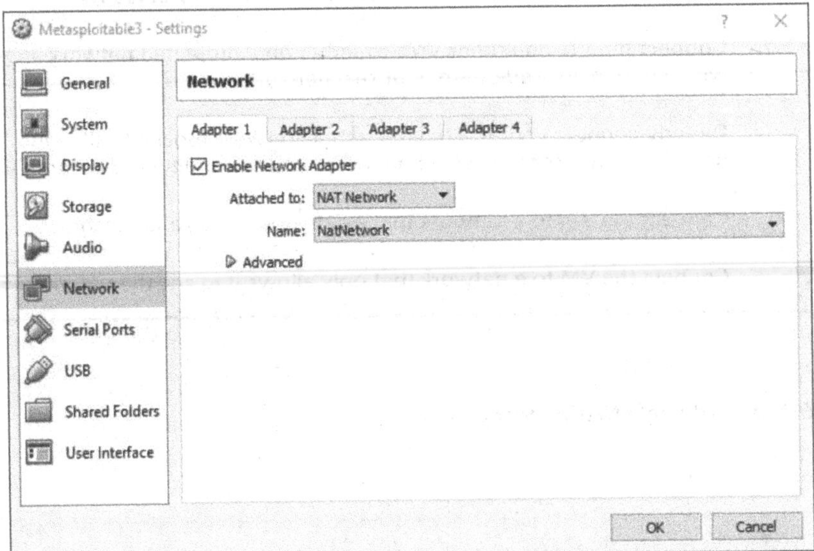

6. Now you're all set! You can start both machines and test that they can see each other. To do this, simply log in to the Metasploitable box and run `ifconfig` to find its IP address. Use SSH to connect from the Kali Linux system to the Metasploitable system using `ssh [ip address] -l msfadmin`. If you connect and can log in, you're ready to run exercises between the two systems!

Assessment Test

If you're considering taking the Cybersecurity Analyst+ exam, you should have already taken and passed the CompTIA Security+ and Network+ exams and should have four years of experience in the field. You may also already hold other equivalent certifications. The following assessment test help to make sure that you have the knowledge that you should have before you tackle the Cybersecurity Analyst+ certification and will help you determine where you may want to spend the most time with this book.

1. After running an nmap scan of a system, you receive scan data that indicates the following three ports are open:

   22/TCP

   443/TCP

   1521/TCP

   What services commonly run on these ports?

   A. SMTP, NetBIOS, MySQL

   B. SSH, Microsoft DS, WINS

   C. SSH, HTTPS, Oracle

   D. FTP, HTTPS, MS-SQL

2. Which of the following tools is best suited to querying data provided by organizations like the American Registry for Internet Numbers (ARIN) as part of a footprinting or reconnaissance exercise?

   A. `nmap`

   B. `traceroute`

   C. `regmon`

   D. `whois`

3. What type of system allows attackers to believe they have succeeded with their attack, thus providing defenders with information about their attack methods and tools?

   A. A honeypot

   B. A sinkhole

   C. A crackpot

   D. A darknet

4. What cybersecurity objective could be achieved by running your organization's web servers in redundant, geographically separate datacenters?

   A. Confidentiality

   B. Integrity

   C. Immutability

   D. Availability

5. Which of the following vulnerability scanning methods will provide the most accurate detail during a scan?
   A. Black box
   B. Authenticated
   C. Internal view
   D. External view
6. Security researchers recently discovered a flaw in the Chakra JavaScript scripting engine in Microsoft's Edge browser that could allow remote execution or denial of service via a specifically crafted website. The CVSS 3.0 score for this vulnerability reads

   ```
   CVSS:3.0/AV:N/AC:H/PR:N/UI:R/S:U/C:H/I:H/A:H
   ```

   What is the attack vector and the impact to integrity based on this rating?
   A. System, 9, 8
   B. Browser, High
   C. Network, High
   D. None, High
7. Alice is a security engineer tasked with performing vulnerability scans for her organization. She encounters a false positive error in one of her scans. What should she do about this?
   A. Verify that it is a false positive, and then document the exception.
   B. Implement a workaround.
   C. Update the vulnerability scanner.
   D. Use an authenticated scan, and then document the vulnerability.
8. Which phase of the incident response process is most likely to include gathering additional evidence such as information that would support legal action?
   A. Preparation
   B. Detection and Analysis
   C. Containment, Eradication, and Recovery
   D. Postincident Activity and Reporting
9. Which of the following descriptions explains an integrity loss?
   A. Systems were taken offline, resulting in a loss of business income.
   B. Sensitive or proprietary information was changed or deleted.
   C. Protected information was accessed or exfiltrated.
   D. Sensitive personally identifiable information was accessed or exfiltrated.
10. Which of the following techniques is an example of active monitoring?
    A. Ping
    B. RMON

C. NetFlows

D. A network tap

11. Abdul's monitoring detects regular traffic sent from a system that is suspected to be compromised and participating in a botnet to a set of remote IP addresses. What is this called?

A. Anomalous pings

B. Probing

C. Zombie chatter

D. Beaconing

12. Which of the following tools is not useful for monitoring memory usage in Linux?

A. `df`

B. `top`

C. `ps`

D. `free`

13. Which of the following tools cannot be used to make a forensic disk image?

A. `xcopy`

B. FTK

C. `dd`

D. EnCase

14. During a forensic investigation, Maria is told to look for information in slack space on the drive. Where should she look, and what is she likely to find?

A. She should look at unallocated space, and she is likely to find file fragments from deleted files.

B. She should look at unused space where files were deleted, and she is likely to find complete files hidden there by the individual being investigated.

C. She should look in the space reserved on the drive for spare blocks, and she is likely to find complete files duplicated there.

D. She should look at unused space left when a file is written, and she is likely to find file fragments from deleted files.

15. What type of system is used to contain an attacker to allow them to be monitored?

A. A white box

B. A sandbox

C. A network jail

D. A VLAN

16. Oscar's manager has asked him to ensure that a compromised system has been completely purged of the compromise. What is Oscar's best course of action?

A. Use an antivirus tool to remove any associated malware

B. Use an antimalware tool to completely scan and clean the system

C. Wipe and rebuild the system

D. Restore a recent backup

17. What level of secure media disposition as defined by NIST SP 800-88 is best suited to a hard drive from a high-security system that will be reused in the same company by an employee of a different level or job type?

A. Clear

B. Purge

C. Destroy

D. Reinstall

18. Which of the following actions is not a common activity during the recovery phase of an incident response process?

A. Reviewing accounts and adding new privileges

B. Validating that only authorized user accounts are on the systems

C. Verifying that all systems are logging properly

D. Performing vulnerability scans of all systems

19. A statement like "Windows workstations must have the current security configuration template applied to them before being deployed" is most likely to be part of which document?

A. Policies

B. Standards

C. Procedures

D. Guidelines

20. Jamal is concerned with complying with the U.S. federal law covering student educational records. Which of the following laws is he attempting to comply with?

A. HIPAA

B. GLBA

C. SOX

D. FERPA

21. A fire suppression system is an example of what type of control?

A. Logical

B. Physical

C. Administrative

D. Operational

22. Suki is concerned that a user might abuse their privileges to create a new vendor in the accounting system and then issue that vendor a check. What security control would best protect against this risk?

A. Dual control

B. Separation of duties

C. Background checks

D. Cross training

23. Joe wants to implement an authentication protocol that is well suited to untrusted networks. Which of the following options is best suited to his needs in its default state?

A. Kerberos

B. RADIUS

C. LDAP

D. TACACS+

24. Which software development life cycle model uses linear development concepts in an iterative, four-phase process?

A. Waterfall

B. Agile

C. RAD

D. Spiral

Answers to the Assessment Test

1. C. These three TCP ports are associated with SSH (22), HTTPS (443), and Oracle databases (1521). Other ports mentioned in the potential answers are SMTP (25), NetBIOS (137–139), MySQL (3306), WINS (1512), FTP (20 and 21), and MS-SQL (1433/1434).

2. D. Regional Internet registries like ARIN are best queried either via their websites or using tools like `whois`. `nmap` is a useful port scanning utility, `traceroute` is used for testing the path packets take to a remote system, and `regmon` is an outdated Windows Registry tool that has been supplanted by Process Monitor.

3. A. Honeypots are systems that are designed to look like attractive targets. When they are attacked, they simulate a compromise, providing defenders with a chance to see how attackers operate and what tools they use. DNS sinkholes provide false information to malicious software, redirecting queries about command and control systems to allow remediation. Darknets are segments of unused network space that are monitored to detect traffic—since legitimate traffic should never be aimed at the darknet, this can be used to detect attacks and other unwanted traffic. Crackpots are eccentric people—not a system you'll run into on a network.

4. D. Redundant systems, particularly when run in multiple locations and with other protections to ensure uptime, can help provide availability.

5. B. An authenticated, or credentialed, scan provides the most detailed view of the system. Black-box assessments presume no knowledge of a system and would not have credentials or an agent to work with on the system. Internal views typically provide more detail than external views, but neither provides the same level of detail that credentials can allow.

6. C. When reading the CVSS 3.0 score, AV is the attack vector. Here, N means network. Confidentiality (C), integrity (I), and availability (A) are listed at the end of the listing, and all three are rated as High in this CVSS rating.

7. A. When Alice encounters a false positive error in her scans, her first action should be to verify it. This may involve running a more in-depth scan like an authenticated scan, but it could also involve getting assistance from system administrators, checking documentation, or other validation actions. Once she is done, she should document the exception so that it is properly tracked. Implementing a workaround is not necessary for false positive vulnerabilities, and updating the scanner should be done before every vulnerability scan. Using an authenticated scan might help but does not cover all the possibilities for validation she may need to use.

8. C. The Containment, Eradication, and Recovery phase of an incident includes steps to limit damage and document what occurred, including potentially identifying the attacker and tools used for the attack. This means that information useful to legal actions is most likely to be gathered during this phase.

9. B. Integrity breaches involve data being modified or deleted. Systems being taken offline is an availability issue, protected information being accessed might be classified as a breach of proprietary information, and sensitive personally identifiable information breaches would typically be classified as privacy breaches.

10. A. Active monitoring sends traffic like pings to remote devices as part of the monitoring process. RMON and NetFlows are both examples of router-based monitoring, whereas network taps allow passive monitoring.

11. D. Regular traffic from compromised systems to command and control nodes is known as beaconing. Anomalous pings could describe unexpected pings, but they are not typically part of botnet behavior, zombie chatter is a made-up term, and probing is part of scanning behavior in some cases.

12. A. The `df` command is used to show the amount of free and used disk space. Each of the other commands can show information about memory usage in Linux.

13. A. FTK, EnCase, and `dd` all provide options that support their use for forensic disk image creation. Since `xcopy` cannot create a bitwise image of a drive, it should not be used to create forensic images.

14. D. Slack space is the space left when a file is written. Since the space may have previously been filled by another file, file fragments are likely to exist and be recoverable. Unallocated space is space that has not been partitioned and could contain data, but looking there isn't part of Maria's task. The reserved space maintained by drives for wear leveling (for SSDs) or to replace bad blocks (for spinning disks) may contain data, but again, this was not part of her task.

15. B. Sandboxes are used to isolate attackers, malicious code, and other untrusted applications. They allow defenders to monitor and study behavior in the sandbox without exposing systems or networks to potential attacks or compromise.

16. C. The most foolproof means of ensuring that a system does not remain compromised is to wipe and rebuild it. Without full knowledge of when the compromise occurred, restoring a backup may not help, and both antimalware and antivirus software packages cannot always ensure that no remnant of the compromise remains, particularly if the attacker created accounts or otherwise made changes that wouldn't be detected as malicious software.

17. B. NIST SP 800-88 defines three levels of action of increasing severity: clear, purge, and destroy. In this case, purging, which uses technical means to make data infeasible to recover, is appropriate for a high-security device. Destruction might be preferable, but the reuse element of the question rules this out. Reinstallation is not an option in the NIST guidelines, and clearing is less secure.

18. A. The recovery phase does not typically seek to add new privileges. Validating that only legitimate accounts exist, that the systems are all logging properly, and that systems have been vulnerability scanned are all common parts of an incident response recovery phase.

19. B. This statement is most likely to be part of a standard. Policies contain high-level statements of management intent; standards provide mandatory requirements for how policies are carried out, including statements like that provided in the question. A procedure would include the step-by-step process, and a guideline describes a best practice or recommendation.

20. D. The Family Educational Rights and Privacy Act (FERPA) requires educational institutions to implement security and privacy controls for student educational records. HIPAA covers security and privacy for healthcare providers, health insurers, and health information clearinghouses; GLBA covers financial institutions; and SOX applies to financial records of publicly traded companies.

21. B. Fire suppression systems are physical controls. Logical controls are technical controls that enforce confidentiality, integrity, and availability. Administrative controls are procedural controls, and operational controls are not a type of security control as used in security design.

22. B. Suki should implement separation of duties in a way that ensures that the same individual does not have rights to both create a new vendor and issue a check to that vendor. This approach would require the collusion of two individuals to defraud the organization.

23. A. Kerberos is designed to run on untrusted networks and encrypts authentication traffic by default. LDAP and RADIUS can be encrypted but are not necessarily encrypted by default (and LDAP has limitations as an authentication mechanism). It is recommended that TACACS+ be run only on isolated administrative networks.

24. D. The Spiral model uses linear development concepts like those used in Waterfall but repeats four phases through its life cycle: requirements gathering, design, build, and evaluation.

Today's Cybersecurity Analyst

THE COMPTIA CYBERSECURITY ANALYST (CYSA+) EXAM OBJECTIVES COVERED IN THIS CHAPTER INCLUDE:

✓ **Domain 3.0: Security Operations and Monitoring**

- 3.4 Compare and contrast automation concepts and technologies.
  - Machine Learning

✓ **Domain 5.0: Compliance and Assessment**

- 5.1 Understand the importance of data privacy and protection.
  - Privacy vs. Security

Cybersecurity analysts are responsible for protecting the confidentiality, integrity, and availability of information and information systems used by their organizations. Fulfilling this responsibility requires a commitment to a defense-in-depth approach to information security that uses multiple, overlapping security controls to achieve each cybersecurity objective. It also requires that analysts have a strong understanding of the threat environment facing their organization in order to develop a set of controls capable of rising to the occasion and answering those threats.

In the first section of this chapter, you will learn how to assess the cybersecurity threats facing your organization and determine the risk that they pose to the confidentiality, integrity, and availability of your operations. In the sections that follow, you will learn about controls that you can put in place to secure networks and endpoints and evaluate the effectiveness of those controls over time.

Cybersecurity Objectives

When most people think of cybersecurity, they imagine hackers trying to break into an organization's system and steal sensitive information, ranging from Social Security numbers and credit cards to top-secret military information. Although protecting sensitive information from unauthorized disclosure is certainly one element of a cybersecurity program, it is important to understand that cybersecurity actually has three complementary objectives, as shown in Figure 1.1.

FIGURE 1.1 The three key objectives of cybersecurity programs are confidentiality, integrity, and availability.

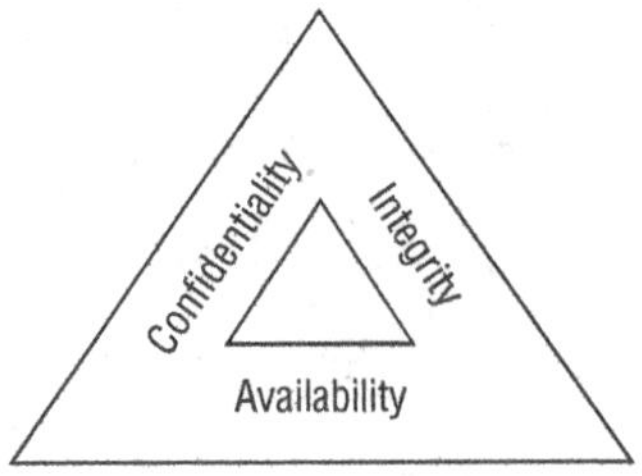

Confidentiality ensures that unauthorized individuals are not able to gain access to sensitive information. Cybersecurity professionals develop and implement security controls, including firewalls, access control lists, and encryption, to prevent unauthorized access to information. Attackers may seek to undermine confidentiality controls to achieve one of their goals: the unauthorized disclosure of sensitive information.

Integrity ensures that there are no unauthorized modifications to information or systems, either intentionally or unintentionally. Integrity controls, such as hashing and integrity monitoring solutions, seek to enforce this requirement. Integrity threats may come from attackers seeking the alteration of information without authorization or nonmalicious sources, such as a power spike causing the corruption of information.

Availability ensures that information and systems are ready to meet the needs of legitimate users at the time those users request them. Availability controls, such as fault tolerance, clustering, and backups, seek to ensure that legitimate users may gain access as needed. Similar to integrity threats, availability threats may come either from attackers seeking the disruption of access or nonmalicious sources, such as a fire destroying a datacenter that contains valuable information or services.

Cybersecurity analysts often refer to these three goals, known as the CIA Triad, when performing their work. They often characterize risks, attacks, and security controls as meeting one or more of the three CIA Triad goals when describing them.

Privacy vs. Security

Privacy and security are closely related concepts. We just discussed the three major components of security: confidentiality, integrity, and availability. These goals are all focused on the ways that an organization can protect its own data. Confidentiality protects data from unauthorized disclosure. Integrity protects data from unauthorized modification. Availability protects data from unauthorized denial of access.

Privacy controls have a different focus. Instead of focusing on ways that an organization can protect its own information, privacy focuses on the ways that an organization can use and share information that it has collected about individuals. This data, known as *personally identifiable information (PII)*, is often protected by regulatory standards and is always governed by ethical considerations. Organizations seek to protect the security of private information and may do so using the same security controls that they use to protect other categories of sensitive information, but privacy obligations extend beyond just security. Privacy extends to include the ways that an organization uses and shares the information that it collects and maintains with others.

Exam Note

Remember that privacy and security are complementary and overlapping, but they have different objectives. This is an important concept on the exam.

The *Generally Accepted Privacy Principles (GAPP)* outline 10 privacy practices that organizations should strive to follow:

- **Management** says that the organization should document its privacy practices in a privacy policy and related documents.
- **Notice** says that the organization should notify individuals about its privacy practices and inform individuals of the type of information that it collects and how that information is used.
- **Choice and consent** says that the organization should obtain the direct consent of individuals for the storage, use, and sharing of PII.
- **Collection** says that the organization should collect PII only for the purposes identified in the notice and consented to by the individual.
- **Use, retention, and disposal** says that the organization should only use information for identified purposes and may not use information collected for one stated purpose for any other nondisclosed purpose.
- **Access** says that the organization should provide individuals with access to any information about that individual in the organization's records, at the individual's request.
- **Disclosure** says that the organization will disclose information to third parties only when consistent with notice and consent.
- **Security** says that PII will be protected against unauthorized access.
- **Quality** says that the organization will maintain accurate and complete information.
- **Monitoring and enforcement** says that the organization will put business processes in place to ensure that it remains compliant with its privacy policy.

The GAPP principles are not mandated by law but are strong best practices for building a privacy program. In Chapter 16, "Policy and Compliance," we will discuss policies in greater detail and cover legal requirements that compel companies operating in certain industries and jurisdictions to implement privacy policies.

Evaluating Security Risks

Cybersecurity risk analysis is the cornerstone of any information security program. Analysts must take the time to thoroughly understand their own technology environments and the external threats that jeopardize their information security. A well-rounded cybersecurity risk assessment combines information about internal and external factors to help analysts understand the threats facing their organization and then design an appropriate set of controls to meet those threats.

Before diving into the world of risk assessment, we must begin with a common vocabulary. You must know three important terms to communicate clearly with other risk analysts: vulnerabilities, threats, and risks.

A *vulnerability* is a weakness in a device, system, application, or process that might allow an attack to take place. Vulnerabilities are internal factors that may be controlled by cybersecurity professionals. For example, a web server that is running an outdated version of the Apache service may contain a vulnerability that would allow an attacker to conduct a denial-of-service (DoS) attack against the websites hosted on that server, jeopardizing their availability. Cybersecurity professionals within the organization have the ability to remediate this vulnerability by upgrading the Apache service to the most recent version that is not susceptible to the DoS attack.

A *threat* in the world of cybersecurity is an outside force that may exploit a vulnerability. For example, a hacker who would like to conduct a DoS attack against a website and knows about an Apache vulnerability poses a clear cybersecurity threat. Although many threats are malicious in nature, this is not necessarily the case. For example, an earthquake may also disrupt the availability of a website by damaging the datacenter containing the web servers. Earthquakes clearly do not have malicious intent. In most cases, cybersecurity professionals cannot do much to eliminate a threat. Hackers will hack and earthquakes will strike whether we like it or not.

A *risk* is the combination of a threat and a corresponding vulnerability. Both of these factors must be present before a situation poses a risk to the security of an organization. For example, if a hacker targets an organization's web server with a DoS attack but the server was patched so that it is not vulnerable to that attack, there is no risk because even though a threat is present (the hacker), there is no vulnerability. Similarly, a datacenter may be vulnerable to earthquakes because the walls are not built to withstand the extreme movements present during an earthquake, but it may be located in a region of the world where earthquakes do not occur. The datacenter may be vulnerable to earthquakes but there is little to no threat of earthquake in its location, so there is no risk.

The relationship between risks, threats, and vulnerabilities is an important one, and it is often represented by this equation:

$$\text{Risk} = \text{Threat} \times \text{Vulnerability}$$

This is not meant to be a literal equation where you would actually plug in values. Instead, it is meant to demonstrate the fact that risks exist only when there is both a threat and a corresponding vulnerability that the threat might exploit. If either the threat or vulnerability is zero, the risk is also zero. Figure 1.2 shows this in another way: risks are the intersection of threats and vulnerabilities.

Organizations should routinely conduct risk assessments to take stock of their existing risk landscape. The National Institute of Standards and Technology (NIST) publishes a guide for conducting risk assessments that is widely used throughout the cybersecurity field as a foundation for risk assessments. The document, designated NIST Special Publication (SP) 800-30, suggests the risk assessment process shown in Figure 1.3.

FIGURE 1.2 Risks exist at the intersection of threats and vulnerabilities. If either the threat or vulnerability is missing, there is no risk.

FIGURE 1.3 The NIST SP 800-30 risk assessment process suggests that an organization should identify threats and vulnerabilities and then use that information to determine the level of risk posed by the combination of those threats and vulnerabilities. Source: NIST SP 800-30

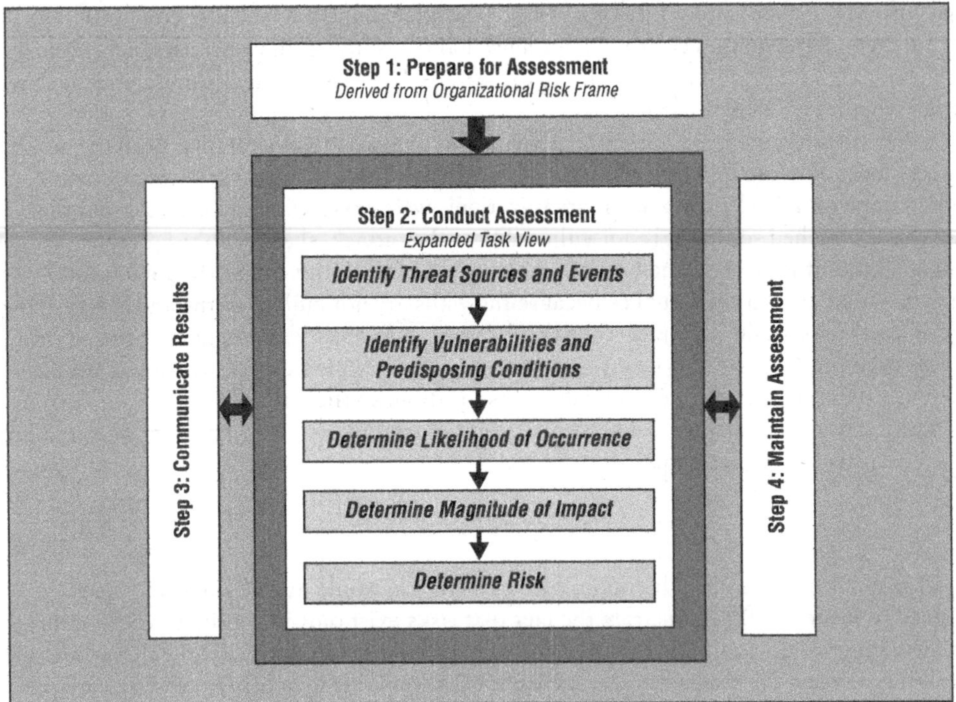

Identify Threats

Organizations begin the risk assessment process by identifying the types of threats that exist in their threat environment. Although some threats, such as malware and spam, affect all organizations, other threats are targeted against specific types of organizations. For example, government-sponsored advanced persistent threat (APT) attackers typically target government agencies, military organizations, and companies that operate in related fields. It is unlikely that an APT attacker would target an elementary school.

NIST identifies four different categories of threats that an organization might face and should consider in its threat identification process:

- **Adversarial threats** are individuals, groups, and organizations that are attempting to deliberately undermine the security of an organization. Adversaries may include trusted insiders, competitors, suppliers, customers, business partners, or even nation-states. When evaluating an adversarial threat, cybersecurity analysts should consider the capability of the threat actor to engage in attacks, the intent of the threat actor, and the likelihood that the threat will target the organization.
- **Accidental threats** occur when individuals doing their routine work mistakenly perform an action that undermines security. For example, a system administrator might accidentally delete a critical disk volume, causing a loss of availability. When evaluating an accidental threat, cybersecurity analysts should consider the possible range of effects that the threat might have on the organization.
- **Structural threats** occur when equipment, software, or environmental controls fail due to the exhaustion of resources (such as running out of gas), exceeding their operational capability (such as operating in extreme heat), or simply failing due to age. Structural threats may come from IT components (such as storage, servers, and network devices), environmental controls (such as power and cooling infrastructure), and software (such as operating systems and applications). When evaluating a structural threat, cybersecurity analysts should consider the possible range of effects that the threat might have on the organization.
- **Environmental threats** occur when natural or man-made disasters occur that are outside the control of the organization. These might include fires, flooding, severe storms, power failures, or widespread telecommunications disruptions. When evaluating environmental threats, cybersecurity analysts should consider common natural environmental threats to their geographic region, as well as how to appropriately prevent or counter man-made environmental threats.

The nature and scope of the threats in each of these categories will vary depending on the nature of the organization, the composition of its technology infrastructure, and many other situation-specific circumstances. That said, it may be helpful to obtain copies of the risk assessments performed by other, similar organizations as a starting point for an organization's own risk assessment or to use as a quality assessment check during various stages of the organization's assessment.

The Insider Threat

When performing a threat analysis, cybersecurity professionals must remember that threats come from both external and internal sources. In addition to the hackers, natural disasters, and other threats that begin outside the organization, rogue employees, disgruntled team members, and incompetent administrators also pose a significant threat to enterprise cybersecurity. As an organization designs controls, it must consider both internal and external threats.

NIST SP 800-30 provides a great deal of additional information to help organizations conduct risk assessments, including detailed tasks associated with each of these steps. This information is outside the scope of the Cybersecurity Analyst (CySA+) exam, but organizations preparing to conduct risk assessments should download and read the entire publication. It is available at `csrc.nist.gov/publications/detail/sp/800-30/rev-1/final`.

Identify Vulnerabilities

During the threat identification phase of a risk assessment, cybersecurity analysts focus on the external factors likely to impact an organization's security efforts. After completing threat identification, the focus of the assessment turns inward, identifying the vulnerabilities that those threats might exploit to compromise an organization's confidentiality, integrity, or availability.

Chapter 4, "Designing a Vulnerability Management Program," and Chapter 5, "Analyzing Vulnerability Scans," of this book focus extensively on the identification and management of vulnerabilities.

Determine Likelihood, Impact, and Risk

After identifying the threats and vulnerabilities facing an organization, risk assessors next seek out combinations of threat and vulnerability that pose a risk to the confidentiality, integrity, or availability of enterprise information and systems. This requires assessing both the likelihood that a risk will materialize and the impact that the risk will have on the organization if it does occur.

When determining the likelihood of a risk occurring, analysts should consider two factors. First, they should assess the likelihood that the threat source will initiate the risk. In the case of an adversarial threat source, this is the likelihood that the adversary will execute an attack against the organization. In the case of accidental, structural, or environmental threats, it is the likelihood that the threat will occur. The second factor that contributes is the likelihood that, if a risk occurs, it will actually have an adverse impact on the organization, given the state of the organization's security controls. After considering each of these criteria, risk assessors assign an overall likelihood rating. This may use categories, such as "low," "medium," and "high," to describe the likelihood qualitatively.

Risk assessors evaluate the impact of a risk using a similar rating scale. This evaluation should assume that a threat actually does take place and cause a risk to the organization and then attempt to identify the magnitude of the adverse impact that the risk will have on the organization. When evaluating this risk, it is helpful to refer to the three objectives of cybersecurity shown in Figure 1.1, confidentiality, integrity, and availability, and then assess the impact that the risk would have on each of these objectives.

The risk assessment process described here, using categories of "high," "medium," and "low," is an example of a qualitative risk assessment process. Risk assessments also may use quantitative techniques that numerically assess the likelihood and impact of risks. Quantitative risk assessments are beyond the scope of the Cybersecurity Analyst (CySA+) exam but are found on more advanced security exams, including the CompTIA Advanced Security Practitioner (CASP+) and Certified Information Systems Security Professional (CISSP) exams.

After assessing the likelihood and impact of a risk, risk assessors then combine those two evaluations to determine an overall risk rating. This may be as simple as using a matrix similar to the one shown in Figure 1.4 that describes how the organization assigns overall ratings to risks. For example, an organization might decide that the likelihood of a hacker attack is medium whereas the impact would be high. Looking this combination up in Figure 1.4 reveals that it should be considered a high overall risk. Similarly, if an organization assesses the likelihood of a flood as medium and the impact as low, a flood scenario would have an overall risk of low.

FIGURE 1.4 Many organizations use a risk matrix to determine an overall risk rating based on likelihood and impact assessments.

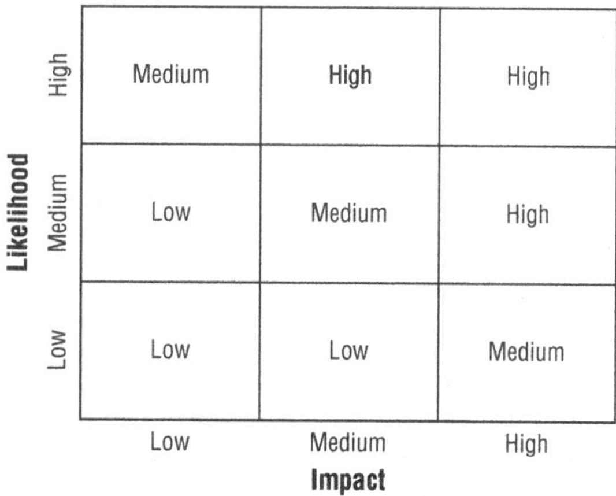

Reviewing Controls

Cybersecurity professionals use risk management strategies, such as risk acceptance, risk avoidance, risk mitigation, and risk transference, to reduce the likelihood and impact of risks identified during risk assessments. The most common way that organizations manage security risks is to develop sets of technical and operational security controls that mitigate those risks to acceptable levels.

Technical controls are systems, devices, software, and settings that work to enforce confidentiality, integrity, and/or availability requirements. Examples of technical controls include building a secure network and implementing endpoint security, two topics discussed later in this chapter. Operational controls are practices and procedures that bolster cybersecurity. Examples of operational controls include conducting penetration testing and using reverse engineering to analyze acquired software. These two topics are also discussed later in this chapter.

Building a Secure Network

Many threats to an organization's cybersecurity exploit vulnerabilities in the organization's network to gain initial access to systems and information. To help mitigate these risks, organizations should focus on building secure networks that keep attackers at bay. Examples of the controls that an organization may use to contribute to building a secure network include network access control (NAC) solutions; network perimeter security controls, such as firewalls; network segmentation; and the use of deception as a defensive measure.

Network Access Control

One of the basic security objectives set forth by most organizations is controlling access to the organization's network. Network access control (NAC) solutions help security professionals achieve two cybersecurity objectives: limiting network access to authorized individuals and ensuring that systems accessing the organization's network meet basic security requirements.

The 802.1x protocol is a common standard used for NAC. When a new device wishes to gain access to a network, either by connecting to a wireless access point or plugging into a wired network port, the network challenges that device to authenticate using the 802.1x protocol. A special piece of software, known as a supplicant, resides on the device requesting to join the network. The supplicant communicates with a service known as the authenticator that runs on either the wireless access point or the network switch. The authenticator does not have the information necessary to validate the user itself, so it passes access requests along to an authentication server using the Remote Access Dial-In User Service (RADIUS) protocol. If the user correctly authenticates and is authorized to access the network, the switch or access point then joins the user to the network. If the user does not successfully complete this process, the device is denied access to the network or may be assigned to a special quarantine network for remediation. Figure 1.5 shows the devices involved in 802.1x authentication.

FIGURE 1.5 In an 802.1x system, the device attempting to join the network runs a NAC supplicant, which communicates with an authenticator on the network switch or wireless access point. The authenticator uses RADIUS to communicate with an authentication server.

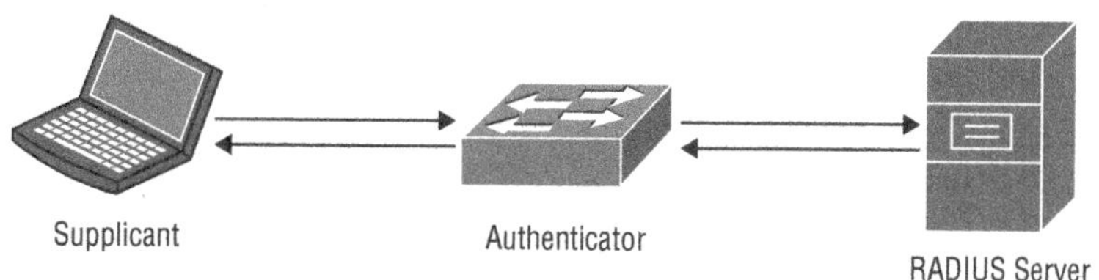

Many different NAC solutions are available on the market, and they differ in two major ways:

Agent-Based vs. Agentless Agent-based solutions, such as 802.1x, require that the device requesting access to the network run special software designed to communicate with the NAC service. Agentless approaches to NAC conduct authentication in the web browser and do not require special software.

In-Band vs. Out-of-Band In-band (or inline) NAC solutions use dedicated appliances that sit in between devices and the resources that they wish to access. They deny or limit network access to devices that do not pass the NAC authentication process. The "captive portal" NAC solutions found in hotels that hijack all web requests until the guest enters a room number are examples of in-band NAC. Out-of-band NAC solutions, such as 802.1x, leverage the existing network infrastructure and have network devices communicate with authentication servers and then reconfigure the network to grant or deny network access, as needed.

NAC solutions are often used simply to limit access to authorized users based on those users successfully authenticating, but they may also make network admission decisions based on other criteria. Some of the criteria used by NAC solutions are as follows:

Time of Day Users may be authorized to access the network only during specific time periods, such as during business hours.

Role Users may be assigned to particular network segments based on their role in the organization. For example, a college might assign faculty and staff to an administrative network that may access administrative systems while assigning students to an academic network that does not allow such access.

Location Users may be granted or denied access to network resources based on their physical location. For example, access to the datacenter network may be limited to systems physically present in the datacenter.

System Health NAC solutions may use agents running on devices to obtain configuration information from the device. Devices that fail to meet minimum security standards, such as having incorrectly configured host firewalls, outdated virus definitions, or missing security patches, may be either completely denied network access or placed on a special quarantine network where they are granted only the limited access required to update the system's security.

Exam Note

NAC criteria are a very testable item. You should be prepared to answer questions about these criteria when you take the CySA+ exam.

Administrators may create NAC rules that limit access based on any combination of these characteristics. NAC products provide the flexibility needed to implement the organization's specific security requirements for network admission.

You'll sometimes see the acronym NAC expanded to "Network Admission Control" instead of "network access control." In both cases, people are referring to the same general technology. Network Admission Control is a proprietary name used by Cisco for its network access control solutions.

Firewalls and Network Perimeter Security

NAC solutions are designed to manage the systems that connect directly to an organization's wired or wireless network. They provide excellent protection against intruders who seek to gain access to the organization's information resources by physically accessing a facility and connecting a device to the physical network. They don't provide protection against intruders seeking to gain access over a network connection. That's where firewalls enter the picture.

Network firewalls sit at the boundaries between networks and provide perimeter security. Much like a security guard might control the physical perimeter of a building, the network firewall controls the electronic perimeter. Firewalls are typically configured in the triple-homed fashion illustrated in Figure 1.6. Triple-homed simply means that the firewall connects to three different networks. The firewall in Figure 1.6 connects to the Internet, the internal network, and a special network known as the demilitarized zone (DMZ). Any traffic that wishes to pass from one zone to another, such as between the Internet and the internal network, must pass through the firewall.

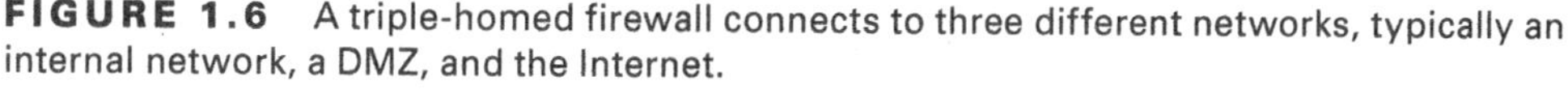

FIGURE 1.6 A triple-homed firewall connects to three different networks, typically an internal network, a DMZ, and the Internet.

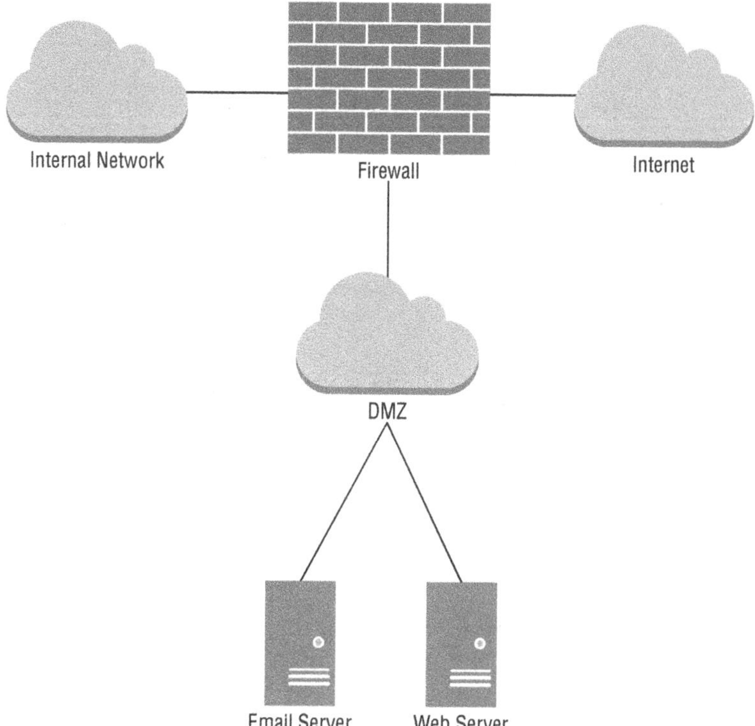

The DMZ is a special network zone designed to house systems that receive connections from the outside world, such as web and email servers. Sound firewall designs place these systems on an isolated network where, if they become compromised, they pose little threat to the internal network because connections between the DMZ and the internal network must still pass through the firewall and are subject to its security policy.

Whenever the firewall receives a connection request, it evaluates it according to the firewall's rule base. This rule base is an access control list (ACL) that identifies the types of traffic permitted to pass through the firewall. The rules used by the firewall typically specify the source and destination IP addresses for traffic as well as the destination port corresponding to the authorized service. A list of common ports appears in Table 1.1. Firewalls follow the default deny principle, which says that if there is no rule explicitly allowing a connection, the firewall will deny that connection.

TABLE 1.1 Common TCP ports

Port	Service
20,21	FTP
22	SSH
23	Telnet
25	SMTP
53	DNS
80	HTTP
110	POP3
123	NTP
143	IMAP
389	LDAP
443	HTTPS
636	LDAPS
1443	SQL Server
1521	Oracle
1720	H.323
1723	PPTP
3389	RDP

Several categories of firewalls are available on the market today, and they vary in both price and functionality:

- Packet filtering firewalls simply check the characteristics of each packet against the firewall rules without any additional intelligence. Packet filtering firewall capabilities are typically found in routers and other network devices and are very rudimentary firewalls.
- Stateful inspection firewalls go beyond packet filters and maintain information about the state of each connection passing through the firewall. These are the most basic firewalls sold as stand-alone products.

- Next-generation firewalls (NGFWs) incorporate even more information into their decision-making process, including contextual information about users, applications, and business processes. They are the current state-of-the-art in network firewall protection and are quite expensive compared to stateful inspection devices.
- Web application firewalls (WAFs) are specialized firewalls designed to protect against web application attacks, such as SQL injection and cross-site scripting. WAFs are discussed in more detail in Chapter 10, "Security Operations and Monitoring."

Network Segmentation

Firewalls use a principle known as network segmentation to separate networks of differing security levels from each other. This principle certainly applies to the example shown in Figure 1.6, where the internal network, DMZ, and Internet all have differing security levels. The same principle may be applied to further segment the internal network into different zones of trust.

For example, imagine an organization that has several hundred employees and a large datacenter located in its corporate headquarters. The datacenter may house many sensitive systems, such as database servers that contain sensitive employee information, business plans, and other critical information assets. The corporate network may house employees, temporary contractors, visitors, and other people who aren't entirely trusted. In this common example, security professionals would want to segment the datacenter network so that it is not directly accessible by systems on the corporate network. This can be accomplished using a firewall, as shown in Figure 1.7.

The network shown in Figure 1.7 uses a triple-homed firewall, just as was used to control the network perimeter with the Internet in Figure 1.6. The concept is identical, except in this case the firewall is protecting the perimeter of the datacenter from the less trusted corporate network.

Notice that the network in Figure 1.7 also contains a DMZ with a server called the jump box. The purpose of this server is to act as a secure transition point between the corporate network and the datacenter network, providing a trusted path between the two zones. System administrators who need to access the datacenter network should not connect devices directly to the datacenter network but should instead initiate an administrative connection to the jump box, using Secure Shell (SSH), the Remote Desktop Protocol (RDP), or a similar secure remote administration protocol. After successfully authenticating to the jump box, they may then connect from the jump box to the datacenter network, providing some isolation between their own systems and the datacenter network. Connections to the jump box should be carefully controlled and protected with strong multifactor authentication technology.

Jump boxes may also be used to serve as a layer of insulation against systems that may only be partially trusted. For example, if you have contractors who bring equipment owned by their employer onto your network or employees bringing personally owned devices, you might use a jump box to prevent those systems from directly connecting to your company's systems.

FIGURE 1.7 A triple-homed firewall may also be used to isolate internal network segments of varying trust levels.

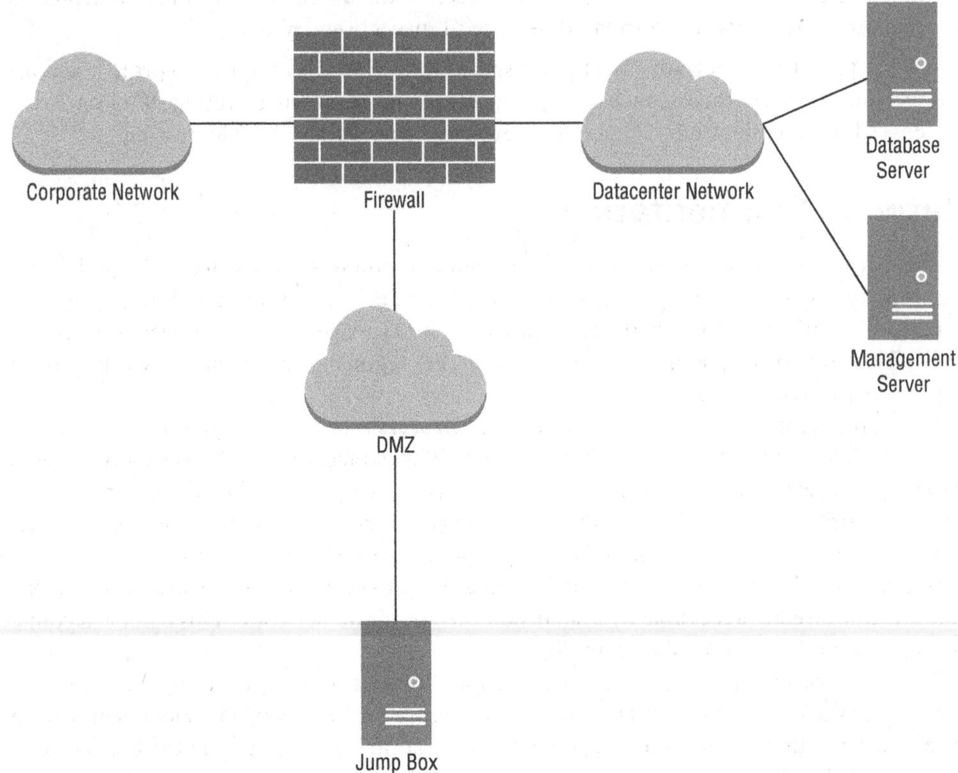

Defense Through Deception

Cybersecurity professionals may wish to go beyond typical security controls and engage in active defensive measures that actually lure attackers to specific targets and seek to monitor their activity in a carefully controlled environment.

Honeypots are systems designed to appear to attackers as lucrative targets due to the services they run, vulnerabilities they contain, or sensitive information that they appear to host. The reality is that honeypots are designed by cybersecurity experts to falsely appear vulnerable and fool malicious individuals into attempting an attack against them. When an attacker tries to compromise a honeypot, the honeypot simulates a successful attack and then monitors the attacker's activity to learn more about his or her intentions. Honeypots may also be used to feed network blacklists, blocking all inbound activity from any IP address that attacks the honeypot.

DNS sinkholes feed false information to malicious software that works its way onto the enterprise network. When a compromised system attempts to obtain information from a DNS server about its command-and-control server, the DNS server detects the suspicious request and, instead of responding with the correct answer, responds with the IP address of a sinkhole system designed to detect and remediate the botnet-infected system.

Secure Endpoint Management

Laptop and desktop computers, tablets, smartphones, and other endpoint devices are a constant source of security threats on a network. These systems interact directly with end users and require careful configuration management to ensure that they remain secure and do not serve as the entry point for a security vulnerability on enterprise networks. Fortunately, by taking some simple security precautions, technology professionals can secure these devices against most attacks.

Hardening System Configurations

Operating systems are extremely complex pieces of software designed to perform thousands of different functions. The large code bases that make up modern operating systems are a frequent source of vulnerabilities, as evidenced by the frequent security patches issued by operating system vendors.

One of the most important ways that system administrators can protect endpoints is by hardening their configurations, making them as attack-resistant as possible. This includes disabling any unnecessary services or ports on the endpoints to reduce their susceptibility to attack, ensuring that secure configuration settings exist on devices and centrally controlling device security settings.

Patch Management

System administrators must maintain current security patch levels on all operating systems and applications under their care. Once the vendor releases a security patch, attackers are likely already aware of a vulnerability and may immediately begin preying on susceptible systems. The longer an organization waits to apply security patches, the more likely it becomes that they will fall victim to an attack. That said, enterprises should always test patches prior to deploying them on production systems and networks.

Fortunately, patch management software makes it easy to centrally distribute and monitor the patch level of systems throughout the enterprise. For example, Microsoft's System Center Configuration Manager (SCCM) allows administrators to quickly view the patch status of enterprise systems and remediate any systems with missing patches.

Compensating Controls

In some cases, security professionals may not be able to implement all of the desired security controls due to technical, operational, or financial reasons. For example, an organization may not be able to upgrade the operating system on retail point-of-sale (POS) terminals due to an incompatibility with the POS software. In these cases, security professionals should seek out compensating controls designed to provide a similar level of security using alternate means. In the POS example, administrators might place the POS terminals on a segmented, isolated network and use intrusion prevention systems to monitor network traffic for any attempt to exploit an unpatched vulnerability and block it from reaching the vulnerable host. This meets the same objective of protecting the POS terminal from compromise and serves as a compensating control.

Group Policies

Group Policies provide administrators with an efficient way to manage security and other system configuration settings across a large number of devices. Microsoft's Group Policy Object (GPO) mechanism allows administrators to define groups of security settings once and then apply those settings to either all systems in the enterprise or a group of systems based on role.

For example, Figure 1.8 shows a GPO designed to enforce Windows Firewall settings on sensitive workstations. This GPO is configured to require the use of Windows Firewall and block all inbound connections.

FIGURE 1.8 Group Policy Objects (GPOs) may be used to apply settings to many different systems at the same time.

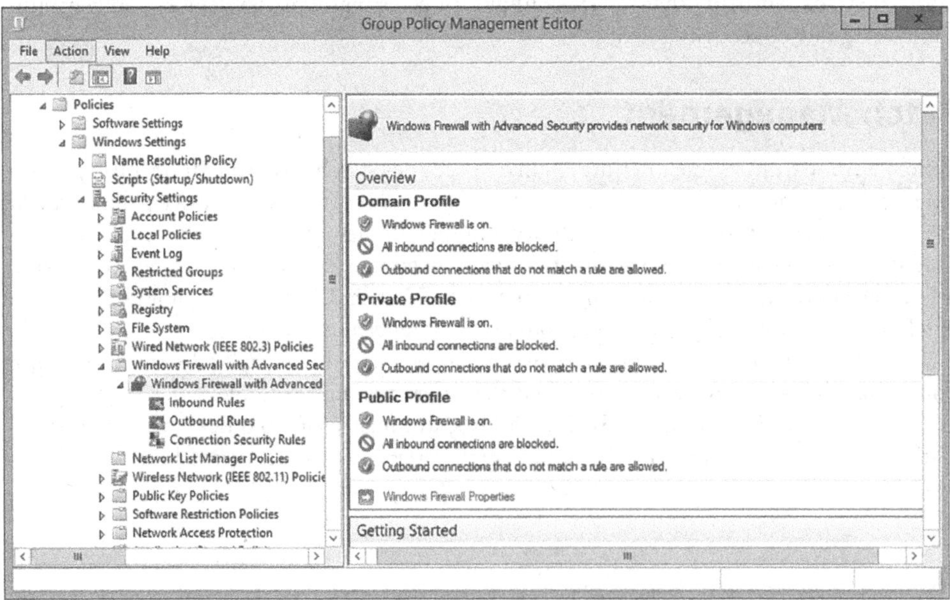

Administrators may use GPOs to control a wide variety of Windows settings and create different policies that apply to different classes of systems.

Endpoint Security Software

Endpoint systems should also run specialized security software designed to enforce the organization's security objectives. At a minimum, this should include antivirus software designed to scan the system for signs of malicious software that might jeopardize the security of the endpoint. Administrators may also choose to install host-based firewall software that serves as a basic firewall for that individual system, complementing network-based firewall controls or host intrusion prevention systems (HIPSs) that block suspicious network activity. Endpoint security software should report its status to a centralized management system that allows security administrators to monitor the entire enterprise from a single location.

Mandatory Access Controls

In highly secure environments, administrators may opt to implement a mandatory access control (MAC) approach to security. In a MAC system, administrators set all security permissions, and end users cannot modify those permissions. This stands in contrast to the discretionary access control (DAC) model found in most modern operating systems where the owner of a file or resource controls the permissions on that resource and can delegate them at their discretion.

MAC systems are very unwieldy and, therefore, are rarely used outside of very sensitive government and military applications. Security-Enhanced Linux (SELinux), an operating system developed by the U.S. National Security Agency, is an example of a system that enforces mandatory access controls.

Penetration Testing

In addition to bearing responsibility for the design and implementation of security controls, cybersecurity analysts are responsible for monitoring the ongoing effectiveness of those controls. Penetration testing is one of the techniques they use to fulfill this obligation. During a penetration test, the testers simulate an attack against the organization using the same information, tools, and techniques available to real attackers. They seek to gain access to systems and information and then report their findings to management. The results of penetration tests may be used to bolster an organization's security controls.

Penetration tests may be performed by an organization's internal staff or by external consultants. In the case of internal tests, they require highly skilled individuals and are quite time-consuming. External tests mitigate these concerns but are often quite expensive to conduct. Despite these barriers to penetration tests, organizations should try to perform them periodically since a well-designed and well-executed penetration test is one of the best measures of an organization's cybersecurity posture.

NIST divides penetration testing into the four phases shown in Figure 1.9.

FIGURE 1.9 NIST divides penetration testing into four phases. Source: NIST SP 800-115: Technical Guide to Information Security Testing and Assessment

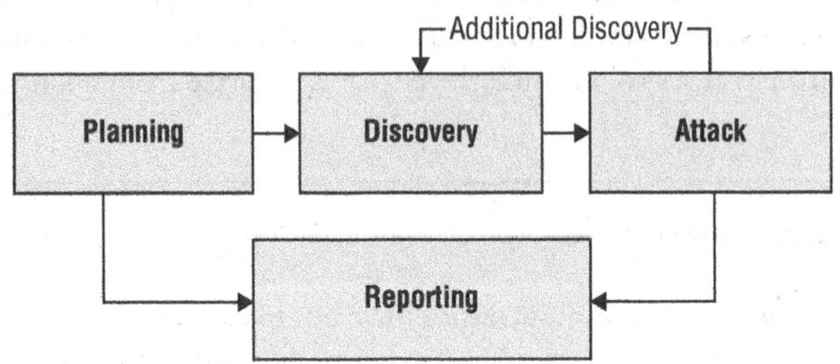

Planning a Penetration Test

The planning phase of a penetration test lays the administrative groundwork for the test. No technical work is performed during the planning phase, but it is a critical component of any penetration test. There are three important rules of engagement to finalize during the planning phase:

Timing When will the test take place? Will technology staff be informed of the test? Can it be timed to have as little impact on business operations as possible?

Scope What is the agreed-on scope of the penetration test? Are any systems, networks, personnel, or business processes off-limits to the testers?

Authorization Who is authorizing the penetration test to take place? What should testers do if they are confronted by an employee or other individual who notices their suspicious activity?

These details are administrative in nature, but it is important to agree on them up front and in writing to avoid problems during and after the penetration test.

You should never conduct a penetration test without permission. Not only is an unauthorized test unethical, it may be illegal.

Conducting Discovery

The technical work of the penetration test begins during the discovery phase when attackers conduct reconnaissance and gather as much information as possible about the targeted network, systems, users, and applications. This may include conducting reviews of publicly available material, performing port scans of systems, using network vulnerability scanners and web application testers to probe for vulnerabilities, and performing other information gathering.

Vulnerability scanning is an important component of penetration testing. This topic is covered extensively in Chapters 4 and 5.

Executing a Penetration Test

During the attack phase, penetration testers seek to bypass the organization's security controls and gain access to systems and applications run by the organization. Testers often follow the NIST attack process shown in Figure 1.10.

In this process, attackers use the information gathered during the discovery phase to gain initial access to a system. Once they establish a foothold, they then seek to escalate their access until they gain complete administrative control of the system. From there, they can scan for additional systems on the network, install additional penetration testing tools, and begin the cycle anew, seeking to expand their footprint within the targeted organization. They continue this cycle until they exhaust the possibilities or the time allotted for the test expires.

FIGURE 1.10 The attack phase of a penetration test uses a cyclical process that gains a foothold and then uses it to expand access within the target organization. Source: NIST SP 800-115: Technical Guide to Information Security Testing and Assessment

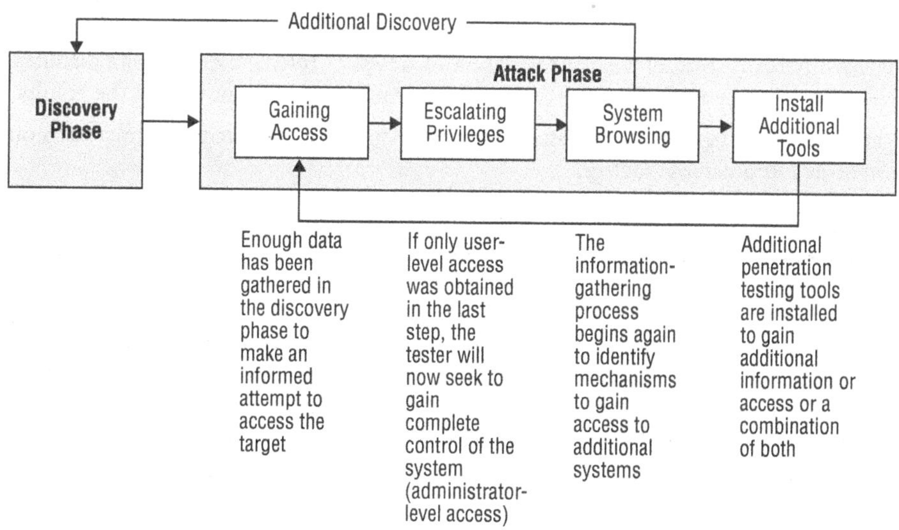

Exam Note

The attack phase of a penetration test is also known as the exploitation phase. Questions on the exam referring to test execution, the attack phase, and the exploitation phase are all referring to the same thing.

Communicating Penetration Test Results

At the conclusion of the penetration test, the testers prepare a detailed report communicating the access they were able to achieve and the vulnerabilities they exploited to gain this access. The results of penetration tests are valuable security planning tools, because they describe the actual vulnerabilities that an attacker might exploit to gain access to a network. Penetration testing reports typically contain detailed appendixes that include the results of various tests and may be shared with system administrators responsible for remediating issues.

Training and Exercises

In addition to performing penetration tests, some organizations choose to run wargame exercises that pit teams of security professionals against one another in a cyberdefense scenario. These exercises are typically performed in simulated environments, rather than on production networks, and seek to improve the skills of security professionals on both sides by exposing them to the tools and techniques used by attackers. Three teams are involved in most cybersecurity wargames:

- The red team plays the role of the attacker and uses reconnaissance and exploitation tools to attempt to gain access to the protected network. The red team's work is similar to that of the testers during a penetration test.
- The blue team is responsible for securing the targeted environment and keeping the red team out by building, maintaining, and monitoring a comprehensive set of security controls.
- The white team coordinates the exercise and serves as referees, arbitrating disputes between the team, maintaining the technical environment, and monitoring the results.

Cybersecurity wargames can be an effective way to educate security professionals on modern attack and defense tactics.

Reverse Engineering

In many cases, vendors do not release the details of how hardware and software work. Certainly, the authors of malicious software don't explain their work to the world. In these situations, security professionals may be in the dark about the security of their environments. Reverse engineering is a technique used to work backward from a finished product to figure out how it works. Security professionals sometimes use reverse engineering to learn the inner workings of suspicious software or inspect the integrity of hardware. Reverse engineering uses a philosophy known as decomposition where reverse engineers start with the finished product and work their way back to its component parts.

Isolation and Sandboxing

One of the most dangerous threats to the security of modern organizations is customized malware developed by APT actors who create specialized tools designed to penetrate a single target. Since they have never been used before, these tools are not detectable with the signature-detection technology used by traditional antivirus software.

Sandboxing is an approach used to detect malicious software based on its behavior rather than its signatures. Sandboxing systems watch systems and the network for unknown pieces of code and, when they detect an application that has not been seen before, immediately isolate that code in a special environment known as a *sandbox* where it does not have access to any other systems or applications. The sandboxing solution then executes the code and watches how it behaves, checking to see if it begins scanning the network for other systems, gathering sensitive information, communicating with a command-and-control server, or performing any other potentially malicious activity.

If the sandboxing solution identifies strange behavior, it blocks the code from entering the organization's network and flags it for administrator review. This process, also known as code detonation, is an example of an automated reverse engineering technique that takes action based on the observed behavior of software.

Reverse-Engineering Software

In most programming languages, developers write software in a human-readable language such as C/C++, Java, Ruby, or Python. Depending on the programming language, the computer may process this code in one of two ways. In interpreted languages, such as Ruby and Python, the computer works directly from the source code. Reverse engineers seeking to analyze code written in interpreted languages can simply read through the code and often get a good idea of what the code is attempting to accomplish.

In compiled languages, such as Java and C/C++, the developer uses a tool called a compiler to convert the source code into binary code that is readable by the computer. This binary code is what is often distributed to users of the software, and it is very difficult, if not impossible, to examine binary code and determine what it is doing, making the reverse engineering of compiled languages much more difficult. Technologists seeking to reverse-engineer compiled code have two options. First, they can attempt to use a specialized program known as a decompiler to convert the binary code back to source code. Unfortunately, however, this process usually does not work very well. Second, they can use a specialized environment and carefully monitor how software responds to different inputs in an attempt to discover its inner workings. In either case, reverse engineering compiled software is extremely difficult.

Fingerprinting Software

Although it is difficult to reverse-engineer compiled code, technologists can easily detect whether two pieces of compiled code are identical or whether one has been modified. *Hashing* is a mathematical technique that analyzes a file and computes a unique fingerprint, known as a message digest or hash, for that file. Analysts using hash functions, such as the Secure Hash Algorithm (SHA), can compute the hashes of two files and compare the output values. If the hashes are identical, the file contents are identical. If the hashes differ, the two files contain at least one difference. Hashing software is covered in more detail in Chapter 13, "Forensic Analysis and Forensic Techniques."

Reverse-Engineering Hardware

Reverse-engineering hardware is even more difficult than reverse-engineering software because the authenticity of hardware often rests in the invisible code embedded within integrated circuits and firmware contents. Although organizations may perform a physical inspection of hardware to detect tampering, it is important to verify that hardware has source authenticity, meaning that it comes from a trusted, reliable source, because it is simply too difficult to exhaustively test hardware.

The U.S. government recognizes the difficulty of ensuring source authenticity and operates a trusted foundry program for critical defense systems. The U.S. Department of Defense (DoD) and National Security Agency (NSA) certify companies as trusted foundries that are approved to create sensitive integrated circuits for government use. Companies seeking trusted foundry status must show that they completely secure the production process, including design, prototyping, packing, assembly, and other elements of the process.

Reverse engineers seeking to determine the function of hardware use some of the same techniques used for compiled software, particularly when it comes to observing behavior. Operating a piece of hardware in a controlled environment and observing how it responds to different inputs provides clues to the functions performed in the hardware. Reverse engineers may also seek to obtain documentation from original equipment manufacturers (OEMs) that provide insight into how components of a piece of hardware function.

Compromising Cisco Routers

According to NSA documents released by Edward Snowden, the U.S. government has engaged in reverse engineering of hardware designed to circumvent security.

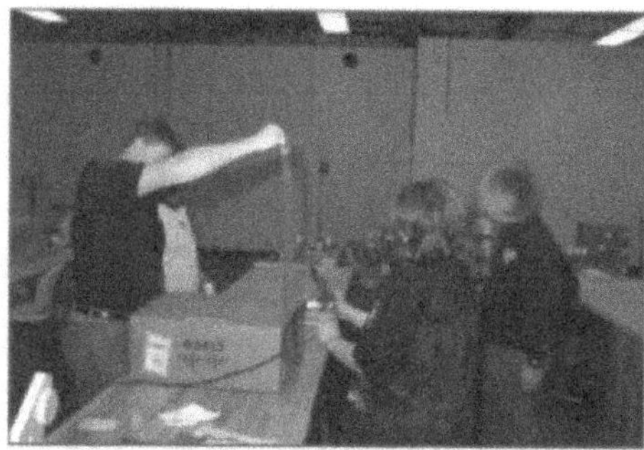

(TS//SI//NF) Left: Intercepted packages are opened carefully; Right: A "load station" implants a beacon

Source: "Spiegel supply chain interdiction: Stealthy techniques can crack some of sigints hardest targets" by `eff.org` licensed under CC By 3.0 US

In a process shown in this photo, NSA employees intercepted packages containing Cisco routers, switches, and other network gear after it left the factory and before it reached the customer. They then opened the packages and inserted covert firmware into the devices that facilitated government monitoring.

The Future of Cybersecurity Analytics

As we continue to develop our cybersecurity analytics capabilities, the tools and techniques available to us advance in sophistication. The area of greatest promise for future cybersecurity analytics tools is the continued adoption of *machine learning* techniques designed to automatically extract knowledge from the voluminous quantity of information generated by security systems.

Machine learning techniques are already incorporated into many security analytics tools, providing automated analysis of data based on the experiences of other users of the tool. Expect to see these capabilities continue to develop as organizations harvest the power of machine learning to reduce the requirements for human analysts to perform burdensome sifting of data and allow them to focus on the output of machine learning algorithms that guide them toward more productive work.

Summary

Cybersecurity professionals are responsible for ensuring the confidentiality, integrity, and availability of information and systems maintained by their organizations. Confidentiality ensures that unauthorized individuals are not able to gain access to sensitive information. Integrity ensures that there are no unauthorized modifications to information or systems, either intentionally or unintentionally. Availability ensures that information and systems are ready to meet the needs of legitimate users at the time those users request them. Together, these three goals are known as the CIA Triad.

As cybersecurity analysts seek to protect their organizations, they must evaluate risks to the CIA Triad. This includes identifying vulnerabilities, recognizing corresponding threats, and determining the level of risk that results from vulnerability and threat combinations. Analysts must then evaluate each risk and identify appropriate risk management strategies to mitigate or otherwise address the risk. They may use machine learning techniques to assist with this work.

Cybersecurity analysts mitigate risks using security controls designed to reduce the likelihood or impact of a risk. Network security controls include network access control (NAC) systems, firewalls, and network segmentation. Secure endpoint controls include hardened system configurations, patch management, Group Policies, and endpoint security software.

Penetration tests and reverse engineering provide analysts with the reassurance that the controls they've implemented to mitigate risks are functioning properly. By following a careful risk analysis and control process, analysts significantly enhance the confidentiality, integrity, and availability of information and systems under their control.

Exam Essentials

Know the three objectives of cybersecurity. *Confidentiality* ensures that unauthorized individuals are not able to gain access to sensitive information. *Integrity* ensures that there are no unauthorized modifications to information or systems, either intentionally or unintentionally. *Availability* ensures that information and systems are ready to meet the needs of legitimate users at the time those users request them.

Know how cybersecurity risks result from the combination of a threat and a vulnerability. A vulnerability is a weakness in a device, system, application, or process that might allow an attack to take place. A threat in the world of cybersecurity is an outside force that may exploit a vulnerability.

Be able to categorize cybersecurity threats as adversarial, accidental, structural, or environmental. Adversarial threats are individuals, groups, and organizations that are attempting to deliberately undermine the security of an organization. Accidental threats occur when individuals doing their routine work mistakenly perform an action that undermines security. Structural threats occur when equipment, software, or environmental controls fail due to the exhaustion of resources, exceeding their operational capability or simply failing due to age. Environmental threats occur when natural or man-made disasters occur that are outside the control of the organization.

Understand how networks are made more secure through the use of network access control, firewalls, and segmentation. Network access control (NAC) solutions help security professionals achieve two cybersecurity objectives: limiting network access to authorized individuals and ensuring that systems accessing the organization's network meet basic security requirements. Network firewalls sit at the boundaries between networks and provide perimeter security. Network segmentation uses isolation to separate networks of differing security levels from each other.

Understand how endpoints are made more secure through the use of hardened configurations, patch management, Group Policy, and endpoint security software. Hardening configurations includes disabling any unnecessary services on the endpoints to reduce their susceptibility to attack, ensuring that secure configuration settings exist on devices, and centrally controlling device security settings. Patch management ensures that operating systems and applications are not susceptible to known vulnerabilities. Group Policy allows the application of security settings to many devices simultaneously, and endpoint security software protects against malicious software and other threats.

Know that penetration tests provide organizations with an attacker's perspective on their security. The NIST process for penetration testing divides tests into four phases: planning, discovery, attack, and reporting. The results of penetration tests are valuable security planning tools, since they describe the actual vulnerabilities that an attacker might exploit to gain access to a network.

Understand how reverse engineering techniques attempt to determine how hardware and software functions internally. Sandboxing is an approach used to detect malicious software based on its behavior rather than its signatures. Other reverse engineering techniques are difficult to perform, are often unsuccessful, and are quite time-consuming.

Know how machine learning technology facilitates cybersecurity analysis. The area of greatest promise for future cybersecurity analytics tools is the continued adoption of *machine learning* techniques designed to automatically extract knowledge from the voluminous quantity of information generated by security systems. Machine learning techniques are already incorporated into many security analytics tools, providing automated analysis of data based on the experiences of other users of the tool.

Lab Exercises

Activity 1.1: Create an Inbound Firewall Rule

In this lab, you will verify that the Windows Defender Firewall is enabled on a server and then create an inbound firewall rule that blocks file and printer sharing.

These lab instructions were written to run on a system running Windows Server 2019. The process for working on other versions of Windows Server is quite similar, although the exact names of services, options, and icons may differ slightly.

You should perform this lab on a test system. Enabling file and printer sharing on a production system may have undesired consequences. The easiest way to get access to a Windows Server 2019 system is to create an inexpensive cloud instance through Amazon Web Services (AWS) or Microsoft Azure.

Part 1: Verify that Windows Defender Firewall is enabled

1. Open the Control Panel for your Windows Server.
2. Choose System and Security.
3. Under Windows Defender Firewall, click Check Firewall Status.
4. Verify that the Windows Defender Firewall state is set to On for Private networks. If it is not on, enable the firewall by using the "Turn Windows Defender Firewall on or off" link on the left side of the window.

Part 2: Create an inbound firewall rule that allows file and printer sharing

1. On the left side of the Windows Defender Firewall control panel, click "Allow an app or feature through Windows Defender Firewall."
2. Scroll down the list of applications and find File and Printer Sharing.
3. Check the box to the left of that entry to block connections related to File and Printer Sharing.
4. Notice that the Private box to the right of that option was automatically selected. This allows File and Printer Sharing only for other systems on the same local network. The box for public access should be unchecked, specifying that remote systems are not able to access this feature.
5. Click OK to apply the setting.

Activity 1.2: Create a Group Policy Object

In this lab, you will create a Group Policy Object and edit its contents to enforce an organization's password policy.

These lab instructions were written to run on a system running Windows Server 2019. The process for working on other versions of Windows Server is quite similar, although the exact names of services, options, and icons may differ slightly. To complete this lab, your Windows Server must be configured as a domain controller.

1. Open the Group Policy Management Console. (If you do not find this console on your Windows Server, it is likely that it is not configured as a domain controller.)
2. Expand the folder corresponding to your Active Directory forest.
3. Expand the Domains folder.
4. Expand the folder corresponding to your domain.
5. Right-click the Group Policy Objects folder and click New on the pop-up menu.
6. Name your new GPO **Password Policy** and click OK.
7. Click on the Group Policy Objects folder.
8. Right-click the new Password Policy GPO and choose Edit from the pop-up menu.
9. When Group Policy Editor opens, expand the Computer Configuration folder.
10. Expand the Policies folder.
11. Expand the Windows Settings folder.
12. Expand the Security Settings folder.
13. Expand the Account Policies folder.
14. Click Password Policy.
15. Double-click Maximum Password Age.
16. In the pop-up window, select the Define This Policy Setting check box and set the expiration value to 90 days.
17. Click OK to close the window.
18. Click OK to accept the suggested change to the minimum password age.
19. Double-click the Minimum Password Length option.
20. As in the prior step, click the box to define the policy setting and set the minimum password length to 12 characters.
21. Click OK to close the window.
22. Double-click the Password Must Meet Complexity Requirements option.
23. Click the box to define the policy setting and change the value to Enabled.
24. Click OK to close the window.
25. Click the X to exit Group Policy Editor.

You have now successfully created a Group Policy Object that enforces the organization's password policy. You can apply this GPO to users and/or groups as needed.

Activity 1.3: Write a Penetration Testing Plan

For this activity, you will design a penetration testing plan for a test against an organization of your choosing. If you are employed, you may choose to use your employer's network. If you are a student, you may choose to create a plan for a penetration test of your school. Otherwise, you may choose any organization, real or fictitious, of your choice.

Your penetration testing plan should cover the three main criteria required before initiating any penetration test:

- Timing
- Scope
- Authorization

One word of warning: You should not conduct a penetration test without permission of the network owner. This assignment only asks you to design the test on paper.

Activity 1.4: Recognize Security Tools

Match each of the security tools listed in this table with the correct description.

Firewall	Determines which clients may access a wired or wireless network
Decompiler	Creates a unique fingerprint of a file
Antivirus	Filters network connections based on source, destination, and port
NAC	System intentionally created to appear vulnerable
GPO	Attempts to recover source code from binary code
Hash	Scans a system for malicious software
Honeypot	Protects against SQL injection attacks
WAF	Deploys configuration settings to multiple Windows systems

Review Questions

1. Which one of the following objectives is *not* one of the three main objectives that information security professionals must achieve to protect their organizations against cybersecurity threats?
   - **A.** Integrity
   - **B.** Nonrepudiation
   - **C.** Availability
   - **D.** Confidentiality

2. Tommy is assessing the security of several database servers in his datacenter and realizes that one of them is missing a critical Oracle security patch. What type of situation has Tommy detected?
   A. Risk
   B. Vulnerability
   C. Hacker
   D. Threat

3. Ben is preparing to conduct a cybersecurity risk assessment for his organization. If he chooses to follow the standard process proposed by NIST, which one of the following steps would come first?
   A. Determine likelihood
   B. Determine impact
   C. Identify threats
   D. Identify vulnerabilities

4. Cindy is conducting a cybersecurity risk assessment and is considering the impact that a failure of her city's power grid might have on the organization. What type of threat is she considering?
   A. Adversarial
   B. Accidental
   C. Structural
   D. Environmental

5. Which one of the following categories of threat requires that cybersecurity analysts consider the capability, intent, and targeting of the threat source?
   A. Adversarial
   B. Accidental
   C. Structural
   D. Environmental

6. Vincent is responding to a security incident that compromised one of his organization's web servers. He does not believe that the attackers modified or stole any information, but they did disrupt access to the organization's website. What cybersecurity objective did this attack violate?
   A. Confidentiality
   B. Nonrepudiation
   C. Integrity
   D. Availability

7. Which one of the following is an example of an operational security control?
   A. Encryption software
   B. Network firewall
   C. Antivirus software
   D. Penetration tests

8. Paul recently completed a risk assessment and determined that his network was vulnerable to hackers connecting to open ports on servers. He implemented a network firewall to reduce the likelihood of a successful attack. What risk management strategy did Paul choose to pursue?
   - A. Risk mitigation
   - B. Risk avoidance
   - C. Risk transference
   - D. Risk acceptance

9. Robert's organization has a Bring Your Own Device (BYOD) policy, and he would like to ensure that devices connected to the network under this policy have current antivirus software. What technology can best assist him with this goal?
   - A. Network firewall
   - B. Network access control (NAC)
   - C. Network segmentation
   - D. Virtual private network

10. When performing 802.1x authentication, what protocol does the authenticator use to communicate with the authentication server?
    - A. 802.11g
    - B. EAP
    - C. PEAP
    - D. RADIUS

11. Juan is configuring a new device that will join his organization's wireless network. The wireless network uses 802.1x authentication. What type of agent must be running on the device for it to join this network?
    - A. Supplicant
    - B. Authenticator
    - C. Authentication server
    - D. Command and control

12. Rick is preparing a firewall rule that will allow network traffic from external systems to a web server running the HTTPS protocol. What TCP port must he allow to pass through the firewall?
    - A. 25
    - B. 80
    - C. 143
    - D. 443

13. What type of firewall provides the greatest degree of contextual information and can include information about users and applications in its decision-making process?

    A. NGFW
    B. WAF
    C. Packet filter
    D. Stateful inspection

14. Wayne is configuring a jump box server that system administrators will connect to from their laptops. Which one of the following ports should definitely not be open on the jump box?

    A. 22
    B. 23
    C. 443
    D. 3389

15. Tom would like to deploy consistent security settings to all of his Windows systems simultaneously. What technology can he use to achieve this goal?

    A. GPO
    B. HIPS
    C. IPS
    D. DNS

16. During what phase of a penetration test should the testers obtain written authorization to conduct the test?

    A. Planning
    B. Attack
    C. Discovery
    D. Reporting

17. Which step occurs first during the attack phase of a penetration test?

    A. Gaining access
    B. Escalating privileges
    C. Browsing the system
    D. Installing additional tools

18. Barry is participating in a cybersecurity wargame exercise. His role is to attempt to break into adversary systems. What team is he on?

    A. Red team
    B. Blue team
    C. White team
    D. Black team

19. Which one of the following techniques might be used to automatically detect and block malicious software that does not match known malware signatures?
    A. MAC
    B. Hashing
    C. Decompiling
    D. Sandboxing
20. Kevin would like to implement a specialized firewall that can protect against SQL injection, cross-site scripting, and similar attacks. What technology should he choose?
    A. NGFW
    B. WAF
    C. Packet filter
    D. Stateful inspection

Using Threat Intelligence

THE COMPTIA CYBERSECURITY ANALYST (CYSA+) EXAM OBJECTIVES COVERED IN THIS CHAPTER INCLUDE:

✓ **Domain 1.0: Threat and Vulnerability Management**

- 1.1: Explain the importance of threat data and intelligence.
- 1.2: Given a scenario, utilize threat intelligence to support organizational security.

✓ **Domain 3.0: Security Operations and Monitoring**

- 3.3: Explain the importance of proactive threat hunting.

Security professionals of all types need to fully understand threats in order to prevent them or limit their impact. In order to do this, you need threat intelligence: data about your adversaries, their motivations, capabilities, tools, and methodologies. In addition, you need information about what to look for when your adversaries succeed.

Threat intelligence gathering relies on real-world information gathering, evidence collection, and analysis. Threat intelligence can be categorized into three levels of intelligence. The first is strategic intelligence, which provides broad information about threats and threat actors allowing organizations to understand and respond to trends. Second, tactical threat intelligence includes more detailed technical and behavioral information that is directly useful to security professionals and others who are tasked with defense and response. Finally, operational threat intelligence is composed of highly detailed information allowing response to a specific threat and often includes information about where it came from, who created it or how it has changed over time, how it is delivered or how it spreads, what it attempts to do, how to remove it, and how to prevent it.

In this chapter, you will learn about the many types of threat intelligence, including sources and means of assessing the relevance and accuracy of a given threat intelligence source. There is a broad threat intelligence community, and we will discuss sources that you can use in your work. We will also talk about threat classification, threat actors, and attack frameworks to help you as you model and describe threats. Finally, you will learn about how to apply threat intelligence across your organization.

Threat Data and Intelligence

There are many sources of threat intelligence, ranging from open source intelligence that you can gather from publicly available sources to commercial services that provide proprietary or closed source intelligence information. An increasing number of products and services have the ability to consume threat feed data, allowing you to leverage it throughout your infrastructure and systems.

Regardless of their source, threat feeds are intended to provide up-to-date details about threats in a way that your organization can leverage. Threat feeds often include details such as IP addresses, hostnames and domains, email addresses, URLs, file hashes, file paths,

CVE numbers, and other details about a threat. Additional information is often included to help make the information relevant and understandable, including details of what may make your organization a target or vulnerable to the threat, descriptions of threat actors, and even details of their motivations and methodologies.

Open Source Intelligence

Open source threat intelligence is threat intelligence that is acquired from publicly available sources. Many organizations have recognized how useful open sharing of threat information can be, and open source threat intelligence has become broadly available. In fact, now the challenge is often around deciding what threat intelligence sources to use, ensuring that they are reliable and up-to-date, and leveraging them well.

A number of sites maintain extensive lists of open source threat information sources:

- Senki.org provides a list: `www.senki.org/operators-security-toolkit/open-source-threat-intelligence-feeds/`
- The Open Threat Exchange operated by AlienVault is part of a global community of security professionals and threat researchers: `www.alienvault.com/open-threat-exchange`
- The MISP Threat Sharing project provides standardized threat feeds from many sources: `www.misp-project.org/feeds/`, with community-driven collections.
- Threatfeeds.io hosts a list of open source threat intelligence feeds with details of when they were added and modified, who maintains them, and other useful information: `threatfeeds.io`

In addition to open source and community threat data sources, there are many government and public sources of threat intelligence data. For example, Figure 2.1 shows a recent alert listing from the CISA website.

Government sites:

- The U.S. Cybersecurity and Infrastructure Security Agency (CISA) site: `www.us-cert.gov`
- The U.S. Department of Defense Cyber Crime Center site: `www.dc3.mil`
- The CISA's Automated Indicator Sharing (AIS) program, `www.dhs.gov/cisa/automated-indicator-sharing-ais`, and their Information Sharing and Analysis Organizations program, `www.dhs.gov/cisa/information-sharing-and-analysis-organizations-isaos`

Vendor websites:

- Microsoft's threat intelligence blog: `www.microsoft.com/security/blog/tag/threat-intelligence/`

FIGURE 2.1 Recent alert listing from the CISA website

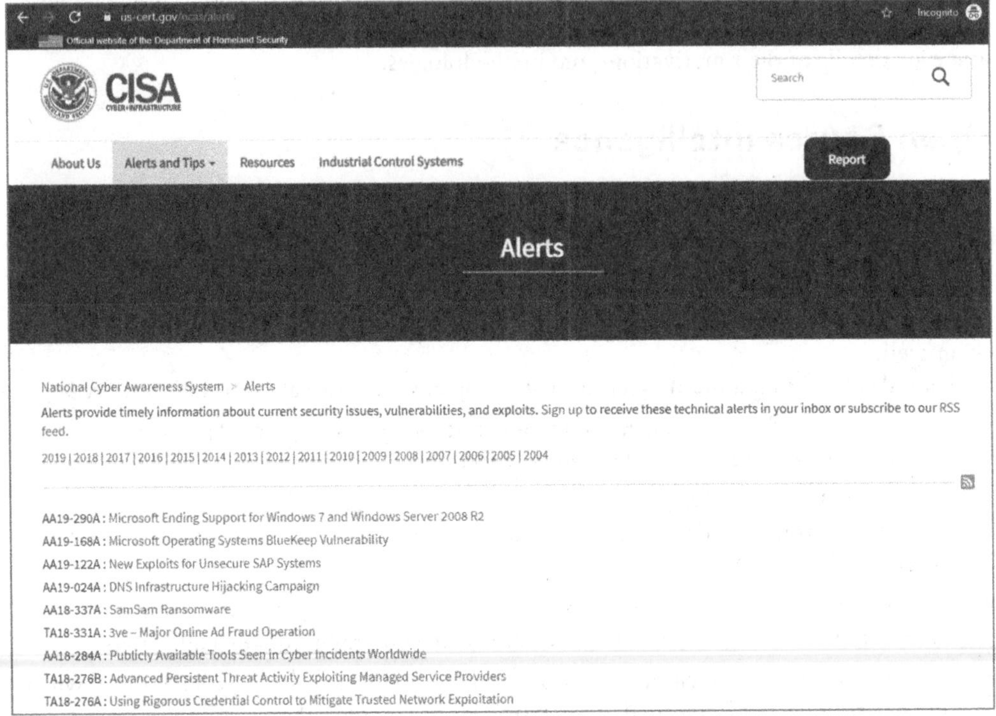

- Cisco's threat security site includes an experts' blog with threat research information, `tools.cisco.com/security/center/home.x`, as well as the Cisco Talos reputation lookup tool, `talosintelligence.com`

Public sources:

- The SANS Internet Storm Center: `isc.sans.org`
- VirusShare contains details about malware uploaded to VirusTotal: `virusshare.com`
- Spamhaus focuses on block lists, including spam via the Spamhaus Block List (SBL), hijacked and compromised computers on the Exploits Block List (XBL), the Policy Block List (PBL), the Don't Route or Peer lists (DROP) listing netblocks that you may not want to allow traffic from, and a variety of other information: `www.spamhaus.org`

Although these are just a small portion of the open source intelligence resources available to security practitioners, they can give you a good idea of what is available.

Many countries provide their own cybersecurity sites, like the Australian Signals Directorate's Cyber Security Centre: `www.cyber.gov.au`. You should become familiar with major intelligence providers, worldwide and for each country you operate in or work with.

Proprietary and Closed Source Intelligence

Commercial security vendors, government organizations, and other security-centric organizations also create and use proprietary, or *closed source, intelligence*. They do their own information gathering and research, and they may use custom tools, analysis models, or other proprietary methods to gather, curate, and maintain their threat feeds.

There are a number of reasons that proprietary threat intelligence may be used. The organization may want to keep their threat data secret, they may want to sell or license it and their methods and sources are their trade secrets, or they may not want to take the chance of the threat actors knowing about the data they are gathering.

Commercial closed source intelligence is often part of a service offering that can be a compelling resource for security professionals. The sheer amount of data available via open source threat intelligence feeds can be overwhelming for many organizations. Combing through threat feeds to identify relevant threats, then ensuring that they are both well defined and applied appropriately for your organization, can require massive amounts of effort. Validating threat data can be difficult in many cases, and once you are done making sure you have high-quality threat data, you still have to do something with it!

When a Threat Feed Fails

The authors of this book learned a lesson about up-to-date threat feeds a number of years ago after working with an IDS and IPS vendor. The vendor promised up-to-date feeds and detects for current issues but tended to run behind other vendors in the marketplace. In one case, a critical Microsoft vulnerability was announced, and exploit code was available and in active use within less than 48 hours. Despite repeated queries, the vendor did not provide detection rules for over two weeks. Unfortunately, manual creation of rules on this vendor's platform did not work well, resulting in exposure of systems that should have been protected.

It is critical that you have reliable, up-to-date feeds to avoid situations like this. You may want to have multiple feeds that you can check against each other—often one feed may be faster or release information sooner, so multiple good-quality, reliable feeds can be a big help.

Assessing Threat Intelligence

Regardless of the source of your threat intelligence information, you need to assess it. A number of common factors come into play when you assess a threat intelligence source or a specific threat intelligence notification:

- Is it timely? A feed that is operating on delay can cause you to miss a threat or to react after the threat is no longer relevant.
- Is the information accurate? Can you rely on what it says, and how likely is it that the assessment is valid? Does it rely on a single source or multiple sources? How often are those sources correct?

- Is the information relevant? If it describes the wrong platform, software, or reason for the organization to be targeted, the data may be very timely, very accurate, and completely irrelevant to your organization.

The CySA+ exam objectives call out timeliness, relevancy, and accuracy of intelligence sources, so you should be prepared to assess threat intelligence based on those factors as well as to explain why they are important.

One way to summarize the threat intelligence assessment data is via a confidence score. Confidence scores allow organizations to filter and use threat intelligence based on how much trust they can give it. That doesn't mean that lower confidence information isn't useful; in fact, a lot of threat intelligence starts with a lower confidence score and that score increases as the information solidifies and as additional sources of information confirm it or are able to do a full analysis. Low confidence threat information shouldn't be completely ignored, but it also shouldn't be relied on to make important decisions without taking the low confidence score into account.

Assessing the Confidence Level of Your Intelligence

Many threat feeds will include a confidence rating, along with a descriptive scale. For example, ThreatConnect uses six levels of confidence:

- Confirmed (90–100) uses independent sources or direct analysis to prove that the threat is real.
- Probable (70–89) relies on logical inference but does not directly confirm the threat.
- Possible (50–69) is used when some information agrees with the analysis, but the assessment is not confirmed and is somewhat logical to infer from the given data.
- Doubtful (30–49) is assigned when the assessment is possible but not the most likely option, or the assessment cannot be proven or disproven by the information that is available.
- Improbable (2–29) means that the assessment is possible but is not the most logical option, or it is refuted by other information that is available.
- Discredited (1) is used when the assessment has been confirmed to be inaccurate or incorrect.

You can read through all of ThreatConnect's rating system at `threatconnect.com/blog/best-practices-indicator-rating-and-confidence/`.

Your organization may use a different scale: 1–5, 1–10, and High/Medium/Low scales are all commonly used to allow threat intelligence users to quickly assess the quality of the assessment and its underlying data.

Threat Indicator Management and Exchange

Managing threat information at any scale requires standardization and tooling to allow the threat information to be processed and used in automated ways. Indicator management can be much easier with a defined set of terms. That's where structured markup languages like STIX and OpenIOC come in.

Structured Threat Information Expression (STIX) is an XML language originally sponsored by the U.S. Department of Homeland Security. STIX 2.0 (its current version as of this writing) defines 12 STIX domain objects, including things like attack patterns, identities, malware, threat actors, and tools. These objects are then related to each other by one of two STIX relationship object models: either as a relationship or as a sighting. A STIX 2.0 JSON description of a threat actor might read

```
{
  "type": "threat-actor",
  "created": "2019-10-20T19:17:05.000Z",
  "modified": "2019-10-21T12:22:20.000Z",
  "labels": [ "crime-syndicate"],
  "name": "Evil Maid, Inc",
  "description": "Threat actors with access to hotel rooms",
  "aliases": ["Local USB threats"],
  "goals": ["Gain physical access to devices", "Acquire data"],
  "sophistication": "intermediate",
  "resource_level": "government",
  "primary_motivation": "organizational-gain"
}
```

Fields like `sophistication` and `resource_level` use defined vocabulary options to allow STIX 2.0 users to consistently use the data as part of automated and manual systems.

Using a single threat feed can leave you in the dark! Many organizations leverage multiple threat feeds to get the most up-to-date information. Thread feed combination can also be challenging since they may not use the same format, classification model, or other elements. You can work around this by finding sources that already combine multiple feeds, or by finding feeds that use the same description frameworks like STIX.

Since its creation, STIX has been handed off to OASIS (the Organization for the Advancement of Structured Information Standards), an international nonprofit consortium that maintains many other projects related to information formatting, including XML and HTML.

A companion to STIX is the *Trusted Automated Exchange of Indicator Information (TAXII)* protocol. TAXII is intended to allow cyberthreat information to be communicated at the application layer via HTTPS. TAXII is specifically designed to support STIX data exchange. You can read more about both STIX and TAXII in detail at the OASIS GitHub documentation site: `oasis-open.github.io/cti-documentation/`.

Another option is the *Open Indicators of Compromise (OpenIOC)* format. Like STIX, OpenIOC is an XML-based framework. The OpenIOC schema was developed by Mandiant, and it uses Mandiant's indicators for its base framework. A typical IOC includes metadata like the author, the name of the IOC, and a description; references to the investigation or case and information about the maturity of the IOC; and the definition for the indicator of compromise, which may include details of the actual compromise.

The Intelligence Cycle

Using threat intelligence well requires planning and forethought. Thus, many organizations adopt a threat intelligence life cycle, as shown in Figure 2.2.

FIGURE 2.2 The threat intelligence cycle

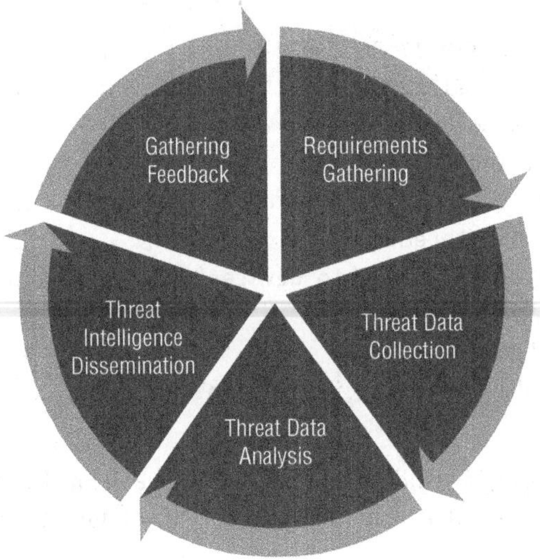

Exam Note

The CySA+ exam objectives call out the Intelligence cycle with five major components: requirements, collection, analysis, dissemination, and feedback. As you read this section, think about how you would answer questions related to each of those requirements.

Planning Threat Intelligence: Requirements Gathering

The first phase in the intelligence cycle is to plan for your intelligence requirements. Your requirements may be created as a result of successful breaches and compromises, industry trends, or risk assessments conducted for your organization. In this step you will typically do the following:

- Assess what security breaches or compromises you have faced

- Assess what information could have prevented or limited the impact of the breach
- Assess what controls and security measures were not in place that would have mitigated the breach

Data Collection

Once you have your information requirements, you can collect data from threat intelligence sources to meet those requirements. This phase may repeat as additional requirements are added or as requirements are refined based on available data and data sources.

Data Processing and Analysis

The threat intelligence data that you gathered in the data collection stage will likely be in several different formats. Some may be in easy-to-access formats that your existing tools and systems can consume. Other data may be in plain-text or written form, or it may be almost entirely unformatted. In this stage you must first process the data to allow it to be consumed by whatever tools or processes you intend to use, and then you must analyze the data itself. The output from this stage could be data fed into automated systems or other tools, or written reports to distribute to leadership or others across your organization.

Intelligence Dissemination

In the dissemination phase of the intelligence cycle, data is distributed to leadership and operational personnel who will use the data as part of their security operations role.

Feedback

The final stage in the threat intelligence cycle is gathering feedback about the reports and data you have gathered. Continuous improvement is a critical element in the process, and it should be used to create better requirements and to improve the overall output of your threat intelligence program.

The Threat Intelligence Community

In addition to threat intelligence vendors and resources, threat intelligence communities have been created to share threat information. In the United States, organizations known as Information Sharing and Analysis Centers (ISACs) help infrastructure owners and operators share threat information, as well as provide tools and assistance to their members. The National Council of ISACs lists the sector-based ISACs at `www.nationalisacs.org/member-isacs`.

The ISAC concept was introduced in 1998 as part of Presidential Decision Directive-63 (PDD-63), which asked critical infrastructure sectors to establish organizations to share information about threats and vulnerabilities. ISACs operate on a trust model, allowing in-depth sharing of threat information for both physical and cyber threats. Most ISACs operate 24/7, providing ISAC members in their sector with incident response and threat analysis.

Exam Note

The CySA+ exam objectives specifically mention three areas in this information sharing grouping: healthcare, financial services, and aviation. There are actually 25 organizations currently in the national council of ISACs, which means there is a good chance your industry may have an ISAC that covers it. You can find specific information about the three ISACs that the exam objectives mention at these sites:

- The healthcare ISAC, H-ISAC: `h-isac.org`
- The financial services ISAC: `fsisac.com`
- The aviation ISAC: `a-isac.com`

In addition to ISACs, there are specific U.S. agencies or department partners for each critical infrastructure area. A list breaking them down by sector can be found here: `www.dhs.gov/cisa/critical-infrastructure-sectors`.

Outside the United States, government bodies and agencies with similar responsibilities exist in many countries. The UK's Centre for Protection of National Infrastructure (`www.cpni.gov.uk`) is tasked with providing threat information as well as resources and guidance to industry and academia, as well as other parts of the government and law enforcement.

Threat Classification

Once you decide to assess the threats to your organization, you will quickly find that you need standard ways to describe them. Fortunately, there are a number of common descriptive schemes and terms used across the industry. Many organizations seek to describe both the threat actors and to classify the threats that they face to better understand the threats themselves.

Threat Actors

The CySA+ exam objectives specifically call out four common threat actors:

- **Nation-state** actors often have the most access to resources, including tools, talent, equipment, and time. Nation-state threat actors have the resources of a country behind them, and their goals are typically those of the country they are sponsored by. Nation-state actors are often associated with advanced persistent threat (APT) organizations, and they have advanced tools and capabilities not commonly seen in the hands of other threat actors.
- **Organized crime** has played a significant role as a threat actor, with focused attacks typically aimed at financial gain. Ransomware attacks are an increasingly common example of this type of threat from organized crime groups.

Exam Note

The CySA+ exam objectives mention *commodity malware*, and organized crime is a major source of it. Commodity malware is malware that is written and then sold on the open (or black) market. Some is sold as part of a toolkit, whereas other commodity malware is sold as stand-alone tools.

- **Hacktivists** are activists who use hacking as a means to a political or philosophical end. Hacktivists range from individual actors to large groups like Anonymous, and their technical capabilities and resources can vary greatly. When you are assessing threats from hacktivists, you need to carefully consider what types of hacktivists are most likely to target your organization and why.
- **Insider threats** are threats from employees or other trusted individuals or groups inside an organization. They may be intentional or unintentional, but in either case, they can pose a significant threat due to the trusted position they have. Insider threats are frequently considered to be one of the most likely causes of breaches and are often difficult to detect.

Exam Note

The CySA+ exam objectives break insider threats into two categories: intentional and unintentional. Make sure that you take that difference into account when you answer questions about insider threats on the exam.

Your organization may want to consider other specific threat actors based on your threat models and profile, so you should not consider this a complete list. You should conduct an organizational threat assessment to determine what types of threat actors are most likely to target your organization and why.

Threat Classification

Although there are many ways to classify threats, common classifications include differentiating between known threats, which you are aware of and are likely to have useful information about, and unknown threats, which you can prepare for only through use of general controls and processes. Zero-day threats, or threats that exploit an unknown security vulnerability, are one of the most common types of unknown threats.

Advanced persistent threat actors, particularly those with nation-state resources, commonly acquire zero-day exploit information and leverage it to their advantage.

Classifying Threats with STRIDE

Microsoft's STRIDE classification model is one method you can use to classify threats based on what they leverage. STRIDE stands for

Spoofing of user identity

Tampering

Repudiation

Information disclosure

Denial of service

Elevation of privilege

Other models include PASTA (Process for Attack Simulation and Threat Analysis), LINDDUN, CVSS (which we discuss in Chapter 5, "Analyzing Vulnerability Scans"), and techniques like using attack trees, security cards, and others.

A classification tool provides two major benefits. First, it allows you to use a common framework to describe threats, allowing others to contribute and manage threat information. Second, models serve as a reminder of the types of threats that exist and can help analysts and security practitioners perform better threat analysis by giving them a list of potential threat options.

Threat Research and Modeling

Organizations actively seek to understand the threats that they are likely to face by conducting threat modeling activities. Threat modeling takes many factors into account, but common elements include the following:

- Assessing *adversary capability*, or the resources, intent, and ability of the likely threat actor or organization.
- The total *attack surface* of the organization you are assessing. This means any system, device, network, application, staff member, or other target that a threat may target.
- Listing possible *attack vectors*, the means by which attackers can gain access to their targets.
- The impact if the attack was successful.
- The likelihood of the attack or threat succeeding.

All of these items can be scored to help assess organizational risk, as well as to help the organization understand the threats it faces.

Once an organization has established a threat model, or has made it part of their threat modeling activities, they will conduct threat research. There are a number of types of threat research that you or your organization may choose to conduct. You may look at the reputation of a site, netblock, or actor to determine whether they have a history or habit of malicious behavior. This is called *threat reputation*, and it is most often paired with IP addresses or domains, but file reputation services and data feeds also exist, as well as other reputation-based tools.

You can see an example of this done via Cisco's Talos Intelligence reputation lookup tools found at `talosintelligence.com/reputation_center` and shown in Figure 2.3. Note that you can see the host's owner and DNS information, as well as email reputation, web reputation, how much spam email it is sending, and if it is on blacklists. In some cases, you may also get information about the content.

FIGURE 2.3 A Talos reputation report for a single host

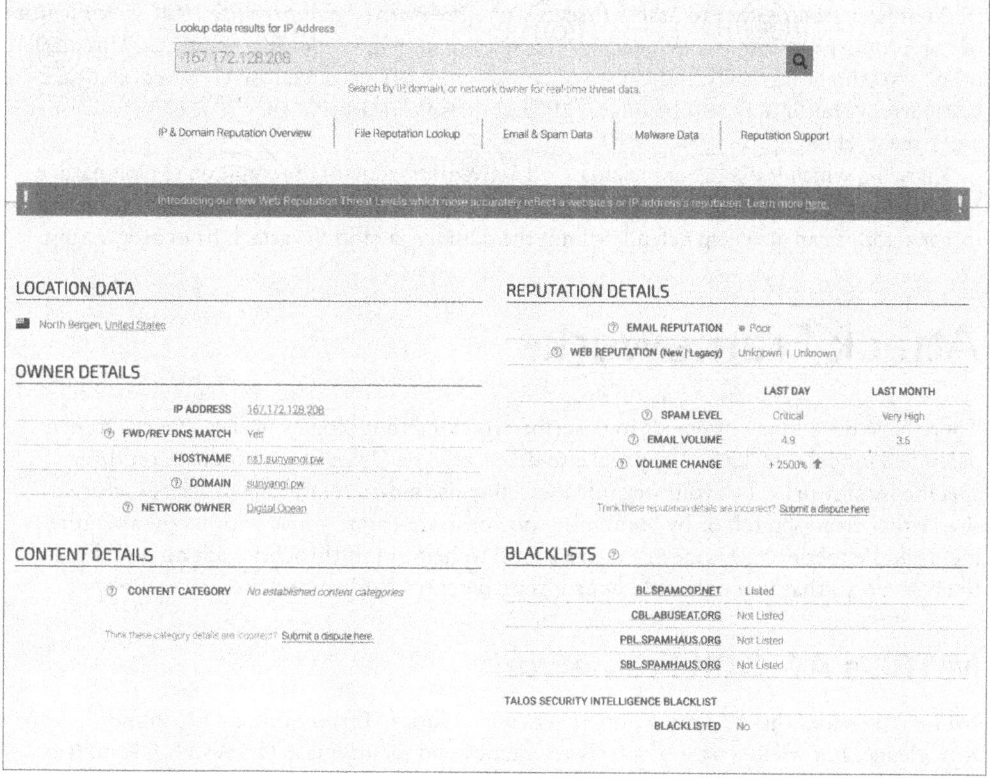

Exam Note

Although the CySA+ exam lists "reputational" as a type of threat research, you're more likely to run into the term in use when describing the impact or damage that a threat can cause. Reputational damage, sometimes called brand damage, is a major concern for many organizations. Thus, if you search for "threat" and "reputational" you won't find a lot about reputational threat research, but you will find a lot about reputational damage.

In addition to reputation research, behavioral assessments are often used to assess a threat. Monitoring for behaviors like those listed in the ATT&CK framework can provide the basis for threat identification and incident response.

Behavioral assessments are particularly useful for insider threats because insider threat behavior is often difficult to distinguish from job- or role-related work. Detecting internal threat behaviors relies heavily on the context of the actions that were performed; a broad view of the insider's actions across all the systems, applications, and networks they interact with; and the availability to provide insight over time. Many insider attacks rely on privileged account abuse, leveraging access to sensitive information, and use of shared passwords. They also often occur outside of normal hours or may require more time, making it possible to identify them through these differences in behavior.

Another measure used to assess threats are *indicators of compromise (IOCs)*. Indicators of compromise are forensic evidence or data that can help to identify an attack. Unlike the other assessment methods, indicators of compromise are used exclusively after an attack has started—but it may still be ongoing! That doesn't mean that they're useless for threat assessment, though.

Knowing which IOCs are associated with a given threat actor, or common exploit path, can help defenders take appropriate steps to prevent further compromise and possibly to identify the threat actor. It can also help defenders limit the damage or stop the attack from progressing.

Attack Frameworks

There have been many attempts to describe attack methodologies in frameworks to help defenders model attacks and appropriate defenses. The CySA+ exam focuses on three specific frameworks, but your organization may use a different model or could create its own either from scratch or by combining one or more frameworks with its own requirements and experience. Frameworks are useful to help think through what an attacker is likely to do so that you can build appropriate defenses against attacks.

MITRE's ATT&CK Framework

MITRE provides the *ATT&CK*, or Adversarial Tactics, Techniques, and Common Knowledge, knowledge base of adversary tactics and techniques. The ATT&CK matrices include detailed descriptions, definitions, and examples for the complete threat life cycle, from initial access through execution, persistence, privilege escalation, and exfiltration. At each level, it lists techniques and components, allowing threat assessment modeling to leverage common descriptions and knowledge.

ATT&CK matrices include preattack, enterprise matrices focusing on Windows, macOS, Linux, and cloud computing, as well as iOS and Android mobile platforms. It also includes details of mitigations, threat actor groups, software, and a host of other useful details. All of this adds up to make ATT&CK the most comprehensive freely available database of adversary techniques, tactics, and related information that the authors of this book are aware of.

Figure 2.4 shows an example of an ATT&CK technique definition for attacks against cloud instances via their metadata APIs. It provides an ID number as well as classification details like the tactic, platforms it applies to, what user permissions are required, the data sources it applies to, who contributed it, and the revision level of the specific technique.

FIGURE 2.4 The ATT&CK definition for Cloud Instance Metadata API attacks

Cloud Instance Metadata API

Adversaries may attempt to access the Cloud Instance Metadata API to collect credentials and other sensitive data.

Most cloud service providers support a Cloud Instance Metadata API which is a service provided to running virtual instances that allows applications to access information about the running virtual instance. Available information generally includes name, security group, and additional metadata including sensitive data such as credentials and UserData scripts that may contain additional secrets. The Instance Metadata API is provided as a convenience to assist in managing applications and is accessible by anyone who can access the instance.[1]

If adversaries have a presence on the running virtual instance, they may query the Instance Metadata API directly to identify credentials that grant access to additional resources. Additionally, attackers may exploit a Server-Side Request Forgery (SSRF) vulnerability in a public facing web proxy that allows the attacker to gain access to the sensitive information via a request to the Instance Metadata API.[2]

The de facto standard across cloud service providers is to host the Instance Metadata API at `http[:]//169.254.169.254`.

ID: T1522

Tactic: Credential Access

Platform: AWS, GCP, Azure

Permissions Required: User

Data Sources: Azure activity logs, AWS CloudTrail logs, Authentication logs

Contributors: Praetorian

Version: 1.0

Mitigations

Mitigation	Description
Filter Network Traffic	Limit access to the Instance Metadata API using a host-based firewall such as iptables. A properly configured Web Application Firewall (WAF) may help prevent external adversaries from exploiting Server-side Request Forgery (SSRF) attacks that allow access to the Cloud Instance Metadata API. [2]

Detection

- Monitor access to the Instance Metadata API and look for anomalous queries.
- It may be possible to detect adversary use of credentials they have obtained. See Valid Accounts for more information.

References

1. AWS. (n.d.). Instance Metadata and User Data. Retrieved July 18, 2019.
2. Higashi, Michael. (2018, May 15). Instance Metadata API: A Modern Day Trojan Horse. Retrieved July 16, 2019.

The October 2019 update for ATT&CK added cloud-focused techniques ranging from the use of application access tokens to unused cloud region exploits. ATT&CK's inclusion of these detailed techniques makes ATT&CK particularly useful for detailed threat analysis of cloud environments.

In addition to the ATT&CK website and materials, a variety of third-party projects leverage ATT&CK to build playbooks, tools, and even commercial software. You can find the ATT&CK website at `attack.mitre.org`.

The Diamond Model of Intrusion Analysis

The *Diamond Model of Intrusion Analysis* describes a sequence where an adversary deploys a capability targeted at an infrastructure against a victim. In this model, activities are called events, and analysts label the vertices as events that are detected or discovered. The model is intended to help analysts discover more information by highlighting the relationship between elements by following the edges between the events.

The Diamond Model uses a number of specific terms:

- *Core Features* of an event, which are the adversary, capability, infrastructure, and victim (the vertices of the diamond).
- The *Meta-Features*, which are start and end timestamps, phase, result, direction, methodology, and resources. These are used to order events in a sequence known as an activity thread, as well as for grouping events based on their features.
- A *Confidence Value*, which is undefined by the model, but which analysts are expected to determine based on their own work.

Figure 2.5 shows an example of an analysis conducted for a compromised system. Note that each element helps to identify additional information or areas to review.

FIGURE 2.5 A Diamond Model analysis of a compromised system

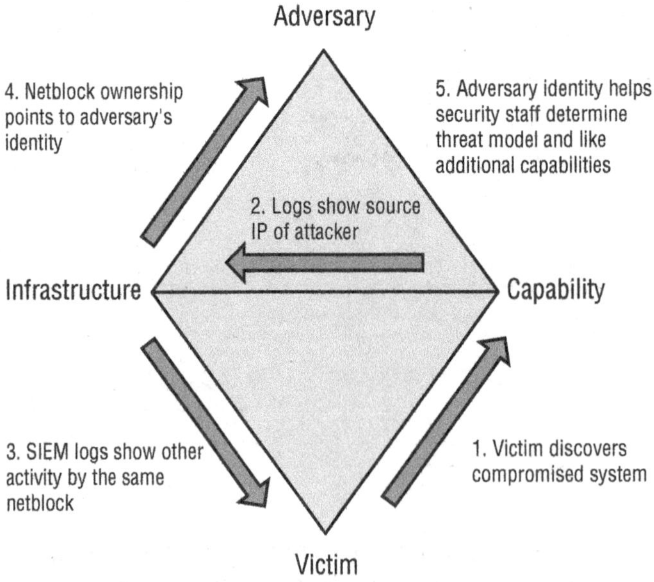

The Diamond Model focuses heavily on understanding the attacker and their motivations, and then uses relationships between these elements to allow security analysts to both understand the threat and consider what other data or information they may need to obtain or may already have available.

You can read the full text of the Diamond Model paper at `apps.dtic.mil/dtic/tr/fulltext/u2/a586960.pdf`.

Lockheed Martin's Cyber Kill Chain

Lockheed Martin's *Cyber Kill Chain* is a seven-stage process, as shown in Figure 2.6.

FIGURE 2.6 The Cyber Kill Chain.

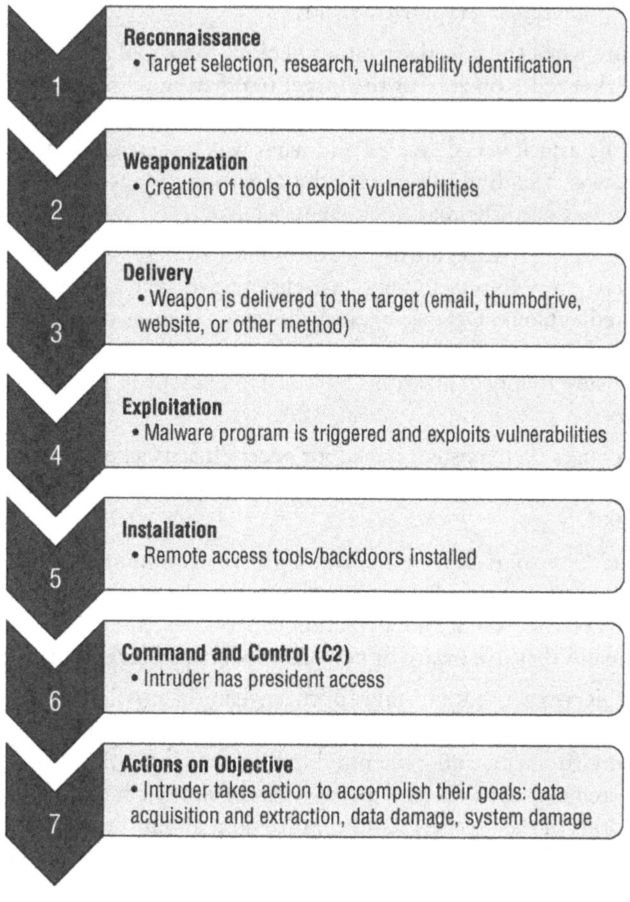

The seven stages are as follows:

1. **Reconnaissance**, which identifies targets. In this phase, adversaries are planning their attacks and will gather intelligence about the target, including both open source intelligence and direct acquisition of target data via scanning. Defenders must gather data about reconnaissance activities and prioritize defenses based on that information.
2. **Weaponization** involves building or otherwise acquiring a weaponizer that combines malware and an exploit into a payload that can be delivered to the target. This may require creating decoy documents, choosing the right command-and-control tool, and other details. The model emphasizes the fact that defenders need to conduct full malware analysis in this stage to understand not only what payload is dropped but how the weaponized exploit was made. Defenders should also build detections for weaponizers, look at the timeline of when malware was created versus its use, and collect both files and metadata to help them see if the tools are widely shared or closely held and thus potentially very narrowly targeted.
3. **Delivery** occurs when the adversary either deploys their tool directly against targets or via release that relies on staff at the target interacting with it such as in an email payload, on a USB stick, or via websites that they visit. Defenders in this stage must observe how the attack was delivered and what was targeted, and then will infer what the adversary was intending to accomplish. Retention of logs is also important in this stage, as defenders need them to track what occurred.
4. **Exploitation** uses a software, hardware, or human vulnerability to gain access. This can involve zero-day exploits and may use either adversary-triggered exploits or victim-triggered exploits. Defense against this stage focuses on user awareness, secure coding, vulnerability scanning, penetration testing, endpoint hardening, and similar activities to ensure that organizations have a strong security posture and very limited attack surface.
5. **Installation** focuses on persistent backdoor access for attackers. Defenders must monitor for typical artifacts of a persistent remote shell or other remote access methodologies.
6. **Command and Control** (C2) access allows two-way communication and continued control of the remote system. Defenders will seek to detect the C2 infrastructure by hardening the network, deploying detection capabilities, and conducting ongoing research to ensure they are aware of new C2 models and technology.
7. **Actions on Objectives**, the final stage, occurs when the mission's goal is achieved. Adversaries will collect credentials, escalate privileges, pivot and move laterally through the environment, and gather and exfiltrate information. They may also cause damage to systems or data. Defenders must establish their incident response playbook, detect the actions of the attackers and capture data about them, respond to alerts, and assess the damage the attackers have caused.

The entire Lockheed Martin Cyber Kill Chain can be found in greater detail at `www.lockheedmartin.com/content/dam/lockheed-martin/rms/documents/cyber/Gaining_the_Advantage_Cyber_Kill_Chain.pdf`.

The Unified Kill Chain

Although the CySA+ exam doesn't specifically mention it, you may find the Unified Kill Chain useful. The Unified Kill Chain combines both Lockheed Martin's Cyber Kill Chain and MITRE's ATT&CK framework (as well as quite a few others!) into a single kill chain model. It uses 18 phases to describe attacks that occur both inside and outside a defended network, addressing complaints about both frameworks. You can read Paul Pols's 2017 proposal for the Unified Kill Chain at `www.csacademy.nl/images/scripties/2018/Paul_Pols_-_The_Unified_Kill_Chain_1.pdf`.

Assessing Attack Frameworks

Before you adopt a conceptual model for attacks, you should read up on the commentary about it. For example, Lockheed Martin's Cyber Kill Chain has been criticized for including actions that occur outside of the defended network, since those are outside of the areas that many defenders can take action on. Other criticisms have included commentary about the focus on perimeter and antimalware-based defensive techniques, as well as a lack of focus on insider threats.

As advanced persistent threats and insider threats continue to be major concerns, simply adopting the Cyber Kill Chain model might not serve your organization's needs. Thus, you should carefully consider what model fits the threats you're most likely to encounter, and either select a model that fits or modify an existing model to meet your organization's needs.

Common Vulnerability Scoring System (CVSS)

While you are reviewing threat frameworks, you are likely to encounter the *Common Vulnerability Scoring System (CVSS)*. Although CVSS does not cover threats directly, it is often used to help describe vulnerabilities using a numerical score. You can read about CVSS, how CVSS scoring works, and how to use CVSS as part of your vulnerability assessment program in Chapter 4, "Designing a Vulnerability Management Program."

Applying Threat Intelligence Organizationwide

Building a comprehensive threat intelligence function requires multiple parts of an organization to work together. Security practitioners, system administrators, auditors, and others need to share data to identify threats, monitor for them, detect them using known activities and fingerprints, then respond to them, and finally use the information you have gained to prepare for future threats.

Threat intelligence should be shared to ensure that incident response, vulnerability management, risk management, and security engineering functions understand the likely threat actors, capabilities, and indicators of compromise you will face.

Proactive Threat Hunting

Searching for threats proactively rather than reactively can help you stay ahead of attackers. Proactive threat hunting is often triggered by new data or tools that inspire threat analysts or security professionals to establish a hypothesis about a new threat, a new threat actor, or a new type of threat.

Once you have a hypothesis, the next step is to investigate the threat. The analytical frameworks we discussed earlier in this chapter can provide a foundation that will allow you to profile threat actors, to analyze malware or other tools by doing things like executable process analysis or reverse engineering, or to otherwise investigate the new threat.

If a new threat is discovered, then some form of action is typically undertaken to counter the threat. You might identify a way to reduce your organization's attack surface area, or you might find other ways to reduce the number of attack vectors available to attackers based on your threat analysis.

Keys to this type of proactive activity are the use of integrated intelligence feeds from multiple sources, and improving your organization's detection capabilities so that you can identity threats before they become a serious issue.

The CySA+ exam groups proactive threat hunting activities into a few bullets:

- Establishing a hypothesis. A hypothesis is needed to test and should have actionable results based on the threat that the hypothesis considers.
- Profiling threat actors and activities. This helps ensure that you have considered who may be a threat, and why, as well as what their typical actions and processes are.
- Threat hunting tactics. These are key to success in threat hunting activities. The skills, techniques, and procedures are where action meets analysis. This step includes executable process analysis, which the CySA+ exam outline specifically mentions.
- Reducing the attack surface area. This allows resources to be focused on the remaining surface area, making protection more manageable.
- Bundling critical assets into groups and protection zones. This helps with managing attack surface area, threat hunting, and response activities, since each asset doesn't need to be individually assessed or managed as a unique item.
- Attack vectors must be understood, assessed, and addressed based on analysis of threat actors and their techniques as well as the surface area that threat actors can target.
- Integrated intelligence combines multiple intelligence sources to provide a better view of threats.

- Improving detection capabilities. This is a continuous process as threats improve their techniques and technology. If you do not improve your detection capabilities, new threats will bypass existing capabilities over time.

As you prepare for the exam, make sure you consider how each of these plays a role in proactive threat hunting activities and what impact they would have in your organization.

Exam Note

Objective 3.3 of the CySA+ exam objectives specifically asks test takers to be prepared to explain the importance of proactive threat hunting. You should bear in mind that staying ahead of advanced adversaries can be extremely difficult, but that continually updating and advancing your security posture by leveraging a mature threat modeling and analysis function is a great way to reduce your organization's overall risk of compromise.

Summary

Understanding the threats that your organization faces is a critical part of your security program and operations. In order to understand those threats, security professionals gather threat intelligence composed of data about your adversaries, their motivations, capabilities, tools, and methodologies.

Open source threat intelligence is acquired from publicly available sources, and closed source threat intelligence is from commercial or other sources that do not make their data available to the public. Both are used by many organizations as part of their threat intelligence efforts. Many open source threat intelligence sources exist, including government sponsored feeds and sites, professional organizations, vendor resources, social media, and even information from individuals.

A source of threat intelligence needs to be assessed, and the level of confidence you have in the data is important to know before you take actions based on it. Threat information also needs to be managed, and standardized formats and languages for describing threat information exist to help make threat information more usable. STIX, ATT&CK, and other tools help to standardize threat information. They also help to classify threats using common terms like nation-state actors and adversary capabilities.

Threat information gathering can be described as a cycle, with requirements gathering, threat data collection, threat data analysis, threat intelligence dissemination or sharing, and feedback and improvement stages all part of the typical threat information process.

Analyzing threats can also be aided by using a framework, and ATT&CK, the Diamond Model, and the Cyber Kill Chain are all common tools intended to assist in threat analysis. Each has advantages and disadvantages, and you should review them carefully to determine whether one is a better fit to your needs than the others.

Once you have built a threat intelligence function, you need to use and maintain it, and that is where organizationwide use of threat intelligence can come in. Many areas within an organization may have a use for threat data or can contribute to the threat intelligence gathering process. That data can be used for proactive threat hunting to identify threats before they successfully complete an attack or exploit.

Exam Essentials

Understand what drives intelligence source choices. Both open source and closed source or proprietary threat intelligence sources are available, and matching your needs to the right resources is important for threat intelligence programs. Intelligence sharing communities can provide threat data specifically targeted at industries or professional groups. Assessing intelligence sources based on their timeliness, how relevant the data is to your needs, and how accurate they are will help guide your choices of which datasets to use and how much you can rely on them.

Know the standards for indicator management that make intelligence data more useful. Using standardized languages like STIX and interchange protocols like TAXII allows threat intelligence information exchange and management. Describing indicators of compromise using OpenIOC provides organizations with a framework to agree on ratings for threats and events and communicate details of compromise in a known and well-defined format.

Describe threats using classification standards and common terms. Threats are often classified using a few common terms; known versus unknown threats, zero-day exploits, and advanced persistent threats are all commonly used. In addition, threats may be described by the threat actor, with nation-states, hacktivists, organized crime, and both intentional and unintentional insiders frequently identified as threat actors by organizations conducting threat intelligence and analysis activities.

Know that the threat intelligence cycle is ongoing. The threat intelligence cycle from requirements to collection of data, analysis, communication and dissemination, and gathering feedback ensures that threat intelligence does not grow stale and that threat data is consistently and continuously updated.

Be able to describe threats and attacks using frameworks and model them using analysis techniques. Frameworks like the Diamond Model, the MITRE ATT&CK framework, and Lockheed Martin's Cyber Kill Chain all provide ways to assess and describe threats. Using a threat model can help to more fully understand a threat by identifying gaps. Tools like ATT&CK also provide a broad standard taxonomy for threats that allow you to use the data in tools compatible with the framework.

Know that the ongoing process of threat management and intelligence sharing should occur organizationwide. The security processes and functions that an organization uses can benefit from threat intelligence. Threat intelligence has a major role to play in risk assessment, as it can influence the probability and impact assessment as well as provide useful information about risks due to specific threat actors. Proactive threat hunting, from forming a hypothesis, to taking actions such as reducing the organization's attack surface, is a critical part of threat intelligence and management activities. Detection and monitoring systems can more accurately detect attacks if they have good threat intelligence, and vulnerability management, incident response, and security engineering all benefit from ongoing sharing of threat details.

Lab Exercises

Activity 2.1: Explore the ATT&CK Framework

In this exercise, you will use the ATT&CK framework to analyze a threat. You may want to select a recent compromise that you have seen in the news, or one that has impacted an organization that you have worked with. If nothing comes to mind, the 2019 Capital One data breach offers a useful example, and you can find details of the exploit in multiple places with a quick search.

You may wonder why we aren't giving you details or a link to a specific article. That's part of the exercise! Threat intelligence requires the ability to find and combine data to perform the analysis. The best articles for this will provide details of how the systems were accessed and how data was exfiltrated, or similar elements.

Part 1: Build a threat profile

1. List what you know about the compromise or exploit, including details about the threat actor, what occurred, what tools were used, and as many other details as you can find.
2. Review your list against the headings for the appropriate ATT&CK matrix. Do you have items that match the headings?
3. If you still lack data, you should continue your search or find another example to work through!

Part 2: Analysis

Now that you have your basic profile, follow the detailed listings in the matrix to match up the threat to its ATT&CK techniques, threat actors, and other details.

1. Match each data point to the appropriate ATT&CK entry.
2. Review the details of each entry so that you become familiar with them.
3. Identify gaps in your knowledge. What information would you look for if you were researching this threat? What information do you think you could reasonably obtain, and what might you be unable to gather?

4. Consider what your report to leadership would contain based on what you have found. What would you include for a technical group, and what would you include for senior leaders like a CIO or CEO?

Activity 2.2: Set Up a STIX/TAXII Feed

Anomali's STAXX community version provides an easy way to consume STIX feeds. In this exercise, you will download and install the STAXX client, and then review the data from one of the included feeds.

1. Visit `www.anomali.com/community/staxx` and download the STAXX Community edition software. STAXX is a 1 GB download and requires an email to get the download link.
2. Install the STAXX client. You will need a virtualization environment like VirtualBox or VMWare to open the OVA file. Follow the Anomali setup and installation guide at `update.anomali.com/staxx/docs/Anomali_STAXX_Installation_&_Administration_Guide.pdf`.

   This guide will help you get Anomali set up. When you connect to the web interface, you will need to accept the insecure connection on most major browsers.
3. When asked, use the Anomali Limo service to gather data for your first feeds.
4. Once you are in and Anomali has ingested its feeds, explore the dashboards. What is the most common indicator type? Does it match what you would expect?
5. Advanced: Identify a STIX feed that isn't part of the STAXX default feed list and add it to STAXX.

Activity 2.3: Intelligence Gathering Techniques

Match each of the activities to the phase of the threat intelligence cycle where it fits.

Requirements gathering	Update requirements for your intelligence gathering program
Threat data collection	Provide information about a threat to an IPS administrator
Threat data analysis	Assess missing controls from a recent breach
Threat intelligence dissemination	Download data via STIX
Gathering feedback	Convert manually gathered threat data to STIX format

Review Questions

1. Which of the following measures is not commonly used to assess threat intelligence?
   A. Timeliness
   B. Detail
   C. Accuracy
   D. Relevance
2. What language is STIX based on?
   A. PHP
   B. HTML
   C. XML
   D. Python
3. Which of the following activities follows threat data analysis in the threat intelligence cycle?
   A. Gathering feedback
   B. Threat data collection
   C. Threat data review
   D. Threat intelligence dissemination
4. Susan wants to start performing intelligence gathering. Which of the following options is frequently conducted in the requirements gathering stage?
   A. Review of security breaches or compromises your organization has faced
   B. Review of current vulnerability scans
   C. Review of current data handling standards
   D. A review of threat intelligence feeds for new threats
5. What organizations did the U.S. government help create to help share knowledge between organizations in specific verticals?
   A. DHS
   B. SANS
   C. CERTS
   D. ISACs
6. Which of the following threat actors typically has the greatest access to resources?
   A. Nation-state actors
   B. Organized crime
   C. Hacktivists
   D. Insider threats

7. Organizations like Anonymous, which target governments and businesses for political reasons, are examples of what type of threat actor?
   - A. Hacktivists
   - B. Military assets
   - C. Nation-state actors
   - D. Organized crime

8. Jason gathers threat intelligence that tells him that an adversary his organization considers a threat likes to use USB key drops to compromise their targets. What is this an example of?
   - A. His organization's attack surface
   - B. A possible attack vector
   - C. An example of adversary capability
   - D. A probability assessment

9. What type of assessment is particularly useful for identifying insider threats?
   - A. Behavioral
   - B. Instinctual
   - C. Habitual
   - D. IOCs

10. Cyn wants to send threat information via a standardized protocol specifically designed to exchange cyberthreat information. What should she choose?
    - A. STIX 1.0
    - B. OpenIOC
    - C. STIX 2.0
    - D. TAXII

11. What phase of the Cyber Kill Chain includes creation of persistent backdoor access for attackers?
    - A. Delivery
    - B. Exploitation
    - C. Installation
    - D. C2

12. What common criticism is leveled at the Cyber Kill Chain?
    - A. Not all threats are aimed at a kill.
    - B. It is too detailed.
    - C. It includes actions outside the defended network.
    - D. It focuses too much on insider threats.

13. Which of the following is not a common technique used to defend against command and control (C2) capabilities deployed by attackers?
    A. Network hardening
    B. Patching against zero-day attacks
    C. Deploying detection capabilities
    D. Tracking new C2 methods and technology
14. What term describes an analysis of threat information that might include details such as whether it is confirmed by multiple independent sources or has been directly confirmed?
    A. Threat quality level
    B. STIX level
    C. Confidence level
    D. Assurance level
15. What drove the creation of ISACs in the United States?
    A. Threat information sharing for infrastructure owners
    B. The Cybersecurity Act of 1994
    C. Threat information collection network providers
    D. The 1998 ISAC Act
16. STRIDE, PASTA, and LINDDUN are all examples of what?
    A. Zero-day rating systems
    B. Vulnerability assessment tools
    C. Adversary analysis tools
    D. Threat classification tools
17. OpenIOC uses a base set of indicators of compromise originally created and provided by which security company?
    A. Mandiant
    B. McAfee
    C. CrowdStrike
    D. Cisco
18. Advanced persistent threats are most commonly associated with which type of threat actor?
    A. Insider threats
    B. Nation-state actors
    C. Organized crime
    D. Hacktivists

19. Gabby wants to select a threat framework for her organization, and identifying threat actor tactics in a standardized way is an important part of her selection process. Which threat model would be her best choice?

    A. The Diamond Model

    B. ATT&CK

    C. The Cyber Kill Chain

    D. The Universal Threat Model

20. Forensic data is most often used for what type of threat assessment data?

    A. STIX

    B. Behavioral

    C. IOCs

    D. TAXII

Reconnaissance and Intelligence Gathering

THE COMPTIA CYBERSECURITY ANALYST (CYSA+) EXAM OBJECTIVES COVERED IN THIS CHAPTER INCLUDE:

✓ **Domain 1.0: Threat and Vulnerability Management**

- 1.4 Given a scenario, analyze the output from common vulnerability assessment tools.

✓ **Domain 3.0: Security Operations and Monitoring**

- 3.1 Given a scenario, analyze data as part of security monitoring activities.

Security analysts, penetration testing professionals, vulnerability and threat analysts, and others who are tasked with understanding the security environment in which an organization operates need to know how to gather information. This process is called reconnaissance or intelligence gathering.

Information gathering is often a requirement of information security standards and laws. For example, the Payment Card Industry Data Security Standard (PCI DSS) requires that organizations handling credit cards perform both internal and external network vulnerability scans at least quarterly, and after any significant change. Gathering internal and external information about your own organization is typically considered a necessary part of understanding organizational risk, and implementing industry best practices to meet required due diligence requirements is likely to result in this type of work.

In this chapter, you will explore active intelligence gathering, including port scanning tools and how you can determine a network's topology from scan data. Then you will learn about passive intelligence gathering, including tools, techniques, and real-world experiences, to help you understand your organization's footprint. Finally, you will learn how to limit a potential attacker's ability to gather information about your organization using the same techniques.

Mapping and Enumeration

The first step when gathering organizational intelligence is to identify an organization's technical footprint. *Host enumeration* is used to create a map of an organization's networks, systems, and other infrastructure. This is typically accomplished by combining information-gathering tools with manual research to identify the networks and systems that an organization uses.

Standards for penetration testing typically include enumeration and reconnaissance processes and guidelines. There are a number of publicly available resources, including the Open Source Security Testing Methodology Manual (OSSTMM), the Penetration Testing Execution Standard, and National Institute of Standards and Technology (NIST) Special Publication 800-115, the Technical Guide to Information Security Testing and Assessment.

- OSSTMM: `www.isecom.org/research.html`
- Penetration Testing Execution Standard: `www.pentest-standard.org/index.php/Main_Page`
- SP 800-115: `csrc.nist.gov/publications/nistpubs/800-115/SP800-115.pdf`

Active Reconnaissance

Information gathered during enumeration exercises is typically used to provide the targets for *active reconnaissance*. Active reconnaissance uses host scanning tools to gather information about systems, services, and vulnerabilities. It is important to note that although reconnaissance does not involve exploitation, it can provide information about vulnerabilities that can be exploited.

Permission and Executive Support

Scanning a network or systems can cause problems for the devices that are scanned. Some services may not tolerate scan traffic well, whereas others may fill their logs or set off security alarms when scanned. This means you should make sure you have permission from the appropriate authorities in your organization before conducting active reconnaissance. You'll likely hear approvals like this referred to as "Get out of jail free cards," as they help to ensure that you won't get into trouble for the scans. You may still want to touch base with system and network administrators to ensure that the scans don't have an unintended impact.

Scanning systems belonging to others may also be illegal without permission or may be prohibited by the terms of use of your Internet service provider. For example, some cloud computing platforms require users to complete a vulnerability or penetration testing request form before conducting scans using their infrastructure, and both apply limits to the types of systems and services that can be scanned.

Mapping Networks and Discovering Topology

Active scans can also provide information about network design and topology. As a scanning tool traverses a network range, it can assess information contained in the responses it receives. This can help a tester take an educated guess about the topology of the network based on the time to live (TTL) of the packets it receives, traceroute information, and responses from network and security devices. Figure 3.1 shows a scan of a simple example network. Routers or gateways are centrally connected to hosts and allow you to easily see where a group of hosts connect. The system that nmap runs from becomes the center of the initial scan and shows its local loopback address, 127.0.0.1. A number of hosts appear on a second network segment behind the 10.0.2.1 router. Nmap (and Zenmap, using nmap) may not discover all systems and network devices—firewalls or other security devices can stop scan traffic, resulting in missing systems or networks.

FIGURE 3.1 Zenmap topology view

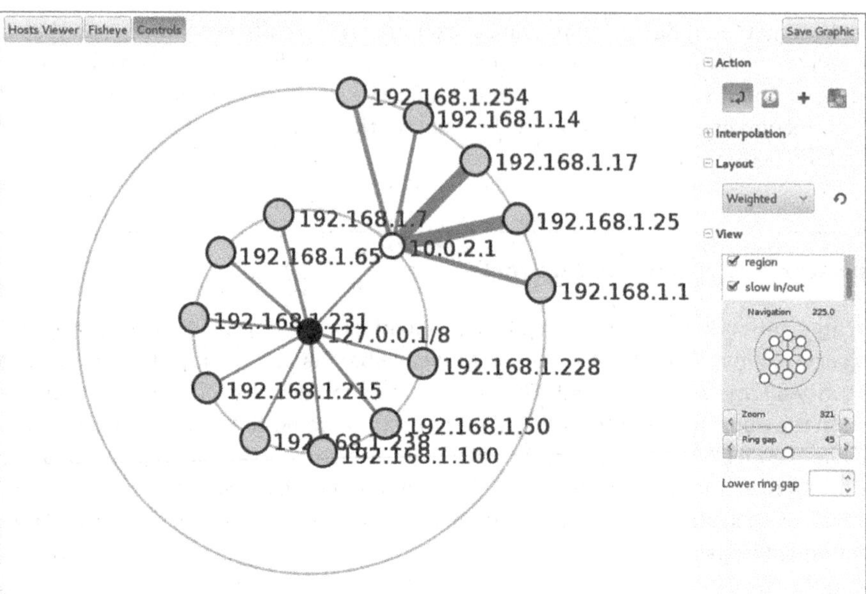

When you are performing network discovery and mapping, it is important to lay out the systems that are discovered based on their network addresses and TTL. These data points can help you assess their relative position in the network. Of course, if you can get actual network diagrams, you will have a much more accurate view of the network design than scans may provide.

The Zenmap graphical user interface to nmap includes a built-in topology discovery tool that provides a visual representation of the scanned network. Remember that this is a best guess and isn't necessarily a perfect match for the actual network.

The topology information gathered by a scanning tool is likely to have flaws and may not match the actual design of the target network. Security and network devices can cause differences in the TTL and traceroute information, resulting in incorrect or missing data. Firewalls can also make devices and systems effectively invisible to scans, resulting in segments of the network not showing up in the topology built from scan results.

In addition to challenges caused by security devices, you may have to account for variables, including differences between wired and wireless networks, virtual networks and virtual environments like VMware and Microsoft Hyper-V, and of course on-premises networks versus cloud-hosted services and infrastructure. If you are scanning networks that you or your organization controls, you should be able to ensure that your scanning systems or devices are placed appropriately to gather the information that you need. If you are scanning as part of a penetration test or a zero-knowledge test, you may need to review your data to ensure that these variables haven't caused you to miss important information.

Mapping and Scanning VMs and the Cloud

Mapping networks, port scanning, service discovery, and many of the other techniques we discuss involve such variables as whether the networks are wired or wireless, whether systems and network devices are virtual or physical, or whether the systems and services are on-premises or in the cloud. This may mean that you need to use a tool that specifically targets wireless networks, or you may need to account for virtual systems that are not visible outside of a virtual host's firewall. You may also have to handle a service differently, such as avoiding scanning a cloud service or system based on contracts or agreements. Remember to document what you know about the networks and systems you are scanning and to consider how these could impact both the data you gather and the techniques you use.

Pinging Hosts

The most basic form of discovery that you can conduct is *pinging* a network address. The `ping` command is a low-level network command that sends a packet called an *echo request* to a remote IP address. If the remote system receives the request, it responds with an *echo reply*, indicating that it is up and running and that the communication path is valid. Ping communications take place using the *Internet Control Message Protocol (ICMP)*.

Here's an example of an echo request sent to a server running on a local network:

```
[~/]$ ping 172.31.48.137
PING 172.31.48.137 (172.31.48.137) 56(84) bytes of data.
64 bytes from 172.31.48.137: icmp_seq=1 ttl=255 time=0.016 ms
64 bytes from 172.31.48.137: icmp_seq=2 ttl=255 time=0.037 ms
64 bytes from 172.31.48.137: icmp_seq=3 ttl=255 time=0.026 ms
64 bytes from 172.31.48.137: icmp_seq=4 ttl=255 time=0.028 ms
64 bytes from 172.31.48.137: icmp_seq=5 ttl=255 time=0.026 ms
64 bytes from 172.31.48.137: icmp_seq=6 ttl=255 time=0.027 ms
64 bytes from 172.31.48.137: icmp_seq=7 ttl=255 time=0.027 ms

--- 172.31.48.137 ping statistics ---
7 packets transmitted, 7 received, 0% packet loss, time 6142ms
rtt min/avg/max/mdev = 0.016/0.026/0.037/0.008 ms
```

In this case, a user used the ping command to query the status of a system located at 172.31.48.137 and received seven replies to the seven requests that were sent.

It's important to recognize that, while an echo reply from a remote host indicates that it is up and running, the lack of a response does not necessarily mean that the remote host is not active. Many firewalls block ping requests and individual systems may be configured to ignore echo request packets.

The hping utility is a more advanced version of the ping command that allows the customization of echo requests in an effort to increase the likelihood of detection. hping can also be used to generate handcrafted packets as part of a penetration test. Here's an example of the hping command in action:

```
[~/]$ hping -p 80 -S 172.31.48.137
HPING 172.31.48.137 (eth0 172.31.48.137): S set, 40 headers + 0 data bytes.
len=44 ip=172.31.48.137 ttl=45 DF id=0 sport=80 flags=SA seq=0 win-29200 rtt=20.0ms
len=44 ip=172.31.48.137 ttl=45 DF id=0 sport=80 flags=SA seq=1 win-29200 rtt=19.7ms
len=44 ip=172.31.48.137 ttl=45 DF id=0 sport=80 flags=SA seq=2 win-29200 rtt=19.8ms
len=44 ip=172.31.48.137 ttl=44 DF id=0 sport=80 flags=SA seq=3 win-29200 rtt=20.1ms
len=44 ip=172.31.48.137 ttl=46 DF id=0 sport=80 flags=SA seq=4 win-29200 rtt=20.2ms
len=44 ip=172.31.48.137 ttl=45 DF id=0 sport=80 flags=SA seq=5 win-29200 rtt=20.5ms
len=44 ip=172.31.48.137 ttl=46 DF id=0 sport=80 flags=SA seq=6 win-29200 rtt=20.2ms
^C
--- 172.31.48.137 hping statistic ---
26 packets transmitted, 26 packets received, 0% packet loss
Round-trip min/avg/max = 19.2/20.0/20.8
```

In this command, the -p 80 flag was used to specify that the probes should take place using TCP port 80. This port is a strong choice because it is used to host web servers. The -S flag indicates that the TCP SYN flag should be set, indicating a request to open a connection. Any remote target running an HTTP web server would be likely to respond to this request because it is indistinguishable from a legitimate web connection request.

The ping command is included by default on all major operating systems. hping, on the other hand, is a separate utility that must be installed. You can download the hping source code from www.hping.org.

Port Scanning and Service Discovery Techniques and Tools

Port scanning tools are designed to send traffic to remote systems and then gather responses that provide information about the systems and the services they provide. They are one of the most frequently used tools when gathering information about a network and the devices that are connected to it. Because of this, port scans are often the first step in an active reconnaissance of an organization.

Port scanners have a number of common features, including the following:

- Host discovery
- Port scanning and service identification
- Service version identification
- Operating system identification

Ports Scanners: A Handy Swiss Army Knife

These capabilities also mean that port scanners are useful for network inventory tasks, security audits to identify new systems and services, and of course testing security devices and systems by sending scanning traffic for them to alert on. Integrating a port scanner into your toolkit (and scripting it!) can be a powerful tool.

An important part of port scanning is an understanding of common ports and services. Ports 0–1023 are referred to as *well-known ports* or *system ports*, but there are quite a few higher ports that are commonly of interest when conducting port scanning. Ports ranging from 1024 to 49151 are *registered ports* and are assigned by the Internet Assigned Numbers Authority (IANA) when requested. Many are also used arbitrarily for services. Since ports can be manually assigned, simply assuming that a service running on a given port matches the common usage isn't always a good idea. In particular, many SSH and HTTP/HTTPS servers are run on alternate ports, either to allow multiple web services to have unique ports or to avoid port scanning that only targets their normal port.

Analysis of scan data can be an art, but basic knowledge of how to read a scan is quite useful since scans can provide information about what hosts are on a network, what services they are running, and clues about whether they are vulnerable to attacks. In Figure 3.2, a vulnerable Linux system with a wide range of services available has been scanned. To read this scan, you can start at the top with the command used to run it. The nmap port scanner (which we will discuss in more depth in a few pages) was run with the `-O` option, resulting in an attempt at operating system identification. The `-P0` flag tells nmap to skip pinging the system before scanning, and the -sS flag performed a TCP SYN scan, which sends connection attempts to each port. Finally, we see the IP address of the remote system. By default, nmap scans 1,000 common ports, and nmap discovered 23 open ports out of that list.

FIGURE 3.2 Nmap scan results

```
root@demo:~# nmap -O -P0 -sS 10.0.2.4

Starting Nmap 7.01 ( https://nmap.org ) at 2016-10-02 12:22 EDT
Nmap scan report for 10.0.2.4
Host is up (0.00017s latency).
Not shown: 977 closed ports
PORT     STATE SERVICE
21/tcp   open  ftp
22/tcp   open  ssh
23/tcp   open  telnet
25/tcp   open  smtp
53/tcp   open  domain
80/tcp   open  http
111/tcp  open  rpcbind
139/tcp  open  netbios-ssn
445/tcp  open  microsoft-ds
512/tcp  open  exec
513/tcp  open  login
514/tcp  open  shell
1099/tcp open  rmiregistry
1524/tcp open  ingreslock
2049/tcp open  nfs
2121/tcp open  ccproxy-ftp
3306/tcp open  mysql
5432/tcp open  postgresql
5900/tcp open  vnc
6000/tcp open  X11
6667/tcp open  irc
8009/tcp open  ajp13
8180/tcp open  unknown
MAC Address: 08:00:27:92:5F:44 (Oracle VirtualBox virtual NIC)
Device type: general purpose
Running: Linux 2.6.X
OS CPE: cpe:/o:linux:linux_kernel:2.6
OS details: Linux 2.6.9 - 2.6.33
Network Distance: 1 hop

OS detection performed. Please report any incorrect results at https://nmap.org/
submit/ .
Nmap done: 1 IP address (1 host up) scanned in 1.77 seconds
```

Next, the scan shows us the ports it found open, whether they are TCP or UDP, their state (which can be open if the service is accessible, closed if it is not, or filtered if there is a firewall or similar protection in place), and its guess about what service the port is. Nmap service identification can be wrong—it's not as full featured as some vulnerability scanners, but the service list is a useful starting place.

Finally, after we see our services listed, we get the MAC address—in this case, indicating that the system is running as a VM under Oracle's VirtualBox virtualization tool and that it is running a 2.6 Linux kernel. This kernel is quite old and reached its end-of-life support date in February 2016, meaning that it's likely to be vulnerable.

The final things to note about this scan are the time it took to run and how many hops there are to the host. This scan completed in less than two seconds, which tells us that the host responded quickly and that the host was only one hop away—it was directly accessible from the scanning host. A more complex network path will show more hops, and scanning more hosts or additional security on the system or between the scanner and the remote target can slow things down.

The viewpoint of active reconnaissance can make a big difference in the data gathered. Internal scans from a trusted system or network will typically provide much more information than an external scan of a well-secured network. If you are attempting to replicate a specific scenario, such as scanning by an external attacker who has no access to an internal system, your scanning viewpoint should match.

OS Fingerprinting

The ability to identify an operating system based on the network traffic that it sends is known as *operating system fingerprinting*, and it can provide useful information when performing reconnaissance. This is typically done using TCP/IP stack fingerprinting techniques that focus on comparing responses to TCP and UDP packets sent to remote hosts. Differences in how operating systems and even operating system versions respond, what TCP options they support, what order they send packets in, and a host of other details can provide a good guess at what OS the remote system is running.

Service and Version Identification

The ability to identify a service can provide useful information about potential vulnerabilities, as well as verify that the service that is responding on a given port matches the service that typically uses that port. Service identification is usually done in one of two ways: either by connecting and grabbing the *banner* or connection information provided by the service or by comparing its responses to the signatures of known services.

Figure 3.3 shows the same system scanned in Figure 3.1 with the nmap `-sV` flag used. The `-sV` flag grabs banners and performs other service version validation steps to capture additional information, which it checks against a database of services.

The basic nmap output remains the same as Figure 3.1, but we have added information in the Version column, including the service name as well as the version and sometimes additional detail about the service protocol version or other details. This information can be used to check for patch levels or vulnerabilities and can also help to identify services that are running on nonstandard ports.

Common Tools

Nmap is the most commonly used command-line port scanner, and it is a free, open source tool. It provides a broad range of capabilities, including multiple scan modes intended to

FIGURE 3.3 Nmap service and version detection

```
Starting Nmap 7.01 ( https://nmap.org ) at 2016-10-02 12:41 EDT
Nmap scan report for 10.0.2.4
Host is up (0.00022s latency).
Not shown: 977 closed ports
PORT     STATE SERVICE     VERSION
21/tcp   open  ftp         vsftpd 2.3.4
22/tcp   open  ssh         OpenSSH 4.7p1 Debian 8ubuntu1 (protocol 2.0)
23/tcp   open  telnet      Linux telnetd
25/tcp   open  smtp        Postfix smtpd
53/tcp   open  domain      ISC BIND 9.4.2
80/tcp   open  http        Apache httpd 2.2.8 ((Ubuntu) DAV/2)
111/tcp  open  rpcbind     2 (RPC #100000)
139/tcp  open  netbios-ssn Samba smbd 3.X (workgroup: WORKGROUP)
445/tcp  open  netbios-ssn Samba smbd 3.X (workgroup: WORKGROUP)
512/tcp  open  exec        netkit-rsh rexecd
513/tcp  open  login?
514/tcp  open  tcpwrapped
1099/tcp open  rmiregistry GNU Classpath grmiregistry
1524/tcp open  shell       Metasploitable root shell
2049/tcp open  nfs         2-4 (RPC #100003)
2121/tcp open  ftp         ProFTPD 1.3.1
3306/tcp open  mysql       MySQL 5.0.51a-3ubuntu5
5432/tcp open  postgresql  PostgreSQL DB 8.3.0 - 8.3.7
5900/tcp open  vnc         VNC (protocol 3.3)
6000/tcp open  X11         (access denied)
6667/tcp open  irc         Unreal ircd
8009/tcp open  ajp13       Apache Jserv (Protocol v1.3)
8180/tcp open  http        Apache Tomcat/Coyote JSP engine 1.1
MAC Address: 08:00:27:92:5F:44 (Oracle VirtualBox virtual NIC)
Device type: general purpose
Running: Linux 2.6.X
OS CPE: cpe:/o:linux:linux_kernel:2.6
OS details: Linux 2.6.9 - 2.6.33
Network Distance: 1 hop
Service Info: Hosts:  metasploitable.localdomain, localhost, irc.Metasploitable.
LAN; OSs: Unix, Linux; CPE: cpe:/o:linux:linux_kernel

OS and Service detection performed. Please report any incorrect results at https
://nmap.org/submit/ .
Nmap done: 1 IP address (1 host up) scanned in 16.37 seconds
```

bypass firewalls and other network protection devices. In addition, it provides support for operating system fingerprinting, service identification, and many other capabilities.

Using nmap's basic functionality is quite simple. Port scanning a system merely requires that nmap be installed and that you provide the target system's hostname or IP address. Figure 3.4 shows an nmap scan of a Windows 10 system with its firewall turned off. The nmap scan provides quite a bit of information about the system—first, we see a series of common Microsoft ports, including 135, 139, and 445, running Microsoft Remote Procedure Call (MSRPC), NetBIOS, and Microsoft's domain services, which are useful indicators that a remote system is a Windows host. The additional ports that are shown also reinforce that assessment, since ICSLAP (the local port opened by Internet Connection Sharing) is used for Microsoft internal proxying, Web Services on Devices API (WSDAPI) is a Microsoft devices API, and each of the other ports can be similarly easily identified by using a quick search for the port and service name nmap provides. This means that you can often correctly guess details about a system even without an OS identification scan.

FIGURE 3.4 Nmap of a Windows 10 system

```
root@demo:~# nmap 192.168.1.14

Starting Nmap 7.01 ( https://nmap.org ) at 2016-08-24 22:49 EDT
Nmap scan report for dynamo (192.168.1.14)
Host is up (1.0s latency).
Not shown: 992 closed ports
PORT     STATE SERVICE
135/tcp  open  msrpc
139/tcp  open  netbios-ssn
445/tcp  open  microsoft-ds
902/tcp  open  iss-realsecure
912/tcp  open  apex-mesh
2869/tcp open  icslap
4242/tcp open  vrml-multi-use
5357/tcp open  wsdapi

Nmap done: 1 IP address (1 host up) scanned in 126.26 seconds
```

A more typical nmap scan is likely to include a number of nmap's command-line flags:

- A scan technique, like TCP `SYN`, which is the most popular scan method because it uses a TCP `SYN` packet to verify a service response, and is quick and unobtrusive. Other connection methods are Connect, which completes a full connection; UDP scans for non-TCP services; ACK scans, which are used to map firewall rules; and a variety of other methods for specific uses.
- A port range, either specifying ports or including the full 1–65535 range. Scanning the full range of ports can be very slow, but it can be useful to identify hidden or unexpected services. Fortunately, nmap's default ports are likely to help find and identify most systems.
- Service version detection using the `-sV` flag, which as shown earlier can provide additional detail but may not be necessary if you intend to use a vulnerability scanner to follow up on your scans.
- OS detection using the `-O` flag, which can help provide additional information about systems on your network.

Nmap also has an official graphical user interface, Zenmap, which provides additional visualization capabilities, including a topology view mode that provides information about how hosts fit into a network.

Angry IP Scanner is a multiplatform (Windows, Linux, and macOS) port scanner with a graphical user interface. In Figure 3.5, you can see a sample scan run with Angry IP Scanner with the details for a single scanned host displayed. Unlike nmap, Angry IP Scanner does not provide detailed identification for services and operating systems, but you can turn on different modules called "fetchers," including ports, TTL, filtered ports, and others. When running Angry IP Scanner, it is important to configure the ports scanned under the Preferences menu; otherwise, no port information will be returned! Unfortunately, Angry IP Scanner requires Java, which means that it may not run on systems where Java is not installed for security reasons.

FIGURE 3.5 Angry IP Scanner

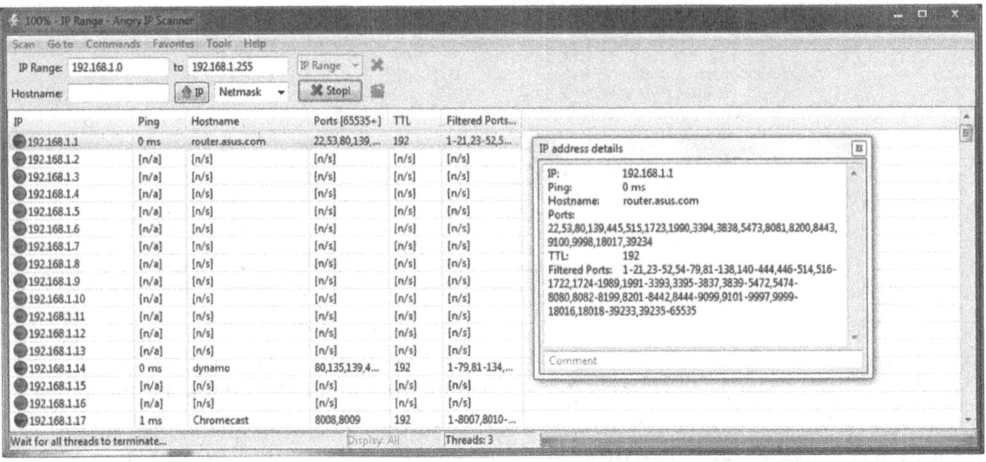

Exam Note

We discuss Angry IP Scanner here as an example, but you don't need to know how to use it on the CySA+ exam.

Angry IP Scanner is not as feature rich as nmap, but the same basic techniques can be used to gather information about hosts based on the port scan results. Figure 3.5 shows the information from a scan of a home router. Note that unlike nmap, Angry IP Scanner does not provide service names or service identification information.

In addition to these two popular scanners, security tools often build in a port scanning capability to support their primary functionality. Metasploit, the Qualys vulnerability management platform, OpenVAS, and Tenable's Nessus vulnerability scanner are all examples of security tools that have built-in port scanning capabilities as part of their suite of tools.

Packet Capture for Pen Testers

Many penetration testers will use packet capture tools during their testing to capture additional data. Not only does this provide a potentially useful dataset for further analysis, but it can also be used to identify problems that result during the scan. Of course, port and vulnerability scanning can create a lot of data, so it pays to make sure you need the packet capture data before running a sniffer during scanning.

Determining an Internal Footprint

Gathering knowledge about the footprint of an organization from the inside is tremendously valuable. Organizations face both insider threats and very capable malicious actors who build malware and other tools designed to get them past external security layers to less protected internal networks and systems. A security professional must have a good understanding of how their organization's networks and defenses are laid out and what systems, devices, and services can be found in each part of the network.

Security practitioners who perform an internal footprinting exercise typically have the advantage of performing a crystal, or white-box, exercise where they have complete access to the knowledge that the organization has about itself. This means that rather than spending time trying to understand network topology, they can spend their time gathering information, scanning networks, and gathering system data. They may still be surprised! Often networks grow organically, and what is shown in an organization's documentation may not be an exact match for what intelligence gathering shows.

The same cautions that apply to using the scanning tools we have discussed in this chapter still hold true for internal testing. Remember to use caution when scanning potentially delicate systems or those that control sensitive processes.

Passive Footprinting

Passive footprinting is far more challenging than active information gathering. Passive analysis relies on information that is available about the organization, systems, or network without performing your own probes. Passive fingerprinting typically relies on logs and other existing data, which may not provide all the information needed to fully identify targets. Its reliance on stored data means that it may also be out of date!

Despite this, you can use a number of common techniques if you need to perform passive fingerprinting. Each relies on access to existing data, or to a place where data can be gathered in the course of normal business operations.

Exam Note

Be sure to understand the differences between active and passive scanning. This is one of the CySA+ exam objectives. Active scanning interacts with a host, whereas passive information gathering simply observes activity and draws conclusions.

Log and Configuration Analysis

Log files can provide a treasure trove of information about systems and networks. If you have access to local system configuration data and logs, you can use the information they contain to build a thorough map of how systems work together, which users and systems exist, and how they are configured. Over the next few pages, we will look at how each of these types of log files can be used and some of the common locations where they can be found.

Network Devices

Network devices log their own activities, status, and events including traffic patterns and usage. Network device information includes network device logs, network device configuration files, and network flows.

Network Device Logs

By default, many network devices log messages to their console ports, which means that only a user logged in at the console will see them. Fortunately, most managed networks also send network logs to a central log server using the *syslog* utility. Many networks also leverage the Simple Network Management Protocol (SNMP) to send device information to a central control system.

Network device log files often have a log level associated with them. Although log level definitions vary, many are similar to Cisco's log levels, which are shown in Table 3.1.

TABLE 3.1 Cisco log levels

Level	Level name	Example
0	Emergencies	Device shutdown due to failure
1	Alerts	Temperature limit exceeded
2	Critical	Software failure
3	Errors	Interface down message
4	Warning	Configuration change
5	Notifications	Line protocol up/down
6	Information	ACL violation
7	Debugging	Debugging messages

Network device logs are often not as useful as the device configuration data when you are focused on intelligence gathering, although they can provide some assistance with topology discovery based on the devices they communicate with. During penetration tests or when you are conducting security operations, network device logs can provide useful warning of attacks or reveal configuration or system issues.

The Cisco router log shown in Figure 3.6 is accessed using the command `show logging` and can be filtered using an IP address, a list number, or a number of other variables. Here, we see a series of entries with a single packet denied from a remote host 10.0.2.50. The remote host is attempting to connect to its target system on a steadily increasing TCP port, likely indicating a port scan is in progress and being blocked by a rule in access list 210.

FIGURE 3.6 Cisco router log

```
002040: Oct 02 2016 13:01:20.450 EDT: %SEC-6-IPACCESSLOGP: list 210 denied tcp 10.0.2.50(15580) -> 192.168.2.1(22), 1 packet
002041: Oct 02 2016 13:01:21.455 EDT: %SEC-6-IPACCESSLOGP: list 210 denied tcp 10.0.2.50(16420) -> 192.168.2.1(23), 1 packet
002044: Oct 02 2016 13:01:21.458 EDT: %SEC-6-IPACCESSLOGP: list 210 denied tcp 10.0.2.50(41283) -> 192.168.2.1(25), 1 packet
002044: Oct 02 2016 13:01:21.462 EDT: %SEC-6-IPACCESSLOGP: list 210 denied tcp 10.0.2.50(7387) -> 192.168.2.1(25), 1 packet
002045: Oct 02 2016 13:01:21.470 EDT: %SEC-6-IPACCESSLOGP: list 210 denied tcp 10.0.2.50(60410) -> 192.168.2.1(26), 1 packet
002046: Oct 02 2016 13:01:22.350 EDT: %SEC-6-IPACCESSLOGP: list 210 denied tcp 10.0.2.50(35542) -> 192.168.2.1(27), 1 packet
002047: Oct 02 2016 13:02:22.375 EDT: %SEC-6-IPACCESSLOGP: list 210 denied tcp 10.0.2.50(32456) -> 192.168.2.1(28), 1 packet
002048: Oct 02 2016 13:02:22.450 EDT: %SEC-6-IPACCESSLOGP: list 210 denied tcp 10.0.2.50(18950) -> 192.168.2.1(29), 1 packet
002049: Oct 02 2016 13:02:24.150 EDT: %SEC-6-IPACCESSLOGP: list 210 denied tcp 10.0.2.50(14430) -> 192.168.2.1(30), 1 packet
002057: Oct 02 2016 13:02:26.250 EDT: %SEC-6-IPACCESSLOGP: list 210 denied tcp 10.0.2.50(11903) -> 192.168.2.1(31), 1 packet
```

Exam Note

The CySA+ exam covers a broad range of networking and security concepts and includes many questions on reviewing and interpreting logs. This is an area where there is no substitute for hands-on experience. Be certain that you've spent significant time reviewing and interpreting real-world log files before attempting to tackle the exam.

Network Device Configuration

Configuration files from network devices can be invaluable when mapping network topology. Configuration files often include details of the network, routes, systems that the devices interact with, and other network details. In addition, they can provide details about syslog and SNMP servers, administrative and user account information, and other configuration items useful as part of information gathering.

Figure 3.7 shows a portion of the SNMP configuration from a typical Cisco router. Reading the entire file shows routing information, interface information, and details that will help you place the router in a network topology. The section shown provides in-depth detail of the SNMP community strings, the contact for the device, as well as what traps are enabled and where they are sent. In addition, you can see that the organization uses Terminal Access Controller Access Control System (TACACS) to control their servers and what the IP addresses of those servers are. As a security analyst, this is useful information—for an attacker, this could be the start of an effective social engineering attack!

FIGURE 3.7 SNMP configuration from a typical Cisco router

```
snmp-server community Example RO
snmp-server community Demo RW 2
snmp-server community Secure RW 51
snmp-server location Europe
snmp-server contact example@demo.org
snmp-server enable traps tty
snmp-server enable traps ike policy add
snmp-server enable traps ike policy delete
snmp-server enable traps ike tunnel start
snmp-server enable traps ike tunnel stop
snmp-server enable traps ipsec cryptomap add
snmp-server enable traps ipsec cryptomap delete
snmp-server enable traps ipsec cryptomap attach
snmp-server enable traps ipsec cryptomap detach
snmp-server enable traps ipsec tunnel start
snmp-server enable traps ipsec tunnel stop
snmp-server enable traps ipsec too-many-sas
snmp-server host 10.16.11.254 *****
snmp-server host 172.16.2.2 *****
snmp-server host 172.16.2.24 *****
!
tacacs-server host 172.16.3.126
tacacs-server host 172.16.65.33
tacacs-server directed-request
tacacs-server *****
```

Netflows

Netflow is a Cisco network protocol that collects IP traffic information, allowing network traffic monitoring. Flow data is used to provide a view of traffic flow and volume. A typical flow capture includes the IP and port source and destination for the traffic and the class of service. Netflows and a netflow analyzer can help identify service problems and baseline typical network behavior and can also be useful in identifying unexpected behaviors.

Vendors other than Cisco have created their own flow monitoring technology, and although "flows" or "netflow" is commonly used, they actually use their own names. Juniper's Jflow and cflowd, Citrix AppFlow, and HP's NetStream, as well as sFlow (an industry term for *sampled flow*), are all terms you may encounter.

Netstat

In addition to network log files, local host network information can be gathered using *netstat* in Windows, Linux, and macOS, as well as most Unix and Unix-like operating systems. Netstat provides a wealth of information, with its capabilities varying slightly between operating systems. It can provide such information as the following:

- Active TCP and UDP connections, filtered by each of the major protocols: TCP, UDP, ICMP, IP, IPv6, and others. Figure 3.8 shows Linux netstat output for `netstat -ta`, showing active TCP connections. Here, an SSH session is open to a remote host. The `-u` flag would work the same way for UDP; `-w` shows RAW, and `-X` shows Unix socket connections.

FIGURE 3.8 Linux `netstat -ta` output

```
root@demo:~# netstat -ta
Active Internet connections (servers and established)
Proto Recv-Q Send-Q Local Address           Foreign Address         State
tcp        0      0 demo:53042              10.0.2.4:ssh            ESTABLISHED
```

- Which executable file created the connection, or its process ID (PID). Figure 3.9 shows a Windows netstat call using the `-o` flag to identify process numbers, which can then be referenced using the Windows Task Manager.

FIGURE 3.9 Windows `netstat -o` output

```
C:\WINDOWS\system32>netstat -o

Active Connections

  Proto  Local Address          Foreign Address        State           PID
  TCP    127.0.0.1:80           dynamo:52964           TIME_WAIT       0
  TCP    127.0.0.1:4243         dynamo:49741           ESTABLISHED     2792
  TCP    127.0.0.1:5354         dynamo:49669           ESTABLISHED     2768
  TCP    127.0.0.1:5354         dynamo:49671           ESTABLISHED     2768
  TCP    127.0.0.1:23560        dynamo:50122           ESTABLISHED     3112
  TCP    127.0.0.1:27015        dynamo:49744           ESTABLISHED     2784
  TCP    127.0.0.1:49669        dynamo:5354            ESTABLISHED     2784
  TCP    127.0.0.1:49671        dynamo:5354            ESTABLISHED     2784
  TCP    127.0.0.1:49692        dynamo:49693           ESTABLISHED     2792
  TCP    127.0.0.1:49693        dynamo:49692           ESTABLISHED     2792
```

- Ethernet statistics on how many bytes and packets have been sent and received. In Figure 3.10, netstat is run on a Windows system with the `-e` flag, providing interface statistics. This tracks the number of bytes sent and received, as well as errors, discards, and traffic sent via unknown protocols.

FIGURE 3.10 Windows `netstat -e` output

```
C:\WINDOWS\system32>netstat -e
Interface Statistics

                           Received            Sent

Bytes                    1802049200       116174058
Unicast packets             1542688          957264
Non-unicast packets           23014          395290
Discards                          0               0
Errors                            0               0
Unknown protocols                 0
```

- Route table information, including IPv4 and IPv6 information, as shown in Figure 3.11. This is retrieved using the `-nr` flag and includes various information depending on the OS, with the Windows version showing the destination network, netmask, gateway, the interface the route is associated with, and a metric for the route that captures link speed and other details to establish preference for the route.

FIGURE 3.11 Windows `netstat -nr` output

```
===========================================================================
IPv4 Route Table
===========================================================================
Active Routes:
Network Destination        Netmask          Gateway       Interface  Metric
          0.0.0.0          0.0.0.0      192.168.1.1    192.168.1.14     25
        127.0.0.0        255.0.0.0         On-link        127.0.0.1    331
        127.0.0.1  255.255.255.255         On-link        127.0.0.1    331
  127.255.255.255  255.255.255.255         On-link        127.0.0.1    331
      169.254.0.0      255.255.0.0         On-link   169.254.71.244    281
      169.254.0.0      255.255.0.0         On-link    169.254.49.12    291
      169.254.0.0      255.255.0.0         On-link   169.254.129.13    291
      169.254.0.0      255.255.0.0         On-link    169.254.31.14    291
      169.254.0.0      255.255.0.0         On-link   169.254.245.26    291
      169.254.0.0      255.255.0.0         On-link   169.254.147.98    291
      169.254.0.0      255.255.0.0         On-link   169.254.107.29    291
      169.254.0.0      255.255.0.0         On-link   169.254.52.253    291
      169.254.0.0      255.255.0.0         On-link    169.254.34.58    291
```

This means that running netstat from a system can provide information about both the machine's network behavior and what the local network looks like. Knowing what machines a system has or is communicating with can help you understand local topology and services. Best of all, because netstat is available by default on so many operating systems, it makes sense to presume it will exist and that you can use it to gather information.

DHCP Logs and DHCP Server Configuration Files

The Dynamic Host Configuration Protocol (DHCP) is a client/server protocol that provides an IP address as well as information such as the default gateway and subnet mask for the network segment that the host will reside on. When you are conducting passive reconnaissance, DHCP logs from the DHCP server for a network can provide a quick way to identify many of the hosts on the network. If you combine DHCP logs with other logs, such as firewall logs, you can determine which hosts are provided with dynamic IP addresses and which hosts are using static IP addresses. As you can see in Figure 3.12, a Linux `dhcpd.conf` file provides information about hosts and the network they are accessing.

FIGURE 3.12 Linux `dhcpd.conf` file

```
#
# DHCP Server Configuration file.
#   see /usr/share/doc/dhcp-server/dhcpd.conf.example
#   see dhcpd.conf(5) man page
#


default-lease-time 600;
max-lease-time 7200;
option subnet-mask 255.255.255.0;
option broadcast-address 192.168.1.255;
option routers 192.168.1.1;
option domain-name-servers 192.168.1.1, 192.168.1.2;
option domain-search "example.com";
subnet 192.168.1.0 netmask 255.255.255.0{
        range 192.168.1.20 192.168.1.240;
}

host demo {
        option host-name "demo.example.com";
        hardware ethernet 08:00:27:fa:25:8e;
        fixed address 192.168.1.241;
}
```

The `dhcpd.conf` and other configuration files can be easily accessed by using the `more` command to display the file. Most, but not all, configuration files are stored in the `/etc` directory for Linux systems, although some applications and services keep their configuration files elsewhere—if you can't find the configuration file in `/etc`, check the documentation.

In this example, the DHCP server provides IP addresses between 192.168.1.20 and 192.168.1.240; the router for the network is 192.168.1.1, and the DNS servers are 192.168.1.1 and 192.168.1.2. We also see a single system named "Demo" with a fixed DHCP address. Systems with fixed DHCP addresses are often servers or systems that need to have a known IP address for a specific function and are thus more interesting when gathering information.

DHCP logs for Linux are typically found in `/var/log/dhcpd.log` or by using the `journalctl` command to view logs, depending on the distribution you are using. DHCP logs can provide information about systems, their MAC addresses, and their IP addresses, as seen in this sample log entry:

```
Oct  5 02:28:11 demo dhcpd[3957]: reuse_lease: lease age 80 (secs) under 25%
threshold, reply with unaltered, existing lease
Oct  5 02:28:11 demo dhcpd[3957]: DHCPREQUEST for 10.0.2.40 (10.0.2.32) from
08:00:27:fa:25:8e via enp0s3
Oct  5 02:28:11 demo dhcpd[3957]: DHCPACK on 10.0.2.40 to 08:00:27:fa:25:8e v
ia enp0s3
Oct  5 02:29:17 demo dhcpd[3957]: reuse_lease: lease age 146 (secs) under 25%
threshold, reply with unaltered, existing lease
Oct  5 02:29:17 demo dhcpd[3957]: DHCPREQUEST for 10.0.2.40 from 08:00:27:fa:
25:8e via enp0s3
Oct  5 02:29:17 demo dhcpd[3957]: DHCPACK on 10.0.2.40 to 08:00:27:fa:25:8e v
ia enp0s3
Oct  5 02:29:38 demo dhcpd[3957]: DHCPREQUEST for 10.0.2.40 from 08:00:27:fa:
25:8e via enp0s3
Oct  5 02:29:38 demo dhcpd[3957]: DHCPACK on 10.0.2.40 to 08:00:27:fa:25:8e
(demo) via enp0s3
```

This log shows a system with IP address 10.0.2.40 renewing its existing lease. The system has a hardware address of 08:00:27:fa:25:8e, and the server runs its DHCP server on the local interface enp0s3.

Servers and network devices are often given either static addresses or permanently configured dynamic addresses set in the DHCP server configuration file. Workstations and other nonserver devices are more likely to receive DHCP addresses, making it easier to take a quick guess about what each device's address may be.

Firewall Logs and Configuration Files

Router and firewall configurations files and logs often contain information about both successful and blocked connections. This means that analyzing router and firewall access control lists (ACLs) and logs can provide useful information about what traffic is allowed and can help with topological mapping by identifying where systems are based on traffic allowed through or blocked. Configuration files make this even easier, since they can be directly read to understand how systems interact with the firewall.

Firewall logs can also allow penetration testers to reverse-engineer firewall rules based on the contents of the logs. Even without the actual configuration files, log files can provide a good view of how traffic flows. Like many other network devices, firewalls often use log levels to separate informational and debugging messages from more important messages. In addition, they typically have a vendor-specific firewall event log format that provides information based on the vendor's logging standards.

Organizations use a wide variety of firewalls, including those from Cisco, Palo Alto, and Check Point, which means that you may encounter logs in multiple formats. Fortunately, all three have common features. Each provides a date/timestamp and details of the event in a format intended to be understandable. For example, Cisco ASA firewall logs can be accessed from the console using the `show logging` command (often typed as `show log`). Entries are reasonably readable, listing the date and time, the system, and the action taken. For example, a log might read

```
Sep 13 10:05:11 10.0.0.1 %ASA-5-111008: User 'ASAadmin' executed the 'enable' command
```

This command indicates that the user ASAadmin ran the Cisco `enable` command, which is typically used to enter privileged mode on the device. If ASAadmin was not supposed to use administrative privileges, this would be an immediate red flag in your investigation.

Cisco firewall logs use identifiers for messages; in the previous code snippet, you can see the six-digit number after %ASA-5-. This identifier matches the command type, and common security mnemonic identifiers for ASAs include 4000xx, 106xxx, and 710003. Other commands may also be of interest depending on what data you are looking for. You can find a list, as well as tips on finding security incidents via ASA firewall logs, at `www.cisco.com/c/en/us/about/security-center/identify-incidents-via-syslog.html`.

A review of router/firewall ACLs can also be conducted manually. A portion of a sample Cisco router ACL is shown here:

```
ip access-list extended inb-lan
 permit tcp 10.0.0.0 0.255.255.255 any eq 22
 permit tcp 172.16.0.0 0.15.255.255 any eq 22
 permit tcp host 192.168.2.1 any eq 22
 deny tcp 8.16.0.0 0.15.255.255 any eq 22
```

This ACL segment names the access list and then sets a series of permitted actions along with the networks that are allowed to perform the actions. This set of rules specifically allows all addresses in the 10.0.0.0 network to use TCP port 22 to send traffic, thus allowing SSH. The 172.16.0.0 network is allowed the same access, as is a host with IP address 192.168.2.1. The final deny rule will prevent the named network range from sending SSH traffic.

If you encounter firewall or router configuration files, log files, or rules on the exam, it may help to rewrite them into language you can read more easily. To do that, start with the action or command; then find the targets, users, or other things that are affected. Finally, find any modifiers that specify what will occur or what did occur. In the previous router configuration, you could write `permit tcp 10.0.0.0 0.255.255.255 any eq 22` as "Allow TCP traffic from the 10.0.0.0 network on any source port to destination port 22." Even if you're not familiar with the specific configuration or commands, this can help you understand many of the entries you will encounter.

System Log Files

System logs are collected by most systems to provide troubleshooting and other system information. Log information can vary greatly depending on the operating system, how it is configured, and what service and applications the system is running.

Log Types

Linux systems typically log to the `/var/log` directory, although individual applications may have their own logging directory. Windows provides several types of event logs:

- Application logs, containing events logged by programs or applications. What is logged varies from program to program.
- Security logs, which can capture login events, resource and rights usage, and events like files being opened, created, or deleted. These options are set by administrators of the Windows system.
- Setup logs are captured when applications are set up.
- System logs contain events logged by Windows components. These are preset as part of Windows.
- Forwarded events logs are set up using event subscriptions and contain events collected from remote computers. They have to be specifically configured.

Log files can provide information about how systems are configured, what applications are running on them, which user accounts exist on the system, and other details, but they are not typically at the top of the list for reconnaissance. They are gathered if they are accessible, but most log files are kept in a secure location and are not accessible without administrative system access.

Exam Note

You'll learn more about log review in Chapter 10, "Security Operations and Monitoring." Be sure that you have a solid understanding of how to locate and interpret system event logs, firewall logs, web application firewall (WAF) logs, proxy server logs, and intrusion detection and prevention logs before you take the exam.

Harvesting Data from DNS and Whois

The Domain Name System (DNS) is often one of the first stops when gathering information about an organization. Not only is DNS information publicly available, it is often easily connected to the organization by simply checking for Whois information about their website. With that information available, you can find other websites and hosts to add to your organizational footprint.

Whois is a tool used to query domain registration data. We'll talk about it more later in this chapter.

DNS and Traceroute Information

DNS converts domain names like `google.com` to IP addresses (as shown in Figure 3.13) or from IP addresses to human-understandable domain names. The command for this on Windows, Linux, and macOS systems is *nslookup*.

FIGURE 3.13 Nslookup for google.com

```
root@demo:~# nslookup google.com
Server:         192.168.1.1
Address:        192.168.1.1#53

Non-authoritative answer:
Name:   google.com
Address: 172.217.4.238
```

Once you know the IP address that a system is using, you can look up information about the IP range it resides in. That can provide information about the company or about the hosting services that they use. Nslookup provides a number of additional flags and capabilities, including choosing the DNS server that you use by specifying it as the second parameter, as shown here with a sample query looking up Microsoft.com via Google's public DNS server 8.8.8.8:

```
nslookup microsoft.com 8.8.8.8
```

Other types of DNS records can be looked up using the `-query` flag, including `MX`, `NS`, `SOA`, and `ANY` as possible entries:

```
nslookup -query=mx microsoft.com
```

This results in a response like that shown in Figure 3.14.

FIGURE 3.14 Nslookup using Google's DNS with `MX` query flag

```
Mikes-MacBook-Air-2:~ mikechapple$ nslookup -query=mx microsoft.com
Server:         172.30.25.8
Address:        172.30.25.8#53

Non-authoritative answer:
microsoft.com   mail exchanger = 10 microsoft-com.mail.protection.outlook.com.

Authoritative answers can be found from:
microsoft-com.mail.protection.outlook.com       internet address = 104.47.54.36
```

The IP address or hostname also can be used to gather information about the network topology for the system or device that has a given IP address. Using traceroute in Linux or macOS (or tracert on Windows systems), you can see the path packets take to the host. Since the Internet is designed to allow traffic to take the best path, you may see several different paths on the way to the system, but you will typically find that the last few responses stay the same. These are often the local routers and other network devices in an organization's network, and knowing how traffic gets to a system can give you insight into the company's internal network topology. Some systems don't respond with hostname data. Traceroute can be helpful, but it often provides only part of the story, as you can see in Figure 3.15, which provides traceroute information to the BBC's website as shown by the asterisks and `request timed out` entries in Figure 3.15, and that the last two systems return only IP addresses.

This traceroute starts by passing through the author's home router, then follows a path through Comcast's network with stops in the South Bend area, and then Chicago. The 4.68.63.125 address without a hostname resolution can be matched to Level 3 communications using a Whois website. The requests that timed out may be due to blocked ICMP responses or other network issues, but the rest of the path remains clear: another Level 3 communications host, then a BBC IP address, and two addresses that are under the control of RIPE, the European NCC. Here we can see details of upstream network providers and backbone networks and even start to get an idea of what might be some of the BBC's production network IP ranges.

The routing information for an organization can provide insight into how their external network connectivity is set up. Fortunately for us, there are public Border Gateway Protocol (BGP) route information servers known as BGP looking glasses. You can find a list of them, including both global and regional servers, at `www.bgp4.as/looking-glasses`.

FIGURE 3.15 Traceroute for bbc.co.uk

```
Tracing route to bbc.co.uk [212.58.244.22]
over a maximum of 30 hops:

  1    <1 ms    <1 ms    <1 ms  router.asus.com [192.168.1.1]
  2     9 ms     8 ms     9 ms  96.120.24.121
  3     9 ms     9 ms     9 ms  Te0-5-0-17-sur01.mishawaka.in.sbend.comcast.net [68.86.118.93]
  4    18 ms    17 ms    16 ms  te-1-7-0-2-ar01.area4.il.chicago.comcast.net [162.151.36.53]
  5     *       13 ms    12 ms  4.68.63.125
  6     *        *        *     Request timed out.
  7   107 ms   111 ms   106 ms  unknown.Level3.net [212.187.139.230]
  8     *        *        *     Request timed out.
  9   101 ms   101 ms   101 ms  ae0.er01.telhc.bbc.co.uk [132.185.254.109]
 10   106 ms   105 ms   108 ms  132.185.255.148
 11   105 ms   107 ms   107 ms  212.58.244.22

Trace complete.
```

Domains and IP Ranges

Domain names are managed by domain name *registrars*. Domain registrars are accredited by generic top-level domain (gTLD) registries and/or country code top-level domain (ccTLD) registries. This means that registrars work with the domain name registries to provide registration services: the ability to acquire and use domain names. Registrars provide the interface between customers and the domain registries and handle purchase, billing, and day-to-day domain maintenance, including renewals for domain registrations.

Domain transfer scams often target organizations whose domains are close to expiration. Make sure that the people responsible for domain registration for your organization know which registrar you work with and what to expect for your renewals.

Registrars also handle transfers of domains, either due to a sale or when a domain is transferred to another registrar. This requires authorization by the current domain owner, as well as a release of the domain to the new registrar.

We Forgot to Renew Our Domain!

If an organization doesn't renew its domain name, someone else can register it. This happens relatively frequently, and there are a number of examples of major companies that forgot to renew their domains. Google, Microsoft, Regions Bank, the Dallas Cowboys, and FourSquare all make the list for domain renewal issues. A story from Google offers a good example of what can happen.

In 2015, Google's domain was not renewed—in fact, google.com was available via Google Domains, Google's own domain registry service. Sanmay Ved, a former Google employee, purchased google.com, and immediately received access to the messages that Google's own domain owners would have normally received. As you might imagine, he could have wreaked havoc if he had decided to abuse the power he suddenly had.

Google Domains quickly canceled the sale and refunded Sanmay's $12. Google later gave Sanmay a "bug bounty" for finding the problem, which Sanmay donated to charity.

If you'd like to read Sanmay's full story, you can find it at `www.linkedin.com/pulse/i-purchased-domain-googlecom-via-google-domains-sanmay-ved`.

The global IP address space is managed by IANA. In addition, IANA manages the DNS Root Zone, which handles the assignments of both gTLDs and ccTLDs. Regional authority over these resources are handled by five regional Internet registries (RIRs):

- African Network Information Center (AFRINIC) for Africa
- American Registry for Internet Numbers (ARIN) for the United States, Canada, parts of the Caribbean region, and Antarctica
- Asia-Pacific Network Information Centre (APNIC) for Asia, Australia, New Zealand, and other countries in the region
- Latin America and Caribbean Network Information Centre (LACNIC) for Latin America and parts of the Caribbean not covered by ARIN
- Réseaux IP Européens Network Coordination Centre (RIPE NCC) for Central Asia, Europe, the Middle East, and Russia

Each of the RIRs provides Whois services to identify the assigned users of the IP space they are responsible for, as well as other services that help to ensure that the underlying IP and DNS foundations of the Internet function for their region.

You may encounter autonomous system (AS) numbers when you're gathering information about an organization. AS numbers are assigned by RIRs to network operators as part of the routing infrastructure of the Internet. For our purposes, the AS number typically isn't a critical piece of information.

DNS Entries

In addition to the information provided using nslookup, DNS entries can provide useful information about systems simply through the hostname. A system named "AD4" is a more likely target for Active Directory–based exploits and Windows Server–specific scans, whereas hostnames that reflect a specific application or service can provide both target information and a clue for social engineering and human intelligence activities.

DNS Discovery

External DNS information for an organization is provided as part of its Whois information, providing a good starting place for DNS-based information gathering. Additional DNS servers may be identified either as part of active scanning or passive information gathering based on network traffic or logs, or even by reviewing an organization's documentation. This can be done using a port scan and searching for systems that provide DNS services on UDP or TCP port 53. Once you have found a DNS server, you can query it using `dig` or other DNS lookup commands, or you can test it to see if it supports zone transfers, which can make acquiring organizational DNS data easy.

Zone Transfers

One way to gather information about an organization is to perform a *zone transfer*. Zone transfers are intended to be used to replicate DNS databases between DNS servers, which makes them a powerful information-gathering tool if a target's DNS servers allow a zone transfer. This means that most DNS servers are set to prohibit zone transfers to servers that aren't their trusted DNS peers, but security analysts, penetration testers, and attackers are still likely to check to see if a zone transfer is possible.

To check if your DNS server allows zone transfers from the command line, you can use either `host` or `dig`:

```
host -t axfr domain.name dns-server
dig axfr @dns-server domain.name
```

Running this against a DNS server that allows zone transfers will result in a large file with data like the following dump from `digi.ninja`, a site that allows practice zone transfers for security practitioners:

```
; <<>> DiG 9.9.5-12.1-Debian <<>> axfr @nsztm1.digi.ninja zonetransfer.me
; (1 server found)
;; global options: +cmd
zonetransfer.me.     7200     IN     SOA     nsztm1.digi.ninja.
robin.digi.ninja. 2014101603 172800 900 1209600 3600
zonetransfer.me.     7200     IN     RRSIG     SOA 8 2 7200 20160330133700
20160229123700 44244 zonetransfer.me. GzQojkYAP8zuTOB9UAx66mTDiEGJ26hVIIP2
ifk2DpbQLrEAPg4M77i4 M0yFWHpNfMJIuuJ8nMxQgFVCU3yTOeT/EMbN98FYC8lVYwEZeWHtb
MmS 88jVlF+cOz2WarjCdyV0+UJCTdGtBJriIczC52EXKkw2RCkv3gtdKKVa fBE=
zonetransfer.me.     7200     IN     NS     nsztm1.digi.ninja.
zonetransfer.me.     7200     IN     NS     nsztm2.digi.ninja.
zonetransfer.me.     7200     IN     RRSIG     NS 8 2 7200 20160330133700
20160229123700 44244 zonetransfer.me. TyFngBk2PMWxgJc6RtgCE/RhE0kqeWfwhYS
BxFxezupFLeiDjHeVXo+S WZxP54Xvwfk7jlFClNZ9lRNkL5qHyxRElhlH1JJI1hjvod0fycq
LqCnx XIqkOzUCkm2Mxr8OcGf2jVNDUcLPDO5XjHgOXCK9tRbVVKIpB92f4Qal ulw=
zonetransfer.me.     7200     IN     A     217.147.177.157
```

This transfer starts with a start of authority (SOA) record, which lists the primary name server; the contact for it, `robin.digi.ninja` (which should be read as `robin@digi.ninja`); and the current serial number for the domain, 2014101603. It also provides the time secondary name servers should wait between changes: 172,800 seconds, the time a primary name server should wait if it fails to refresh; 900 seconds, the time in seconds that a secondary name server can claim to have authoritative information; 1,209,600 seconds, the expiration of the record (two weeks); and 3,600 seconds, the minimum TTL for the domain. Both of the primary name servers for the domain are also listed—`nsztm1` and `nsztm2`—and MX records and other details are contained in the file. These details, plus the full list of DNS entries for the domain, can be very useful when gathering information about an organization, and they are a major reason that zone transfers are turned off for most DNS servers.

DigiNinja provides DNS servers that allow zone transfers to demonstrate how dangerous this can be. You can try out domain zone transfers using the domain `zonetransfer.me` with name servers `nsztm1.digi.ninja` and `nsztm2.digi.ninja`. Full details of how to read the file are also available at `digi.ninja/projects/zonetransferme.php`.

DNS Brute Forcing

If a zone transfer isn't possible, DNS information can still be gathered from public DNS by brute force. Simply sending a manual or scripted DNS query for each IP address that the organization uses can provide a useful list of systems. This can be partially prevented by using an IDS or IPS with a rule that will prevent DNS brute-force attacks. Sending queries at a slow rate or from a number of systems can bypass most prevention methods.

Whois

Whois, as mentioned earlier, allows you to search databases of registered users of domains and IP address blocks, and it can provide useful information about an organization or individual based on their registration information. In the sample Whois query for Google shown in Figure 3.16, you can see that information about Google, such as the company's headquarters location, contact information, and its primary name servers, is returned by the Whois query. This information can provide you with additional hints about the organization by looking for other domains registered with similar information, email addresses to contact, and details you can use during the information-gathering process.

Other information can be gathered by using the `host` command in Linux. This command will provide information about a system's IPv4 and IPv6 addresses as well as its email servers, as shown in Figure 3.17.

FIGURE 3.16 Whois query data for google.com

```
Domain Name: google.com
Registry Domain ID: 2138514_DOMAIN_COM-VRSN
Registrar WHOIS Server: whois.markmonitor.com
Registrar URL: http://www.markmonitor.com
Updated Date: 2015-06-12T10:38:52-0700
Creation Date: 1997-09-15T00:00:00-0700
Registrar Registration Expiration Date: 2020-09-13T21:00:00-0700
Registrar: MarkMonitor, Inc.
Registrar IANA ID: 292
Registrar Abuse Contact Email: abusecomplaints@markmonitor.com
Registrar Abuse Contact Phone: +1.2083895740
Domain Status: clientUpdateProhibited (https://www.icann.org/epp#clientUpdateProhibited)
Domain Status: clientTransferProhibited (https://www.icann.org/epp#clientTransferProhibited)
Domain Status: clientDeleteProhibited (https://www.icann.org/epp#clientDeleteProhibited)
Domain Status: serverUpdateProhibited (https://www.icann.org/epp#serverUpdateProhibited)
Domain Status: serverTransferProhibited (https://www.icann.org/epp#serverTransferProhibited)
Domain Status: serverDeleteProhibited (https://www.icann.org/epp#serverDeleteProhibited)
Registry Registrant ID:
Registrant Name: Dns Admin
Registrant Organization: Google Inc.
Registrant Street: Please contact contact-admin@google.com, 1600 Amphitheatre Parkway
Registrant City: Mountain View
Registrant State/Province: CA
Registrant Postal Code: 94043
Registrant Country: US
Registrant Phone: +1.6502530000
Registrant Phone Ext:
Registrant Fax: +1.6506188571
Registrant Fax Ext:
Registrant Email: dns-admin@google.com
Registry Admin ID:
Admin Name: DNS Admin
Admin Organization: Google Inc.
Admin Street: 1600 Amphitheatre Parkway
Admin City: Mountain View
Admin State/Province: CA
Admin Postal Code: 94043
Admin Country: US
Admin Phone: +1.6506234000
Admin Phone Ext:
Admin Fax: +1.6506188571
Admin Fax Ext:
Admin Email: dns-admin@google.com
Registry Tech ID:
Tech Name: DNS Admin
Tech Organization: Google Inc.
Tech Street: 2400 E. Bayshore Pkwy
```

FIGURE 3.17 `host` command response for google.com

```
root@demo:~# host google.com
google.com has address 216.58.216.238
google.com has IPv6 address 2607:f8b0:4009:809::200e
google.com mail is handled by 50 alt4.aspmx.l.google.com.
google.com mail is handled by 20 alt1.aspmx.l.google.com.
google.com mail is handled by 10 aspmx.l.google.com.
google.com mail is handled by 40 alt3.aspmx.l.google.com.
google.com mail is handled by 30 alt2.aspmx.l.google.com.
```

It can also be useful to know the history of domain ownership for a domain when conducting reconnaissance. Various services like the Domain Tools history service (`research.domaintools.com/research/whoishistory/`) provide a historical view of the domain registration information provided by Whois. Many domain owners reduce the amount of visible data after their domains have been registered for some time, meaning that historical domain registration information can be a treasure trove of useful details.

Responder

Responder is a Python script that is an interesting hybrid between active and passive information gathering. It begins by passively monitoring the network, waiting for other systems to send out broadcast requests intended for devices running networked services. Once Responder passively identifies one of these requests, it switches into active mode and responds, attempting to hijack the connection and gather information from the broadcasting system and its users.

Figure 3.18 provides a look at the Responder start-up screen, showing the variety of services that Responder monitors.

FIGURE 3.18 Responder start-up screen

```
           NBT-NS, LLMNR & MDNS Responder 2.3

  Author: Laurent Gaffie (laurent.gaffie@gmail.com)
  To kill this script hit CRTL-C


[+] Poisoners:
    LLMNR                      [ON]
    NBT-NS                     [ON]
    DNS/MDNS                   [ON]

[+] Servers:
    HTTP server                [ON]
    HTTPS server               [ON]
    WPAD proxy                 [OFF]
    SMB server                 [ON]
    Kerberos server            [ON]
    SQL server                 [ON]
    FTP server                 [ON]
    IMAP server                [ON]
    POP3 server                [ON]
    SMTP server                [ON]
    DNS server                 [ON]
    LDAP server                [ON]

[+] HTTP Options:
    Always serving EXE         [OFF]
    Serving EXE                [OFF]
    Serving HTML               [OFF]
    Upstream Proxy             [OFF]

[+] Poisoning Options:
    Analyze Mode               [OFF]
    Force WPAD auth            [OFF]
    Force Basic Auth           [OFF]
    Force LM downgrade         [OFF]
    Fingerprint hosts          [OFF]

[+] Generic Options:
    Responder NIC              [eth0]
    Responder IP               [172.31.25.248]
    Challenge set              [1122334455667788]


[+] Listening for events...
```

Responder is available for download from the GitHub repository at `github.com/SpiderLabs/Responder`.

Information Aggregation and Analysis Tools

A variety of tools can help with aggregating and analyzing information gathering. Examples include theHarvester, a tool designed to gather emails, domain information, hostnames, employee names, and open ports and banners using search engines; Maltego, which builds relationship maps between people and their ties to other resources; and the Shodan search engine for Internet-connected devices and their vulnerabilities. Using a tool like the Harvester can help simplify searches of large datasets, but it's not a complete substitute for a human's creativity.

Information Gathering Using Packet Capture

A final method of passive information gathering requires access to the target network. This means that internal security teams can more easily rely on packet capture as a tool, whereas penetration testers (or attackers!) typically have to breach an organization's security to capture network traffic.

Packet capture utilities are also often called sniffers or packet analyzers.

Once you have access, however, packet capture can provide huge amounts of useful information. A capture from a single host can tell you what systems are on a given network by capturing broadcast packets, and OS fingerprinting can give you a good guess about a remote host's operating system. If you are able to capture data from a strategic location in a network using a network tap or span port, you'll have access to far more network traffic, and thus even more information about the network.

In Figure 3.19, you can see filtered packet capture data during an nmap scan. Using packet capture can allow you to dig into specific responses or to verify that you did test a specific host at a specific time. Thus, packet capture can be used both as an analysis tool and as proof that a task was accomplished.

Gathering Organizational Intelligence

The CySA+ exam objectives focus on technical capabilities, but an understanding of non-technical information gathering can give you a real edge when conducting penetration testing or protecting your organization. Organizational data can provide clues to how systems and networks may be structured, useful information for social engineering, or details of specific platforms or applications that could be vulnerable.

FIGURE 3.19 Packet capture data from an nmap scan

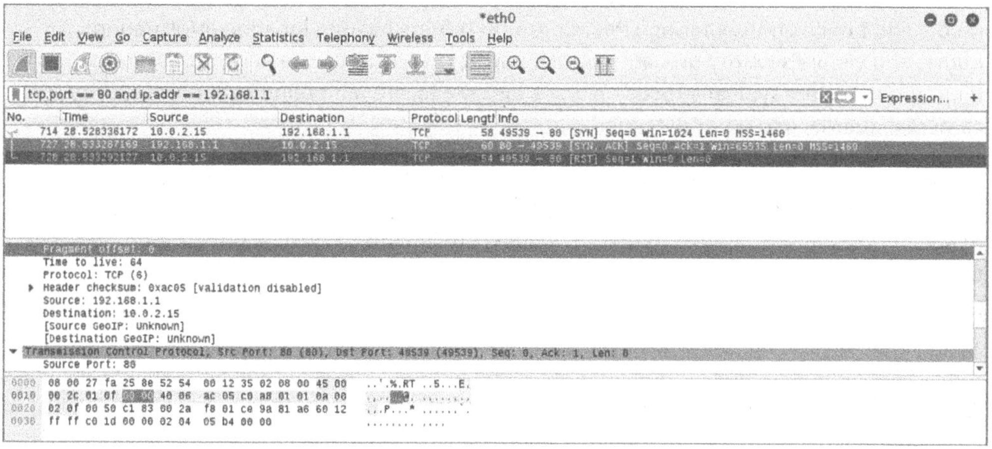

Organizational Data

Gathering organizational data takes on many forms, from reviewing websites to searching through databases like the EDGAR financial database, gathering data from social networks, and even social-engineering staff members to gather data.

Organizational data covers a broad range of information. Penetration testers often look for such information as

- Locations, including where buildings are, how they are secured, and even the business hours and workflow of the organization
- Relationships between departments, individuals, and even other organizations
- Organizational charts
- Document analysis—metadata and marketing
- Financial data
- Individuals

The type of organizational data gathered and the methods used depend on the type of assessment or evaluation being conducted. A no-holds-barred external penetration test may use almost all the techniques we will discuss, whereas an internal assessment may only verify that critical information is not publicly available.

Gathering Information About Physical Facilities

Reconnaissance isn't limited to only electronic means. Physical reconnaissance activities are also on the menu for penetration testers and attackers. Physical reconnaissance often starts with open data about the target, including satellite imagery, images of the exterior of buildings provided by tools like Google's Street View, public records, and information provided online about the organization's physical facilities, including data from social media and public photo-sharing sites. Common targets include location information; hours; and visible security precautions like fences, gates, and access control systems. Penetration testers typically focus on ways into the facility and blind spots for security cameras, guards, and other defenses.

Much like active network reconnaissance, physical testing will then move on to on-site information gathering through observation and actual nonintrusive testing. Once all the needed information has been gathered, a plan is built, and a physical penetration test can be conducted.

Electronic Document Harvesting

Documents can provide a treasure trove of information about an organization. Document metadata often includes information like the author's name and information about the software used to create the document, and at times it can even include revisions, edits, and other data that you may not want to expose to others who access the files. Cell phone photos may have location data, allowing you to know when and where the photo was taken.

Tag data from photos, known as Exif data, is part of the Exchangeable Image File format and can easily be read using Exif data reading tools. One of the authors of this book demonstrates the power of tools like Exiftool, a metadata viewing tool, by asking students to email an innocuous photo during their spring break. A simple photo of a tasty lunch can result in identifying the restaurant that the student ate at—simply by plugging the photo's GPS metadata into an online mapping application.

Analytical data based on documents and email can also provide useful information about an organization. In Figure 3.20, an MIT Media Labs tool called Immersion provides information about the people who the demo email account emails regularly. This type of analysis can help identify key contacts and topics quickly, providing leads for further investigation.

Fortunately, *metadata scrubbing* is easily handled by using a metadata scrubber utility or by using built-in tools like the Document Inspector built into Microsoft Word or the Examine Document tool in Adobe Acrobat. Many websites automatically strip sensitive metadata like location information.

FIGURE 3.20 Demonstration account from `immersion.media.mit.edu`

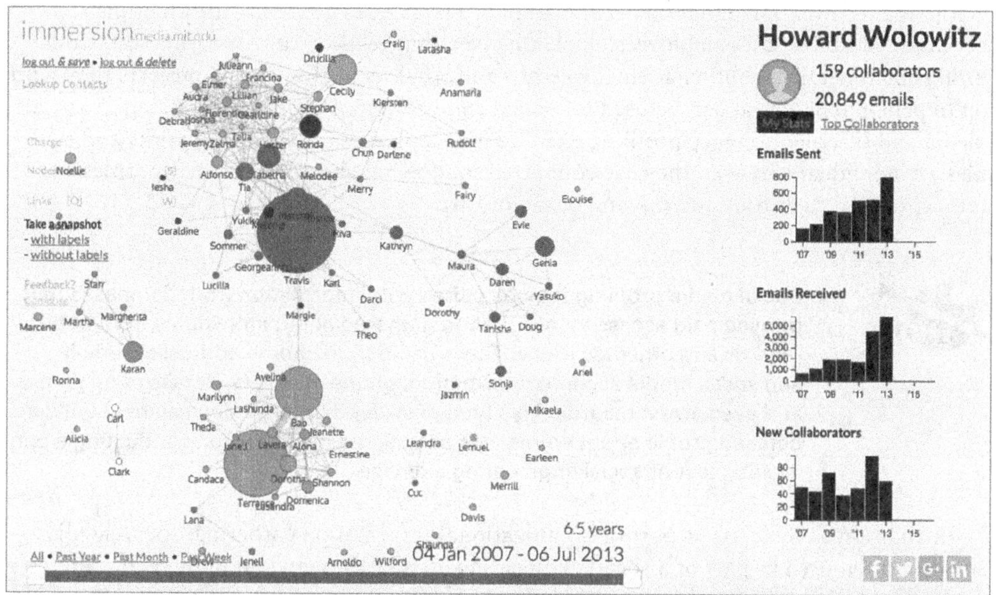

The advent of file sharing and collaboration cloud services means that organizational perimeters are even more porous than they were when employees tended to rely on internal file servers. If you can find an employee or a department that has publicly shared their Google Drive, Dropbox, or other working space, you (or an attacker!) may find yourself with internal information that the company has no way to monitor.

Websites

It might seem obvious to include an organization's website when gathering electronic documents, but simply gathering the current website's information doesn't provide a full view of the data that might be available. The Internet Archive (`archive.org`) and the Time Travel Service (`timetravel.mementoweb.org`) both provide a way to search historic versions of websites. You can also directly search Google and other caches using a site like `cachedview.com`.

Historical and cached information can provide valuable data, including details that the organization believes are no longer accessible. Finding every instance of a cached copy and ensuring that they are removed can be quite challenging!

Social Media Analysis

Gathering information about an organization often includes gathering information about the organization's employees. Social media can provide a lot of information, from professional details about what employees do and what technologies and projects they work on to personal data that can be used for social engineering or password guessing. A social media and Internet presence profiling exercise may look at what social networks and profiles an individual has, who they are connected to, how much metadata their profiles contain, and what their tone and posting behaviors are.

Social media profiling may be paired with information from databases that provide paid access to information gathered about individuals from public records and other locations. These can provide home addresses, email and social media account information, phone numbers, details of relatives, and even arrest records. This type of in-depth information can help build a detailed profile about employees and can be helpful when conducting a penetration test or social engineering exercise.

In addition to their use as part of organizational information gathering, social media sites are often used as part of a social engineering attack. Knowing an individual's interests or details of their life can provide a much more effective way to ensure that they are caught by a social engineering attack.

Social Engineering

Social engineering, or exploiting the human element of security, targets individuals to gather information. This may be via phone, email, social media, or in person. Typically, social engineering targets specific access or accounts, but it may be more general in nature.

A number of toolkits are available to help with social engineering activities:

- The Social Engineering Toolkit (SET), which provides technical tools to enable social engineering attacks
- Creepy, a geolocation tool that uses social media and file metadata about individuals to provide better information about them
- Metasploit, which includes phishing and other tools to help with social engineering

Phishing, which targets account information or other sensitive information by pretending to be a reputable entity or organization via email or other channels, is commonly used as part of a social engineering process. Targeting an organization with a well-designed phishing attack is one of the most common ways to get credentials for an organization.

Detecting, Preventing, and Responding to Reconnaissance

Although reconnaissance doesn't always result in attacks, limiting the ability of potential attackers to gather information about your organization is a good idea. Unfortunately, organizations that are connected to the Internet are almost constantly being scanned, and that background noise can make it difficult to detect directed attacks. That means that detecting reconnaissance at your Internet border may be a process filled with a lot of background noise. Fortunately, the same techniques apply to limiting both casual and directed reconnaissance activities.

Capturing and Analyzing Data to Detect Reconnaissance

The first step in detecting reconnaissance is to capture data. In order to prioritize where data collection should occur, you first need to understand your own network topology. Monitoring at the connection points between network zones and where data sensitivity or privilege zones meet will provide the most benefit. Since most internal networks should be well protected, monitoring for internal scans is usually a lot easier than monitoring for external data gathering.

Data Sources

Typical data sources for analysis include the following:

- Network traffic analysis using intrusion detection systems (IDSs), intrusion prevention systems (IPSs), host intrusion detection systems (HIDSs), network intrusion detection systems (NIDSs), firewalls, or other network security devices. These devices often provide one or more of the following types of analysis capabilities:
  - Packet analysis, with inspection occurring at the individual packet level to detect issues with the content of the packets, behaviors related to the content of the packet, or signatures of attacks contained in them.
  - Protocol analysis, which examines traffic to ensure that protocol-level attacks and exploits are not being conducted.
  - Traffic and flow analysis intended to monitor behavior based on historic traffic patterns and behavior-based models.

Wireless analysis uses the same types of tools and adds support for wireless specific protocols and features. Since wireless networks can be accessed from a distance, they are sometimes an easier target for local attackers.

- Device and system logs that can help identify reconnaissance and attacks when analyzed manually or using a tool.
- Port and vulnerability scans conducted internally to identify potential issues. These can help match known vulnerabilities to attempted exploits, alerting administrators to attacks that are likely to have succeeded.
- Security device logs that are designed to identify problems and that often have specific detection and/or response capabilities that can help limit the impact of reconnaissance.
- Security information and event management (SIEM) systems that centralize and analyze data, allowing reporting, notification, and response to security events based on correlation and analysis capabilities.

Hosted Services and Reconnaissance

Outsourced services can make detecting reconnaissance activities aimed at your organization's systems and data harder to detect. In some cases you will still be able to deploy security monitoring tools, but in most software as a service (SaaS) and platform as a service (PaaS) environments, you will have to rely on the outsourced provider. If that's the case, ensuring that they have a strong security program and regular external security audits is vital to a secure outsourced environment.

Data Analysis Methods

Collecting data isn't useful unless you can correlate and analyze it. Understanding the techniques available to analyze data can help you decide how to handle data and what tools you want to apply.

- *Anomaly analysis* looks for differences from established patterns or expected behaviors. Anomaly detection requires knowledge of what "normal" is to identify differences to build a base model. IDSs and IPSs often use anomaly detection as part of their detection methods.
- *Trend analysis* focuses on predicting behaviors based on existing data. Trend analysis can help to identify future outcomes such as network congestion based on usage patterns and observed growth. It is not used as frequently as a security analysis method but can be useful to help guarantee availability of services by ensuring that they are capable of handling an organization's growth or increasing needs.
- *Signature analysis* uses a fingerprint or signature to detect threats or other events. This means that a signature has to exist before it can be detected, but if the signature is well designed, it can reliably detect the specific threat or event.
- *Heuristic*, or *behavioral analysis*, is used to detect threats based on their behavior. Unlike signature detection, heuristic detection can detect unknown threats since it focuses on what the threat does rather than attempting to match it to a known fingerprint.

- *Manual analysis* is also frequently performed. Human expertise and instinct can be useful when analyzing data and may detect something that would otherwise not be seen.

Your choice of analysis methods will be shaped by the tools you have available and the threats your organization faces. In many cases, you may deploy multiple detection and analysis methods in differing locations throughout your network and systems. Defense-in-depth remains a key concept when building a comprehensive security infrastructure.

Preventing Reconnaissance

Denying attackers information about your organization is a useful defensive strategy. Now that you have explored how to perform reconnaissance, you may want to review how to limit the effectiveness of the same strategies.

As you consider defenses against reconnaissance, remember that network defense-in-depth should implement many of the defenses needed to limit active reconnaissance. Passive reconnaissance and social engineering are less likely to be dealt with in a network security–centered defensive design.

Preventing Active Reconnaissance

Active reconnaissance can be limited by employing network defenses, but it cannot be completely stopped if you provide any services to the outside world. Active reconnaissance prevention typically relies on a few common defenses:

- Limiting external exposure of services and ensuring that you know your external footprint
- Using an IPS or similar defensive technology that can limit or stop probes to prevent scanning
- Using monitoring and alerting systems to notify you about events that continue despite these preventive measures

Detecting active reconnaissance on your internal network should be a priority, and policy related to the use of scanning tools should be a priority to ensure that attackers cannot probe your internal systems without being detected.

Preventing Passive Information Gathering

Preventing passive information gathering relies on controlling the information that you release. Reviewing passive information gathering techniques, then making sure that your organization has intentionally decided what information should be available, is critical to ensuring that passive information gathering is not a significant risk.

Each passive information gathering technique has its own set of controls that can be applied. For example, DNS antiharvesting techniques used by domain registrars can help prevent misuse. These include the following:

- Blacklisting systems or networks that abuse the service
- Using CAPTCHAs to prevent bots
- Providing privacy services that use third-party registration information instead of the actual person or organization registering the domain
- Implementing rate limiting to ensure that lookups are not done at high speeds
- Not publishing zone files if possible, but gTLDs are required to publish their zone files, meaning this works for only some ccTLDs

Other types of passive information gathering each require a thorough review of exposed data and organization decisions about what should (or must) be exposed and what can be limited either by technical or administrative means.

Protecting social media information can be a challenge since most of the social media targets of an information gathering exercise will be individual accounts. If social media information gathering is a particular concern for your organization, an awareness campaign on social media security is typically the best option.

Summary

Reconnaissance is performed by both attackers and defenders. Both sides seek to gather information about potential targets using port scans, vulnerability scans, and information gathering, thus creating a view of an organization's networks and systems. Security professionals may use the information they gather to improve their defensive posture or to identify potential issues. Attackers may find the information they need to attack vulnerable infrastructure.

Organizational intelligence gathering is often performed in addition to the technical information that is frequently gathered during footprinting and active reconnaissance activities. Organizational intelligence focuses on information about an organization, such as its physical location and facilities security, internal hierarchy and structure, social media and web presence, and how policies and procedures work. This information can help attackers perform social engineering attacks or better leverage the information they gained during their technical reconnaissance activities.

Detecting reconnaissance typically involves instrumenting networks and systems using tools like IDSs, IPSs, and network traffic flow monitors. Scans and probes are common on public networks, but internal networks should experience scanning only from expected locations and times set by internal policies and procedures. Unexpected scans are often an indication of compromise or a flaw in the organization's perimeter security.

As a security practitioner, you need to understand how to gather information by port and vulnerability scanning, log review, passive information gathering, and organizational intelligence gathering. You should also be familiar with common tools like nmap; vulnerability scanners; and local host utilities like dig, netstat, and traceroute. Together these skills will provide you with the abilities you need to understand the networks, systems, and other organizational assets that you must defend.

Exam Essentials

Explain how active reconnaissance is critical to understanding system and network exposure. Active reconnaissance involves probing systems and networks for information. Port scanning is a frequent first step during reconnaissance, and nmap is a commonly used tool for system, port, OS, and service discovery for part scanning. Active reconnaissance can also help determine network topology by capturing information and analyzing responses from network devices and systems. It is important to know common port and service pairings to help with analyzing and understanding discovered services.

Know how passive footprinting provides information without active probes. Passive footprinting relies on data gathered without probing systems and networks. Log files, configuration files, and published data from DNS and Whois queries can all provide valuable data without sending any traffic to a system or network. Packet capture is useful when working to understand a network and can help document active reconnaissance activities as well as providing diagnostic and network data.

Know how gathering organizational intelligence is important to perform or prevent social engineering attacks. Organizational intelligence includes information about the organization like its location, org charts, financial data, business relationships, and details about its staff. This data can be gathered through electronic data harvesting, social media analysis, and social engineering, or by gathering data in person.

Describe how detecting reconnaissance can help identify security flaws and warn of potential attacks. Detecting reconnaissance relies on capturing evidence of the intelligence gathering activities. This is typically done using tools like IDSs, IPSs, and log analysis, and by correlating information using a SIEM system. Automated data analysis methods used to detect reconnaissance look for anomalies, trends, signatures, and behaviors, but having a human expert in the process can help identify events that a program may miss.

Describe what preventing, and responding to, reconnaissance relies on. Preventing information gathering typically requires limiting your organizational footprint, as well as detecting and preventing information gathering using automated means like an IPS or firewall. Proactive measures such as penetration testing and self-testing can help ensure that you know and understand your footprint and potential areas of exposure. Each technology and service that is in place requires a distinct plan to prevent or limit information gathering.

Lab Exercises

Activity 3.1: Port Scanning

In this exercise, you will use a Kali Linux virtual machine to

- Perform a port scan of a vulnerable system using nmap
- Identify the remote system's operating system and version
- Capture packets during the port scan

Part 1: Set up virtual machines

Information on downloading and setting up the Kali Linux and Metasploitable virtual machines can be found in the introduction of this book. You can also substitute your own system if you have one already set up to run nmap.

1. Boot the Kali Linux and Metasploitable virtual machines and log into both. The username/password pair for Kali Linux is `root/toor`, and Metasploitable uses `msfadmin /msfadmin`.
2. Run `ifconfig` from the console of the Metasploitable virtual machine. Take note of the IP address assigned to the system.

Part 2: Perform a port scan

Now we will perform a port scan of the Metasploitable virtual machine. Metasploitable is designed to be vulnerable, so we should anticipate seeing many services that might not otherwise be available on a properly secured Linux system.

1. Open a Terminal window using the menu bar at the top of the screen.
2. To run nmap, simply type **nmap** and the IP address of the target system. Use the IP address of the Metasploitable system: **nmap** [*target IP*].

   What ports are open, and what services are identified? Do you believe that you have identified all the open ports on the system?
3. Now we will identify the operating system of the Metasploitable virtual machine. This is enabled using the `-O` flag in nmap. Rerun your nmap, but this time type **nmap -O** [*target IP*] and add **-p 1-65535** to capture all possible ports.

   Which operating system and version is the Metasploitable virtual machine running? Which additional ports showed up?

Activity 3.2: Write an Intelligence Gathering Plan

For this activity, design a passive intelligence gathering plan for an organization of your choice. You may want to reference a resource like OSSTMM, NIST SP 800-115, or `pentest-standard.org` before you write the plan.

Your intelligence gathering plan should identify the following:

- The target
- How you would gather passive data, including what data you would look for
- What tools you would use

Once you are done, use one or more of the references listed earlier to review your plan. Identify what you missed and what additional data you could gather.

Repeat the activity, documenting how you would perform active intelligence gathering, including how you would determine network topology, what operating systems are in use, and what services are accessible. Remember to account for variables like wired and wireless networks, on-site and cloud hosting, and virtual versus physical hosts.

Activity 3.3: Intelligence Gathering Techniques

Match each of the information types in the following chart to the tool that can help gather it.

Route to a system	netstat
Open services via a network	Whois
IP traffic flow and volume	traceroute
Organizational contact information associated with domain registration	Wireshark
Connections listed by protocol	Nmap
Packet capture	Creepy
Zone transfer	dig
Social media geotagging	netflow

Review Questions

1. What method is used to replicate DNS information for DNS servers but is also a tempting exploit target for attackers?
   - A. DNSSEC
   - B. AXR
   - C. DNS registration
   - D. Zone transfers

2. What flag does nmap use to enable operating system identification?

   A. `-os`

   B. `-id`

   C. `-o`

   D. `-osscan`

3. What command-line tool can be used to determine the path that traffic takes to a remote system?

   A. Whois

   B. traceroute

   C. nslookup

   D. routeview

4. What type of data can frequently be gathered from images taken on smartphones?

   A. Extended Graphics Format

   B. Exif

   C. JPIF

   D. PNGrams

5. Which Cisco log level is the most critical?

   A. 0

   B. 1

   C. 7

   D. 10

6. During passive intelligence gathering, you are able to run netstat on a workstation located at your target's headquarters. What information would you not be able to find using netstat on a Windows system?

   A. Active TCP connections

   B. A list of executables by connection

   C. Active UDP connections

   D. Route table information

7. Which of the following options is the most likely used for the host listed in the `dhcpd.conf` entry?

```
host db1 {
      option host-name "sqldb1.example.com";
      hardware ethernet 8a:00:83:aa:21:9f
      fixed address 10.1.240.10
```

A. Active Directory server
B. Apache web server
C. Oracle database server
D. Microsoft SQL Server

8. Which type of Windows log is most likely to contain information about a file being deleted?
   A. `httpd` logs
   B. Security logs
   C. System logs
   D. Configuration logs

9. What organization manages the global IP address space?
   A. NASA
   B. ARIN
   C. WorldNIC
   D. IANA

10. Before Ben sends a Word document, he uses the built-in Document Inspector to verify that the file does not contain hidden content. What is this process called?
    A. Data purging
    B. Data remanence insurance
    C. Metadata scrubbing
    D. File cleansing

11. What type of analysis is best suited to identify a previously unknown malware package operating on a compromised system?
    A. Trend analysis
    B. Signature analysis
    C. Heuristic analysis
    D. Regression analysis

12. Which of the following is not a common DNS antiharvesting technique?
    A. Blacklisting systems or networks
    B. Registering manually
    C. Rate limiting
    D. CAPTCHAs

13. What technique is being used in this command?

```
dig axfr @dns-server example.com
```

  A. DNS query
  B. nslookup
  C. dig scan
  D. Zone transfer

14. Which of the following is not a reason that penetration testers often perform packet capture while conducting port and vulnerability scanning?
  A. Work process documentation
  B. To capture additional data for analysis
  C. Plausible deniability
  D. To provide a timeline

15. What process uses information such as the way that a system's TCP stack responds to queries, what TCP options it supports, and the initial window size it uses?
  A. Service identification
  B. Fuzzing
  C. Application scanning
  D. OS detection

16. What tool would you use to capture IP traffic information to provide flow and volume information about a network?
  A. libpcap
  B. netflow
  C. netstat
  D. pflow

17. What method used to replicate DNS information between DNS servers can also be used to gather large amounts of information about an organization's systems?
  A. traceroute
  B. Zone transfer
  C. DNS sync
  D. dig

18. Selah believes that an organization she is penetration testing may have exposed information about their systems on their website in the past. What site might help her find an older copy of their website?
  A. The Internet Archive
  B. WikiLeaks
  C. The Internet Rewinder
  D. TimeTurner

19. During an information gathering exercise, Chris is asked to find out detailed personal information about his target's employees. What is frequently the best place to find this information?
    A. Forums
    B. Social media
    C. The company's website
    D. Creepy
20. Which lookup tool provides information about a domain's registrar and physical location?
    A. nslookup
    B. host
    C. Whois
    D. traceroute

Designing a Vulnerability Management Program

THE COMPTIA CYBERSECURITY ANALYST (CYSA+) EXAM OBJECTIVES COVERED IN THIS CHAPTER INCLUDE:

✓ **Domain 1.0: Threat and Vulnerability Management**

- 1.3 Given a scenario, perform vulnerability management activities.
- 1.4 Given a scenario, analyze the output from common vulnerability assessment tools.

✓ **Domain 3.0: Security Operations and Monitoring**

- 3.4 Compare and contrast automation concepts and technologies.

Cybersecurity is a cat-and-mouse game where information technology professionals seek to combat the new vulnerabilities discovered by adversaries on an almost daily basis. Modern enterprises consist of hardware and software of almost unfathomable complexity, and buried within those systems are thousands of undiscovered security vulnerabilities waiting for an attacker to exploit them. *Vulnerability management programs* seek to identify, prioritize, and remediate these vulnerabilities before an attacker exploits them to undermine the confidentiality, integrity, or availability of enterprise information assets. Effective vulnerability management programs use an organized approach to scanning enterprise assets for vulnerabilities, using a defined workflow to remediate those vulnerabilities and performing continuous assessment to provide technologists and managers with insight into the current state of enterprise cybersecurity.

Identifying Vulnerability Management Requirements

As an organization begins developing a vulnerability management program, it should first undertake the identification of any internal or external requirements for vulnerability scanning. These requirements may come from the regulatory environments in which the organization operates and/or internal policy-driven requirements.

Regulatory Environment

Many organizations find themselves bound by laws and regulations that govern the ways they store, process, and transmit different types of data. This is especially true when the organization handles sensitive personal information or information belonging to government agencies.

Many of these laws are not overly prescriptive and do not specifically address the implementation of a vulnerability management program. For example, the Health Insurance Portability and Accountability Act (HIPAA) regulates the ways that healthcare providers, insurance companies, and their business associates handle protected health information. Similarly, the Gramm–Leach–Bliley Act (GLBA) governs how financial institutions handle customer financial records. Neither of these laws specifically requires that covered organizations conduct vulnerability scanning.

Two regulatory schemes, however, do specifically mandate the implementation of a vulnerability management program: the Payment Card Industry Data Security Standard (PCI DSS) and the Federal Information Security Management Act (FISMA).

Payment Card Industry Data Security Standard (PCI DSS)

PCI DSS prescribes specific security controls for merchants who handle credit card transactions and service providers who assist merchants with these transactions. This standard includes what are arguably the most specific requirements for vulnerability scanning of any standard.

Contrary to what some believe, PCI DSS is *not* a law. The standard is maintained by an industry group known as the Payment Card Industry Security Standards Council (PCI SSC), which is funded by the industry to maintain the requirements. Organizations are subject to PCI DSS due to contractual requirements rather than a law.

PCI DSS prescribes many of the details of vulnerability scans. These include the following:

- Organizations must run both internal and external vulnerability scans (PCI DSS requirement 11.2).
- Organizations must run scans on at least a quarterly basis and "after any significant change in the network (such as new system component installations, changes in network topology, firewall rule modifications, product upgrades)" (PCI DSS requirement 11.2).
- Internal scans must be conducted by qualified personnel (PCI DSS requirement 11.2.1).
- Organizations must remediate any high-risk vulnerabilities and repeat scans to confirm that they are resolved until they receive a "clean" scan report (PCI DSS requirement 11.2.1).
- External scans must be conducted by an Approved Scanning Vendor (ASV) authorized by PCI SSC (PCI DSS requirement 11.2.2).

Vulnerability scanning for PCI DSS compliance is a thriving and competitive industry, and many security consulting firms specialize in these scans. Many organizations choose to conduct their own scans first to assure themselves that they will achieve a passing result before requesting an official scan from an ASV.

You should *never* conduct vulnerability scans unless you have explicit permission to do so. Running scans without permission can be a serious violation of an organization's security policy and may also be a crime.

Federal Information Security Management Act (FISMA)

The *Federal Information Security Management Act (FISMA)* requires that government agencies and other organizations operating on behalf of government agencies comply with a series of security standards. The specific controls required by these standards depend on whether the government designates the system as low impact, moderate impact, or high impact, according to the definitions shown in Figure 4.1. Further guidance on system classification is found in Federal Information Processing Standard (FIPS) 199: Standards for Security Categorization of Federal Information and Information Systems.

FIGURE 4.1 FIPS 199 Standards (Source: FIPS 199)

	POTENTIAL IMPACT		
Security Objective	**LOW**	**MODERATE**	**HIGH**
Confidentiality Preserving authorized restrictions on information access and disclosure, including means for protecting personal privacy and proprietary information. [44 U.S.C., SEC. 3542]	The unauthorized disclosure of information could be expected to have a **limited** adverse effect on organizational operations, organizational assets, or individuals.	The unauthorized disclosure of information could be expected to have a **serious** adverse effect on organizational operations, organizational assets, or individuals.	The unauthorized disclosure of information could be expected to have a **severe or catastrophic** adverse effect on organizational operations, organizational assets, or individuals.
Integrity Guarding against improper information modification or destruction, and includes ensuring information non-repudiation and authenticity. [44 U.S.C., SEC. 3542]	The unauthorized modification or destruction of information could be expected to have a **limited** adverse effect on organizational operations, organizational assets, or individuals.	The unauthorized modification or destruction of information could be expected to have a **serious** adverse effect on organizational operations, organizational assets, or individuals.	The unauthorized modification or destruction of information could be expected to have a **severe or catastrophic** adverse effect on organizational operations, organizational assets, or individuals.
Availability Ensuring timely and reliable access to and use of information. [44 U.S.C., SEC. 3542]	The disruption of access to or use of information or an information system could be expected to have a **limited** adverse effect on organizational operations, organizational assets, or individuals.	The disruption of access to or use of information or an information system could be expected to have a **serious** adverse effect on organizational operations, organizational assets, or individuals.	The disruption of access to or use of information or an information system could be expected to have a **severe or catastrophic** adverse effect on organizational operations, organizational assets, or individuals.

All federal information systems, regardless of their impact categorization, must meet the basic requirements for vulnerability scanning found in NIST Special Publication 800-53: Security and Privacy Controls for Federal Information Systems and Organizations. These require that each organization subject to FISMA do the following:

a. Scan for vulnerabilities in the information system and hosted applications and, when new vulnerabilities potentially affecting the system/application are identified, report them.
b. Employ vulnerability scanning tools and techniques that facilitate interoperability among tools and automate parts of the vulnerability management process by using standards for
    1. Enumerating platforms, software flaws, and improper configurations
    2. Formatting checklists and test procedures
    3. Measuring vulnerability impact
c. Analyze vulnerability scan reports and results from security control assessments.
d. Remediate legitimate vulnerabilities in accordance with an organizational assessment of risk.
e. Share information obtained from the vulnerability scanning process and security control assessments to help eliminate similar vulnerabilities in other information systems (i.e., systemic weaknesses or deficiencies).

These requirements establish a baseline for all federal information systems. NIST 800-53 then describes eight control enhancements that may be required depending on the circumstances:

1. The organization employs vulnerability scanning tools that include the capability to readily update the information system vulnerabilities to be scanned.
2. The organization updates the information system vulnerabilities scanned prior to a new scan (and/or) when new vulnerabilities are identified and reported.
3. The organization employs vulnerability scanning procedures that can identify the breadth and depth of coverage (i.e., information system components scanned and vulnerabilities checked).
4. The organization determines what information about the information system is discoverable by adversaries and subsequently takes organization-defined corrective actions.
5. The information system implements privileged access authorization to information system components for selected vulnerability scanning activities.
6. The organization employs automated mechanisms to compare the results of vulnerability scans over time to determine trends in information system vulnerabilities.
7. (Requirement 7 was withdrawn.)
8. The organization reviews historic audit logs to determine if a vulnerability identified in the information system has been previously exploited.
9. (Requirement 9 was withdrawn.)
10. The organization correlates the output from vulnerability scanning tools to determine the presence of multi-vulnerability/multi-hop attack vectors.

Note that requirements 7 and 9 were control enhancements that were previously included in the standard but were later withdrawn.

In cases where a federal agency determines that an information system falls into the moderate impact category, it must implement control enhancements 1, 2, and 5, at a minimum. If the agency determines a system is high impact, it must implement at least control enhancements 1, 2, 4, and 5.

Corporate Policy

The prescriptive security requirements of PCI DSS and FISMA cover organizations involved in processing retail transactions and operating government systems, but those two groups constitute only a fraction of enterprises. Cybersecurity professionals widely agree that vulnerability management is a critical component of any information security program, and for this reason, many organizations mandate vulnerability scanning in corporate policy, even if this requirement is not imposed by regulatory requirements.

Identifying Scan Targets

Once an organization decides that it wishes to conduct vulnerability scanning and determines which, if any, regulatory requirements apply to their scans, they move on to the more detailed phases of the planning process. The next step is to identify the systems that will be covered by the vulnerability scans. Some organizations choose to cover all systems in their scanning process whereas others scan systems differently (or not at all) depending on the answers to many different questions, including

- What is the *data classification* of the information stored, processed, or transmitted by the system?
- Is the system exposed to the Internet or other public or semipublic networks?
- What services are offered by the system?
- Is the system a production, test, or development system?

Organizations also use automated techniques to identify the systems that may be covered by a scan. Cybersecurity professionals use scanning tools to search the network for connected systems, whether they were previously known or unknown, and build an *asset inventory*. Figure 4.2 shows an example of an asset map developed using the Qualys vulnerability scanner's asset inventory functionality.

Administrators may then supplement this inventory with additional information about the type of system and the information it handles. This information then helps make determinations about which systems are critical and which are noncritical. Asset inventory and *asset criticality* information helps guide decisions about the types of scans that are performed, the frequency of those scans, and the priority administrators should place on remediating vulnerabilities detected by the scan.

FIGURE 4.2 Qualys asset map

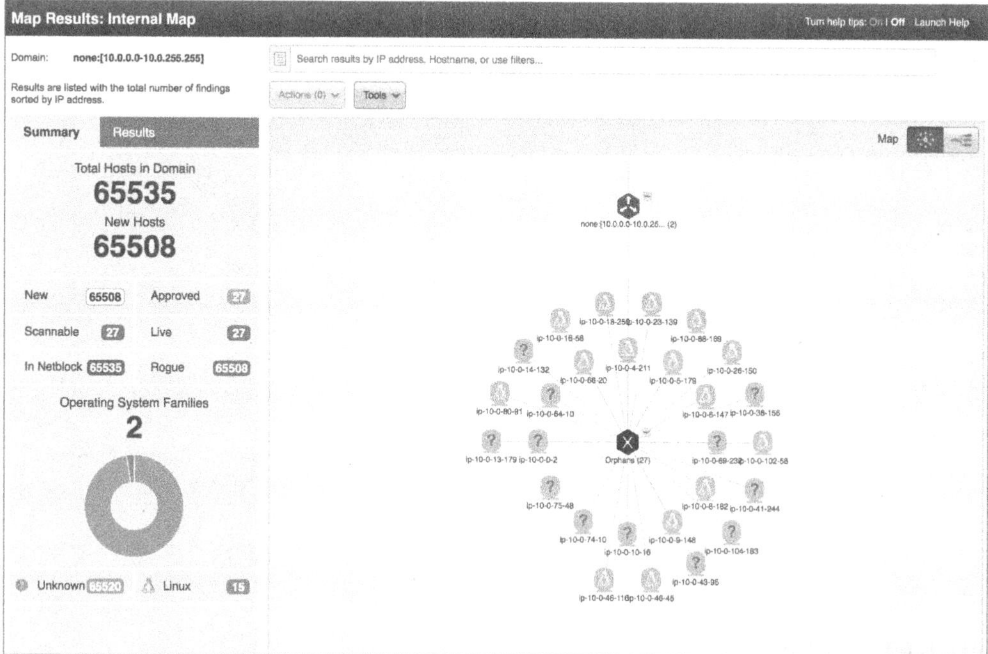

Determining Scan Frequency

Cybersecurity professionals depend on automation to help them perform their duties in an efficient, effective manner. Vulnerability scanning tools allow the automated scheduling of scans to take the burden off administrators. Figure 4.3 shows an example of how these scans might be configured in Tenable's Nessus product. Nessus was one of the first vulnerability scanners on the market and remains widely used today. Administrators may designate a schedule that meets their security, compliance, and business requirements.

Administrators should configure these scans to provide automated alerting when they detect new vulnerabilities. Many security teams configure their scans to produce automated email reports of scan results, such as the report shown in Figure 4.4.

Many different factors influence how often an organization decides to conduct vulnerability scans against its systems:

- The organization's *risk appetite* is its willingness to tolerate risk within the environment. If an organization is extremely risk averse, it may choose to conduct scans more frequently to minimize the amount of time between when a vulnerability comes into existence and when it is detected by a scan.
- *Regulatory requirements,* such as PCI DSS or FISMA, may dictate a minimum frequency for vulnerability scans. These requirements may also come from corporate policies.

FIGURE 4.3 Configuring a Nessus scan

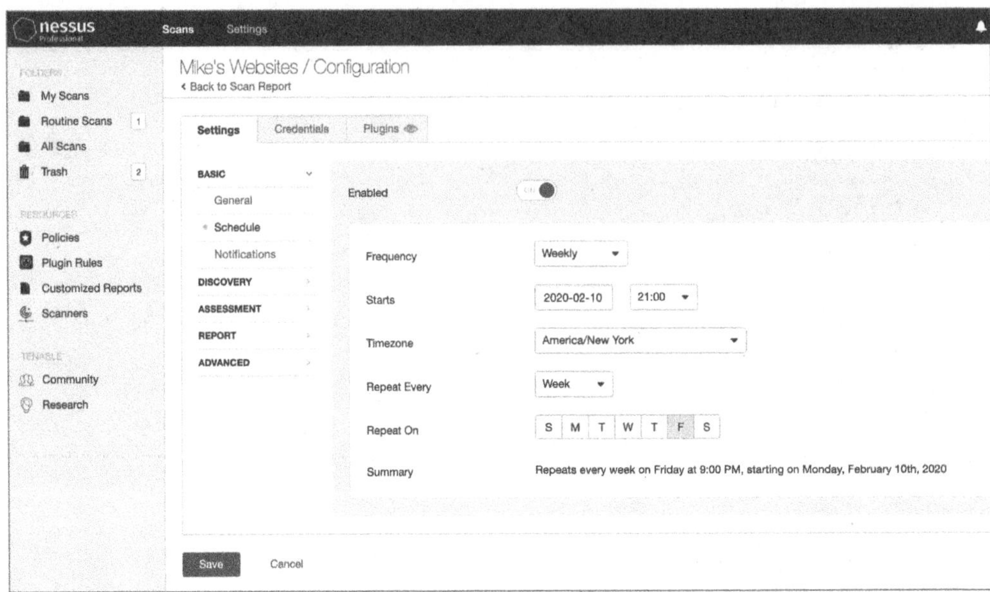

FIGURE 4.4 Sample Nessus scan report

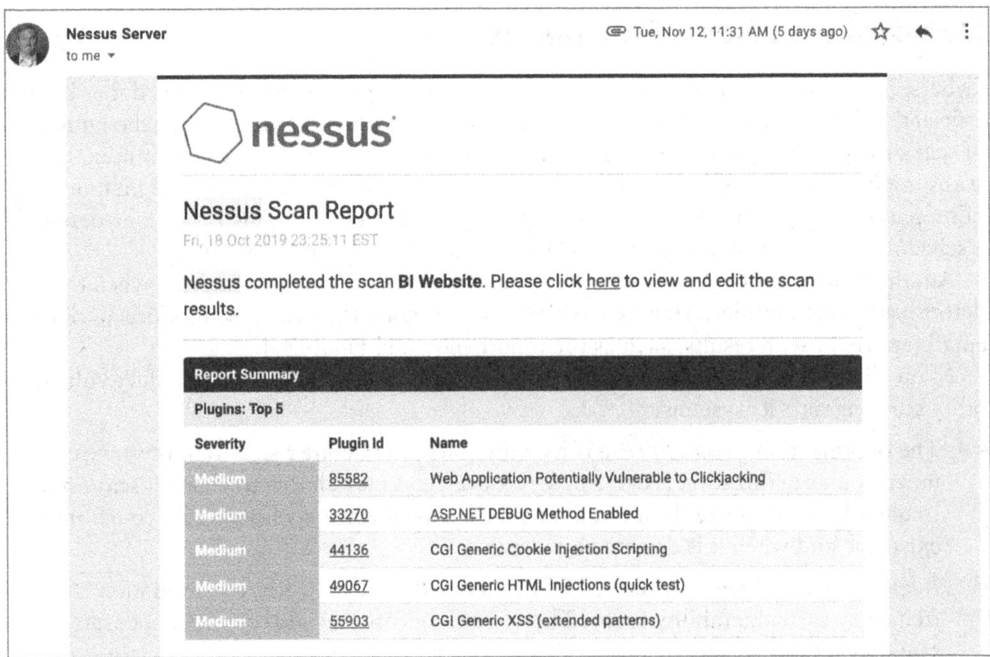

- *Technical constraints* may limit the frequency of scanning. For example, the scanning system may only be capable of performing a certain number of scans per day, and organizations may need to adjust scan frequency to ensure that all scans complete successfully.
- *Business constraints* may limit the organization from conducting resource-intensive vulnerability scans during periods of high business activity to avoid disruption of critical processes.
- *Licensing limitations* may curtail the bandwidth consumed by the scanner or the number of scans that may be conducted simultaneously.

Cybersecurity professionals must balance each of these considerations when planning a vulnerability scanning program. It is usually wise to begin small and slowly expand the scope and frequency of vulnerability scans over time to avoid overwhelming the scanning infrastructure or enterprise systems.

Active vs. Passive Scanning

Most vulnerability scanning tools perform *active vulnerability scanning*, meaning that the tool actually interacts with the scanned host to identify open services and check for possible vulnerabilities. Active scanning does provide high-quality results, but those results come with some drawbacks:

- Active scanning is noisy and will likely be detected by the administrators of scanned systems. This may not be an issue in environments where administrators have knowledge of the scanning, but active scanning is problematic if the scan is meant to be stealthy.
- Active scanning also has the potential to accidentally exploit vulnerabilities and interfere with the functioning of production systems. Although active scanners often have settings that you can use to minimize this risk, the reality is that active scanning can cause production issues.
- Active scans may also completely miss some systems if they are blocked by firewalls, intrusion prevention systems, network segmentation, or other security controls.

Passive vulnerability scanning takes a different approach that supplements active scans. Instead of probing systems for vulnerabilities, passive scanners monitor the network, similar to the technique used by intrusion detection systems. But instead of watching for intrusion attempts, they look for the telltale signatures of outdated systems and applications, reporting results to administrators.

Passive scans have some very attractive benefits, but they're only capable of detecting vulnerabilities that are reflected in network traffic. They're not a replacement for active scanning, but they are a very strong complement to periodic active vulnerability scans.

Configuring and Executing Vulnerability Scans

Once security professionals have determined the basic requirements for their vulnerability management program, they must configure vulnerability management tools to perform scans according to the requirements-based scan specifications. These tasks include identifying the appropriate scope for each scan, configuring scans to meet the organization's requirements, and maintaining the currency of the vulnerability scanning tool.

Scoping Vulnerability Scans

The *scope* of a vulnerability scan describes the extent of the scan, including answers to the following questions:

- What systems and networks will be included in the vulnerability scan?
- What technical measures will be used to test whether systems are present on the network?
- What tests will be performed against systems discovered by a vulnerability scan?

Administrators should first answer these questions in a general sense and ensure that they have consensus from technical staff and management that the scans are appropriate and unlikely to cause disruption to the business. Once they've determined that the scans are well designed and unlikely to cause serious issues, they may then move on to configuring the scans within the vulnerability management tool.

Scoping for Compliance Purposes

Scoping is an important tool in the cybersecurity analyst's toolkit because it allows analysts to reduce problems to a manageable size. For example, an organization that processes credit cards may face the seemingly insurmountable task of achieving PCI DSS compliance across their entire network that consists of thousands of systems.

Through judicious use of network segmentation and other techniques, administrators may isolate the handful of systems involved in credit card processing, segregating them from the vast majority of systems on the organization's network. When done properly, this segmentation reduces the scope of PCI DSS compliance to the much smaller isolated network that is dedicated to payment card processing.

When the organization is able to reduce the scope of the PCI DSS network, it also reduces the scope of many of the required PCI DSS controls, including vulnerability scanning. Instead of contracting with an approved scanning vendor to conduct quarterly compliance scans of the organization's entire network, they may reduce the scope of that scan to those systems that actually engage in card processing. This will dramatically reduce the cost of the scanning engagement and the remediation workload facing cybersecurity professionals after the scan completes.

Configuring Vulnerability Scans

Vulnerability management solutions provide administrators with the ability to configure many different parameters related to scans. In addition to scheduling automated scans and producing reports, administrators can customize the types of checks performed by the scanner, provide credentials to access target servers, install scanning agents on target servers, and conduct scans from a variety of network perspectives.

Scan Sensitivity Levels

Cybersecurity professionals configuring vulnerability scans should pay careful attention to the configuration settings related to the scan sensitivity level. These settings determine the types of checks that the scanner will perform and should be customized to ensure that the scan meets its objectives while minimizing the possibility of disrupting the target environment.

Typically, administrators create a new scan by beginning with a template. This may be a template provided by the vulnerability management vendor and built into the product, such as the Nessus templates shown in Figure 4.5, or it may be a custom-developed template created for use within the organization. As administrators create their own scan configurations, they should consider saving common configuration settings in templates to allow efficient reuse of their work, saving time and reducing errors when configuring future scans.

FIGURE 4.5 Nessus scan templates

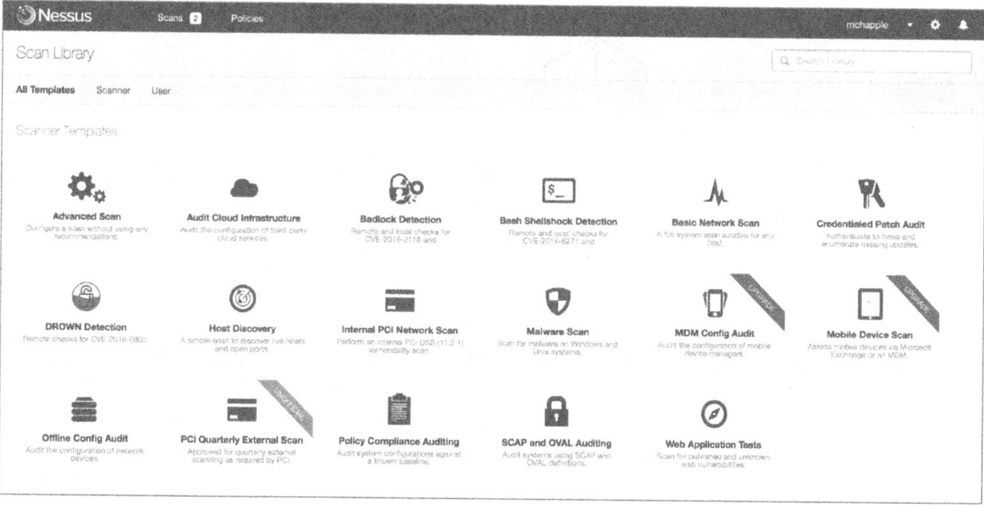

Administrators may also improve the efficiency of their scans by configuring the specific plug-ins that will run during each scan. Each plug-in performs a check for a specific vulnerability, and these plug-ins are often grouped into families based on the operating system, application, or device that they involve. Disabling unnecessary plug-ins improves the speed of the scan by bypassing unnecessary checks and also may reduce the number of false positive results detected by the scanner.

For example, an organization that does not use the Amazon Linux operating system may choose to disable all checks related to Amazon Linux in their scanning template. Figure 4.6 shows an example of disabling these plug-ins in Nessus.

FIGURE 4.6 Disabling unused plug-ins

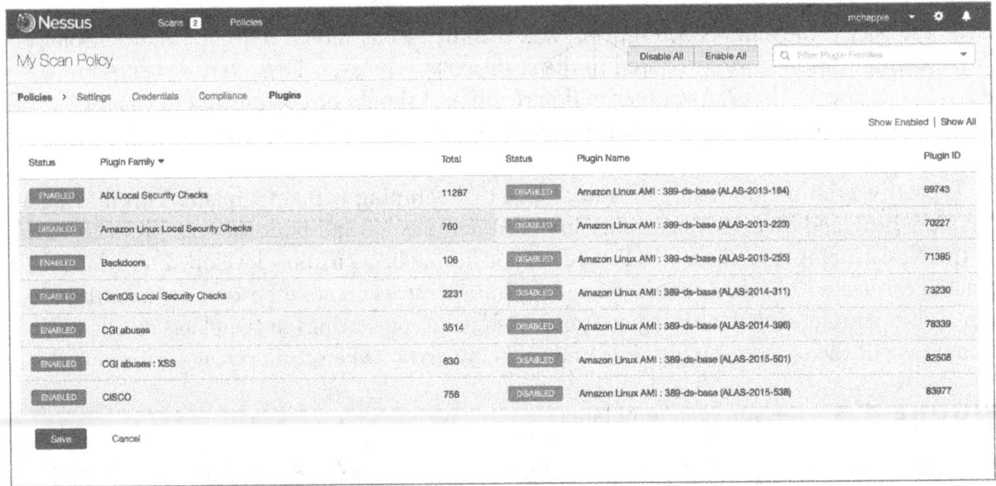

Some plug-ins perform tests that may disrupt activity on a production system or, in the worst case, damage content on those systems. These plug-ins are a tricky situation. Administrators want to run these scans because they may identify problems that could be exploited by a malicious source. At the same time, cybersecurity professionals clearly don't want to *cause* problems on the organization's network!

One way around this problem is to maintain a test environment containing copies of the same systems running on the production network and running scans against those test systems first. If the scans detect problems in the test environment, administrators may correct the underlying causes on both test and production networks before running scans on the production network.

Supplementing Network Scans

Basic vulnerability scans run over a network, probing a system from a distance. This provides a realistic view of the system's security by simulating what an attacker might see from another network vantage point. However, the firewalls, intrusion prevention systems, and other security controls that exist on the path between the scanner and the target server may affect the scan results, providing an inaccurate view of the server's security independent of those controls.

Additionally, many security vulnerabilities are difficult to confirm using only a remote scan. Vulnerability scans that run over the network may detect the possibility that a vulnerability exists but be unable to confirm it with confidence, causing a false positive result that requires time-consuming administrator investigation.

Modern vulnerability management solutions can supplement these remote scans with trusted information about server configurations. This information may be gathered in two ways. First, administrators can provide the scanner with credentials that allow the scanner to connect to the target server and retrieve configuration information. This information can then be used to determine whether a vulnerability exists, improving the scan's accuracy over noncredentialed alternatives. For example, if a vulnerability scan detects a potential issue that can be corrected by an operating system update, the credentialed scan can check whether the update is installed on the system before reporting a vulnerability.

Figure 4.7 shows an example of the *credentialed scanning* options available within Qualys. Credentialed scans may access operating systems, databases, and applications, among other sources.

Credentialed scans typically only retrieve information from target servers and do not make changes to the server itself. Therefore, administrators should enforce the principle of least privilege by providing the scanner with a read-only account on the server. This reduces the likelihood of a security incident related to the scanner's credentialed access.

FIGURE 4.7 Configuring authenticated scanning

Authentication

Authentication enables the scanner to log into hosts at scan time to extend detection capabilities. See the online help to learn how to configure this option.

- [x] Windows
- [x] Unix/Cisco IOS
- [x] Oracle
- [ ] Oracle Listener
- [ ] SNMP
- [ ] VMware
- [ ] DB2
- [ ] HTTP
- [ ] MySQL

In addition to credentialed scanning, some scanners supplement the traditional *server-based scanning* approach to vulnerability scanning with a complementary *agent-based scanning* approach. In this approach, administrators install small software agents on each target server. These agents conduct scans of the server configuration, providing an "inside-out" vulnerability scan, and then report information back to the vulnerability management platform for analysis and reporting.

System administrators are typically wary of installing agents on the servers that they manage for fear that the agent will cause performance or stability issues. If you choose to use an agent-based approach to scanning, you should approach this concept conservatively, beginning with a small pilot deployment that builds confidence in the agent before proceeding with a more widespread deployment.

Scan Perspective

Comprehensive vulnerability management programs provide the ability to conduct scans from a variety of *scan perspectives*. Each scan perspective conducts the scan from a different location on the network, providing a different view into vulnerabilities. For example, an external scan is run from the Internet, giving administrators a view of what an attacker located outside the organization would see as potential vulnerabilities. Internal scans might run from a scanner on the general corporate network, providing the view that a malicious insider might encounter. Finally, scanners located inside the datacenter and agents located on the servers offer the most accurate view of the real state of the server by showing vulnerabilities that might be blocked by other security controls on the network. Controls that might affect scan results include

- Firewall settings
- Network segmentation
- Intrusion detection systems (IDSs)
- Intrusion prevention systems (IPSs)

The internal and external scans required by PCI DSS are a good example of scans performed from different perspectives. The organization may conduct its own internal scans but must supplement them with external scans conducted by an approved scanning vendor.

Vulnerability management platforms have the ability to manage different scanners and provide a consolidated view of scan results, compiling data from different sources. Figure 4.8 shows an example of how the administrator may select the scanner for a newly configured scan using Qualys.

FIGURE 4.8 Choosing a scan appliance

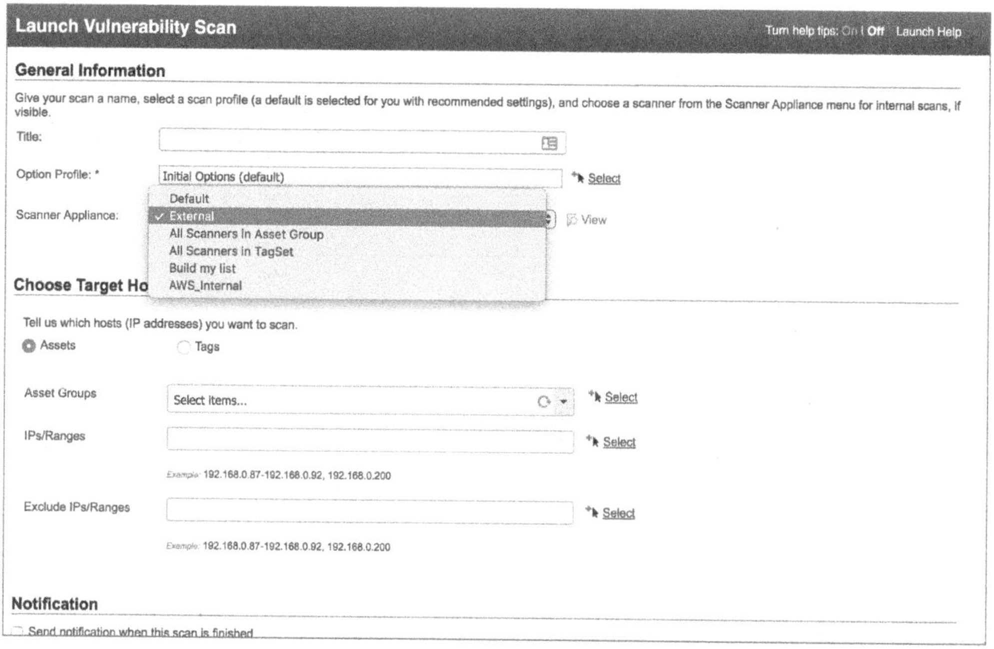

Scanner Maintenance

As with any technology product, vulnerability management solutions require care and feeding. Administrators should conduct regular maintenance of their vulnerability scanner to ensure that the scanning software and *vulnerability feeds* remain up-to-date.

Scanning systems do provide automatic updating capabilities that keep the scanner and its vulnerability feeds up to date. Organizations can and should take advantage of these features, but it is always a good idea to check in once in a while and manually verify that the scanner is updating properly.

Scanner Software

Scanning systems themselves aren't immune from vulnerabilities. As shown in Figure 4.9, even vulnerability scanners can have security issues! Regular patching of scanner software protects an organization against scanner-specific vulnerabilities and also provides important bug fixes and feature enhancements to improve scan quality.

FIGURE 4.9 Nessus vulnerability in the NIST National Vulnerability Database (Source: NIST)

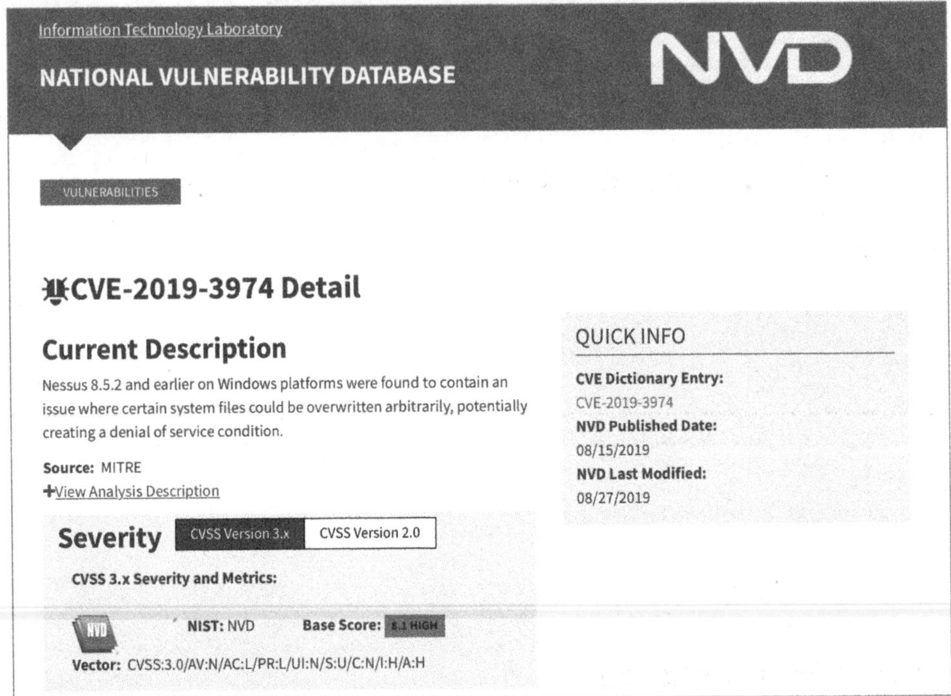

Vulnerability Plug-in Feeds

Security researchers discover new vulnerabilities every week, and vulnerability scanners can be effective against these vulnerabilities only if they receive frequent updates to their plug-ins. Administrators should configure their scanners to retrieve new plug-ins on a regular basis, preferably daily. Fortunately, as shown in Figure 4.10, this process is easily automated.

Security Content Automation Protocol (SCAP)

The Security Content Automation Protocol (SCAP) is an effort by the security community, led by the National Institute of Standards and Technology (NIST), to create a standardized approach for communicating security-related information. This standardization is important to the automation of interactions between security components. The SCAP standards include the following:

Common Configuration Enumeration (CCE) Provides a standard nomenclature for discussing system configuration issues

Common Platform Enumeration (CPE) Provides a standard nomenclature for describing product names and versions

Common Vulnerabilities and Exposures (CVE) Provides a standard nomenclature for describing security-related software flaws

Common Vulnerability Scoring System (CVSS) Provides a standardized approach for measuring and describing the severity of security-related software flaws

Extensible Configuration Checklist Description Format (XCCDF) A language for specifying checklists and reporting checklist results

Open Vulnerability and Assessment Language (OVAL) A language for specifying low-level testing procedures used by checklists

For more information on SCAP, see NIST SP 800-117: Guide to Adopting and Using the Security Content Automation Protocol (SCAP) Version 1.0 or the SCAP website (`csrc.nist.gov/projects/security-content-automation-protocol/`).

FIGURE 4.10 Nessus Automatic Updates

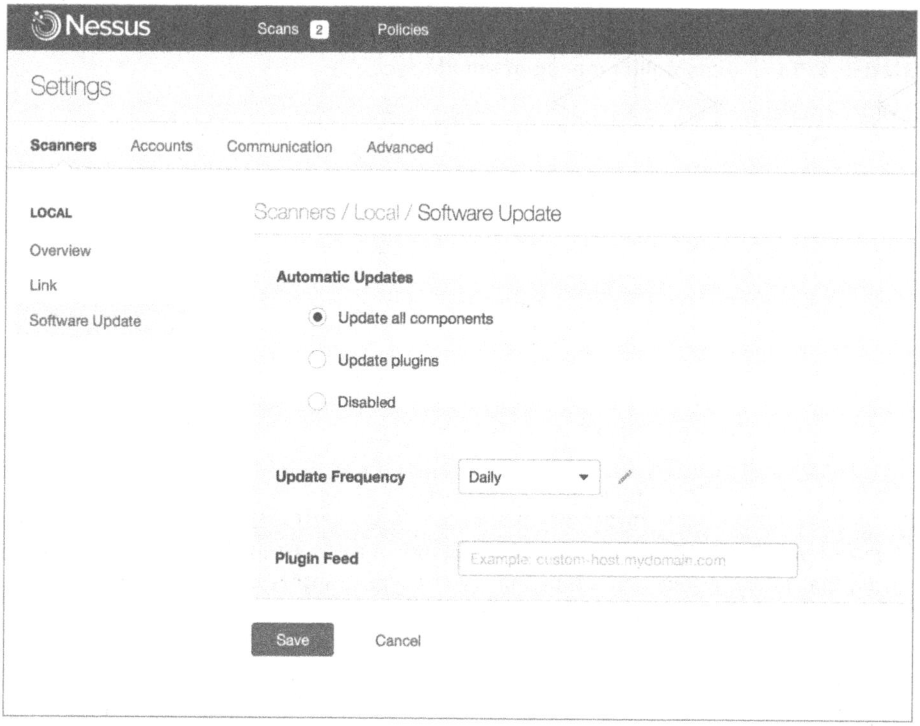

Developing a Remediation Workflow

Vulnerability scans often produce a fairly steady stream of security issues that require attention from cybersecurity professionals, system engineers, software developers, network engineers, and other technologists. The initial scans of an environment can produce an overwhelming number of issues requiring prioritization and eventual *remediation*. Organizations should develop a remediation workflow that allows for the prioritization of vulnerabilities and the tracking of remediation through the cycle of detection, remediation, and testing shown in Figure 4.11.

This remediation workflow should be as automated as possible, given the tools available to the organization. Many vulnerability management products include a built-in workflow mechanism that allows cybersecurity experts to track vulnerabilities through the remediation process and automatically close out vulnerabilities after testing confirms that the remediation was successful. Although these tools are helpful, other organizations often choose not to use them in favor of tracking vulnerabilities in the IT service management (ITSM) tool that the organization uses for other technology issues. This approach avoids asking technologists to use two different issue tracking systems and improves compliance with the remediation process. However, it also requires selecting vulnerability management tools that integrate natively with the organization's ITSM tool (or vice versa) or building an integration between the tools if one does not already exist.

FIGURE 4.11 Vulnerability management life cycle

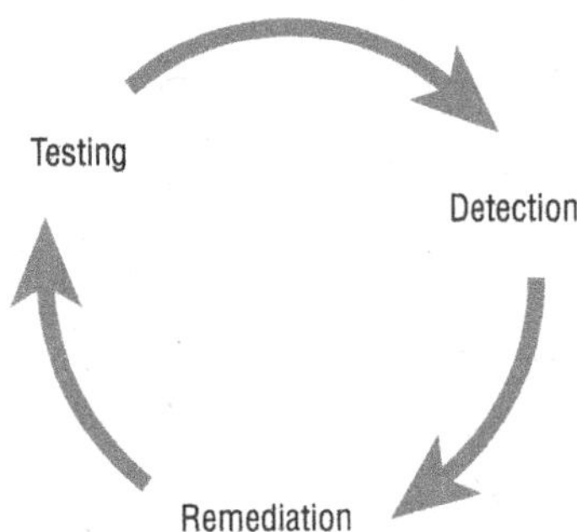

An important trend in vulnerability management is a shift toward *ongoing scanning* and *continuous monitoring*. Ongoing scanning moves away from the scheduled scanning approach that tested systems on a scheduled weekly or monthly basis and instead configures scanners to simply scan systems on a rotating basis, checking for vulnerabilities as often as scanning resources permit. This approach can be bandwidth and resource intensive, but it does provide earlier detection of vulnerabilities. Continuous monitoring incorporates data from agent-based approaches to vulnerability detection and reports security-related configuration changes to the vulnerability management platform as soon as they occur, providing the ability to analyze those changes for potential vulnerabilities.

Reporting and Communication

Communicating vulnerability scan results to technologists who have the ability to remediate them and managers responsible for the security of the environment is a critical component of vulnerability management. After all, if the team members who can correct the issue never see the results, vulnerability scanning is a waste of time!

Modern vulnerability management tools provide very strong reporting capabilities. These reports may be manually generated on demand to answer specific questions, or administrators may set up automated reports that generate on a scheduled basis and are pushed out to those who need to see them. Additionally, administrators may set up alerting mechanisms to immediately notify key personnel of critical new vulnerabilities as soon as they are detected.

Management-level dashboards provide a very high-level summary of the cybersecurity health of the environment. This type of report is often used to give leaders a quick snapshot of the environment. An example of a dashboard from Qualys appears in Figure 4.12.

FIGURE 4.12 Qualys dashboard example

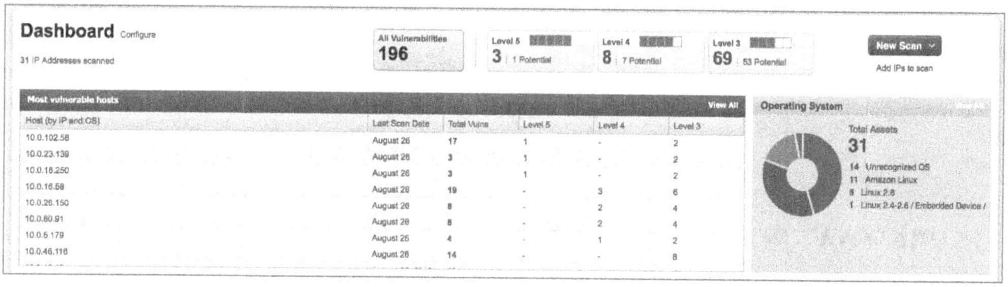

As cybersecurity analysts drill deeper into the vulnerability management system, they can see summary technical reports that show the specific vulnerabilities detected on the network and sort them by vulnerability type, severity, host group, and other factors. An example of this type of report from Nessus appears in Figure 4.13. These reports are useful in identifying the widespread issues that require attention from cybersecurity professionals.

System engineers are typically more interested in detailed reports listing all the vulnerabilities on the systems they administer. Figure 4.14 shows a Nessus report listing all the vulnerabilities that exist on a single system scanned by the tool. The report provides a full listing of vulnerabilities, sorted by severity, and can serve as a checklist that system engineers can use to prioritize their remediation efforts for a system.

The final level of drill-down provides the nitty-gritty details required to fix an individual vulnerability on a system. Figure 4.15 shows an example of this type of reporting. The report identifies the vulnerability that was detected, explains the significance and cause of the vulnerability, and provides remediation instructions to help guide the administrator's efforts in correcting the underlying security issue.

FIGURE 4.13 Nessus report example by IP address

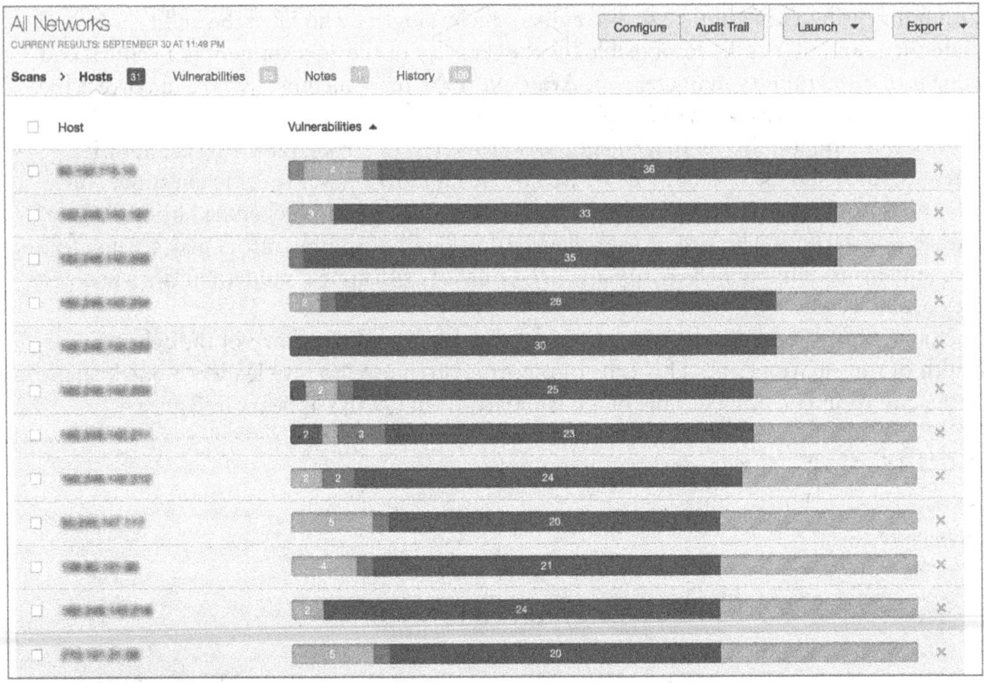

FIGURE 4.14 Nessus report example by criticality

Severity	Plugin Name	Plugin Family	Count
CRITICAL	MS14-066: Vulnerability in Schannel Could Allow Remote Code Execution (2992611) (uncre...	Windows	1
CRITICAL	MS15-034: Vulnerability in HTTP.sys Could Allow Remote Code Execution (3042553) (uncre...	Windows	1
MEDIUM	Microsoft Exchange Client Access Server Information Disclosure	Windows	1
LOW	Web Server HTTP Header Internal IP Disclosure	Web Servers	2
LOW	SSL RC4 Cipher Suites Supported (Bar Mitzvah)	General	1
INFO	Service Detection	Service detection	3
INFO	HyperText Transfer Protocol (HTTP) Information	Web Servers	2
INFO	Nessus SYN scanner	Port scanners	2
INFO	Web Server No 404 Error Code Check	Web Servers	2
INFO	Additional DNS Hostnames	General	1
INFO	Common Platform Enumeration (CPE)	General	1
INFO	Device Type	General	1
INFO	Host Fully Qualified Domain Name (FQDN) Resolution	General	1

FIGURE 4.15 Detailed vulnerability report

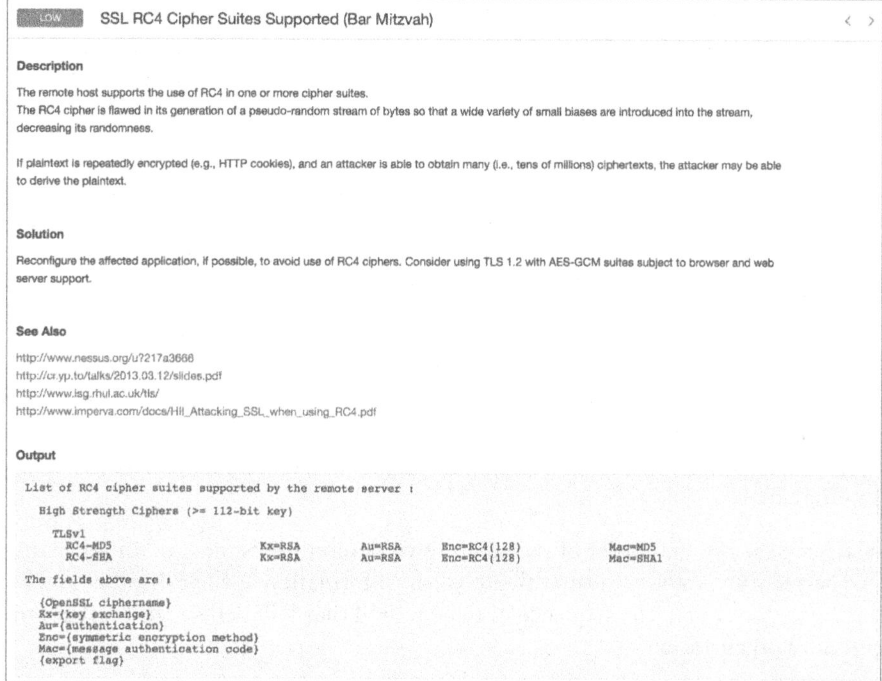

LOW SSL RC4 Cipher Suites Supported (Bar Mitzvah)

Description

The remote host supports the use of RC4 in one or more cipher suites.
The RC4 cipher is flawed in its generation of a pseudo-random stream of bytes so that a wide variety of small biases are introduced into the stream, decreasing its randomness.

If plaintext is repeatedly encrypted (e.g., HTTP cookies), and an attacker is able to obtain many (i.e., tens of millions) ciphertexts, the attacker may be able to derive the plaintext.

Solution

Reconfigure the affected application, if possible, to avoid use of RC4 ciphers. Consider using TLS 1.2 with AES-GCM suites subject to browser and web server support.

See Also

http://www.nessus.org/u?217a3666
http://cr.yp.to/talks/2013.03.12/slides.pdf
http://www.isg.rhul.ac.uk/tls/
http://www.imperva.com/docs/HII_Attacking_SSL_when_using_RC4.pdf

Output

```
List of RC4 cipher suites supported by the remote server :

  High Strength Ciphers (>= 112-bit key)

    TLSv1
      RC4-MD5              Kx=RSA     Au=RSA     Enc=RC4(128)          Mac=MD5
      RC4-SHA              Kx=RSA     Au=RSA     Enc=RC4(128)          Mac=SHA1

The fields above are :

  {OpenSSL ciphername}
  Kx={key exchange}
  Au={authentication}
  Enc={symmetric encryption method}
  Mac={message authentication code}
  {export flag}
```

Prioritizing Remediation

As cybersecurity analysts work their way through vulnerability scanning reports, they must make important decisions about prioritizing remediation to use their limited resources to resolve the issues that pose the greatest danger to the organization. There is no cut-and-dried formula for prioritizing vulnerabilities. Rather, analysts must take several important factors into account when choosing where to turn their attention first.

Some of the most important factors in the remediation prioritization decision-making process include the following:

Criticality of the Systems and Information Affected by the Vulnerability Criticality measures should take into account confidentiality, integrity, and availability requirements, depending on the nature of the vulnerability. For example, if the vulnerability allows a denial-of-service attack, cybersecurity analysts should consider the impact to the organization if the system became unusable due to an attack. If the vulnerability allows the theft of stored information from a database, cybersecurity analysts should consider the impact on the organization if that information were stolen.

Difficulty of Remediating the Vulnerability If fixing a vulnerability will require an inordinate commitment of human or financial resources, that fact should be factored into the decision-making process. Cybersecurity analysts may find that they can fix five issues rated numbers 2 through 6 in priority order for the same investment that would be required to address the top issue. This doesn't mean that they should necessarily choose to make that decision based on cost and difficulty alone, but it is a consideration in the prioritization process.

Severity of the Vulnerability The more severe an issue is, the more important it is to correct that issue. Analysts may turn to the Common Vulnerability Scoring System (CVSS) to provide relative severity rankings for different vulnerabilities. Remember from earlier in this chapter that CVSS is a component of SCAP.

Exposure of the Vulnerability Cybersecurity analysts should also consider how exposed the vulnerability is to potential exploitation. For example, if an internal server has a serious SQL injection vulnerability but that server is accessible only from internal networks, remediating that issue may take a lower priority than remediating a less severe issue that is exposed to the Internet and, therefore, more vulnerable to external attack.

Identifying the optimal order of remediating vulnerabilities is more of an art than a science. Cybersecurity analysts must evaluate all the information at their disposal and make informed decisions about the sequence of remediation that will deliver the most security value to their organization.

Testing and Implementing Fixes

Before deploying any remediation activity, cybersecurity professionals and other technologists should thoroughly test their planned fixes in a sandbox environment. This allows technologists to identify any unforeseen side effects of the fix and reduces the likelihood that remediation activities will disrupt business operations or cause damage to the organization's information assets.

After deploying a fix by patching or hardening the affected system(s), you should take steps to verify that the mitigation was effective. This typically involves repeating the vulnerability scan that initially identified the vulnerability and confirming that the issue does not appear in the new scan results.

When you do perform mitigation activities, it's important to remember to update your configuration baseline as well. For example, if you apply a security patch to your systems, you should also modify your configuration baseline to ensure that future systems are patched against that same vulnerability from the start.

Delayed Remediation Options

It's not always possible to remediate every vulnerability. In cases where you can't correct the problem immediately, you have two basic options available to you.

First, you can implement a *compensating control*. Compensating controls are additional security measures that you take to address a vulnerability without remediating the underlying issue. For example, if you have a web application that is vulnerable to SQL injection but you can't correct the web application itself, you might use a web application firewall to block SQL injection attack attempts. The web application firewall serves as a compensating control.

Second, you can decide that the risk is acceptable and that you will continue business as usual, acknowledging the risk and moving on.

Overcoming Risks of Vulnerability Scanning

Vulnerability scanning is often a high priority for cybersecurity professionals, but other technologists in the organization may not see it as an important activity. Cybersecurity analysts should be aware of the barriers raised by others to vulnerability scanning and ways to address those concerns. Some common barriers to overcome include the following:

Service Degradations This is the most common barrier to vulnerability scanning raised by technology professionals. Vulnerability scans consume network bandwidth and tie up the resources on systems that are the targets of scans. This may degrade system functionality and pose a risk of interrupting business processes. This risk increases when scans involve *legacy systems* or *proprietary systems* that might exhibit unpredictable behavior in the face of an automated vulnerability scan. Cybersecurity professionals can address these concerns by tuning scans to consume less bandwidth and coordinating scan times with operational schedules. Figure 4.16 shows ways that administrators can adjust scan intensity in Qualys.

Customer Commitments They can create barriers to vulnerability scanning. *Memorandums of understanding (MOUs)* and *service-level agreements (SLAs)* with customers may create expectations related to uptime, performance, and security that the organization must fulfill. If scanning will negatively impact the organization's ability to meet customer commitments, customers may need to participate in the decision-making process.

FIGURE 4.16 Qualys scan performance settings

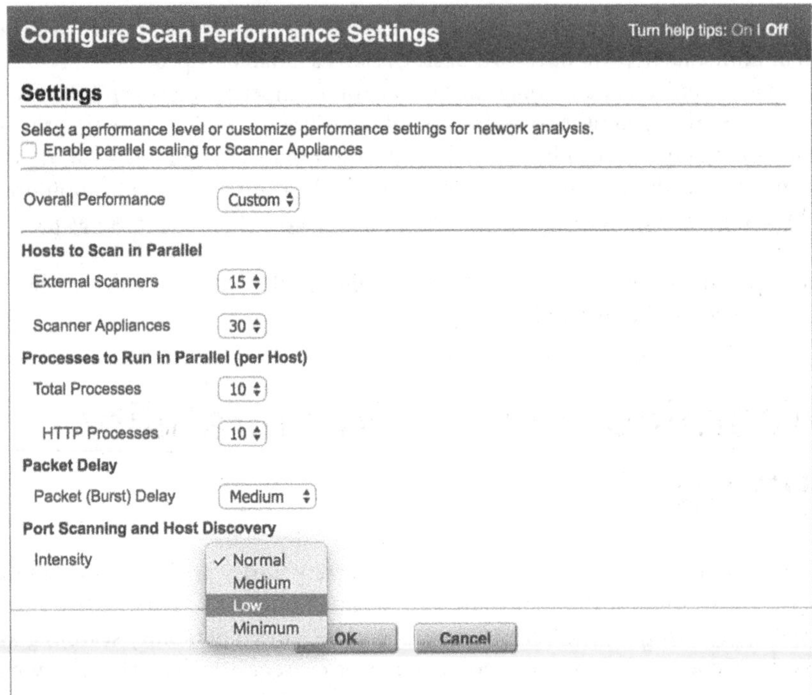

Cybersecurity professionals can avoid issues with MOUs and SLAs by ensuring that they are involved in the creation of those agreements in the first place. Many concerns can be avoided if customer agreements include language that anticipates vulnerability scans and acknowledges that they may have an impact on performance. Most customers will understand the importance of conducting vulnerability scans as long as you provide them with advanced notice of the timing and potential impact of scans.

IT Governance and Change Management Processes They can create bureaucratic hurdles to making the configuration changes required to support scanning. Cybersecurity analysts should work within these organizational governance processes to obtain the resources and support required to support a vulnerability management program.

Vulnerability Scanning Tools

As you fill out your cybersecurity toolkit, you will want to have both a network vulnerability scanner and a web application scanner available for use. Vulnerability scanners are often leveraged for preventive scanning and testing and are also found in penetration testers toolkits, where they help identify systems that testers can exploit. This also means they're a favorite tool of attackers!

Infrastructure Vulnerability Scanning

As you prepare for the CySA+ exam, you should be familiar with the major infrastructure vulnerability scanning tools used by cybersecurity analysts. The following tools are examples of network vulnerability scanners:

- Tenable's *Nessus* is a well-known and widely respected network vulnerability scanning product that was one of the earliest products in this field.
- *Qualys's* vulnerability scanner is a more recently developed commercial network vulnerability scanner that offers a unique deployment model using a software-as-a-service (SaaS) management console to run scans using appliances located both in on-premises datacenters and in the cloud.
- Rapid7's *Nexpose* is another commercial vulnerability management system that offers capabilities similar to those of Nessus and Qualys.
- The open source *OpenVAS* offers a free alternative to commercial vulnerability scanners.

These four products are the network vulnerability scanners that you are required to know for the CySA+ exam. Many other examples of network vulnerability scanners are on the market today, and every mature organization should have at least one scanner in their toolkit. Many organizations choose to deploy two different vulnerability scanning products in the same environment as a defense-in-depth control.

Web Application Scanning

Web application scanners are specialized tools used to examine the security of web applications. These tools test for web-specific vulnerabilities, such as SQL injection, cross-site scripting (XSS), and cross-site request forgery (CSRF) vulnerabilities. They work by combining traditional network scans of web servers with detailed probing of web applications using such techniques as sending known malicious input sequences and fuzzing in attempts to break the application.

Nikto is one of the two open source web application scanning tools that are required knowledge for the CySA+ exam. As an open source tool, it is freely available for anyone to use. As shown in Figure 4.17, Nikto uses a command-line interface and is somewhat difficult to use.

FIGURE 4.17 Nikto web application scanner

```
 Scripting (XSS). http://www.cert.org/advisories/CA-2000-02.html.
+ /servlet/org.apache.catalina.ContainerServlet/<script>alert('Vulnerable')</script>: Apache-Tomcat is vulnerab
le to Cross Site Scripting (XSS) by invoking java classes. http://www.cert.org/advisories/CA-2000-02.html.
+ /servlet/org.apache.catalina.Context/<script>alert('Vulnerable')</script>: Apache-Tomcat is vulnerable to Cro
ss Site Scripting (XSS) by invoking java classes. http://www.cert.org/advisories/CA-2000-02.html.
+ /servlet/org.apache.catalina.Globals/<script>alert('Vulnerable')</script>: Apache-Tomcat is vulnerable to Cro
ss Site Scripting (XSS) by invoking java classes. http://www.cert.org/advisories/CA-2000-02.html.
+ /servlet/org.apache.catalina.servlets.WebdavStatus/<script>alert('Vulnerable')</script>: Apache-Tomcat is vul
nerable to Cross Site Scripting (XSS) by invoking java classes. http://www.cert.org/advisories/CA-2000-02.html.
+ /nosuchurl/><script>alert('Vulnerable')</script>: JEUS is vulnerable to Cross Site Scripting (XSS) when reque
sting non-existing JSP pages. http://securitytracker.com/alerts/2003/Jun/1007004.html
+ /~/<script>alert('Vulnerable')</script>.aspx?aspxerrorpath=null: Cross site scripting (XSS) is allowed with .
aspx file requests (may be Microsoft .net). http://www.cert.org/advisories/CA-2000-02.html
+ /~/<script>alert('Vulnerable')</script>.aspx: Cross site scripting (XSS) is allowed with .aspx file requests
(may be Microsoft .net). http://www.cert.org/advisories/CA-2000-02.html
+ /~/<script>alert('Vulnerable')</script>.asp: Cross site scripting (XSS) is allowed with .asp file requests (m
ay be Microsoft .net). http://www.cert.org/advisories/CA-2000-02.html
+ /node/view/666\"><script>alert(document.domain)</script>: Drupal 4.2.0 RC is vulnerable to Cross Site Scripti
ng (XSS). http://www.cert.org/advisories/CA-2000-02.html.
+ /mailman/listinfo/<script>alert('Vulnerable')</script>: Mailman is vulnerable to Cross Site Scripting (XSS).
Upgrade to version 2.0.8 to fix. http://www.cert.org/advisories/CA-2000-02.html.
+ OSVDB-27095: /bb000001.pl<script>alert('Vulnerable')</script>: Actinic E-Commerce services is vulnerable to C
ross Site Scripting (XSS). http://www.cert.org/advisories/CA-2000-02.html.
+ OSVDB-54589: /a.jsp/<script>alert('Vulnerable')</script>: JServ is vulnerable to Cross Site Scripting (XSS) w
hen a non-existent JSP file is requested. Upgrade to the latest version of JServ. http://www.cert.org/advisorie
s/CA-2000-02.html.
+ /<script>alert('Vulnerable')</script>.thtml: Server is vulnerable to Cross Site Scripting (XSS). http://www.c
ert.org/advisories/CA-2000-02.html.
+ /<script>alert('Vulnerable')</script>.shtml: Server is vulnerable to Cross Site Scripting (XSS). http://www.c
ert.org/advisories/CA-2000-02.html.
+ /<script>alert('Vulnerable')</script>.jsp: Server is vulnerable to Cross Site Scripting (XSS). http://www.cer
t.org/advisories/CA-2000-02.html.
+ /<script>alert('Vulnerable')</script>.aspx: Cross site scripting (XSS) is allowed with .aspx file requests (m
ay be Microsoft .net). http://www.cert.org/advisories/CA-2000-02.html.
```

The other open source tool available for web application scanning is Arachni. This tool, shown in Figure 4.18, is a packaged scanner available for Windows, macOS, and Linux operating systems.

Most organizations use web application scanners, but they choose to use commercial products that offer advanced capabilities and user-friendly interfaces. Although there are dedicated web application scanners, such as Acunetix, on the market, many firms use the web application scanning capabilities of traditional network vulnerability scanners, such as Nessus, Qualys, and Nexpose. Figure 4.19 shows an example of Nessus used in a web scanning role.

Interception Proxies

Interception proxies are valuable tools for penetration testers and others seeking to evaluate the security of web applications. As such, they can be classified as exploit tools. They run on the tester's system and intercept requests being sent from the web browser to the web server before they are released onto the network. This allows the tester to manually manipulate the request to attempt the injection of an attack.

Figure 4.20 shows the popular open source Zed Attack Proxy (ZAP). ZAP is a community development project coordinated by the Open Web Application Security Project (OWASP). Users of ZAP can intercept requests sent from any web browser and alter them before passing them to the web server.

FIGURE 4.18 Arachni web application scanner

FIGURE 4.19 Nessus web application scanner

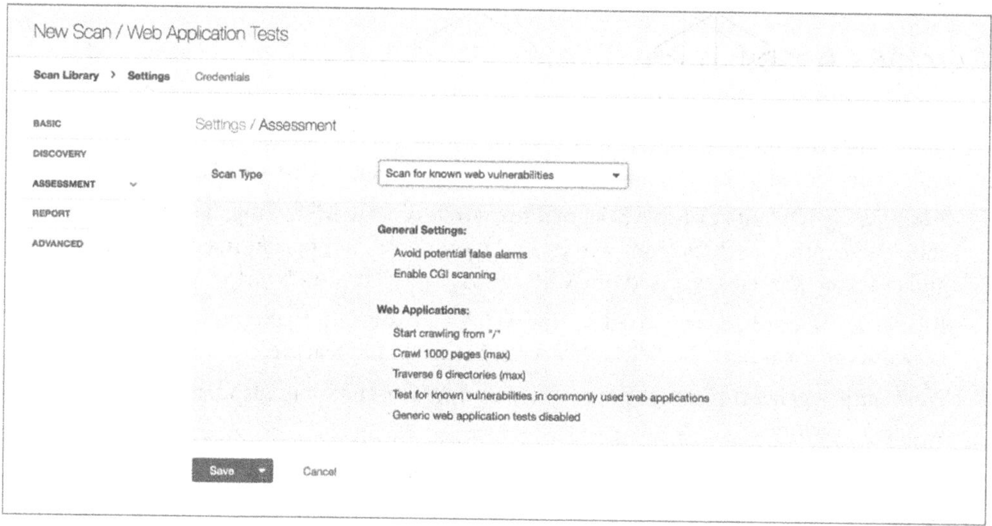

The Burp Proxy, shown in Figure 4.21, is another option available to cybersecurity analysts seeking an interception proxy. It is part of a commercial web application security toolkit called the Burp Suite from PortSwigger. While the full Burp Suite requires a paid license, Burp Proxy is currently available as part of a free edition of the product.

FIGURE 4.20 Zed Attack Proxy (ZAP)

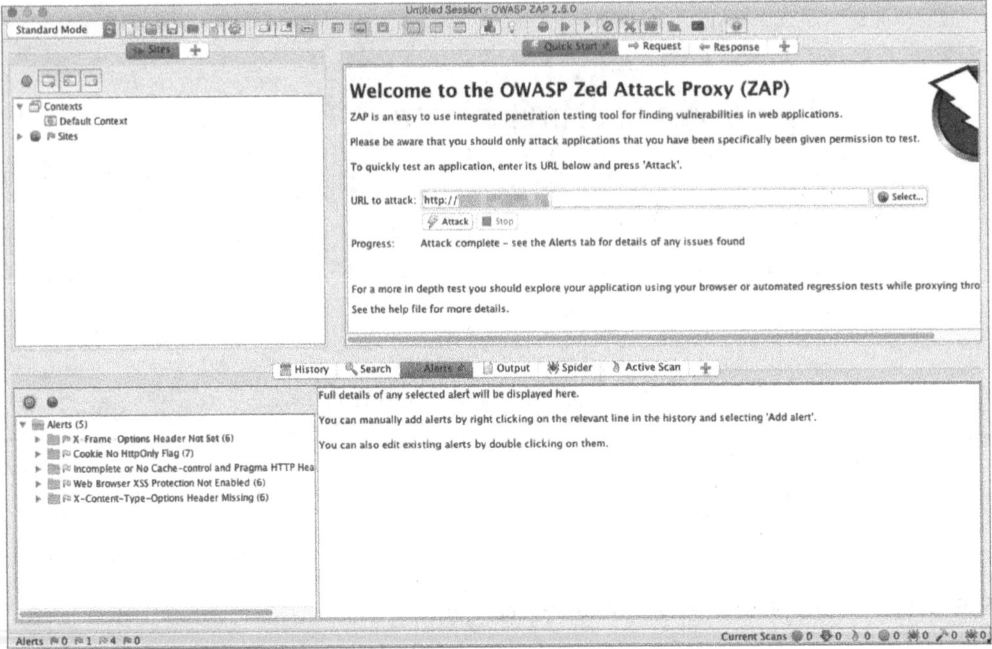

Wireless Assessment Tools

If you are tasked with performing a vulnerability assessment of a wireless network, there are three tools covered on the CySA+ exam that you might find useful. As you prepare for the exam, you should know the names and purposes of each of these tools:

- *Aircrack-ng* is a suite of tools designed for wireless network testing. The tools in this suite can capture packets from wireless networks, conduct packet injection attacks, and crack preshared keys used on WEP, WPA, and WPA2 networks.
- *Reaver* is a specialized tool used to find WPA and WPA2 passphrases specifically on networks that support the Wi-Fi Protected Setup (WPS) feature.
- *Hashcat* is a general-purpose password cracking tool that may also be used on wireless networks.

Exam Note

The CySA+ exam objectives do not reference Hashcat directly. Instead, they reference an older version of the tool called oclHashcat. This name used to refer to a specialized version of Hashcat designed to support graphics processing unit (GPU) computation. oclHashcat no longer exists as a separate tool, as the main Hashcat tool now supports GPUs. You should be aware of this in the event that you encounter an exam question referencing the older oclHashcat tool.

FIGURE 4.21 Burp Proxy

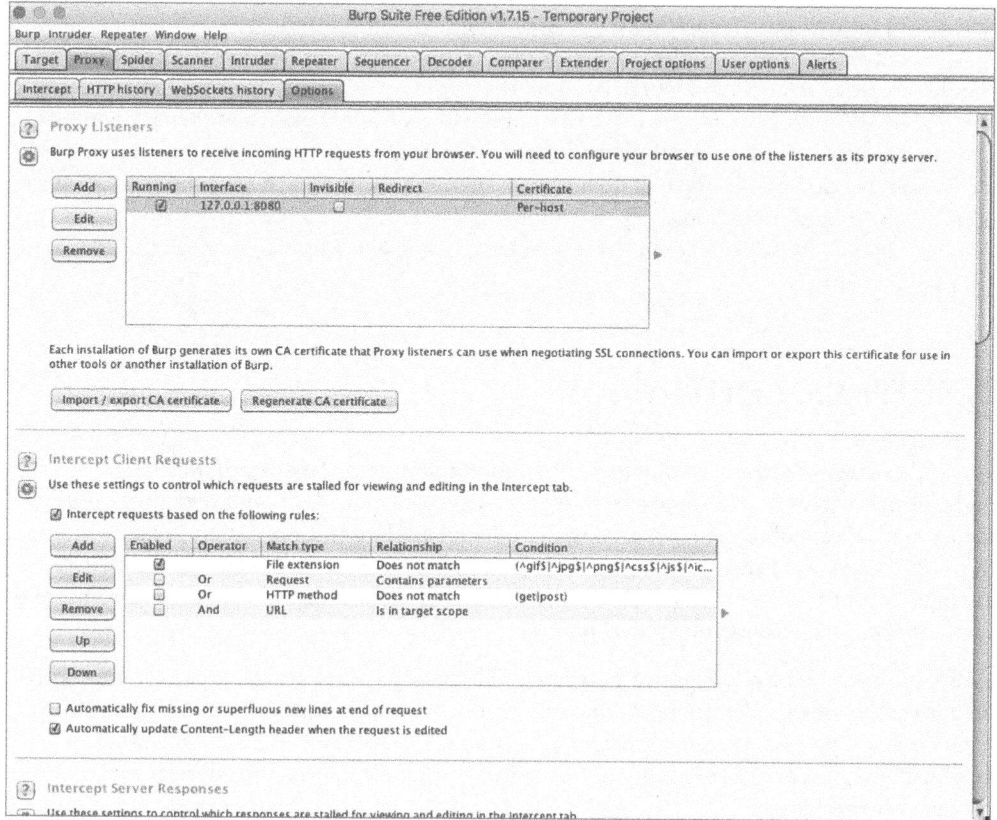

Summary

Vulnerability management programs allow cybersecurity professionals to identify and remediate gaps in the security of systems, applications, and devices under their control. Organizations that operate in highly regulated environments may be required to conduct vulnerability scanning by law or regulation, but many organizations outside those industries implement vulnerability management programs as a security best practice.

Cybersecurity analysts building a vulnerability management program should begin by identifying the scan requirements. This includes a review of possible scan targets and the selection of scan frequencies. Once these early decisions are made, analysts may configure and execute vulnerability scans on a regular basis, preferably through the use of automated scan scheduling systems.

Each vulnerability detected during a scan should be fed into a vulnerability remediation workflow that assigns tasks to the appropriate engineers, tracks completion of remediation effort, and follows up remediation work with a final vulnerability scan.

Working through the initial scan results may be an overwhelming task. Organizations should prioritize remediation work based on the criticality of the systems and information affected by the vulnerability, the difficulty of remediation, the severity of the vulnerability, and the exposure of the vulnerability to outside networks. As an organization cleans up its initial scan results, it may move on to an ongoing scanning approach that embraces continuous monitoring to quickly identify new vulnerabilities.

In Chapter 5, "Analyzing Vulnerability Scans," you'll learn how to analyze the results of vulnerability scans.

Exam Essentials

Know that requirements for vulnerability scanning may come from both internal and external sources. In some cases, organizations may face legal and regulatory requirements to conduct vulnerability scanning. The Payment Card Industry Data Security Standard (PCI DSS) and Federal Information Security Management Act (FISMA) are two examples of these external requirements. In other cases, scanning may be driven by internal requirements, such as organizational policy.

Know the criteria for selecting scan targets. Discovery scans provide organizations with an automated way to identify hosts that exist on the network and build an asset inventory. Cybersecurity professionals may then select scan targets based on data classification, system exposure, services offered, and the status of the system as a test, development, or production environment.

Describe how scan frequency will vary based on the needs of the organization. Administrators may choose to run scans on a daily, weekly, or monthly basis depending on the organization's risk appetite, regulatory requirements, licensing limitations, and business and technical constraints. Some organizations may choose to adopt continuous monitoring approaches to vulnerability detection.

Explain how configuring scan settings allows customization to meet the organization's security requirements. Cybersecurity professionals may customize scans by configuring the sensitivity level, including and excluding plug-ins, and supplementing basic network scans with information gathered from credentialed scans and server-based agents. Security teams may also conduct scans from more than one scan perspective, providing different views of the network.

Name the tasks administrators who are responsible for maintaining vulnerability scanning systems should perform. Administrators responsible for maintaining vulnerability scanning systems should perform two important administrative tasks. First, they should update the scanner software on a regular basis to correct security issues and add new functionality. Second, they should update plug-ins frequently to provide the most accurate and up-to-date vulnerability scans of their environment.

Describe the remediation workflow organizations should use to identify, remediate, and test vulnerabilities. Remediation workflows should be as automated as possible and integrate with other workflow technology used by the IT organization. As technologists correct vulnerabilities, they should validate that the remediation was effective through security testing and close out the vulnerability in the tracking system. The vulnerability management system should provide a range of reporting and alerting tools to supplement these efforts.

Know that cybersecurity professionals should prioritize remediation activities to make effective use of limited resources. It simply isn't possible to correct every vulnerability immediately. Security teams should prioritize their work based on the criticality of the systems and information affected by the vulnerability, the difficulty of remediating the vulnerability, the severity of the vulnerability, and the exposure of the affected system.

Know how cybersecurity professionals must prepare to overcome objections to scanning from other members of the IT team. Common objections to vulnerability scanning include the effect that service degradation caused by scanning will have on IT services, commitments to customers in MOUs and SLAs, and the use of IT governance and change management processes.

Lab Exercises

Activity 4.1: Install a Vulnerability Scanner

In this lab, you will install the Nessus vulnerability management package on a system.

This lab requires access to a Linux system that you can use to install Nessus (preferably Ubuntu, Debian, Red Hat, SUSE, or Fedora).

Part 1: Obtain a Nessus Essentials activation code

- Visit the Nessus website (`www.tenable.com/products/nessus/nessusessentials`) and fill out the form to obtain an activation code.

  Save the email containing the code for use during the installation and activation process.

Part 2: Download Nessus and install it on your system

1. Visit the Nessus download page (`www.tenable.com/products/nessus/select-your-operating-system#download`) and download the appropriate version of Nessus for your system.
2. Install Nessus following the documentation available at `docs.tenable.com/nessus/8_8/Content/Install.htm`.
3. Verify that your installation was successful by logging into your Nessus server.

Activity 4.2: Run a Vulnerability Scan

In this lab, you will run a vulnerability scan against a server of your choice. It is important to note that you should *never* run a vulnerability scan without permission.

You will need access to both your vulnerability scanning server that you built in Activity 4.1 and a target server for your scan. If you do not have a server that you currently have permission to scan, you may build one using a cloud service provider, such as Amazon Web Services (AWS), Microsoft Azure, or Google Compute Platform.

Conduct a vulnerability scan against your server and save the resulting report. If you need assistance, consult the Nessus documentation. You will need the report from this vulnerability scan to complete the activities in the next chapter.

Review Questions

1. What federal law requires the use of vulnerability scanning on information systems operated by federal government agencies?
   - **A.** HIPAA
   - **B.** GLBA
   - **C.** FISMA
   - **D.** FERPA
2. Gary is the system administrator for a federal agency and is responsible for a variety of information systems. Which systems must be covered by vulnerability scanning programs?
   - **A.** Only high-impact systems
   - **B.** Only systems containing classified information
   - **C.** High- or moderate-impact systems
   - **D.** High-, moderate-, and low-impact systems
3. What tool can administrators use to help identify the systems present on a network prior to conducting vulnerability scans?
   - **A.** Asset inventory
   - **B.** Web application assessment
   - **C.** Router
   - **D.** DLP
4. Tonya is configuring vulnerability scans for a system that is subject to the PCI DSS compliance standard. What is the minimum frequency with which she must conduct scans?
   - **A.** Daily
   - **B.** Weekly
   - **C.** Monthly
   - **D.** Quarterly

5. Which one of the following is *not* an example of a vulnerability scanning tool?
   A. Qualys
   B. Snort
   C. Nessus
   D. OpenVAS

6. Bethany is the vulnerability management specialist for a large retail organization. She completed her last PCI DSS compliance scan in March. In April, the organization upgraded their point-of-sale system, and Bethany is preparing to conduct new scans. When must she complete the new scan?
   A. Immediately
   B. June
   C. December
   D. No scans are required

7. Renee is configuring her vulnerability management solution to perform credentialed scans of servers on her network. What type of account should she provide to the scanner?
   A. Domain administrator
   B. Local administrator
   C. Root
   D. Read-only

8. Jason is writing a report about a potential security vulnerability in a software product and wishes to use standardized product names to ensure that other security analysts understand the report. Which SCAP component can Jason turn to for assistance?
   A. CVSS
   B. CVE
   C. CPE
   D. OVAL

9. Bill would like to run an internal vulnerability scan on a system for PCI DSS compliance purposes. Who is authorized to complete one of these scans?
   A. Any employee of the organization
   B. An approved scanning vendor
   C. A PCI DSS service provider
   D. Any qualified individual

10. Which type of organization is the most likely to face a statutory requirement to conduct vulnerability scans?
    A. Bank
    B. Hospital
    C. Government agency
    D. Doctor's office

11. What minimum level of impact must a system have under FISMA before the organization is required to determine what information about the system is discoverable by adversaries?
    A. Low
    B. Moderate
    C. High
    D. Severe

12. What term describes an organization's willingness to tolerate risk in their computing environment?
    A. Risk landscape
    B. Risk appetite
    C. Risk level
    D. Risk adaptation

13. Which one of the following factors is least likely to impact vulnerability scanning schedules?
    A. Regulatory requirements
    B. Technical constraints
    C. Business constraints
    D. Staff availability

14. Barry placed all of his organization's credit card processing systems on an isolated network dedicated to card processing. He has implemented appropriate segmentation controls to limit the scope of PCI DSS to those systems through the use of VLANs and firewalls. When Barry goes to conduct vulnerability scans for PCI DSS compliance purposes, what systems must he scan?
    A. Customer systems
    B. Systems on the isolated network
    C. Systems on the general enterprise network
    D. Both B and C

15. Ryan is planning to conduct a vulnerability scan of a business-critical system using dangerous plug-ins. What would be the best approach for the initial scan?
    A. Run the scan against production systems to achieve the most realistic results possible.
    B. Run the scan during business hours.
    C. Run the scan in a test environment.
    D. Do not run the scan to avoid disrupting the business.

16. Which one of the following activities is *not* part of the vulnerability management life cycle?
    A. Detection
    B. Remediation
    C. Reporting
    D. Testing
17. What approach to vulnerability scanning incorporates information from agents running on the target servers?
    A. Continuous monitoring
    B. Ongoing scanning
    C. On-demand scanning
    D. Alerting
18. Brian is seeking to determine the appropriate impact categorization for a federal information system as he plans the vulnerability scanning controls for that system. After consulting management, he discovers that the system contains information that, if disclosed improperly, would have a serious adverse impact on the organization. How should this system be categorized?
    A. Low impact
    B. Moderate impact
    C. High impact
    D. Severe impact
19. Jessica is reading reports from vulnerability scans run by different parts of her organization using different products. She is responsible for assigning remediation resources and is having difficulty prioritizing issues from different sources. What SCAP component can help Jessica with this task?
    A. CVSS
    B. CVE
    C. CPE
    D. XCCDF
20. Sarah would like to run an external vulnerability scan on a system for PCI DSS compliance purposes. Who is authorized to complete one of these scans?
    A. Any employee of the organization
    B. An Approved Scanning Vendor
    C. A PCI DSS service provider
    D. Any qualified individual

Analyzing Vulnerability Scans

THE COMPTIA CYBERSECURITY ANALYST (CYSA+) EXAM OBJECTIVES COVERED IN THIS CHAPTER INCLUDE:

✓ **Domain 1.0: Threat and Vulnerability Management**

- 1.3 Given a scenario, perform vulnerability management activities.
- 1.4 Given a scenario, analyze the output from common vulnerability assessment tools.
- 1.5 Explain the threats and vulnerabilities associated with specialized technology.
- 1.7 Given a scenario, implement controls to mitigate attacks and software vulnerabilities.

Cybersecurity analysts spend a significant amount of time analyzing and interpreting the reports generated by vulnerability scanners. Although scanners are extremely effective at automating the manual work of vulnerability identification, the results that they generate require interpretation by a trained analyst to eliminate false positive reports, prioritize remediation activities, and delve into the root causes of vulnerability reports. In this chapter, you will learn how cybersecurity analysts apply their knowledge and experience to the review of vulnerability scan reports.

Reviewing and Interpreting Scan Reports

Vulnerability scan reports provide analysts with a significant amount of information that assists with the interpretation of the report. In addition to the high-level report examples shown in Chapter 4, "Designing a Vulnerability Management Program," vulnerability scanners provide detailed information about each vulnerability that they identify. Figure 5.1 shows an example of a single vulnerability reported by the Nessus vulnerability scanner.

Let's take a look at this report, section by section, beginning in the top left and proceeding in a counterclockwise fashion.

At the very top of the report, we see two critical details: the *name of the vulnerability*, which offers a descriptive title, and the *overall severity* of the vulnerability, expressed as a general category, such as low, medium, high, or critical. In this example report, the scanner is reporting that a server is running an outdated and insecure version of the SSL protocol. It is assigned to the high severity category.

Next, the report provides a *detailed description* of the vulnerability. In this case, the report provides a detailed description of the flaws in the SSL protocol and explains that SSL is no longer considered acceptable for use.

The next section of the report provides a *solution* to the vulnerability. When possible, the scanner offers detailed information about how system administrators, security professionals, network engineers, and/or application developers may correct the vulnerability. In this case, the reader is instructed to disable SSL 2.0 and 3.0 and replace their use with a secure version of the TLS protocol.

FIGURE 5.1 Nessus vulnerability scan report

HIGH SSL Version 2 and 3 Protocol Detection

Description

The remote service accepts connections encrypted using SSL 2.0 and/or SSL 3.0. These versions of SSL are affected by several cryptographic flaws, including:

- An insecure padding scheme with CBC ciphers.

- Insecure session renegotiation and resumption schemes.

An attacker can exploit these flaws to conduct man-in-the-middle attacks or to decrypt communications between the affected service and clients.

Although SSL/TLS has a secure means for choosing the highest supported version of the protocol (so that these versions will be used only if the client or server support nothing better), many web browsers implement this in an unsafe way that allows an attacker to downgrade a connection (such as in POODLE). Therefore, it is recommended that these protocols be disabled entirely.

NIST has determined that SSL 3.0 is no longer acceptable for secure communications. As of the date of enforcement found in PCI DSS v3.1, any version of SSL will not meet the PCI SSC's definition of 'strong cryptography'.

Solution

Consult the application's documentation to disable SSL 2.0 and 3.0.
Use TLS 1.1 (with approved cipher suites) or higher instead.

See Also

https://www.schneier.com/academic/paperfiles/paper-ssl.pdf
http://www.nessus.org/u?b06c7e95
http://www.nessus.org/u?247c4540
https://www.openssl.org/~bodo/ssl-poodle.pdf
http://www.nessus.org/u?5d15ba70
https://www.imperialviolet.org/2014/10/14/poodle.html
https://tools.ietf.org/html/rfc7507
https://tools.ietf.org/html/rfc7568

Output

```
- SSLv3 is enabled and the server supports at least one cipher.
      Explanation: TLS 1.0 and SSL 3.0 cipher suites may be used with SSLv3

  High Strength Ciphers (>= 112-bit key)

    RC4-MD5                  Kx=RSA      Au=RSA    Enc=RC4(128)        Mac=MD5
    RC4-SHA                  Kx=RSA      Au=RSA    Enc=RC4(128)
 Mac=SHA1

 The fields above are :

  {OpenSSL ciphername}
  Kx={key exchange}
  Au={authentication}
  Enc={symmetric encryption method}
  Mac={message authentication code}
  {export flag}
```

Port -	Hosts
4433 / tcp / www	
443 / tcp / www	

Plugin Details

Severity:	High
ID:	20007
Version:	1.32
Type:	remote
Family:	Service detection
Published:	October 12, 2005
Modified:	March 27, 2019

Risk Information

Risk Factor: High
CVSS v3.0 Base Score 7.5
CVSS v3.0 Vector:
CVSS:3.0/AV:N/AC:L/PR:N/UI:N/S:U/C:H/I:N/A:N
CVSS Base Score: 7.1
CVSS Vector:
CVSS2#AV:N/AC:M/Au:N/C:C/I:N/A:N

Vulnerability Information

In the news: true

In the section of the report titled "See Also," the scanner provides *references* where administrators can find more details on the vulnerability described in the report. In this case, the scanner refers the reader to several blog posts, Nessus documentation pages, and Internet Engineering Task Force (IETF) documents that provide more details on the vulnerability.

The *output* section of the report shows the detailed information returned by the remote system when probed for the vulnerability. This information can be extremely valuable to an analyst because it often provides the verbatim output returned by a command. Analysts can use this to better understand why the scanner is reporting a vulnerability, identify the location of a vulnerability, and potentially identify false positive reports. In this case, the output section shows the specific insecure ciphers being used.

The *port/hosts* section provides details on the server(s) that contain the vulnerability as well as the specific services on that server that have the vulnerability. In this case, the server's IP address is obscured for privacy reasons, but we can see that the server is running insecure versions of SSL on both ports 443 and 4433.

The *vulnerability information* section provides some miscellaneous information about the vulnerability. In this case, we see that the SSL vulnerability has appeared in news reports.

The *risk information* section includes useful information for assessing the severity of the vulnerability. In this case, the scanner reports that the vulnerability has an overall risk factor of High (consistent with the tag next to the vulnerability title). It also provides details on how the vulnerability rates when using the Common Vulnerability Scoring System (CVSS). You'll notice that there are two different CVSS scores and vectors. We will use the CVSS version 3 information, since it is the more recent rating scale. In this case, the vulnerability has a CVSS base score of 7.5 and has the CVSS vector

```
CVSS:3.0/AV:N/AC:L/PR:N/UI:N/S:U/C:H/I:N/A:N
```

We'll discuss the details of CVSS scoring in the next section of this chapter.

The final section of the vulnerability report provides details on the vulnerability scanner plug-in that detected the issue. This vulnerability was reported by Nessus plug-in ID 20007, which was published in October 2005 and updated in March 2019.

Although this chapter focuses on interpreting the details of a Nessus vulnerability scan, the process is extremely similar for other vulnerability scanners. The format of the reports generated by different products may vary, but they generally contain the same information. For example, Figure 5.2 shows the output of a Qualys vulnerability report.

Understanding CVSS

The *Common Vulnerability Scoring System (CVSS)* is an industry standard for assessing the severity of security vulnerabilities. It provides a technique for scoring each vulnerability on a variety of measures. Cybersecurity analysts often use CVSS ratings to prioritize response actions.

Analysts scoring a new vulnerability begin by rating the vulnerability on eight different measures. Each measure is given both a descriptive rating and a numeric score. The first four measures evaluate the exploitability of the vulnerability, whereas the last three evaluate the impact of the vulnerability. The eighth metric discusses the scope of the vulnerability.

FIGURE 5.2 Qualys vulnerability scan report

4 OpenSSL oracle padding vulnerability(CVE-2016-2107) port 443/tcp over SSL

QID: 38626
Category: General remote services
CVE ID: CVE-2016-2107
Vendor Reference OpenSSL Security Advisory 20160503
Bugtraq ID: 91787
Service Modified: 05/24/2016
User Modified: -
Edited: No
PCI Vuln: No
Ticket State:

THREAT:
The OpenSSL Project is an Open Source toolkit implementing the Secure Sockets Layer (SSL v2/v3) and Transport Layer Security (TLS) protocols as well as a general purpose cryptography library.
OpenSSL contains the following vulnerability:
A MITM attacker can use a padding oracle attack to decrypt traffic when the connection uses an AES CBC cipher and the server support AES-NI. Affected Versions:
OpenSSL 1.0.2 prior to OpenSSL 1.0.2h OpenSSL 1.0.1 prior to OpenSSL 1.0.1t

IMPACT:
A MITM attacker can use a padding oracle attack to decrypt traffic.

SOLUTION:
OpenSSL version 1.0.2h and 1.0.1t have been released to address these issues. Refer to OpenSSL Advisory to obtain more information.
Patch:
Following are links for downloading patches to fix the vulnerabilities:
OpenSSL Security Advisory 3rd May 2016

COMPLIANCE:
Not Applicable

EXPLOITABILITY:
The Exploit-DB
Reference: CVE-2016-2107
Description: OpenSSL - Padding Oracle in AES-NI CBC MAC Check - The Exploit-DB Ref : 39768
Link: http://www.exploit-db.com/exploits/39768

ASSOCIATED MALWARE:
There is no malware information for this vulnerability.

RESULTS:
No results available

Attack Vector Metric

The *attack vector metric* describes how an attacker would exploit the vulnerability and is assigned according to the criteria shown in Table 5.1.

TABLE 5.1 CVSS attack vector metric

Value	Description	Score
Physical (P)	The attacker must physically touch the vulnerable device.	0.20
Local (L)	The attacker must have physical or logical access to the affected system.	0.55
Adjacent Network (A)	The attacker must have access to the local network that the affected system is connected to.	0.62
Network (N)	The attacker can exploit the vulnerability remotely over a network.	0.85

Attack Complexity Metric

The *attack complexity metric* describes the difficulty of exploiting the vulnerability and is assigned according to the criteria shown in Table 5.2.

TABLE 5.2 CVSS attack complexity metric

Value	Description	Score
High (H)	Exploiting the vulnerability requires "specialized" conditions that would be difficult to find.	0.44
Low (L)	Exploiting the vulnerability does not require any specialized conditions.	0.77

Privileges Required Metric

The *privileges required metric* describes the type of account access that an attacker would need to exploit a vulnerability and is assigned according to the criteria in Table 5.3.

TABLE 5.3 CVSS privileges required metric

Value	Description	Score
High (H)	Attackers require administrative privileges to conduct the attack.	0.270 (or 0.50 if Scope is Changed)
Low (L)	Attackers require basic user privileges to conduct the attack.	0.62 (or 0.68 if Scope is Changed)
None (N)	Attackers do not need to authenticate to exploit the vulnerability.	0.85

User Interaction Metric

The *user interaction metric* describes whether the attacker needs to involve another human in the attack. The user interaction metric is assigned according to the criteria in Table 5.4.

Confidentiality Metric

The *confidentiality metric* describes the type of information disclosure that might occur if an attacker successfully exploits the vulnerability. The confidentiality metric is assigned according to the criteria in Table 5.5.

TABLE 5.4 CVSS user interaction metric

Value	Description	Score
None (N)	Successful exploitation does not require action by any user other than the attacker.	0.85
Required (R)	Successful exploitation does require action by a user other than the attacker.	0.62

TABLE 5.5 CVSS confidentiality metric

Value	Description	Score
None (N)	There is no confidentiality impact.	0.00
Low (L)	Access to some information is possible, but the attacker does not have control over what information is compromised.	0.22
High (H)	All information on the system is compromised.	0.56

Integrity Metric

The *integrity metric* describes the type of information alteration that might occur if an attacker successfully exploits the vulnerability. The integrity metric is assigned according to the criteria in Table 5.6.

TABLE 5.6 CVSS integrity metric

Value	Description	Score
None (N)	There is no integrity impact.	0.00
Low (L)	Modification of some information is possible, but the attacker does not have control over what information is modified.	0.22
High (H)	The integrity of the system is totally compromised, and the attacker may change any information at will.	0.56

Availability Metric

The *availability metric* describes the type of disruption that might occur if an attacker successfully exploits the vulnerability. The availability metric is assigned according to the criteria in Table 5.7.

TABLE 5.7 CVSS availability metric

Value	Description	Score
None (N)	There is no availability impact.	0.00
Low (L)	The performance of the system is degraded.	0.22
High (H)	The system is completely shut down.	0.56

Scope Metric

The *scope metric* describes whether the vulnerability can affect system components beyond the scope of the vulnerability. The scope metric is assigned according to the criteria in Table 5.8. Note that the scope metric table does not contain score information. The value of the scope metric is reflected in the values for the privileges required metric, shown earlier in Table 5.3.

TABLE 5.8 CVSS scope metric

Value	Description
Unchanged (U)	The exploited vulnerability can only affect resources managed by the same security authority.
Changed (C)	The exploited vulnerability can affect resources beyond the scope of the security authority managing the component containing the vulnerability.

The current version of CVSS is version 3.1, which is a minor update from version 3.0. You will find that attack vectors normally cite version 3.0. This chapter uses CVSS version 3.1 as the basis of our conversation, but 3.0 and 3.1 are functionally equivalent for our purposes. You may still find documentation that references CVSS version 2, which uses a similar methodology but has different ratings.

Interpreting the CVSS Vector

The CVSS vector uses a single-line format to convey the ratings of a vulnerability on all eight of the metrics described in the preceding sections. For example, recall the CVSS vector presented in Figure 5.1:

`CVSS:3.0/AV:N/AC:L/PR:N/UI:N/S:U/C:H/I:N/A:N`

This vector contains nine components. The first section, `CVSS:3.0`, simply informs the reader (human or system) that the vector was composed using CVSS version 3. The next eight sections correspond to each of the eight CVSS metrics. In this case, the SSL vulnerability in Figure 5.1 received the following ratings:

- Attack Vector: Network (score: 0.85)
- Attack Complexity: Low (score: 0.77)
- Privileges Required: None (score: 0.85)
- User Interaction: None (score: 0.85)
- Scope: Unchanged
- Confidentiality: High (score: 0.56)
- Integrity: None (score: 0.00)
- Availability: None (score: 0.00)

Summarizing CVSS Scores

The CVSS vector provides good detailed information on the nature of the risk posed by a vulnerability, but the complexity of the vector makes it difficult to use in prioritization exercises. For this reason, analysts can calculate the *CVSS base score*, which is a single number representing the overall risk posed by the vulnerability. Arriving at the base score requires first calculating the *exploitability score*, *impact score*, and *impact function.*

Calculating the Impact Sub-Score (ISS)

The first calculation analysts perform is computing the impact sub-score (ISS). This metric summarizes the three impact metrics using the formula:

$$ISS = 1 - \left[\left(1 - \text{Confidentiality}\right) \times \left(1 - \text{Integrity}\right) \times \left(1 - \text{Availability}\right)\right]$$

Plugging in the values for our SSL vulnerability, we obtain

$$ISS = 1 - \left[\left(1 - 0.56\right) \times \left(1 - 0.00\right) \times \left(1 - 0.00\right)\right]$$

$$ISS = 1 - \left[0.44 \times 1.00 \times 1.00\right]$$

$$ISS = 1 - 0.44$$

$$ISS = 0.56$$

Calculating the Impact Score

To obtain the impact score from the impact sub-score, we must take the value of the scope metric into account. If the scope metric is Unchanged, as it is in our example, we multiply the ISS by 6.42:

$$Impact = 6.42 * ISS$$

$$Impact = 6.42 * 0.56$$

$$Impact = 3.60$$

If the scope metric is Changed, we use a more complex formula:

$$Impact = 7.52 \times (ISS - 0.029) - 3.25 \times (ISS - 0.02)^{15}$$

Calculating the Exploitability Score

Analysts may calculate the exploitability score for a vulnerability using this formula:

$$Exploitability = 8.22 \times AttackVector \times AttackComplexity \times PrivilegesRequired \times UserInteraction$$

Plugging in values for our SSL vulnerability, we get

$$Exploitability = 8.22 \times 0.85 \times 0.77 \times 0.85 \times 0.85$$
$$Exploitability = 3.89$$

Calculating the Base Score

With all of this information at hand, we can now determine the CVSS base score using the following rules:

- If the impact is 0, the base score is 0.
- If the scope metric is Unchanged, calculate the base score by adding together the impact and exploitability scores.

- If the scope metric is Changed, calculate the base score by adding together the impact and exploitability scores and multiplying the result by 1.08.
- The highest possible base score is 10. If the calculated value is greater than 10, set the base score to 10.

In our example, the impact score is 3.60 and the exploitability score rounds to 3.9. Adding these together, we get a base score of 7.5, which is the same value found in Figure 5.1.

Now that you understand the math behind CVSS scores, the good news is that you don't need to perform these calculations by hand. NIST offers a CVSS calculator at `nvd.nist.gov/vuln-metrics/cvss/v3-calculator`, where you can easily compute the CVSS base score for a vulnerability.

Categorizing CVSS Base Scores

Many vulnerability scanning systems further summarize CVSS results by using risk categories rather than numeric risk ratings. These are usually based on the CVSS Qualitative Severity Rating Scale, shown in Table 5.9.

TABLE 5.9 CVSS Qualitative Severity Rating Scale

CVSS Score	Rating
0.0	None
0.1–3.9	Low
4.0–6.9	Medium
7.0–8.9	High
9.0–10.0	Critical

Continuing with the SSL vulnerability example from Figure 5.1, we calculated the CVSS score for this vulnerability as 7.5. This places it into the High risk category, as shown in the header of Figure 5.1.

Validating Scan Results

Cybersecurity analysts interpreting reports often perform their own investigations to confirm the presence and severity of vulnerabilities. These investigations may include the use of external data sources that supply additional information valuable to the analysis.

False Positives

Vulnerability scanners are useful tools, but they aren't foolproof. Scanners do sometimes make mistakes for a variety of reasons. The scanner might not have sufficient access to the target system to confirm a vulnerability, or it might simply have an error in a plug-in that generates an erroneous vulnerability report. When a scanner reports a vulnerability that does not exist, this is known as a *false positive error.*

When a vulnerability scanner reports a vulnerability, this is known as a *positive report.* This report may either be accurate (a *true positive* report) or inaccurate (a *false positive* report). Similarly, when a scanner reports that a vulnerability is not present, this is a *negative report.* The negative report may either be accurate (a *true negative* report) or inaccurate (a *false negative* report).

Exam Note

One of the CySA+ exam objectives requires that you be able to validate scan results. Be certain that you understand the four different types of report: true positive, false positive, true negative, and false negative.

Cybersecurity analysts should confirm each vulnerability reported by a scanner. In some cases, this may be as simple as verifying that a patch is missing or an operating system is outdated. In other cases, verifying a vulnerability requires a complex manual process that simulates an exploit. For example, verifying a SQL injection vulnerability may require actually attempting an attack against a web application and verifying the result in the back-end database.

When verifying a vulnerability, analysts should draw on their own expertise as well as the subject matter expertise of others throughout the organization. Database administrators, system engineers, network technicians, software developers, and other experts have domain knowledge that is essential to the evaluation of a potential false positive report.

Documented Exceptions

In some cases, an organization may decide not to remediate a vulnerability for one reason or another. For example, the organization may decide that business requirements dictate the use of an operating system that is no longer supported. Similarly, development managers may decide that the cost of remediating a vulnerability in a web application that is exposed only to the internal network outweighs the security benefit.

Unless analysts take some action to record these exceptions, vulnerability scans will continue to report them each time a scan runs. It's good practice to document exceptions in the vulnerability management system so that the scanner knows to ignore them in future reports. This reduces the level of noise in scan reports and increases their usefulness to analysts.

Be careful when deciding to allow an exception. As discussed in Chapter 4, many organizations are subject to compliance requirements for vulnerability scanning. Creating an exception may violate those compliance obligations or go against best practices for security.

Understanding Informational Results

Vulnerability scanners often supply very detailed information when run using default configurations. Not everything reported by a vulnerability scanner represents a significant security issue. Nevertheless, scanners provide as much information as they are able to determine to show the types of information that an attacker might be able to gather when conducting a reconnaissance scan.

Figure 5.3 provides an example of a high-level report generated from a vulnerability scan run against a web server. Note that about two-thirds of the vulnerabilities in this report fit into the "Info" risk category. This indicates that the plug-ins providing results are not even categorized according to the CVSS. Instead, they are simply informational results. Most organizations do not go to the extent of removing all possible sources of information about a system because it can be difficult, if not impossible, to do so.

FIGURE 5.3 Scan report showing vulnerabilities and best practices

Severity ▲	Plugin Name	Plugin Family	Count
HIGH	CGI Generic SQL Injection (blind, time based)	CGI abuses	1
MEDIUM	Web Application Potentially Vulnerable to Clickjacking	Web Servers	2
MEDIUM	ASP.NET DEBUG Method Enabled	CGI abuses	1
MEDIUM	CGI Generic Cookie Injection Scripting	CGI abuses	1
MEDIUM	CGI Generic HTML Injections (quick test)	CGI abuses : XSS	1
MEDIUM	CGI Generic XSS (comprehensive test)	CGI abuses : XSS	1
MEDIUM	CGI Generic XSS (extended patterns)	CGI abuses : XSS	1
MEDIUM	CGI Generic XSS (quick test)	CGI abuses : XSS	1
INFO	CGI Generic Tests Load Estimation (all tests)	CGI abuses	2
INFO	CGI Generic Tests Timeout	CGI abuses	2
INFO	External URLs	Web Servers	2
INFO	HTTP Methods Allowed (per directory)	Web Servers	2
INFO	HTTP Server Type and Version	Web Servers	2
INFO	HyperText Transfer Protocol (HTTP) Information	Web Servers	2
INFO	Missing or Permissive Content-Security-Policy HTTP Res...	CGI abuses	2
INFO	Missing or Permissive X-Frame-Options HTTP Response ...	CGI abuses	2

Scan Details

Name:	Main Website
Status:	Completed
Policy:	Web Application Tests
Scanner:	Local Scanner
Folder:	My Scans
Start:	Today at 1:30 AM
End:	Today at 3:20 AM
Elapsed:	2 hours
Targets:	

Vulnerabilities

High
Medium
Info

A cybersecurity analyst encountering the scan report in Figure 5.3 should first turn their attention to the high-severity SQL injection vulnerability that exists. Once that is remediated, seven medium-severity vulnerabilities require attention. The remaining informational vulnerabilities can likely be left alone. Many organizations will adopt a formal policy regarding how they handle these informational messages. For example, some organizations may decide that once a message appears in two or three consecutive scans, they will create a journal entry documenting the actions they took in response to the message or the reasons they chose not to take actions. This approach is particularly important for highly audited organizations that have stringent compliance requirements. Creating a formal record of the decision-making process satisfies auditors that the organization conducted due diligence.

Reconciling Scan Results with Other Data Sources

Vulnerability scans should never take place in a vacuum. Cybersecurity analysts interpreting these reports should also turn to other sources of security information as they perform their analysis. Valuable information sources for this process include the following:

- *Logs* from servers, applications, network devices, and other sources that might contain information about possible attempts to exploit detected vulnerabilities
- *Security information and event management (SIEM)* systems that correlate log entries from multiple sources and provide actionable intelligence
- *Configuration management systems* that provide information on the operating system and applications installed on a system

Each of these information sources can prove invaluable when an analyst attempts to reconcile a scan report with the reality of the organization's computing environment.

Trend Analysis

Trend analysis is also an important part of a vulnerability scanning program. Managers should watch for overall trends in vulnerabilities, including the number of new vulnerabilities arising over time, the age of existing vulnerabilities, and the time required to remediate vulnerabilities. Figure 5.4 shows an example of the trend analysis reports available in Nessus SecurityCenter.

Common Vulnerabilities

Each vulnerability scanning system contains plug-ins able to detect thousands of possible vulnerabilities, ranging from major SQL injection flaws in web applications to more mundane information disclosure issues with network devices. Though it's impossible to discuss each of these vulnerabilities in a book of any length, cybersecurity analysts should be familiar with the most commonly detected vulnerabilities and some of the general categories that cover many different vulnerability variants.

FIGURE 5.4 Vulnerability trend analysis Source: Tenable Network Security, Inc.

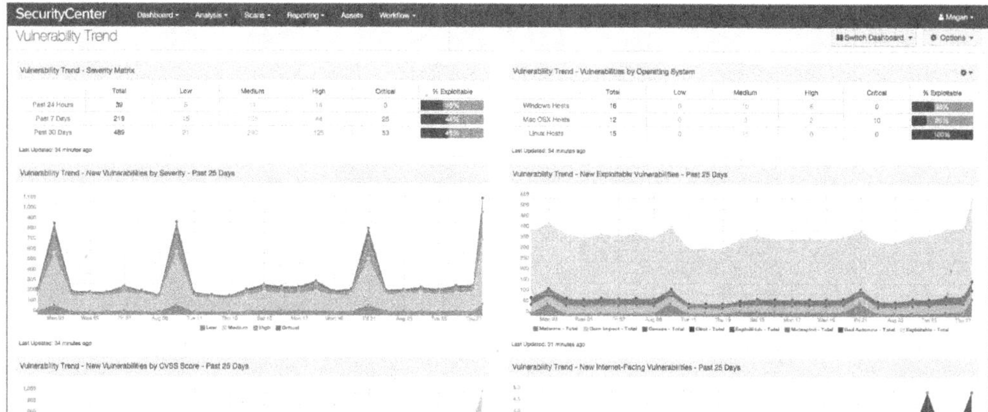

Chapter 4 discussed the importance of regularly updating vulnerability scanners to make them effective against newly discovered threats. Although this is true, it is also important to note that even old vulnerabilities can present significant issues to the security of organizations. Each year Verizon conducts a widely respected analysis of all the data breaches they investigated over the course of the prior year. Figure 5.5 shows some of the results from the 2016 Data Breach Investigations Report. (Note that Verizon does continue to produce these reports on an annual basis, but they no longer include year of discovery data.)

Figure 5.5 underscores the importance of addressing old vulnerabilities and the stark reality that many organizations fail to do so. Many of the vulnerabilities exploited during data breaches in 2015 exploited vulnerabilities discovered more than a *decade* earlier. That's an astounding statistic.

Server and Endpoint Vulnerabilities

Computer systems are quite complex. The operating systems run on both servers and endpoints comprising millions of lines of code, and the differing combinations of applications they run make each system fairly unique. It's no surprise, therefore, that many of the vulnerabilities detected by scans exist on server and endpoint systems, and these vulnerabilities are often among the most complex to remediate.

FIGURE 5.5 Vulnerabilities exploited in 2015 by year of initial discovery

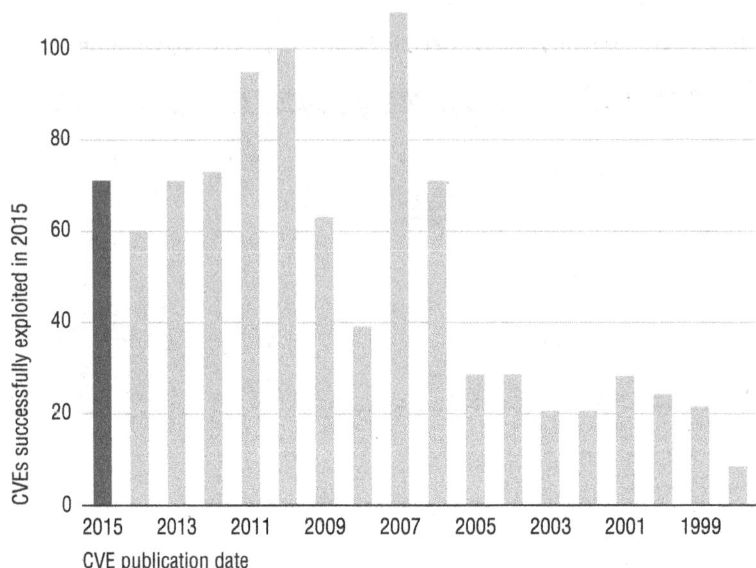

Missing Patches

Applying security patches to systems should be one of the core practices of any information security program, but this routine task is often neglected due to a lack of resources for preventive maintenance. One of the most common alerts from a vulnerability scan is that one or more systems on the network are running an outdated version of an operating system or application and require security patches.

Figure 5.6 shows an example of one of these scan results. The server located at 10.64.142.211 has a remote code execution vulnerability. Though the scan result is fairly brief, it does contain quite a bit of helpful information:

- The description tells us that this is a flaw in the Windows HTTP stack.
- The service information in the Output section of the report confirms that the server is running an HTTPS service on TCP port 443.
- We see in the header that this is a critical vulnerability, and this is confirmed in the Risk Information section, where we see that it has a CVSS base score of 10.

Fortunately, there is an easy way to fix this problem. The Solution section tells us that Microsoft released patches for the affected operating systems, and the See Also section provides a direct link to the Microsoft security bulletin (MS15-034) that describes the issue and solution in greater detail.

FIGURE 5.6 Missing patch vulnerability

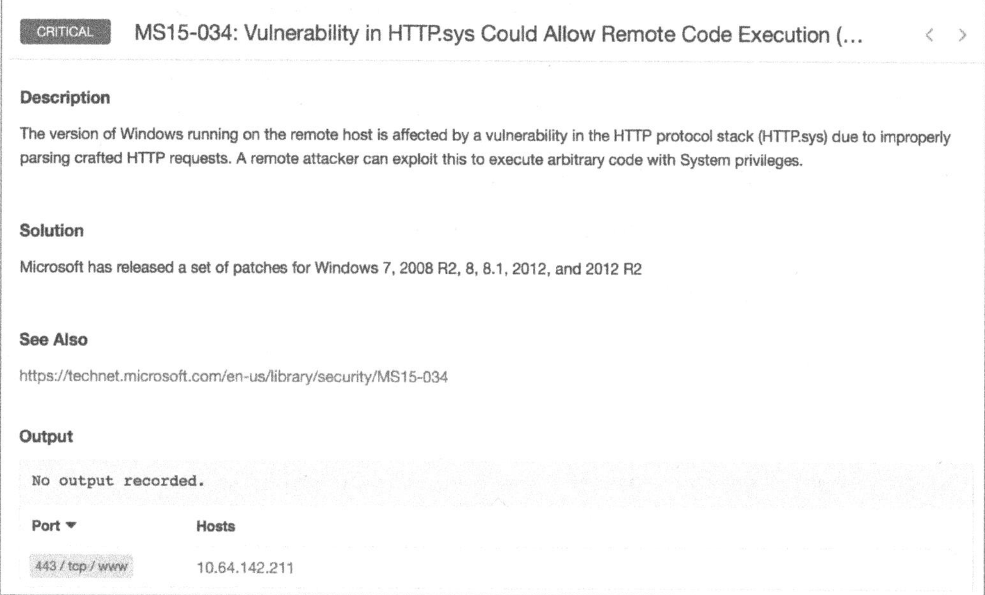

> **Mobile Device Security**
>
> This section refers to the vulnerabilities typically found on traditional servers and endpoints, but it's important to note that mobile devices have a host of security issues of their own and must be carefully managed and patched to remain secure.
>
> The administrators of mobile devices can use a mobile device management (MDM) solution to manage the configuration of those devices, automatically installing patches, requiring the use of encryption, and providing remote wiping functionality. MDM solutions may also restrict the applications that can be run on a mobile device to those that appear on an approved list.
>
> That said, mobile devices do not typically show up on vulnerability scans because they are not often sitting on the network when those scans run. Therefore, administrators should pay careful attention to the security of those devices even when they do not show up as requiring attention after a vulnerability scan.

Unsupported Operating Systems and Applications

Software vendors eventually discontinue support for every product they make. This is true for operating systems as well as applications. Once they announce the final end of support for a product, organizations that continue running the outdated software put themselves at a significant risk of attack. The vendor simply will not investigate or correct security flaws that arise in the product after that date. Organizations continuing to run the unsupported product are on their own from a security perspective, and unless you happen to maintain a team of operating system developers, that's not a good situation to find yourself in.

Perhaps the most famous end of support for a major operating system occurred in July 2015 when Microsoft discontinued support for the more-than-a-decade-old Windows Server 2003. Figure 5.7 shows an example of the report generated by Nessus when it identifies a server running this outdated operating system.

FIGURE 5.7 Unsupported operating system vulnerability

We can see from this report that the scan detected two servers on the network running Windows Server 2003. The description of the vulnerability provides a stark assessment of what lies in store for organizations continuing to run any unsupported operating system:

> Lack of support implies that no new security patches for the product will be released by the vendor. As a result, it is likely to contain security vulnerabilities. Furthermore, Microsoft is unlikely to investigate or acknowledge reports of vulnerabilities.

The solution for organizations running unsupported operating systems is simple in its phrasing but complex in implementation. "Upgrade to a version of Windows that is currently supported" is a pretty straightforward instruction, but it may pose a significant challenge for organizations running applications that simply can't be upgraded to newer versions of Windows. In cases where the organization simply must continue using an unsupported operating system, best practice dictates isolating the system as much as possible, preferably not connecting it to any network, and applying as many compensating security controls as possible, such as increased monitoring and implementation of strict network firewall rules.

Buffer Overflows

Buffer overflow attacks occur when an attacker manipulates a program into placing more data into an area of memory than is allocated for that program's use. The goal is to overwrite other information in memory with instructions that may be executed by a different process running on the system.

Buffer overflow attacks are quite commonplace and tend to persist for many years after they are initially discovered. For example, the 2016 Verizon Data Breach Investigation Report identified 10 vulnerabilities that were responsible for 85 percent of the compromises in their study. Among the top 10 were four overflow issues:

- CVE 1999-1058: Buffer overflow in Vermillion FTP Daemon
- CVE 2001-0876: Buffer overflow in Universal Plug and Play (UPnP) on Windows 98, 98SE, ME, and XP
- CVE 2002-0126: Buffer overflow in BlackMoon FTP Server 1.0 through 1.5
- CVE 2003-0818: Multiple integer overflows in Microsoft ASN.1 library

Exam Note

One of the listed vulnerabilities is an *integer overflow*. This is simply a variant of a buffer overflow where the result of an arithmetic operation attempts to store an integer that is too large to fit in the specified buffer.

The four-digit number following the letters CVE in each vulnerability title indicates the year that the vulnerability was discovered. In a study of breaches that took place in 2015, four of the top 10 issues causing breaches were exploits of overflow vulnerabilities that were between 12 and 16 years old!

Cybersecurity analysts discovering a buffer overflow vulnerability during a vulnerability scan should seek out a patch that corrects the issue. In most cases, the scan report will directly identify an available patch.

Exam Note

Buffer overflows may target two different types of memory. Stack overflows target the stack, which stores variable values and is managed by the operating system. *Heap* overflows target the heap, which stores objects created by code and must be managed by application developers.

Privilege Escalation

Privilege escalation attacks seek to increase the level of access that an attacker has to a target system. They exploit vulnerabilities that allow the transformation of a normal user account into a more privileged account, such as the root superuser account.

In October 2016, security researchers announced the discovery of a Linux kernel vulnerability dubbed Dirty COW. This vulnerability, present in the Linux kernel for nine years, was extremely easy to exploit and provided successful attackers with administrative control of affected systems.

In an attempt to spread the word about this vulnerability and encourage prompt patching of Linux kernels, security researchers set up the dirtycow.ninja website, shown in Figure 5.8. This site provides details on the flaw and corrective measures.

Rootkits are hacking tools designed to automate privilege escalation attacks. An attacker who gains access to a normal user account may use a rootkit to exploit a vulnerability and perform a privilege escalation attack, seeking to gain administrative privileges.

FIGURE 5.8 Dirty COW website

Arbitrary Code Execution

Arbitrary code execution vulnerabilities allow an attacker to run software of their choice on the targeted system. This can be a catastrophic event, particularly if the vulnerability allows the attacker to run the code with administrative privileges. *Remote code execution* vulnerabilities are an even more dangerous subset of code execution vulnerabilities because the attacker can exploit the vulnerability over a network connection without having physical or logical access to the target system.

Figure 5.9 shows an example of a remote code execution vulnerability detected by Nessus. Notice that the CVSS access vector shows that the access vector for this vulnerability is network based. This is consistent with the description of a remote code execution vulnerability. The impact metrics in the vector show that the attacker can exploit this vulnerability to completely compromise the system.

Fortunately, as with most vulnerabilities detected by scans, there is an easy fix for the problem. Microsoft issued patches for the versions of Windows affected by the issue and describes them in Microsoft Security Bulletin MS14-066.

FIGURE 5.9 Code execution vulnerability

CRITICAL MS14-066: Vulnerability in Schannel Could Allow Remote Code Execution (...

Description

The remote Windows host is affected by a remote code execution vulnerability due to improper processing of packets by the Secure Channel (Schannel) security package. An attacker can exploit this issue by sending specially crafted packets to a Windows server.

Note that this plugin sends a client Certificate TLS handshake message followed by a CertificateVerify message. Some Windows hosts will close the connection upon receiving a client certificate for which it did not ask for with a CertificateRequest message. In this case, the plugin cannot proceed to detect the vulnerability as the CertificateVerify message cannot be sent.

Solution

Microsoft has released a set of patches.

See Also

https://technet.microsoft.com/library/security/ms14-066

Output

No output recorded.

Port	Hosts
443 / tcp / www	10.64.142.203

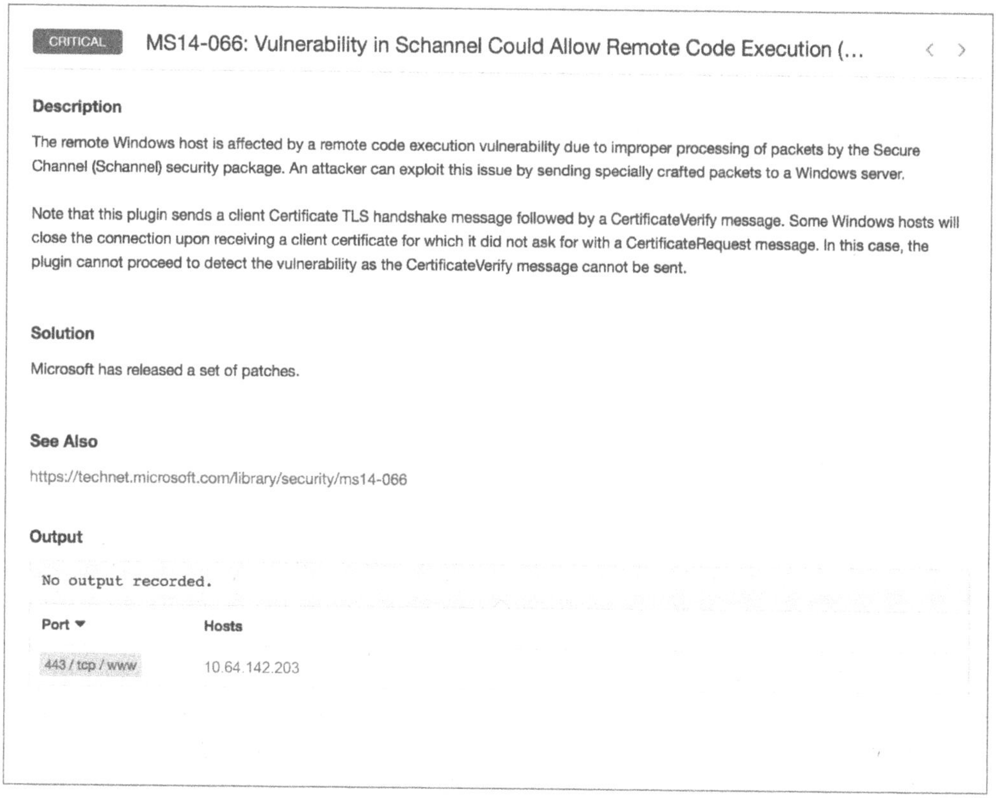

Insecure Protocol Use

Many of the older protocols used on networks in the early days of the Internet were designed without security in mind. They often failed to use encryption to protect usernames, passwords, and the content sent over an open network, exposing the users of the protocol to eavesdropping attacks. Telnet is one example of an insecure protocol used to gain command-line access to a remote server. The File Transfer Protocol (FTP) provides the ability to transfer files between systems but does not incorporate security features. Figure 5.10 shows an example of a scan report that detected a system that supports the insecure FTP protocol.

The solution for this issue is to simply switch to a more secure protocol. Fortunately, encrypted alternatives exist for both Telnet and FTP. System administrators can use Secure Shell (SSH) as a secure replacement for Telnet when seeking to gain command-line access to a remote system. Similarly, the Secure File Transfer Protocol (SFTP) and FTP-Secure (FTPS) both provide a secure method to transfer files between systems.

FIGURE 5.10 FTP cleartext authentication vulnerability

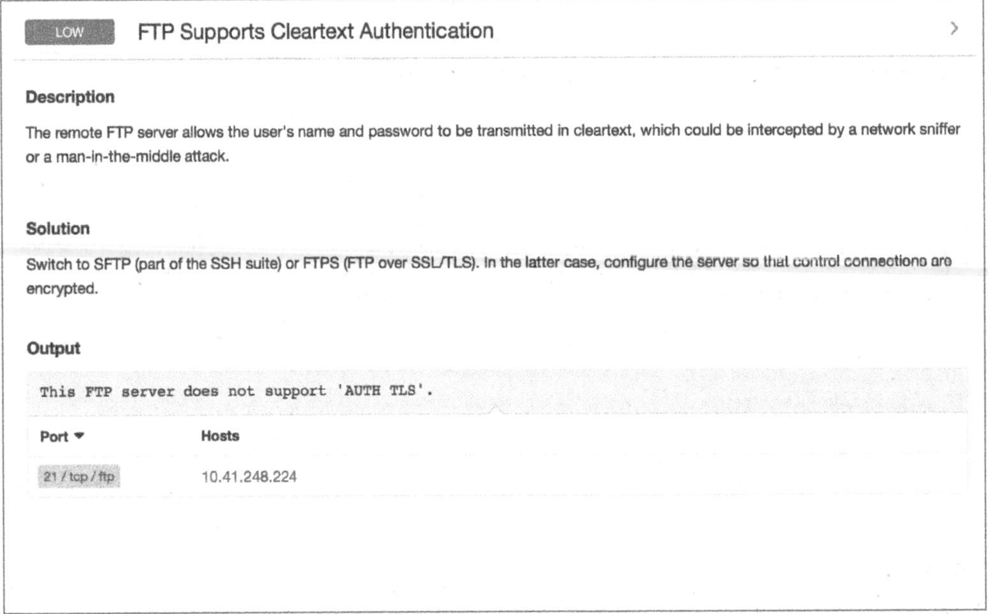

Debugging Modes

Many application development platforms support *debug modes* that give developers crucial information needed to troubleshoot applications in the development process. Debug mode typically provides detailed information on the inner workings of an application and a server, as well as supporting databases. Although this information can be useful to developers, it can inadvertently assist an attacker seeking to gain information about the structure of a database, authentication mechanisms used by an application, or other details. For this reason, vulnerability scans do alert on the presence of debug mode on scanned servers. Figure 5.11 shows an example of this type of scan result.

FIGURE 5.11 Debug mode vulnerability

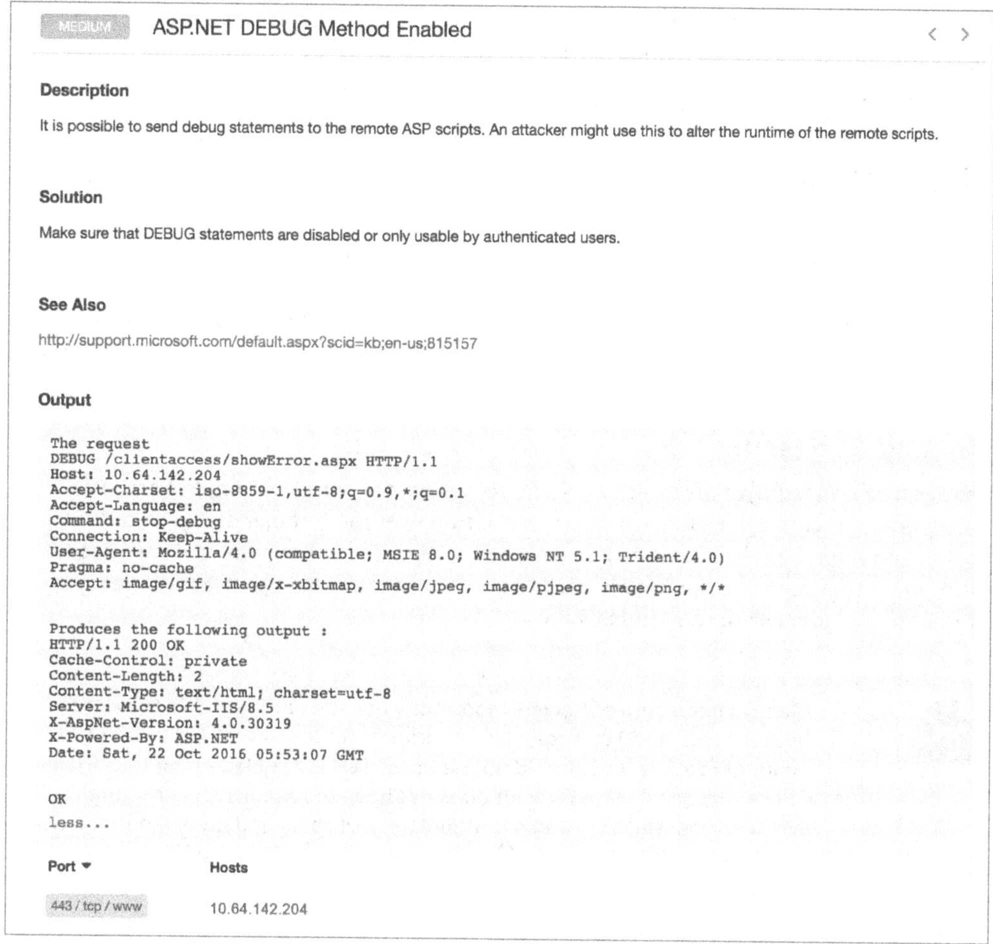

MEDIUM ASP.NET DEBUG Method Enabled

Description

It is possible to send debug statements to the remote ASP scripts. An attacker might use this to alter the runtime of the remote scripts.

Solution

Make sure that DEBUG statements are disabled or only usable by authenticated users.

See Also

http://support.microsoft.com/default.aspx?scid=kb;en-us;815157

Output

```
The request
DEBUG /clientaccess/showError.aspx HTTP/1.1
Host: 10.64.142.204
Accept-Charset: iso-8859-1,utf-8;q=0.9,*;q=0.1
Accept-Language: en
Command: stop-debug
Connection: Keep-Alive
User-Agent: Mozilla/4.0 (compatible; MSIE 8.0; Windows NT 5.1; Trident/4.0)
Pragma: no-cache
Accept: image/gif, image/x-xbitmap, image/jpeg, image/pjpeg, image/png, */*

Produces the following output :
HTTP/1.1 200 OK
Cache-Control: private
Content-Length: 2
Content-Type: text/html; charset=utf-8
Server: Microsoft-IIS/8.5
X-AspNet-Version: 4.0.30319
X-Powered-By: ASP.NET
Date: Sat, 22 Oct 2016 05:53:07 GMT

OK
less...
```

Port ▾	Hosts
443 / tcp / www	10.64.142.204

In this example, the target system appears to be a Windows Server supporting the ASP .NET development environment. The Output section of the report demonstrates that the server responds when sent a DEBUG request by a client.

Solving this issue requires the cooperation of developers and disabling debug modes on systems with public exposure. In mature organizations, software development should always take place in a dedicated development environment that is only accessible from private networks. Developers should be encouraged (or ordered!) to conduct their testing only on systems dedicated to that purpose, and it would be entirely appropriate to enable debug mode on those servers. There should be no need for supporting this capability on public-facing systems.

Network Vulnerabilities

Modern interconnected networks use a complex combination of infrastructure components and network appliances to provide widespread access to secure communications capabilities. These networks and their component parts are also susceptible to security vulnerabilities that may be detected during a vulnerability scan.

Missing Firmware Updates

Operating systems and applications aren't the only devices that require regular security updates. Vulnerability scans may also detect security problems in network devices that require firmware updates from the manufacturer to correct. These vulnerabilities result in reports similar to the operating system missing patch report in Figure 5.6 and typically direct administrators to the location on the vendor's site where the firmware update is available for download.

SSL and TLS Issues

The *Secure Sockets Layer (SSL)* protocol and its successor, *Transport Layer Security (TLS)*, offer a secure means to exchange information over the Internet and private networks. Although these protocols can be used to encrypt almost any type of network communication, they are most commonly used to secure connections to web servers and are familiar to end users as the "S" in HTTPS.

Many cybersecurity analysts incorrectly use the acronym SSL to refer to both the SSL and TLS protocols. It's important to understand that SSL is no longer secure and should not be used. TLS is a replacement for SSL that offers similar functionality but does not have the security flaws contained in SSL. Be careful to use this terminology precisely and question those who use the term SSL about whether they are really referring to TLS to avoid ambiguity.

Outdated SSL/TLS Versions

SSL is no longer considered secure and should not be used on production systems. The same is true for early versions of TLS. Vulnerability scanners may report that web servers are using these protocols, and cybersecurity analysts should understand that any connections making use of these outdated versions of SSL and TLS may be subject to eavesdropping attacks. Figure 5.12 shows an example of a scan report from a network containing multiple systems that support the outdated SSL version 3.

The administrators of servers supporting outdated versions of SSL and TLS should disable support for these older protocols on their servers and support only newer protocols, such as TLS version 1.2.

FIGURE 5.12 Outdated SSL version vulnerability

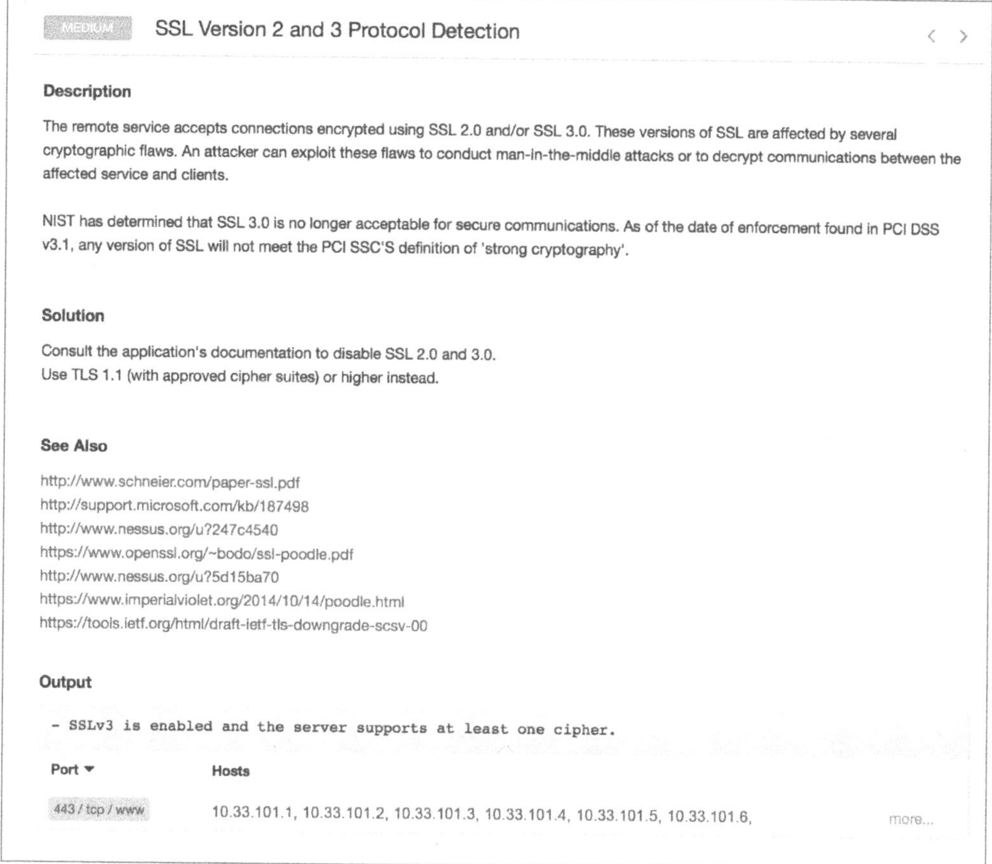

Insecure Cipher Use

SSL and TLS are commonly described as cryptographic algorithms, but in fact, this is not the case. The SSL and TLS protocols describe how cryptographic ciphers may be used to secure network communications, but they are not cryptographic ciphers themselves. Instead, they allow administrators to designate the cryptographic ciphers that can be used with those protocols on a server-by-server basis. When a client and server wish to communicate using SSL/TLS, they exchange a list of ciphers that each system supports and agree on a mutually acceptable cipher.

Some ciphers contain vulnerabilities that render them insecure because of their susceptibility to eavesdropping attacks. For example, Figure 5.13 shows a scan report from a system that supports the insecure RC4 cipher.

Solving this common problem requires altering the set of supported ciphers on the affected server and ensuring that only secure ciphers are used.

FIGURE 5.13 Insecure SSL cipher vulnerability

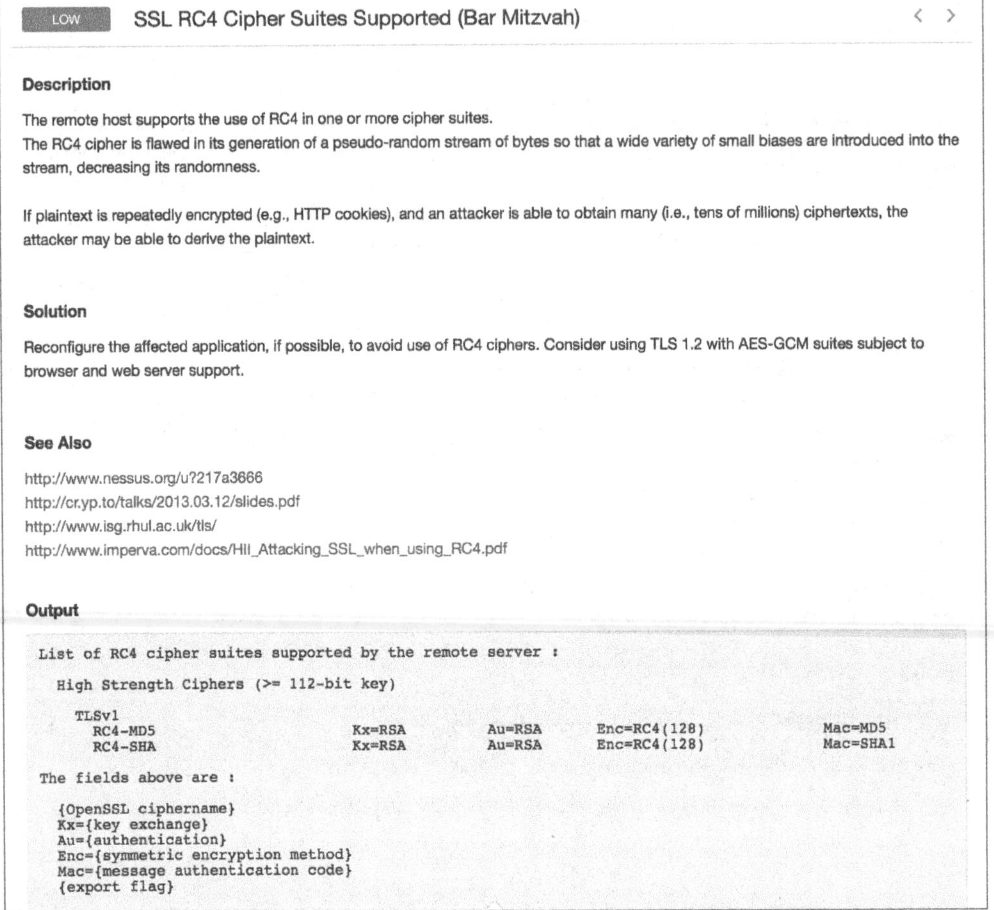

LOW SSL RC4 Cipher Suites Supported (Bar Mitzvah)

Description

The remote host supports the use of RC4 in one or more cipher suites.
The RC4 cipher is flawed in its generation of a pseudo-random stream of bytes so that a wide variety of small biases are introduced into the stream, decreasing its randomness.

If plaintext is repeatedly encrypted (e.g., HTTP cookies), and an attacker is able to obtain many (i.e., tens of millions) ciphertexts, the attacker may be able to derive the plaintext.

Solution

Reconfigure the affected application, if possible, to avoid use of RC4 ciphers. Consider using TLS 1.2 with AES-GCM suites subject to browser and web server support.

See Also

http://www.nessus.org/u?217a3666
http://cr.yp.to/talks/2013.03.12/slides.pdf
http://www.isg.rhul.ac.uk/tls/
http://www.imperva.com/docs/HII_Attacking_SSL_when_using_RC4.pdf

Output

```
List of RC4 cipher suites supported by the remote server :

  High Strength Ciphers (>= 112-bit key)

    TLSv1
      RC4-MD5          Kx=RSA    Au=RSA    Enc=RC4(128)    Mac=MD5
      RC4-SHA          Kx=RSA    Au=RSA    Enc=RC4(128)    Mac=SHA1

The fields above are :

  {OpenSSL ciphername}
  Kx={key exchange}
  Au={authentication}
  Enc={symmetric encryption method}
  Mac={message authentication code}
  {export flag}
```

Certificate Problems

SSL and TLS rely on the use of digital certificates to validate the identity of servers and exchange cryptographic keys. Website users are familiar with the error messages displayed in web browsers, such as that shown in Figure 5.14. These errors often contain extremely important information about the security of the site being accessed but, unfortunately, are all too often ignored.

Vulnerability scans may also detect issues with the certificates presented by servers that support SSL and/or TLS. Common errors include the following:

Mismatch Between the Name on the Certificate and the Name of the Server This is a very serious error because it may indicate the use of a certificate taken from another site. It's the digital equivalent of someone using a fake ID "borrowed" from a friend.

FIGURE 5.14 Invalid certificate warning

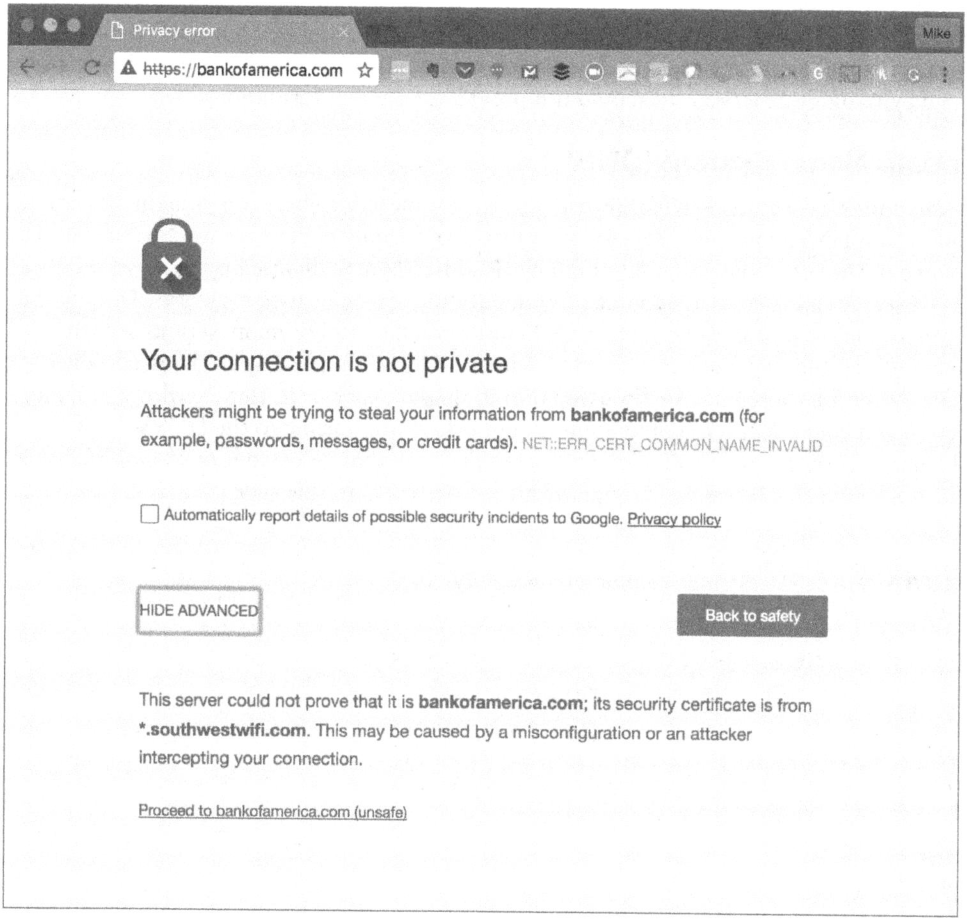

Expiration of the Digital Certificate Digital certificates have validity periods and expiration dates. When you see an expired certificate, it most likely means that the server administrator failed to renew the certificate in a timely manner.

Unknown Certificate Authority (CA) Anyone can create a digital certificate, but digital certificates are useful only if the recipient of a certificate trusts the entity that issued it. Operating systems and browsers contain instructions to trust well-known CAs but will show an error if they encounter a certificate issued by an unknown or untrusted CA.

The error shown in Figure 5.14 indicates that the user is attempting to access a website that is presenting an invalid certificate. From the URL bar, we see that the user is attempting to access `bankofamerica.com`. However, looking in the details section, we see that the certificate being presented was issued to `southwestwifi.com`. This is a typical occurrence on networks that use a captive portal to authenticate users joining a public wireless network. This example is from the in-flight Wi-Fi service offered by Southwest Airlines. The error points out to the user that they are not communicating with the intended website owned by Bank of America and should not provide sensitive information.

Domain Name System (DNS)

The *Domain Name System (DNS)* provides a translation service between domain names and IP addresses. DNS allows end users to remember user-friendly domain names, such as `apple.com`, and not worry about the mind-numbing IP addresses actually used by those servers.

DNS servers are a common source of vulnerabilities on enterprise networks. Despite the seemingly simple nature of the service, DNS has a track record of many serious security vulnerabilities and requires careful configuration and patching. Many of the issues with DNS services are those already discussed in this chapter, such as buffer overflows, missing patches, and code execution vulnerabilities, but others are specific to the DNS service.

Figure 5.15 shows an example of a vulnerability scan that detected a *DNS amplification* vulnerability on two servers on an organization's network. In this type of attack, the

FIGURE 5.15 DNS amplification vulnerability

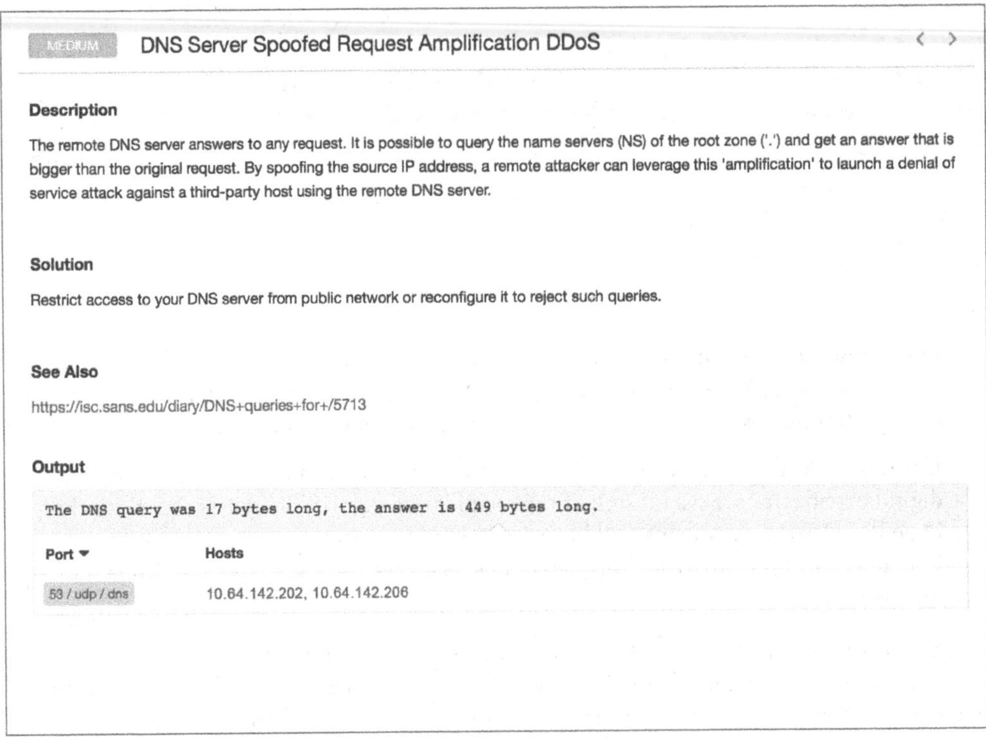
MEDIUM DNS Server Spoofed Request Amplification DDoS

Description

The remote DNS server answers to any request. It is possible to query the name servers (NS) of the root zone ('.') and get an answer that is bigger than the original request. By spoofing the source IP address, a remote attacker can leverage this 'amplification' to launch a denial of service attack against a third-party host using the remote DNS server.

Solution

Restrict access to your DNS server from public network or reconfigure it to reject such queries.

See Also

https://isc.sans.edu/diary/DNS+queries+for+/5713

Output

```
The DNS query was 17 bytes long, the answer is 449 bytes long.
```

Port ▾	Hosts
53 / udp / dns	10.64.142.202, 10.64.142.206

attacker sends spoofed DNS requests to a DNS server that are carefully designed to elicit responses that are much larger in size than the original requests. These large response packets then go to the spoofed address where the DNS server believes the query originated. The IP address used in the spoofed request is actually the target of a denial-of-service attack and is bombarded by very large responses from DNS servers all over the world to queries that it never sent. When conducted in sufficient volume, DNS amplification attacks can completely overwhelm the targeted systems, rendering them inoperable.

Internal IP Disclosure

IP addresses come in two variants: public IP addresses, which can be routed over the Internet, and private IP addresses, which can be used only on local networks. Any server that is accessible over the Internet must have a public IP address to allow that access, but that address is typically managed by a firewall that uses *network address translation (NAT)* to map that public address to the server's true, private IP address. Systems on the local network can use the server's private address to access it directly, but remote systems should never be aware of that address.

Servers that are not properly configured may leak their private IP addresses to remote systems. This can occur when the system includes its own IP address in the header information returned in the response to an HTTP request. The server is not aware that NAT is in use, so it uses the private address in its response. Attackers can use this information to learn more about the internal configuration of a firewalled network. Figure 5.16 shows an example of this type of information disclosure vulnerability.

Virtual Private Network Issues

Many organizations use *virtual private networks (VPNs)* to provide employees with secure remote access to the organization's network. As with any application protocol, administrators must ensure that the VPN services offered by the organization are fully patched to current levels. In addition, VPNs require the use of cryptographic ciphers and suffer from similar issues as SSL and TLS when they support the use of insecure ciphers.

Virtualization Vulnerabilities

Most modern datacenters make extensive use of *virtualization* technology to allow multiple guest systems to share the same underlying hardware. In a virtualized datacenter, the virtual host hardware runs a special operating system known as a *hypervisor* that mediates access to the underlying hardware resources. Virtual machines then run on top of this virtual infrastructure provided by the hypervisor, running standard operating systems such as Windows and Linux variants. The virtual machines may not be aware that they are running in a virtualized environment because the hypervisor tricks them into thinking that they have normal access to the underlying hardware when, in reality, that hardware is shared with other systems.

FIGURE 5.16 Internal IP disclosure vulnerability

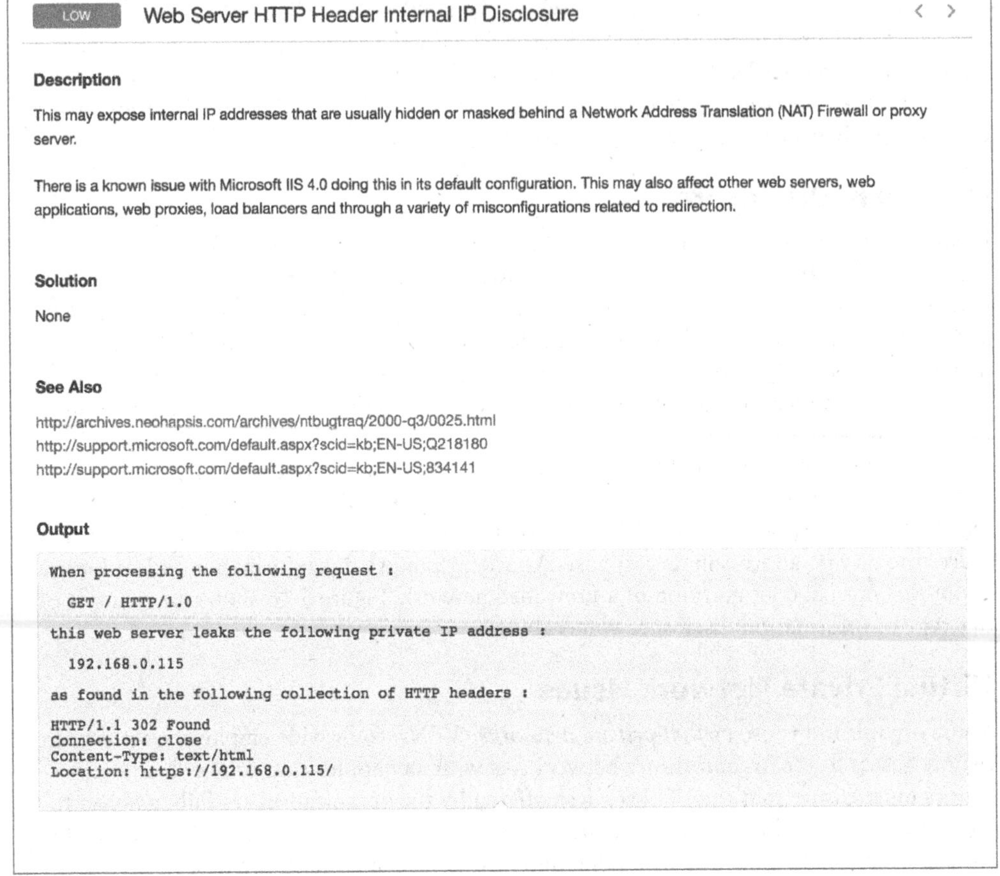

LOW Web Server HTTP Header Internal IP Disclosure

Description

This may expose internal IP addresses that are usually hidden or masked behind a Network Address Translation (NAT) Firewall or proxy server.

There is a known issue with Microsoft IIS 4.0 doing this in its default configuration. This may also affect other web servers, web applications, web proxies, load balancers and through a variety of misconfigurations related to redirection.

Solution

None

See Also

http://archives.neohapsis.com/archives/ntbugtraq/2000-q3/0025.html
http://support.microsoft.com/default.aspx?scid=kb;EN-US;Q218180
http://support.microsoft.com/default.aspx?scid=kb;EN-US;834141

Output

```
When processing the following request :

  GET / HTTP/1.0

this web server leaks the following private IP address :

  192.168.0.115

as found in the following collection of HTTP headers :

HTTP/1.1 302 Found
Connection: close
Content-Type: text/html
Location: https://192.168.0.115/
```

Figure 5.17 provides an illustration of how a hypervisor mediates access to the underlying hardware resources in a virtual host to support multiple virtual guest machines.

FIGURE 5.17 Inside a virtual host

The example described in this chapter, where the hypervisor runs directly on top of physical hardware, is known as bare-metal virtualization. This is the approach commonly used in datacenter environments. There is another type of virtualization, known as hosted virtualization, where a host operating system sits between the hardware and the hypervisor. This is commonly used in cases where the user of an endpoint system wants to simultaneously run multiple operating systems on that device. Parallels is a popular hosted virtualization platform for the Mac.

VM Escape

Virtual machine escape vulnerabilities are the most serious issue that may exist in a virtualized environment, particularly when a virtual host runs systems of differing security levels. In an escape attack, the attacker has access to a single virtual host and then manages to leverage that access to intrude on the resources assigned to a different virtual machine (VM). The hypervisor is supposed to prevent this type of access by restricting a VM's access to only those resources assigned to that machine. Escape attacks allow a process running on the VM to "escape" those hypervisor restrictions.

Management Interface Access

Virtualization engineers use the management interface for a virtual infrastructure to configure the virtualization environment, set up new guest machines, and regulate access to resources. This management interface is extremely sensitive from a security perspective, and access should be tightly controlled to prevent unauthorized individuals from gaining access. In addition to using strong multifactor authentication on the management interface, cybersecurity professionals should ensure that the interface is never directly accessible from a public network. Vulnerability scans that detect the presence of an accessible management interface will report this as a security concern.

Virtual Host Patching

This chapter already discussed the importance of promptly applying security updates to operating systems, applications, and network devices. It is equally important to ensure that virtualization platforms receive security updates that may affect the security of virtual guests or the entire platform. Patches may correct vulnerabilities that allow VM escape attacks or other serious security flaws.

Virtual Guest Issues

Cybersecurity analysts should think of each guest machine running in a virtualized environment as a separate server that requires the same security attention as any other device on the network. Guest operating systems and applications running on the guest OS must be promptly patched to correct security vulnerabilities and be otherwise well maintained. There's no difference from a security perspective between a physical server and a virtualized server.

Virtual Network Issues

As datacenters become increasingly virtualized, a significant amount of network traffic never actually touches a network! Communications between virtual machines that reside on the same physical hardware can occur in memory without ever touching a physical network. For this reason, virtual networks must be maintained with the same attention to security that administrators would apply to physical networks. This includes the use of virtual firewalls to control the flow of information between systems and the isolation of systems of differing security levels on different virtual network segments.

Internet of Things (IoT)

In some environments, cybersecurity analysts may encounter the use of *supervisory control and data acquisition (SCADA)* systems, *industrial control systems (ICSs)*, and other examples of the *Internet of Things (IoT)*. These systems allow the connection of physical devices and processes to networks and provide tremendous sources of data for organizations seeking to make their business processes more efficient and effective. However, they also introduce new security concerns that may arise on vulnerability scans.

The IoT world also extends to include systems related to the management of physical infrastructure. For example, physical access control systems often interact with IoT devices at turnstiles, doors, gates, and other facility entry points. Building automation systems interact with heating, ventilation, and air conditioning (HVAC) systems, fire suppression systems, and other building controls. All of these systems tie together with workflow and process automation systems designed to reduce the burden on human staff.

Industrial control systems rely on a series of sensors and controllers distributed throughout the organization, collecting information and controlling activities. *Programmable logic controllers (PLCs)* are specialized hardware controllers designed to operate in an IoT environment. PLCs often use a specialized communication protocol called *Modbus* to communicate with sensors and other IoT components over wired serial interfaces. In addition to PLCs, you should be familiar with some other technology components that make up IoT deployments as you prepare for the CySA+ exam:

- *Embedded systems* are computers integrated into the operation of another device, such as a vehicle, camera, or multifunction printer.
- *Real-time operating systems (RTOSs)* are slimmed-down operating systems designed to work quickly on IoT devices in a low-power environment.
- *A system on a chip (SoC)* is an entire embedded system packaged onto a single chip, often including a processor, memory, networking interfaces, and power management on the chip.
- *Field-programmable gate arrays (FPGAs)* are computer chips that allow the end user to reprogram their function, making them quite useful for embedded systems.
- *Controller Area Network bus (CAN bus)* networks are specialized networks designed to facilitate communication between embedded systems without the overhead of a TCP/IP network.

Some of the most critical IoT deployments are those found on vehicles and drones. These systems have a dramatic impact on the safety of human life and should be carefully monitored for security issues.

As with any other device on a network, IoT devices may have security vulnerabilities and are subject to network-based attacks. However, it is often more difficult to patch IoT devices than their traditional server counterparts because it is difficult to obtain patches. IoT device manufacturers may not use automatic update mechanisms, and the only way that cybersecurity analysts may become aware of an update is through a vulnerability scan or by proactively subscribing to the security bulletins issued by IoT device manufacturers.

IoT Uprising

On October 21, 2016, a widespread distributed denial-of-service (DDoS) attack shut down large portions of the Internet, affecting services run by Amazon, *The New York Times,* Twitter, Box, and other providers. The attack came in waves over the course of the day and initially mystified technologists seeking to bring systems back online.

Investigation later revealed that the outages occurred when Dyn, a global provider of DNS services, suffered a debilitating attack that prevented it from answering DNS queries. Dyn received massive amounts of traffic that overwhelmed its servers.

The source of all of that traffic? Attackers used an IoT botnet named Mirai to leverage the bandwidth available to baby monitors, DVRs, security cameras, and other IoT devices in the homes of normal people. Those botnetted devices received instructions from a yet-unknown attacker to simultaneously bombard Dyn with requests, knocking it (and a good part of the Internet!) offline.

Web Application Vulnerabilities

Web applications are complex environments that often rely not only on web servers but also on backend databases, authentication servers, and other components to provide services to end users. These web applications may also contain security holes that allow attackers to gain a foothold on a network, and modern vulnerability scanners are able to probe web applications for these vulnerabilities.

Injection Attacks

Injection attacks occur when an attacker is able to send commands through a web server to a backend system, bypassing normal security controls and fooling the backend system into believing that the request came from the web server. The most common form of this attack is the *SQL injection attack*, which exploits web applications to send unauthorized commands to a backend database server.

Web applications often receive input from users and use it to compose a database query that provides results that are sent back to a user. For example, consider the search function on an e-commerce site. If a user enters **orange tiger pillows** into the search box, the web server needs to know what products in the catalog might match this search term. It might send a request to the backend database server that looks something like this:

```
SELECT ItemName, ItemDescription, ItemPrice
FROM Products
WHERE ItemName LIKE '%orange%' AND
ItemName LIKE '%tiger%' AND
ItemName LIKE '%pillow%'
```

This command retrieves a list of items that can be included in the results returned to the end user. In a SQL injection attack, the attacker might send a very unusual-looking request to the web server, perhaps searching for

```
orange tiger pillow'; SELECT CustomerName, CreditCardNumber FROM Orders; --
```

If the web server simply passes this request along to the database server, it would do this (with a little reformatting for ease of viewing):

```
SELECT ItemName, ItemDescription, ItemPrice
FROM Products
WHERE ItemName LIKE '%orange%' AND
ItemName LIKE '%tiger%' AND
ItemName LIKE '%pillow';
SELECT CustomerName, CreditCardNumber
FROM Orders;
--%'
```

This command, if successful, would run two different SQL queries (separated by the semicolon). The first would retrieve the product information, and the second would retrieve a listing of customer names and credit card numbers.

The two best ways to protect against SQL injection attacks are input validation and the enforcement of least privilege restrictions on database access. Input validation ensures that users don't provide unexpected text to the web server. It would block the use of the apostrophe that is needed to "break out" of the original SQL query. Least privilege restricts the tables that may be accessed by a web server and can prevent the retrieval of credit card information by a process designed to handle catalog information requests.

Exam Note

Injection attacks are not limited to SQL and databases. Cybersecurity professionals should also be vigilant for similar attacks that seek to introduce user-supplied, malicious content into Extensible Markup Language (XML) documents and Lightweight Directory Access Protocol (LDAP) queries.

Vulnerability scanners can detect injection vulnerabilities, such as the one shown in Figure 5.18. When cybersecurity analysts notice a potential injection vulnerability, they should work closely with developers to validate that the vulnerability exists and fix the affected code.

Cross-Site Scripting

In a *cross-site scripting (XSS)* attack, an attacker embeds scripting commands on a website that will later be executed by an unsuspecting visitor accessing the site. The idea is to trick a user visiting a trusted site into executing malicious code placed there by an untrusted third party.

FIGURE 5.18 SQL injection vulnerability

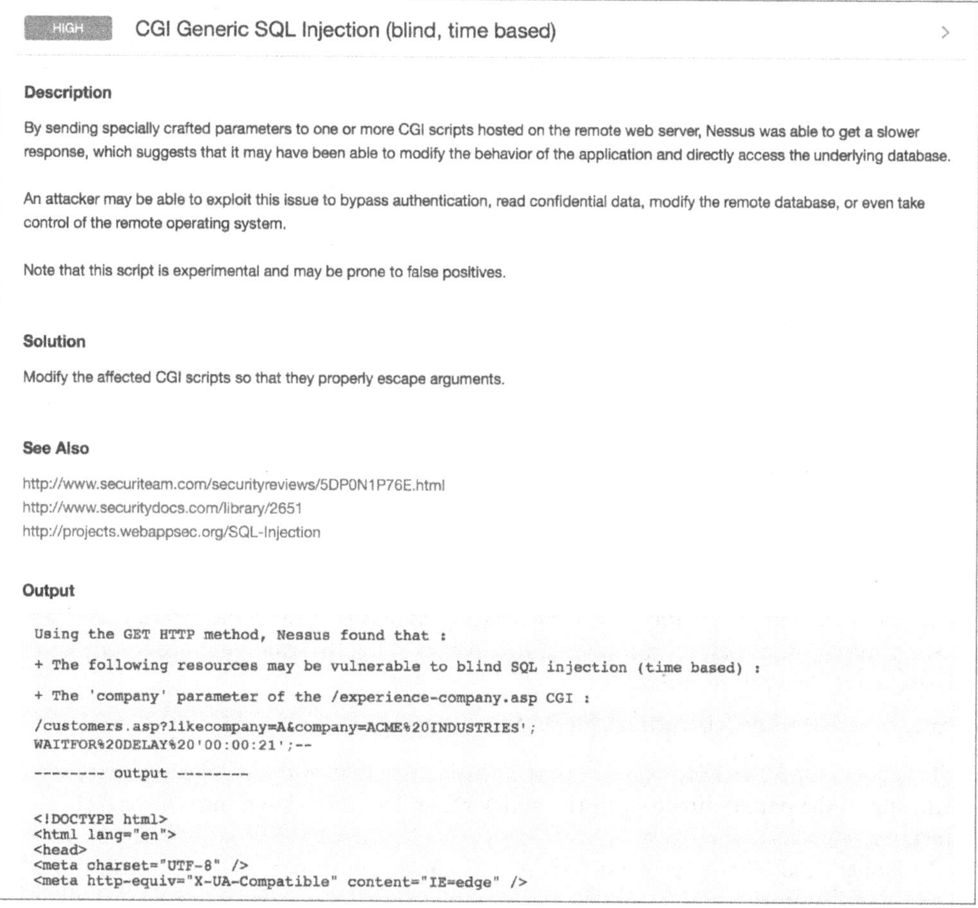

Cross-site scripting attacks arise in three different forms:

- *Persistent XSS* attacks occur when the attacker is able to actually store the attack code on a server. This code remains on the server, waiting for a user to request the affected content. These attacks are also known as stored XSS attacks.
- *Reflected XSS* attacks occur when the attacker tricks a user into sending the attack to the server as part of a query string or other content. The server then sends the attack back to the user (reflecting it), causing the code to execute.
- *Document Object Model (DOM)-based XSS* attacks occur within a database maintained by the user's web browser. These attacks are particularly insidious because they occur entirely on the user's computer and are never seen by the remote web server.

Exam Note

Each of these XSS attack types is covered separately in the CySA+ exam objectives. Make certain that you understand the differences between them as you prepare for the exam.

Figure 5.19 shows an example of an XSS vulnerability detected during a Nessus vulnerability scan.

Cybersecurity analysts discovering potential XSS vulnerabilities during a scan should work with developers to assess the validity of the results and implement appropriate controls to prevent this type of attack, such as input validation.

Directory Traversal

In a *directory traversal* attack, the attacker inserts filesystem path values into a query string, seeking to navigate to a file located in an area not normally authorized for public access. These attacks may occur when filenames are included in query strings. For example, if a web application retrieves policy documents from a remote storage device, it might include the name of the policy in a query string, such as this one:

```
http://www.myserver.com/policy?document='aup.pdf'
```

The web application might see this query string and then go to the policy store and retrieve a document called `aup.pdf`. If an attacker knows that the policy store is located on the same server as payroll records, they might try using the following query string to retrieve Mike's payroll records:

```
http://www.myserver.com/policy?document='../payroll/mike.pdf'
```

This query string seeks to traverse the directory structure of the storage server, navigating up to the parent directory of the policy folder and then down into the payroll directory.

Developers and security professionals should implement three types of controls to protect against directory traversal attacks. First, application designs should avoid including

FIGURE 5.19 Cross-site scripting vulnerability

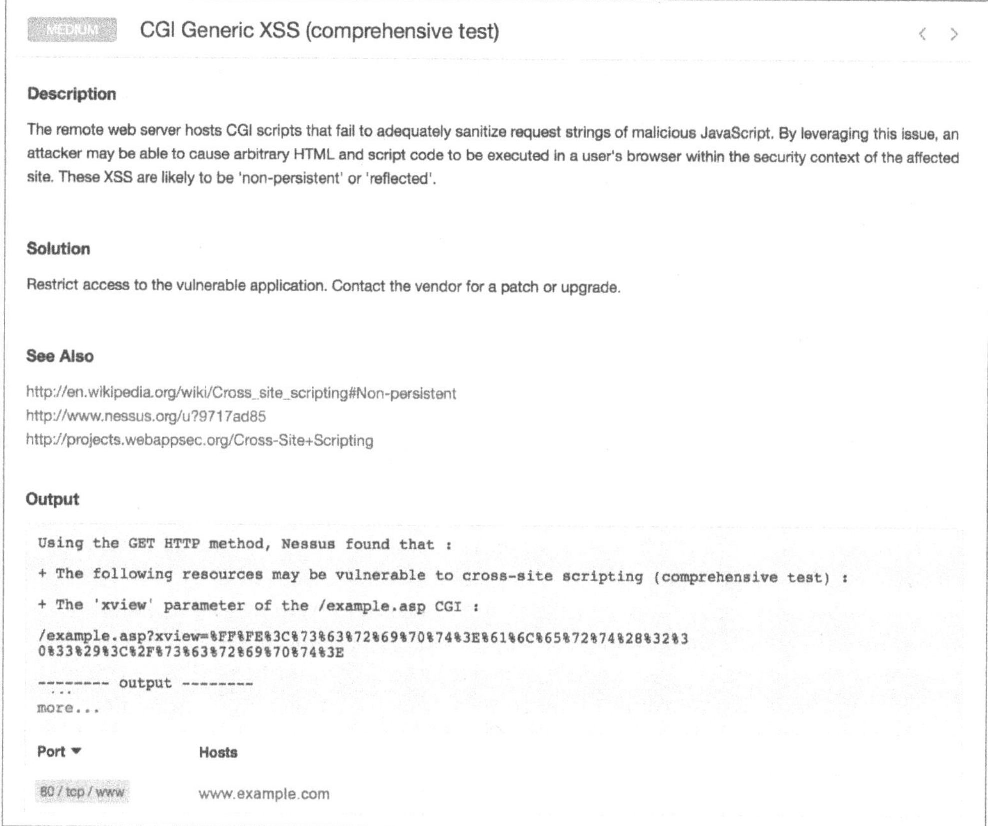

filenames in user-manipulatable fields, such as query strings. Second, input validation should prevent the use of special characters required to perform directory traversal. Finally, access controls on storage servers should restrict the web server's access to files authorized for public access.

Authentication Vulnerabilities

There are a few common methods of targeting identity and access management systems as well as the use of identity information, each with common protection methods that can help to remediate them. These include password spraying, credential stuffing, impersonation, man-in-the-middle, and session hijacking attacks.

Password Reuse

Two common authentication vulnerabilities arise because of the propensity of users to reuse the same passwords across multiple sites:

- *Password spraying* attacks occur when an attacker uses a list of common passwords and attempts to log into many different user accounts with those common passwords. The attacker only needs to find one valid username/password combination to gain access to the system. This attack is successful when users do not choose sufficiently unique passwords.
- *Credential stuffing* attacks occur when an attacker takes a list of usernames and passwords that were stolen in the compromise of one website and uses them to attempt to gain access to a different, potentially unrelated, website. Credential stuffing attacks are successful when users reuse the same password across many different sites.

In addition to encouraging strong password management practices, administrators can further protect themselves against password reuse vulnerabilities by requiring the use of multifactor authentication on sensitive systems.

Impersonation

Impersonation attacks occur when an attacker takes on the identity of a legitimate user. Security issues like OAuth open redirects, discussed in Chapter 8, "Identity and Access Management Security," can allow impersonation to occur. Preventing impersonation may require stronger session handling techniques like those found in the OWASP session management cheat sheet at `cheatsheetseries.owasp.org/cheatsheets/Session_Management_Cheat_Sheet.html`. Other types of impersonation may be prevented by securing session identifiers that attackers might otherwise acquire, either on the local workstation or via the network.

Man-in-the-Middle

Man-in-the-middle (MitM) attacks occur when an attacker is able to interfere in the communication flow between two systems. For example, imagine that a user named Alice is seeking to communicate with her bank's web server, as shown in Figure 5.20.

Figure 5.20 shows the normal communication, where Alice sets up an HTTPS connection and then communicates securely with the web server. If an eavesdropper sees the network traffic related to this connection, they cannot read the communications because they are encrypted.

However, if an attacker is able to impersonate the bank's web server, as shown in Figure 5.21, the attacker can accept Alice's connection request and then establish their own connection to the legitimate bank server. The attacker then sees all of the requests coming from Alice and passes them on to the legitimate server, impersonating Alice. The attacker then sends the bank's responses to Alice. The attacker is serving as the man-in-the-middle.

End-to-end encryption of sessions or network links can help reduce the chance of a successful MitM attack, unless attackers control endpoints or have the encryption keys.

FIGURE 5.20 Alice communicating with a bank web server

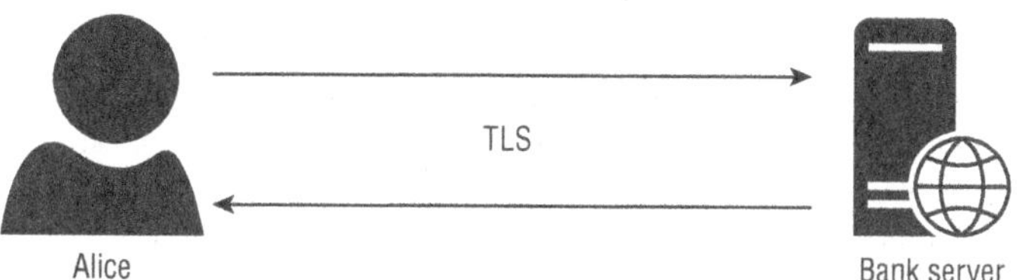

FIGURE 5.21 Man-in-the-middle attack

Session Hijacking

Session hijacking focuses on taking over an already existing session, either by acquiring the session key or cookies used by the remote server to validate the session or by causing the session to pass through a system the attacker controls, allowing them to participate in the session. Much like impersonation and MitM attacks, securing the data that an attacker needs to acquire to hijack the session, either via encrypting network sessions or links or on the local system, can help limit opportunities for session hijacking.

Summary

Vulnerability management programs produce a significant amount of information that requires analysis by trained cybersecurity professionals. Cybersecurity analysts must be familiar with the interpretation of vulnerability scan results and the prioritization of remediation efforts to provide value to their organizations.

Vulnerability scanners usually rank detected issues using the Common Vulnerability Scoring System (CVSS). CVSS provides six measures of each vulnerability: the access vector metric, the access complexity metric, the authentication metric, the confidentiality metric, the integrity metric, and the availability metric. Together, these metrics provide a look at the potential that a vulnerability will be successfully exploited and the impact it could have on the organization.

As analysts interpret scan results, they should be careful to watch for common issues. False positive reports occur when the scanner erroneously reports a vulnerability that does not actually exist. If an analyst is suspicious about the accuracy of a result, they should verify it manually. When verifying a vulnerability, analysts should draw on their own expertise as well as the subject matter expertise of others throughout the organization.

To successfully interpret vulnerability reports, analysts must be familiar with the vulnerabilities that commonly occur. Common server and endpoint vulnerabilities include missing patches, unsupported operating systems and applications, buffer overflows, privilege escalation, arbitrary code execution, insecure protocol usage, and the presence of debugging modes. Common network vulnerabilities include missing firmware updates, SSL/TLS issues, DNS misconfigurations, internal IP disclosures, and VPN issues. Virtualization vulnerabilities include virtual machine escape vulnerabilities, management interface access, missing patches on virtual hosts, and security misconfigurations on virtual guests and virtual networks.

Exam Essentials

Explain how vulnerability scan reports provide critical information to cybersecurity analysts. In addition to providing details about the vulnerabilities present on a system, vulnerability scan reports also offer crucial severity and troubleshooting information. The report typically includes the request and response that triggered a vulnerability report as well as a suggested solution to the problem. Analysts must understand how to identify, validate, and remediate vulnerabilities that occur.

Know the purpose of the Common Vulnerability Scoring System (CVSS). The CVSS base score computes a standard measure on a 10-point scale that incorporates information about the access vector required to exploit a vulnerability, the complexity of the exploit, and the authentication required to execute an attack. The base score also considers the impact of the vulnerability on the confidentiality, integrity, and availability of the affected system.

Explain how servers and endpoint devices are a common source of vulnerability. Missing patches and outdated operating systems are two of the most common vulnerability sources and are easily corrected by proactive device maintenance. Buffer overflow, privilege escalation, and arbitrary code execution attacks typically exploit application flaws. Devices supporting insecure protocols are also a common source of vulnerabilities.

Know that network devices also suffer from frequent vulnerabilities. Network administrators should ensure that network devices receive regular firmware updates to patch security issues. Improper implementations of SSL and TLS encryption also cause vulnerabilities when they use outdated protocols, insecure ciphers, or invalid certificates.

Explain how specialized technologies add complexity to vulnerability scanning. Cybersecurity analysts should understand how to conduct and interpret scans against mobile devices and Internet of Things components. They should also include specialized systems, such as embedded devices, RTOS, SoC, and FPGA technology. Recognize the difficulty added by scanning vehicles, drones, building automation systems, physical access control systems, and industrial control systems.

Know that software vulnerabilities require cooperation between analysts and developers. Web applications, in particular, are susceptible to SQL and XML injection attacks. All software may contain buffer, integer, and heap overflow vulnerabilities. Correcting these problems often requires rewriting code and rescanning vulnerable applications to confirm proper remediation.

Understand how virtualized infrastructures add another layer of potential vulnerability. Administrators responsible for virtualized infrastructure must take extra care to ensure that the hypervisor is patched and protected against virtual machine escape attacks. Additionally, administrators should carefully restrict access to the virtual infrastructure's management interface to prevent unauthorized access attempts.

Lab Exercises

Activity 5.1: Interpret a Vulnerability Scan

In Activity 4.2, you ran a vulnerability scan of a network under your control. In this lab, you will interpret the results of that vulnerability scan.

Review the scan results carefully and develop a remediation plan for your network. This plan should carefully consider the severity of each vulnerability, the potential that each may be a false positive result, and the time required to complete the remediation.

Activity 5.2: Analyze a CVSS Vector

In this lab, you will interpret the CVSS vectors found in a vulnerability scan report to assess the severity and impact of two vulnerabilities.

Review the vulnerability reports in Figures 5.22 and 5.23.

Explain the components of the CVSS vector for each of these vulnerabilities. Which vulnerability is more serious? Why?

Activity 5.3: Remediate a Vulnerability

In this lab, you will remediate one of the vulnerabilities that you identified in Activity 5.1.

1. Review the scan report from Activity 5.1 and select a vulnerability that is a high remediation priority where you have the ability to correct the issue yourself.
2. Perform the remediation.
3. Run a new vulnerability scan to confirm that the vulnerability was successfully remediated.

FIGURE 5.22 First vulnerability report

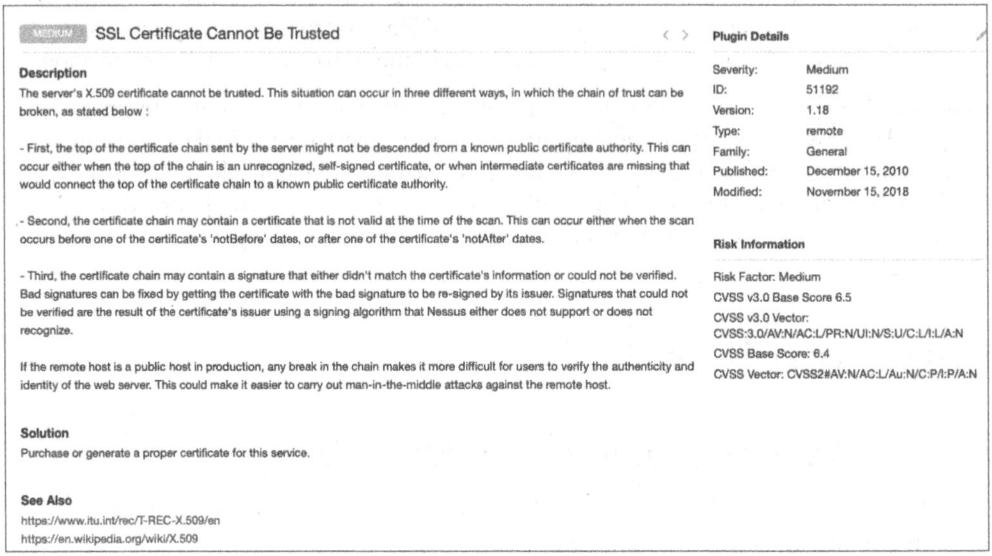

MEDIUM SSL Certificate Cannot Be Trusted

Description

The server's X.509 certificate cannot be trusted. This situation can occur in three different ways, in which the chain of trust can be broken, as stated below :

- First, the top of the certificate chain sent by the server might not be descended from a known public certificate authority. This can occur either when the top of the chain is an unrecognized, self-signed certificate, or when intermediate certificates are missing that would connect the top of the certificate chain to a known public certificate authority.

- Second, the certificate chain may contain a certificate that is not valid at the time of the scan. This can occur either when the scan occurs before one of the certificate's 'notBefore' dates, or after one of the certificate's 'notAfter' dates.

- Third, the certificate chain may contain a signature that either didn't match the certificate's information or could not be verified. Bad signatures can be fixed by getting the certificate with the bad signature to be re-signed by its issuer. Signatures that could not be verified are the result of the certificate's issuer using a signing algorithm that Nessus either does not support or does not recognize.

If the remote host is a public host in production, any break in the chain makes it more difficult for users to verify the authenticity and identity of the web server. This could make it easier to carry out man-in-the-middle attacks against the remote host.

Solution

Purchase or generate a proper certificate for this service.

See Also

https://www.itu.int/rec/T-REC-X.509/en
https://en.wikipedia.org/wiki/X.509

Plugin Details

Severity: Medium
ID: 51192
Version: 1.18
Type: remote
Family: General
Published: December 15, 2010
Modified: November 15, 2018

Risk Information

Risk Factor: Medium
CVSS v3.0 Base Score 6.5
CVSS v3.0 Vector: CVSS:3.0/AV:N/AC:L/PR:N/UI:N/S:U/C:L/I:L/A:N
CVSS Base Score: 6.4
CVSS Vector: CVSS2#AV:N/AC:L/Au:N/C:P/I:P/A:N

FIGURE 5.23 Second vulnerability report

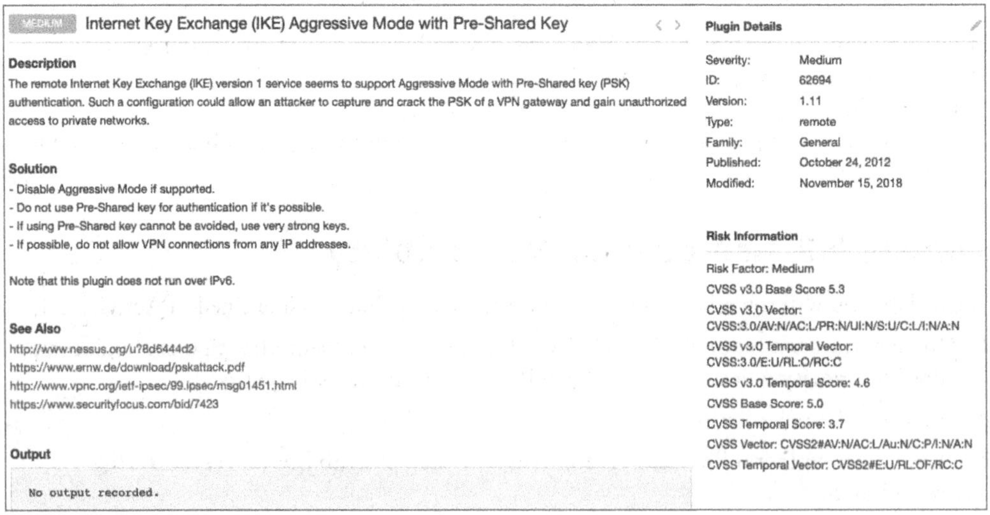

MEDIUM Internet Key Exchange (IKE) Aggressive Mode with Pre-Shared Key

Description

The remote Internet Key Exchange (IKE) version 1 service seems to support Aggressive Mode with Pre-Shared key (PSK) authentication. Such a configuration could allow an attacker to capture and crack the PSK of a VPN gateway and gain unauthorized access to private networks.

Solution

- Disable Aggressive Mode if supported.
- Do not use Pre-Shared key for authentication if it's possible.
- If using Pre-Shared key cannot be avoided, use very strong keys.
- If possible, do not allow VPN connections from any IP addresses.

Note that this plugin does not run over IPv6.

See Also

http://www.nessus.org/u?8d6444d2
https://www.ernw.de/download/pskattack.pdf
http://www.vpnc.org/ietf-ipsec/99.ipsec/msg01451.html
https://www.securityfocus.com/bid/7423

Output

```
No output recorded.
```

Plugin Details

Severity: Medium
ID: 62694
Version: 1.11
Type: remote
Family: General
Published: October 24, 2012
Modified: November 15, 2018

Risk Information

Risk Factor: Medium
CVSS v3.0 Base Score 5.3
CVSS v3.0 Vector: CVSS:3.0/AV:N/AC:L/PR:N/UI:N/S:U/C:L/I:N/A:N
CVSS v3.0 Temporal Vector: CVSS:3.0/E:U/RL:O/RC:C
CVSS v3.0 Temporal Score: 4.6
CVSS Base Score: 5.0
CVSS Temporal Score: 3.7
CVSS Vector: CVSS2#AV:N/AC:L/Au:N/C:P/I:N/A:N
CVSS Temporal Vector: CVSS2#E:U/RL:OF/RC:C

Review Questions

1. Tom is reviewing a vulnerability scan report and finds that one of the servers on his network suffers from an internal IP address disclosure vulnerability. What technology is likely in use on this network that resulted in this vulnerability?
   A. TLS
   B. NAT
   C. SSH
   D. VPN

2. Which one of the CVSS metrics would contain information about the type of account access that an attacker must have to execute an attack?
   A. AV
   B. C
   C. PR
   D. AC

3. Which one of the following values for the CVSS attack complexity metric would indicate that the specified attack is simplest to exploit?
   A. High
   B. Medium
   C. Low
   D. Severe

4. Which one of the following values for the confidentiality, integrity, or availability CVSS metric would indicate the potential for total compromise of a system?
   A. N
   B. L
   C. M
   D. H

5. What is the most recent version of CVSS that is currently available?
   A. 1.0
   B. 2.0
   C. 2.5
   D. 3.1

6. Which one of the following metrics is not included in the calculation of the CVSS exploitability score?

   A. Attack vector

   B. Vulnerability age

   C. Attack complexity

   D. Privileges required

7. Kevin recently identified a new security vulnerability and computed its CVSS base score as 6.5. Which risk category would this vulnerability fall into?

   A. Low

   B. Medium

   C. High

   D. Critical

8. Tara recently analyzed the results of a vulnerability scan report and found that a vulnerability reported by the scanner did not exist because the system was actually patched as specified. What type of error occurred?

   A. False positive

   B. False negative

   C. True positive

   D. True negative

9. Which one of the following is not a common source of information that may be correlated with vulnerability scan results?

   A. Logs

   B. Database tables

   C. SIEM

   D. Configuration management system

10. Which one of the following operating systems should be avoided on production networks?

    A. Windows Server 2003

    B. Red Hat Enterprise Linux 7

    C. CentOS 7

    D. Ubuntu 16

11. In what type of attack does the attacker place more information in a memory location than is allocated for that use?

    A. SQL injection

    B. LDAP injection

    C. Cross-site scripting

    D. Buffer overflow

12. The Dirty COW attack is an example of what type of vulnerability?
    - **A.** Malicious code
    - **B.** Privilege escalation
    - **C.** Buffer overflow
    - **D.** LDAP injection

13. Which one of the following protocols should never be used on a public network?
    - **A.** SSH
    - **B.** HTTPS
    - **C.** SFTP
    - **D.** Telnet

14. Betty is selecting a transport encryption protocol for use in a new public website she is creating. Which protocol would be the best choice?
    - **A.** SSL 2.0
    - **B.** SSL 3.0
    - **C.** TLS 1.0
    - **D.** TLS 1.1

15. Which one of the following conditions would not result in a certificate warning during a vulnerability scan of a web server?
    - **A.** Use of an untrusted CA
    - **B.** Inclusion of a public encryption key
    - **C.** Expiration of the certificate
    - **D.** Mismatch in certificate name

16. What software component is responsible for enforcing the separation of guest systems in a virtualized infrastructure?
    - **A.** Guest operating system
    - **B.** Host operating system
    - **C.** Memory controller
    - **D.** Hypervisor

17. In what type of attack does the attacker seek to gain access to resources assigned to a different virtual machine?
    - **A.** VM escape
    - **B.** Management interface brute force
    - **C.** LDAP injection
    - **D.** DNS amplification

18. Which one of the following terms is not typically used to describe the connection of physical devices to a network?
    A. IoT
    B. IDS
    C. ICS
    D. SCADA
19. Monica discovers that an attacker posted a message in a web forum that she manages that is attacking users who visit the site. Which one of the following attack types is most likely to have occurred?
    A. SQL injection
    B. Malware injection
    C. LDAP injection
    D. Cross-site scripting
20. Alan is reviewing web server logs after an attack and finds many records that contain semicolons and apostrophes in queries from end users. What type of attack should he suspect?
    A. SQL injection
    B. LDAP injection
    C. Cross-site scripting
    D. Buffer overflow

Cloud Security

THE COMPTIA CYBERSECURITY ANALYST (CYSA+) EXAM OBJECTIVES COVERED IN THIS CHAPTER INCLUDE:

✓ **Domain 1.0: Threat and Vulnerability Management**

- 1.4 Given a scenario, analyze the output from common vulnerability assessment tools.
- 1.6 Explain the threats and vulnerabilities associated with operating in the cloud.

✓ **Domain 2.0: Software and Systems Security**

- 2.1 Given a scenario, apply security solutions for infrastructure management.

Almost every modern organization uses the cloud as part of their technology infrastructure to some extent. Some have abandoned their datacenters and shifted technology operations entirely to the cloud. Others are "cloud native" organizations that began in the cloud as start-ups and never operated their own physical IT infrastructure. Those who haven't made this type of large-scale shift likely use at least one software-as-a-service (SaaS) offering for email, calendaring, customer relationship management, videoconferencing, or other critical tasks. The widespread adoption of cloud computing dramatically impacts the work of cybersecurity analysts who must now understand how to gather, correlate, and interpret information coming from many different cloud sources.

Understanding Cloud Environments

Cloud computing is an umbrella term that covers almost any computing service delivered to customers over a network. It encompasses everything from building complete technology infrastructures in Amazon Web Services (AWS) or Microsoft Azure to deploying office productivity tools through Google's G Suite. Although many might define cloud computing as simply delivering computing services over a network, the National Institute of Standards and Technology (NIST) offers a more robust definition:

> Cloud computing is a model for enabling ubiquitous, convenient, on-demand network access to a shared pool of configurable computing resources (e.g., networks, servers, storage, applications, and services) that can be rapidly provisioned and released with minimal management effort or service provider interaction.

Take the time to read through that definition carefully. You'll find that it goes far beyond simply defining cloud computing and encompasses many of the characteristics and benefits of the cloud in very concise language. Let's pick apart some of the more critical pieces of this definition:

- Cloud computing is ubiquitous and convenient. It's designed so that customers can quickly and easily request services and have their needs met immediately. Those services are then accessible from anywhere with a network connection.
- The on-demand nature of cloud computing means that customer requests are fulfilled immediately. They don't need to call up the service provider and ask for capacity or

request services with a long lead time. From the customer's perspective, there is an essentially infinite pool of resources waiting for their requests made through a self-service portal.

- Cloud computing environments draw on a shared pool of resources. They use an approach called *multitenancy* where many different customers share access to the same physical resources. The cloud provider is responsible for implementing *isolation* controls that prevent the actions of one customer from interfering with or accessing data from another customer.
- Cloud environments are highly configurable. The customer can tailor their use of cloud resources to meet their own specific business objectives.
- Cloud resources are not only rapidly provisioned, they can also be rapidly released. When a customer no longer requires a specific cloud resource, they can release that resource and, typically, stop paying for the use of that resource immediately.
- Cloud environments require minimal management effort from the customer. One of the core benefits of the cloud is that customers may transfer many responsibilities from their own IT teams to the cloud provider.

These characteristics broadly describe cloud services. As you will see, the exact implementation of them differs depending on the specific cloud service models and deployment models used by an organization.

The Case for Cloud Computing

Organizations adopting the cloud do so for a wide variety of reasons. They often initiate cloud efforts in response to a specific need but eventually find that they realize many other benefits as well. Some of the core benefits of the cloud include the following:

Disruptive Innovation Cloud providers can generally develop and/or adopt new technologies at a much faster rate than organizations attempting to build their own infrastructures. After all, providing technology services is their core mission, whereas most organizations leverage technology in pursuit of another mission.

Agility and Elasticity Cloud operations facilitate agility within the customer's organization. When new IT resources are required, they can be provisioned at a moment's notice. When they are no longer needed, they can be released, stopping the billing clock. This allows developers to experiment with new solutions in a cost-effective and agile fashion.

Scalability Solutions built on cloud architectures have almost limitless scalability. Computing, storage, and networking resources may be added and removed as needed to meet changing demand. This scalability can be automated to shift dynamically with changing requirements.

Cost Effectiveness Although it might seem counterintuitive that adding another provider to the mix reduces costs, this is generally the case for most organizations. Cloud providers operate massive datacenters that have an economy of scale that is untouchable by all but the very largest organizations.

Security Cloud providers dedicate tremendous resources to cybersecurity. Later in this chapter, you'll learn about the shared responsibility model of cloud computing. Under this model, some responsibilities rest with the cloud service provider whereas others remain the responsibility of the customer. Most cloud service providers are able to do far more to meet their responsibilities than is possible for smaller organizations.

Each organization needs to analyze their own business requirements and develop their own justification for the adoption of cloud computing services, but these core benefits exist in almost every environment.

Cloud Service Models

The services offered by cloud providers fit into three *cloud service models*. Each of these models describes a different level of service delivered through the cloud and creates varying levels of responsibility for both the service provider and the customer.

Software as a Service (SaaS)

Software as a service (SaaS) offerings provide a customer with a complete application that is built and maintained by the service provider and runs in an infrastructure that is either operated or procured by the service provider. The customer of an SaaS offering typically accesses the service through a web browser and performs only limited application configuration. Almost all the responsibility for operating the service rests in the hands of the cloud service provider and, possibly, other cloud service providers who offer the SaaS provider access to underlying infrastructure resources.

Almost every modern organization makes use of at least one SaaS offering, and most organizations rely on a diverse bundle of services that meet a variety of business needs. SaaS offerings provide common productivity applications, such as Google's Gmail (shown in Figure 6.1) and Microsoft's Office 365. Other SaaS providers build industry-specific and function-specific offerings designed to appeal to a specific set of customers. For example, the Slate customer relationship management (CRM) tool, shown in Figure 6.2, is designed specifically for the administration of higher education admissions offices.

Infrastructure as a Service (IaaS)

Infrastructure as a service (IaaS) offerings operate under a very different service model. SaaS offerings endeavor to hide implementation details from the customer, but IaaS offerings expose basic infrastructure building blocks that customers may use to design and implement their own service offerings. These offerings include compute processing, storage, networking, and other basic components of a technology infrastructure.

FIGURE 6.1 Google's Gmail is an example of SaaS computing.

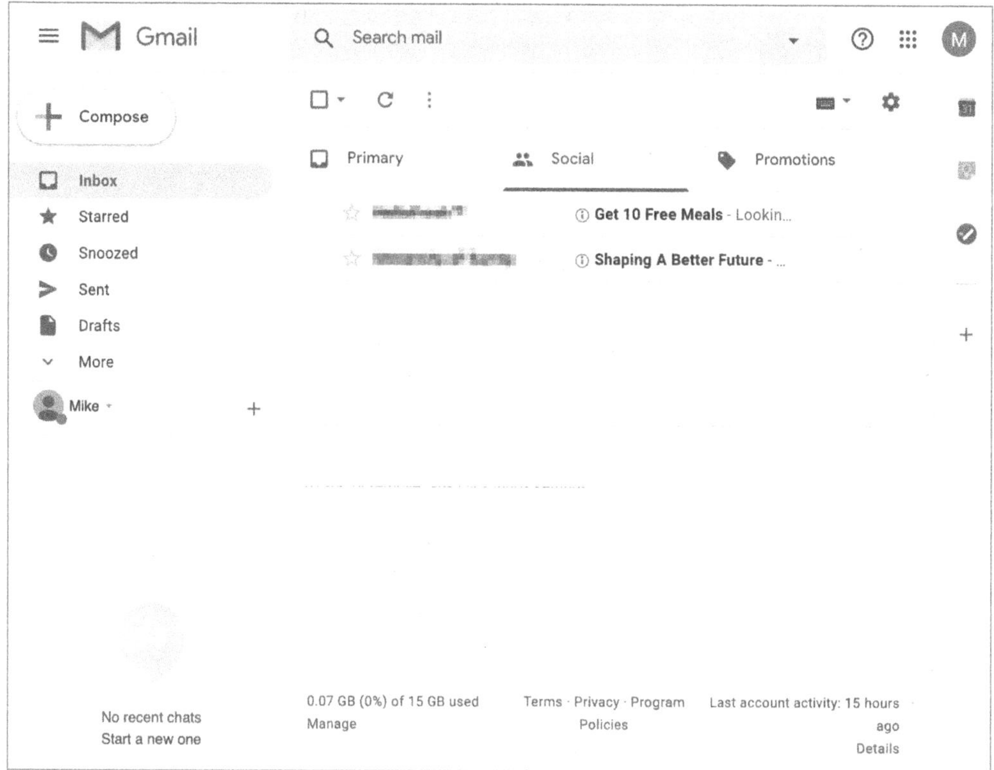

In an IaaS environment, the customer is able to choose and assemble basic cloud offerings to create the services they need to meet their business objectives. In an IaaS environment, the customer retains far more control of the infrastructure than they do in an SaaS environment and, therefore, has greater responsibility for monitoring, management, and security. These customer responsibilities include maintaining and upgrading the operating system as well as software running in the environment. Figure 6.3 shows an example of the AWS dashboard used to manage Elastic Compute Cloud (EC2) server instances.

IaaS cloud providers retain responsibility for maintaining the physical environment, enforcing isolation, and operating the underlying cloud infrastructure.

There are many IaaS providers offering services in today's marketplace, but three major providers dominate the market. The largest is AWS, followed by Microsoft Azure and Google Compute Platform.

FIGURE 6.2 Slate is a CRM tool designed specifically for higher education admissions teams.

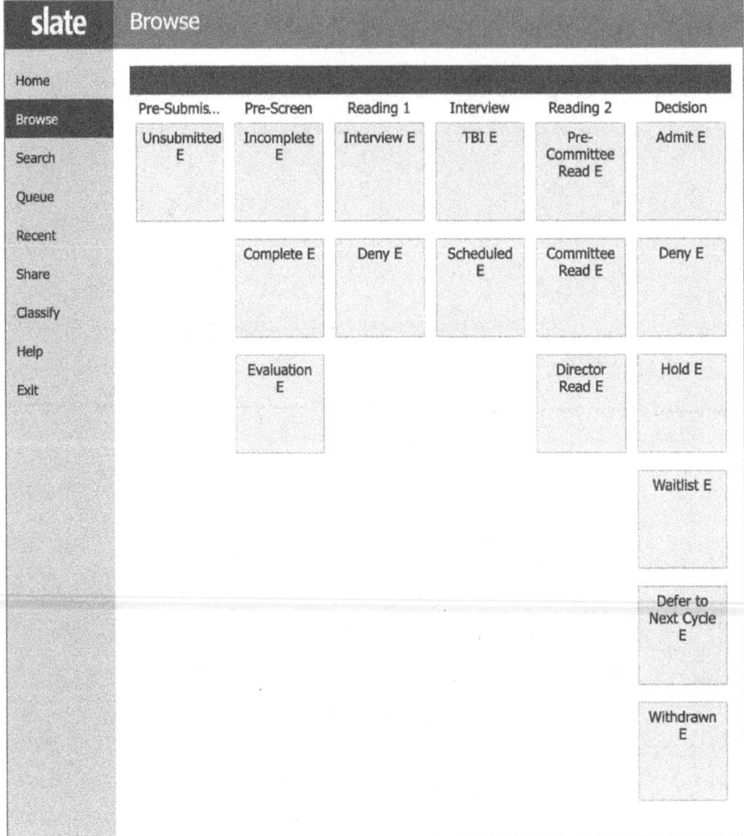

Platform as a Service (PaaS)

Platform as a service (PaaS) approaches occupy a middle ground between SaaS and IaaS services. In this approach, the service provider operates an infrastructure that is fully managed and configurable to run customer applications. Customers then deploy applications that they either developed themselves or purchased from vendors onto the service provider's platform, where they run with minimal customer management.

PaaS platforms support a variety of application types and programming languages. For example, the Heroku PaaS offering shown in Figure 6.4 supports the deployment of customer applications written in Python, Java, Ruby, Node.js, PHP, and other common programming languages.

PaaS offerings allow customers to execute code without managing the underlying servers, but customers typically still need to be involved in provisioning appropriate levels of infrastructure, usually by specifying the number of servers they wish to use. PaaS offerings are then billed based on this provisioned capacity.

FIGURE 6.3 AWS provides customers with access to IaaS computing resources.

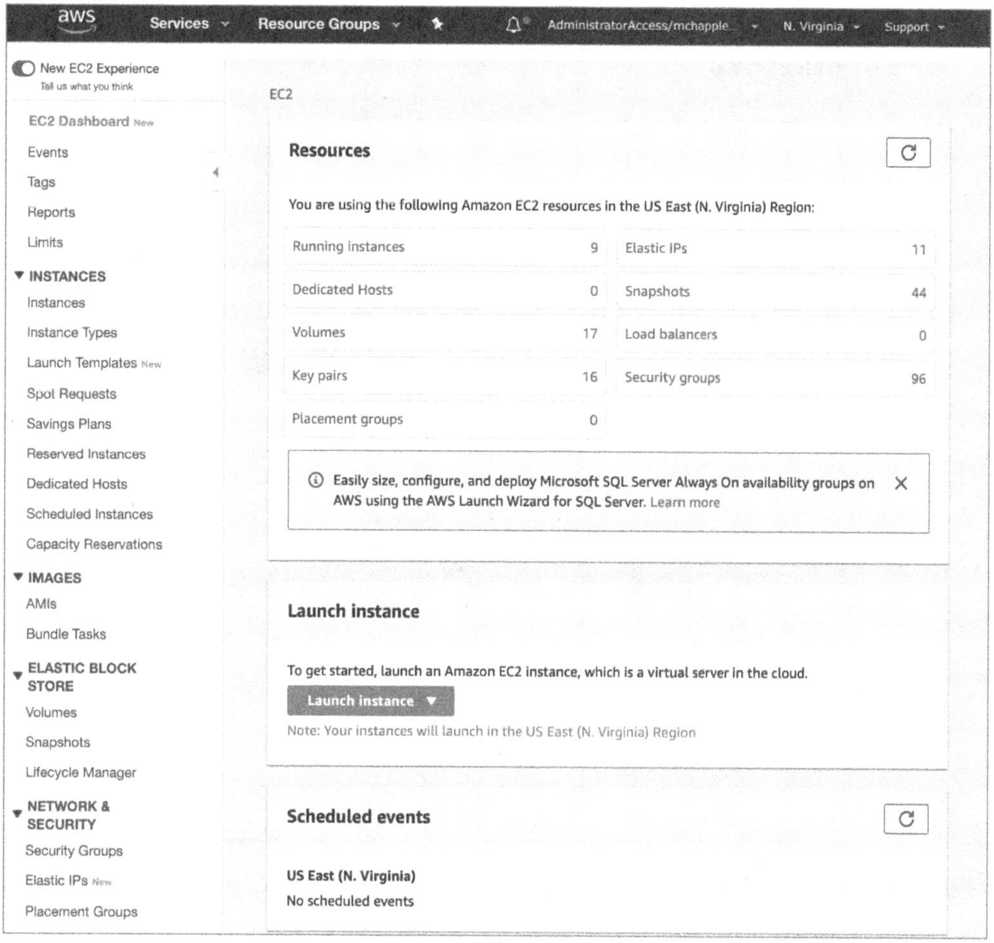

aws Services Resource Groups AdministratorAccess/mchapple... N. Virginia Support

New EC2 Experience
Tell us what you think

EC2 Dashboard New
Events
Tags
Reports
Limits
▼ INSTANCES
Instances
Instance Types
Launch Templates New
Spot Requests
Savings Plans
Reserved Instances
Dedicated Hosts
Scheduled Instances
Capacity Reservations
▼ IMAGES
AMIs
Bundle Tasks
▼ ELASTIC BLOCK STORE
Volumes
Snapshots
Lifecycle Manager
▼ NETWORK & SECURITY
Security Groups
Elastic IPs New
Placement Groups

EC2

Resources

You are using the following Amazon EC2 resources in the US East (N. Virginia) Region:

Running instances	9	Elastic IPs	11
Dedicated Hosts	0	Snapshots	44
Volumes	17	Load balancers	0
Key pairs	16	Security groups	96
Placement groups	0		

Easily size, configure, and deploy Microsoft SQL Server Always On availability groups on AWS using the AWS Launch Wizard for SQL Server. Learn more

Launch instance

To get started, launch an Amazon EC2 instance, which is a virtual server in the cloud.

Launch instance ▼

Note: Your instances will launch in the US East (N. Virginia) Region

Scheduled events

US East (N. Virginia)
No scheduled events

Exam Note

Know the differences between SaaS, PaaS, and IaaS before you take the CySA+ exam.

FIGURE 6.4 Heroku is a popular PaaS offering that supports many popular programming languages.

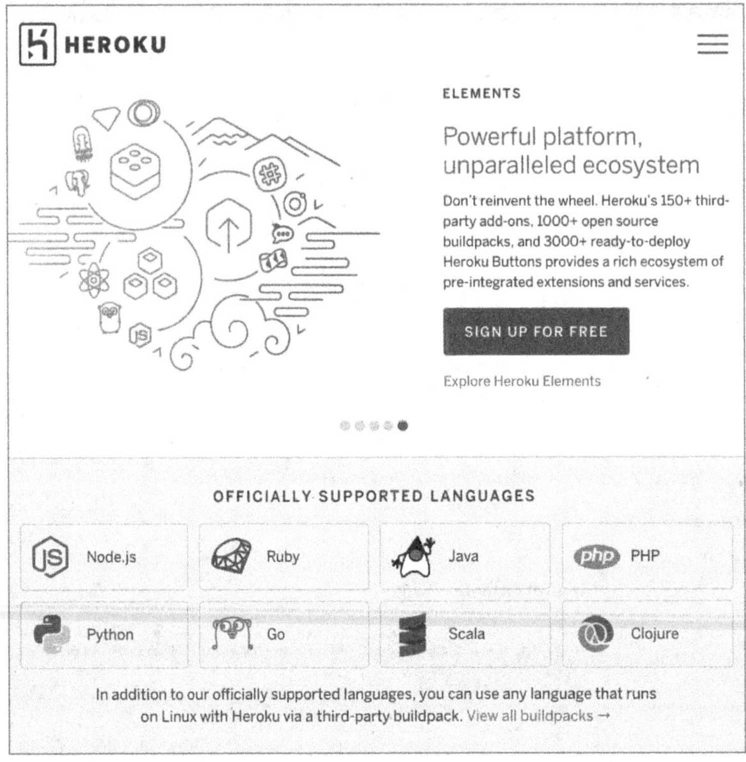

Function as a Service (FaaS)

Cloud customers are increasingly embracing a technology known as function as a service (FaaS) that allows for a serverless application architecture. Developers write functions in common programming languages and can then configure the FaaS platform to execute (or "trigger") those functions in response to events. Functions deployed in this manner are discrete units of code that are easily scaled to millions, or even billions, of executions per day.

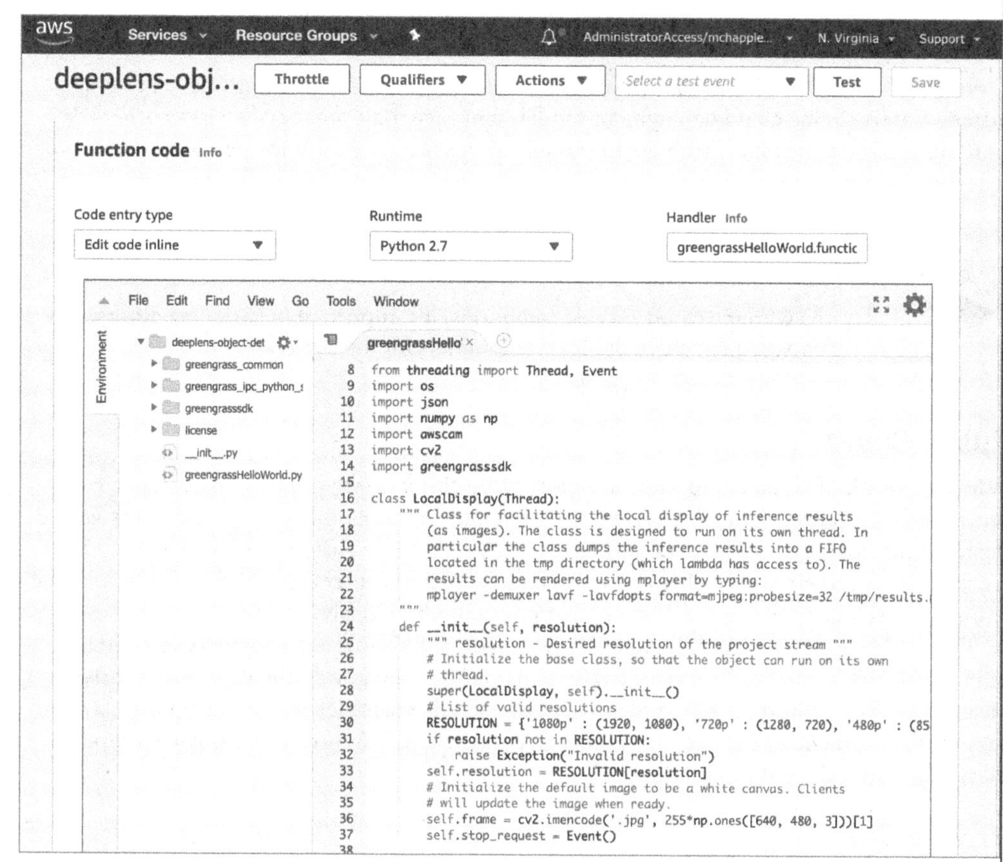

The most popular FaaS offering is Amazon's Lambda service, shown here. Lambda supports the deployment of functions written in Python, Node.js, C#, Ruby, Go, and PowerShell. Developers can also use the Lambda Runtime API to execute code written in other languages. Other popular FaaS offerings include Microsoft Azure Functions and Google Cloud Functions.

FaaS offerings typically completely abstract the infrastructure from developers, billing customers for the actual computing power and memory consumed during function executions.

Cloud Deployment Models

Cloud deployment models describe how cloud infrastructure is (or is not) shared among different users. Some cloud deployment models embrace multitenancy, whereas others dedicate resources to specific customers in pursuit of physical isolation for performance and/or security reasons.

Exam Note

As with the cloud service categories, it's important to know the differences between the cloud deployment models for the CySA+ exam.

Public Cloud

When we think of cloud computing, we most often think of the *public cloud*. Public cloud service providers deploy infrastructure and then make it accessible to any customers who wish to take advantage of it in a multitenant model. A single customer may be running workloads on servers spread throughout one or more datacenters, and those servers may be running workloads for many different customers simultaneously.

The public cloud supports all cloud service models. Public cloud providers may offer IaaS, PaaS, SaaS, and FaaS services to their customers. The key distinction is that those services do not run on infrastructure dedicated to a single customer but rather on infrastructure that is available to the general public. AWS, Microsoft Azure, and Google Compute Platform all use the public cloud model.

Private Cloud

The term *private cloud* is used to describe any cloud infrastructure that is provisioned for use by a single customer. This infrastructure may be built and managed by the organization that will be using the infrastructure, or it may be built and managed by a third party. The key distinction here is that only one customer uses the environment. For this reason, private cloud services tend to have excess unused capacity to support peak demand and, as a result, are not as cost efficient as public cloud services.

The Intelligence Community Leverages a "Private Public" Cloud

The U.S. Intelligence Community (IC) has long been one of the largest, if not *the* largest, users of computing power in the world. In fact, many advances in computing began as projects in support of IC customers. As the private sector began a rapid migration to the public cloud, IC technologists took note but lamented that strict security requirements prevented them from using any multitenant environment for classified national security activities.

IC technologists worked with AWS to address this problem and, in 2014, launched the AWS Commercial Cloud Services (C2S) region that provides dedicated AWS services to IC customers. The region is operated by AWS but physically resides at a Central Intelligence Agency (CIA) facility and is completely air-gapped from the Internet, providing an incredibly high level of security.

The interesting thing about this approach is that it fits the definition of private cloud because AWS is operating the C2S region specifically for the IC but it runs with the same tools and services available in the AWS public cloud, presumably at much greater cost.

In 2017, AWS announced the launch of the AWS Secret Region, an even broader effort designed to support any classified work across the U.S. government. Microsoft also announced the availability of Azure Government Secret for the same purpose. The broad availability of those regions across government agencies makes the Secret regions fit the definition of community cloud rather than private cloud.

Community Cloud

A *community cloud* service shares characteristics of both the public and private models. Community cloud services run in a multitenant environment, but the tenants are limited to members of a specifically designed community. Community membership is normally defined based on shared mission, similar security and compliance requirements, or other commonalities.

The HathiTrust digital library, shown in Figure 6.5, is an example of community cloud in action. Academic research libraries joined together to form a consortium that provides access to their collections of books. Students and faculty at HathiTrust member institutions may log into the community cloud service to access resources.

FIGURE 6.5 HathiTrust is an example of community cloud computing.

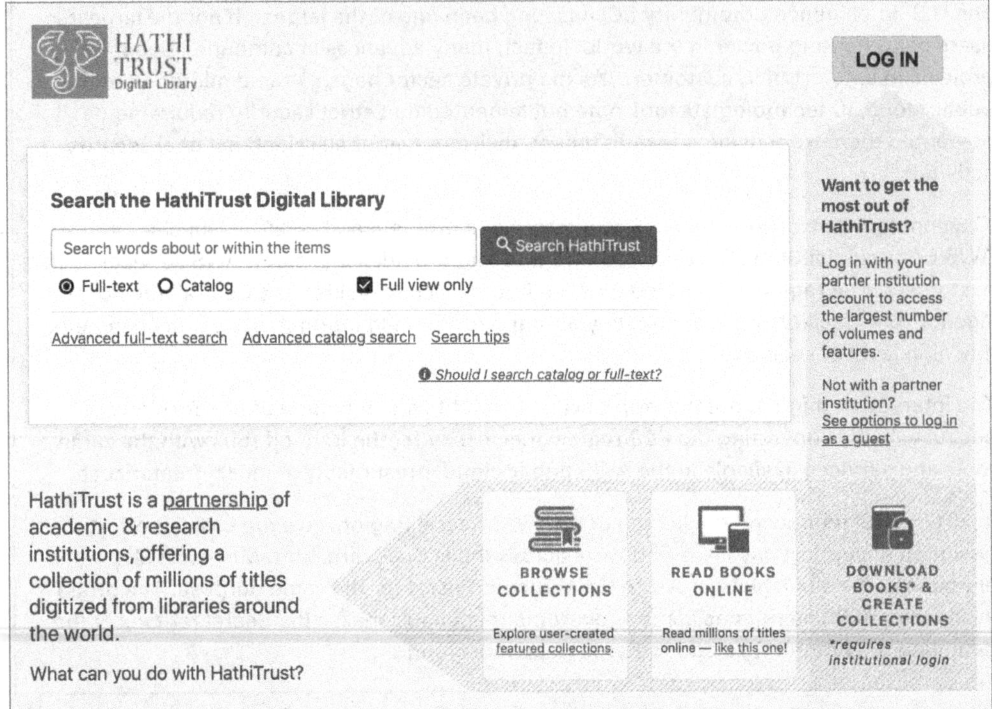

Hybrid Cloud

Hybrid cloud is a catch-all term used to describe cloud deployments that blend public, private, and/or community cloud services together. It is not simply purchasing both public and private cloud services and using them together. Hybrid cloud requires the use of technology that unifies the different cloud offerings into a single coherent platform.

For example, a firm might operate their own private cloud for the majority of their workloads and then leverage public cloud capacity when demand exceeds the capacity of their private cloud infrastructure. This approach is known as public cloud *bursting*.

AWS Outposts, shown in Figure 6.6, are examples of hybrid cloud computing. Customers of this service receive a rack of computing equipment that they install in their own datacenters. The equipment in the rack is maintained by AWS but provisioned by the customer in the same manner as their AWS public cloud resources. This approach qualifies as hybrid cloud because customers can manage both their on-premises AWS Outposts private cloud deployment and their public cloud AWS services through the same management platform.

FIGURE 6.6 AWS Outposts offer hybrid cloud capability.

Image property of Amazon Web Services; used with permission

Operating in the Cloud

In some ways, cybersecurity work in a cloud-centric environment is quite similar to on-premises cybersecurity. No matter where our systems are hosted, we still need to think about the confidentiality, integrity, and availability of our data and implement strong access controls and other mechanisms that protect those primary objectives.

However, cloud security operations also differ significantly from on-premises environments because cloud customers must divide responsibilities between one or more service providers and the customers' own cybersecurity teams. This type of operating environment is known as the *shared responsibility model*. Figure 6.7 shows the common division of responsibilities in IaaS, PaaS, and SaaS environments.

FIGURE 6.7 Shared responsibility model for cloud computing

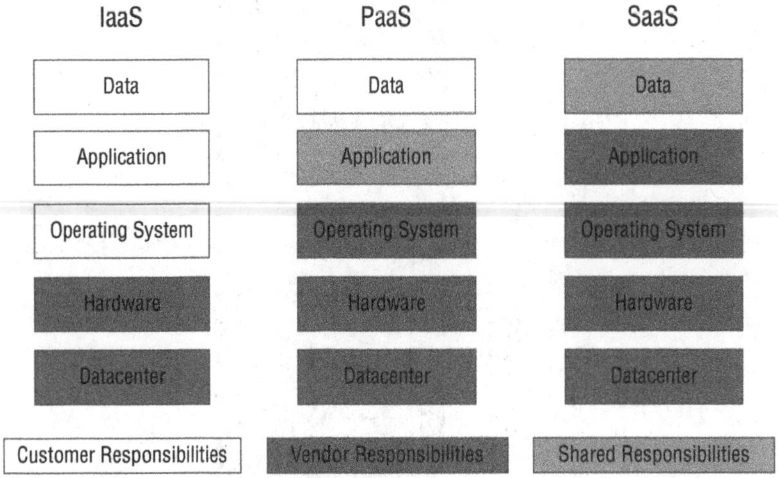

IaaS	PaaS	SaaS
Data	Data	Data
Application	Application	Application
Operating System	Operating System	Operating System
Hardware	Hardware	Hardware
Datacenter	Datacenter	Datacenter

Customer Responsibilities | Vendor Responsibilities | Shared Responsibilities

In some cases, this division of responsibility is straightforward. Cloud providers, by their nature, are always responsible for the security of both hardware and the physical data center environment. If the customer was handling either of these items, the solution would not fit the definition of cloud computing.

The differences in responsibility come higher up in the stack and vary depending on the nature of the cloud service being used. In an IaaS environment, the customer takes over security responsibility for everything that isn't infrastructure—the operating system, applications, and data that they run in the IaaS environment.

In a PaaS solution, the vendor also takes on responsibility for the operating system, whereas the customer retains responsibility for the data being placed into the environment and configuring its security. Responsibility for the application layer is shared between the service provider and the customer, and the exact division of responsibilities shifts based on the nature of the service. For example, if the PaaS platform provides runtime interpreters for customer code, the cloud provider is responsible for the security of those interpreters.

In an SaaS environment, the provider takes on almost all security responsibility. The customer retains some shared control over the data that they place in the SaaS environment and the configuration of access controls around that data, but the SaaS provider is being paid to take on the burden of most operational tasks, including cybersecurity.

Be sure to clearly document the division of responsibilities for cybersecurity tasks. This is particularly important in situations requiring compliance with external regulations. For example, organizations subject to the Payment Card Industry Data Security Standard (PCI DSS) should work with cloud providers to document the specific controls and responsibilities for meeting each one of the many PCI DSS requirements. Cloud providers are familiar with this process, and many host websites provide detailed mappings of their controls to common compliance regimes.

DevOps Strategies

Traditional approaches to organizing and running technology teams focused on building silos of expertise centered on technology roles. In particular, software development and technology operations were often viewed as quite disconnected. Developers worked on creating the software applications that the business desired and had their own processes for specifying requirements, designing interfaces, writing code, testing applications, and maintaining the code base. When they completed testing of a new version of an application, they then handed it off to the technology operations team, who managed the servers and other infrastructure supporting the application.

Separating the development and operations worlds provides technologists with a comfortable working environment where they have their tasks clearly defined and are surrounded by a community of their peers. It also, however, brings significant disadvantages, including the following:

- Isolating operations teams from the development process inhibits their understanding of business requirements.
- Isolating developers from operational considerations leads to designs that are wasteful in terms of processor, memory, and network consumption.
- Requiring clear hand-offs from development to operations reduces agility and flexibility by requiring a lengthy transition phase.
- Increasing the overhead associated with transitions encourages combining many small fixes and enhancements into one major release, increasing the time to requirement satisfaction.

Recognizing the inherent disadvantages of separating development and operational teams, many organizations now embrace a *DevOps* approach to technology management. This approach brings together development and operations teams in a unified process where they work together in an agile approach to software development. The software testing and release process becomes highly automated and collaborative, enabling organizations to move from lengthy release management processes to a world where they might release dozens of updates on a daily basis.

Infrastructure as Code (IaC)

Infrastructure as code (IaC) is one of the key enabling technologies behind the DevOps movement and is also a crucial advantage of cloud computing solutions. IaC is the process of automating the provisioning, management, and deprovisioning of infrastructure services through scripted code rather than human intervention. IaC is one of the key features of all major IaaS environments, including AWS, Microsoft Azure, and Google Cloud Platform.

IaC takes many forms and may be either a feature offered by a cloud service provider or a functionality enabled by a third-party cloud management platform. In most cases, the same actions available to operations teams through the cloud provider's web interface are also available for implementation in code. For example, Figure 6.8 shows the process of creating an EC2 server instance through the AWS graphical interface.

FIGURE 6.8 Creating an EC2 instance through the AWS web interface

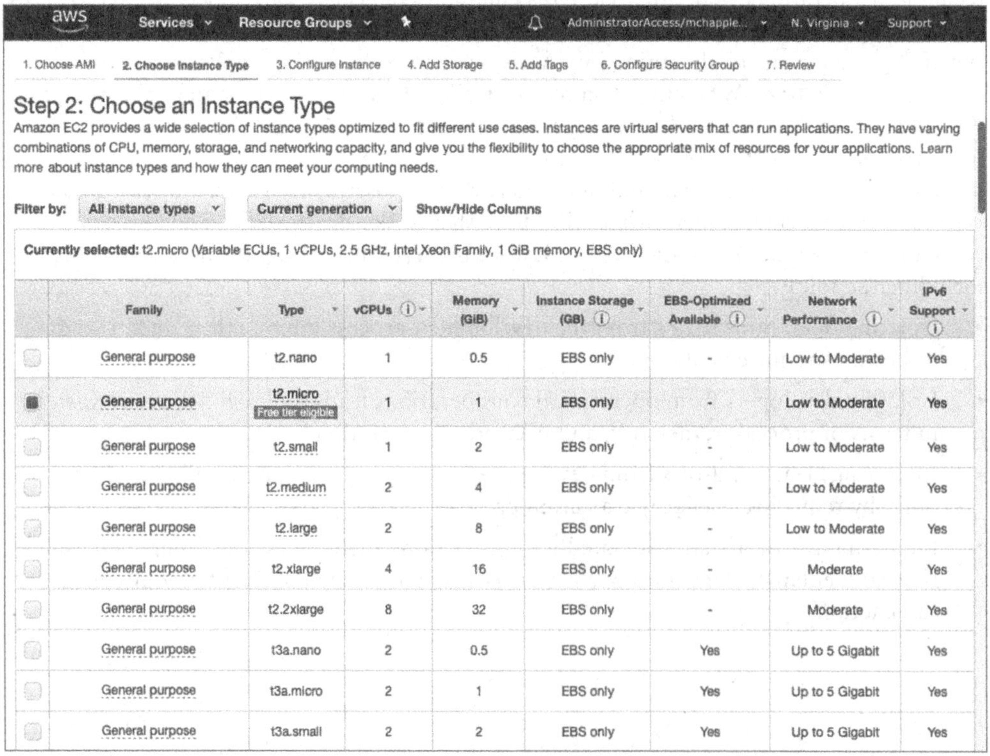

aws Services Resource Groups AdministratorAccess/mchapple... N. Virginia Support

1. Choose AMI 2. Choose Instance Type 3. Configure Instance 4. Add Storage 5. Add Tags 6. Configure Security Group 7. Review

Step 2: Choose an Instance Type

Amazon EC2 provides a wide selection of instance types optimized to fit different use cases. Instances are virtual servers that can run applications. They have varying combinations of CPU, memory, storage, and networking capacity, and give you the flexibility to choose the appropriate mix of resources for your applications. Learn more about instance types and how they can meet your computing needs.

Filter by: All instance types Current generation Show/Hide Columns

Currently selected: t2.micro (Variable ECUs, 1 vCPUs, 2.5 GHz, Intel Xeon Family, 1 GiB memory, EBS only)

	Family	Type	vCPUs	Memory (GiB)	Instance Storage (GB)	EBS-Optimized Available	Network Performance	IPv6 Support
	General purpose	t2.nano	1	0.5	EBS only	-	Low to Moderate	Yes
	General purpose	t2.micro Free tier eligible	1	1	EBS only	-	Low to Moderate	Yes
	General purpose	t2.small	1	2	EBS only	-	Low to Moderate	Yes
	General purpose	t2.medium	2	4	EBS only	-	Low to Moderate	Yes
	General purpose	t2.large	2	8	EBS only	-	Low to Moderate	Yes
	General purpose	t2.xlarge	4	16	EBS only	-	Moderate	Yes
	General purpose	t2.2xlarge	8	32	EBS only	-	Moderate	Yes
	General purpose	t3a.nano	2	0.5	EBS only	Yes	Up to 5 Gigabit	Yes
	General purpose	t3a.micro	2	1	EBS only	Yes	Up to 5 Gigabit	Yes
	General purpose	t3a.small	2	2	EBS only	Yes	Up to 5 Gigabit	Yes

AWS offers a service called CloudFormation that allows developers to specify their infrastructure requirements in several formats, including JavaScript Object Notation (JSON) and Yet Another Markup Language (YAML). Figure 6.9 shows an example of the JSON specification for an EC2 instance.

FIGURE 6.9 Creating an EC2 instance with CloudFormation JSON

```
"Ec2Instance" : {
  "Type" : "AWS::EC2::Instance",
  "Properties" : {
    "ImageId" : { "Fn::FindInMap" : [ "AWSRegionArch2AMI", { "Ref" : "AWS::Region" },
                                      { "Fn::FindInMap" : [ "AWSInstanceType2Arch", { "Ref" : "InstanceType" }, "Arch" ] } ] },
    "KeyName" : { "Ref" : "KeyName" },
    "InstanceType" : { "Ref" : "InstanceType" },
    "SecurityGroups" : [{ "Ref" : "Ec2SecurityGroup" }],
    "BlockDeviceMappings" : [
      {
        "DeviceName" : "/dev/sda1",
        "Ebs" : { "VolumeSize" : "50" }
      },{
        "DeviceName" : "/dev/sdm",
        "Ebs" : { "VolumeSize" : "100" }
      }
    ]
  }
}
```

The major advantages to using an IaC approach are

- Increasing the reusability of code
- Reducing the time spent by operations team creating infrastructure components
- Increasing the speed of infrastructure creation
- Reducing the likelihood of configuration errors by leveraging common templates

Application Programming Interfaces

IaC approaches require that developers interact directly with a cloud service through their code rather than requiring an individual to work within a web interface. As you saw in the previous section, this is sometimes done through a provider interface, such as the AWS CloudFormation service. Developers may wish, however, to write code that executes in their own environment and still interacts with the cloud service. That's where *application programming interfaces (APIs)* come into play.

APIs are standard interfaces used to interact with web-based services in a programmatic fashion. Cloud service providers create APIs and then expose them to their customers to allow customer code to provision, manage, and deprovision services.

Security is paramount when cloud providers expose APIs, as they must ensure that users requesting action through an API are authorized to do so. APIs manage this through the use of *API keys*, which are similar to passwords. When a user sends a request through an API, they also send their API key to authenticate the request. The cloud provider validates the API key and checks that the user, system, or application associated with that key is authorized to perform the requested action.

Insecure APIs are one of the key risks associated with operating in the cloud. Cloud providers generally manage their APIs well to enforce security requirements, but the security of a user's account depends on the security of their API key. Cloud service customers must ensure that they safeguard their keys using the following best practices:

- Limit exposure of the API key to the smallest set of individuals possible.
- Use different API keys for different users, applications, and services.
- Restrict the rights associated with each API key to the specific rights needed by the user, application, or service associated with the key.
- Never transmit API keys over unencrypted channels.
- Never store API keys in unencrypted form.
- Ensure that API keys are removed from any code that is placed in public code repositories or is otherwise at risk of unauthorized access.

Organizations should treat their API keys with the same level of security used to protect encryption keys. Improper key management practices can lead to devastating security consequences.

Cloud Monitoring

In Chapter 10, "Security Operations and Monitoring," you'll discover the importance of monitoring in the world of cybersecurity operations. Security teams require access to historic information in order to detect policy violations, investigate incidents, troubleshoot tools, and perform a variety of other important tasks. The inability to access logs prevents security operations teams from achieving their objectives.

These concerns become paramount in a cloud-centric environment because most log records are generated within the providers' ecosystem. Security operations teams should ensure that they understand the logging and monitoring mechanisms available to them and integrate them with the other tools used within their security operations centers (SOCs). Insufficient logging and monitoring may lead to insufficient information in the wake of a security incident.

Cloud Infrastructure Security

Security analysts working in a cloud-centric environment use many of the same security tools and techniques used in traditional on-premises environments. After all, securing an operating system in the public cloud is not much different than securing one running on a server under your desk.

In addition to these controls, cybersecurity analysts also use cloud-specific tools that are designed to assess and improve the security of the cloud environment itself. These include cloud infrastructure security tools and cloud access security brokers (CASBs).

Using these tools can help protect organizations against cloud-specific risks. For example, unprotected storage environments pose a much greater security risk in the public cloud than they do in a private data center environment. In a private datacenter, firewall controls generally restrict direct access to storage, limiting the exposure of an unprotected file to users who already have access to datacenter systems. In the public cloud, on the other hand, an improperly managed storage bucket may be exposed to the entire Internet with only a few clicks. Cloud infrastructure security tools can help detect and mitigate these risks.

Cloud Infrastructure Security Tools

Cloud infrastructure assessment tools reach into a cloud environment, retrieve security information, and deliver a report showing the relative security of the environment. They might detect issues that would not appear on other vulnerability scans. For example, a cloud-focused tool might be able to reach into the cloud provider's API and identify the fact that a security key has not been rotated for years. Similarly, a tool might be able to retrieve a list of all security groups applied to an instance and determine the instance's network exposure without conducting an exhaustive port scan.

Cloud providers offer many tools to their customers, often at no charge or for very low cost, as it is in the provider's interest to ensure that resources in their environment are operated securely. For example, Figure 6.10 shows a scan run against an AWS environment using the AWS Inspector tool.

Exam Note

The CySA+ exam does not require that you be familiar with tools offered by cloud providers themselves, but it does require that you know three open source cloud assessment tools: ScoutSuite, Pacu, and Prowler.

ScoutSuite

ScoutSuite is a multicloud auditing tool that reaches into the user's accounts with cloud service providers and retrieves configuration information using those services' APIs. It is capable of auditing accounts with AWS, Microsoft Azure, Google Compute Platform, Alibaba Cloud, and Oracle Cloud Infrastructure.

ScoutSuite deeply probes the service configuration and searches for potential security issues. Figure 6.11 shows an example of the high-level dashboard generated by a ScoutSuite scan. It displays the number of issues detected in each cloud service used by the customer.

Detailed reports for each service then drill into the specific issues that exist in the environment. For example, Figure 6.12 shows the AWS EC2 service issues in one account. Expanding each item in the report shows details about the potential problem. In Figure 6.12, you see that this account has 18 Elastic Block Store (EBS) disk volumes that do not use encryption to protect data in transit or at rest.

FIGURE 6.10 Results of an AWS Inspector scan.

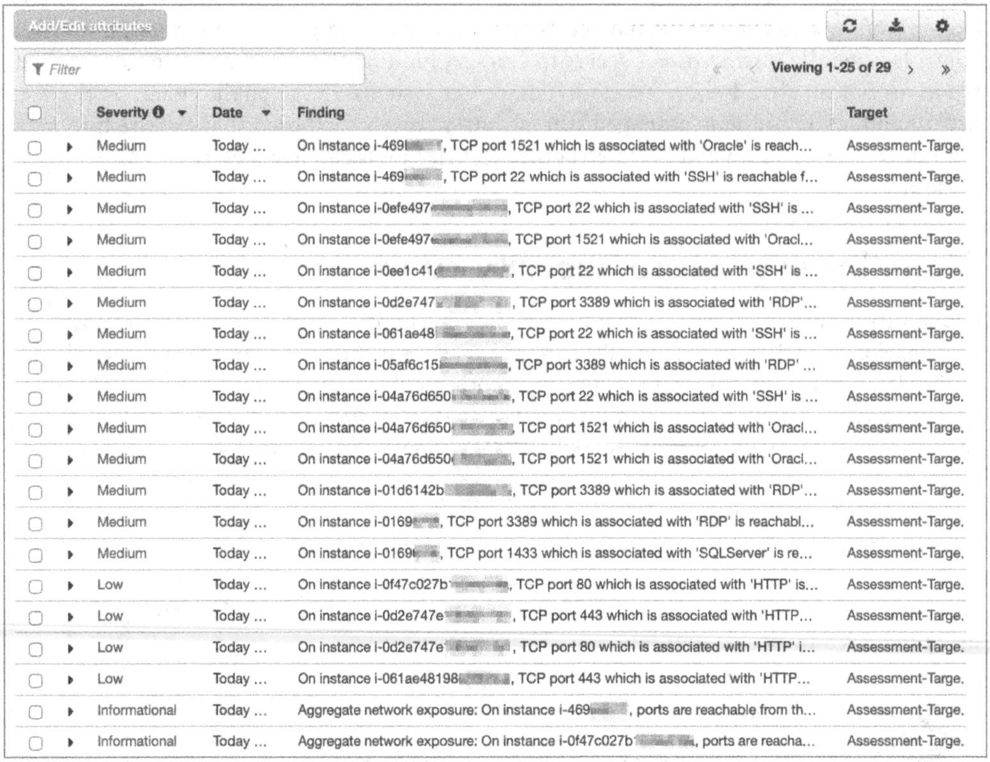

Add/Edit attributes

Filter

Viewing 1-25 of 29

		Severity	Date	Finding	Target
☐	▸	Medium	Today ...	On instance i-469, TCP port 1521 which is associated with 'Oracle' is reach...	Assessment-Targe.
☐	▸	Medium	Today ...	On instance i-469, TCP port 22 which is associated with 'SSH' is reachable f...	Assessment-Targe.
☐	▸	Medium	Today ...	On instance i-0efe497, TCP port 22 which is associated with 'SSH' is ...	Assessment-Targe.
☐	▸	Medium	Today ...	On instance i-0efe497, TCP port 1521 which is associated with 'Oracl...	Assessment-Targe.
☐	▸	Medium	Today ...	On instance i-0ee1c41, TCP port 22 which is associated with 'SSH' is ...	Assessment-Targe.
☐	▸	Medium	Today ...	On instance i-0d2e747, TCP port 3389 which is associated with 'RDP'...	Assessment-Targe.
☐	▸	Medium	Today ...	On instance i-061ae48, TCP port 22 which is associated with 'SSH' is ...	Assessment-Targe.
☐	▸	Medium	Today ...	On instance i-05af6c15, TCP port 3389 which is associated with 'RDP' ...	Assessment-Targe.
☐	▸	Medium	Today ...	On instance i-04a76d650, TCP port 22 which is associated with 'SSH' is ...	Assessment-Targe.
☐	▸	Medium	Today ...	On instance i-04a76d650, TCP port 1521 which is associated with 'Oracl...	Assessment-Targe.
☐	▸	Medium	Today ...	On instance i-04a76d650, TCP port 1521 which is associated with 'Oracl...	Assessment-Targe.
☐	▸	Medium	Today ...	On instance i-01d6142b, TCP port 3389 which is associated with 'RDP'...	Assessment-Targe.
☐	▸	Medium	Today ...	On instance i-0169, TCP port 3389 which is associated with 'RDP' is reachabl...	Assessment-Targe.
☐	▸	Medium	Today ...	On instance i-0169, TCP port 1433 which is associated with 'SQLServer' is re...	Assessment-Targe.
☐	▸	Low	Today ...	On instance i-0f47c027b, TCP port 80 which is associated with 'HTTP' is...	Assessment-Targe.
☐	▸	Low	Today ...	On instance i-0d2e747e, TCP port 443 which is associated with 'HTTP...	Assessment-Targe.
☐	▸	Low	Today ...	On instance i-0d2e747e, TCP port 80 which is associated with 'HTTP' i...	Assessment-Targe.
☐	▸	Low	Today ...	On instance i-061ae48198, TCP port 443 which is associated with 'HTTP...	Assessment-Targe.
☐	▸	Informational	Today ...	Aggregate network exposure: On instance i-469, ports are reachable from th...	Assessment-Targe.
☐	▸	Informational	Today ...	Aggregate network exposure: On instance i-0f47c027b, ports are reacha...	Assessment-Targe.

Pacu

Pacu is not a scanning tool but rather a cloud-focused exploitation framework, similar to Metasploit. It works specifically with AWS accounts and is designed to help attackers determine what they can do with the access they have to an existing AWS account. For this reason, it is a favorite tool of AWS penetration testers.

Working with Pacu is quite similar to working with Metasploit in that Pacu offers a modular framework of plug-ins that test and probe various information sources. Figure 6.13 provides a partial listing of the AWS exploitation plug-ins available for Pacu.

FIGURE 6.11 ScoutSuite dashboard from an AWS account scan

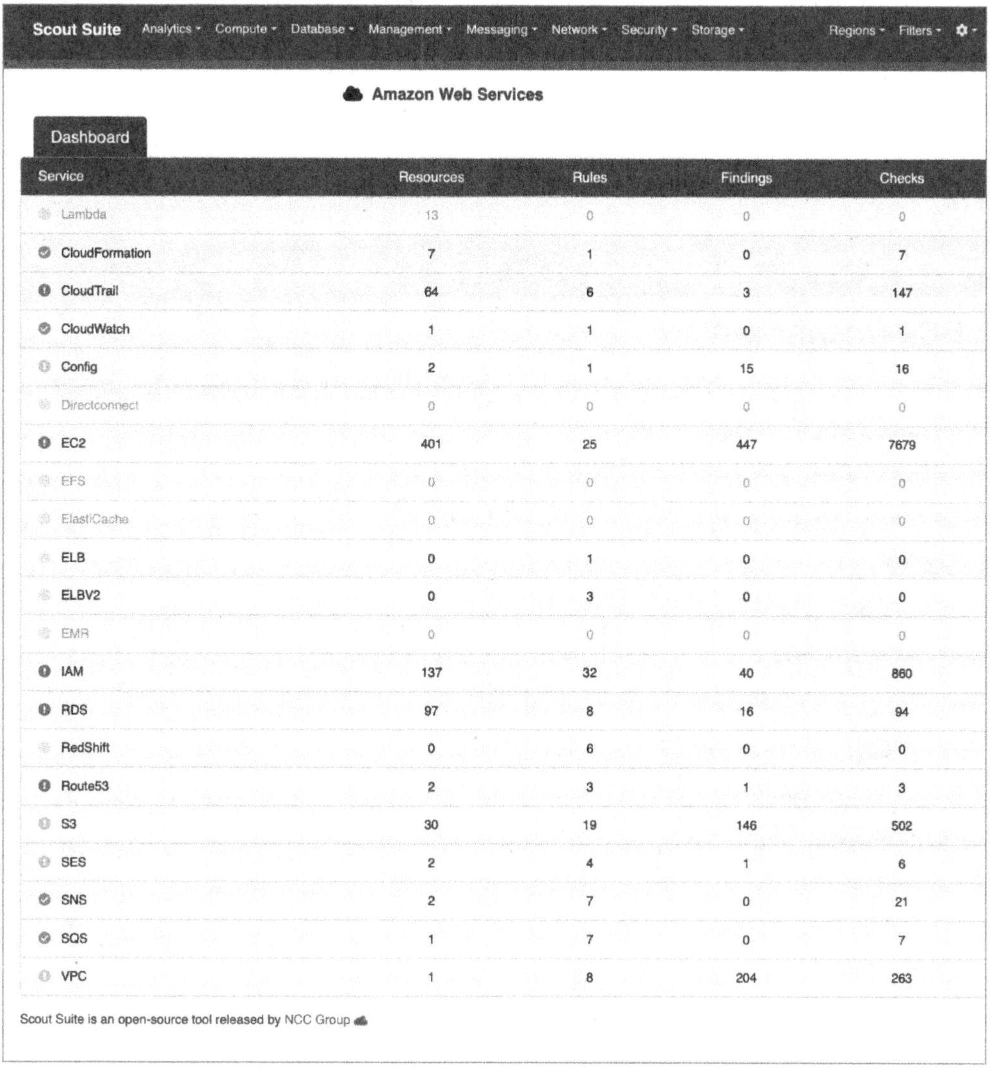

Scout Suite Analytics Compute Database Management Messaging Network Security Storage Regions Filters

Amazon Web Services

Dashboard

Service	Resources	Rules	Findings	Checks
Lambda	13	0	0	0
CloudFormation	7	1	0	7
CloudTrail	64	6	3	147
CloudWatch	1	1	0	1
Config	2	1	15	16
Directconnect	0	0	0	0
EC2	401	25	447	7679
EFS	0	0	0	0
ElastiCache	0	0	0	0
ELB	0	1	0	0
ELBV2	0	3	0	0
EMR	0	0	0	0
IAM	137	32	40	860
RDS	97	8	16	94
RedShift	0	6	0	0
Route53	2	3	1	3
S3	30	19	146	502
SES	2	4	1	6
SNS	2	7	0	21
SQS	1	7	0	7
VPC	1	8	204	263

Scout Suite is an open-source tool released by NCC Group

Prowler

Prowler is a security configuration testing tool, quite similar to ScoutSuite in purpose. Prowler performs deeper testing of some parameters, but it is limited to scanning AWS environments. Figure 6.14 shows the partial result of a Prowler scan against an AWS account.

FIGURE 6.12 EC2 security issues reported during a ScoutSuite scan

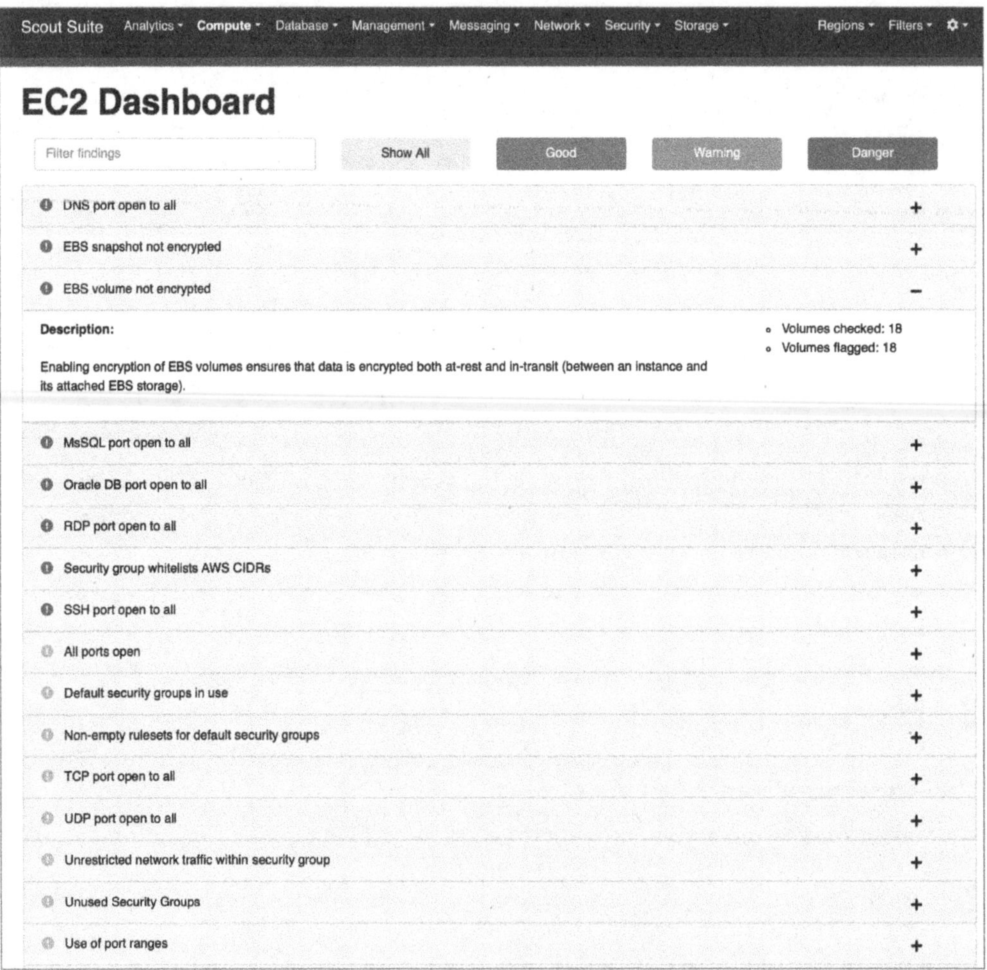

FIGURE 6.13 Partial listing of the exploits available in Pacu

```
Pacu (test:No Keys Set) > list

[Category: RECON_UNAUTH]

  iam__enum_roles
  iam__enum_users
  s3__bucket_finder

[Category: ENUM]

  aws__enum_account
  aws__enum_spend
  codebuild__enum
  ebs__enum_volumes_snapshots
  ec2__check_termination_protection
  ec2__download_userdata
  ec2__enum
  glue__enum
  iam__bruteforce_permissions
  iam__detect_honeytokens
  iam__enum_permissions
  iam__enum_users_roles_policies_groups
  iam__get_credential_report
  inspector__get_reports
  lambda__enum
  lightsail__enum

[Category: ESCALATE]

  iam__privesc_scan

[Category: LATERAL_MOVE]

  cloudtrail__csv_injection
  vpc__enum_lateral_movement
```

Cloud Access Security Brokers (CASB)

Most organizations use a variety of cloud service providers for different purposes. It's not unusual to find that a large organization purchases cloud services from dozens, or even hundreds, of different providers. This is especially true when organizations use highly specialized SaaS products. Managing security policies consistently across these services poses a major challenge for cybersecurity analysts.

Cloud access security brokers (CASBs) are software tools that serve as intermediaries between cloud service users and cloud service providers. This positioning allows them to monitor user activity and enforce policy requirements. CASBs operate using two different approaches:

- Inline CASB solutions physically or logically reside in the connection path between the user and the service. They may do this through a hardware appliance or an endpoint agent that routes requests through the CASB. This approach requires configuration of the network and/or endpoint devices. It provides the advantage of seeing requests before they are sent to the cloud service, allowing the CASB to block requests that violate policy.

- API-based CASB solutions do not interact directly with the user but rather interact directly with the cloud provider through the provider's API. This approach provides direct access to the cloud service and does not require any user device configuration. However, it also does not allow the CASB to block requests that violate policy. API-based CASBs are limited to monitoring user activity and reporting on or correcting policy violations after the fact.

FIGURE 6.14 Partial results of a Prowler scan against an AWS account

```
1.5  [check15] Ensure IAM password policy requires at least one uppercase letter (Scored)
      FAIL! Password Policy missing upper-case requirement

1.6  [check16] Ensure IAM password policy require at least one lowercase letter (Scored)
      FAIL! Password Policy missing lower-case requirement

1.7  [check17] Ensure IAM password policy require at least one symbol (Scored)
      FAIL! Password Policy missing symbol requirement

1.8  [check18] Ensure IAM password policy require at least one number (Scored)
      FAIL! Password Policy missing number requirement

1.9  [check19] Ensure IAM password policy requires minimum length of 14 or greater (Scored)
      FAIL! Password Policy missing or weak length requirement

1.10  [check110] Ensure IAM password policy prevents password reuse: 24 or greater (Scored)
      FAIL! Password Policy missing reuse requirement

1.11  [check111] Ensure IAM password policy expires passwords within 90 days or less (Scored)
      FAIL! Password expiration is not set

1.12  [check112] Ensure no root account access key exists (Scored)
      PASS! No access key 1 found for root
      PASS! No access key 2 found for root

1.13  [check113] Ensure MFA is enabled for the root account (Scored)
      PASS! Virtual MFA is enabled for root

1.14  [check114] Ensure hardware MFA is enabled for the root account (Scored)
      FAIL! Only Virtual MFA is enabled for root

1.15 [check115] Ensure security questions are registered in the AWS account (Not Scored)
      INFO! No command available for check 1.15
      INFO! Login to the AWS Console as root & click on the Account
      INFO! Name -> My Account -> Configure Security Challenge Questions
```

Summary

Cloud computing plays a crucial role in the technology strategies of modern organizations. Cybersecurity analysts must be familiar with the various cloud service and deployment models and understand how the use of cloud services impacts their organizations. They must be able to validate cloud configurations and ensure that they implement strong security controls, including key management, access controls, and logging and monitoring.

They must also understand how to use cloud security assessment tools to verify the integrity of the cloud environment and remediate any security gaps that might exist.

Exam Essentials

Explain how the cloud service models differ in the type of service offered. Infrastructure as a service (IaaS) offerings provide customers with access to storage, computing, and networking capabilities—the basic building blocks of technology solutions. Software as a service (SaaS) offerings provide customers with a complete application, built and managed by the provider. Platform as a service (PaaS) offerings allow customers to run their own applications on an infrastructure managed by the provider. Function as a service (FaaS) offerings allow customers to execute discrete units of code on the provider's infrastructure.

Explain how cloud deployment models differ in how cloud infrastructure is shared. Public cloud services use the multitenancy model and are open to all customers. Private cloud services are restricted to use by a single customer. Community cloud services offer services to members of a defined, closed community. Hybrid environments combine aspects of public, private, and/or community cloud in a unified platform.

Know how cloud environments embrace automation to improve agility. The DevOps approach to technology unifies software development and technology operations practices. Cloud services enable DevOps by offering infrastructure as code (IaC) capabilities through their application programming interfaces (APIs). Cybersecurity analysts must understand how to secure these APIs and manage both API and encryption keys.

Be aware that operating in the cloud introduces new technology risks. Cybersecurity analysts must understand the controls implemented by cloud service providers and how security duties are divided according to the shared responsibility model. They must understand the risks associated with managing those controls and work to prevent undesirable situations, such as unprotected storage.

Know how to integrate cloud services into the organization's SOC. Cybersecurity analysts must ensure that cloud providers offer sufficient logging and monitoring capabilities and that the SOC has the ability to access logs through their existing security tools.

Be familiar with how cloud assessment tools supplement standard security controls. ScoutSuite offers cybersecurity analysts the ability to probe the security configurations of many different cloud providers, whereas Prowler performs the same function only in AWS environments. Pacu is an exploitation framework for use in cloud service penetration tests.

Define the purpose of CASB solutions. Cloud access security brokers (CASBs) serve as an intermediary between users and providers, allowing cybersecurity teams to monitor user activity and consistently enforce security policies. CASB solutions may either exist directly inline with user connections or interact with the provider through the provider's API.

Lab Exercises

Activity 6.1: Run a ScoutSuite Assessment

ScoutSuite is a Python script available for free download. In this activity, you will download and run the tool. Note that running ScoutSuite requires read-only access to a cloud account. You should only run this scan against an account that you have permission to scan.

1. Download ScoutSuite from the GitHub repository at `github.com/nccgroup/ScoutSuite`.
2. Run it on a system that has Python installed using the command `python3 scout.py`. Review the instructions presented to you to configure and run ScoutSuite against the cloud provider of your choice.
3. Analyze the findings from your ScoutSuite report. What are the most pressing vulnerabilities that you found? How would you address them?

Activity 6.2: Explore the Exploits Available with Pacu

Pacu is also a Python script available for free download. In this activity, you will download and run the tool. Running Pacu requires access to an AWS account. You should only run Pacu against an account that you have permission to scan.

1. Download Pacu from the GitHub repository at `github.com/RhinoSecurityLabs/pacu`.
2. Install and configure Pacu on your system using the command `bash install.sh`.
3. Run it on a system that has Python installed using the command `python3 pacu.py`. Review the instructions presented to you to configure and run ScoutSuite against the cloud provider of your choice.
4. Run the `list` command to determine the modules currently available in Pacu. Which of these seem most valuable to you? How might you use them in a penetration test?

Activity 6.3: Scan an AWS Account with Prowler

Prowler is a command-line tool available for free download. In this activity, you will download and run the tool. Note that running Prowler requires read-only access to an AWS account. You should only run this scan against an account that you have permission to scan.

1. Download Prowler from the GitHub repository at `github.com/toniblyx/prowler`.
2. Install it on your system, configure it, and run a scan. This is a fairly complex process, but you will find a document walking you through the current steps to do so in the `README.md` file in the Prowler GitHub repository.
3. Analyze the findings from your Prowler report. What are the most pressing vulnerabilities that you found? How would you address them?

Review Questions

1. Which one of the following statements about cloud computing is incorrect?
   A. Cloud computing offers ubiquitous, convenient access.
   B. Cloud computing customers store data on hardware that is shared with other customers.
   C. Cloud computing customers provision resources through the service provider's sales team.
   D. Cloud computing resources are accessed over a network.
2. Under the shared responsibility model, in which tier of cloud computing is the customer responsible for securing the operating system?
   A. IaaS
   B. PaaS
   C. SaaS
   D. All of the above
3. Helen designed a new payroll system that she offers to her customers. She hosts the payroll system in AWS and her customers access it through the web. What tier of cloud computing best describes Helen's service?
   A. PaaS
   B. SaaS
   C. FaaS
   D. IaaS
4. Tony purchases virtual machines from Microsoft Azure and uses them exclusively for use by his organization. What model of cloud computing is this?
   A. Public cloud
   B. Private cloud
   C. Hybrid cloud
   D. Community cloud
5. Amanda would like to run a security configuration scan of her Microsoft Azure cloud environment. Which one of the following tools would be most appropriate for her needs?
   A. Inspector
   B. ScoutSuite
   C. Prowler
   D. Pacu

6. Kevin is using a service where a cloud provider offers a platform that executes his code in response to discrete events. He is billed based on the actual resources consumed during each code execution event. What term best describes this service?

   A. PaaS

   B. SaaS

   C. FaaS

   D. IaaS

7. Under the shared responsibility model, which component always remains the responsibility of the customer, regardless of the cloud service model used?

   A. Application

   B. Hardware

   C. Datacenter

   D. Data

8. Which one of the following services is *not* an example of FaaS computing?

   A. Lambda

   B. DeepLens

   C. Google Cloud Functions

   D. Azure Functions

9. Which cloud computing deployment model requires the use of a unifying technology platform to tie together components from different providers?

   A. Public cloud

   B. Private cloud

   C. Community cloud

   D. Hybrid cloud

10. Which one of the following would not commonly be available as an IaaS service offering?

    A. CRM

    B. Storage

    C. Networking

    D. Computing

11. Which one of the following is a characteristic of DevOps approaches to technology?

    A. Isolating operations teams from development teams

    B. Requiring clear hand-offs between development and production

    C. Increasing the frequency of application releases

    D. Eliminating the need for developers to understand business requirements

12. Which one of the following is *not* an example of infrastructure as code?
    A. Defining infrastructure in JSON
    B. Writing code to interact with a cloud provider's API
    C. Using a cloud provider's web interface to provision resources
    D. Defining infrastructure in YAML
13. Which one of the following conditions is *not* likely to trigger an alert during an automated cloud security assessment?
    A. Presence of an API key in a public repository
    B. Unrestricted API keys
    C. Transmission of an API key over unsecured channels
    D. Sharing of API keys among different developers
14. Brian is selecting a CASB for his organization and he would like to use an approach that interacts with the cloud provider directly. Which CASB approach is most appropriate for his needs?
    A. Inline CASB
    B. Outsider CASB
    C. Comprehensive CASB
    D. API-based CASB
15. A coalition of universities banded together and created a cloud computing environment that is open to all member institutions. The services provided are basic IaaS components. What term best describes this cloud model?
    A. Public cloud
    B. Private cloud
    C. Community cloud
    D. Hybrid cloud
16. In which cloud computing service model does the customer share responsibility with the cloud provider for datacenter security?
    A. IaaS
    B. SaaS
    C. PaaS
    D. None of the above
17. Which one of the following statements about inline CASB is incorrect?
    A. Inline CASB solutions often use software agents on endpoints.
    B. Inline CASB solutions intercept requests from users to cloud providers.
    C. Inline CASB solutions can monitor activity but cannot actively enforce policy.
    D. Inline CASB solutions may require network reconfiguration.

18. What type of credential is commonly used to restrict access to an API?

    A. Encryption key

    B. API key

    C. Password

    D. Biometrics

19. Gina gained access to a client's AWS account during a penetration test. She would like to determine what level of access she has to the account. Which one of the following tools would best meet her need?

    A. ScoutSuite

    B. Inspector

    C. Prowler

    D. Pacu

20. In which of the following cloud categories are customers typically charged based on the number of virtual server instances dedicated to their use?

    A. IaaS only

    B. SaaS only

    C. IaaS and PaaS

    D. IaaS, SaaS, and PaaS

Infrastructure Security and Controls

THE COMPTIA CYBERSECURITY ANALYST (CYSA+) EXAM OBJECTIVES COVERED IN THIS CHAPTER INCLUDE:

✓ **Domain 2.0: Software and Systems Security**

- 2.1 Given a scenario, apply security solutions for infrastructure management.

✓ **Domain 3.0: Security Operations and Monitoring**

- 3.2 Given a scenario, implement configuration changes to existing controls to improve security.

A well-designed security architecture design seeks to eliminate, or at least minimize, the number of points where a single failure in infrastructure security and controls can lead to a breach. The controls that make up each of the layers of security for an organization can include technical controls, administrative controls, and physical controls that prevent, detect, or correct issues.

In the first half of this chapter, we will explore defense-in-depth designs and layered security concepts. We will then look at how those concepts are implemented via network architecture designs, asset and change management, segmentation, and a variety of other methods. Together, these techniques and design elements can create a complete layered security design, resulting in an effective defense-in-depth strategy.

In the second part of this chapter, we will explore operational security controls ranging from permissions to technical controls like network access control and malware signature development.

Understanding Defense-in-Depth

The foundation of most security designs relies on the concept of defense-in-depth. In other words, a single defensive measure should not be the only control preventing an attacker (or a mistake!) from creating a problem. Since there are many potential ways for a security breach to occur, a wide range of defenses must be layered together to ensure that a failure in one does not endanger sensitive data, systems, or networks.

Layered Security

One of the most important concepts for defense-in-depth is the idea of *layered security*. This means that each layer of security includes additional protections that help prevent a hole or flaw in another layer from allowing an attacker in. Figure 7.1 shows a high-level conceptual diagram of a sample layered security approach. In this design, data security is at the core where policies, practices, and data classification would be implemented. Each additional layer adds protections, from application layer security which protects the methods used to access the data to endpoint system security like data loss prevention software.

As you can see, a layered approach can combine technologies that are specifically appropriate to the layer where they reside with technologies that are a fit for multiple layers. Configurations may differ based on the specific needs found at that layer in the security model. For example, data security might require full disk encryption for laptops and mobile devices, whereas desktops might only leverage data loss prevention software.

FIGURE 7.1 Layered security network design

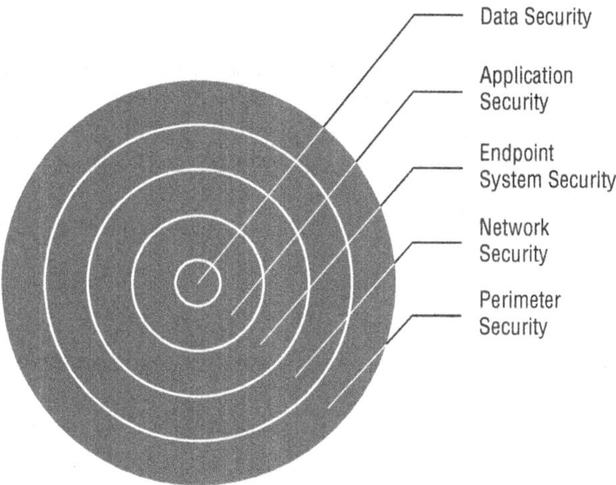

Defense-in-depth should address all three elements of the CIA Triad—confidentiality, integrity, and availability. Depth in availability can take the form of redundant systems or network devices, multiple network paths and providers, or backup power systems, whereas integrity defenses may include file integrity checking or system configuration validation tools.

Layered security can be complex to design. The interactions between security controls, organizational business needs, and usability all require careful attention during the design of a layered security approach.

Zero Trust

One major concept in modern security architecture design is the idea of zero trust. The zero trust concept removes the trust that used to be placed in systems, services, and individuals inside security boundaries. In a zero trust environment, each action requested and allowed must be verified and validated before being allowed to occur.

Zero trust moves away from the strong perimeter as the primary security layer and instead moves even further toward a deeply layered security model where individual devices and applications, as well as user accounts, are part of the security design. As perimeters have become increasingly difficult to define, zero trust designs have become more common to address the changing security environment that modern organizations exist in.

Implementing zero trust designs requires a blend of technologies, processes, and policies to manage, monitor, assess, and maintain a complex environment.

Exam Note

The CySA+ exam outline doesn't mention zero trust architecture, but it is a major topic in modern network design. You don't need to study the concept to pass the exam, but you will need to be familiar with it in your professional life—in fact, the authors of this book were surprised it wasn't included in this version of the exam!

Segmentation

Providing a layered defense often involves the use of segmentation, or separation. *Physical segmentation* involves running on separate physical infrastructure or networks. *System isolation* is handled by ensuring that the infrastructure is separated, and can go as far as using an *air gap*, which ensures that there is no connection at all between the infrastructures.

Air gaps may feel like the ultimate in segmentation-based security, but even a carefully air-gapped system can be compromised. The Stuxnet malware was introduced to air-gapped systems in Iran's nuclear program on a thumb drive carried in by an engineer who didn't know that the malware had transferred to the drive. The authors of this book have seen consultants and staff bring infected systems and malware into physically protected networks, and have also seen data extracted from air-gapped systems by staff members who wanted to work on the data after hours. An air gap is only as effective as the enforcement and monitoring of what bypasses it!

Virtual segmentation takes advantage of virtualization capabilities to separate functions to virtual machines or containers, although some implementations of segmentation for virtualization also run on separate physical servers in addition to running separate virtual machines.

Network segmentation or compartmentalization is a common element of network design. It provides a number of advantages:

- The number of systems that are exposed to attackers (commonly called the organization's *attack surface*) can be reduced by compartmentalizing systems and networks.
- It can help to limit the scope of regulatory compliance efforts by placing the systems, data, or unit that must be compliant in a more easily maintained environment separate from the rest of the organization.

- In some cases, segmentation can help increase availability by limiting the impact of an issue or attack.
- Segmentation is used to increase the efficiency of a network. Larger numbers of systems in a single segment can lead to network congestion, making segmentation attractive as networks increase in size.

Exam Note

The CySA+ exam outline covers two major segmentation concepts: physical and virtual, and then specific solutions in the form of system isolation—particularly air gaps, and focuses on jump boxes as an access method. There are other options, but those are what you should make sure you understand for the exam.

Network segmentation can be accomplished in many ways, but for security reasons, a firewall with a carefully designed ruleset is typically used between network segments with different levels of trust or functional requirements. Network segmentation also frequently relies on routers and switches that support VLAN tagging. In some cases where segmentation is desired and more nuanced controls are not necessary, segmentation is handled using only routers or switches.

One common solution for access into segmented environments like these is the use of a *jump box* (sometimes called a jump server), which is a system that resides in a segmented environment and is used to access and manage the devices in the segment where it resides. Jump boxes span two different security zones and should thus be carefully secured, managed, and monitored.

The Case for Product Diversity

Product diversity (using products from multiple vendors) is sometimes used to create an additional layer of security. The intent of using diverse products is to eliminate a single point of failure by ensuring that a vulnerability or design flaw found in one product does not make an entire network or system vulnerable to exploit. For example, in a network design, this might mean using Juniper border routers, Cisco core routers, and Palo Alto security devices. If a vulnerability existed in the Cisco core routers, the other devices would be less likely to suffer from the same issue, meaning that attackers should not be able to exploit them, thus potentially limiting the impact of an attack.

Unfortunately, using multiple products rather than settling on a single vendor or product for a solution adds additional overhead and costs for maintenance, training, and support, potentially resulting in more vulnerabilities! The right choice varies from organization to organization and design to design, but diversity may be a useful design choice if your organization is worried about a single vulnerability affecting your entire network, platform, or other environment.

In addition to jump boxes, another common means of providing remote access as well as access into segmented networks from different security zones is through a *virtual private network* (VPN). Although VPNs do not technically have to provide an encryption layer to protect the traffic they carry, almost all modern implementations will use encryption while providing a secure connection that makes a remote network available to a system or device.

Figure 7.2 shows an example of a segmented network with a protected network behind security devices, with a VPN connection to a jump box allowing access to the protected segment.

FIGURE 7.2 Network segmentation with a protected network

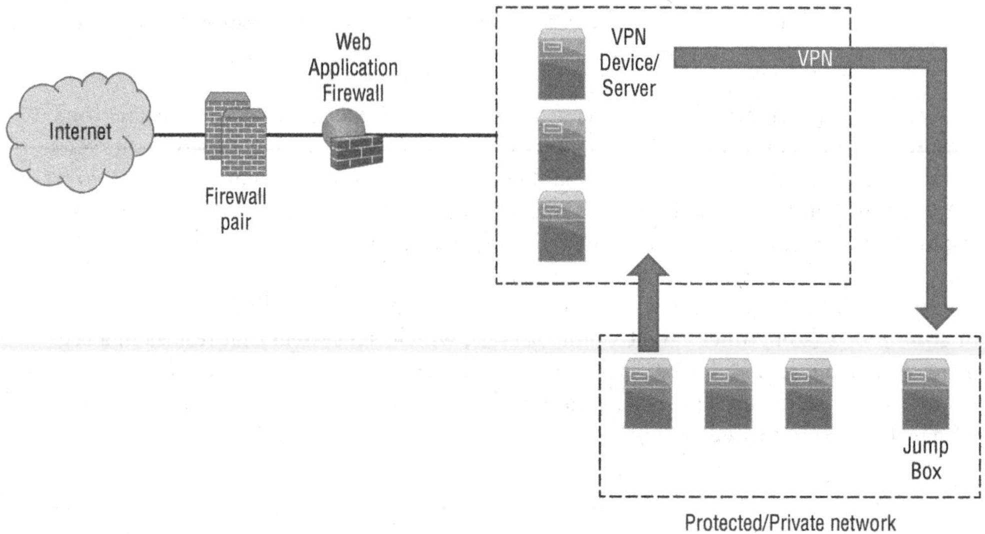

Network Architecture

Understanding how your network is designed, what devices exist on it and what their purposes and capabilities are, and what controls you can apply using the devices is critical to securing a network. Traditional physical networks, software-defined networks, and virtual networks exist in parallel in many organizations, and you will need to understand how each of these technologies can impact the architecture and security posture of your organization.

Exam Note

The CySA+ exam outline puts quite a few technologies under the heading of "network architecture," including physical, software-defined, virtual private cloud, virtual private networks, and serverless. We've separated out serverless into the next section as part of virtualization, and we also cover cloud-specific options in additional depth at the end of this section.

Physical Network Architectures

Physical network architecture is composed of the routers, switches, security devices, cabling, and all the other network components that make up a traditional network. You can leverage a wide range of security solutions on a physical network, but common elements of a security design include the following:

- Firewalls that control traffic flow between networks or systems.
- Intrusion prevention systems (IPSs), which can detect and stop attacks, and intrusion detection systems (IDSs), which only alarm or notify when attacks are detected.
- Content filtering and caching devices that are used to control what information passes through to protected devices.
- Network access control (NAC) technology that controls which devices are able to connect to the network and which may assess the security state of devices or require other information before allowing a connection.
- Network scanners that can identify systems and gather information about them, including the services they are running, patch levels, and other details about the systems.
- Unified threat management (UTM) devices that combine a number of these services often including firewalls, IDSs/IPSs, content filtering, and other security features.

As you prepare for the CySA+ exam, you should familiarize yourself with these common devices and their basic functions so that you can apply them in a network security design.

Software-Defined Networks

Software-defined networking (SDN) makes networks programmable. Using SDN, you can control networks centrally, which allows management of network resources and traffic with more intelligence than a traditional physical network infrastructure. Software-defined networks provide information and control via APIs (application programming interfaces) like OpenFlow, which means that network monitoring and management can be done across disparate hardware and software vendors.

Since SDN allows control via APIs, API security as well as secure code development practices are both important elements of an SDN implementation.

In addition to organizationally controlled SDN implementations, software-defined network wide area networks (SDN-WANs) are an SDN-driven service model where providers use SDN technology to provide network services. They allow blended infrastructures that may combine a variety of technologies behind the scenes to deliver network connectivity to customers. SDN-WAN implementations often provide encryption but introduce risks, including vulnerabilities of the SDN orchestration platform, risks related to multivendor network paths and control, and of course, availability and integrity risks as traffic flows through multiple paths.

Virtualization

Virtualization uses software to run virtual computers on underlying real hardware. This means that you can run multiple systems, running multiple operating systems, all of which act like they are on their own hardware. This approach provides additional control of things like resource usage and what hardware is presented to the guest operating systems, and it allows efficient use of the underlying hardware because you can leverage shared resources.

Virtualization is used in many ways. It is used to implement *virtual desktop infrastructure* (VDI), which runs desktop operating systems like Windows 10 on central hardware and streams the desktops across the network to systems. Many organizations virtualize almost all their servers, running clusters of virtualization hosts that host all their infrastructure. Virtual security appliances and other vendor-provided virtual solutions are also part of the virtualization ecosystem.

The advantages of virtualization also come with some challenges for security professionals who must now determine how to monitor, secure, and respond to issues in a virtual environment. Much like the other elements of a security design that we have discussed, this requires preplanning and effort to understand the architecture and implementation that your organization will use.

Containerization provides an alternative to virtualizing an entire system, and instead permits applications to be run in their own environment with their own required components, such as libraries, configuration files, and other dependencies, in a dedicated container. Kubernetes and Docker are examples of containerization technologies.

Containerization allows for a high level of portability, but it also creates new security challenges. Traditional host-based security may work for the underlying containerization server, but the containers themselves need to be addressed differently. At the same time, since many containers run on the same server, threats to the host OS can impact many containerized services. Fortunately, tools exist to sign container images and to monitor and patch containers. Beyond these tools, traditional hardening, application and service monitoring, and auditing tools can be useful.

When addressing containerized systems, bear in mind the shared underlying host as well as the rapid deployment models typically used with containers. Security must be baked into the service and software development life cycle as well as the system maintenance and management process.

Serverless computing in a broad sense describes cloud computing, but much of the time when it is used currently it describes technology sometimes called function as a service (FaaS). In essence, serverless computing relies on a system that executes functions as they are called. Amazon's AWS Lambda, Google's App Engine, and Azure Functions are all examples of serverless computing FaaS implementations. In these cases, security models typically address the functions like other code, meaning that the same types of controls used for software development need to be applied to the function-as-a-service environment. In addition, controls appropriate to cloud computing environments such as access controls and rights, as well as monitoring and resource management capabilities, are necessary to ensure a secure deployment.

Exam Note

Other serverless technologies exist, including serverless databases, but they are often viewed as cloud services rather than serverless computing. The CySA+ exam outline doesn't specify, so you should make sure you understand the concept and the ideas behind how to implement security for serverless deployments rather than focusing on a specific implementation.

Networking in virtual environments may combine traditional physical networks between virtualization or containerization hosts, and then virtual networking that runs inside the virtual environment. If you don't plan ahead, this can make segments of your network essentially invisible to your monitoring tools and security systems. As you design virtualized environments, make sure that you consider who controls the virtual network connectivity and design, how you will monitor it, and use the same set of security controls that you would need to apply on a physical network.

Asset and Change Management

Securing assets effectively requires knowing what assets you have and what their current state is. Those paired requirements drive organizations to implement *asset management* tools and processes, and to apply change management methodology and tools to the software and systems that they have in their asset inventory.

In addition to having an inventory of what devices, systems, and software they have, organizations often use asset tagging to ensure that their assets can be inventoried and in some cases, may be returned if they are misplaced or stolen. *Asset tagging* can help discourage theft, help identify systems more easily, and can make day-to-day support work easier for support staff who can quickly look up a system or device in an asset inventory list to determine what it is, who the device was issued to, and what its current state should be.

Logging, Monitoring, and Validation

Layered security requires appropriate monitoring, alerting, and validation. Logging systems in a well-designed layered security architecture should ensure that logs are secure and are available centrally for monitoring. Monitoring systems need to have appropriate alert thresholds set and notification capabilities that match the needs of the organization.

Most security designs implement a separate log server, either in the form of a security information and event management (SIEM) device or as a specialized log server. This design allows the remote log server to act as a bastion host, preserving unmodified copies of logs in case of compromise and allowing for central analysis of the log data.

In addition to monitoring and logging capabilities, configuration management and validation capabilities are important. Tools like Microsoft's Endpoint Manager or Jamf's Jamf Pro offer the ability to set and validate system settings across networks of varying types of devices, thus ensuring that their configurations and installed software match institutional expectations.

Encryption

Both encryption and hashing are critical to many of the controls found at each of the layers we have discussed. They play roles in network security, host security, and data security, and they are embedded in many of the applications and systems that each layer depends on.

This makes using current, secure encryption techniques and ensuring that proper key management occurs critical to a layered security design. When reviewing security designs, it is important to identify where encryption (and hashing) are used, how they are used, and how both the encryption keys and their passphrases are stored. It is also important to understand when data is encrypted and when it is unencrypted—security designs can fail because the carefully encrypted data that was sent securely is unencrypted and stored in a cache or by a local user, removing the protection it relied on during transit.

Certificate Management

Managing digital security certificates used to mostly be an issue for system and application administrators who were responsible for the SSL certificates that their web and other services used. As digital certificates have become more deeply integrated into service architectures, including the use of certificates for workstations and other endpoints and for access to cloud service providers, certificate management has become a broader issue.

The basic concepts behind certificate management remain the same, however:

- Keeping private keys and passphrases secure is of the utmost importance.
- Ensuring that systems use and respect certificate revocations is necessary.
- Managing certificate life cycles helps to prevent expired certificates causing issues and ensures that they are replaced when necessary.
- Central management makes responses to events like compromised keys or changes in certificate root vendors less problematic.

If your organization uses certificates, you should ensure that they are tracked and managed, and that you have a plan in place for what would happen if you needed to change them or if they were compromised.

The authors of this book encountered a worst-case scenario with a broadly deployed certificate. The certificate authority (CA) that signed the certificate for an organizationwide wireless deployment changed after a sale, and the certificate couldn't be renewed. Much to the organization's dismay, the only way to change the certificate for the wide range of clients was to require every user to install a new certificate either by hand or through a tool. This caused massive disruption for tens of thousands of users on very short notice.

Active Defense

Active defense describes offensive actions taken to counter adversaries. These might include active responses to incursions to limit damage by shutting down systems, removing accounts, or otherwise responding to attacks and compromises. They can also include incident response and forensic activities that can provide additional information about how the attackers breached your defenses.

Threat intelligence, threat hunting, and countermeasure design and implementation are also part of active defenses. Continuously evaluating your security posture and controls and adjusting them to meet the threats that your organization faces over time is the best approach to building a strong foundation for active defense.

Active defense does not include attacks against adversaries. In fact, attacks against adversaries may be against the law or may have other consequences, and thus isn't part of most organizations' security operations. If you are asked to take offensive action, make sure you understand the legal and ethical implications of what you are being asked to do.

Honeypots

One technology used in some active defenses is a *honeypot*. Honeypots are systems that are designed to look like an attractive target for an attacker. They capture attack traffic, techniques, and other information as attackers attempt to compromise them. This provides both insight into attacker tools and methodologies as well as clues to what attackers and threats might target your organization.

Exam Note

The CySA+ exam objectives specifically call out honeypots, so make sure you are familiar with the concept. Interestingly, they don't mention honeynets, which are networks set up as a network honeypot, or darknets, which are unused network space monitored for scanning and other attacks.

Infrastructure Security and the Cloud

The shift to use of cloud services throughout organizations has not only shifted the perimeter and driven the need for zero trust environments, but has also created a need for organizations to update their security practices for a more porous, more diverse operating environment.

Unlike on-premises systems, the underlying environment provided by cloud service providers is not typically accessible to security practitioners to configure, test, or otherwise control. That means that securing cloud services requires a different approach.

With most software as a service (SaaS) and platform as a service (PaaS) vendors, security will primarily be tackled via contractual obligations. Configurations and implementation options can create security challenges, and identity and access management is also important in these environments.

Infrastructure as a service (IaaS) vendors like AWS, Azure, Google, and others provide more access to infrastructure, and thus some of the traditional security concerns around operating system configuration, management, and patching will apply. Similarly, services and applications need to be installed, configured, and maintained in a secure manner. Cloud providers often provide additional security-oriented services that may be useful in their environment and which may replace or supplement the tools that you might use on-premises.

Many cloud vendors will provide audit and assessment results upon request, often with a required nondisclosure agreement before they will provide the information.

When considering on-premises versus cloud security, you should review what options exist in each environment, and what threats are relevant and which are different, if any. Assessing the security capabilities, posture, threats, and risks that apply to or are specific to your cloud service provider is also an important task.

Virtual private cloud (VPC) is an option delivered by cloud service providers that builds an on-demand semi-isolated environment. A VPC typically exists on a private subnet and may have additional security to ensure that intersystem communications remain secure.

Another cloud security tool is a *cloud access security broker* (CASB). CASB tools are policy enforcement points that can exist either locally or in the cloud, and enforce security policies when cloud resources and services are used. CASBs can help with data security, antimalware functionality, service usage and access visibility, and risk management. As you might expect with powerful tools, a CASB can be very helpful but requires careful configuration and continued maintenance.

Assessing the Cloud

Although control of SaaS and PaaS solutions lies with the vendor, you can take some additional action to help ensure your organization's security. Many cloud vendors offer access to third-party security audit information like an SSAE-16 Type 1 or Type 2 report. In addition, you may want to conduct a security assessment to determine whether the vendor meets your own expected security best practices. Tools like the shared risk assessment tools provided by `www.sharedassessments.org` can help you conduct an assessment before engaging with a cloud or outsourced IT vendor. While you're at it, you should also ensure that the contract covers any legal or regulatory issues that would impact your outsourced solution.

Improving Security by Improving Controls

Security designs rely on controls that can help prevent, detect, counteract, or limit the impact of security risks. Controls are typically classified based on two categorization schemes: how they are implemented, or when they react relative to the security incident or threat. Classifying controls based on implementation type is done using the following model:

- *Technical controls* include firewalls, intrusion detection and prevention systems, network segmentation, authentication and authorization systems, and a variety of other systems and technical capabilities designed to provide security through technical means.
- *Administrative controls* (sometimes called procedural controls) involve processes and procedures like those found in incident response plans, account creation and management, as well as awareness and training efforts.
- *Physical controls* include locks, fences, and other controls that control or limit physical access, as well as controls like fire extinguishers that can help prevent physical harm to property.

Some control classification schemes add a fourth type of control: legal controls. These are controls put in place by law. Some simply count legal controls as a type of administrative control that is put in place by the legal system.

Classification by when the control acts uses the following classification scheme:

- *Preventive controls* are intended to stop an incident from occurring by taking proactive measures to stop the threat. Preventive controls include firewalls, training, and security guards.
- *Detective controls* work to detect an incident and to capture information about it, allowing a response, like alarms or notifications.
- *Corrective controls* either remediate an incident or act to limit how much damage can result from an incident. Corrective controls are often used as part of an incident response process. Examples of corrective controls include patching, antimalware software, and system restores from backups.

Controls that satisfy a requirement that isn't able to be met by an existing security measure—either because it is too difficult to implement or because it does not fully meet the needs—are known as *compensating controls*. Additional control types that you may occasionally encounter include deterrent controls that warn attackers that they shouldn't attack, directive controls that are intended to lead to a desired outcome, and recovery controls that provide ways to respond to a breach.

Layered Host Security

Endpoint systems, whether they are laptops, desktop PCs, or mobile devices, can also use a layered security approach. Since individual systems are used by individual users for their day-to-day work, they are often one of the most at-risk parts of your infrastructure and can create significant threat if they are compromised.

Layered security at the individual host level typically relies on a number of common security controls:

- Passwords or other strong authentication help ensure that only authorized users access hosts.
- Host firewalls and host intrusion prevention software limit the network attack surface of hosts and can also help prevent undesired outbound communication in the event of a system compromise.
- Data loss prevention software monitors and manages protected data.
- Whitelisting or blacklisting software can allow or prevent specific software packages and applications from being installed or run on the system.
- Antimalware and antivirus packages monitor for known malware as well as behavior that commonly occurs due to malicious software.
- Patch management and vulnerability assessment tools are used to ensure that applications and the operating system are fully patched and properly secured.
- System hardening and configuration management ensures that unneeded services are turned off, that good security practices are followed for operating system–level configuration options, and that unnecessary accounts are not present.
- Encryption, either at the file level or full-disk encryption, may be appropriate to protect the system from access if it is lost or stolen or if data at rest needs additional security.
- File integrity monitoring tools monitor files and directories for changes and can alert an administrator if changes occur.
- Logging of events, actions, and issues is an important detective control at the host layer.

The host security layer may also include physical security controls to help prevent theft or undesired access to the systems themselves.

Permissions

Permissions are the access rights or privileges given to users, systems, applications, or devices. Permissions are often granted based on roles in organizations to make rights management easier. You are likely familiar with permissions like read, write, and execute.

Linux permissions can be seen using the `ls` command. In Figure 7.3 you can see a file listing. At the left is a `-`, which means this is a file rather than `d` for a directory. Next are three sets of three characters, which can be `r` for read, `w` for write, `x` for execute, or `a` for no permission. These three settings define what the user can do, what the group can do, and what all or everyone can do.

FIGURE 7.3 Linux permissions

```
root@kali:~/example# ls -l
total 4
-rw-r--r-- 1 root root 18 Jan 11 18:12 example.txt
root@kali:~/example# █
```

Exam Note

You should be familiar with how to check and read both Windows and Linux permissions using the Windows `attrib` command, the Windows GUI, and `chmod` in Linux.

Permissions exist in many places such as software packages, operating systems, and cloud services. Building appropriate permissions models for users and their roles is a critical part of a strong security control model.

Whitelisting and Blacklisting

Whitelisting and *blacklisting* are important concepts for security professionals who are implementing controls. Whitelisting techniques rely on building a list of allowed things, whether they are IP addresses in firewall ruleset, software packages, or something else. Blacklisting takes the opposite approach and specifically prohibits things based on entries in a list.

Whitelisting can be difficult in some scenarios because you have to have a list of all possible needed entries on your permitted list. Whitelisting software packages for an entire enterprise can be challenging for this reason. Blacklisting has its own challenges, particularly in cases where using broad definitions in entries can lead to inadvertent blocks.

Despite these challenges, whitelisting and blacklisting are both commonly used techniques.

Technical Controls

Technical controls use technology to implement safeguards. Technical controls can be implemented in software, hardware, or firmware, and they typically provide automated protection to the systems where they are implemented.

Exam Note

Although there are many technical controls, the CySA+ exam calls out a few specifically, including whitelisting and blacklisting, firewalls, IPS rules, DLP systems, endpoint detection and response capabilities, network access controls, sinkholing, malware signatures, sandboxing, and port security. We've covered those here, so you'll be ready for the exam.

For the CySA+ exam, you should be familiar with the basics of the following types of security devices and controls:

- *Firewalls* that block or allow traffic based on rules that use information like the source or destination IP address, port, or protocol used by traffic. They are typically used between different trust zones. There are a number of different types of firewall technologies, as well as both host and network firewall devices.
- *Intrusion prevention systems* (IPSs) are used to monitor traffic and apply rules based on behaviors and traffic content. Like firewalls, IPSs and IDSs (intrusion detection systems) rely on rules, but both IPSs and IDSs typically inspect traffic at a deeper level, paying attention to content and other details inside the packets themselves. Although the CySA+ exam materials reference only IPSs that can stop unwanted traffic, IDSs that can only detect traffic and alert or log information about it are also deployed as a detective control. Or an IPS may be configured with rules that do not take action when such an action might cause issues.
- *Data loss prevention* (DLP) systems and software work to protect data from leaving the organization or systems where it should be contained. A complete DLP system targets data in motion, data at rest and in use, and endpoint systems where data may be accessed or stored. DLP relies on identifying the data that should be protected and then detecting when leaks occur, which can be challenging when encryption is frequently used between systems and across networks. This means that DLP installations combine endpoint software and various means of making network traffic visible to the DLP system.
- *Endpoint detection and response* (EDR) is a relatively new term for systems that provides continuous monitoring and response to advanced threats. They typically use endpoint data gathering and monitoring capabilities paired with central processing and analysis to provide high levels of visibility into what occurs on endpoints. This use of data gathering, search, and analysis tools is intended to help detect and respond to suspicious activity. The ability to handle multiple threat types, including ransomware, malware, and data exfiltration, is also a common feature for EDR systems.

- *Network access control (NAC)* is a technology that requires a system to authenticate or provide other information before it can connect to a network. NAC operates in either a preadmission or postadmission mode, either checking systems before they are connected or checking user actions after systems are connected to the network. NAC solutions may require an agent or software on the connecting system to gather data and handle the NAC connection process, or they may be agentless. When systems do not successfully connect to a NAC-protected network, or when an issue is detected, they may be placed into a quarantine network where they may have access to remediation tools or an information portal, or they may simply be prevented from connecting.
- *Sinkholing* redirects traffic from its original destination to a destination of your choice. Although the most common implementation of sinkholing is done via DNS to prevent traffic from being sent to malicious sites, you may also encounter other types of sinkholing as well.
- *Port security* is a technology that monitors the MAC (hardware) addresses of devices connecting to switch ports and allows or denies them access to the network based on their MAC address. A knowledgeable attacker may spoof a MAC address from a trusted system to bypass port security.
- *Sandboxing* refers to a variety of techniques that place untrusted software or systems into a protected and isolated environment. Sandboxing is often used for software testing and will isolate an application from the system, thus preventing it from causing issues if something goes wrong. Virtualization technologies can be used to create sandboxes for entire systems, and organizations that test for malware often use heavily instrumented sandbox environments to determine what a malware package is doing.

Malware Signatures

Malware signatures used to be simply composed of recognizable file patterns or hashes that could be checked to see if a given file or files matched those from known malware. As malware has become more complex, techniques that help obfuscate the malware by changing it to prevent this via techniques like mutation, expanding or shrinking code, or register renaming have made traditional signature-based identification less successful.

Exam Note

This version of the CySA+ exam specifically calls out malware signatures, how they are developed, and how rules using them are written, as well as the role of automated malware signature development, so make sure you're familiar with this topic before you tackle the exam.

Signatures can be created by analyzing the malware and creating hashes or other comparators that can be checked to see if packages match.

Malware identification now relies on multiple layers of detection capabilities that look at more than just file signatures. Behavior-based detection looks at the actions that an executable takes such as accessing memory or the filesystem, changing rights, or otherwise performing suspicious actions. Looking at behaviors also helps identify polymorphic viruses, which change themselves so that simply hashing their binaries will not allow them to be identified. Now antimalware software may even roll back actions that the malware took while it was being monitored. This type of monitoring is often called dynamic analysis.

In both traditional malware signature creation scenarios and behavior-based detection creation scenarios, malware samples are placed into an isolated sandbox with instrumentation that tracks what the malware does. That information is used to help create both signatures from files or other materials the malware creates, installs, or modifies, and the actions that it takes. In many cases, *automated malware signature creation* is done using these techniques so that antimalware providers can provide signatures more quickly.

If you want to try this out yourself, you can submit suspected malware to sites like `VirusTotal.com` or `jotti.com`.

Policy, Process, and Standards

Administrative controls that involve policies, processes, and standards are a necessary layer when looking at a complete layered security design. In addition to controls that support security at the technology layer, administrative controls found in a complete security design include

- Change control
- Configuration management
- Monitoring and response policies
- Personnel security controls
- Business continuity and disaster recovery controls
- Human resource controls like background checks and terminations

Personnel Security

In addition to technical and procedural concerns, the human layer of a design must be considered. Staff members need to be trained for the tasks they perform and to ensure that they react appropriately to security issues and threats. Critical personnel controls should be put in place where needed to provide separation of duties and to remove single points of failure in staffing.

Exam Note

Personnel controls are important for you to know about, but version 2 of the CySA+ exam outline dropped the entire section on personnel security! If you're only studying for the exam, you don't need to spend as much time here. If you're working to become a practitioner, we encourage you to keep these in mind, as the human side of security is one of the most common failure points in security designs.

A wide variety of personnel controls can be implemented as part of a complete security program, ranging from training to process and human resources–related controls. The most common personnel controls are as follows:

Separation of Duties When individuals in an organization are given a role to perform, they can potentially abuse the rights and privileges that that role provides. Properly implemented separation of duties requires more than one individual to perform elements of a task to ensure that fraud or abuse do not occur. A typical separation of duties can be found in financially significant systems like payroll or accounts payable software. One person should not be able to modify financial data without being detected, so they should not have modification rights and also be charged with monitoring for changes.

Succession Planning This is important to ensure continuity for roles, regardless of the reason a person leaves your organization. A departing staff member can take critical expertise and skills with them, leaving important duties unattended or tasks unperformed. When a manager or supervisor leaves, not having a succession plan can also result in a lack of oversight for functions, making it easier for other personnel issues to occur without being caught.

Background Checks These are commonly performed before employees are hired to ensure that the candidates are suitable for employment with the organization.

Termination When an employee quits or is terminated, it is important to ensure that their access to organizational resources and accounts is also terminated. This requires reviewing their access and ensuring that the organization's separation process properly handles retrieving any organizational property like laptops, mobile devices, and data. In many organizations, accounts are initially disabled (often by changing the password to one the current user does not know). This ensures that data is not lost and can be accessed by the organization if needed. Once you know that any data associated with the account is no longer needed, you can then delete the account itself.

Cross Training Cross training focuses on teaching employees skills that enable them to take on tasks that their coworkers and other staff members normally perform. This can help to prevent single points of failure due to skillsets and can also help to detect issues caused by an employee or a process by bringing someone who is less familiar with the task or procedure into the loop. Cross training is commonly used to help ensure that critical capabilities have backups in place since it can help prevent issues with employee separation when an indispensable employee leaves. It is also an important part of enabling other security controls. Succession planning and mandatory vacation are made easier if appropriate cross training occurs.

Dual Control Dual control is useful when a process is so sensitive that it is desirable to require two individuals to perform an action together. The classic example of this appears in many movies in the form of a dual-control system that requires two military officers to insert and turn their keys at the same time to fire a nuclear weapon.

Of course, this isn't likely to be necessary in your organization, but dual control may be a useful security control when sensitive tasks are involved because it requires both parties to collude for a breach to occur. This is often seen in organizations that require two signatures for checks over a certain value. Dual control can be implemented as either an administrative control via procedures or via technical controls.

Mandatory Vacation This process requires staff members to take vacation, allowing you to identify individuals who are exploiting the rights they have. Mandatory vacation prevents employees from hiding issues or taking advantage of their privileges by ensuring that they are not continuously responsible for a task.

When mandatory vacation is combined with separation of duties, it can provide a highly effective way to detect employee collusion and malfeasance. Sending one or more employees involved in a process on vacation offers an opportunity for a third party to observe any issues or irregularities in the processes that the employees on vacation normally handle.

Analyzing Security Architecture

The key to analyzing a security infrastructure for an organization is to identify where defenses are weak, or where an attacker may be able to exploit flaws in architectural design, processes, procedures, or in the underlying technology like vulnerabilities or misconfigurations. Control gaps, single points of failure, and improperly implemented controls are all common issues that you are likely to encounter.

Penetration testers also perform security architecture analysis when they are working to find ways through an organization's security. It can help to think like a penetration tester (or an attacker!) when you're reviewing a security architecture for flaws.

Analyzing Security Requirements

Security architectures can be analyzed based on their attributes by reviewing the security model and ensuring that it meets a specific requirement. For example, if you were asked to review a workstation security design that used antimalware software to determine if it would prevent unwanted software from being installed, you might identify three scenarios:

Success Antimalware software can successfully prevent unwanted software installation if the software is known malware or if it behaves in a way that the antimalware software will detect as unwanted.

Failure It will not detect software that is not permitted by organizational policy but that is not malware.

Failure It may not prevent unknown malware, or malware that does not act in ways that are typical of known malware.

This type of attribute-based testing can be performed based on a risk assessment and control plan to determine whether the security architecture meets the control objectives. It can also be directly applied to each control by determining the goal of each control and then reviewing whether it meets that goal.

Reviewing Architecture

In addition to a requirement-based analysis method, a number of formal architectural models rely on views, or viewpoints, from which the architecture and controls can be reviewed. Common views that can be taken when reviewing an architecture include the following:

- *Operational views* describe how a function is performed, or what it accomplishes. This view typically shows how information flows but does not capture the technical detail about how data is transmitted, stored, or captured. Operational views are useful for understanding what is occurring and often influence procedural or administrative controls.
- *Technical views* (sometimes called service-oriented, or systems-based, views) focus on the technologies, settings, and configurations used in an architecture. This can help identify incorrect configurations and insecure design decisions. An example of a technical view might include details like the TLS version of a connection, or the specific settings for password length and complexity required for user accounts.
- A *logical view* is sometimes used to describe how systems interconnect. It is typically less technically detailed than a technical view but conveys broader information about how a system or service connects or works. The network diagrams earlier in this chapter are examples of logical views.

Security architecture reviews may need any or all of these viewpoints to provide a complete understanding of where issues may exist.

Formal security frameworks have different views, adding specific viewpoints based on their requirements. The British Ministry of Defense's Architecture Framework (MODAF) uses seven categories: strategic, operational, service oriented, systems, acquisition, technical, and the "all viewpoint," which describes the architecture. The U.S. Department of Defense (DoD) uses a similar set of views for architectural review: all, capability, data and information, project, services, standards, and systems viewpoints are considered in the DoD model.

Common Issues

Analyzing security architectures requires an understanding of the design concepts and controls they commonly use as well as the issues that are most frequently encountered in those designs. Four of the most commonly encountered design issues are single points of failure, data validation and trust problems, user issues, and authentication and authorization security and process problems.

Single Points of Failure

A key element to consider when analyzing a layered security architecture is the existence of single points of failure—a single point of the system where, if that component, control, or system fails, the entire system will not work or will fail to provide the desired level of security.

Figure 7.4 shows a fully redundant network design with fault-tolerant firewalls, routers, and core switches. Each device communicates with its partner via a heartbeat link, which provides status and synchronization information. If a device's partner fails, it will take over, providing continuity of service. Each device is also cross-linked, allowing any component to send traffic to the devices in front of and behind it via multiple paths, removing a failed wire as a potential point of failure. Similar protections would be in place for power protection, and the devices would typically be physically located in separate racks or even rooms to prevent a single physical issue from disrupting service.

FIGURE 7.4 A fully redundant network edge design

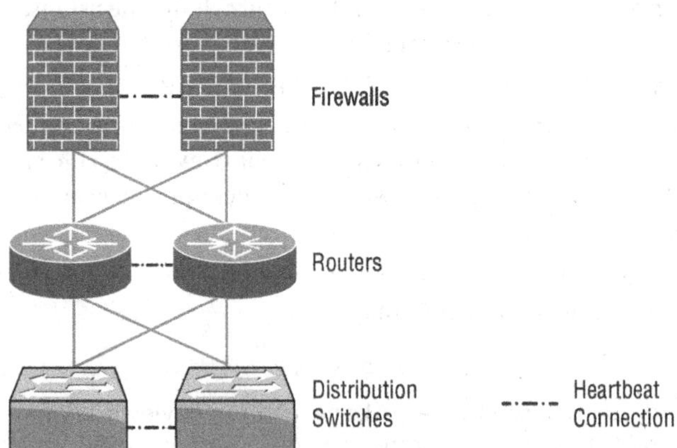

Network and infrastructure design diagrams can make spotting a potential single point of failure much easier. In Figure 7.5, the same redundant network's internal design shows a single point of failure (Point A) at the distribution router and edge switch layers. Here, a failure of a link, the router, or the switches might take down a section of the network, rather than the organization's primary Internet link. In situations like this, a single point of failure may be acceptable based on the organization's risk profile and functional requirements.

FIGURE 7.5 Single points of failure in a network design

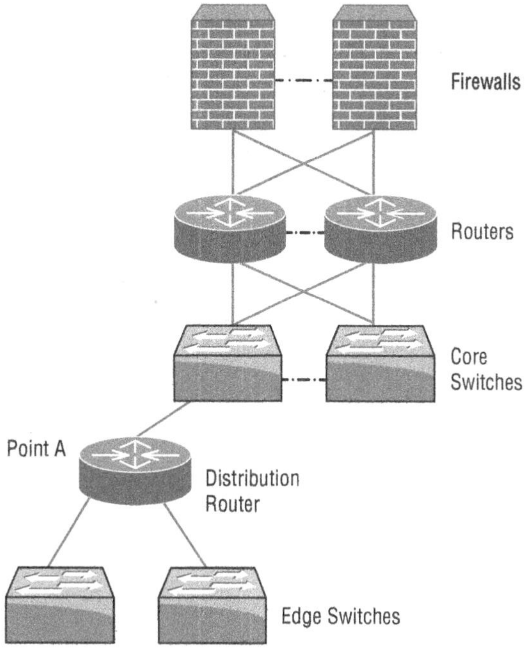

Redundant Layers of Failure

Having a redundant system doesn't guarantee that systems will work. The authors of this book worked with a redundant firewall system that used a heartbeat function for an active/passive pair. In this design, one firewall was always active, and if it failed, the secondary firewall would take over as the active partner. If the primary firewall then resumed function, it would determine that it should then take the passive role, and normal function would continue.

At least, that's how the system was designed. Unfortunately, a software update caused the heartbeat system to fail, resulting in both firewalls determining that their partner was offline. Both firewalls then set themselves to active mode, resulting in network traffic being routed erratically through each firewall as they wrestled for control of the traffic that was supposed to flow through them. Some traffic did make it through, but the failure of the partnering system essentially stopped all traffic into and out of a production datacenter.

In this scenario, the firewall administrators were able to turn off the secondary firewall and then worked to revert it to the software version before the flaw was introduced. They then restored the firewall, failed over to it manually from the primary, and then reverted the broken patch back on the primary firewall to return to a known good state.

The same analysis process can be used to identify issues with applications, processes, and control architectures. A block diagram is created that includes all the critical components or controls, and the flow that the diagram supports is traced through the diagram. Figure 7.6 shows a sample flow diagram for an account creation process. Note that at point A, an authorized requester files a request for a new account, and at point B, a manager approves the account creation. During process analysis a flaw would be noted if the manager can both request and approve an account creation. If the review at point D is also performed by the manager, this process flaw would be even more severe. This provides a great case for separation of duties as an appropriate and useful control!

FIGURE 7.6 Single points of failure in a process flow

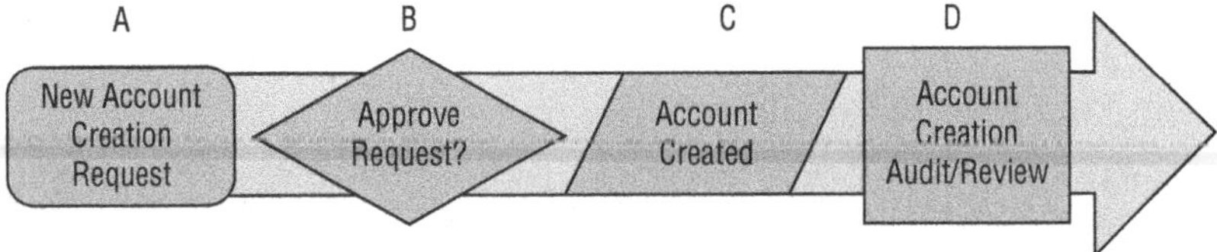

Data Validation and Trust

The ability to trust data that is used for data processing or to make decisions is another area where security issues frequently occur. Data is often assumed to be valid, and incorrect or falsified data can result in significant issues. The ability to rely on data can be enhanced by

- Protecting data at rest and in transit using encryption
- Validating data integrity using file integrity checking tools, or otherwise performing data integrity validation
- Implementing processes to verify data in an automated or a manual fashion
- Profiling or boundary checking data based on known attributes of the data

Web application security testers are very familiar with exploiting weaknesses in data validation schemes. Insecure web applications often trust that the data they receive from a page that they generate is valid and then use that data for further tasks. For example, if an item costs $25 and the application pulls that data from a hidden field found in a web form but does not validate that the data it receives matches a value it should accept, an attacker could change the value to $0 and might get the item for free! Validating that the data you receive either matches the specific dataset you expect or is at least in a reasonable range is a critical step in layered security design.

When analyzing data flows, storage, and usage, remember to look for places where data issues could cause high-impact failures. Data validation issues at some points in a design can be far more critical to the overall design than they are at other points, making effective control placement extremely important in those locations.

When assessing data validation and trust controls, it can help to work backward by asking yourself "What would happen if the data were incorrect, or worse, if it an attacker could change it to anything they wanted to?"

Users

Human error is a frequent cause of failure in security architectures. Mistakes, malfeasance, or social engineering attacks that target staff members can all break security designs. Layered security designs should be built with the assumption that the humans who carry out the procedures and processes that it relies on may make mistakes and should be designed to identify and alert if intentional violations occur.

Failures due to users are often limited by

- Using automated monitoring and alerting systems to detect human error
- Constraining interfaces to only allow permitted activities
- Implementing procedural checks and balances like separation of duties and the other personnel controls previously discussed in this chapter
- Training and awareness programs designed to help prepare staff for the types of threats they are likely to encounter

Identifying possible issues caused by users is often useful to brainstorm with experts on the systems or processes. When that isn't possible, reviewing how user actions are monitored and controlled can help point to possible gaps.

A practical example of this type of review occurs in grocery stores where it is common practice to issue a cashier a cash drawer to take to their station. Sometimes, the cashier counts out their own drawer before starting a shift; in other cases they are given a cash drawer with a standard and verified amount of money. During their shift, they are the only users of that drawer, and at the end of the shift, they count out the drawer and have it verified or work with a manager to count it out. If there continued to be loss at grocery store, you might walk through the cashier's tasks, asking them at each step what task they are performing and how it is validated. When you identify an area where an issue could occur, you can then work to identify controls to prevent that issue.

Authentication and Authorization

User credentials, passwords, and user rights are all areas that often create issues in security designs. Common problems include inappropriate or overly broad user rights, poor credential security or management, embedded and stored passwords and keys, as well as reliance on passwords to protect critical systems. Security designs that seek to avoid these issues often implement solutions like

- Multifactor authentication
- Centralized account and privilege management and monitoring
- Privileged account usage monitoring
- Training and awareness efforts

When analyzing a security design for potential authentication and authorization issues, the first step is to identify where authentication occurs, how authorization is performed, and what rights are needed and provided to users. Once you understand those, you can focus on the controls that are implemented and where those controls may leave gaps. Remember to consider technical, process, and human factors.

Cloud computing and other outsourcing models can make security designs even more complex. Fortunately, sample cloud security architecture models have started to become available. NIST, the U.S. National Institute of Standards and Technology, released the NIST Cloud Computing Security Reference Architecture in 2013, providing a useful reference for organizations that need to design or assess cloud security designs. You can find it at `collaborate.nist.gov/twiki-cloud-computing/pub/CloudComputing/CloudSecurity/NIST_Security_Reference_Architecture_2013.05.15_v1.0.pdf`.

Reviewing a Security Architecture

Reviewing a security architecture requires step-by-step analysis of the security needs that influenced a design and the controls that were put in place. Figure 7.7 shows a high-level design for a web application with a database backend. To analyze this, we can first start with a statement of the design requirements for the service:

> The web application is presented to customers via the Internet, and contains customer business sensitive data. It must be fault-tolerant, secure against web application attacks, and should provide secure authentication and authorization, as well as appropriate security monitoring and system security.

From this, we can review the design for potential flaws. Starting from the left, we will step through each section looking for possible issues. It's important to note that this example won't cover every possible flaw with this design. Instead, this is meant as an example of how a review might identify flaws based on a network logical diagram.

- The Internet connection, as shown, has a single path. This could cause an availability issue.

- There is no IDS or IPS between the Internet and the web server layer. This may be desirable to handle attacks that the WAF and the firewall layer cannot detect.
- The diagram does not show how the network security devices like firewalls and the WAF are managed. Exposure of management ports via public networks is a security risk.
- The web application firewall and the load balancers are shown as clustered devices. This may indicate an availability issue.
- There is no active detection security layer between the web server and the databases. A SQL-aware security device would provide an additional layer of security.

FIGURE 7.7 Sample security architecture

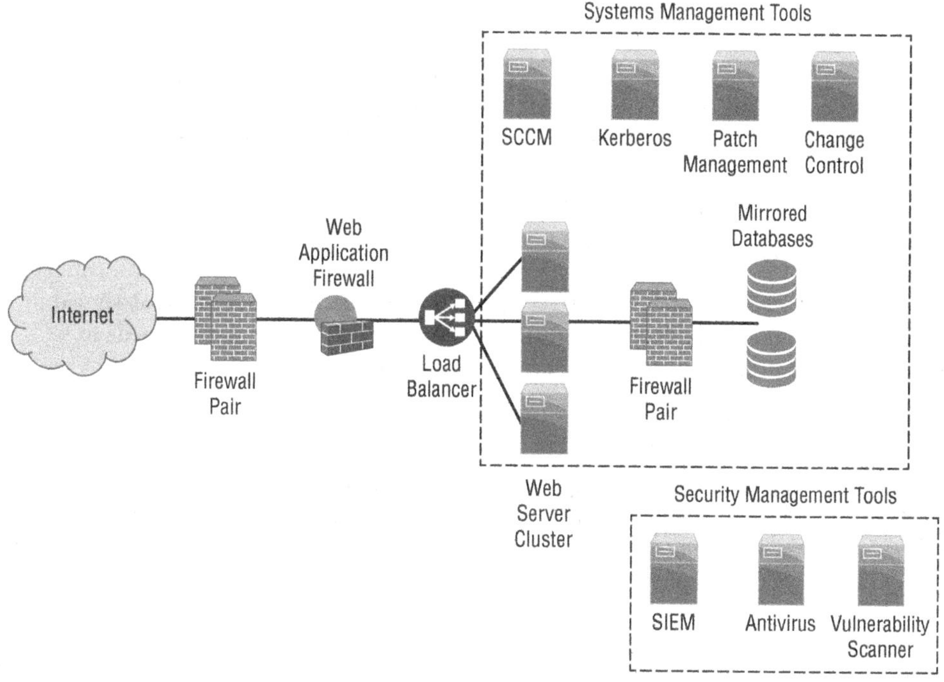

In addition to the information that the logical diagram shows, review of a dataflow diagram, configurations, processes, and procedures would each provide useful views to ensure this design provides an appropriate level of security.

Maintaining a Security Design

Security designs need to continue to address the threats and requirements that they were built to address. Over time, new threats may appear, old threats may stop being a concern, technology will change, and organizational capabilities will be different. That means that they need to be reviewed, improved, and eventually retired.

Scheduled Reviews

A security design should undergo periodical, scheduled reviews. The frequency of the reviews may vary depending on how quickly threats that the organization faces change; how often its systems, networks, and processes change; if regulator or contractual requirements change; and if a major security event occurs that indicates that a review may be needed.

It may seem obvious, but recording the last change date for a security design or program can help track when a review was done. A date in the header of a design file is useful when you are quickly reviewing what has been done.

Continual Improvement

Continual improvement processes (sometimes called CIP or CI processes) are designed to provide incremental improvements over time. A security program or design needs to be assessed on a recurring basis, making a continuous improvement process important to ensure that the design does not become outdated.

Another word frequently used in improvement processes is *kaizen*, a Japanese word that translates to "good change." A kaizen continuous improvement approach is often used in manufacturing and in lean programming and places the responsibility for improvement in the hands of all employees, not just an improvement group or team.

Retirement of Processes

Security processes and policies may become outdated, and instead of updating, they may need to be retired. This is often the case for one of a few reasons:

- The process or policy is no longer relevant.
- It has been superseded by a newer policy or process.
- The organization no longer wants to use the policy or process.

Retirement of processes and policies should be documented and recorded in the document that describes it. Once a decision has been made, appropriate communication needs to occur to ensure that it is no longer used and that individuals and groups who used the process or policy are aware of its replacement if appropriate.

Summary

Security controls should be layered to ensure that the failure of a control does not result in the failure of the overall security architecture of an organization, system, or service. Layered security designs may provide uniform protection or may implement design choices that place more sensitive systems or data in protected enclaves. It may also use analysis of threats or data classifications as the foundation for design decisions. In any complete security design, multiple controls are implemented together to create a stronger security design that can prevent attacks, detect problems, and allow for appropriate response and recovery in the event that a failure does occur.

Layered security designs often use segmentation and network security devices to separate networks and systems based on functional or other distinctions. Systems also require layered security, and tools like host firewalls, data loss prevention software, antivirus and antimalware software, and system configuration and monitoring tools, all providing parts of the host security puzzle. Other common parts of a layered security design include encryption, logging and monitoring, and personnel security, as well as policies, processes, and standards. Attribute-based assessments of security models rely on verifying that a design meets security requirements. Views of the architecture should be used to ensure that the design holds up from multiple perspectives, including operational, technical, and logical paths through the security design. Single points of failure, trust and data validation problems, authentication and authorization issues, and user-related concerns are all important to consider when looking for flaws. All of this means that security designs should undergo regular review and updates to stay ahead of changing needs and new security threats.

Exam Essentials

Know why security solutions are an important part of infrastructure management. Layered security, including segmentation at the physical and/or virtual level, as well as use of concepts like system isolation and air gapping, is part of a strong defensive design. The network architecture for physical, virtual, and cloud environments must leverage secure design concepts as well as security tools like honeypots, firewalls, and other technologies.

Explain what implementing defense-in-depth requires. Common designs use segmentation to separate different security levels or areas where security needs differ. Network architecture in many organizations needs to take into account physical network devices and design, cloud options, and software-defined networks. Cloud tools like virtual private clouds and tools like cloud access security brokers should be considered where appropriate. A wide range of controls can help with this, ranging from use of appropriate permissions, whitelisting, and blacklisting to technical controls like firewalls, intrusion prevention and detection systems, data loss prevention (DLP) tools, and endpoint detection and response.

Know that understanding requirements and identifying potential points of failure are part of security architecture analysis. Single points of failure are design elements where a single failure can cause the design to fail to function as intended. Other common issues include data validation issues, problems caused by trust and requirements for trust versus whether the data or system can be trusted, user-related failures, and authentication and authorization processes and procedures.

Know that maintaining layered security designs requires continual review and validation. Scheduled reviews help to ensure that the design has not become outdated. Continual improvement processes keep layered defense designs current while helping to engage staff and provide ongoing awareness. At the end of their life cycle, processes, procedures, and technical designs must be retired with appropriate notification and documentation.

Lab Exercises

Activity 7.1: Review an Application Using the OWASP Attack Surface Analysis Cheat Sheet

In this exercise you will use the Open Web Application Security Project Application Attack Surface Analysis Cheat Sheet. If you are not completely familiar with an application in your organization, you may find it helpful to talk to an application administrator, DevOps engineer, or developer.

Part 1: Review the OWASP Attack Surface Analysis Cheat Sheet. The cheat sheet can be found at `cheatsheetseries.owasp.org/cheatsheets/Attack_Surface_Analysis_Cheat_Sheet.html`.

Review the cheat sheet, and make sure that you understand how application attack surfaces are mapped. If you're not familiar with the topic area, spend some time researching it.

Part 2: Select an application you are familiar with and follow the cheat sheet to map the application's attack surface. Select an application that you have experience with from your professional experience and follow the cheat sheet. If you do not know an answer, note that you cannot identify the information and move on.

Part 3: Measure the application's attack surface. Use your responses to analyze the application's attack surface. Answer the following questions:

1. What are the high-risk attack surface areas?
2. What entry points exist for the application?
3. Can you calculate the Relative Attack Surface Quotient for the application using the data you have? If not, why not?
4. What did you learn by doing this mapping?

Part 4: Manage the attack surface. Using your mapping, identify how (and if!) you should modify the application's attack surface. What would you change and why? Are there controls or decisions that you would make differently in different circumstances?

Activity 7.2: Review a NIST Security Architecture

The graphic on the next page shows the NIST access authorization information flow and its control points in a logical flow diagram as found in NIST SP1800-5b. This NIST architecture uses a number of important information gathering and analytical systems:

- Fathom, a system that provides anomaly detection
- BelManage, which monitors installed software
- Bro, an IDS
- Puppet, an open source configuration management tool that is connected to the organization's change management process
- Splunk, for searching, monitoring, and analyzing machine-generated big data, via a web-style interface
- Snort, an IDS
- WSUS for Windows updates
- OpenVAS, an open source vulnerability management tool
- Asset Central, an asset tracking system
- CA ITAM, which also tracks physical assets
- iSTAR Edge, a physical access control system

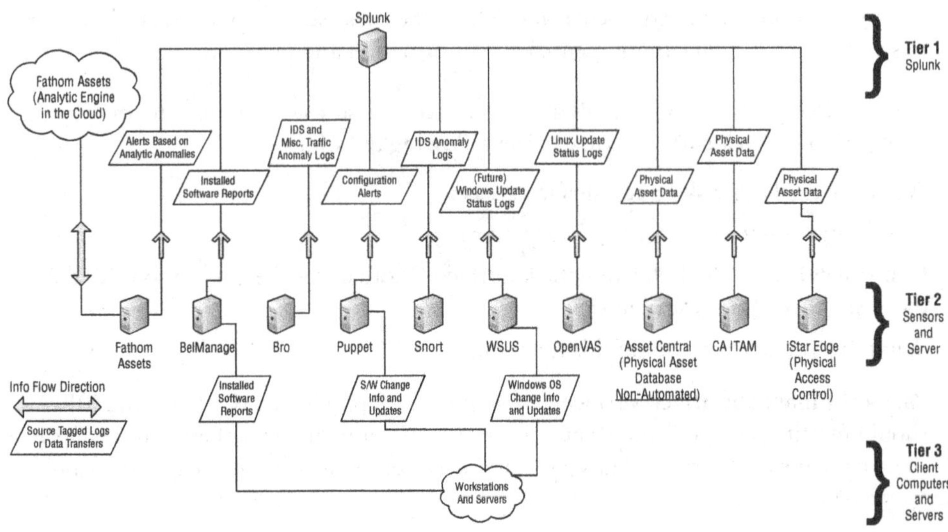

Make note of potential issues with this diagram, marking where you would apply additional controls or where a single failure might lead to a systemwide failure. Additional details about the specific systems and capabilities can be found in the NIST ITAM draft at `nccoe.nist.gov/sites/default/files/library/sp1800/fs-itam-nist-sp1800-5b-draft.pdf`.

Activity 7.3: Security Architecture Terminology

Match each of the following terms to the correct description.

Air gap	A logically isolated segment of a cloud that provides you with control of your own environment.
Containerization	An access control mechanism that allows through all things except those that are specifically blocked.
VPC	A physical separation between devices or networks to prevent access.
Cloud access security broker	A system that scans outbound traffic and prevents it from being transmitted if it contains specific content types.
Blacklisting	A system that validates systems and sometimes users before they connect to a network.
Asset tagging	Software or a service that enforces security for cloud applications.

Air gap	A logically isolated segment of a cloud that provides you with control of your own environment.
NAC	A technology that bundles together an application and the files, libraries, and other dependencies it needs to run, allowing the application to be deployed to multiple platforms or systems.
Data loss prevention	Labeling or otherwise identifying systems, devices, or other items.

Review Questions

1. Susan needs to explain what a jump box is to a member of her team. What should she tell them?
   A. It is a secured system that is exposed in a DMZ.
   B. It is a system used to access and manage systems or devices in the same security zone.
   C. It is a system used to skip revisions during updates.
   D. It is a system used to access and manage systems or devices in another security zone.
2. Ben sets up a system that acts like a vulnerable host in order to observe attacker behavior. What type of system has he set up?
   A. A sinkhole
   B. A blackhole
   C. A honeypot
   D. A beehive
3. Cameron builds a malware signature using a hash of the binary that he found on an infected system. What problem is he likely to encounter with modern malware when he tries to match hashes with other infected systems?
   A. The malware may be polymorphic.
   B. The hashes may match too many malware packages.
   C. The attackers may have encrypted the binary.
   D. The hash value may be too long.
4. Ric is reviewing his organization's network design and is concerned that a known flaw in the border router could let an attacker disable their Internet connectivity. Which of the following is an appropriate compensatory control?
   A. An identical second redundant router set up in an active/passive design
   B. An alternate Internet connectivity method using a different router type

- **C.** An identical second redundant router set up in an active/active design
- **D.** A firewall in front of the router to stop any potential exploits that could cause a failure of connectivity

5. Fred wants to ensure that only software that has been preapproved runs on workstations he manages. What solution will best fit this need?
   - **A.** Blacklisting
   - **B.** Antivirus
   - **C.** Whitelisting
   - **D.** Virtual desktop infrastructure (VDI)

6. A member of Susan's team recently fell for a phishing scam and provided his password and personal information to a scammer. What layered security approach is not an appropriate layer for Susan to implement to protect her organization from future issues?
   - **A.** Multifactor authentication
   - **B.** Multitiered firewalls
   - **C.** An awareness program
   - **D.** A SIEM monitoring where logins occur

7. Chris is in charge of his organization's Windows security standard, including their Windows 7 security standard, and has recently decommissioned the organization's last Windows 7 system. What is the next step in his security standard's life cycle?
   - **A.** A scheduled review of the Windows standards
   - **B.** A final update to the standard, noting that Windows 7 is no longer supported
   - **C.** Continual improvement of the Windows standards
   - **D.** Retiring the Windows 7 standard

8. Example Corporation has split their network into network zones that include sales, HR, research and development, and guest networks, each separated from the others using network security devices. What concept is Example Corporation using for their network security?
   - **A.** Segmentation
   - **B.** Multiple-interface firewalls
   - **C.** Single-point-of-failure avoidance
   - **D.** Zoned routing

9. Which of the following layered security controls is commonly used at the WAN, LAN, and host layer in a security design?
   - **A.** Encryption of data at rest
   - **B.** Firewalls
   - **C.** DMZs
   - **D.** Antivirus

10. After a breach that resulted in attackers successfully exfiltrating a sensitive database, Jason has been asked to deploy a technology that will prevent similar issues in the future. What technology is best suited to this requirement?

    A. Firewalls

    B. IDS

    C. DLP

    D. EDR

11. Michelle has been asked to review her corporate network's design for single points of failure that would impact the core network operations. The following graphic shows a redundant network design with a critical fault: a single point of failure that could take the network offline if it failed. Where is this single point of failure?

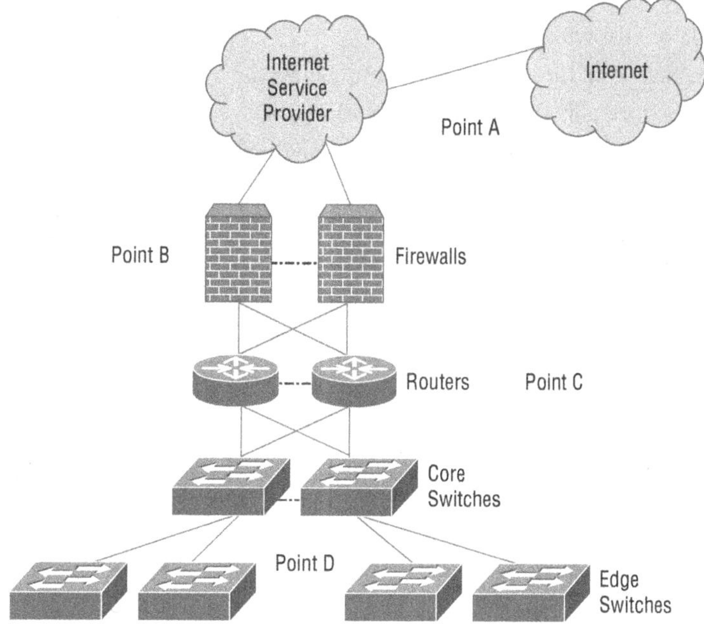

    A. Point A

    B. Point B

    C. Point C

    D. Point D

12. During a penetration test of Anna's company, the penetration testers were able to compromise the company's web servers and deleted their log files, preventing analysis of their attacks. What compensating control is best suited to prevent this issue in the future?

    A. Using full-disk encryption

    B. Using log rotation

C. Sending logs to a syslog server

D. Using TLS to protect traffic

13. Which of the following controls is best suited to prevent vulnerabilities related to software updates?

A. Operating system patching standards

B. Centralized patch management software

C. Vulnerability scanning

D. An IPS with appropriate detections enabled

14. Ben's organization uses data loss prevention software that relies on metadata tagging to ensure that sensitive files do not leave the organization. What compensating control is best suited to ensuring that data that does leave is not exposed?

A. Mandatory data tagging policies

B. Encryption of all files sent outside the organization

C. DLP monitoring of all outbound network traffic

D. Network segmentation for sensitive data handling systems

15. James is concerned that network traffic from his datacenter has increased and that it may be caused by a compromise that his security tools have not identified. What SIEM analysis capability could he use to look at the traffic over time sent by his datacenter systems?

A. Automated reporting

B. Trend analysis

C. BGP graphing

D. Log aggregation

16. Angela needs to implement a control to ensure that she is notified of changes to important configuration files on her server. What type of tool should she use for this control?

A. Antimalware

B. Configuration management

C. File integrity checking

D. Logging

17. Megan has recently discovered that the Linux server she is responsible for maintaining is affected by a zero-day exploit for a vulnerability in the web application software that is needed by her organization. Which of the following compensating controls should she implement to best protect the server?

A. A WAF

B. Least privilege for accounts

C. A patch from the vendor

D. An IDS

18. Mike installs a firewall in front of a previously open network to prevent the systems behind the firewall from being targeted by external systems. What did Mike do?

A. Reduced the organization's attack surface

B. Implemented defense-in-depth

C. Added a corrective control

D. Added an administrative control

19. Port security refers to what type of security control?

A. Allowing only specific MAC addresses to access a network port

B. The controls used to protect port when oceangoing vessels dock

C. A technical control that requires authentication by a user before a port is used

D. A layer 3 filter applied to switch ports

20. Tony configures his network to provide false DNS responses for known malware domains. What technique is he using?

A. Blacklisting

B. Whitelisting

C. Sinkholing

D. Honeypotting

Identity and Access Management Security

THE COMPTIA CYBERSECURITY ANALYST (CYSA+) EXAM OBJECTIVES COVERED IN THIS CHAPTER INCLUDE:

✓ **Domain 2.0: Software and Systems Security**

- 2.1 Given a scenario, apply security solutions for infrastructure management.

Identities—the collection of user information, credentials, rights, roles, group memberships, and other attributes and information about individuals and accounts—are among the most critical assets that an organization owns. Identities, and the access and rights that we grant to them, provide the keys to systems, services, and data, making them targets for both internal and external attackers.

As organizational security has improved, the ability of attackers to simply target unpatched or unprotected systems exposed to the Internet has decreased, making it increasingly necessary for them to obtain accounts to gain and maintain access to their targets. Now, attackers frequently need to have valid user credentials to compromise systems, networks, or services. This means you need to understand both the threats that identity and access systems and technologies face and how to defend against them.

In this chapter, we will explore the major threats to identities, credentials, and the authentication, authorization, and accounting systems behind them. We will look at the ways in which identity can be used as a security layer to provide an important part of a defense-in-depth plan and will review how identity management integrates into a security operations design. Finally, we will discuss federated identities and single sign-on security, an increasingly important element of both cloud services and many organizational support strategies.

Understanding Identity

Identities, or the set of claims made about an individual or account holder that are made about one party to another party (such as a service provider, application, or system), are a key part of authentication, authorization, and accounting. The user accounts we use to log in require the ability to uniquely identify individuals and other *subjects* such as services to allow for permissions, rights, group memberships, and attributes to be associated with them.

The attributes associated with an identity include information about a subject and often include their name, address, title, contact information, and other details about the individual. These attributes may be used as part of authentication processes, may be used to populate *directory* information, or could be collected to help meet other organizational needs or business purposes.

Some schemes call out traits and preferences separately from attributes. In those designs, traits are inherent parts of the subject like their hair color, nationality, or birthday. Preferences are based on a person's choices like their favorite color or band.

Identities are used as part of the *authentication*, *authorization*, and *accounting* (*AAA*) framework that is used to control access to computers, networks, and services. AAA systems authenticate users by requiring credentials like a username, a password, and possibly a biometric or token-based authenticator. Once individuals have proven who they are, they are then authorized to access or use resources or systems. Authorization applies policies based on the user's identity information and rules or settings, allowing the owner of the identity to perform actions or to gain access to systems. The ongoing management of these rights is known as *privilege management*. The accounting element of the AAA process is the logging and monitoring that goes with the authentication and authorization. Accounting monitors usage and provides information about how and what users are doing.

Exam Note

Pay particular attention to the concept of privilege management—it shows up in the exam objectives, and we discuss it throughout the chapter.

Central management of identities normally occurs in *identity and access management* (*IAM*) systems. IAM systems are built to create, store, and manage identity information as well as the permissions, groups, and other information needed to support the use of identities. Figure 8.1 shows a high-level view of identity management for an organization. The data to create identities comes from systems of record like the organization's ERP, HR systems, or customer databases. The data is supplied to the identity management systems and services, which provide account creation, provisioning, management, and oversight for the organization. Those systems then offer authentication and authorization services to identity consumers like servers, workstations, services, and third-party service providers.

Identity Systems and Security Design

Identity systems provide a number of common functions: identity creation and management, authentication and authorization, and in some cases, federation of identity information to allow use of identities outside of their home organization. To enable this, a number of common technologies are used: directories, authentication services, identity management platforms, and federated identity tools.

FIGURE 8.1 A high-level logical view of identity management infrastructure

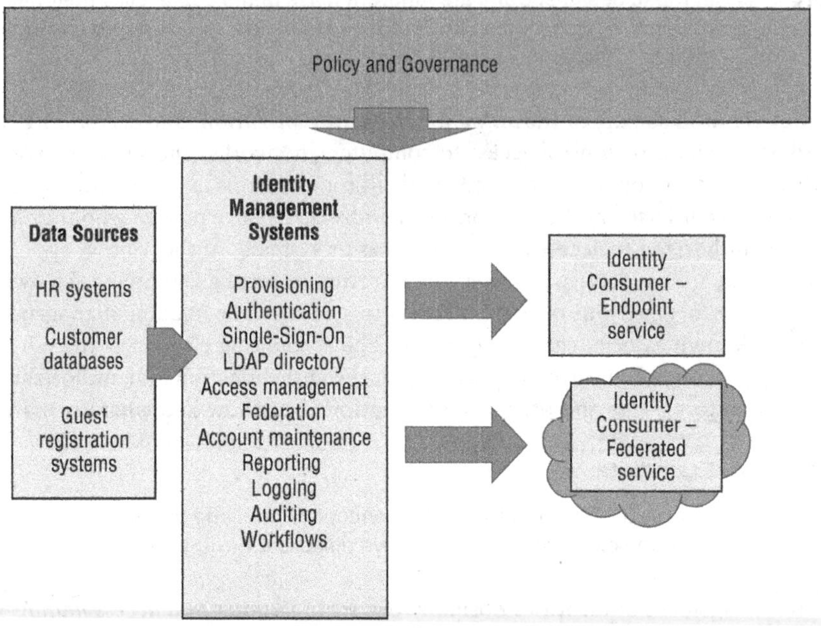

Exam Note

The CySA+ exam objectives for the CS-002 version of the exam removed many of the IAM-related topics found in the CS-001 first exam edition, and in fact reduced identity down to a sub-bullet. So why is there a whole chapter on identity management? After a lot of discussion, we wanted to make sure that we provided context for the elements that remain. Identity is a critical security layer for most organizations. To help you with the exam, we'll call out the specific areas that are in the exam objectives throughout the chapter.

Directories

Directory services are used in networks to provide information about systems, users, and other information about an organization. Directory services like *LDAP* (the Lightweight Directory Access Protocol) are commonly deployed as part of an identity management infrastructure and offer hierarchically organized information about the organization. They are frequently used to make available an organizational directory for email and other contact information.

Figure 8.2 shows an example LDAP directory hierarchy for `example.com`, where there are two organizational units (OUs): security and human resources. Each of those units includes a number of entries labeled with a common name (CN). In addition to the structure shown in the diagram, each entry would have additional information not shown in this simplified diagram, including a distinguished name, an email address, phone numbers, office location, and other details.

FIGURE 8.2 LDAP directory structure

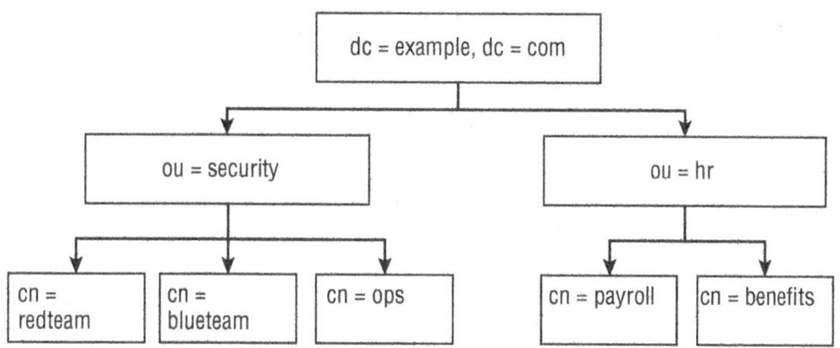

There are a number of open source LDAP server implementations, including OpenLDAP, 389 Directory Server, ApacheDS, and OpenDJ, as well as commercial software like Oracle's Internet Directory, Microsoft's Active Directory, IBM's Security Directory Server, and CA Directory. Thus, steps required to implement a secure LDAP server will vary, but some of the common considerations remain the same. These include the following:

- Enabling and requiring TLS to keep LDAP queries and authentication secure.
- Setting password storage to use a secure method. LDAP passwords are often stored in plain text, but additional methods are supported and should be used if possible.

While LDAP implementations vary, OpenLDAP has historically been one of the most common choices. When using OpenLDAP, the SSHA password storage scheme uses a salted SHA (Secure Hash Algorithm) hash for password storage. This is stronger than the CRYPT, MD5, SHA, and Simple Authentication and Security Layer (SASL) schemes that OpenLDAP supports. Understanding details of how your specific LDAP server works can make a major difference in how secure it is in practice.

- Using password-based authentication and requiring TLS. LDAP provides three modes of operation: anonymous, unauthenticated, and username/password authenticated. When authenticated sessions are turned on, unauthenticated mode should be disabled to prevent issues with unsecured connections.

- Replication of LDAP servers, which can help to prevent denial-of-service attacks and other service outages.
- Access control lists for LDAP, which offer the ability to limit access to specific objects in the directory as well as overall rules for how entries are created, modified, and deleted.

Since directories contain significant amounts of organizational data and may be used to support a range of services, including directory-based authentication, they must be well protected. The same set of needs often means that directory servers should be publicly exposed to provide services to systems or business partners who need to access the directory information. In those cases, additional security, tighter access controls, or even an entirely separate public directory service may be needed.

One of the most common attacks on web services that use LDAP is LDAP injection, which uses improperly filtered user input via web applications to send arbitrary LDAP queries. Details, and a cheat sheet on how to avoid it, can be found at `cheatsheetseries.owasp.org/cheatsheets/LDAP_Injection_Prevention_Cheat_Sheet.html`.

Authentication Protocols

Centralized authentication services allow clients to authenticate to a central authentication service, which then supplies verification of the user's identity to the relying system. Central authentication services may also provide authorization information for the user to the relying party, or they may match the identity with their own authorization and rules.

Common authentication protocols include

- *TACACS+*, a Cisco-designed extension to TACAS, the Terminal Access Controller Access Control System. It uses TCP traffic to provide authentication, authorization, and accounting services. TACACS+ suffers from a number of flaws, including a lack of integrity checking for the data it sends, allowing an attacker with access to the traffic it sends to make arbitrary changes or to use replay attacks against the TACACS+ service. TACACS+ also has encryption flaws that can lead to compromise of the encryption key. This means TACACS+ systems that provide AAA services for network devices should operate on an isolated administrative network if possible.
- *RADIUS*, the Remote Authentication Dial-in User Service, is one of the most common AAA systems for network devices, wireless networks, and other services. RADIUS can operate via TCP or UDP and operates in a client-server model. RADIUS sends passwords that are obfuscated by a shared secret and MD5 hash, meaning that its password security is not very strong. RADIUS traffic between the RADIUS network access server and the RADIUS server is typically encrypted using IPSec tunnels or other protections to protect the traffic.

- *Kerberos,* which unlike TACACS+ and RADIUS, is designed to operate on untrusted networks and uses encryption to protect its authentication traffic. Users in Kerberos, called principals, are composed of three elements: the primary (frequently the username), the instance (used to differentiate similar primaries), and the realm, which consists of groups of principals. Realms are often separated on trust boundaries and have distinct key distribution centers (KDCs). Figure 8.3 shows the basic Kerberos authentication flow.

FIGURE 8.3 Kerberos authentication flow

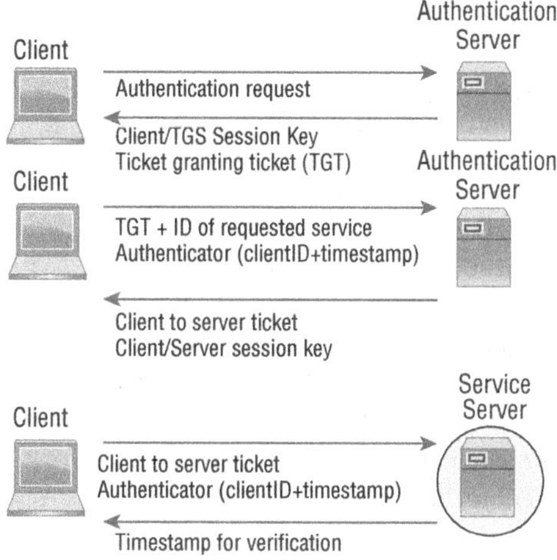

Active Directory (AD) uses the Kerberos protocol for authentication. Older versions of Windows relied on NTLM authentication; however, NTLM is outdated and you are unlikely to encounter it in modern environments. If you do, you'll likely have a lot of other major security worries too!

Single Sign-On and Shared Authentication Schemes

Many web applications rely on *single sign-on (SSO)* systems to allow users to authenticate once and then to use multiple systems or services without having to use different usernames or passwords. *Shared authentication* schemes are somewhat similar to single sign-on and allow an identity to be reused on multiple sites while relying on authentication via a single identity provider. Shared authentication systems require users to enter credentials when authenticating to each site, unlike SSO systems.

Exam Note

The CySA+ exam objectives mention SSO but don't list specific technologies. As you prepare for the exam, make sure you understand the general concept of SSO, why your organization might want to use it, and what security issues it can bring with it.

Common SSO technologies include LDAP and the *Central Authentication Service (CAS)*. Shared authentication technologies include the following:

- *OpenID*, an open source standard for decentralized authentication. OpenID is broadly used by major websites like Google, Amazon, and Microsoft. Users create credentials with an identity provider like Google; then sites (relying parties) use that identity.
- *OAuth*, an open authorization standard. OAuth is used by Google, Microsoft, Facebook, and other sites to allow users to share elements of their identity or account information while authenticating via the original identity provider. OAuth relies on access tokens, which are issued by an authorization server and then presented to resource servers like third-party web applications by clients.
- *OpenID Connect* is an authentication layer built using the OAuth protocol.
- *Facebook Connect,* also known as Login with Facebook, is a shared authentication system that relies on Facebook credentials for authentication.

One of SSO's most significant security benefits is the potential to reduce the occurrence of password reuse. This may also reduce the likelihood of credential exposure via third-party sites when users reuse credential sets. In addition, SSO is popular due to the potential cost savings from fewer password resets and support calls.

Shared authentication systems share some of the same benefits, allowing users to use their credentials without having to create new accounts on each site, thus reducing password fatigue. In addition, users are typically informed about the types of data that will be released to the relying party, such as email account, contact information, gender, or other personal information. Shared authentication systems do not necessarily provide a single sign-on experience.

Of course, SSO systems create risks as well—since SSO makes it easier to access multiple systems and services, it makes it easier for attackers who obtain credentials to access them. SSO may also make it easier for an attacker to exploit additional systems once they control a user's browser or system, as the user will not be required to log in again. This can be partially countered by requiring reauthentication and the use of two-factor authentication for critical systems. Although SSO does create dangers, it is the most common solution for most organizations because of the ease of use it creates.

Access Control Models

In addition to authenticating and authorizing subjects, managing who can access or use resources is a critical part of IAM systems and privilege management. Organizations typically choose an access control model based on such factors as the level of control they need, their security and compliance requirements, and their technical and administrative capability to implement and maintain them.

Exam Note

The updated CySA+ exam objectives removed many of the identity and access control items contained in the first version of the exam but specifically added role-based, attribute-based, and mandatory access control models. If you're focusing solely on what the exam objectives cover, you may want to spend a little extra time right here in the chapter. The outline does not mention rule-based or discretionary access control, although both models are in common use.

You may have noticed that this chapter covers identity in far more depth than the exam objectives give it. That is for two reasons: First, identity and access management is a complex subject both from a security and a technology perspective, and a useful understanding of the topic needs deeper coverage for you to have all the context you need. Second, we cover the topic in more depth because you will likely encounter many of these issues in your security career.

Role-Based Access Control

Often called *RBAC* (and thus, sometimes confused with rule-based access control which can also sometimes be called RBAC), *role-based access control* uses roles associated with job functions or other criteria. Roles are matched to permission sets appropriate to those roles, and then users or other objects like a system or software package are assigned roles.

A subject can have more than one role and may even have more than one active role. On top of this, three common constraints are frequently implemented within role-based access control systems:

- Subjects can only use permissions if they have a role.
- The subject's active role must be one it is authorized to have.
- Subjects can use permissions only if the subject's active role is authorized to use it.

Role-based access control systems can implement both discretionary access control and mandatory access control.

Attribute-Based Access Control

Attribute-based access control (ABAC) gives users rights based on policies. Policies use collections of attributes to determine which access rights to grant, thus building logic-based collections of rights.

ABAC tends to be used when a flexible, context-sensitive access control model is required. Combining attributes that describe the subject (like their role, division, or other personal attributes), the action they are trying to perform, attributes of the object that they are attempting to access or use, and environmental attributes like time of day or location allows complex access control logic with fine-grained control.

Mandatory Access Control

Mandatory access control (MAC) systems rely on the operating system to control what subjects can access and what actions they can perform. Due to this design, MAC usually relies on a system administrator to implement access control policies. Since it is relatively rigid, MAC implementations have typically been associated with military systems, although an increasing number of operating systems and security packages implement MAC capabilities.

Rule-Based Access Control

Rule-based access control systems use a set of rules implemented by an administrator. Access control lists (ACLs) are typically associated with each object, and rules are checked against that ACL when access is requested.

While rule-based access control is sometimes also called RBAC, in most cases it is safe to assume that RBAC means role-based access control unless otherwise specified.

Discretionary Access Control

Discretionary access control (DAC) systems delegate control to the administrators or owners of protected resources like systems or data. This allows delegated control but requires trust in the choices that owners and administrators make, and it can also cause issues due to a lack of central access control.

Validating Access

Ensuring that users don't have more rights than they should is an important part of identity management. In many cases, organizations use *manual review* processes to validate roles and rights, particularly when staff members change jobs or take on a new role. Staff who are charged with permissions management cringe when they hear a request for rights like "Just make my new employee's rights match the person currently in the role" because that person may have other rights that are not appropriate to the role.

The process of manual review can be time consuming and, like any other manual process, can be error prone. Those issues, as well as the use of identity as an effective security layer for organizations, has driven a significant growth in capabilities of identity management solutions that have built-in validation and monitoring tools. Automated tools can remove much of the burden that manual validation creates, especially when paired with tools that look for out-of-the-ordinary user behavior, overly broad privileges, and role grants that do not match the organizational structure.

Exam Note

Manual review is specifically called out in the CySA+ exam objectives, but automated review isn't! Here, it is important to understand that manual reviews are useful and sometimes necessary as part of access control schemes but can require significant effort and time and may be error prone. In most organizations, a combination of manual and automated review processes is likely the best bet to ensure that access control is properly managed.

Threats to Identity and Access

Identity threats can be broadly classified into a handful of major areas. First, threats to the underlying authentication and authorization systems seek to exploit vulnerabilities in the way that users log in, how their credentials are handled, or how they are authorized. Second, attackers may also target the account life cycle by creating credentials, preventing them from being removed, or causing them to have greater privileges associated with them. Third, attackers may focus on accounts themselves, either via phishing or compromising systems where credentials may be stored. Over the next few pages, we will explore attacks on identity repositories and supporting systems, targeting identity management process flaws via the account creation, provisioning, and maintenance process; exploits against identity and authorization systems; how credentials are acquired by attackers; and defenses against these attacks.

Understanding Security Issues with Identities

Identities, including credentials, roles, rights, and permissions, and related data, can face a multitude of security issues. As you consider them, it can help to divide them into a few categories:

- *Personnel*-based identity security, which includes training and awareness, as well as threats like insider attacks, phishing, and social engineering
- *Endpoints* and their role in attacks on identity, including capturing credentials via local exploits; screen capture and keyboard capture applications; local administrative rights; and how password stores, tokens, and other credentials are stored on local systems and devices like phones and tablets
- *Server*-based exploits, which can target the systems that run identity services, or which can attack the servers and send identity and authentication data to AAA services
- *Applications* and *services* that provide, consume, and interact with identity systems
- *Roles,* rights, and permissions that are associated with users or groups

Exam Note

As you prepare for the exam, remember to consider identity security issues from each of these viewpoints. If you are answering questions about a topic like phishing, you may want to consider multiple controls like a training and awareness program and technical measures, including two-factor authentication, email filtering, and reputation-based sender rules.

Attacking AAA Systems and Protocols

Identity repositories like directory systems, authentication systems, and single sign-on services are all attractive targets for attackers. Attacks against identity repositories and systems may target the specific software via vulnerabilities or misconfigurations; they can be aimed at the protocol itself or at how the protocol is implemented.

Attacks at the underlying systems, such as denial-of-service attacks and system compromises, are also common, since taking over the host system can provide full control over an authorization system, giving attackers the keys to the entire kingdom. Since there are a multitude of potential attacks against the many types of identity repositories and authorization systems, we will take a brief look at some of the most common protocols and services to gain an understanding of common threats.

LDAP Attacks

LDAP services are used in many organizations for authentication and directory information. This makes them targets for attackers who want to obtain organizational information or to access systems or applications that rely on LDAP-based authentication.

Attacks against LDAP directory servers typically focus on

- Attacks against insecure binding (connection) methods that target unencrypted LDAP traffic, either to capture the traffic or to exploit LDAP as an authentication service
- Improper LDAP access controls that allow attackers to harvest directory information or to make modifications to directory entries that they should not be able to change
- LDAP injection, which exploits web applications that build LDAP queries using user input, allowing attackers to gather additional information or to make changes they should not be authorized to make by operating as the web service
- Denial-of-service (DsoS) attacks, which can disrupt authentication services that rely on LDAP or cause applications and services that rely on LDAP to fail

Each of these attacks can be prevented or mitigated through careful design and implementation of LDAP services and access methods. Requiring secure binding methods, setting appropriate access controls (and verifying them!), using good web application development practices, and designing a scalable LDAP directory service can all reduce the likelihood of LDAP-related security issues.

LDAP as an Attack Tool

In 2016, the Connectionless LDAP service (CLDAP) was found to be a potential attack vector allowing amplification attacks because it would respond to spoofed addresses, resulting in amplification rates up to 55 times higher than the source traffic. That means that your otherwise innocent-appearing LDAP service could issue a DoS attack on your critical infrastructure without an attacker even making it through other network defenses! You can read more about it at `www.securityweek.com/ldap-attack-vector-makes-terabit-scale-ddos-attacks-possible`.

OAuth, OpenID, and OpenID Connect

OAuth and OpenID are implemented on a per-provider basis, resulting in flaws unique to each party. One of the most common attacks based on this is the use of open redirects. When redirects and forwards are not validated, untrusted user input can be sent to the relying web application, resulting in users being redirected to untrusted sites, allowing phishing scams or permitting attackers to bypass security layers.

The OpenID Connect implementer's guide can be found at `openid.net/connect` and OAuth 2.0 guides can be found at `oauth.net/getting-started`.

Figure 8.4 shows where this occurs in an OAuth flow. If a user accesses a website that is an open redirect endpoint, it will allow URLs at point A to be any redirect URL, instead of a specific URL associated with that site, and if the site also passes that URL forward at point B, attackers can exploit the authorization flow. Fortunately, this won't cause the account associated with the service provider to be compromised—it only causes issues for the site with the open redirect endpoint, since the redirect can result in the phishing scams and similar issues related to untrusted redirects mentioned earlier occurring.

In addition to individual implementation issues, OAuth's broad adoption for cloud services and mobile applications makes it a particularly tempting target for attackers. Poor session management, reliance on a central shared secrets file for OAuth servers, and inadvertent use of plain-text OAuth sessions are all potential issues for OAuth providers.

FIGURE 8.4 OAuth covert redirects

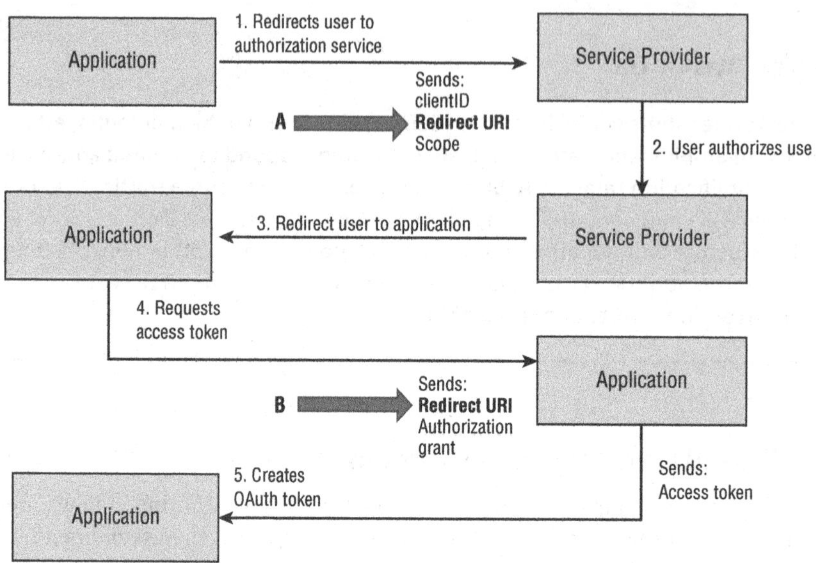

Real World Scenario

OAuth Security and Threat Models

OAuth does not set specific requirements for how the backend of OAuth authentication applications interact with third-party applications, leading to issues with single sign-on applications. To read more about recent exposures, visit `threatpost.com/oauth-2-0-hack-exposes-1-billion-mobile-apps-to-account-hijacking/121889/`. An in-depth discussion of the OAuth 2.0 threat model can be found in RFC 6819, "OAuth 2.0 Threat Model and Security Considerations," at `tools.ietf.org/html/rfc6819`.

Many attacks against OpenID have been aimed at protocol vulnerabilities, including a 2012 discovery related to the ability of attackers to forge OpenID requests in a way that resulted in relying parties allowing arbitrary logins to their services. In addition to protocol attacks, OAuth2 can be vulnerable to cross-site request forgery (CSRF) attacks, which focus on getting a user to click a link that causes that user's browser to perform an action at that user. OpenID Connect offers additional protections for encryption and signing, which, if properly implemented, can help prevent many of the exploits conducted against OpenID services.

Kerberos

Kerberos relies on a central key distribution center (KDC). Compromise of the KDC would allow an attacker to impersonate any user. Kerberos attacks have received significant attention over the past few years due to local attacks against compromised KDCs resulting in complete compromise of Kerberos authenticated systems. Common Kerberos attacks include the following:

- Administrator account attacks.
- Kerberos ticket reuse, including pass-the-ticket attacks, which allows impersonation of legitimate users for the lifespan of the ticket, and pass-the-key attacks, which reuse a secret key to acquire tickets.
- Ticket-granting ticket (TGT)-focused attacks. TGTs are incredibly valuable and can be created with extended lifespans. When attackers succeed in acquiring TGTs, the TGTs are often called "golden tickets" because they allow complete access to the Kerberos-connected systems, including creation of new tickets, account changes, and even falsification of accounts or services.

Automated monitoring of authentication and authorization systems can help detect anomalous behaviors like the creation of a golden ticket—a normal ticket-generating ticket wouldn't have a lifespan of months or years, making behavior-based monitoring an important part of defense against advanced attackers. Details of this attack can be found here: `www.blackhat.com/docs/us-15/materials/us-15-Metcalf-Red-Vs-Blue-Modern-Active-Directory-Attacks-Detection-And-Protection-wp.pdf`.

RADIUS

RADIUS is commonly used for authentication of network devices, including VPNs, network hardware, and similar services. This makes it a tempting target for attackers who want to penetrate the network infrastructure of their targets. RADIUS attacks often focus on the following:

- Session replay of server responses by matching known traffic and replaying previous responses or replaying server responses to authenticate client without valid credentials
- Targeting the RADIUS shared secret, since RADIUS uses a fixed shared secret that can be compromised at the client level
- DoS attacks aimed to preventing users from authenticating
- Credential-based attacks that rely on the use of a RADIUS-shared secret to brute-force the shared secret given a known password

Using TLS to protect RADIUS authentication instead of relying on the protections built into RADIUS can help mitigate many of these attacks; however, doing so requires consistent implementation throughout an organization.

Active Directory

Active Directory (AD) is the core identity store and AAA service for many Windows-centric organizations. That makes AD a popular target for attackers, and the prevalence of Windows workstations in corporate environments means that many exploit tools are built to target both Windows and Active Directory.

Common Active Directory attacks include the following:

- Malware-focused attacks that seek to place credential capturing or exploit-based malware onto Windows systems or AD servers
- Credential theft via phishing or other techniques
- Privilege escalation attacks using known or new Windows exploits
- Service accounts that are an often forgotten element of Active Directory environments and may suffer from both privilege creep and overly permissive rights
- Domain administrator rights that exist for more staff than is necessary, creating more targets for attackers and a greater likelihood that an AD admin account will not be properly maintained or that its password will be exposed
- The use of down-level versions of protocols used in Windows domains like NTLM v1 and LANMAN, NetBIOS, and unsigned LDAP and SMB to capture credentials or to conduct other attacks

Windows domains often include older systems or have settings configured to support them. Combined with the many exploit tools that are aimed at Windows systems, these make Windows domains a tempting target for attackers.

Handling Active Directory GPO Credential Storage

Some specific behaviors of AD and Group Policy are targeted by attackers. Group Policy Preferences can be used to perform a number of actions, but unfortunately, they also store the credentials they use in XML files in the SYSVOL share of every domain controller in the domain. The password storage method used can be easily reversed, making this a significant flaw. The issue is so common that Microsoft provided remediation tools here: `support.microsoft.com/en-us/kb/2962486`.

Targeting Account Creation, Provisioning, and Deprovisioning

The steps from account request to creation, provisioning of accounts, maintenance during the life cycle of the account, and the eventual deprovisioning and deletion of the account are known as the account life cycle. Figure 8.5 shows a typical account life cycle, from start to finish.

FIGURE 8.5 A sample account life cycle

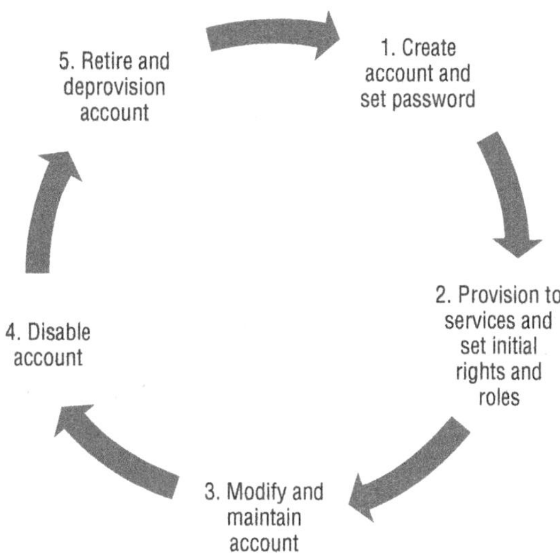

Both internal and external threats target the systems, services, and procedures that make up the account life cycle in order to gain access to accounts, or to gain privileges for the accounts that they already have access to.

The account creation process is an important target for attackers who have either gained access to systems in a trusted environment or are able to use social engineering attacks to persuade someone with appropriate rights to create an account for them. Internal threats may also seek to create accounts for their use to avoid detection.

Once an account exists, attackers will focus on gaining access to it. Social engineering, phishing, and attacks against credential stores and locations where credentials are used and could be compromised in transit or in use are all frequent methods of attack. Compromising credentials can provide the rights and access that the account is provisioned with and may allow attackers to operate in trusted areas where they can attempt attacks that are unlikely to succeed in more protected areas.

Attackers may also focus on accounts that have fallen through the cracks in an identity management system. Major threats from unused or improperly maintained accounts include

- Unused accounts, which attackers can compromise and use without the owner noticing something is amiss.
- Accounts that were not properly deprovisioned and abandoned on systems because they were missed during normal account removal or end-of-life processes. Accounts that are not properly deleted can often indicate an issue with management of the system, and may not be logged or monitored.
- Permissions, group memberships, and other privileges often accrue to accounts during a staff member's employment with an organization and may not be updated properly. Attackers, particularly insider threats, may be able to leverage rights that they, or others, have accrued over time without knowing that they still have them.

Rights and Roles

Maintaining rights, roles, and group memberships is another key element in identity management, and an important feature in identity management systems. User accounts are normally managed using the principle of *least privilege,* which states that users should be provided only with the least set of privileges or permissions required to perform their job function. This helps prevent users (or attackers who acquire their credentials) from performing actions that they should not and limits the exposure that they can cause.

Many accounts experience *privilege creep*, or the steady accrual of additional rights over time as account owners change roles, positions, or responsibilities. Privilege creep directly conflicts with the concept of least privilege since accounts should not have rights that aren't required for their current role. Unfortunately, this can be hard to track—new managers may not be aware of the user's old rights, or the user may even be asked to continue to perform their old duties on occasion.

Fortunately, centralized identity management suites provide monitoring and privilege management tools designed to monitor for privilege creep and can be set to identify accounts that end up with excessive privileges or which have privileges beyond what their role requires. Identity management systems like Centrify, Okta, SailPoint, and Ping Identity have account life cycle maintenance and monitoring features designed to fight this type of issue.

Preventing Common Exploits of Identity and Authorization

There are a few common methods of targeting identity and access management systems as well as the use of identity information, each with common protection methods that can help to remediate them. These include the following:

- *Impersonation* attacks occur when an attacker takes on the identity of a legitimate user. Security issues like OAuth open redirects discussed earlier in this chapter can allow impersonation to occur. Preventing impersonation may require stronger session handling techniques like those found in the OWASP session management cheat sheet at `www.owasp.org/index.php/Session_Management_Cheat_Sheet`. Other types of impersonation may be prevented by securing session identifiers that attackers might otherwise acquire, either on the local workstation or via the network.

- *Man-in-the-middle* (MitM) attacks rely on accessing information flow between systems or services. End-to-end encryption of sessions or network links can help reduce the chance of a successful MitM attack, unless attackers control endpoints or have the encryption keys.
- *Session hijacking* focuses on taking over an already existing session, either by acquiring the session key or cookies used by the remote server to validate the session or by causing the session to pass through a system the attacker controls, allowing them to participate in the session. Much like impersonation and MitM attacks, securing the data that an attacker needs to acquire to hijack the session, either via encrypting network sessions or links or on the local system, can help limit opportunities for session hijacking.
- *Privilege escalation* attacks focus on exploiting flaws to gain elevated permissions or access. A successful privilege escalation attack can allow a normal or an untrusted user to use administrator or other privileged access. Privilege escalation frequently relies on software vulnerabilities, requiring administrators to ensure that local applications, services, and utilities are not vulnerable.
- *Rootkits* combine multiple malicious software tools to provide continued access to a computer while hiding their own existence. Fighting rootkits requires a full suite of system security practices, ranging from proper patching and layered security design to antimalware techniques like whitelisting, heuristic detection techniques, and malicious software detection tools.

Exam Note

Privilege escalation, impersonation, man-in-the-middle attacks, session hijacking, and rootkits all appear in Domain 1.0 under Objective 1.7. As you review them, think about how you would implement controls to prevent these attacks against identity management systems as well as in other scenarios.

Acquiring Credentials

In addition to attacks against AAA and identity management infrastructure, attacks designed to acquire identities and credentials are common, and they can be easier to accomplish from outside an organization. Attacks against credentials commonly occur in the form of phishing attacks, compromises of other services, and brute-force attacks.

Phishing

Phishing attacks aimed at credentials often use replicas of legitimate authentication portals to trick their victims into entering their username and password. More advanced versions will even replay those entries into the legitimate site to prevent their targets from noticing that their login did not work.

Figure 8.6 shows an example of a phishing email that targets a recipient's PayPal ID. If the potential victim did not notice that the URL was wrong or that the site was not exactly the same as the site they normally log into, they could send their credentials to the attacker.

FIGURE 8.6 Phishing for a PayPal ID

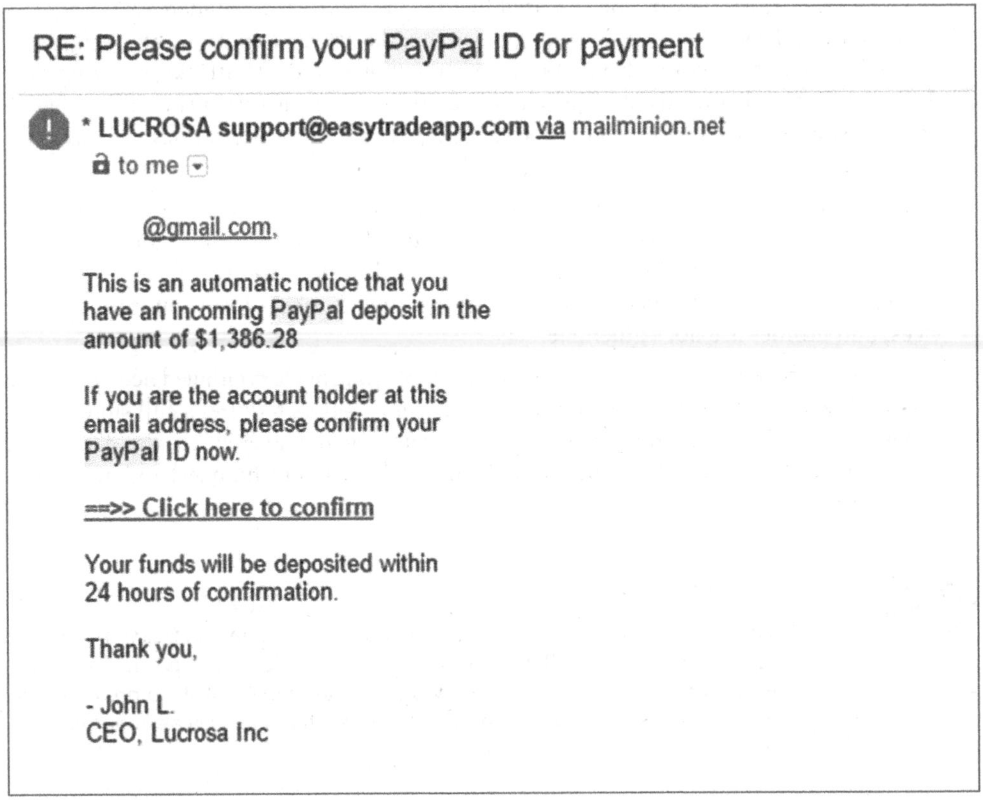

RE: Please confirm your PayPal ID for payment

 * LUCROSA support@easytradeapp.com via mailminion.net

to me

@gmail.com,

This is an automatic notice that you have an incoming PayPal deposit in the amount of $1,386.28

If you are the account holder at this email address, please confirm your PayPal ID now.

==>> Click here to confirm

Your funds will be deposited within 24 hours of confirmation.

Thank you,

- John L.
CEO, Lucrosa Inc

Multifactor authentication can help limit the impact of a successful phishing attack by requiring users to take an additional action and by providing an authenticator with a limited lifespan. User education and training including how to detect phishing and avoiding password reuse are also an important part of anti-phishing defenses.

Compromise of Other Services

Attacking third-party services to obtain passwords that may have been reused is another common threat vector. Attackers who obtain plain-text or recoverable passwords can then reuse those passwords on other accounts the users may have had. Unfortunately, many sites do not use strong password hashing algorithms, allowing attackers to easily crack the hashes for passwords stored using MD5 and other weak mechanisms.

Sites like haveibeenpwned.com now track major breaches and allow users to check if an email address or username has been exposed in public breaches.

This type of attack means that password reuse is a significant danger, particularly when passwords are used as the only factor for authentication. Breaches of major sites, like the two major Yahoo breaches from 2013 (announced in 2016), have resulted in passwords only minimally protected by MD5 hashes being available for almost a billion potential users. This makes a potential target for exploit any other services those users used that can be matched with their email or other identifiers.

Preventing other sites from being compromised isn't a reasonable expectation for a security professional. That's where technologies like multifactor authentication can provide a useful security layer. Even if users use the same password on multiple sites, their additional factors should remain secure, preventing lost passwords from causing an immediate problem. Training and awareness are still important, since password reuse remains a bad idea.

Brute-Force Attacks

Although having passwords available is preferable for attackers, sites that do not prevent repeated login attempts can still be attacked using brute-force methods by simply attempting to log in using password dictionaries or other brute-force methods. Preventing brute-force attacks requires building in back-off algorithms that prevent repeated logins after failure or other similar solutions like the use of CAPTCHA-style methods to verify that the logins are not being attempted by a script or bot. Some organizations choose to implement account lockout techniques to help with brute-force attacks, although lockouts can increase the workload for support teams unless users have an easy method of unlocking their accounts.

As you might expect, connecting authentication events to your security management and logging tools can help detect brute-force attacks, allowing you to take action to prevent the system or systems that are conducting the brute-force attack from attempting to authenticate. If you are considering this option, be sure to identify appropriate thresholds for what you consider brute force—otherwise you may lock out legitimate but forgetful users!

CAPTCHA is an acronym for Completely Automated Public Turing test to tell Computers and Humans Apart. CAPTCHAs use a variety of methods to try to prevent bots from performing actions, including requiring users to identify numbers, or to differentiate pictures of kittens from pictures of puppies. If you're looking to prevent brute-force web activity, OWASP's "Blocking Brute Force Attacks" guide can offer useful advice: `www.owasp.org/index.php/Blocking_Brute_Force_Attacks`.

Identity as a Security Layer

Identity is a critical part of most defense-in-depth designs. User and service accounts are crucial to controlling access to systems and services and also allow detailed monitoring and auditing of usage. Since rights and permissions are assigned either to roles that accounts are associated with or to individual users, identity is also critical to ensuring that rights management is handled properly.

Identity and Defense-in-Depth

The account lifecycle offers a number of opportunities for defense-in-depth designs. Although identity management processes will vary from organization to organization, a few critical parts of the identity management life cycle are consistent from a defense-in-depth design perspective. These process requirements occur at the major phases of an account's life cycle:

- Identity creation must ensure that only valid accounts are created and that the correct owner receives the account. At this phase in the account life cycle, it is important to avoid duplicate account creation, to ensure that initial authentication factors are delivered or set securely, and that accounts are added to a central identity management system for monitoring and auditing.
- Account provisioning and rights management needs to be consistent—pockets of unmanaged systems or systems that do not integrate can result in unmanaged accounts. Rights management is typically role-based, preventing individual accounts from accruing specialized permissions.
- Account modification and maintenance should track the individual's changing roles and group memberships to prevent privilege creep.
- Account termination needs to ensure that accounts are terminated properly and that they are removed from all systems that they were provisioned to.

Exam Note

Defense-in-depth for identity should address all three elements of the CIA Triad. That means ensuring that credentials and credential stores remain confidential in motion and at rest and that their integrity is monitored to ensure that unauthorized changes do not occur. Availability is also a critical concern—centralized identity and authorization services are wonderful until they allow an entire organization's ability to log in to fail due to a failed service or DoS attack!

Securing Authentication and Authorization

Securing the authentication process requires a combination of technical and procedural elements. Technological controls focus on protecting both the systems that provide authentication services and the traffic between clients and those servers. Providing a secure means of validating the identity of users is also critical, since attackers are more likely to have advanced capabilities that result in them successfully obtaining valid usernames and passwords via phishing, malware, or other means. Figure 8.7 shows a sample authentication flow with security considerations at each point in the flow, including use of TLS, multifactor authentication, and redundant authentication servers. Note that authentication security requires design or process security considerations throughout the flow.

FIGURE 8.7 Authentication security model

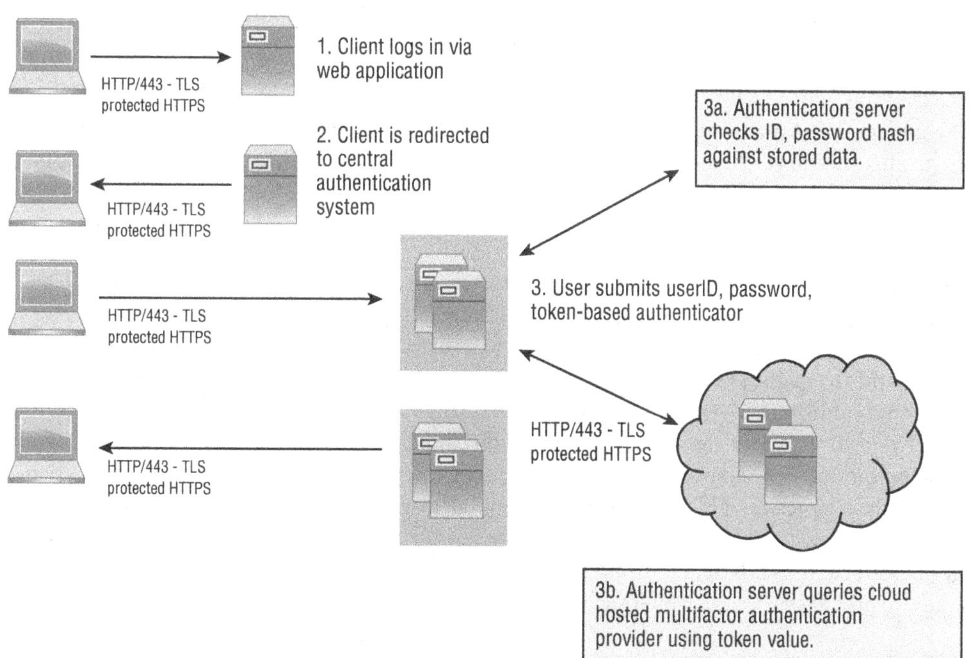

Password management is also a design concern for organizations. Users are asked to remember a large number of passwords, and password reuse is a continuing threat. This means that organizationally sponsored adoption of *password safes* or password storage utilities can have a significant impact on password security. Tools like KeePass, Password Safe, Dashlane, 1Password, and LastPass, as well as enterprise-centric password storage and management tools, can provide a useful means of maintaining distinct passwords without large numbers of support calls.

Moving Beyond Password Complexity Requirements

Password complexity guidelines that included a requirement for specific types of characters and complexity were common until very recently, due in large part to the limited length of passwords supported by many systems. Recommendations for strong passwords have largely changed to be length-based, and users are often advised to use a passphrase instead of a password. NIST's SP 800-63-3 "Digital Identity Guidelines" (`pages.nist.gov/800-63-3/`) released in mid-2017 reflect major changes in digital authentication standards from previous versions.

Authorization and Rights Management

Matching users with their rights, roles, and group membership is the next step of identity-based security. Rights management allows *access control* by matching users with the access they should have. Building a rights management security layer relies on the following:

- Building a set of policies that describe what rights are allocated to each role or task
- Implementing a management system to ensure that rights are granted to accounts and groups that need them and removed from groups and users that do not hold the appropriate role
- Monitoring and reporting to ensure that rights management occurs according to policy

In addition to managing rights for normal users, organizations need to pay particular attention to *privileged user management*, the management of administrative and super-user rights. Privileged users often have the ability to override system policies, to make changes to logging and oversight systems, or to otherwise impact systems in very powerful ways. This means that additional oversight needs to be placed around who can use privileged accounts and how administrative rights are granted and removed. Additional monitoring and logging is also common, and separation of administrative accounts from personal accounts is considered a best practice. This ensures that administrative actions can be logged by requiring users to specifically log in to an administrative account or to activate administrative privileges before their use. Since administrative accounts shouldn't be used constantly, this also makes misuse easy to detect by looking for administrative accounts that are constantly logged in. As always, appropriate training is required to make sure that administrators understand this.

Multifactor Authentication

One of the most important security measures put in place to authenticate users is *multi-factor authentication (MFA)*. MFA relies on two or more distinct authentication factors like a password, a token or smartcard, a biometric factor, or even the location that the individual is authenticating from. A key part of this is that the factors should be different; two passwords do not make an effective MFA scheme.

Exam Note

Multifactor authentication is one of the identity topics that are specifically called out in the exam objectives. Make sure you have a good understanding of multifactor authentication, what factors exist, why it is useful, and what issues exist with MFA solutions.

MFA relies on a few common types of authentication factors or methods:

- *Knowledge factors* are something you know. Passwords and passphrases are the most common knowledge factors, but authentication systems also sometimes use other data that you may know. Examples include systems that build questions from personal data the organization has about you such as your current mortgage payment, your residence a decade ago, or other things that you will know but that someone else is unlikely to.
- *Possession factors* are something you have. The most common examples of this are authenticator applications, security tokens, and smartcards. Figure 8.8 shows an example of the Google Authenticator application, a smartphone-based onetime password generator tool. Having the application that provides the code is the possession factor when using this type of token.
- *Biometric factors* are something that you are. They include fingerprints, retina scans, voiceprints, and a host of other methods of measuring features of the human body.
- *Location factors,* which are less frequently used, rely on physical location, determined either by where a system or network is located, or by using GPS or other data to verify that you are in a place that is trusted or allowed to access a system.

Since the token in Figure 8.8 is a onetime token, it's safe to publish in the book with its associated email address. To access the account, you would need both the current password and the current Google Authenticator code. The authors created a throwaway account for this screenshot anyway!

FIGURE 8.8 Google Authenticator token

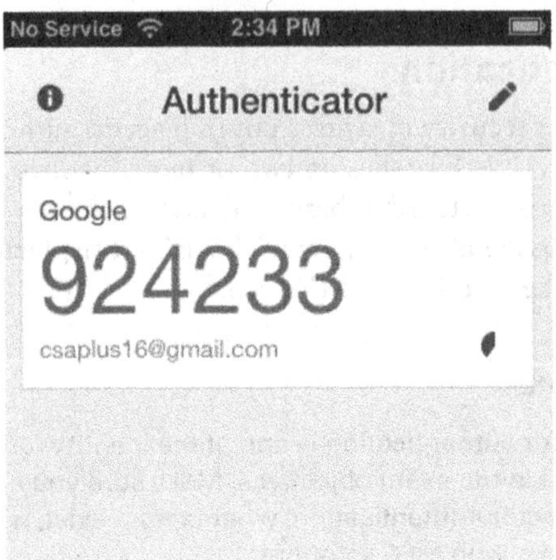

MFA helps prevent attackers from authenticating using stolen credentials by making it significantly less likely they will have both (or more!) of the factors that are required to authenticate to a user account. If an attacker manages to phish a password or conducts a successful brute-force password guessing attack, they probably won't have access to that individual's cell phone or token or have access to a biometric factor like their fingerprint.

This security advantage means that MFA is increasingly considered a necessary default security control for systems and services that require a greater level of security than a simple password. Major e-commerce, banking, social networks, and other service providers now have two-factor functionality available, and an increasing number are requiring it by default. That doesn't mean that MFA is perfect; a lost phone or token, an insecure method of delivering a second factor, or a backup access method that allows users to bypass the second factor by talking to a support person can all result in a failure of a multifactor system.

Context-Based Authentication

A key concept in authentication systems is the idea of context-based authentication. Context-based authentication allows authentication decisions to be made based on information about the user, the system the user is connecting from, or other information that is relevant to the system or organization performing the authentication.

Common data used for context-based authentication includes the following:

- User roles and group memberships related to application or service access
- IP address and/or IP reputation, providing information on whether the remote IP is known to be part of a botnet or other IP range with known bad behavior

- Time of day, often related to a job role or working hours
- Location-based information like their IP address or GPS location
- Frequency of access, which may be combined with behavioral data like keystroke patterns, browsing habits, or other details that can help uniquely identify a user
- *Device-based, including information about the web browser in use and other data that can provide a device fingerprint such as its IP address, time zone, screen resolution, cookies or cookie settings, installed fonts, and language*

Figure 8.9 shows an example of context-based authentication flow. A user logs in via the organization's VPN where a network access control (NAC) system profiles the user's device, identifying device-based fingerprint information. The user provides their username and password, which in this example do not match the device—the user has never logged in from it before. Due to this, the user is asked to provide a onetime password code from a security token and is then authenticated, having proven that they are who they say they are. The NAC server records the new device as a valid, trusted device and adds its unique profile to its database, and the user is connected via the VPN to the organization's internal network.

FIGURE 8.9 Context-based authentication

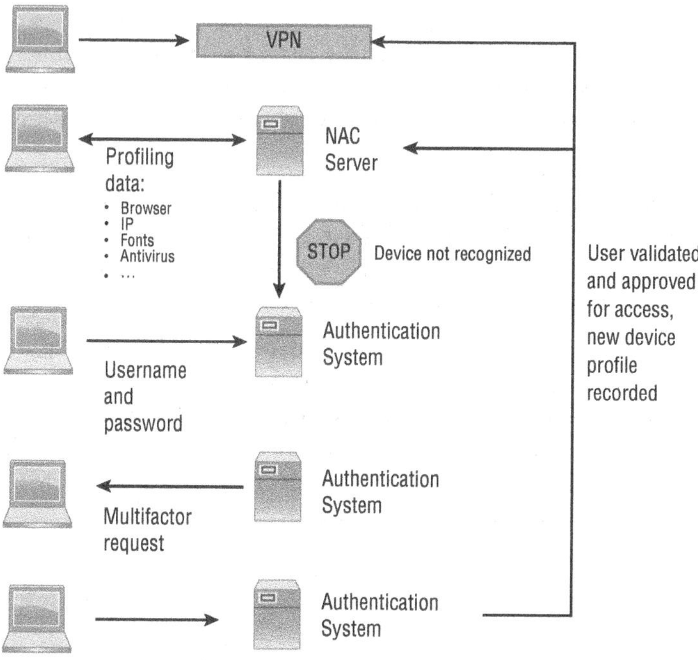

Organizations often use multiple types of contextual information to help to authenticate their users and may use it either in parallel with or in place of other MFA schemes.

Context-based authentication can be combined with multifactor authentication, allowing you to require users to provide enhanced authentication when additional verification is needed or desired.

The Problem with SMS

You have probably encountered SMS (text message)-based second factors in your daily life—Amazon, among many other major websites, uses it to verify your identity. The idea behind SMS as a second factor is that people will almost always have possession of their phone and that SMS provides a useful second factor when added to a password since it will prevent an attacker who only knows a password from logging in.

Unfortunately, SMS isn't a very secure protocol. In fact, NIST's Special Publication 800-63-3: Digital Identity Guidelines recommends that SMS be deprecated. Not only have successful attacks against SMS-based onetime passwords increased, but there are a number of ways that it can be successfully targeted with relative ease. One of the major areas in which this is prevalent is via VoIP systems, where SMS messages are relatively easily stolen, or where the password that an attacker has may have been reused for a given user's account controls, allowing attackers to see SMS messages or redirect them.

Another recent attack against SMS-based multifactor implementations is SIM swapping, which typically relies on bribed employees at cellular carriers. SIM swaps occur when attackers manage to get a new SIM card added to an account, taking over from the old SIM. This directs all activity to the attacker's phone instead of the legitimate owner's phone, allowing them to bypass SMS and other validation systems.

Fortunately, reasonable alternatives exist in the form of authenticator applications like Google Authenticator that generate onetime codes on an ongoing basis or by using hardware fobs. Does this mean that SMS will stop being used? Probably not, but it does mean that security professionals need to be aware that SMS probably isn't suitable for high-security environments.

Identity as a Service

Identity as a service (IDaaS) services provide authentication services, typically as a cloud-hosted service. IDaaS solutions typically provide features that include the following:

- Identity life cycle management, which consists of technologies and processes to create, provision, and manage identities for systems, services, and even other cloud services
- Directory services, using LDAP, Active Directory, or another directory technology
- Access management with both authentication and authorization capabilities
- Single sign-on support via technologies like Security Assertion Markup Language (SAML) integrations, OAuth, or other standards
- Privileged account management and monitoring
- Reporting, auditing, and other management capabilities to provide oversight and visibility into the identity life cycle

Identity as a service can create new security concerns for an organization due to hosting an identity store or an authorization system outside its internal network. Understanding how the IDaaS provider handles and secures identity information, what their incident response practices and notification policy is, and performing due diligence when selecting a provider are all important parts of an IDaaS implementation.

Implementing a cloud-hosted identity service can mean significant changes to internal AAA system designs. Major elements include

- Deciding whether the organization will centralize their directory services or whether internal and third-party hosted directories will both exist.
- Similarly, a decision must be made to centralize authentication or to federate multiple authentication and authorization systems.
- The location for the organization's authoritative credential store may be local or cloud-based.

IDaaS also has significant potential security benefits for organizations that do not have a strong in-house identity management capability or that need to better integrate with third-party services. In organizations without strong internal identity practices, an IDaaS solution can provide a more secure, better managed, and more capable toolset. Automated monitoring and reporting services can also help identify security issues earlier than might occur with a noncentralized system.

Detecting Attacks and Security Operations

Security information and event management (SIEM) systems can be used to leverage identity information as well as the other types of security information we have discussed in this book. Using identity information provides the "who" when reviewing events and incidents; when paired with other SIEM data and event logs, it provides a complete view of what occurred and what the user, service, or account's behavior was. Human or automated analysis can determine whether the actions were appropriate.

Configuring a SIEM or other security monitoring device to look for the following types of events can provide significant security benefits:

- Privileged account usage
- Privilege changes and grants
- Account creation and modification
- Employee termination and terminated account usage
- Account life cycle management events
- Separation-of-duty violations

Centralizing both IAM and user authentication and authorization systems helps ensure that accounts and privileges are well understood and managed throughout an organization. Attackers who can find a system that uses distinct accounts, or that does not centrally log authentication and authorization events, can far more easily take advantage of that system's isolation without their exploits being detected.

Much like other security events, detecting identity attacks requires that organizations have well-defined security policies and standards for use of credentials and privileges. Once those are in place, baselines can be set, and anomaly detection can be implemented to sound the alarm when unexpected behaviors occur.

The final layer for any identity-based security system is active monitoring and administration by knowledgeable administrators. Having humans analyze the reports and other information provided by central monitoring and security systems will help identify events that might be missed by automated systems.

Federation and Single Sign-On

The ability to federate identity, which is the process of linking an identity and its related attributes between multiple identity management systems, has become increasingly common. You have probably already seen or used a federated identity system if you use your Microsoft, Google, Facebook, or LinkedIn accounts to access sites that aren't hosted by those service providers. Each site allows use of their credentials, as well as a set of attributes by third-party sites.

Exam Note

The CySA+ exam objectives specifically call out federation, but without any further detail. Make sure you pay attention to what federation is, why you might want to use it, and what security concerns it brings, and know a bit about the common technologies associated with it.

Federated Identity Security Considerations

Federated identities move trust boundaries outside of your own organization, resulting in new concerns when designing, implementing, or using federated identity. This leads to the need to look at federated security from three points of view:

- As an *identity provider (IDP)*, members of a *federation* must provide identities, make assertions about those identities to relying parties, and release information to relying parties about identity holders. The identities and related data must be kept secure. Identities (and sometimes attributes) have to be validated to a level that fits the needs of the federation, and may have user-level controls applied to their release. In addition, service providers may be responsible for providing incident response coordination for the federation, communication between federation members, or other tasks due to their role in the federation.
- As the *relying party (RP)* or *service provider (SP)*, members of a federation must provide services to members of the federation, and should handle the data from both users and identity providers securely.
- The *consumer* or user of federated services may be asked to make decisions about attribute release, and to provide validation information about their identity claims to the IDP.

Each of these roles appears in Figure 8.10, which shows an example of the trust relationships and authentication flow that are required for federated identities to work.

FIGURE 8.10 Federated identity high-level design

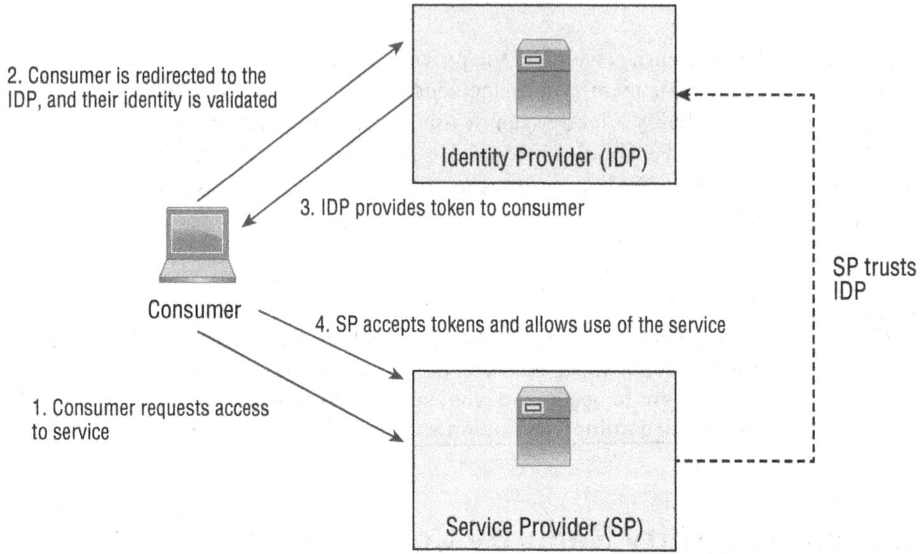

Real World Scenario

Hacking from Inside a Federation

Federated identities can be very useful, but federations are only as strong as their weakest member's security. In the past, one of the authors of this book was involved in the incident response process between members of a large-scale federation.

A successful hacker used compromised credentials to log in to systems at various federation member sites. There, he used the credentials to access systems used for research efforts. Although the credentials he had were not administrative credentials, they did have local system access, allowing the attacker to identify and exploit local privilege escalation flaws. Once he had exploited those flaws, he replaced the SSH Daemon running on the systems and captured credentials belonging to other federation members as well as local users. That provided him with enough new credentials to continue his exploits throughout other member sites.

The hacker was eventually tracked back through a series of systems around the world and was arrested after a massive coordinated effort between system administrators, security professionals, and law enforcement. The federation continued to operate, but the hacker's attacks led to additional security controls being put into place to ensure that future attacks of the same nature would be harder.

If you are part of a federation, you should consider how much you trust the organizational security practices and policies of the other federation members. That should drive the rights and access that you provide to holders of federated identities, as well as how you monitor their actions.

If you'd like to read more about this, the U.S. Federal Bureau of Investigation wrote a case study about the event that is available here: `publish.illinois.edu/kericker/files/2013/09/NCDIR-TR-2008-01.pdf`.

Federated Identity Design Choices

Using federated identity creates new security design concerns that you will have to plan and design around. If you are intending to leverage federated identity, the first question to answer is what trust model you want to use with the federated identity provider. Common providers of federated identity include Google, LinkedIn, and Amazon, but a broad range of commercial and private federations exist, including those operated by governments and higher education.

If you are using an existing federated identity provider such as Google, you are likely interested in allowing consumers to bring their own identity, which you will then map internally to your own privilege and rights structures. This model presumes that you do not care that a user is probably who they claim to be—instead, you only care that they own the account they are using.

In federation models that rely on verifiable identities, a greater level of assurance about the user's identity claims is needed, requiring additional trust between the federated identity providers and the relying parties. Examples of this include research federations that have identity vetting and assertion requirements between multiple identity providers within the federation.

Trust decisions will also influence organizational decisions about manual provisioning versus automatic provisioning and deprovisioning. Integration with third-party federated identity services works best when provisioning occurs when users request access with immediate account provisioning occurring once the federated identity has been validated. Manual provisioning provides greater security by allowing for additional oversight but can cause delays for user access.

Provisioning can also involve attribute release, as relying parties in a federation need some basic information for a user account to provide authorization and to contact the user.

The amount of information released by an identity provider can vary, from complete attribute release with all data about the account potentially available to very limited release such as the request shown in Figure 8.11.

FIGURE 8.11 Attribute release request for LoginRadius.com

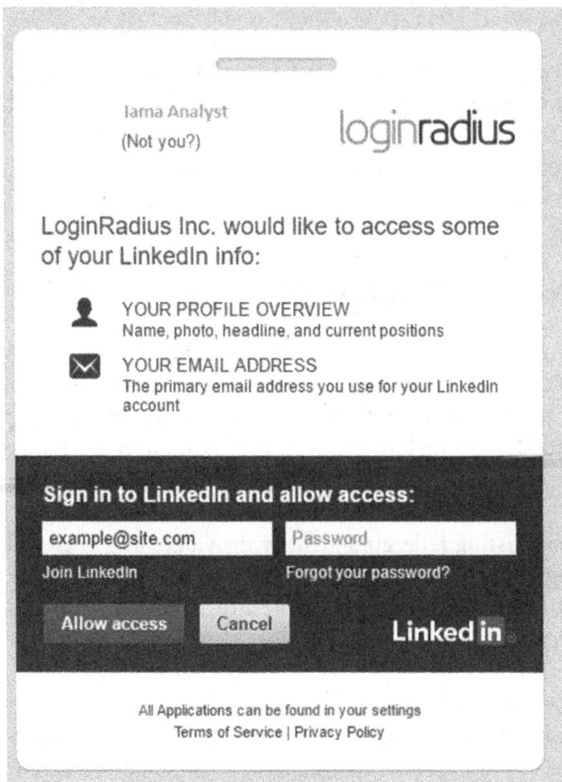

Figure 8.11 shows an example of an attribute release request for `LoginRadius.com`, a site that supports both LinkedIn and Google with federated identities for their users. Implementation decisions for each of these technologies will vary, but design requirements for data handling, storage, and release of attributes are all important.

Similar concerns exist for self-service password resets and other user-initiated account options. Allowing users to change these settings typically results in a lower support load, but it may also allow attackers to use poor security questions or other methods to change user passwords and other data without the user being involved.

Once you have identified the appropriate trust requirements for the identities you intend to use for your federated identities, you will either have to adopt the underlying technologies that they use or select the technology that fits your needs. This is particularly true if you are federating your own organization, rather than using a federated identity provider like LinkedIn or Google. Technologies like SAML, OAuth, OpenID Connect, and Facebook Connect are all potentially part of the solutions you may adopt.

The type of federation you intend to implement also influences the security requirements you can expect, or may require, from federation members, including both identity providers and relying parties. In a loosely bound federation like sites using Google accounts, the underlying security model for Google accounts is not as significant of a concern since any owner of a Google account can typically use services that federate with Google.

In federations that require a higher trust level, vetting of the security practices of both identity providers and relying parties is necessary. Identity providers must validate the identity of the users they support, they must secure their credential store, and they should have a strong handling and notification process in place for security issues that might impact the federation's members. Relying parties need to ensure that their credential handling is properly secured and that they are meeting any security or operational requirements that the federation presents.

Federated Identity Technologies

Four major technologies serve as the core of federated identity for current federations: SAML, ADFS, OAuth, and OpenID Connect. These technologies provide ways for identity providers to integrate with service providers in a secure manner without having to know details about how the service provider implements their service or their own use of the identity.

Table 8.1 compares SAML, OpenID, OAuth2, and ADFS, including their support for authorization and authentication, some of their most common potential security risks, and how they are often used.

TABLE 8.1 Comparison of federated identity technologies

	SAML	OpenID	OAuth2	ADFS
Authorization	Yes	No	Yes	Yes
Authentication	Yes	Yes	Partial	Yes
Potential security risks	Message confidentiality Protocol usage and processing risks Denial of service	Redirect manipulation Message confidentiality Replay attacks CSRF/XSS attacks Phishing	Redirect manipulation Message confidentiality Authorization or resource server impersonation	Token attacks (replay, capture)

TABLE 8.1 Comparison of federated identity technologies *(continued)*

	SAML	OpenID	OAuth2	ADFS
Common uses	Enterprise authentication and authorization, particularly in Linux-centric environments	Authentication	API and service authorization	Enterprise authentication and authorization, particularly in Windows-centric environments

SAML

SAML is an XML-based language used to send authentication and authorization data between identity providers and service providers. It is frequently used to enable single sign-on for web applications and services because SAML allows identity providers to make assertions about principals to service providers so that they can make decisions about that user. SAML allows authentication, attribute, and authorization decision statements to be exchanged.

Figure 8.12 shows a very simple sample SAML authentication process. In this flow, a user attempts to use a SAML authenticated service and is referred to the identity provider to authenticate their identity. After a successful login, the browser returns to the relying party with an appropriate SAML response, which it verifies. With these steps done, the user can now use the application they initially wanted to access.

OWASP provides a comprehensive SAML security cheat sheet at cheatsheetseries.owasp.org/cheatsheets/SAML_Security_Cheat_Sheet.html.

ADFS

Active Directory Federation Services (ADFS) is the Microsoft answer to federation. ADFS provides authentication and identity information as *claims* to third-party partner sites. Partner sites then use *trust policies* to match claims to claims supported by a service, and then it uses those claims to make authorization decisions.

ADFS uses a similar process to an OAuth authentication process:

1. The user attempts to access an ADFS–enabled web application hosted by a resource partner.
2. The ADFS web agent on the partner's web server checks for the ADFS cookie; if it is there, access is granted. If the cookie is not there, the user is sent to the partner's ADFS server.

3. The resource partner's ADFS checks for an SAML token from the account partner, and if it's not found, ADFS performs home realm discovery.
4. Home realm discovery identifies the federation server associated with the user and then authenticates the user via that home realm.
5. The account partner then provides a security token with identity information in the form of claims, and sends the user back to the resource partner's ADFS server.
6. Validation then occurs normally and uses its trust policy to map the account partner claims to claims the web application supports.
7. A new SAML token is created by ADFS that contains the resource partner claims, and this cookie is stored on the user's computer. The user is then redirected to the web application, where the application can read the cookie and allow access supported by the claims.

FIGURE 8.12 Simple SAML transaction

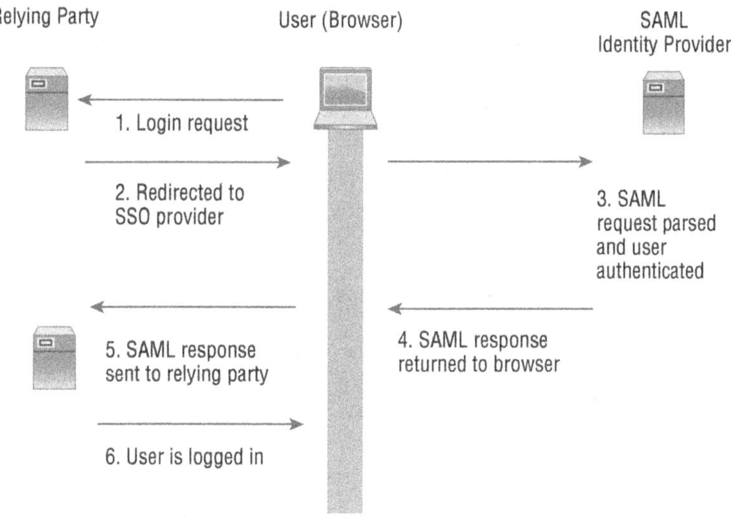

ADFS can be controlled using the ADFS MMC snap-in, `adfs.msc`. The ADFS console allows you to add resource partners and account partners, map partner claims, manage account stores, and configure web applications that support federation. Microsoft provides a useful overview of ADFS at `msdn.microsoft.com/en-us/library/bb897402.aspx`.

OAuth

The OAuth 2.0 protocol provides an authorization framework designed to allow third-party applications to access HTTP-based services. It was developed via the Internet Engineering Task Force (IETF) and supports web clients, desktops, mobile devices, and a broad range of other embedded and mobile technologies, as well as the service providers that they connect to. OAuth provides access delegation, allowing service providers to perform actions for you.

OAuth flows recognize four parties:

- **Clients** The applications that users want to use
- **Resource Owners** The end users
- **Resource Servers** Servers provided by a service that the resource owner wants the application to use
- **Authorization Servers** Servers owned by the identity provider

Figure 8.13 shows how authentication flows work with OAuth. In this chain, the client is attempting to access a third-party service. The third-party site, which is the consumer, is directed to a service provider to authenticate. To request authentication, the consumer sends a request for a request token. The service provider validates the user's identity, grants a request token, and then directs the consumer back to the service provider. There, the service provider obtains the user authorization and sends the user to the third-party site. The consumer requests an access token, the service provider grants it, and then the consumer can access resources.

FIGURE 8.13 OAuth authentication process

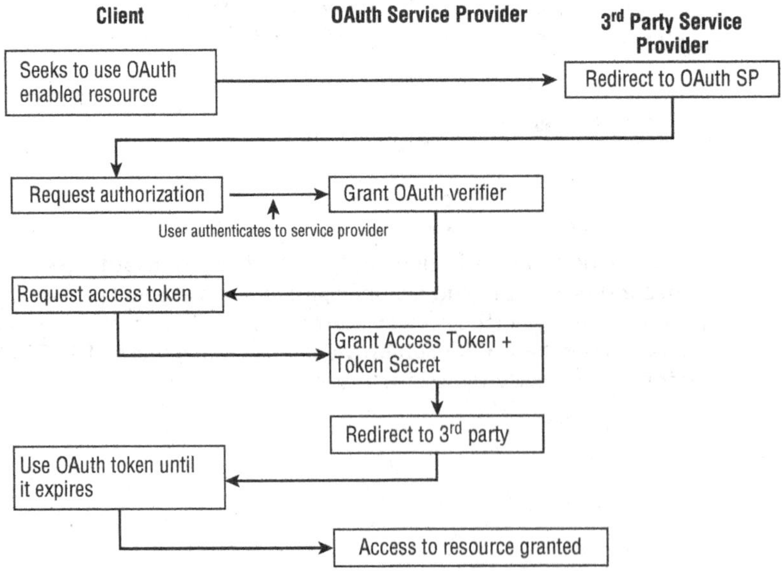

OpenID Connect

OpenID Connect is often paired with OAuth to provide authentication. It allows the authorization server to issue an ID token in addition to the authorization token provided by OAuth. This allows services to know that the action was authorized and that the user authenticated with the identity provider.

Federation Incident Response

Incident response with federated identities can be a complex topic. The amount of information released by identity providers, service providers, and relying parties will vary due to the contractual agreements (if any!) or the federation operating agreements between them.

Building a response plan for federated identity varies based on the role your organization holds in the federation:

- Identity providers are typically responsible for notifying account owners and may be responsible for notifying relying parties. Incident response policies need to envision compromise of the identity provider itself, as well as what events such as a required password reset for all users would entail.
- Service providers need to determine what their response would be if the identity provider was compromised, as well as a range of smaller incidents, including compromise of their own authorization systems or a limited compromise of accounts provided by the identity provider.

Consumers must consider what the impact would be if their accounts were inaccessible—if they used a Google account for many sites, and Google were compromised or unavailable, what would they do?

As with all incident response policies and procedures, a strong communications plan and testing of the response plan itself, either via practice scenarios or walk-throughs, is strongly recommended.

Summary

Identity and authorization are key elements in a security design. Authentication, authorization, and accounting (AAA) systems are part of an identity and access management (IAM) infrastructure. IAM systems manage user account life cycles, as well as rights and privileges, and provide oversight of identity to ensure that accounts and the rights they have are not misused or abused.

Common AAA systems include LDAP directory servers, Kerberos, RADIUS, and Active Directory. In addition, federated identity systems are increasingly important as organizations connect with cloud-hosted services using onsite and third-party identity and authorization services. Securing each of these systems requires careful configuration and understanding of its security models and uses in the organization.

There are a number of common access control methods. They include role-based access control (RBAC), attribute-based access control (ABAC), mandatory access control (MAC) and others. Review of the rights granted to subjects is an important part of identity and access management oversight. Both automated and manual review processes can help prevent privilege creep, overly broad privileges, and other problems associated with rights and role management.

Attackers target identity and identity systems to gain access to organizational resources and data. They target personnel to acquire their credentials via phishing attacks, malware, and social engineering. At the same time, endpoints like mobile devices and workstations, as well as servers, are targeted for compromise to acquire user IDs, passwords, or even entire identity stores. Applications and services may also be targeted, due to weaknesses in their implementation of authorization or authentication technologies or due to compromised credentials.

Despite the many attacks aimed at identity, it can also provide a useful security layer. Centralized management of authentication and authorization combined with logging and auditing can help prevent attacks, or identify attacks as they occur. Behavioral analysis, policy-based monitoring, and other techniques used in SIEM and other security technologies can be applied to identity systems to detect issues and attacks.

Federated identity adds new complexity to identity-based security design. Federated identity may be as simple as allowing users to bring their own account, thus simplifying account maintenance for the relying organization, but it can also be a complex trust-based relationship with broad attribute release and rights based on those attributes. Responding to federation-based incidents requires an understanding of the trust relationships, privileges, and reporting relationships within the federation.

Exam Essentials

Explain how identities are the core of authentication, authorization, and accounting (AAA) systems. AAA systems authenticate users by using a user ID, password, or other factors. Central management of identities is handled by identity and access management (IAM) systems. IAM systems create, store, manage, and monitor identities and authorization through organizations. Rights and roles are managed via role-based, attributed-based, mandatory, and other access control schemes. Key elements of IAM systems include directories, authentication systems and protocols, single sign-on (SSO) and shared authentication services, and federated identity systems.

Name some threats to identities. Identity threats target not only the credentials issued to users and services, but also identity management systems, the protocols and applications used to manage and consume identity data, and the account life cycle itself. Personnel are targets of phishing and social engineering attacks, and the roles and privileges they have are targeted for abuse. Malware compromises target servers, systems, and devices. Applications and services are targeted via misconfigurations, protocol vulnerabilities, design issues, and compromise.

Explain why identity is a critical security layer. The account life cycle is the core of identity-based security and relies on secure creation, provisioning, maintenance, and removal at the end of the account's life to ensure security. The rights and privileges that accounts are assigned require strong policy-based management and oversight, as well as monitoring to avoid privilege creep via privilege management. Credential and password management, and the use of multifactor authentication (MFA), are important due to increased targeting of credentials by advanced attackers.

Know how federated identity technologies are broadly used for cloud services and interorganizational authentication and authorization. Identity providers provide both identities and authentication services to federations. Relying parties and service providers use identities to authorize users to make use of their services or applications. Consumers may use social identities like Google or Facebook credentials to access a broad range of services using protocols like OpenID Connect and OAuth. Incident response in federations requires additional preparation to ensure that new models for reporting, notification, and handling are ready when needed.

Explain how identity can provide a useful control layer. Implementing defenses against privilege escalation, impersonation, man-in-the-middle attacks, and other threats can involve identity and access management techniques. Session hijacking, cross-site scripting, and even rootkits can have their impact limited by controlling the privileges, ensuring proper authentication and authorization, and logging and tracking account access and privileges account activity. Remember to consider identity as a security layer in your control plans.

Lab Exercises

Activity 8.1: Federated Security Scenario

In this exercise, you will be provided with two different federated identity scenarios. For each, you should research the technology or situation described and then write a written recommendation to handle the issue described.

Part 1: Google OAuth integration

Example Corp.'s development team has implemented an OAuth integration with Google. The internal development team has written their own libraries for the company's OAuth endpoint and has implemented their server via HTTP between Example Corp.'s servers.

What security issues would you identify with this design, and what fixes would you recommend?

Part 2: High security federation incident response

Example Corp. is considering using Facebook Login to allow users to bring their own identity for its customer support website. This would remove the need for Example Corp. to handle its own identity management in most cases and is seen as an attractive option to remove expensive user support for this type of account.

Answer the following questions:

1. What recommendations and advice would you provide to the implementation team?
2. What should Example Corp.'s incident response plan include to handle issues involving Facebook Login?
3. Does using Facebook Login create more or less risk for Example Corp.? Why?

Part 3: Analyze your responses

To analyze your response to Part 1, use the OWASP Authentication cheat sheet found at `cheatsheetseries.owasp.org/cheatsheets/Authentication_Cheat_Sheet.html`. You will find tips on OAuth and application communications.

To analyze your response to Part 2, review federation-aware incident response policies like `doi.org/10.26869/TI.100.1` and `www.btaa.org/docs/default-source/technology/federated_security_incident_response.pdf`.

Activity 8.2: On-site Identity Issues Scenario

In this exercise, you will be provided with two different local identity scenarios. For each, you should research the technology or situation described, and then write a written recommendation to handle the issue described. In Part 3, you will review your answers and look for potential flaws that remain.

Part 1: Emergency privilege escalation

At Example Corp., administrative accounts are created and managed using a central identity and access management suite. This suite, as well as the company's central AAA servers, are hosted in redundant datacenters, and site-to-site VPNs normally connect those datacenters to multiple locations around the country.

Example Corp.'s systems engineering department recently dealt with a major Internet connectivity outage, which also resulted in engineers being unable to log in to the systems at the sites where they worked. This meant that they were unable to work to fix the issues.

The engineers have requested that you identify a secure way to provide emergency, on-demand privileged access to local servers when the central AAA services are unavailable. You have been asked to provide a solution to central IT management that is both secure and flexible enough to allow authentication for network devices, servers, and workstations.

Part 2: Managing privilege creep

A recent audit of Example Corp.'s file shares shows that many long-term employees have significantly broader rights to files and folders than their current roles should allow. In fact, in some cases employees could see sensitive data that could result in negative audit findings in a pending external audit.

How would you recommend that Example Corp. handle both the current issue of privilege creep and the ongoing problem of ensuring that it does not occur in the future without seriously disrupting the company's operations?

Part 3: Review

Review your recommendations to ensure that confidentiality, integrity, and availability are maintained. Did you provide a solution that covers each of these three areas?

1. Does your solution cover each of these areas (if appropriate)?
   - Personnel
   - Endpoint devices
   - Servers
   - Services and applications
   - Roles and groups
2. If you were asked to conduct a penetration test of an organization that had implemented your recommendations, how would you approach attacking your solution?

Activity 8.3: Identity and Access Management Terminology

Match each of the following terms to the correct description.

TACACS+	LDAP is deployed in this role.
Identity	The practice of managing and controlling identities and rights.
ADFS	An open standard for authorization used for websites and applications.
Privilege creep	Access control based on elements like things that describe the user (role, title), what action is being attempted, or other similar data.
Directory service	This issue occurs when accounts gain more rights over time due to role changes.
OAuth 2.0	The set of claims made about an account holder.
SAML	A technical system that allows access to many different systems or services with a single authentication event.
RADIUS	A Cisco-designed authentication protocol.
Privilege management	An access control scheme where the operating system constrains the ability of the user or subject to take action.

Multifactor authentication (MFA)	An access control scheme based on an individual's job duties or other position in an organization.
Single sign-on (SSO)	A common AAA system for network devices.
Federation	Checking rights without an automated system.
Role-based	Microsoft's identity federation service.
Attribute-based	The linking of an individual's identity across multiple identity management systems.
Mandatory	An XML-based protocol used to exchange authentication and authorization data.
Manual review	The combination of multiple means of proving an identity to authenticate.

Review Questions

1. Gabby is designing a multifactor authentication system for her company. She has decided to use a passphrase, a time-based code generator, and a PIN to provide additional security. How many distinct factors will she have implemented when she is done?
   A. One
   B. Two
   C. Three
   D. Four
2. Susan wants to manage access based on the job titles of members of her organization's staff. What kind of access control is best suited to this requirement?
   A. Role-based access control
   B. Attribute-based access control
   C. Mandatory access control
   D. Discretionary access control
3. During an incident response process, Michelle discovers that the administrative credentials for her organization's Kerberos server have been compromised and that attackers have issued themselves a TGT without an expiration date. What is this type of ticket called?
   A. A master ticket
   B. A golden ticket
   C. A KDC
   D. A MGT
4. Which of the following technologies is NTLM associated with?
   A. SAML
   B. Active Directory
   C. OAuth
   D. RADIUS
5. Jim was originally hired into the helpdesk at his current employer but has since then moved into finance. During a rights audit, it is discovered that he still has the ability to change passwords for other staff members. What is this issue called?
   A. Rights mismanagement
   B. Least privilege
   C. Permission misalignment
   D. Privilege creep

6. What type of attack occurs when an attacker takes advantage of OAuth open redirects to take on the identity of a legitimate user?
   A. Impersonation
   B. Session hijacking
   C. MitM
   D. Protocol analysis

7. The 2013 Yahoo breach resulted in almost 1 billion MD5 hashed passwords being exposed. What user behavior creates the most danger when this type of breach occurs?
   A. Insecure password reset questions
   B. Use of federated credentials
   C. Password reuse
   D. Unencrypted password storage

8. Authentication that uses the IP address, geographic location, and time of day to help validate the user is known as what type of authentication?
   A. Token-based
   B. Context-based
   C. NAC
   D. System-data contextual

9. Which of the following is not a common attack against Kerberos?
   A. Administrator account attacks
   B. Ticket reuse attacks
   C. Open redirect-based attacks
   D. TGT-focused attacks

10. Which of the following technologies is not a shared authentication technology?
    A. OpenID Connect
    B. LDAP
    C. OAuth
    D. Facebook Connect

11. Angela is concerned about attackers enumerating her organization's LDAP directory. What LDAP control should she recommend to help limit the impact of this type of data gathering?
    A. LDAP replication
    B. ACLs
    C. Enable TLS
    D. Use MD5 for storage of secrets

12. What security design is best suited to protect authentication and authorization for a network that uses TACACS+?
    A. Use TACACS+ built-in encryption to protect traffic
    B. Implement TACACS++
    C. Enable accounting services to detect issues
    D. Route management traffic over a dedicated network

13. Jason has user rights on his Linux workstation, but he wants to read his department's financial reports, which he knows are stored in a directory that only administrators can access. He executes a local exploit, which gives him the ability to act as root. What type of attack is this?
    A. Privilege escalation
    B. Zero-day
    C. Rootkit
    D. Session hijacking

14. Chris is responsible for monitoring his organization's file shares and security and has discovered that employees are consistently retaining access to files after they change positions. Where should he focus his efforts if his organization's account life cycle matches the following?

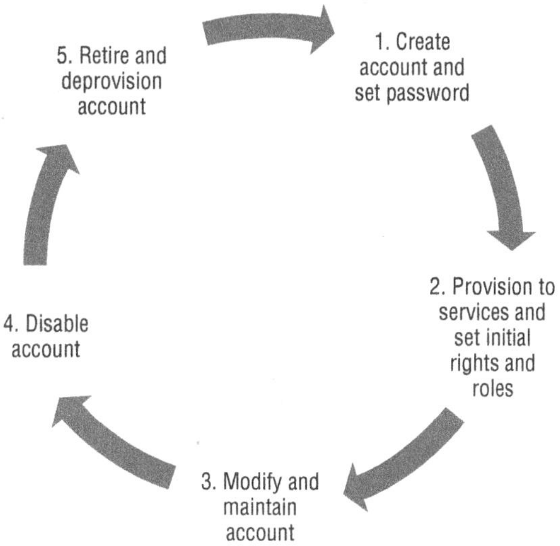

    A. Step 1
    B. Step 2
    C. Step 3
    D. Step 5

15. Which of the following methods is not an effective method for preventing brute-force password guessing attacks via login portals?

    A. CAPTCHAs

    B. Returning an HTTP error

    C. Login throttling

    D. Failed login account lockout

16. Which party in a federated identity service model makes assertions about identities to service providers?

    A. RPs

    B. CDUs

    C. IDPs

    D. APs

17. Which of the following is not a reason to avoid using SMS as a second factor for authentication?

    A. SMS via VoIP is easy to target.

    B. SMS is insecure.

    C. SMS cannot send unique tokens.

    D. VoIP management often uses the same password as the account.

18. Ben's successful attack on an authenticated user required him to duplicate the cookies that the web application put in place to identify the legitimate user. What type of attack did Ben conduct?

    A. Impersonation

    B. MitM

    C. Session hijacking

    D. Privilege escalation

19. Gabby connects to a Linux web server and executes an attack that gives her access to the account that the Apache web server runs as. If her next attack is aimed at a script that runs with root privileges, what type of attack has she attempted?

    A. A brute-force attack

    B. A dictionary attack

    C. A pass-the-hash attack

    D. A privilege escalation attack

20. Michelle has a security token that her company issues to her. What type of authentication factor does she have?

    A. Biometric

    B. Possession

    C. Knowledge

    D. Inherence

Software and Hardware Development Security

THE COMPTIA CYBERSECURITY ANALYST (CYSA+) EXAM OBJECTIVES COVERED IN THIS CHAPTER INCLUDE:

✓ **Domain 1.0 Threat and Vulnerability Management**

- 1.7 Given a scenario, implement controls to mitigate attacks and software vulnerabilities.

✓ **Domain 2.0: Software and Systems Security**

- 2.2 Explain software assurance best practices.
- 2.3 Explain hardware assurance best practices.

✓ **Domain 3.0: Security Operations and Monitoring**

- 3.4 Compare and contrast automation concepts and technologies.

Software ranging from customer-facing applications and services to smaller programs, down to the smallest custom scripts written to support business needs, is everywhere in our organizations. That software runs on hardware that brings its own security requirements and risks. Ensuring that that software and hardware is secure is an important part of a security professional's skillset.

The process of designing, creating, supporting, and maintaining that software is known as the software development life cycle (SDLC). As a security practitioner, you need to understand the SDLC and its security implications to ensure that the software your organization uses is well written and secure throughout its lifespan.

In this chapter you will learn about major SDLC models and the reasons for choosing them, as well as the architectures they are implemented to support. You will learn about secure coding best practices and tools, and software assessment methods and techniques. As part of this, you will see how software is tested and reviewed and how these processes fit into the SDLC. You will learn about code review and inspection methodologies like pair programming and over-the-shoulder code reviews as well as Fagan inspection that can help ensure that the code your organization puts into production is ready to face both users and attackers.

In addition, you will learn about hardware assurance best practices ranging from trusted foundries and supply chain security to secure processing and specific hardware security concepts and techniques.

Software Assurance Best Practices

Building, deploying, and maintaining software requires security involvement throughout the software's life cycle. The CySA+ exam objectives focus on the software development life cycle, software assessment methods and tools, coding practices, platforms, and architectures.

Exam Note

Although the CySA+ exam objectives don't list specific SDLC models, the exam expects you to understand how security plugs into the SDLC. That means you need to know that different models exist and understand how those differences can impact where and how security integration occurs. We have attempted to give you a good overview of modern SDLC models, as well as the overall SDLC concept as context for security operations and integration.

The Software Development Life Cycle

The software development life cycle (SDLC) describes the steps in a model for software development throughout its life. As shown in Figure 9.1, it maps software creation from an idea to requirements gathering and analysis to design, coding, testing, and rollout. Once software is in production, it also includes user training, maintenance, and decommissioning at the end of the software package's useful life.

Software development does not always follow a formal model, but most enterprise development for major applications does follow most, if not all, of these phases. In some cases, developers may even use elements of an SDLC model without realizing it!

FIGURE 9.1 High-level SDLC view

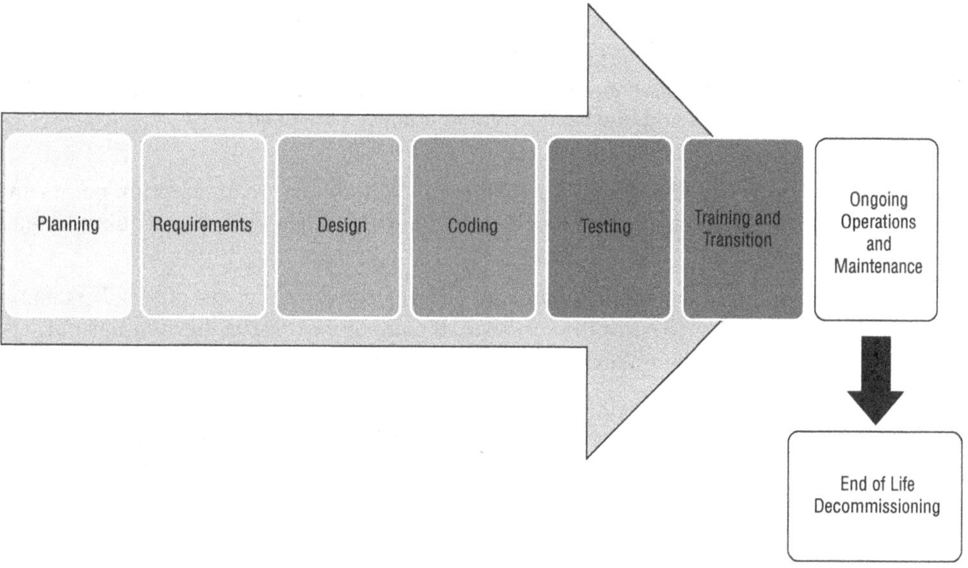

The SDLC is useful for organizations and for developers because it provides a consistent framework to structure workflow and to provide planning for the development process. Despite these advantages, simply picking an SDLC model to implement may not always be the best choice. Each SDLC model has certain types of work and projects that it fits better than others, making choosing an SDLC model that fits the work an important part of the process.

In this chapter, we refer to the output of the SDLC as "software" or as an "application," but the SDLC may be run for a service, a system, or other output. Feel free to substitute the right phrasing that is appropriate for you.

Software Development Phases

Regardless of which SDLC or process is chosen by your organization, a few phases appear in most SDLC models:

1. The *feasibility* phase is where initial investigations into whether the effort should occur are conducted. Feasibility also looks at alternative solutions and high-level costs for each solution proposed. It results in a recommendation with a plan to move forward.
2. Once an effort has been deemed feasible, it will typically go through an *analysis and requirements definition* phase. In this phase customer input is sought to determine what the desired functionality is, what the current system or application currently does and doesn't do, and what improvements are desired. Requirements may be ranked to determine which are most critical to the success of the project.

Security requirements definition is an important part of the analysis and requirements definition phase. It ensures that the application is designed to be secure and that secure coding practices are used.

3. The *design* phase includes design for functionality, architecture, integration points and techniques, dataflows, business processes, and any other elements that require design consideration.
4. The actual coding of the application occurs during the *development* phase. This phase may involve testing of parts of the software, including *unit testing* (testing of small components individually to ensure they function properly) and *code analysis*.
5. Although some testing is likely to occur in the development phase, formal testing with customers or others outside of the development team occurs in the *testing and integration* phase. Individual units or software components are integrated and then tested to ensure proper functionality. In addition, connections to outside services, data sources, and other integration may occur during this phase. During this phase *user acceptance testing* (UAT) occurs to ensure that the users of the software are satisfied with its functionality.
6. The important task of ensuring that the end users are trained on the software and that the software has entered general use occurs in the *training and transition* phase. This phase is sometimes called the acceptance, installation, and deployment phase.
7. Once a project reaches completion, the application or service will enter what is usually the longest phase: *ongoing operations and maintenance*. This phase includes patching, updating, minor modifications, and other work that goes into daily support.
8. The *disposition* phase occurs when a product or system reaches the end of its life. Although disposition is often ignored in the excitement of developing new products, it is an important phase for a number of reasons: shutting down old products can produce cost savings, replacing existing tools may require specific knowledge or additional effort, and data and systems may need to be preserved or properly disposed of.

The order of the phases may vary, with some progressing in a simple linear fashion and others taking an iterative or parallel approach. You will still see some form of each of these phases in successful software life cycles.

Development, Test, and Production—Oh, My!

Many organizations use multiple environments for their software and systems development and testing. The names and specific purposes for these systems vary depending on organizational needs, but the most common environments are as follows:

- *Development,* typically used for developers or other "builders" to do their work. Some workflows provide each developer with their own development environment; others use a shared development environment.
- *Test,* an environment where the software or systems can be tested without impacting the production environment. In some schemes, this is preproduction, whereas in others a separate preproduction staging environment is used.
- *Production,* the live system. Software, patches, and other changes that have been tested and approved move to production.

Change management processes are typically followed to move through these environments. This provides accountability and oversight and may be required for audit or compliance purposes as well.

Software Development Models

The SDLC can be approached in many ways, and over time a number of formal models have been created to help provide a common framework for development. While formal SDLC models can be very detailed, with specific practices, procedures, and documentation, many organizations choose the elements of one or more models that best fit their organizational style, workflow, and requirements.

Waterfall

The *Waterfall* methodology is a sequential model in which each phase is followed by the next phase. Phases do not overlap, and each logically leads to the next. A typical six-phase Waterfall process is shown in Figure 9.2. In Phase 1, requirements are gathered and documented. Phase 2 involves analysis intended to build business rules and models. In Phase 3, a software architecture is designed, and coding and integration of the software occurs in Phase 4. Once the software is complete, Phase 5 occurs, with testing and debugging being completed in this phase. Finally the software enters an operational phase, with support, maintenance, and other operational activities happening on an ongoing basis.

FIGURE 9.2 The Waterfall SDLC model

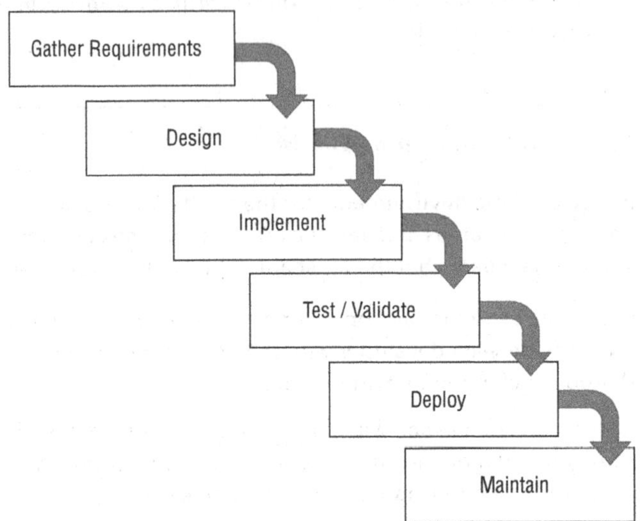

Waterfall has been replaced in many organizations because it is seen as relatively inflexible, but it remains in use for complex systems. Since Waterfall is not highly responsive to changes and does not account for internal iterative work, it is typically recommended for development efforts that involve a fixed scope and a known timeframe for delivery and that are using a stable, well-understood technology platform.

Spiral

The *Spiral* model uses the linear development concepts from the Waterfall model and adds an iterative process that revisits four phases multiple times during the development life cycle to gather more detailed requirements, design functionality guided by the requirements, and build based on the design. In addition, the Spiral model puts significant emphasis on risk assessment as part of the SDLC, reviewing risks multiple times during the development process.

The Spiral model shown in Figure 9.3 uses four phases, which it repeatedly visits throughout the development life cycle:

1. Identification, or requirements gathering, which initially gathers business requirements, system requirements, and more detailed requirements for subsystems or modules as the process continues.
2. Design, conceptual, architectural, logical, and sometimes physical or final design.
3. Build, which produces an initial proof of concept and then further development releases until the final production build is produced.

4. Evaluation, which involves risk analysis for the development project intended to monitor the feasibility of delivering the software from a technical and managerial viewpoint. As the development cycle continues, this phase also involves customer testing and feedback to ensure customer acceptance.

FIGURE 9.3 The Spiral SDLC model

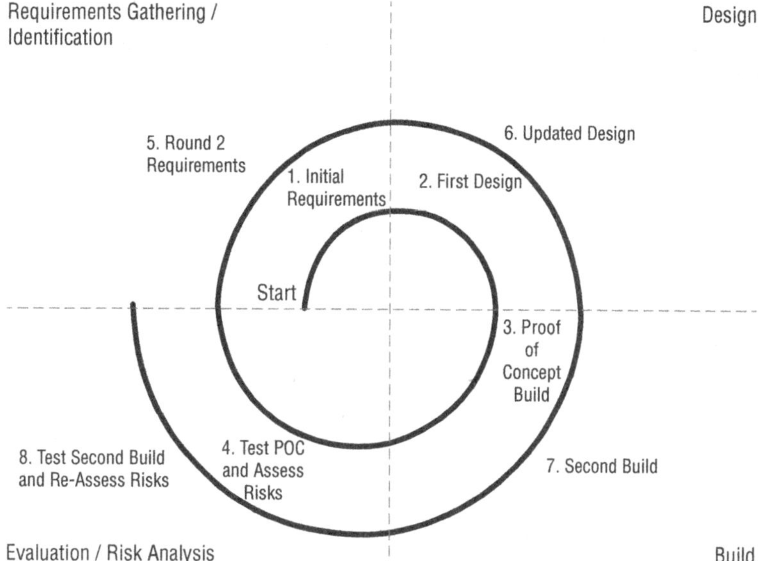

The Spiral model provides greater flexibility to handle changes in requirements as well as external influences such as availability of customer feedback and development staff. It also allows the software development life cycle to start earlier in the process than Waterfall does. Because Spiral revisits its process, it is possible for this model to result in rework or to identify design requirements later in the process that require a significant design change due to more detailed requirements coming to light.

Agile

Agile software development is an iterative and incremental process, rather than the linear processes that Waterfall and Spiral use. Agile is rooted in the Manifesto for Agile Software Development, a document that has four basic premises:

- Individuals and interactions are more important than processes and tools.
- Working software is preferable to comprehensive documentation.
- Customer collaboration replaces contract negotiation.
- Responding to change is key, rather than following a plan.

If you are used to a Waterfall or Spiral development process, Agile is a significant departure from the planning, design, and documentation-centric approaches that Agile's predecessors use. Agile methods tend to break work up into smaller units, allowing work to be done more quickly and with less up-front planning. It focuses on adapting to needs, rather than predicting them, with major milestones identified early in the process but subject to change as the project continues to develop.

Work is typically broken up into short working sessions, called *sprints*, that can last days to a few weeks. Figure 9.4 shows a simplified view of an Agile project methodology with multiple sprints conducted. When the developers and customer agree that the task is done or when the time allocated for the sprints is complete, the development effort is completed.

FIGURE 9.4 Agile sprints

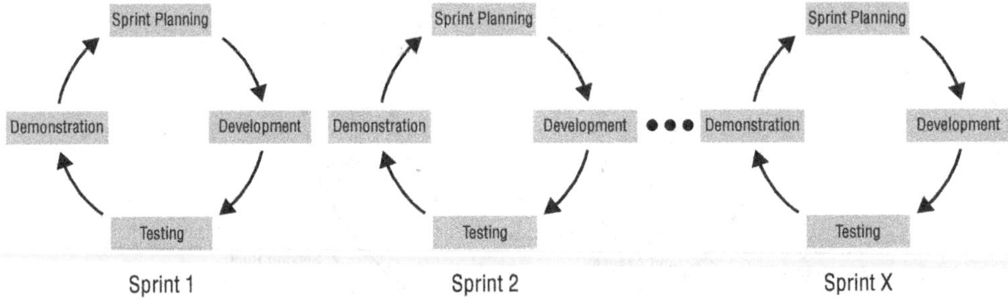

The Agile methodology is based on 12 principles:

1. Ensure customer satisfaction via early and continuous delivery of the software.
2. Welcome changing requirements, even late in the development process.
3. Deliver working software frequently (in weeks rather than months).
4. Ensure daily cooperation between developers and businesspeople.
5. Projects should be built around motivated individuals who get the support, trust, and environment they need to succeed.
6. Face-to-face conversations are the most efficient way to convey information inside the development team.
7. Progress is measured by having working software.
8. Development should be done at a sustainable pace that can be maintained on an ongoing basis.
9. Pay continuous attention to technical excellence and good design.
10. Simplicity—the art of maximizing the amount of work not done—is essential.

11. The best architectures, requirements, and designs emerge from self-organizing teams.
12. Teams should reflect on how to become more effective and then implement that behavior at regular intervals.

These principles drive an SDLC process that is less formally structured than Spiral or Waterfall but that has many opportunities for customer feedback and revision. It can react more nimbly to problems and will typically allow faster customer feedback—an advantage when security issues are discovered.

Agile development uses a number of specialized terms:

- *Backlogs* are lists of features or tasks that are required to complete a project.
- *Planning poker* is a tool for estimation and planning used in Agile development processes. Estimators are given cards with values for the amount of work required for a task. Estimators are asked to estimate, and each reveals their "bid" on the task. This is done until agreement is reached, with the goal to have estimators reach the same estimate through discussion.
- *Timeboxing*, a term that describes the use of timeboxes. Timeboxes are a previously agreed-on time that a person or team uses to work on a specific goal. This limits the time to work on a goal to the timeboxed time, rather than allowing work until completion. Once a timebox is over, the completed work is assessed to determine what needs to occur next.
- *User stories* are collected to describe high-level user requirements. A user story might be "Users can change their password via the mobile app," which would provide direction for estimation and planning for an Agile work session.
- Velocity tracking is conducted by adding up the estimates for the current sprint's effort and then comparing that to what was completed. This tells the team whether they are on track, faster, or slower than expected.

Rapid Application Development

The RAD (Rapid Application Development) model is an iterative process that relies on building prototypes. Unlike many other methods, there is no planning phase; instead, planning is done as the software is written. RAD relies on functional components of the code being developed in parallel and then integrated to produce the finished product. Much like Agile, RAD can provide a highly responsive development environment.

RAD involves five phases, as shown in Figure 9.5.

1. *Business modeling*, which focuses on the business model, including what information is important, how it is processed, and what the business process should involve.
2. *Data modeling*, including gathering and analyzing all datasets and objects needed for the effort and defining their attributes and relationships.
3. *Process modeling* for dataflows based on the business model, as well as process descriptions for how data is handled.

4. *Application generation* through coding and use of automated tools to convert data and process models into prototypes.
5. *Testing and turnover*, which focuses on the dataflow and interfaces between components since prototypes are tested at each iteration for functionality.

RAD is best suited to development efforts where the application can be modularized and where support for automated code generation exists. It works better for efforts where the ability to handle change is required and where the customer or experts with strong business process domain knowledge are available.

FIGURE 9.5 Rapid Application Development prototypes

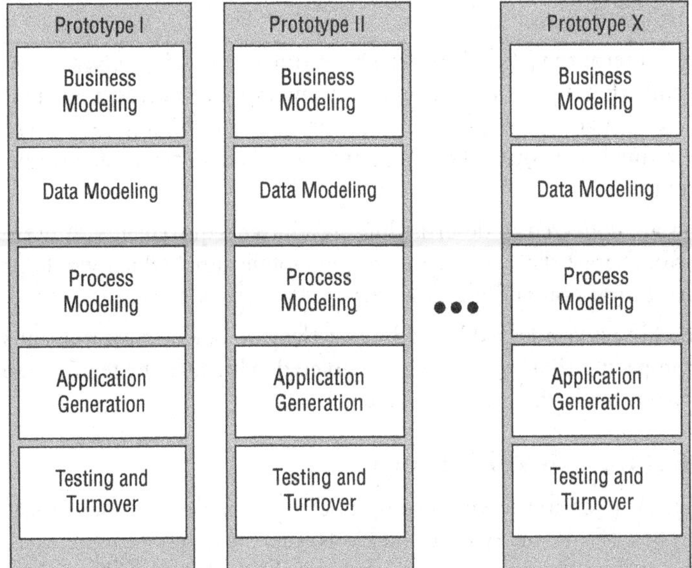

Other Models

While we have discussed some of the most common models for software development, others exist, including the following:

- The V model, which is an extension of the Waterfall model that pairs a testing phase with each development stage. Each phase starts only after the testing for the previous phase is done. Thus, at the requirements phase the requirements are reviewed (or tested), and at design phase, a test phase for the system design is completed before starting coding.

- The Big Bang SDLC model relies on no planning or process. Instead, it focuses on making resources available and simply starting coding based on requirements as they are revealed. Obviously the Big Bang model doesn't scale, but it is a common model for individual developers working on their own code.

New SDLC models spread quickly and often influence existing models with new ideas and workflows. Understanding the benefits and drawbacks of each SDLC model can help you provide input at the right times to ensure that the software that is written meets the security requirements of your organization.

DevSecOps and DevOps

DevOps combines software development and IT operations with the goal of optimizing the SDLC. This is done by using collections of tools called toolchains to improve the coding, building and test, packaging, release, configuration and configuration management, and monitoring elements of a software development life cycle.

Of course, DevOps should have security baked into it as well. The term *DevSecOps* describes security as part of the DevOps model. In this model, security is a shared responsibility that is part of the entire development and operations cycle. That means integrating security into the design, development, testing, and operational work done to produce applications and services.

The role of security practitioners in a DevSecOps model includes threat analysis and communications, planning, testing, providing feedback, and of course ongoing improvement and awareness responsibilities. To do this requires a strong understanding of the organization's risk tolerance, as well as awareness of what the others involved in the DevSecOps environment are doing and when they are doing it. DevOps and DevSecOps are often combined with continuous integration and continuous deployment methodologies where they can rely on automated security testing, and integrated security tooling including scanning, updates, and configuration management tools to help ensure security.

Exam Note

DevSecOps specifically appears in the CySA+ exam objectives, so you should be aware of what it is and what it would take to implement, but DevOps doesn't appear in the list. Outside of the exam, you're more likely to hear the term DevOps in daily use. Fortunately, most organizations are building in security integration even if they don't use the term DevSecOps.

Continuous Integration and Continuous Deployment

Continuous integration (*CI*) is a development practice that checks code into a shared repository on a consistent ongoing basis. In continuous integration environments, this can range from a few times a day to a very frequent process of check-ins and automated builds.

Since continuous integration relies on an automated build process, it also requires automated testing. It is also often paired with *continuous deployment* (CD) (sometimes called continuous delivery), which rolls out tested changes into production automatically as soon as they have been tested.

Figure 9.6 shows a view of the continuous integration/continuous deployment pipeline.

FIGURE 9.6 The CI/CD pipeline

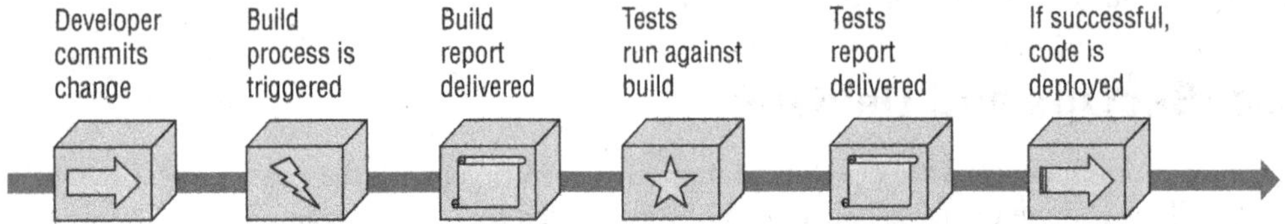

Using continuous integration and continuous deployment methods requires building automated security testing into the pipeline testing process. It can result in new vulnerabilities being deployed into production, and could allow an untrusted or rogue developer to insert flaws into code that is deployed, then remove the code as part of a deployment in the next cycle. This means that logging, reporting, and monitoring must all be designed to fit the CI/CD process.

Exam Note

Continuous integration and continuous deployment/delivery show up in Objective 3.4 in the CS0-002 exam objectives. Make sure you know the differences between them for the exam!

Designing and Coding for Security

Participating in the SDLC as a security professional provides significant opportunities to improve the security of applications. The first chance to help with software security is in the requirements gathering and design phases when security can be built in as part of the requirements and then designed in based on those requirements. Later, during the development process, secure coding techniques, code review, and testing can improve the quality and security of the code that is developed.

During the testing phase, fully integrated software can be tested using tools like web application security scanners or penetration testing techniques. This also provides the foundation for ongoing security operations by building the baseline for future security scans and regression testing during patching and updates. Throughout these steps, it helps to understand the common security issues that developers face, create, and discover.

Common Software Development Security Issues

A multitude of development styles, languages, frameworks, and other variables may be involved in the creation of an application, but many of the same security issues are the same regardless of which you use. In fact, despite many development frameworks and languages providing security features, the same security problems continue to appear in applications all the time! Fortunately, a number of common best practices are available that you can use to help ensure software security for your organization.

Exam Note

If you don't know what a pointer is, or if other terms here aren't familiar to you, we suggest spending some time on the OWASP website. The Attacks category alone contains 73 entries, and it is worth your time to read through many of them. You can find the Attacks category at `www.owasp.org/index.php/Category:Attack`.

Since the list of software vulnerabilities in the CS0-002 version of the exam is a new addition, we wouldn't be surprised if entries on this list were changed in the next version of the exam to more closely match resources like OWASP's top 10 lists.

There are many software flaws that you may encounter as a security practitioner, but the CySA+ exam focuses on some of the most common, such as the following:

- *Improper error handling*, which often results in error messages that shouldn't be exposed outside of a secure environment being accessible to attackers or the general public. Since errors often include detailed information about what is going on at the moment the error occurs, attackers can use them to learn about the application, databases, or even to get stack trace information providing significant detail they can leverage in further attacks. Errors that don't appear to provide detailed information can still allow attackers to learn more about the application, as differing responses can give attackers clues about how successful their efforts are. As a security practitioner, you should pay careful attention to application vulnerability reports that show accessible error messages, as well as the content of those messages.
- *Dereferencing* issues are often due to null pointer dereferences. This means that a pointer with a value of NULL (in other words, one that isn't set) is used as though it contains an expected value. This type of error almost always leads to a crash unless caught by an error handler. Race conditions, like those mentioned in a moment, are also a common place to find a dereferencing issue.
- *Insecure object references* occur when applications expose information about internal objects, allowing attackers to see how the object is identified and stored in a backend storage system. Once an attacker knows that, they may be able to leverage the information to gain further access, or to make assumptions about other data objects that they cannot view in this way.

- *Race conditions* rely on timing. An application that needs to take action on an object may be sensitive to what is occurring or has occurred to that object. Although race conditions are not always reliable, they can be very powerful, and repeated attacks against a race condition can result in attackers succeeding.
- *Broken authentication* is exactly what it sounds like. Improperly implemented authentication may allow attackers who are not logged in, or who are not logged in as a user with the correct rights, access to resources. Implementing a strong and reliable authentication (and authorization!) system is an important part of application coding.
- *Sensitive data exposure* may occur when any of a number of flaws are exploited. The simplest version of this is when the application does not properly protect sensitive data, allowing attackers to access it.
- *Insecure components* include a broad range of issues introduced when a component of an application or service is vulnerable and thus it introduces that vulnerability to the application. Understanding all of the components and modules that make up an application is critical to determining whether it may have known vulnerabilities that exist due to those components.
- *Insufficient logging and monitoring* will result in being unable to determine what occurred when something does go wrong. Part of a strong security design is determining what should be logged and monitored, ensuring that it is appropriately captured, and then building processes and systems to handle those logs and events so that the right thing happens when they occur.
- *Weak or default configurations* are common when applications and services are not properly set up or when default settings are used. One common example of this is using a default password for a service or database connection. Many application vulnerability scanners look for these default configurations, making it even easier for attackers to find them.
- *Use of insecure functions* can make it much harder to secure code. Functions like `strcpy`, which don't have critical security features built in, can result in code that is easier for attackers to target. In fact, *strcpy* is the only specific function that the CySA+ objectives call out, likely because of how commonly it is used for buffer overflow attacks in applications written in C. `strcpy` allows data to be copied without caring whether the source is bigger than the destination. If this occurs, attackers can place arbitrary data in memory locations past the original destination, possibly allowing a buffer overflow attack to succeed.

Exam Note

The CySA+ exam objectives mention strcpy, so you should be sure you know why it is a concern. Outside of the exam, we suggest reading more about buffer overflows instead of just knowing about strcpy. As with many code security vulnerabilities, OWASP provides a thorough explanation at `https://owasp.org/www-community/attacks/Buffer_overflow_attack`

Security Implications of Target Platforms

There are many factors that need to be taken into account when looking at software development security. The language that is used, the modules and frameworks that are part of the development process, how testing and validation are done, and of course, the underlying platform that the code will run on are all important. The platform helps to determine what tools you can use, which security capabilities are built in, and many other conditions that impact the software development process.

Exam Note

As you prepare for the exam, make sure you are familiar with each of the following platforms, including their similarities and their differences.

Mobile platforms have their own operating systems, and their own platform security controls. They also have their own security tools like the iOS Keychain and Face ID. They store data in ways that can be specific to the device, with Android devices often offering both on-board storage and storage via microSD cards, which can make tampering easier for attackers. Most of the common issues for mobile platforms, however, are similar to those found in other platforms. As of this writing, OWASP's most recent mobile vulnerability list includes insecure communication, insecure authentication and authorization, insufficient cryptography, code quality, and reverse engineering—all issues with other platforms.

Embedded systems, or computer systems that are part of a larger system with a small number of dedicated functions, and *system-on-chip* (*SOC*) systems, which embed a complete computer in a chip, can provide additional security because they're not as accessible, but that often comes with less frequent updates or an inability to update them easily. Both embedded systems and SOC devices may have hardware, firmware, and software vulnerabilities, and their pervasive nature means that broadly deployed systems are attractive targets for attackers who find them built into the Internet of Things (IoT) or the control planes of utilities, factories, and other infrastructure or critical targets.

One of the most common platforms for applications is the *client-server* application model. In this model, clients (web browsers, applications, or other clients) communicate with one or more servers that provide information to them. Web applications work this way, and security practitioners need to understand that attacks may be conducted against the clients, against the network, against the traffic sent between the client and server, and against the server itself. Thus, the attack surface of a client-server application is broad, and appropriate security measures must be implemented for each component.

The final platform that the CySA+ 2.2 exam objectives consider is firmware. *Firmware* is the embedded software used by a computer or hardware device. Firmware flaws can be hard to fix, since not all devices are designed to update their firmware. Attackers who want to target firmware will often seek to acquire a copy of the firmware, either by directly connecting to the device and downloading it or by acquiring the firmware itself from a download site or other means. After that, standard reverse engineering and other software exploitation techniques can be applied to it to identify flaws that may be worth exploiting.

Real World Scenario

Removing the Seatbelts and Airbags

A number of years ago, one of the authors of this book was hired to perform a web application security test for a new website. During testing, the website proved to be massively vulnerable to a multitude of common issues, ranging from SQL injection to session hijacking. Many of the issues that were found should have been prevented by default by the web application development environment that the team who built the website was using. In fact, signs pointed to those controls being purposefully removed instead of inadvertently disabled.

When asked about why those controls weren't there, the development team responded that "those controls slowed us down" and "we can build in better security ourselves." In essence, the team had removed every built-in safety feature that they had gotten for free by choosing the development tools they had. The reason that "Leverage Security Frameworks and Libraries" is on the OWASP top 10 controls is to prevent issues like this!

Secure Coding Best Practices

The best practices for producing secure code will vary depending on the application, its infrastructure and backend design, and what framework or language it is written in. Despite that, many of the same development, implementation, and design best practices apply to most applications. These include the following:

- *Have a secure coding policy* to serve as a foundation for secure development practices and standards.
- *Risk assessment* is important to understand what risks the application faces and how to prioritize remediation of those issues. Continuous assessment is recommended for applications using regularly scheduled testing tools that can inform the application risk assessment process.
- *Input validation* helps prevent a wide range of problems, from cross-site scripting (XSS) to SQL injection attacks.
- *Output encoding* translates special characters into an equivalent but safe version before a target application or interpreter reads it. This helps to prevent XSS attacks by preventing special characters from being inserted that cause the target application to perform an action.
- *Web application firewalls (WAFs)* can prevent attacks against vulnerable applications and offer a line of defense for applications that don't have an available patch or that cannot be taken offline for patching.

- *Error message management*, particularly ensuring that error messages do not leak information, is important to ensure that attackers can't use error messages to learn about your applications or systems.
- *Database security* at both the application and database can help ensure that data leaks don't occur.
- Using *parameterized queries*, which are precompiled SQL that takes input variables before it is executed. This helps prevent SQL injection attacks.
- *Securing sensitive information* by encrypting it or storing it using appropriate secure mechanisms (like password hashes for passwords) helps ensure that a breach of a system does not result in broader issues. The CySA+ exam calls this *data protection*.
- *Ensuring availability* by performing load and stress testing and designing the application infrastructure to be scalable can prevent outages and may limit the impact of denial-of-service attacks.
- *Monitoring and logging* should be enabled, centralized, and set to identify both application and security issues.
- *Authentication* limits access to applications to only authenticated users or systems.
- *Use multifactor authentication* to help limit the impact of credential compromises.
- *Use secure session management* to ensure that attackers cannot hijack user sessions or that session issues don't cause confusion among users.
- *Cookie management* is important for web applications that rely on cookie-based information.
- *Secure all network traffic*. Encryption of all traffic is a viable option with modern hardware, and it prevents network-based attacks from easily capturing data that could be sensitive.

Exam Note

The CySA+ exam objectives mention six specific coding best practices: input validation, output encoding, session management, authentication, data protection, and parameterized queries. This is a smaller and less developed list than what OWASP and other organizations maintain, but it is what you can expect to be tested on. Our list includes a broader range of practices to help prepare you for real-world work as well as the exam!

One of the best resources for secure coding practices is the Open Web Application Security Project (OWASP). OWASP is the home of a broad community of developers and security practitioners, and it hosts many community-developed standards, guides, and best practice documents, as well as a multitude of open source tools. OWASP provides a regularly updated list of proactive controls that is useful to review not only as a set of useful best practices, but also as a way to see how web application security threats change from year to year.

Here are OWASP's current top proactive controls (updated in 2018) with brief descriptions:

Define Security Requirements Document what security the software needs and how it should be implemented.

Leverage Security Frameworks and Libraries Use existing security tools to make it easier to develop securely.

Secure Database Access Databases contain most of the important data in modern applications, making database security a key concern.

Encode and Escape Data Ensure that attackers can't embed code or special characters in ways that will be executed or otherwise may cause harm to the application.

Validate All Inputs Treat user input as untrusted and filter appropriately.

Implement Digital Identity Identity is a core security layer, including things like using multifactor authentication, secure password storage and recovery, and session handling.

Enforce Access Controls Require all requests to go through access control checks, deny by default, and apply the principle of least privilege.

Protect Data Everywhere Use encryption in transit and at rest.

Implement Security Logging and Monitoring This helps detect problems and allows investigation after the fact.

Handle All Errors and Exceptions Errors should not provide sensitive data, and applications should be tested to ensure that they handle problems gracefully.

You can find OWASP's Proactive Controls list at `www.owasp.org/index.php/OWASP_Proactive_Controls`, and a useful quick reference guide to secure coding practices is available at `www.owasp.org/index.php/OWASP_Secure_Coding_Practices_-_Quick_Reference_Guide`.

In addition to the resources provided by OWASP, SANS maintains a list of the top 25 software errors in three categories:

- *Insecure Interaction Between Components*, which includes issues like SQL and operating system command injection, file upload path issues, cross-site request forgery, and cross-site scripting.
- *Risky Resource Management* problems, which deal with buffer overflows, path traversal attacks, and other ways that software fails to properly guard system resources.
- *Porous Defenses*, including not using or misusing defensive techniques like overly permissive rights, hard-coded credentials, missing authorization and authentication, and use of unsalted hashes.

Unfortunately, the SANS/CIS top 25 resources have not been updated since 2011. OWASP's list is regularly updated, but it is web-centric.

Top listings of common controls and problems are useful as a reminder, but understanding the set of controls that are appropriate to your environment is critical. A thorough assessment with developers and other experts who understand not only the business requirements and process but also the development language or framework will help keep your organization secure.

API Security

Application programming interfaces (APIs) are interfaces between clients and servers or applications and operating systems that define how the client should ask for information from the server and how the server will respond. This definition means that programs written in any language can implement the API and make requests.

APIs are tremendously useful for building interfaces between systems, but they can also be a point of vulnerability if they are not properly secured. API security relies on authentication, authorization, proper data scoping to ensure that too much data isn't released, rate limiting, input filtering, and appropriate monitoring and logging to remain secure. Of course, securing the underlying systems, configuring the API endpoint server or service, and providing normal network layer security to protect the service are also important.

OWASP's API Security Project provides a useful breakdown of API security techniques. You can read more at `www.owasp.org/index.php/OWASP_API_Security_Project`.

Many security tools and servers provide APIs, and security professionals are often asked to write scripts or programs that can access an API to pull data. In fact, the TAXII and STIX protocol and language we described in Chapter 2, "Using Threat Intelligence," are a great example of an interface that might be accessed via an API call.

Service-Oriented Architectures

Service-oriented architecture (SOA) is a software design that provides services to components of a system or service via communication protocols on a network. The intent of a SOA design is to allow loosely coupled components to communicate in a standardized way, allowing them to consume and provide data to other components. Developers abstract the service, hiding the complexity of the service and its inner workings, instead providing ways to access the data. Typical components of a service-oriented architecture include service providers, service registries or service brokers that provide listings and information about service providers, and consumers who access the services.

Exam Note

The CySA+ exam looks at three protocols for this—SAML, SOAP, and REST. While there are other protocols that may be used for SOA, these three are what you need to focus on for the exam.

SOAP (Simple Object Access Protocol) is an XML-based messaging protocol that was frequently used for web services. SOAP defines how messages should be formatted and exchanged, how transport of the messages occurs, as well as models for processing them. Like other XML-based protocols, SOAP is extensible, so it can be customized as needed.

We covered SAML in depth in Chapter 8, "Identity and Access Management Security," so we will focus on SOAP and REST here.

RESTful HTTP (REST stands for Representational State Transfer) has largely supplanted SOAP in many use cases because of its greater flexibility. *REST* APIs follow six architectural constraints: they use a uniform interface, they separate clients and servers, they are stateless (in other words they don't use server-side sessions), they mark whether server responses are cacheable, they are designed to allow layering of services between clients and servers, and they may include client executable code in their responses.

Both REST and SOAP allow developers to create their own APIs, but unlike SOAP, REST is not a protocol—instead, it defines how a RESTful architecture should be designed and built.

As a security professional, you need to know that public and private APIs exist and may be built using various technologies, frameworks, and protocols, including these. The APIs may themselves be vulnerable, and the underlying services, servers, and protocols may be part of the attack surface you need to assess.

What Happens When Services Team Up?

Another way to approach service-oriented architectures is to build a service entirely out of a set of loosely coupled services. *Microservices* rely on independently deployable services that are connected together to provide a business service. These services are small and decentralized, and are often built and maintained using a continuous development/continuous deployment model. Of course, this means that security professionals need to ensure that each service is properly security tested, and that the data and access that the microservice creates in aggregate is secure.

Application Testing

Application testing can be conducted in one of four ways: as a scan using a tool, via an automated vulnerability scanner, through manual penetration testing, or via code review. OWASP's Code Review guide notes that code reviews provide the best insight into all the common issues that applications face: availability, business logic, compliance, privacy, and vulnerabilities. Combining code review with a penetration test based on the code review's output (which then drives further code review, known as a 360 review) can provide even more insight into an application's security.

Information Security and the SDLC

Software defects can have a significant impact on security, but creating secure software requires more than just security scans and reviewing code when it is complete. Information security needs to be involved at each part of the SDLC process.

1. During the *Feasibility phase* security practitioners may be asked to participate in initial assessments or cost evaluations.
2. The *Analysis and Requirements Definition phase* should include security requirements and planning for requirements like authentication, data security, and technical security needs.
3. Security artifacts created during the *Design phase* often include security architecture documentation, dataflow diagrams, and other useful information.
4. The *Development (Implementation) phase* involves security testing of the code, code review, and other development-centric security operations.
5. *Testing and Integration phase* tasks include vulnerability testing and additional code review of the completed product. This also occurs when testing of a completely integrated solution can be conducted to ensure that no security issues show up once components are integrated.
6. While it may not be immediately evident, there is a security aspect to the *Training and Transition phase* as well. User training is part of the security posture of an application, and proper training can help ensure that both the users and administrators of an application are using it correctly.
7. *Operations and Maintenance* activities require ongoing scans, patching, and regression testing when upgrades occur.
8. *Disposition* of the systems and data that the application used when its life is over ensures that the end of operations for the application is not the start of a data breach.

Implementing security controls through the software development life cycle can help ensure that the applications that enter production are properly secured and maintained throughout their life cycle. Being fully involved in the SDLC requires security professionals to learn about the tools, techniques, and processes that development teams use, so be ready to learn about how software is created in your organization.

NIST's "Systems Security Engineering" SP 800-160 is the current reference that includes coverage of software development as well as system development. It can be found at `nvlpubs.nist.gov/nistpubs/SpecialPublications/NIST.SP.800-160v1.pdf`.

Version Control and Source Code Management

Once the SDLC reaches the development phase, code starts to be generated. That means that the ability to control the version of the software or component that your team is working on, combined with check-in/check-out functionality and revision histories, is a necessary and powerful tool when developing software. Fortunately, version control and *source control management* tools fill that role.

A strong SDLC requires the ability to determine that the code that is being deployed or tested is the correct version and that fixes that were previously applied have not been dropped from the release that is under development. Popular version control systems include Git, Subversion, and CVS, but there are dozens of different tools in use.

Code Review Models

Reviewing the code that is written for an application provides a number of advantages. It helps to share knowledge of the code, and the experience gained by writing is better than simple documentation alone since it provides personal understanding of the code and its functions. It also helps detect problems while enforcing coding best practices and standards by exposing the code to review during its development cycle. Finally, it ensures that multiple members of a team are aware of what the code is supposed to do and how it accomplishes its task.

There are a number of common *code review* processes, including both formal and Agile processes like pair programming, over-the-shoulder, and Fagan code reviews.

OWASP's Code Review guide provides in-depth technical information on specific vulnerabilities and how to find them, as well as how to conduct a code review. It can be found here: `www.owasp.org/index.php/Category:OWASP_Code_Review_Project`.

Pair Programming

Pair programming is an Agile software development technique that places two developers at one workstation. One developer writes code, while the other developer reviews their code as they write it. This is intended to provide real-time code review, and it ensures that multiple developers are familiar with the code that is written. In most pair programming environments, the developers are expected to change roles frequently, allowing both of them to spend time thinking about the code while at the keyboard and to consider the design and any issues in the code while reviewing it.

Pair programming adds additional cost to development since it requires two full-time developers. At the same time, it provides additional opportunities for review and analysis of the code and directly applies more experience to coding problems, potentially increasing the quality of the code.

Over-the-Shoulder

Over-the-shoulder code review also relies on a pair of developers, but rather than requiring constant interaction and hand-offs, over-the-shoulder requires the developer who wrote the code to explain the code to the other developer. This allows peer review of code and can also assist developers in understanding how the code works, without the relatively high cost of pair programming.

Pass-Around Code Reviews

Pass-around code review, sometimes known as email pass-around code review, is a form of manual peer review done by sending completed code to reviewers who check the code for issues. Pass-around reviews may involve more than one reviewer, allowing reviewers with different expertise and experience to contribute their expertise. Although pass-around reviews allow more flexibility in *when* they occur than an over-the-shoulder review, they don't provide the same easy opportunity to learn about the code from the developer who wrote it that over-the-shoulder and pair programming offer, making documentation more important.

Tool-Assisted Reviews

Tool-assisted code reviews rely on formal or informal software-based tools to conduct code reviews. Tools like Atlassian's Crucible collaborative code review tool, Codacy's static code review tool, and Phabricator's Differential code review tool are all designed to improve the code review process. The wide variety of tools used for code review reflects not only the multitude of software development life cycle options but also how organizations set up their design and review processes.

Choosing a Review Method

Table 9.1 compares the four informal code review methods and formal code review. Specific implementations may vary, but these comparisons will generally hold true between each type of code review. In addition, the theory behind each method may not always reflect the reality of how an organization will use it. For example, pair programming is intended to provide the same speed of development as two developers working on their own while increasing the quality of the code. This may be true for experienced programmers who work well together, but lack of training, personality differences, and variation in work styles can make pair programming less effective than expected.

TABLE 9.1 Code review method comparison

	Cost	When does review happen	Ability to explain the code	Skill required
Pair programming	Medium	Real time	High	Users must know how to pair program
Over-the-shoulder	Medium	Real time	High	No additional skill
Pass-around code review	Low/Medium	Asynchronous	Low	No additional skill
Tool assisted review	Medium	Tool/process dependent	Typically low	Training to use the tool may be required
Formal code review	High	Asynchronous	Typically low	Code review process training

Exam Note

The CySA+ exam objectives simply list "code review" without mentioning the review methods we have covered here. You'll want to have the concept of code reviews in mind as you take the exam, but you may not be asked to explain all of the methods in depth. As with some of the other topics we cover, we think that it is useful to be aware of these techniques as security professionals who may encounter them or may need to help your organization choose the right option.

When code requires more in-depth review than the relatively lightweight Agile processes like pass-around and over-the-shoulder reviews, formal code review processes are sometimes used. As you might imagine from the name, formal code reviews are an in-depth, often time-consuming process intended to fully review code using a team of experts. The primary form of formal code review is Fagan inspection.

Fagan Inspection

Fagan inspection is a form of structured, formal code review intended to find a variety of problems during the development process. Fagan inspection specifies entry and exit criteria for processes, ensuring that a process is not started before appropriate diligence has been performed, and also making sure that there are known criteria for moving to the next phase.

The Fagan inspection process in Figure 9.7 shows the six typical phases:

1. Planning, including preparation of materials, attendees, and location
2. Overview, which prepares the team by reviewing the materials and assigning roles such as coder, reader, reviewer, and moderator
3. Preparation, which involves reviewing the code or other item being inspected and documents any issues or questions they may have
4. Meeting to identify defects based on the notes from the preparation phase
5. Rework to resolve issues
6. Follow-up by the moderator to ensure that all issues identified have been found and that no new defects were created during the resolution process

FIGURE 9.7 Fagan code review

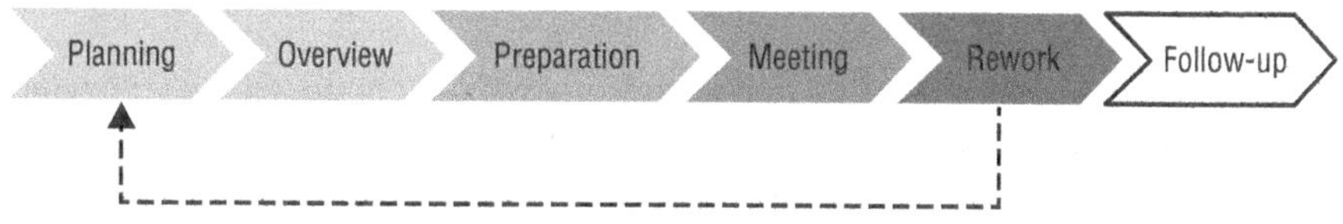

Formal methods for verification of software like Fagan inspection and similar formal review processes can sound very expensive, but catching problems early can result in significant savings in time and cost. Fagan code reviews remain relatively rare since many of the "lightweight" review options are easier to implement, offer many of the same benefits, and are far less costly.

Software Security Testing

No matter how talented the development team for an application is, there will be some form of flaws in the code. Veracode's 2019 metrics for applications based on their testing showed that 83 percent of the 1.4 million applications they scanned had at least one security flaw in the initial scan. That number points to a massive need for software security testing to continue to be better integrated into the software development life cycle.

Veracode provides a useful yearly review of the state of software security. You can read more of the most recent report at www.veracode.com/state-of-software-security-report.

A broad variety of manual and automatic testing tools and methods are available to security professionals and developers. Fortunately, automated tools have continued to improve, providing an easier way to verify that code is more secure. Over the next few pages, we will review some of the critical software security testing methods and tools.

Software Assessment: Testing and Analyzing Code

The source code that is the basis of every application and program can contain a variety of bugs and flaws, from programming and syntax errors to problems with business logic, error handling, and integration with other services and systems. It is important to be able to analyze the code to understand what it does, how it performs that task, and where flaws may occur in the program itself. This is often done via static or dynamic code analysis, along with testing methods like fuzzing, fault injection, mutation testing, and stress testing. Once changes are made to code and it is deployed, it must be regression tested to ensure that the fixes put in place didn't create new security issues.

Static Code Analysis

Static code analysis (sometimes called source code analysis) is conducted by reviewing the code for an application. Since static analysis uses the source code for an application, it can be seen as a type of white-box testing with full visibility to the testers. This can allow testers to find problems that other tests might miss, either because the logic is not exposed to other testing methods or because of internal business logic problems.

Unlike many other methods, static analysis does not run the program; instead, it focuses on understanding how the program is written and what the code is intended to do. Static code analysis can be conducted using automated tools or manually by reviewing the code—a process sometimes called "code understanding." Automated static code analysis can be very effective at finding known issues, and manual static code analysis helps identify programmer-induced errors.

OWASP provides static code analysis tools for .NET, Java, PHP, C, and JSP, as well as a list of other static code analysis tools, at www.owasp.org/index.php/Static_Code_Analysis.

Dynamic Code Analysis

Dynamic code analysis relies on execution of the code while providing it with input to test the software. Much like static code analysis, dynamic code analysis may be done via automated tools or manually, but there is a strong preference for automated testing due to the volume of tests that need to be conducted in most dynamic code testing processes.

Exam Note

Both static and dynamic analysis tools show up in Objective 2.2. You'll need to know the differences between the two types of tools.

Fuzzing

Fuzz testing, or *fuzzing*, involves sending invalid or random data to an application to test its ability to handle unexpected data. The application is monitored to determine if it crashes, fails, or responds in an incorrect manner. Because of the large amount of data that a fuzz test involves, fuzzing is typically automated, and it is particularly useful for detecting input validation and logic issues as well as memory leaks and error handling. Unfortunately, fuzzing tends to identify only simple problems; it does not account for complex logic or business process issues and may not provide complete code coverage if its progress is not monitored.

Fault Injection

Unlike fuzzing, fault injection directly inserts faults into error handling paths, particularly error handling mechanisms that are rarely used or might otherwise be missed during normal testing. Fault injection may be done in one of three ways:

- Compile-time injection, which inserts faults by modifying the source code of the application
- Protocol software fault injection, which uses fuzzing techniques to send unexpected or protocol noncompliant data to an application or service that expects protocol-compliant input
- Runtime injection of data into the running program, either by inserting it into the running memory of the program or by injecting the faults in a way that causes the program to deal with them

Fault injection is typically done using automated tools due to the potential for human error in the fault injection process.

Mutation Testing

Mutation testing is related to fuzzing and fault injection, but rather than changing the inputs to the program or introducing faults to it, mutation testing makes small modifications to the program itself. The altered versions, or mutants, are then tested and rejected if they cause failures. The mutations themselves are guided by rules that are intended to create common errors as well as to replicate the types of errors that developers might introduce during their normal programing process. Much like fault injection, mutation testing helps identify issues with code that is infrequently used, but it can also help identify problems with test data and scripts by finding places where the scripts do not fully test for possible issues.

Stress Testing and Load Testing

Performance testing for applications is as important as testing for code flaws. Ensuring that applications and the systems that support them can stand up to the full production load they are anticipated to need is part of a typical SDLC process. When an application is ready to be tested, *stress test applications* and *load testing tools* are used to simulate a full application load, and in the case of stress testing, to go beyond any normal level of load to see how the application or system will respond when tested to the breaking point.

Stress and load testing should typically test for a worst-case scenario. In fact, many organizations load-test to the infrastructure's breaking point so that they know what their worst-case scenario is. With automatically scaling applications becoming more common, this is a lot harder to do, so setting a reasonable maximum load to test to is recommended if you have a scalable application or infrastructure.

Stress testing can also be conducted against individual components of an application to ensure that they are capable of handling load conditions. During integration and component testing, fault injection may also be used to ensure that problems during heavy load are properly handled by the application.

Security Regression Testing

Regression testing focuses on testing to ensure that changes that have been made do not create new issues. From a security perspective, this often comes into play when patches are installed or when new updates are applied to a system or application. *Security regression testing* is performed to ensure that no new vulnerabilities, misconfigurations, or other issues have been introduced.

Automated testing using tools like web application vulnerability scanners and other vulnerability scanning tools are often used as part of an automated or semiautomated regression testing process. Reports are generated to review the state of the application (and its underlying server and services) before and after changes are made to ensure that it remains secure.

It isn't uncommon for a vulnerability to be introduced by a patch or fix. Coders who are not following best practices for code commits and other good habits for version control may accidentally put code that was previously fixed back into a new release without noticing the problem. Change control as well as version and source code management practices are critical to preventing this.

Hardware Assurance Best Practices

While we often think about software security, the security of the underlying hardware can also be a concern. Checking the individual components built into every device in your organization is likely beyond the capabilities that you will have, but you should know the concepts behind hardware assurance and what to look for if you need to have high assurance levels for your devices and systems.

Cryptographic Hardware

Modern hardware assurance often begins with the *hardware root of trust*. The hardware root of trust for a system contains the cryptographic keys that secure the boot process. This means that the system or device inherently trusts the hardware root of trust, and that it needs to be secure! One common implementation of a hardware root of trust is the *Trusted Platform Module (TPM)* chip built into many computers. TPM chips are frequently used to provide built-in encryption, and they provide three major functions:

- Remote attestation, allowing hardware and software configurations to be verified
- Binding, which encrypts data
- Sealing, which encrypts data and sets requirements for the state of the TPM chip before decryption

While TPM chips are one common solution, others include serial numbers that cannot be modified or cloned, and physically unclonable functions (PUFs), which are unique to the specific hardware device that provides a unique identifier or digital fingerprint for the device.

A PUF is based on the unique features of a microprocessor that are created when it is manufactured and are not intentionally created or replicated.

An additional security feature intended to help prevent boot-level malware is *measured boot*. Measured boot processes measure each component, starting with the firmware and ending with the boot start drivers. The data gathered is stored in a TPM module, and the logs can be validated remotely to let security administrators know the boot state of the system. This allows comparison against known good states, and administrators can take action if the measured boot shows a difference from the accepted or secure known state.

A related technology is hardware security modules (HSMs). Hardware security modules are typically external devices or plug-in cards used to create, store, and manage digital keys for cryptographic functions and authentication, as well as to offload cryptographic processing. HSMs are often used in high-security environments and are normally certified to meet standards like FIPS 140 or Common Criteria standards.

Firmware Security

Other defensive technologies can also help to secure systems. IBM's eFuse technology has a number of uses that can help with tuning performance or responding to system degradation, but it also has some interesting security applications. For example, an eFuse can be set at the chip level to monitor firmware levels. This is implemented in the Nintendo Switch, which uses eFuse checking to validate whether the firmware that is being installed is older than the currently installed firmware, preventing downgrading of firmware. When newer firmware is installed, eFuses are "burned," indicating the new firmware level that is installed.

Most modern computers use a version of the Unified Extensible Firmware Interface (UEFI). UEFI provides for the ability to secure boot, which will load only drivers and operating system loaders that have been signed using an accepted digital signature. Since these keys have to be loaded into the UEFI firmware, UEFI security has been somewhat contentious, particularly with the open source community. UEFI remains one way to provide additional security if your organization needs to have a greater level of trust in the software a system is loading.

You may be used to hearing the term BIOS (basic input/output system) firmware that computers used to boot from. UEFI is the replacement for BIOS and provides a wide range of more modern features.

If you rely on firmware to provide security, you also need a method to ensure that the firmware is secure and that updates to the firmware are secure. Trusted firmware updates can help, with validation done using methods like checksum validation, cryptographic signing, and similar techniques. This technique is frequently used to validate updates like those for network devices, motherboards, phones, printers, and other hardware that receives firmware updates.

Exam Note

The CySA+ exam outline calls out "trusted firmware updates," but trusted firmware itself is more commonly described as part of *trusted execution environments (TEEs)*. Trusted firmware is signed by a chip vendor or other trusted party, and then used to access keys to help control access to hardware. TEEs like those used by ARM processors leverage these technologies to protect the hardware by preventing unsigned code from using privileged features.

Hardware Security

Securing hardware can start at the supply chain level. The U.S. government started the Trusted Foundry Program to validate microelectronic suppliers throughout the supply chain. The program assesses the integrity and processes of the companies, staff, distribution chain, and other factors involved in the delivery of microelectronics components and devices. This provides a chain of custody for classified and unclassified integrated circuits, and helps to ensure that reasonable threats to the supply chain are prevented such as tampering, reverse engineering, or modification. You can read about the DMEA and its role with trusted foundry accreditation at `https://www.dmea.osd.mil/TrustedIC.aspx`

The security of hardware is also done at the underlying design level. A number of these concepts are part of the CySA+:

- *Secure processing* can mean a number of things, but in the context of hardware security it typically refers to trusted execution environments. Much like other low-level hardware protections, secure processing often starts with boot processes and may include monitoring, privileged execution management, and other protections. Secure processing can leverage or allow access to a trusted execution environment.
- *Processor security extensions* exist in many different CPUs, including ARM, Intel, and AMD CPUs. They provide security-related functions implemented in the CPU hardware. Extensions typically recognize secure and nonsecure states and have memory allocated as secure memory, but implementations may vary.
- *Atomic execution* describes a type of operation during which a processor both reads and writes a location during the same bus operation. Since this happens in the same operation, it prevents other processors or devices from accessing or modifying the location during the operation, helping to ensure the integrity of the operation.
- *Secure enclaves* in modern Apple mobile devices are hardware components that provide cryptographic operations and user authentication, and are designed to remain secure even if the operating system is compromised. They run their own micro-kernel, and their own secure boot process, allowing secure processing separate from the rest of the operating system and CPU. Secure enclaves on Apple devices generate an encryption key at boot, then pair it with a userID to encrypt, validate, and use the secure enclave's portion of system memory. The secure enclave also handles things like Face ID, allowing authentication to be handled in a secure partition.

Exam Note

The CySA+ exam outline specifically calls out a small subset of hardware assurance best practices and technologies, including anti-tamper, self-encrypting drives, trusted firmware updates, measured boot and attestation, and bus encryption. Make sure you know what they are and why they might be used so that you can answer questions about them.

Finally, there are a number of techniques that can help to protect devices. The CySA+ exam outline calls out a few that you may encounter:

- *Anti-tamper* protection comes in many varieties from mechanical means like anti-tamper screws and holographic stickers to electronic detection methods. Tamper-proofing microprocessors often takes the form of encasing electronics or otherwise securing them, while attackers use techniques like physically probing or modifying them, freezing devices, and applying out-of-spec power or signals.
- *Self-encrypting drives (SEDs)* provide built-in encryption capabilities. When the drive needs to be accessed, the user must present a cryptographic key. Once the key is provided, the drive is unlocked and accessible, transparently encrypting and decrypting data as it is needed. This means that if the drive is removed or the key is not available, all of the contents of the drive will remain encrypted and secure.
- *Bus encryption* is used to protect data traveling inside as system or device. Bus encryption relies on built-in cryptographic processing capabilities to secure information as it flows from one component to another, often from the CPU to other elements of the device. Using an encrypted bus can protect data that is being processed and help to prevent reverse engineering efforts conducted against the hardware or CPU.

Summary

The software development life cycle describes the path that software takes from planning and requirements gathering to design, coding, testing, training, and deployment. Once software is operational, it also covers the ongoing maintenance and eventual decommissioning of the software. That means that participating in the SDLC as a security professional can have a significant impact on organizational software security.

There are many SDLC models, including the linear Waterfall method, Spiral's iterative process-based design, and Agile methodologies that focus on sprints with timeboxed working sessions and greater flexibility to meet changing customer needs. Other models include Rapid Application Development's iterative prototype-based cycles, the V model with parallel test cycles for each stage, and the Big Bang model, a model without real planning or process. Each SDLC model offers advantages and disadvantages, meaning that a single model may not fit every project.

Coding for information security requires an understanding of common software coding best practices. These include performing risk assessments, validating all user input to applications, ensuring that error messages don't reveal internal information, and securing sessions, traffic, and cookies if they are used. OWASP and other organizations provide up-to-date guidance on common issues as well as current best practices, allowing security professionals and developers to stay up to date.

Security testing and code review can help to improve an application's security and code quality. Pair programming, over-the-shoulder code review, pass-around code reviews, and tool-assisted code reviews are all common, but for formal review Fagan inspection remains the primary, but time-intensive, solution. Security testing may involve static or dynamic code analysis, fuzzing, fault injection, mutation testing, stress or load testing, or regression testing, with each providing specific functionality that can help ensure the security of an application.

Finally, web application security testing is conducted using both automated scanners known as web application vulnerability scanners, and by penetration testers and web application security testing professionals. Much like vulnerability scanning, using application-scanning tools provides a recurring view of the application's security profile and monitors for changes due to patches, configuration changes, or other new issues.

Exam Essentials

Be familiar with the software development life cycle (SDLC). SDLC models include Waterfall, Spiral, Agile, and RAD. Each model covers phases like feasibility, requirements gathering, design, development, testing and integration, deployment and training, operations, and eventual decommissioning, although they may not always occur in the same order or at the same time.

Explain how designing information security into applications occurs in each phase of the SDLC. Coding best practices and understanding common software issues are important to prevent security flaws. Version control helps to prevent issues that exist in older code versions from reappearing in new code. Code review models like over-the-shoulder and pair programming, as well as formal review using Fagan inspection, are used to validate the quality and security of code.

Define the purpose of security testing. The majority of code has critical flaws, making testing a necessity. Static testing targets source code, whereas dynamic testing tests the application itself. Fuzzing, fault injection, mutation testing, stress and load testing, as well as security regression testing are all common testing methods. Web applications are tested using web application vulnerability scanners as well as via manual methods to ensure that they are secure and that no new vulnerabilities have been added by configuration changes or patches.

Know how hardware security interacts with software to provide a trusted computing environment. Hardware trust starts at the foundry or manufacturer. Hardware modules like HSM and TPM modules can provide cryptographic and other security services to help systems remain secure. Firmware and hardware security features like eFuse, trusted execution environments, and secure enclaves provide ways for hardware and software developers to leverage security features.

Lab Exercises

Activity 9.1: Review an Application Using the OWASP Application Security Architecture Cheat Sheet

In this exercise you will use the Acunetix web vulnerability scanner to scan a sample site and then review the data generated.

Part 1: Download and install the Acunetix scanner

Acunetix provides their Web Vulnerability scanner as a 14-day limited term trial download. You can download it at `www.acunetix.com/vulnerability-scanner/download/`.

Part 2: Select an application and scan it

When you download the Acunetix scanner, you will receive an email listing Acunetix-hosted vulnerable sites. Select one of these sites and use the vulnerability scanner to scan it. Once it is complete, review the report that was generated by the scan.

Part 3: Analyze the scan results

Review the scan results and answer the following questions.

1. What is the most critical vulnerability? How can it be remediated?
2. What is the most common vulnerability (which occurs most often)? Is there a coding change you would recommend to the developers of this application to prevent it?
3. How would you protect this application if you were not able to change the code?

Activity 9.2: Learn About Web Application Exploits from WebGoat

OWASP in partnership with Mandiant provides the OWASP Broken Web Applications project virtual machine. This VM includes very vulnerable web applications as a VMware VM, including WebGoat, OWASP's web application vulnerability learning environment.

Step 1: Download the VMware VM

Go to `sourceforge.net/projects/owaspbwa/files/1.2/`.

Step 2: Run the VMware VM and start WebGoat

Run the virtual machine using VMware —you can use the free vSphere Hypervisor from `www.vmware.com/products/vsphere-hypervisor.html`, or the 30-day demo of Workstation Player from `www.vmware.com/products/player/playerpro-evaluation.html`.

Once the VM starts, log in as root with the password **owaspbwa** and run **`ifconfig`** to determine your system's IP address.

Step 3: Succeed with an attack

WebGoat includes a multitude of vulnerable web application modules. Select one (or more!) and follow the instructions to attack the application. If you need help, review the WebGoat lesson plans and solutions at `https://github.com/WebGoat/WebGoat/wiki/(Almost)-Fully-Documented-Solution-(en)`, or visit YouTube, where you'll find numerous videos that show step-by-step guides to the solutions.

Activity 9.3: SDLC Terminology

Match each of the following terms to the correct description.

Subversion	The first SDLC model, replaced in many organizations but still used for very complex systems
Agile	A formal code review process that relies on specified entry and exit criteria for each phase
Dynamic code analysis	An Agile term that describes the list of features needed to complete a project
Fuzzing	A source control management tool
Fagan inspection	A code review process that requires one developer to explain their code to another developer
Over-the-shoulder	An SDLC model that relies on sprints to accomplish tasks based on user stories
Waterfall	A code analysis done using a running application that relies on sending unexpected data to see if the application fails
Backlog	A code analysis that is done using a running application

Review Questions

1. What term describes a chip that is built into a computer that stores encryption keys specific to the system that is used for hardware authentication?
   A. Trusted foundry
   B. TPM
   C. HSM
   D. SED
2. During a Fagan code inspection, which process can redirect to the planning stage?
   A. Overview
   B. Preparation
   C. Meeting
   D. Rework
3. Adam is conducting software testing by reviewing the source code of the application. What type of code testing is Adam conducting?
   A. Mutation testing
   B. Static code analysis
   C. Dynamic code analysis
   D. Fuzzing
4. After a major patch is released for the web application that he is responsible for, Sam proceeds to run his web application security scanner against the web application to verify that it is still secure. What is the term for the process Sam is conducting?
   A. Code review
   B. Regression testing
   C. Stress testing
   D. Whiffing
5. During testing, Tiffany slowly increases the number of connections to an application until it fails. What is she doing?
   A. Regression testing
   B. Unit testing
   C. Stress testing
   D. Fagan testing
6. Charles is worried about users conducting SQL injection attacks. Which of the following solutions will best address his concerns?
   A. Using secure session management
   B. Enabling logging on the database

C. Performing user input validation

D. Implementing TLS

7. Susan's team has been writing code for a major project for a year and recently released their third version of the code. During a postimplementation regression test, an issue that was originally seen in version 1 reappeared. What type of tool should Susan implement to help avoid this issue in the future?

 A. Stress testing

 B. A WAF

 C. Pair programming

 D. Source control management

8. Precompiled SQL statements that only require variables to be input are an example of what type of application security control?

 A. Parameterized queries

 B. Encoding data

 C. Input validation

 D. Appropriate access controls

9. What process checks to ensure that functionality meets customer needs?

 A. CNA

 B. Stress testing

 C. UAT

 D. Unit testing

10. Matt wants to prevent attackers from capturing data by directly connecting to the hardware communications components of a device he is building. What should he use to make sure that communications between the processor and other chips are not vulnerable?

 A. Bus encryption

 B. A HSM

 C. A TPM module

 D. LAMP encryption

11. Using TLS to protect application traffic helps satisfy which of the OWASP best practices?

 A. Parameterize queries

 B. Encode data

 C. Validate all inputs

 D. Protect data

12. Kristen wants to implement a code review but has a distributed team that works at various times during the day. She also does not want to create any additional support load for her team with new development environment applications. What type of review process will work best for her needs?
    - A. Pair programming
    - B. Pass-around
    - C. Over-the-shoulder
    - D. Tool-assisted
13. What type of attack is typically associated with the `strcpy` function?
    - A. Pointer dereferencing
    - B. A race condition
    - C. SQL injection
    - D. Buffer overflow
14. Kathleen wants to build a public API for a modern service-oriented architecture. What model is likely her best choice?
    - A. REST
    - B. SOAP
    - C. SAML
    - D. RAD
15. During a web application test, Ben discovers that the application shows SQL code as part of an error provided to application users. What should he note in his report?
    - A. Improper error handling
    - B. Code exposure
    - C. SQL injection
    - D. A default configuration issue
16. What process is used to ensure that an application can handle very high numbers of concurrent users or sessions?
    - A. Fuzzing
    - B. Fault injection
    - C. Mutation testing
    - D. Load testing
17. Gabby wants to insert data into the response from her browser to a web application. What type of tool should she use if she wants to easily make manual changes in what her browser sends out as she interacts with the website?
    - A. An interception proxy
    - B. A fuzzer

C. A WAF

D. A sniffer

18. What type of testing focuses on inserting problems into the error handling processes and paths in an application?

    A. Fuzzing

    B. Stress testing

    C. Dynamic code analysis

    D. Fault injection

19. The application that Scott is writing has a flaw that occurs when two operations are attempted at the same time, resulting in unexpected results when the two actions do not occur in the expected order. What type of flaw does the application have?

    A. Dereferencing

    B. A race condition

    C. An insecure function

    D. Improper error handling

20. Every time Susan checks code into her organization's code repository it is tested, validated, then if accepted it is immediately put into production. What is the term for this?

    A. Continuous integration

    B. Continuous delivery

    C. A security nightmare

    D. Agile development

Security Operations and Monitoring

THE COMPTIA CYBERSECURITY ANALYST (CYSA+) EXAM OBJECTIVES COVERED IN THIS CHAPTER INCLUDE:

✓ **Domain 3.0: Security Operations and Monitoring**

- 3.1: Given a scenario, analyze data as part of security monitoring activities.
- 3.4: Compare and contrast automation concepts and technologies.

Monitoring systems, devices, and events throughout an organization can be a monumental task. Endpoint devices, servers, applications, and almost every other connected devices in your organization can, and likely do, log what happens on them and to them. Those logs can be an invaluable resource for security analysts, allowing detection of misuse and compromise, but they can also bury important information in mountains of operational data.

Learning how to analyze data from the many sources is a critical part of being a security analyst. Techniques like email header analysis, rule writing for event management systems, and basic scripting and query writing techniques should all be part of your toolkit.

In this chapter, you will explore how security monitoring data is captured and analyzed. You will learn the details of how endpoint and network monitoring techniques and technologies are applied as well as some of the artifacts that security analysts commonly look for. Along the way, you will explore logging tools, how to access common logs on Windows and Linux systems, and the log review concepts that are used to analyze firewall, IDS/IPS, system, and event logs.

Security Monitoring

The foundation of most security designs relies on the concept of *defense-in-depth*. In other words, a single defensive measure should not be the only control preventing an attacker (or a mistake!) from creating a problem. Since there are many potential ways for a security breach to occur, a wide range of defenses must be layered together to ensure that a failure in one does not endanger sensitive data, systems, or networks.

Analyzing Security Data

Organizations can end up with a massive volume of security data from monitoring and logging various systems and services. Security analysts are often asked to help analyze that data to identify security issues and to respond to security events.

This means that analysts need to know how to quickly assess the *organizational impact* of an event and must be able to determine if the event is localized or if it has a broader scope. Analyzing the impact of an event requires the following:

- Knowing if other events are correlated with the initial event
- Understanding what systems, users, services, or other assets were involved or impacted

- Data classification for any data assets that are part of the event
- Other information that may influence organizational decisions about the event

Analyzing data will also require the ability to sort through it, either using a security information and event management (SIEM) tool, through logging and aggregation technologies like Splunk or an ELK (Elasticsearch, Logstash, and Kibana) stack implementation, or using more manual techniques.

In addition to assessing organizational impact versus *localized impact*, analysts must determine what the immediate impact of an event or incident is versus the total impact. A single incident may result in little or no harm, but it may also be a sign of a larger compromise or a broad scale attack against an organization.

Understanding what is occurring across an organization may involve *trend analysis* techniques that help analysts see changes from a baseline or normal levels for events. They can also help analysts compare events against industry norms or historic patterns.

Logs

Applications, services, systems, and many other assets in your organization's infrastructure will either generate logs or will have the ability to generate logs if you configure them properly. The sheer volume of logs and logging sources can quickly become overwhelming, and finding meaningful data in logs from even a small organization may feel impossible.

Security analysts need to know what logs exist by default on systems, how to access them, how to find information about the content of those logs, and how to interpret that content. In addition, you need to understand how the organization uses logs, whether those logs are properly secured, and what gaps exist in log collecting and analysis infrastructure.

Exam Note

The CySA+ exam objectives list a few specific items for log review: event logs, syslog, firewall logs, web application firewall (WAF) logs, proxy logs, and intrusion detection and prevention system logs. We will discuss the basics of each of those types of logs in this chapter. If you haven't encountered an example of one or more of these types of logs, you may want to dig a little deeper outside of this book to familiarize yourself with that type of log data and the specifics of how to analyze it.

Event Logs

The Windows event log can be viewed directly on workstations using the Event Viewer from the Start menu. By default, Windows includes Application, Security, Setup, and System logs, which can all be useful for analysts. In Figure 10.1, you can see an example of the Application log showing installer events. Tracking when a specific package was installed and by whom is a common part of many investigations into malware events and other forensic or incident response processes.

FIGURE 10.1 Windows Event Viewer entries

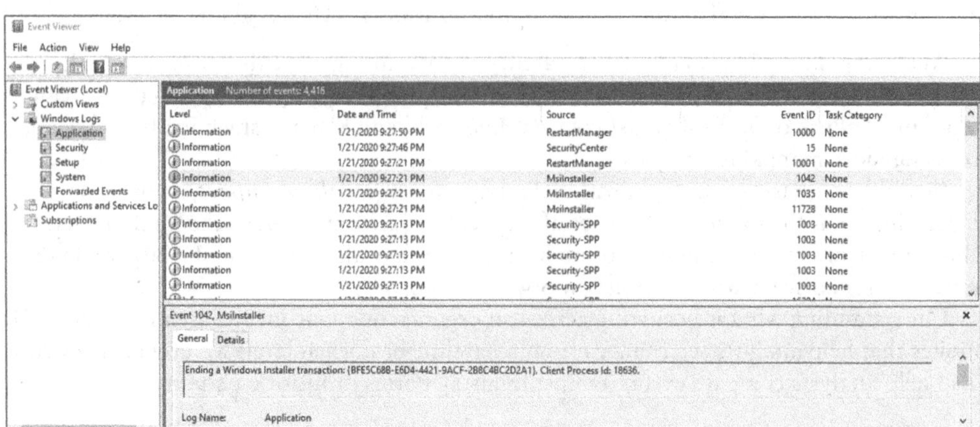

Event Viewer also works for Active Directory logs, although you'll quickly find that even a moderately sized domain can generate more logs than you may want to directly view in Event Viewer. Exporting your logs to a purpose-built log aggregation and analysis system can be an attractive option.

Syslog

Linux maintains information about the state of the system, events, and many other details, typically in the `/var/log` directory. Additional logs may be in application-specific directories, or other locations on the system based on specific configurations or application and service defaults.

Figure 10.2 shows the `auth.log` file on an Ubuntu server with a variety of `sudo` events that occurred. Searching for known events that include the use of administrative privileges is a common part of incident investigations.

Security Device Logs

Security devices capture information about security events, system events, and other details that can be useful to security analysts. While most devices are capable of sending syslog compatible messages, what those messages contain and the way they are formatted can vary significantly from vendor to vendor.

Exam Note

The CySA+ exam is vendor neutral, which means you're not expected to be an expert in any specific vendor's log format, messages, or error codes. That also means that you need to understand how to read log entries without knowing the specifics of the log format. Here, we focus on log entry concepts and provide a handful of examples for you to review. If you find these challenging, you should spend some additional time with logs from sources you're not familiar with so that reading new types of logs becomes more natural to you.

FIGURE 10.2 Linux syslog entries in `auth.log` with sudo events

```
example@cysa_demo: /var/log
Jan 26 18:35:28 cysa_demo sudo: pam_unix(sudo:session): session closed for user root
Jan 26 18:35:37 cysa_demo sudo:   example : TTY=tty1 ; PWD=/home/example ; USER=root ; COMMAND=/usr/sbin/ufw all
ow Apache
Jan 26 18:35:37 cysa_demo sudo: pam_unix(sudo:session): session opened for user root by example(uid=0)
Jan 26 18:35:37 cysa_demo sudo: pam_unix(sudo:session): session closed for user root
Jan 26 18:35:44 cysa_demo sshd[1334]: Received signal 15; terminating.
Jan 26 18:35:44 cysa_demo sshd[6096]: Server listening on 0.0.0.0 port 22.
Jan 26 18:35:44 cysa_demo sshd[6096]: Server listening on :: port 22.
Jan 26 18:35:59 cysa_demo sudo:   example : TTY=tty1 ; PWD=/home/example ; USER=root ; COMMAND=/usr/sbin/ufw sta
tus
Jan 26 18:35:59 cysa_demo sudo: pam_unix(sudo:session): session opened for user root by example(uid=0)
Jan 26 18:35:59 cysa_demo sudo: pam_unix(sudo:session): session closed for user root
Jan 26 18:36:14 cysa_demo sudo:   example : TTY=tty1 ; PWD=/home/example ; USER=root ; COMMAND=/usr/sbin/ufw ?
Jan 26 18:36:14 cysa_demo sudo: pam_unix(sudo:session): session opened for user root by example(uid=0)
Jan 26 18:36:14 cysa_demo sudo: pam_unix(sudo:session): session closed for user root
Jan 26 18:36:20 cysa_demo sudo:   example : TTY=tty1 ; PWD=/home/example ; USER=root ; COMMAND=/usr/sbin/ufw ena
ble
Jan 26 18:36:20 cysa_demo sudo: pam_unix(sudo:session): session opened for user root by example(uid=0)
Jan 26 18:36:21 cysa_demo sudo: pam_unix(sudo:session): session closed for user root
Jan 26 18:36:25 cysa_demo sudo:   example : TTY=tty1 ; PWD=/home/example ; USER=root ; COMMAND=/usr/sbin/ufw sta
tus
Jan 26 18:36:25 cysa_demo sudo: pam_unix(sudo:session): session opened for user root by example(uid=0)
Jan 26 18:36:26 cysa_demo sudo: pam_unix(sudo:session): session closed for user root
--More--(35%)
```

Regardless of the type of log that you are reviewing, you should bear in mind what type of event you are looking for and what identifiers appear in it that match the event or entry that you're searching for. In many cases, you should look for related entries based on what you find in your initial search. For example, if you're looking for blocked traffic to a host with IP address 10.1.10.4, you may also want to look at other entries for that host, and you may choose to broaden your search to search for all entries for 10.1.10.4.

Similarly, if you were looking at blocked traffic and found that a host at 192.168.1.172 was sending traffic to 10.1.10.4, and that you saw hundreds of attempts on different ports, all of which were blocked, you might then search the logs to see if 192.168.1.172 was port-scanning your entire network.

Firewall Logs

Although there are many types of firewall logs, most have some similarities. They typically identify the source and destination IP address, the port and protocol, and what action was taken on the traffic. They may also include data like the role that was matched, if there is a specific threat identifier associated with a block, which interface or port the traffic entered or exited the firewall on, and details of how much traffic was sent.

In Figure 10.3, you can see an example of firewall entries for the Ubuntu UFW firewall. Note that the entries show the source and destination hosts, and that the service that was being accessed was on port 22. In this case, the firewall was blocking access to the OpenSSH service, and a client was retrying access until it failed.

FIGURE 10.3 UFW blocked connection firewall log entry examples

```
Jan 26 18:54:12 cysa_demo kernel: [ 1422.549524] [UFW BLOCK] IN=enp0s3 OUT= MAC=08:00:27:14:3d:56:34:e8:94:5f:fa:d6:08:00 SRC=192.168.1.24 D
ST=192.168.1.33 LEN=52 TOS=0x00 PREC=0x00 TTL=128 ID=57179 DF PROTO=TCP SPT=58487 DPT=22 WINDOW=64240 RES=0x00 SYN URGP=0
Jan 26 18:54:13 cysa_demo kernel: [ 1423.549180] [UFW BLOCK] IN=enp0s3 OUT= MAC=08:00:27:14:3d:56:34:e8:94:5f:fa:d6:08:00 SRC=192.168.1.24 D
ST=192.168.1.33 LEN=52 TOS=0x00 PREC=0x00 TTL=128 ID=57180 DF PROTO=TCP SPT=58487 DPT=22 WINDOW=64240 RES=0x00 SYN URGP=0
Jan 26 18:54:15 cysa_demo kernel: [ 1425.549174] [UFW BLOCK] IN=enp0s3 OUT= MAC=08:00:27:14:3d:56:34:e8:94:5f:fa:d6:08:00 SRC=192.168.1.24 D
ST=192.168.1.33 LEN=52 TOS=0x00 PREC=0x00 TTL=128 ID=57181 DF PROTO=TCP SPT=58487 DPT=22 WINDOW=64240 RES=0x00 SYN URGP=0
Jan 26 18:54:19 cysa_demo kernel: [ 1429.549957] [UFW BLOCK] IN=enp0s3 OUT= MAC=08:00:27:14:3d:56:34:e8:94:5f:fa:d6:08:00 SRC=192.168.1.24 D
ST=192.168.1.33 LEN=52 TOS=0x00 PREC=0x00 TTL=128 ID=57182 DF PROTO=TCP SPT=58487 DPT=22 WINDOW=64240 RES=0x00 SYN URGP=0
Jan 26 18:54:27 cysa_demo kernel: [ 1437.549836] [UFW BLOCK] IN=enp0s3 OUT= MAC=08:00:27:14:3d:56:34:e8:94:5f:fa:d6:08:00 SRC=192.168.1.24 D
ST=192.168.1.33 LEN=52 TOS=0x00 PREC=0x00 TTL=128 ID=57183 DF PROTO=TCP SPT=58487 DPT=22 WINDOW=64240 RES=0x00 SYN URGP=0
example@cysa_demo:/var/log/apache2$
```

WAF Logs

Web application firewalls are a specialized type of firewall that operates at the application layer to filter out attacks against web applications. Many WAF systems have default rulesets that look for attacks that match the OWASP Top 10 (`owasp.org/www-project-top-ten/`) or other common application security risks, allowing administrators to quickly enable a common ruleset.

Figure 10.4 shows an example of a ModSecurity entry for an OWASP Top 10 match, which found a request for the bash shell (`/bin/bash`) in the arguments for the request. This type of log entry can help identify active attacks based on content in the logs.

FIGURE 10.4 ModSecurity log entry examples

```
example@cysa_demo: /var/log/apache2
--b4e35a32-E--
<!DOCTYPE HTML PUBLIC "-//IETF//DTD HTML 2.0//EN">
<html><head>
<title>403 Forbidden</title>
</head><body>
<h1>Forbidden</h1>
<p>You don't have permission to access this resource.</p>
<hr>
<address>Apache/2.4.29 (Ubuntu) Server at 192.168.1.33 Port 80</address>
</body></html>

--b4e35a32-H--
Message: Warning. Pattern match "^[\\d.:]+$" at REQUEST_HEADERS:Host. [file "/usr/share/modsecurity-crs/rules/REQUEST-920-PROTOCOL-ENFORCEME
NT.conf"] [line "708"] [id "920350"] [msg "Host header is a numeric IP address"] [data "192.168.1.33"] [severity "WARNING"] [ver "OWASP_CRS/
3.2.0"] [tag "application-multi"] [tag "language-multi"] [tag "platform-multi"] [tag "attack-protocol"] [tag "paranoia-level/1"] [tag "OWASP
_CRS"] [tag "OWASP_CRS/PROTOCOL_VIOLATION/IP_HOST"] [tag "WASCTC/WASC-21"] [tag "OWASP_TOP_10/A7"] [tag "PCI/6.5.10"]
Message: Warning. Matched phrase "bin/bash" at ARGS:exec. [file "/usr/share/modsecurity-crs/rules/REQUEST-932-APPLICATION-ATTACK-RCE.conf"]
[line "518"] [id "932160"] [msg "Remote Command Execution: Unix Shell Code Found"] [data "Matched Data: bin/bash found within ARGS:exec: /bi
n/bash"] [severity "CRITICAL"] [ver "OWASP_CRS/3.2.0"] [tag "application-multi"] [tag "language-shell"] [tag "platform-unix"] [tag "attack-r
ce"] [tag "paranoia-level/1"] [tag "OWASP_CRS"] [tag "OWASP_CRS/WEB_ATTACK/COMMAND_INJECTION"] [tag "WASCTC/WASC-31"] [tag "OWASP_TOP_10/A1"
] [tag "PCI/6.5.2"]
Message: Access denied with code 403 (phase 2). Operator GE matched 5 at TX:anomaly_score. [file "/usr/share/modsecurity-crs/rules/REQUEST-9
49-BLOCKING-EVALUATION.conf"] [line "91"] [id "949110"] [msg "Inbound Anomaly Score Exceeded (Total Score: 8)"] [severity "CRITICAL"] [tag "
```

Proxy Logs

Much like firewall logs, proxy logs can provide useful information about connections and traffic. Proxies are often used to either centralize access traffic or to filter traffic. Thus, proxy logs will contain the source and destination IP address, the source and destination port, the requested resource, the date and time, and often the content type and HTTP referrer as well as details about the content, such as the amount of traffic that was sent.

When analyzing proxy logs, you should look for data such as the following:

- Target host IP, hostname, and what was requested.
- The amount of content requested. This may help indicate a compromise or match a known malicious package.
- The HTTP request method, which can provide details of the query string with `GET` requests (`POST` requests carry this in the body of the message, requiring you to read the full payload, which is more complex).
- Unusual user agents and protocol versions, which may be useful for identifying applications, malware, or other targets.

Intrusion Detection System (IDS) and Intrusion Prevention System (IPS) Logs

IDS and IPS systems rely on rules to identify unwanted traffic. That means that when a rule is triggered on an IDS and IPS, the logs will contain information about the rule that was activated and information about the traffic that was captured and analyzed to trigger the rule. Since IDS and IPS systems often analyze the content of packets and look at traffic across multiple packets or entire conversations to perform their functions, more data about what is occurring at the application level is often available. For example, if you are tracking a malware that uses an Internet Relay Chat (IRC)-based command and control network, you could search for rule hits that included a specific channel name or a nickname that was used.

Much like the other logs types we have discussed, finding the first log entry of interest will often lead to other interesting log entries. It helps to annotate the log entries, capturing details about what you need to pursue further and what other searches you should perform with what you know as you proceed through your log review.

Security Information and Event Management Systems

As the number of security appliances, software packages, and services that create security related logs have grown, tools to centralize, correlate, analyze, and alert on items found in those logs have proliferated. Modern security information and event management (SIEM) systems like Splunk, LogRhythm, QRadar, and other tools are a common part of security infrastructures.

Figure 10.5 shows a high-level view of the role of a SIEM system. Note the multiple sources of threat information, including analysts, threat feeds, and vendor-provided information, all of which helps to define the rules applied to the data the SIEM ingests, thus determining what the SIEM will search for. Log data is aggregated and centralized, and once the analysis is complete, alerts and/or active responses are the output of the SIEM device.

Adding additional data sources beyond your own is a form of *data enrichment*. Other data enrichment techniques include processes that improve or refine your original data. The analysts shown in Figure 10.5 will spend time reviewing data, ensuring that the right data is being logged and that the logs contain all the information needed to address issues they find. Data enrichment activities can also involve pruning or removing raw data, ensuring that resources are not spent on needless information.

Writing rules is a common task for security analysts tasked with managing a SIEM. Rule writing for most SIEM devices focuses on correlation rules, which look at activities or events and then match them to unwanted behaviors. A simple correlation rule may look for failed logins for administrative accounts, whereas a more complex version of the same rule might look for those failures and then a success paired with the use of escalated privileges or data leaving the system.

FIGURE 10.5 SIEM data acquisition, rule creation, and automation

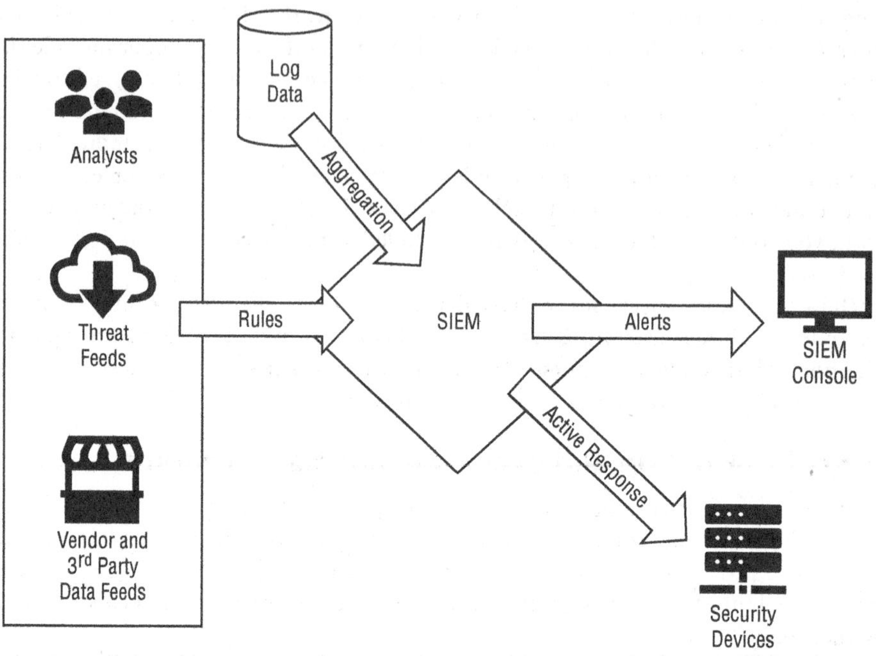

A common example of correlation rules involves use of *known-bad Internet protocol (IP) addresses* from IP reputation lists with suspected malicious behavior. The high-level description of a rule that uses information from a DNS or IP address blacklist that uses an active response might look like this:

```
Block traffic from internal hosts if an outbound attempt to connect to
a known bad IP address is made, then alert the responsible
administrator or security analyst via a ticket, email, or text message.
```

When writing SIEM rules, you need to balance the desire to alarm on unexpected or unwanted actions and events and the likelihood of false positives. If you create a rule that creates too many false positives, you will quickly find that the rule is ignored, resulting in events that should have been noticed being missed.

Exam Note

The CySA+ exam objectives specifically call out known-bad Internet protocol as an item in this section. That's a bit vague, but you should be aware of IP and domain reputation services as well as manual identification of known-bad IPs and domains. Some organizations also block entire netblocks because of malicious behavior. While this can help, the huge increase in the availability of cloud computing and VPNs means that attackers have a much easier path to getting an IP address that you will be less likely to block.

SIEM systems typically provide the ability to create a *dashboard,* which shows the status of rules, data sources, actions taken, and other critical operational and analytic information that the SIEM provides. If you haven't worked with a SIEM before, you can view them, and in some cases try hands-on online demos, from many of the major SIEM vendors. Simply search for a demo for tools like Splunk, Fortinet's SIEM, or others to give them a try and to see what the dashboards and rules look like. Some vendors also provide trial editions and/or limited-functionality versions that you can set up and use in your home lab.

Security Orchestration, Automation, and Response

Security orchestration, automation, and response (SOAR) is a concept that relies on a stack of security tools to collect data from a variety of security sources and then automatically respond. While SIEM tools include many of these components and capabilities, Gartner coined the term to describe a set of tools that are often put in place to complement SIEM tools. Garner describes SOAR's three major components as

Threat and Vulnerability Management Components include threat management tools and vulnerability scanners as well as workflow, reporting, and collaboration tools that support them.

Security Incident Response IR suites that provide the tools to manage incidents from start to finish.

Security Operations Automation Orchestration and workflow tools fit into this category, as well as reporting, policy, and process management tools.

SOAR systems and services tend to add a layer of workflow management. That means that SOAR deployments may actually ingest SIEM alerts and other data and then apply workflows and automation to them.

SIEM and SOAR tools can be difficult to distinguish from each other, with one current difference being the broader range of tools that SOAR services integrate with. The same vendors who provide SIEM capabilities also provide SOAR systems in many cases with Splunk, Rapid7, and IBM (QRadar) all included. There are differences, however, as ITSM tools like ServiceNow play in the space as well.

As an analyst, you need to know that SOAR services and tools exist and can be leveraged to cover additional elements beyond what traditional SIEM systems have historically handled.

Exam Note

SOAR is a relatively new concept, and the technologies and players in the space are changing very quickly. Gartner's 2019 SOAR market report noted that fewer than 5% of organizations used SOAR tools when the report came out. While they predict that 30% of organizations with more than five employees will use SOAR tools by 2022, SOAR is still a very new market. Thus, you'll most likely need to know the concepts behind SOAR and what it is rather than a specific technical question for the exam.

Endpoint Data Analysis

Endpoints of all types are found throughout organizations. From desktops and laptops to mobile devices, IoT (Internet of Things) sensors, and many other types of endpoint devices, all gather data, including logs and other information. Security analysts need to consider what data may exist on an endpoint device, how to access it, whether that data should be sent to a central log collection and analysis point, and what you would do with that data if you need to monitor for security issues or to investigate an incident.

Malware Analysis

Security analysts often encounter malware as part of their practice, whether it is detected by antimalware tools or discovered as part of an incident response process. In-depth malware analysis is a complex skillset, but analysts should know about the approaches that are commonly used to analyze malware. These include reverse engineering, applying heuristic analysis techniques, and using tools to identify malware packages.

Reverse Engineering

Reverse engineering malware requires using tools like disassemblers, debuggers, monitoring tools, unpackers, and code and binary analysis tools to pull apart malware packages to determine what they do, who wrote them, and other details of their functionality and construction. Reverse engineering tends to be a specialized discipline, with generalist security analysts rarely doing more than cursory analysis. You should, however, be aware of the common types of tools used for reverse engineering:

- Debuggers allow you to run programs in a controlled environment, modifying variables and how the program is running, including adding stop points and monitoring what it is doing.
- Disassemblers are used to convert machine code into assembly language, whereas decompilers attempt to convert machine code into a high-level language like C or Java.
- Unpackers and packer identifiers are used to identify what packing and encryption techniques were used to obfuscate a program and then to undo the packing process.
- System monitoring tools are used to monitor impact to a system like changes to the filesystem, registry, or other settings or configuration changes.

Since this is a test preparation book, we won't go into great depth on malware reverse engineering techniques and tools. If you'd like to learn about this topic, classes like the SANS FOR610 course and books like Monnappa K. A.'s *Learning Malware Analysis* (Packt Publishing, 2018) and Michael Sikorski and Andrew Honig's *Practical Malware Analysis* (No Starch Press, 2012) are good places to learn a lot more.

Heuristics

Antimalware tools often use heuristic analysis to analyze suspected malware. They may do things like decompile a binary to see if the code is similar to existing samples, or they may run the program and analyze its behavior while looking for things that malware often does, like modifying the Windows registry or creating hooks to the filesystem to conceal files. This may be done by running the code in a container or in a virtual environment, but in all cases, it relies on heavily instrumenting the environment in which the code is executed to be able to detect changes and actions that the code takes.

Heuristics can be exceptionally valuable because they can detect unknown malware. That advantage comes with a potential downfall, however: heuristic analysis tools can have a hard time separating malware behavior from that of legitimate software. A common example is one antimalware package detecting another antimalware package because of the techniques they use to capture malware behavior!

Exam Note

If you're following the CySA+ exam objectives, you may wonder why we put heuristics here instead of under its own heading. In most cases, heuristics are most closely aligned with antimalware activities, where they are used to monitor for malware-like behavior. Heuristic techniques may be used elsewhere, but you're most likely to encounter them in antimalware tools.

Tool-Based Analysis

For many analysts, most of your day-to-day malware analysis will be done via submissions to third-party tools like VirusTotal (`virustotal.com`), VirSCAN (`virscan.org`), Jotti (`virsscan.jotti.com`), and others that use multiple antivirus and antimalware engines to test submitted files against known malware profiles and signatures.

Locally installed tools and commercial antivirus and antimalware packages are a common part of the antimalware toolkit for endpoint protection and analysis.

Memory Analysis

Gaining insight into which services and applications are using memory, how much memory they are using, and what else they are connected to can be helpful when gathering information about systems.

For Windows systems, the Resource Monitor (`resmon`), can be a useful built-in tool. Figure 10.6 shows a typical Resource Monitor window, including applications like Chrome and Discord with their process ID (PID), memory that is being used, and a view of the total memory available to the system itself. The charts at the right also show usage over time, which can help you understand trends or see spikes in usage. Note that Resource Monitor can also show CPU, disk, and network usage, allowing analysts to check multiple data points in one interface.

FIGURE 10.6 The Windows 10 Resource Monitor

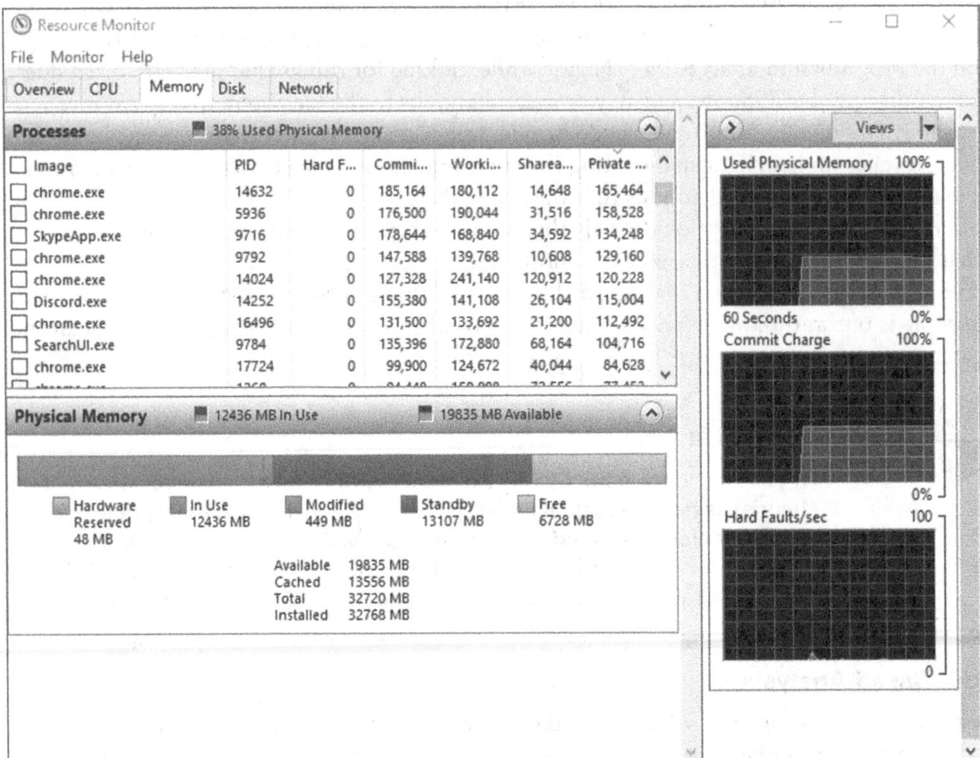

Linux and Unix systems provide a number of command-line tools that can also help with memory analysis, including `top`, which shows processes, their PIDs, the user who is executing the process, and the command executed to start it. That's a lot of useful data when hunting threats, especially if you see a binary running that doesn't make sense for the user who is running it.

The Linux `ps` command provides information about processes and their CPU and memory utilization. Figure 10.7 shows a typical `ps` output.

In this section we specifically cover operational memory analysis rather than forensic memory analysis. You will find more about memory forensics in Chapter 13, "Performing Forensic Analysis and Techniques."

Antimalware and endpoint security solutions automatically scan memory for artifacts of malicious software and typically monitor memory for behavior that matches typical behavior patterns for malicious activities as well. That means that manual analysis is often reserved for cases where specific information is needed or when troubleshooting is required.

FIGURE 10.7 Linux ps output

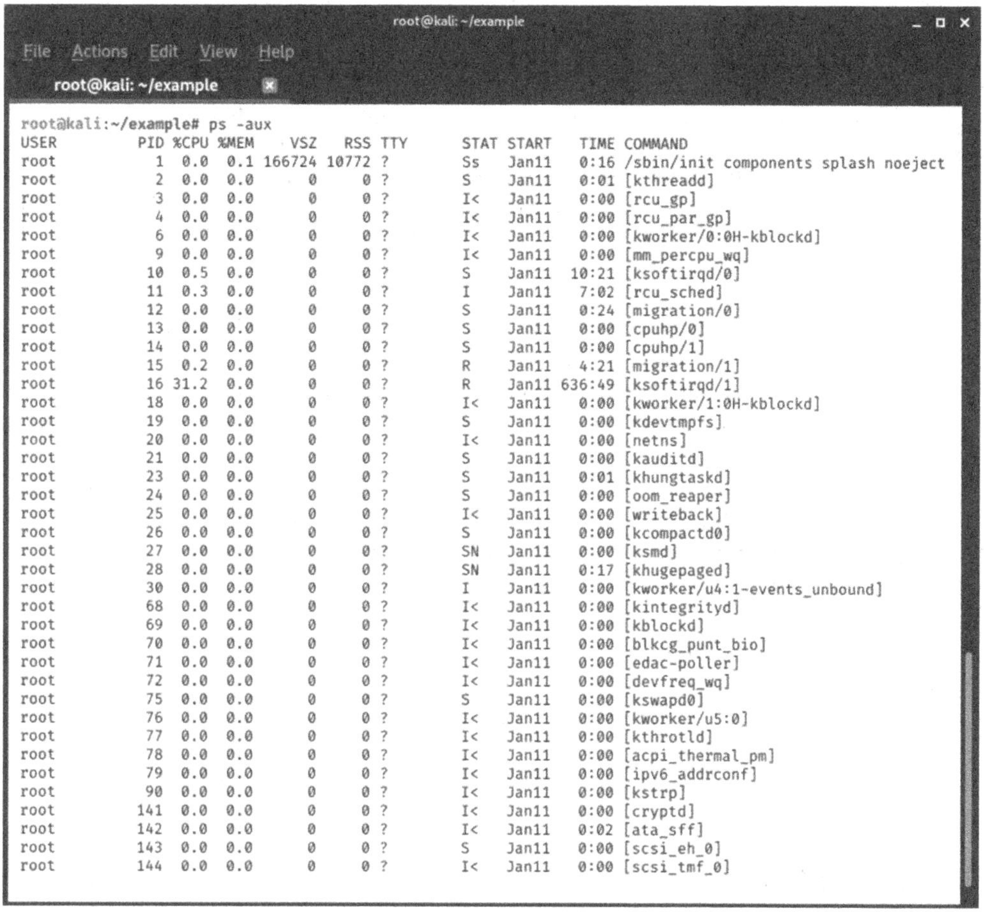

```
root@kali: ~/example
File  Actions  Edit  View  Help
root@kali: ~/example

root@kali:~/example# ps -aux
USER       PID %CPU %MEM    VSZ   RSS TTY      STAT START   TIME COMMAND
root         1  0.0  0.1 166724 10772 ?        Ss   Jan11   0:16 /sbin/init components splash noeject
root         2  0.0  0.0      0     0 ?        S    Jan11   0:01 [kthreadd]
root         3  0.0  0.0      0     0 ?        I<   Jan11   0:00 [rcu_gp]
root         4  0.0  0.0      0     0 ?        I<   Jan11   0:00 [rcu_par_gp]
root         6  0.0  0.0      0     0 ?        I<   Jan11   0:00 [kworker/0:0H-kblockd]
root         9  0.0  0.0      0     0 ?        I<   Jan11   0:00 [mm_percpu_wq]
root        10  0.5  0.0      0     0 ?        S    Jan11  10:21 [ksoftirqd/0]
root        11  0.3  0.0      0     0 ?        I    Jan11   7:02 [rcu_sched]
root        12  0.0  0.0      0     0 ?        S    Jan11   0:24 [migration/0]
root        13  0.0  0.0      0     0 ?        S    Jan11   0:00 [cpuhp/0]
root        14  0.0  0.0      0     0 ?        S    Jan11   0:00 [cpuhp/1]
root        15  0.2  0.0      0     0 ?        R    Jan11   4:21 [migration/1]
root        16 31.2  0.0      0     0 ?        R    Jan11 636:49 [ksoftirqd/1]
root        18  0.0  0.0      0     0 ?        I<   Jan11   0:00 [kworker/1:0H-kblockd]
root        19  0.0  0.0      0     0 ?        S    Jan11   0:00 [kdevtmpfs]
root        20  0.0  0.0      0     0 ?        I<   Jan11   0:00 [netns]
root        21  0.0  0.0      0     0 ?        S    Jan11   0:00 [kauditd]
root        23  0.0  0.0      0     0 ?        S    Jan11   0:01 [khungtaskd]
root        24  0.0  0.0      0     0 ?        S    Jan11   0:00 [oom_reaper]
root        25  0.0  0.0      0     0 ?        I<   Jan11   0:00 [writeback]
root        26  0.0  0.0      0     0 ?        S    Jan11   0:00 [kcompactd0]
root        27  0.0  0.0      0     0 ?        SN   Jan11   0:00 [ksmd]
root        28  0.0  0.0      0     0 ?        SN   Jan11   0:17 [khugepaged]
root        30  0.0  0.0      0     0 ?        I    Jan11   0:00 [kworker/u4:1-events_unbound]
root        68  0.0  0.0      0     0 ?        I<   Jan11   0:00 [kintegrityd]
root        69  0.0  0.0      0     0 ?        I<   Jan11   0:00 [kblockd]
root        70  0.0  0.0      0     0 ?        I<   Jan11   0:00 [blkcg_punt_bio]
root        71  0.0  0.0      0     0 ?        I<   Jan11   0:00 [edac-poller]
root        72  0.0  0.0      0     0 ?        I<   Jan11   0:00 [devfreq_wq]
root        75  0.0  0.0      0     0 ?        S    Jan11   0:00 [kswapd0]
root        76  0.0  0.0      0     0 ?        I<   Jan11   0:00 [kworker/u5:0]
root        77  0.0  0.0      0     0 ?        I<   Jan11   0:00 [kthrotld]
root        78  0.0  0.0      0     0 ?        I<   Jan11   0:00 [acpi_thermal_pm]
root        79  0.0  0.0      0     0 ?        I<   Jan11   0:00 [ipv6_addrconf]
root        90  0.0  0.0      0     0 ?        I<   Jan11   0:00 [kstrp]
root       141  0.0  0.0      0     0 ?        I<   Jan11   0:00 [cryptd]
root       142  0.0  0.0      0     0 ?        I<   Jan11   0:02 [ata_sff]
root       143  0.0  0.0      0     0 ?        S    Jan11   0:00 [scsi_eh_0]
root       144  0.0  0.0      0     0 ?        I<   Jan11   0:00 [scsi_tmf_0]
```

System and Application Behavior

Understanding typical system and application behavior helps security professionals compare known-good behavior to suspected malicious or abnormal behavior. Tracking behavior requires a combination of tools that show things like CPU, memory, network, and disk usage as well as logs and real-time analysis tools. In addition to manual review, many tools provide automated capabilities to assess behaviors. Some also provide the ability to use heuristic detection methodologies.

Many heuristic tools start by building a baseline of information of *known-good behavior* by monitoring normal behaviors over a period of time and then tracking differences from those behaviors. Tools like Amazon's AWS Inspector tool check for expected behaviors and settings and then flag when they aren't correct. This also means that the tool needs to know about the *anomalous behavior*, or the behavior that doesn't match the normal behavior of the system or network. Much like antivirus systems, anomalous behavior detection systems and tools may rely on heuristics and signature-based detections in addition to using checklists of configuration information and likely problems.

If you capture a baseline for your organization, you're likely to be asked, "What if we're already compromised when we run it?" That's a valid question, but in most cases even small-scale malware infections won't invalidate the baseline's overall usefulness. Of course, if you do believe you have significant security breaches in progress, you should capture a baseline only on trusted systems.

Knowing which exploit techniques are most commonly used and how to find artifacts of those exploits helps analysts detect compromises. The ATT&CK framework discussed in Chapter 2, "Using Threat Intelligence," provides a good starting point to better understand the many types of techniques that can be used, ranging from injecting code into Windows dynamic linked libraries (DLLs) to stealing web session cookies. You can read through them along with descriptions at `attack.mitre.org`.

Detecting these exploit techniques in action requires a combination of active detection tools, logging and analysis, and forensic and incident response tools for those occasions when something gets through your defenses.

Filesystem Monitoring

Monitoring *filesystems* can help detect unauthorized or unexpected changes. Tools like Tripwire, OSSEC, and commercial host intrusion detection system (HIDS) tools are used to monitor and report on filesystem changes. Some tools can actively capture changes and either provide the ability to roll back the changes that were made at will or prevent them from happening.

User and Entity Behavior Analytics

User and entity behavior analytics (UEBA) is a type of tool that is used to analyze normal user behavior and to detect anomalous behavior. It utilizes automated rule creation using machine learning and statistical analysis techniques to perform its detection work, making it a powerful tool. UEBA can be implemented as part of a SIEM or endpoint tool or as a separate application. The key differentiator for UEBA tools is the focus on user and entity behaviors and a focus on anomalous behavior based on previous normal behavior combined with typical indicators of compromise.

Network Data Analysis

Security practitioners need to know how to analyze network traffic, including the contents of packets that are sent, the destinations that traffic is sent to or where traffic is coming from, the overall flow of traffic, and the individual packets and protocols in use. While we can't cover all of those details in a study guide, we can point you to some of the high points for the CySA+ exam.

The first element that the CySA+ exam outline focuses on is URL and domain name analysis. URLs (uniform resource locators) are used to point web browsers and other tools to their destinations. That means that you need to know how to identify suspect URLs and the domains that they may point to.

Manual analysis starts with a review of the URL itself. Does it appear to be a legitimate domain name, or does it have suspect elements like a deceptive hostname or domain name, or an uncommon top-level domain (TLD) that may be easy to confuse with the normal TLD used for a legitimate service?

Google's Safe Browsing tool (`safebrowsing.google.com`) is one example of a tool that analyzes URLs. It also provides information about malicious content hosted on domains, allowing domain administrators to receive notifications if their domains are hosting malware.

The CySA+ exam outline calls out "dynamically generated algorithms" as a subset of URL and domain name analysis. Sometimes called DGAs (domain generation algorithms), these tools are used as part of malware packages to generate domain names from a known seed. The bot control infrastructure can then dynamically generate domain names knowing that bots will use the same seed to know where to send their traffic.

Threat hunters need access to DNS query logs from the DNS servers in their organization to identify bots acting like this. Feeding DNS query information into a SIEM or other tool that uses IP and domain reputation data as well as correlation capabilities can help to detect behaviors that indicate use of a DGA infrastructure.

In addition to dynamic domain name generation algorithms, techniques that automatically register and deregister DNS entries as part of botnets and other malicious activities are commonly used as part of botnets and control infrastructure and are called *fast flux DNS*. There are two major models of fast flux DNS:

- **Single flux** continuously registers addresses as part of the DNS address A record for a DNS entry. When combined with a very short time to live for the records and a round-robin DNS that points to different systems as the record is called, this can help disguise malicious systems.
- **Double flux** is more complex, although similar. Double flux uses a similar technique to register and deregister DNS servers for the DNS zone, adding another layer of confusion when attempting to pin down malicious systems.

Since many systems will be pointed to over a relatively short period of time for a single DNS entry, fast flux DNS makes it hard to use traditional tools to identify malicious IP addresses and domains.

Exam Note

The CySA+ exam outline includes DGAs but doesn't call out fast flux DNS. We've included detail on fast flux because you're likely to encounter it as part of many botnets.

Network flows work a lot like telephone records: they capture data about which host talked to which host, via what protocol and which port, and how much data was transferred. Flow analysis can be helpful for detecting abnormal traffic patterns, as well as for providing a high-level overview of where traffic flows within your network.

NetFlow tools like those shown in Figure 10.8 typically allow visualization as well as drill-down detail views of traffic so that you can analyze what is happening on your network. Flow data is typically captured by network devices like switches, routers, and security devices but can also be captured by a wide range of devices if they are configured to do so. If you haven't spent time with flows, companies like SolarWinds provide demo flow analysis environments that you can explore to learn more about flows (`oriondemo.solarwinds.com/Orion/SummaryView.aspx?ViewID=1`).

FIGURE 10.8 SolarWinds network flow console

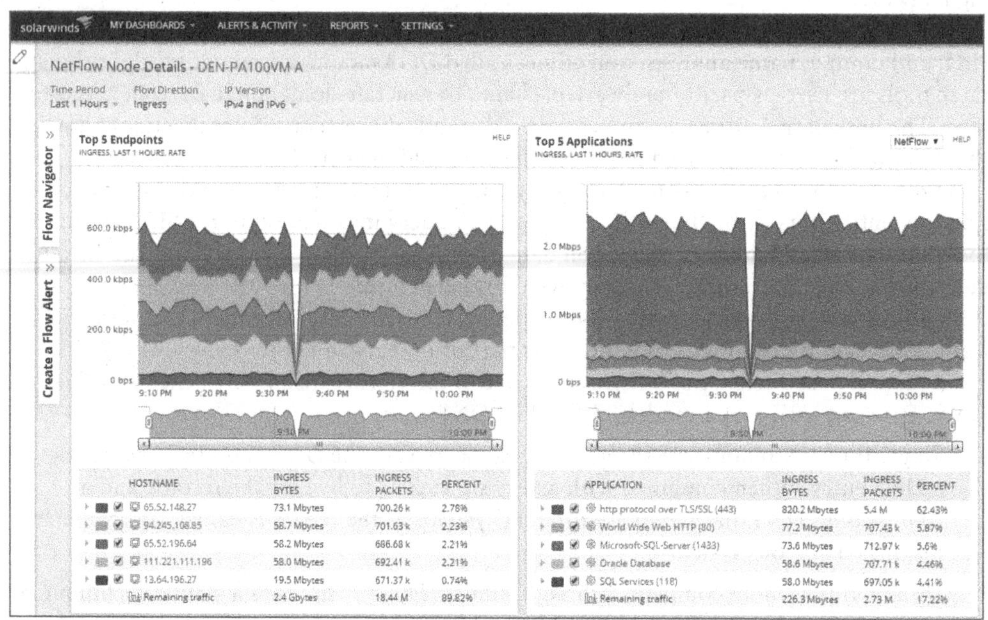

Packet and protocol analysis are performed using automated tools like IPS and IDS systems, as well as with manual analysis tools like Wireshark. As a security analyst, you will need to know the basics of using Wireshark or similar packet analyzer tools, as well as common protocols like DHCP, DNS, HTTP, and others.

Figure 10.9 shows some of the deep detail you can obtain using Wireshark. In this case, you can determine the user agent for the device that is browsing a website, what site was browsed, and details of the content. Note that the host is `cdn.iphonehacks.com` and that the device being used is identified as an iPad running iOS 13.2.2.

FIGURE 10.9 Wireshark packet analysis with packet content detail

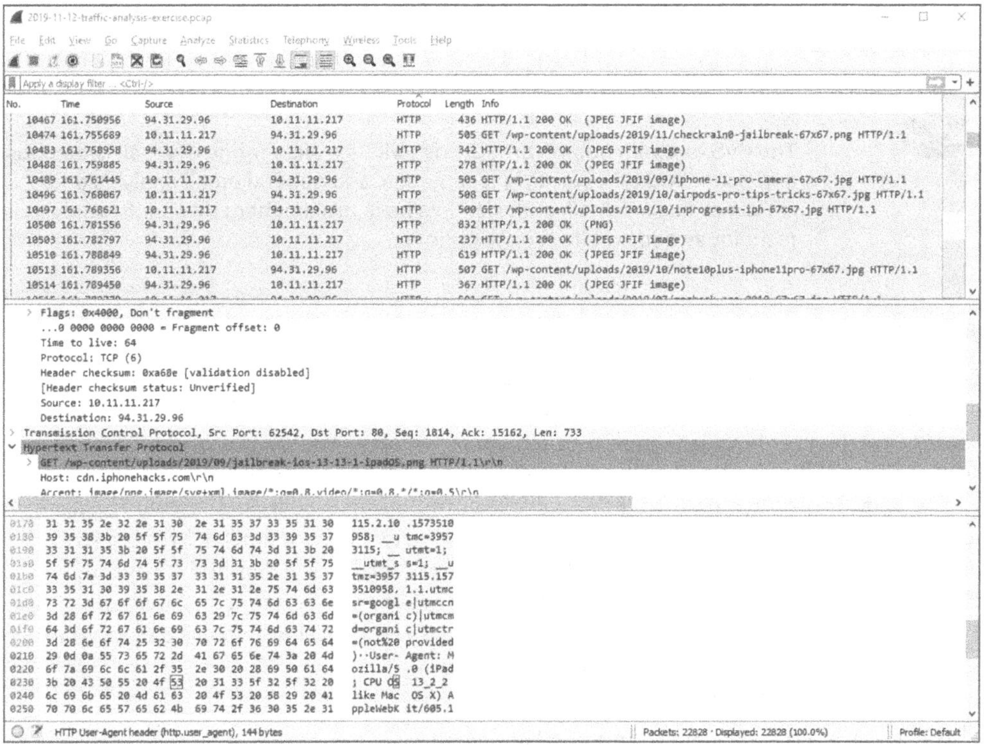

Identifying malware on your network through packet and protocol analysis relies on a strong knowledge of what traffic should look like and what behaviors and content are abnormal. Packet lengths, destination IP addresses, ports, and protocols can all provide useful information if you know what you are looking for or what normal and abnormal traffic looks like. Finding malware traffic when you can't see the content of the packets due to encryption can be more challenging. In cases where packets are encrypted, you may have to rely on behavior-based analysis by looking at traffic patterns that are indicative of malware like visiting known-bad sites, sending unexpected traffic on uncommon ports, or other abnormal behaviors.

Although we can't teach you in-depth techniques for malware identification, you can practice using some great resources. Check out `www.malware-traffic-analysis.net/`, which provides examples and tutorials, including traffic captures that you can work with.

Protecting and Analyzing Email

Email remains a frequent vector for attacks, ranging from phishing attacks to spreading malware as email attachments or via other techniques. Security analysts need to know the basics of email analysis, including how to analyze email headers, how to identify common attack techniques, and the most common security techniques intended to prevent email attacks.

Exam Note

The CySA+ exam outline broadly describes a wide range of email protection, anti-spam and anti-phishing techniques, and general email analysis and review skills as "email analysis." We have broken them down into analysis techniques and email security options.

Analyzing Email

Most organizations use automated email analysis as a first line of defense against malicious and spam emails. Automated tools look for indicators like known malicious or spam senders, often using blacklists built using information from around the world. They also scan every email looking for malicious payloads like malware or other unwanted files.

The same tools often perform header analysis and message content analysis. Header analysis looks at the content of the email's header. An example of a header from a spam email is shown in Figure 10.10. Note that the first two lines state that SPF is neutral. Further down we see that a domain `notes.langdale.com` is mentioned as well as a received from header entry that shows as `efianalytics.com`. The extensive reply-to list is strange, as is the message ID found later in the email.

FIGURE 10.10 Headers from a phishing email

```
ARC-Authentication-Results: i=1; mx.google.com;
       spf=neutral (google.com: 54.245.238.56 is neither permitted nor denied by best guess record for domain of bounce@notes.langdale.com.au)
smtp.mailfrom=bounce@notes.langdale.com.au
Return-Path: <bounce@notes.langdale.com.au>
Received: from notes.langdale.com.au (ec2-54-245-238-56.us-west-2.compute.amazonaws.com. [54.245.238.56])
        by mx.google.com with ESMTP id r4si14295947plo.397.2020.01.28.05.30.37
        for
        Tue, 28 Jan 2020 05:30:38 -0800 (PST)
Received-SPF: neutral (google.com: 54.245.238.56 is neither permitted nor denied by best guess record for domain of bounce@notes.langdale.com.au)
client-ip=54.245.238.56;
Authentication-Results: mx.google.com;
       spf=neutral (google.com: 54.245.238.56 is neither permitted nor denied by best guess record for domain of bounce@notes.langdale.com.au)
smtp.mailfrom=bounce@notes.langdale.com.au
Received: from efianalytics.com (efianalytics.com. 216.244.76.116)
List-Unsubscribe: <kmCudKmfngEhbQY5FH7-iZKAoOiOoApIEMVVNzN8@amazonaws.com>
From: _SecurityAlert <ivhdyRcNK@hstepielyczrwkuppr.com>
Reply-To: reply@memorably.site, jamila.badaoui@yandex.com, narine.simade@yandex.com.ge, rabab.bajira@yandex.by, narine.simade@yandex.com,
farge1939@yandex.kz, undon1955@yandex.com, jamila.badaoui@yandex.ee, maram.ounis@yandex.com, sara@bestforever.best, lama.sindih@yandex.com,
wittand54@yandex.by, undon1955@yandex.az, yassin_akel@aol.com, chadi.william@yandex.com.ge, tolly1983@yandex.md, farge1939@yandex.lv,
lama.sindih@yandex.co.il, inarencee@yandex.ee, chima.fandy@yandex.md, samir.azzi@yandex.tj, inarencee@yandex.kg, juststart2@asia.com,
undon1955@yandex.co.il, chima.fandy@yandex.com, chima.fandy@yandex.co.il, andso1958@yandex.com, farge1939@yandex.ee, bq@liderg.site,
db@overcharge.club, chadi.william@yandex.com, werseemse@yandex.com, farge1939@yandex.lt, narine.simade@yandex.co.il, tolly1983@yandex.lt,
john.jacob@juno.com, lisa@memorably.site, marco@ostracize.club, dankofran@yandex.ru, undon1955@yandex.ru, mido.farisi@yandex.kg, 1368864469@qq.com,
rabab.bajira@yandex.com, narine.simade@yandex.by, farge1939@yandex.com, mido.farisi@yandex.com, inarencee@yandex.md, support@laelaps.website,
lama.sindih@yandex.by, werseemse@yandex.ua, aploshian@yandex.ru, farge1939@yandex.kg, tolly1983@yandex.com, werseemse@yandex.ru, tolly1983@yandex.ru,
inarencee@yandex.ru, rabab.bajira@yandex.md, andso1958@yandex.tm, hasta@distancegroup.asia, samir.azzi@yandex.tm, lama.sindih@yandex.az,
apursa@yandex.com, yep@absence.website, samir.azzi@yandex.com, wittand54@yandex.com, maram.ounis@yandex.ua, mido.farisi@yandex.kz,
edward.akel@aol.com, bbouchta@mail.com, werseemse@yandex.by, samir.azzi@yandex.ua, yessju3st4u@usa.com, labodala@foxmail.com, wittand54@yandex.com.ge,
werseemse@yandex.kz, wittand54@yandex.com.tr, alexghandor@yandex.ru, andso1958@yandex.tj, andso1958@yandex.ru, rabab.bajira@yandex.kg,
wittand54@yandex.ee, cust552@tynker.com, tolly1983@yandex.lv, rabab.bajira@yandex.lt
Date: Tue, 28 Jan 2020 12:48:44 +0100
Subject: ??
  unusual activity
To: <iZKAoOiOoApIEMVVNzN8@itlgopk.uk>
Message-ID: <-SR4ecqCkbBFb29B.sunset.stroulaea.com@clsco.com>
X-EMMAIL: dseidl@gmail.com
Content-Type: text/html; charset=utf-8
```

This email was a very obvious phishing attempt; however, more elaborate and skilled attackers will have fewer obvious issues in both the body of the message and the headers themselves. Legitimate accounts are popular targets of attackers because they can be used to bypass many spam filters and will be more likely to be successful in phishing attacks.

If you're not familiar with the contents of an email header, you can review them at `mediatemple.net/community/products/dv/204643950/understanding-an-email-header` or `https://blog.mailfence.com/email-header/`, among many other sites. Email header analysis tools can also be handy, and many sites provide them, including `www.whatismyip.com/email-header-analyzer/` and `dnschecker.org/email-header-analyzer.php`. You won't have access to automated tools like these on the CySA+ exam, so make sure you know how to read a header without help!

It is important for analysts to know that forwarded email messages will not include the original headers. *Forwarding* an email places the message content into a new mail "envelope," removing the header information that you may need to investigate it. Most modern email clients do allow users to view headers if desired, but that is normally a manual process and isn't something most users will know how to do without instructions.

SPF, which we talk about in a moment, breaks when email is forwarded because the forwarding sender will now be the sender and SPF checks may fail at the new destination.

In addition to the information that can be lost when an email is forwarded, automatic email forwarding is a security concern that organizations need to address as well. Automatic forwarding is sometimes used by attackers who have successfully compromised an account to send all the emails received by that account to a destination of their choosing. Even if the account hasn't been compromised, forwarding can cause internal data that your organization doesn't want to leave to be outside your security perimeter.

Email Elements

In addition to the header, a number of elements may be of concern while performing email analysis. The first, and most common, element to review is an embedded link. Embedded links are often used as part of phishing scams because many users do not check where the link leads before clicking on them. Since an embedded link can differ from the text that it is linked to, many users fall for this technique. Even more sophisticated users may fall for URLs that appear to be legitimate at first glance. Fortunately, email security tools can scan for malicious links and will block many, though not all, links like this.

Email signature blocks can be useful to help identify phishing attacks, although more sophisticated attackers will simply clone legitimate signatures. Since email signatures often contain images and embedded links, they may also contain other dangerous elements that tell attackers if an email was opened or may actually be part of the attack.

Digital signatures rely on digital certificates and public key encryption and can help prove that the actual claimed sender was the real sender of the message and that the content of the message was not changed. When an email is digitally signed, a hash is created; then that hash is encrypted with the signer's private key to create the digital signature. The sender's digital certificate and signature are attached to the email. Recipients can then validate the hash against the email they received and can also decrypt the signature using the sender's public key, verifying that it matches. Many email services provide support for digital signatures and tools like S/MIME, but relatively few organizations make broad use of this capability.

Email Attacks

The most common forms of email attacks include phishing, impersonation, and the inclusion of malicious attachments. Phishing attacks focus on attempts to get unsuspecting users to click through to a site where they will provide their username and password, or other techniques that are focused on getting credentials or other information through deception.

Impersonation attacks are increasingly common, and they often include an email purporting to be from a trusted coworker or manager. The recipient is typically asked to perform an action like buying gift cards, changing banking information, or otherwise doing something that will benefit the attacker.

Malware is also spread via email, either as an attachment or via a clickable download link. Although antimalware software can help with this, there is a constant battle between attackers and defenders, and new techniques and tools appear all the time that help attackers get malicious software through the defenses that organizations have put into place.

Email Security Options

In addition to header analysis, additional technologies can be used to help provide greater protection to emails. These include the DomainKeys Identified Mail (DKIM), the Sender Policy Framework (SPF), and Domain-based Message Authentication, Reporting, and Conformance (DMARC).

DKIM allows organizations to add content to messages to identify them as being from their domain. DKIM signs both the body of the message and elements of the header, helping to ensure that the message is actually from the organization it claims to be from. It adds a DKIM-Signature header, which can be checked against the public key that is stored in public DNS entries for DKIM-enabled organizations.

SPF is an email authentication technique that allows organizations to publish a list of their authorized email servers. SPF records are added to the DNS information for your domain, and they specify which systems are allowed to send email from that domain. Systems not listed in SPF will be rejected.

SPF records in DNS are limited to 255 characters. This can make it tricky to use SPF for organizations that have a lot of email servers or that work with multiple external senders. In fact, SPF has a number of issues you can run into—you can read more about some of them at `www.dmarcanalyzer.com/spf/`.

DMARC, or Domain-based Message Authentication, Reporting, and Conformance, is a protocol that uses SPF and DKIM to determine if an email message is authentic. Like SPF and DKIM, DMARC records are published in DNS, but unlike DKIM and SPF, DMARC can be used to determine if you should accept a message from a sender. Using DMARC, you can choose to reject or quarantine messages that are not sent by a DMARC-supporting sender. You can read an overview of DMARC at `dmarc.org/overview/`.

If you want to see an example of a DMARC record, you can check out the DMARC information for SendGrid by using a `dig` command from a Linux command prompt: **`dig`** `txt_dmarc.sendgrid.net`. You should see something that looks like the following graphic.

```
root@kali:~# dig txt_dmarc.sendgrid.net

; <<>> DiG 9.11.5-P4-5.1+b1-Debian <<>> txt_dmarc.sendgrid.net
;; global options: +cmd
;; Got answer:
;; ->>HEADER<<- opcode: QUERY, status: SERVFAIL, id: 58714
;; flags: qr rd ra; QUERY: 1, ANSWER: 0, AUTHORITY: 1, ADDITIONAL: 1

;; OPT PSEUDOSECTION:
; EDNS: version: 0, flags:; udp: 4096
;; QUESTION SECTION:
;txt_dmarc.sendgrid.net.         IN      A

;; AUTHORITY SECTION:
sendgrid.net.           18      IN      SOA     ns10.dnsmadeeasy.com. dns.dnsmadeeasy.com. 2011181322 144
00 600 1728000 180

;; Query time: 82 msec
;; SERVER: 192.168.1.1#53(192.168.1.1)
;; WHEN: Sun Jan 26 12:45:52 UTC 2020
;; MSG SIZE  rcvd: 111
```

If you do choose to implement DMARC, you should set it up with the none flag for policies and review your data reports before going further to make sure you won't be inadvertently blocking important email. Although many major email services are already using DMARC, smaller providers and organizations may not be.

Scripting, Searching, and Text Manipulation

The ability to write and use basic scripts to search for specific items in logs, as well as to do basic text manipulation and other tasks, is required in many security analyst roles. Python is one of the most popular languages right now, but other languages like Perl and even shell scripting like Bash scripting are still quite common. You should be familiar with a few basic techniques for the CySA+ exam.

Performing string (text) searches with `grep` is a frequent task for security analysts. You might be able to use the `find` command inside a graphical text editor, but text output from `grep` is often fed to other commands or used to quickly find text inside a large file.

A basic `grep` command calls `grep` and then provides the text you are searching for and the filename.

```
grep cysa example.txt
```

You can search multiple files by separating the filenames with commas, search an entire directory by using a `-w` flag, and use an asterisk as a wildcard. You can even search for all the lines in a file that don't contain a specific set of text. Table 10.1 lists some commonly used `grep` flags.

TABLE 10.1 grep flags

`grep` **flag**	**Function**
`-c`	Counts the number of occurrences
`-i`	Matches both lower and upper case
`-n`	Shows the matching line and line number
`-v`	Shows all lines that do not match the string
`-r`	Reads all files under each directory recursively
`-e`	When followed by a pattern, uses the pattern for a search (allows multiple patterns)

Regular expressions are also commonly used in `grep` searches to match a more flexible set of entries. Using letters between square brackets will match any of a set of characters, whereas an * will match any number occurrences of the previous character. Thus, to match all occurrences of text that matches cysa, cysb, and cysc, you could use the following command:

```
grep "cys[abc]" example.txt
```

`grep` is a powerful tool and is frequently combined with other command-line functions to perform complex searches or to prepare data to feed to other tools.

You can find a multitude of grep tutorials online. If you haven't used grep much, or if you're rusty, you may want to take a bit of time to practice. Grab a large file, like the syslog file from a Linux system, find some text, and build a search query for it. Try matching case-sensitive and case-insensitive versions of your query, try it against multiple files, and for the more advanced use cases, you may want to play around with regular expressions.

To send data from one command-line tool to another, you can use a pipe, represented by the | symbol. For example, if you grep for a string and know that you will see multiple pages of output and want to paginate the output, you can pipe the output of grep into the more command:

```
grep cysa example.txt | more
```

Knowing how to use pipes to combine data from multiple commands is a useful skill for security analysts.

Summary

Security analysts need to know how to analyze the data that security monitoring solutions and systems generate. That means understanding trends and how heuristics (behavior-based) analysis tools work. You also need to understand what you can detect on endpoint systems, networks, and email and how to review the logs that devices and applications generate. Once you know what is going on, you must assess the impact to the organization and what it may mean, both in the moment and in the long term.

Analysts also need skills that enable them to work with large volumes of log data. You should be familiar with the basics of rule writing for SIEM and other devices, configuration of dashboards, and how to write queries using common tools like grep and Bash.

Finally, you should understand the role of automation in log analysis and information gathering activities. Scripting, workflow automation, and other tools play a key role in dealing with the sheer volume of data found in a typical security environment.

Exam Essentials

Know the purpose of security monitoring. Capturing information about what is occurring throughout your organization allows you to identify security issues and to monitor the overall health of your systems and devices. Using behavior, or heuristics-based techniques, can allow organizations to find abnormal activities. Trend analysis uses monitoring data over time to identify directional changes. Data must be captured from endpoints, servers, network equipment, and any other important part of your infrastructure. Complete data can help with a full impact analysis when events do occur, letting you determine whether there is an organizationwide or localized impact, and whether the immediate impact is different from the long-term total impact.

Explain why log review is a critical component of security operations activities. Analyzing event logs, system logs, security device logs, and proxy logs can help you detect exploits, attacks, and compromises, as well as provide the information needed to create new rules and signatures. Centralizing logs to a SIEM or other log aggregation and analysis technology helps provide a broader view of your organization's status and activities and allows for correlation across multiple systems.

Define the purpose of email analysis. Email headers contain useful information that can help prevent phishing and impersonation attacks while also helping to identify where malicious email is coming from. Tools like DKIM, SPF, and DMARC are part of a modern email security infrastructure and help identify trusted senders, systems, and domains. Analysts should be able to use tools to identify malicious email payloads.

Explain why automation and scripting are part of security monitoring and log review. Security analysts need to know the basics of scripting and automation. Searching for text using `grep` and other text manipulation tools, use of regular expressions, and the ability to pipe data from one command-line tool to another are all useful skills when dealing with large volumes of text data.

Lab Exercises

Activity 10.1: Analyze a Network Capture File

Analyzing malicious network traffic is an important skill for security professionals. You will need Wireshark or a similar network packet analyzer for this exercise. Once you have Wireshark set up, visit `www.malware-traffic-analysis.net/` to download a packet capture file.

Part 1: Select a packet capture

Select and download a packet capture exercise from `www.malware-traffic-analysis.net/training-exercises.html` and load it into Wireshark. Then review the questions that are matched with the exercise.

Part 2: Analyze the traffic

Using Wireshark, find as many answers as you can. If you don't know how to find those answers, you may need to start with a tutorial: `www.malware-traffic-analysis.net/tutorials/index.html`.

Part 3: Check your answers

Use the provided answers to check your analysis. Did you get everything right? Were there items you did not know how to find or were unable to find? If so, try another exercise!

Activity 10.2: Analyze a Phishing Email

You probably already have great source material for this lab exercise: simply open your email spam folder and find a likely phishing attack email.

Part 1: Manually analyze an email header

Once you have identified a suspected phishing email, you will need to open the headers for the email. If you're not familiar with the process, most email providers have help available on how to access the headers.

It can help to print the headers out for analysis or to import them into your favorite text editor to allow for markup as you track what you have found.

Review the headers and identify what clues you can find about where it was sent from, who sent it, and what path it traveled before you received it. What red flags stand out, and what would you do to identify future phishing emails based on the header information?

Part 2: Analyze the email content

Now that you have reviewed the header, you can move on to the body of the email. In this phase, review the content of the message, paying particular attention to common artifacts found in phishing emails. You should look for embedded links and record any deceptive links or embeds. You can also identify typos, poor grammar, and other typical elements of a phishing email.

Once you have identified these components, check the links against a tool like those found at `zeltser.com/lookup-malicious-websites/`. Is the link or domain a known-bad link?

Part 3: Use an automated tool

Use one or more automated email header analyzers to review the header from part 1. Note if you identify additional useful data and what that data is.

Many sites are available; you can start with `www.whatismyip.com/email-header-analyzer/` or `mxtoolbox.com/EmailHeaders.aspx`.

Activity 10.3: Security Architecture Terminology

Match each of the following terms to the correct description.

Heuristics	The process of disassembling or decompiling a malware package to understand what it does
DMARC	An email authentication technique that detects forged sender addresses
Reverse engineering	A technology designed to monitor end user behavior to prevent targeted attacks and insider threats

Digital signature	An email authentication, policy, and reporting protocol
UEBA	An email authentication method designed to detect forged sender addresses
DKIM	A means of providing assurance that an email has not been modified and that it was sent by the correct sender that relies on a certificate and public key cryptography
SOAR	A technique used to find previously unknown malware by observing behaviors common to malicious software
SPF	An email authentication method designed to detect forged sender addresses

Review Questions

1. Susan wants to use an email security protocol to determine the authenticity of an email. Which of the following options will ensure that her organization's email server can determine if it should accept email from a sender?
   A. DMARC
   B. SPF
   C. DKIM
   D. POP3
2. Ben wants to reverse-engineer a malware sample. Which of the following tools will allow him to view assembly code for the program if he only has a binary executable?
   A. A debugger
   B. A compiler
   C. `grep`
   D. A disassembler
3. Angela wants to review the syslog on a Linux system. What directory should she check to find it on most Linux distributions?
   A. `/home/log`
   B. `/var/log`
   C. `/log`
   D. `/var/syslog`

4. Charles is reviewing flow logs for his organization and notices that traffic has seen a 20 percent increase on the second Thursday of each month, after which the traffic returns to normal. What type of analysis is Charles conducting?

   A. Timeline-based analysis

   B. Threat hunting

   C. Trend analysis

   D. Heuristic analysis

5. Ian wants to view all of the data about current memory consumption on his Linux system but wants to be able to read it one page at a time. Which of the following commands will allow him to do so?

   A. `top | more`

   B. `top | grep`

   C. `top -p`

   D. `top - n`

6. Ben works with a team that includes a dozen security analysts who all write detection rules for his organization's IPS devices for multiple divisions around the world. What type of system could he implement to ensure that releases follow the proper testing and implementation processes?

   A. A CD pipeline

   B. A SIEM

   C. A workflow orchestration system

   D. A fuzzer

7. Chris is reviewing NetFlow logs while monitoring for systems that are participating in a botnet. Which of the following types of data will he not be able to see in his NetFlow records?

   A. Packet payload

   B. Source IP address

   C. Protocol

   D. Destination IP address

8. Alaina wants to deploy a tool that can monitor the behavior of users while correlating that behavior centrally to determine if a security incident has occurred. What type of tool should she acquire?

   A. A network analyzer

   B. A UEBA tool

   C. Antimalware with heuristics

   D. A DMARC tool

9. Chris wants to decrease the threat of malicious email links in email. What technique can he use to decrease their likelihood of success without having a significant business impact?
   A. Block all links in email
   B. Implement DNS blackholing using a DNS reputation service
   C. Turn on SPF and DKIM for all email
   D. Use a proxy to filter all web traffic from email links

10. Tim has assigned an analyst to add third-party threat data feeds to his organization's SIEM. Once the analyst is done, they will spend time reviewing syslog data feeds to ensure that they contain the information that is needed for responses. What is the analyst doing?
    A. Threat feed grooming
    B. Workflow orchestration
    C. Syslog combing
    D. Data enrichment

11. Michelle is analyzing a Wireshark traffic capture, and follows the TCP stream for a TIFF file download. What concern should she raise from the information displayed in the stream viewer?

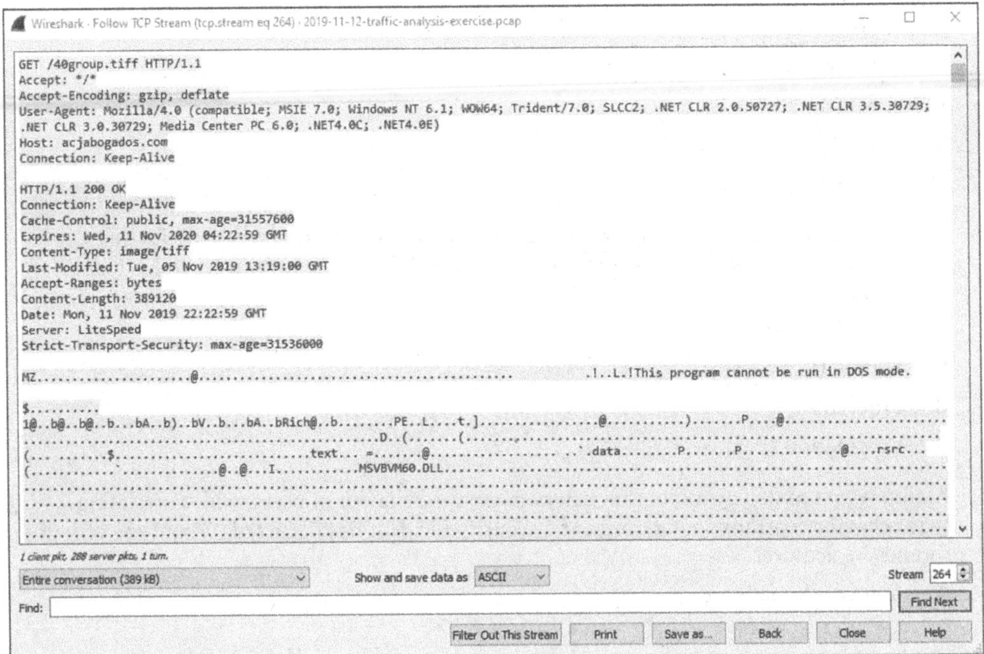

    A. The file cannot be run in DOS mode.
    B. The file is an executable.
    C. The file was gzipped.
    D. The file is actually a JPEG.

12. Elaine wants to check for user logins on a Linux system. What log location should she check first?
    A. `/var/log/syslog`
    B. `/var/log/auth.log`
    C. `/var/log/logins`
    D. `/var/log/messages`
13. While analyzing a malware infection, Joseph notes that the malware has encrypted files, thereby preventing the organization's main web application server from serving files. What type of impact has he noted?
    A. Localized, immediate impact
    B. Organizational total impact
    C. Organizational, immediate impact
    D. Localized total impact
14. Ben's organization uses an IP reputation service to block outbound access to all sites that are flagged with a negative reputation score. What issue could this cause?
    A. Customers may be unable to access the organization's website.
    B. Inadvertent blocking of sites due to false positives.
    C. Too many SIEM entries due to blacklisted sites being accessed.
    D. This will not lead to any problems.
15. James wants to monitor a Linux system's filesystem for unauthorized changes. What open source tool can he use to perform this task?
    A. Tripwire
    B. Filemon
    C. Filecatcher
    D. ftracker
16. Charlene executes the following command against the file shown. What entries will it return?

    ```
    grep -v error /var/log/boot.log
    ```

    A. All lines with the string `"error"` in them
    B. All lines with successful boot messages
    C. All lines without the string `"error"` in them
    D. All lines without successful boot messages
17. Megan is trying to prevent impersonation attacks from impacting her company but receives a "No DMARC record found" error when she checks a frequent business partner's DNS information. What do they need to do to enable DMARC?
    A. Publish a SPF record
    B. Publish a DMARC record

C. Set up DKIM authentication

D. All of the above

18. While reviewing a Wireshark traffic capture, Mike discovers the following information. What does he know about the user's device based on this TCP stream?

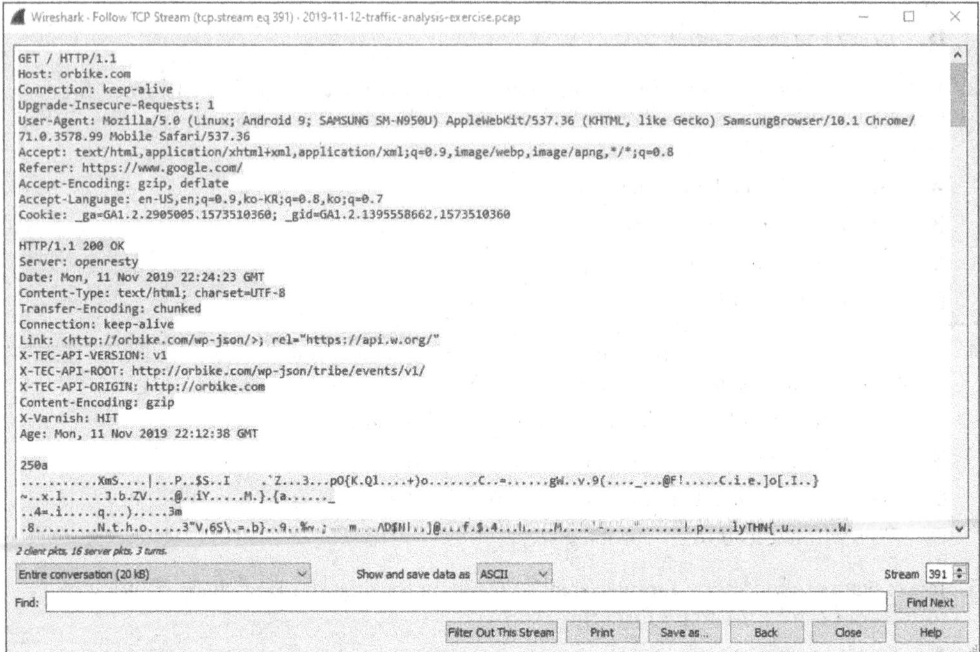

A. The device is an iOS device using Safari.

B. The device is downloading a file.

C. The device is a Samsung SM-N950U.

D. The device is uploading a file.

19. Ian finds entries in `/var/log/faillog` on a Linux system. What types of events will be in the log file?

A. Application start failures

B. System errors resulting in reboots

C. Failed login attempts

D. Failed privilege escalation attempts

20. Tony wants to check the digital signature of an email. What key does he need verify that an email is from his friend Mal?

A. Mal's private key

B. Tony's private key

C. Mal's public key

D. Tony's public key

Building an Incident Response Program

THE COMPTIA CYBERSECURITY ANALYST (CYSA+) EXAM OBJECTIVES COVERED IN THIS CHAPTER INCLUDE:

✓ **Domain 4.0: Incident Response**

- 4.1 Explain the importance of the incident response process.
- 4.2 Given a scenario, apply the appropriate incident response procedure.

No matter how well an organization prepares its cybersecurity defenses, the time will come that it suffers a computer security incident that compromises the confidentiality, integrity, and availability of information or systems under its control. This incident may be a minor virus infection that is quickly remediated or a serious breach of personal information that comes into the national media spotlight. In either event, the organization must be prepared to conduct a coordinated, methodical response effort. By planning in advance, business leaders, technology leaders, cybersecurity experts, and technologists can decide how they will handle these situations and prepare a well-thought-out response.

Security Incidents

Many IT professionals use the terms *security event* and *security incident* casually and interchangeably, but this is not correct. Members of a cybersecurity incident response team should use these terms carefully and according to their precise definitions within the organization. The National Institute for Standards and Technology (NIST) offers the following standard definitions for use throughout the U.S. government, and many private organizations choose to adopt them as well:

- An event is any observable occurrence in a system or network. A security event includes any observable occurrence that relates to a security function. For example, a user accessing a file stored on a server, an administrator changing permissions on a shared folder, and an attacker conducting a port scan are all examples of security events.
- An adverse event is any event that has negative consequences. Examples of adverse events include a malware infection on a system, a server crash, and a user accessing a file that they are not authorized to view.
- A security incident is a violation or imminent threat of violation of computer security policies, acceptable use policies, or standard security practices. Examples of security incidents include the accidental loss of sensitive information, an intrusion into a computer system by an attacker, the use of a keylogger on an executive's system to steal passwords, and the launch of a denial-of-service attack against a website.

Every security incident includes one or more security events, but not every security event is a security incident.

Computer security incident response teams (CSIRTs) are responsible for responding to computer security incidents that occur within an organization by following standardized response procedures and incorporating their subject matter expertise and professional judgment.

For brevity's sake, we will use the term *incident* as shorthand for *computer security incident* in the remainder of this book.

Phases of Incident Response

Organizations depend on members of the CSIRT to respond calmly and consistently in the event of a security incident. The crisis-like atmosphere that surrounds many security incidents may lead to poor decision making unless the organization has a clearly thought-out and refined process that describes how it will handle cybersecurity incident response. Figure 11.1 shows the simple incident response process advocated by NIST.

FIGURE 11.1 Incident response process

Source: NIST SP 800-61: Computer Security Incident Handling Guide

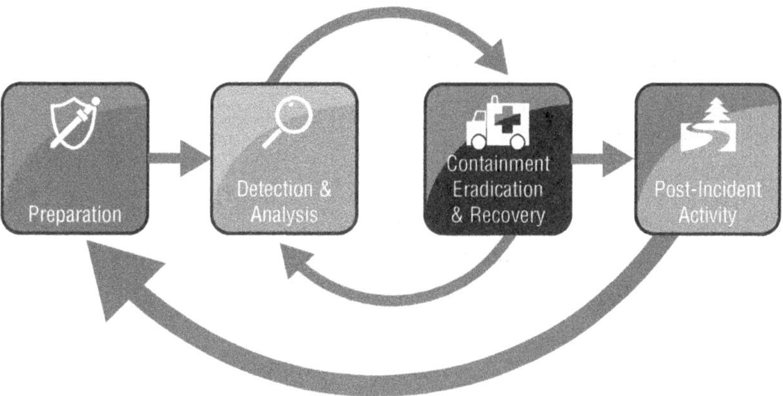

Notice that this process is not a simple progression of steps from start to finish. Instead, it includes loops that allow responders to return to prior phases as needed during the response. These loops reflect the reality of responses to actual cybersecurity incidents. Only in the simplest of incidents would an organization detect an incident, analyze data, conduct a recovery, and close out the incident in a straightforward sequence of steps. Instead, the containment process often includes several loops back through the detection and analysis phase to identify whether the incident has been successfully resolved. These loops are a normal part of the cybersecurity incident response process and should be expected.

Preparation

CSIRTs do not spring up out of thin air. As much as managers may wish it were so, they cannot simply will a CSIRT into existence by creating a policy document and assigning staff members to the CSIRT. Instead, the CSIRT requires careful preparation to ensure that the CSIRT has the proper policy foundation, has operating procedures that will be effective in the organization's computing environment, receives appropriate training, and is prepared to respond to an incident.

The next two sections of this chapter, "Building the Foundation for Incident Response" and "Creating an Incident Response Team," describe the preparation phase in greater detail.

The preparation phase also includes building strong cybersecurity defenses to reduce the likelihood and impact of future incidents. This process of building a defense-in-depth approach to cybersecurity often includes many personnel who might not be part of the CSIRT.

The preparation phase of incident response includes training, testing, and documentation of procedures.

During the preparation phase, the organization should also assemble the hardware, software, and information required to conduct an incident investigation. NIST recommends that every organization's incident response toolkit should include, at a minimum, the following:

- Digital forensic workstations
- Backup devices
- Laptops for data collection, analysis, and reporting
- Spare server and networking equipment
- Blank removable media
- Portable printer
- Forensic and packet capture software
- Bootable USB media containing trusted copies of forensic tools
- Office supplies and evidence collection materials

You'll learn more about the tools used to conduct the incident response process in Chapters 12, 13, and 14.

The preparation phase of the incident response plan is not a "one and done" planning process. Notice in Figure 11.1 that there is a loop from the post-incident activity phase back to the preparation phase. Whenever the organization is not actively involved in an incident response effort, it should be planning for the next incident.

Detection and Analysis

The detection and analysis phase of incident response is one of the trickiest to commit to a routine process. Although cybersecurity analysts have many tools at their disposal that may assist in identifying that a security incident is taking place, many incidents are only detected because of the trained eye of an experienced analyst.

NIST 800-61 describes four major categories of security event indicators:

- *Alerts* that originate from intrusion detection and prevention systems, security information and event management systems, antivirus software, file integrity checking software, and/or third-party monitoring services
- *Logs* generated by operating systems, services, applications, network devices, and network flows
- *Publicly available information* about new vulnerabilities and exploits detected "in the wild" or in a controlled laboratory environment
- *People* from inside the organization or external sources who report suspicious activity that may indicate a security incident is in progress

When any of these information sources indicate that a security incident may be occurring, cybersecurity analysts should shift into the initial validation mode, where they attempt to determine whether an incident is taking place that merits further activation of the incident response process. This analysis is often more art than science and is very difficult work. NIST recommends the following actions to improve the effectiveness of incident analysis:

Profile networks and systems to measure the characteristics of expected activity. This will improve the organization's ability to identify abnormal activity during the detection and analysis process.

Understand normal behavior of users, systems, networks, and applications. This behavior will vary between organizations, at different times of the day, week, and year and with changes in the business cycle. A solid understanding of normal behavior is critical to recognizing deviations from those patterns.

Create a logging policy that specifies the information that must be logged by systems, applications, and network devices. The policy should also specify where those log records should be stored (preferably in a centralized log management system) and the retention period for logs.

Perform event correlation to combine information from multiple sources. This function is typically performed by a *security information and event management (SIEM) system.*

Synchronize clocks across servers, workstations, and network devices. This is done to facilitate the correlation of log entries from different systems. Organizations may easily achieve this objective by operating a *Network Time Protocol (NTP)* server.

Maintain an organizationwide knowledge base that contains critical information about systems and applications. This knowledge base should include information about system profiles, usage patterns, and other information that may be useful to responders who are not familiar with the inner workings of a system.

Capture network traffic as soon as an incident is suspected. If the organization does not routinely capture network traffic, responders should immediately begin packet captures during the detection and analysis phase. This information may provide critical details about an attacker's intentions and activity.

Filter information to reduce clutter. Incident investigations generate massive amounts of information, and it is basically impossible to interpret it all without both inclusion and exclusion filters. Incident response teams may wish to create some predefined filters during the preparation phase to assist with future analysis efforts.

Seek assistance from external resources. Responders should know the parameters for involving outside sources in their response efforts. This may be as simple as conducting a Google search for a strange error message, or it may involve full-fledged coordination with other response teams.

Although it isn't part of the NIST recommendations, you may also find yourself using reverse engineering techniques to investigate the origins and/or intent of malware used in a security incident. You learned about reverse engineering in Chapter 1, "Today's Cybersecurity Analyst."

You'll learn more about the process of detecting and analyzing a security incident in Chapter 12, "Analyzing Indicators of Compromise."

The detection and analysis phase of incident response includes the initial identification and investigation of a security incident.

Containment, Eradication, and Recovery

During the incident detection and analysis phase, the CSIRT engages in primarily passive activities designed to uncover and analyze information about the incident. After completing this assessment, the team moves on to take active measures designed to contain the effects of the incident, eradicate the incident from the network, and recover normal operations. At a high level, the containment, eradication, and recovery phase of the process is designed to achieve these objectives:

1. Select a containment strategy appropriate to the incident circumstances.
2. Implement the selected containment strategy to limit the damage caused by the incident.

3. Gather additional evidence as needed to support the response effort and potential legal action.
4. Identify the attackers and attacking systems.
5. Eradicate the effects of the incident and recover normal business operations.

You'll learn more about the techniques used during the containment, eradication, and recovery phase of incident response in Chapter 14, "Containment, Eradication, and Recovery."

The containment, eradication, and recovery phase of incident response includes isolating systems to contain the damage caused by an incident, eradicating the effects of the incident, and recovering normal business operations.

Postincident Activity

Security incidents don't end after security professionals remove attackers from the network or complete the recovery effort to restore normal business operations. Once the immediate danger passes and normal operations resume, the CSIRT enters the postincident activity phase of incident response. During this phase, team members conduct a lessons learned review and ensure that they meet internal and external evidence retention requirements.

Lessons Learned Review

During the lessons learned review, responders conduct a thorough review of the incident and their response, with an eye toward improving procedures and tools for the next incident. This review is most effective if conducted during a meeting where everyone is present for the discussion (physically or virtually). Although some organizations try to conduct lessons learned reviews in an offline manner, this approach does not lead to the back-and-forth discussion that often yields the greatest insight.

The lessons learned review should be facilitated by an independent facilitator who was not involved in the incident response and is perceived by everyone involved as an objective outsider. This allows the facilitator to guide the discussion in a productive manner without participants feeling that the facilitator is advancing a hidden agenda. NIST recommends that lessons learned processes answer the following questions:

- Exactly what happened and at what times?
- How well did staff and management perform in responding to the incident?
- Were the documented procedures followed? Were they adequate?
- What information was needed sooner?
- Were any steps or actions taken that might have inhibited the recovery?

- What would the staff and management do differently the next time a similar incident occurs?
- How could information sharing with other organizations have been improved?
- What corrective actions can prevent similar incidents in the future?
- What precursors or indicators should be watched for in the future to detect similar incidents?
- What additional tools or resources are needed to detect, analyze, and mitigate future incidents?

Once the group answers these questions, management must ensure that the organization takes follow-up actions, as appropriate. Lessons learned reviews are only effective if they surface needed changes and those changes then occur to improve future incident response efforts.

Evidence Retention

At the conclusion of an incident, the CSIRT has often gathered large quantities of evidence. The team leader should work with staff to identify both internal and external evidence retention requirements. If the incident may result in civil litigation or criminal prosecution, the team should consult attorneys prior to discarding any evidence. If there is no likelihood that the evidence will be used in court, the team should follow any retention policies that the organization has in place.

If the organization does not have an existing evidence retention policy for cybersecurity incidents, now would be a good time to create one. Many organizations choose to implement a two-year retention period for evidence not covered by other requirements. This allows incident handlers time to review the evidence at a later date during incident handling program reviews or while handling future similar incidents.

At the conclusion of the postincident activity phase, the CSIRT deactivates, and the incident-handling cycle returns to the preparation, detect, and analyze phases.

U.S. federal government agencies must retain all incident-handling records for at least three years. This requirement appears in the National Archives General Records Schedule 3.2, Item 20. See `www.archives.gov/files/records-mgmt/grs/grs03-2.pdf` for more information.

You'll read more about the activities undertaken during the postincident activity phase in Chapter 14.

Building the Foundation for Incident Response

One of the major responsibilities that organizations have during the preparation phase of incident response is building a solid policy and procedure foundation for the program. This creates the documentation required to support the program's ongoing efforts.

Policy

The incident response policy serves as the cornerstone of an organization's incident response program. This policy should be written to guide efforts at a high level and provide the authority for incident response. The policy should be approved at the highest level possible within the organization, preferably by the chief executive officer. For this reason, policy authors should attempt to write the policy in a manner that makes it relatively timeless. This means that the policy should contain statements that provide authority for incident response, assign responsibility to the CSIRT, and describe the role of individual users and state organizational priorities. The policy is *not* the place to describe specific technologies, response procedures, or evidence-gathering techniques. Those details may change frequently and should be covered in more easily changed procedure documents.

NIST recommends that incident response policies contain these key elements:

- Statement of management commitment
- Purpose and objectives of the policy
- Scope of the policy (to whom it applies and under what circumstances)
- Definition of cybersecurity incidents and related terms
- Organizational structure and definition of roles, responsibilities, and level of authority
- Prioritization or severity rating scheme for incidents
- Performance measures for the CSIRT
- Reporting and contact forms

Including these elements in the policy provides a solid foundation for the CSIRT's routine and crisis activities.

Procedures and Playbooks

Procedures provide the detailed, tactical information that CSIRT members need when responding to an incident. They represent the collective wisdom of team members and subject matter experts collected during periods of calm and are ready to be applied in the event of an actual incident. CSIRT teams often develop *playbooks* that describe the specific procedures that they will follow in the event of a specific type of cybersecurity incident. For example, a financial institution CSIRT might develop playbooks that cover

- Breach of personal financial information
- Web server defacement
- Phishing attack targeted at customers
- Loss of a laptop
- General security incident not covered by another playbook

This is clearly not an exhaustive list, and each organization will develop playbooks that describe their response to both high severity and frequently occurring incident categories. The idea behind the playbook is that the team should be able to pick it up and find an operational plan for responding to the security incident that they may follow. Playbooks are especially important in the early hours of incident response to ensure that the team has a planned, measured response to the first reports of a potential incident.

For good examples of real-world cybersecurity incident playbooks, see the Ransomware Playbook published by Demisto (`www.demisto.com/playbook-for-handling-ransomware-infections/`) or the Windows incident response playbook from the University of Central Florida (`infosec.ucf.edu/wp-content/uploads/sites/2/2019/07/Procedure_for_Windows_Incident_Response.pdf`).

Playbooks are designed to be step-by-step recipe-style responses to cybersecurity incidents. They should guide the team's response, but they are not a substitute for professional judgment. The responders handling an incident should have appropriate professional expertise and the authority to deviate from the playbook when circumstances require a different approach.

Documenting the Incident Response Plan

When developing the incident response plan documentation, organizations should pay particular attention to creating tools that may be useful during an incident response. These tools should provide clear guidance to response teams that may be quickly read and interpreted during a crisis situation. For example, the incident response checklist shown in Figure 11.2 provides a high-level overview of the incident response process in checklist form. The CSIRT leader may use this checklist to ensure that the team doesn't miss an important step in the heat of the crisis environment.

FIGURE 11.2 Incident response checklist
Source: NIST SP 800-61: Computer Security Incident Handling Guide

	Action	Completed
	Detection and Analysis	
1.	Determine whether an incident has occurred	
1.1	Analyze the precursors and indicators	
1.2	Look for correlating information	
1.3	Perform research (e.g., search engines, knowledge base)	
1.4	As soon as the handler believes an incident has occurred, begin documenting the investigation and gathering evidence	
2.	Prioritize handling the incident based on the relevant factors (functional impact, information impact, recoverability effort, etc.)	
3.	Report the incident to the appropriate internal personnel and external organizations	
	Containment, Eradication, and Recovery	
4.	Acquire, preserve, secure, and document evidence	
5.	Contain the incident	
6.	Eradicate the incident	
6.1	Identify and mitigate all vulnerabilities that were exploited	
6.2	Remove malware, inappropriate materials, and other components	
6.3	If more affected hosts are discovered (e.g., new malware infections), repeat the Detection and Analysis steps (1.1, 1.2) to identify all other affected hosts, then contain (5) and eradicate (6) the incident for them	
7.	Recover from the incident	
7.1	Return affected systems to an operationally ready state	
7.2	Confirm that the affected systems are functioning normally	
7.3	If necessary, implement additional monitoring to look for future related activity	
	Post-Incident Activity	
8.	Create a follow-up report	
9.	Hold a lessons learned meeting (mandatory for major incidents, optional otherwise)	

The National Institute of Standards and Technology publishes a Computer Security Incident Handling Guide (SP 800-61) that contains a wealth of information that is useful to both government agencies and private organizations developing incident response plans. The current version of the guide, NIST SP 800-61 revision 2, is available online at `nvlpubs.nist.gov/nistpubs/SpecialPublications/NIST.SP.800-61r2.pdf`.

Creating an Incident Response Team

There are many different roles that should be represented on a CSIRT. Depending on the organization and its technical needs, some of these roles may be core team members who are always activated, whereas others may be called in as needed on an incident-by-incident basis. For example, a database administrator might be crucial when investigating the aftermath of a SQL injection attack but would probably not be very helpful when responding to a stolen laptop.

The core incident response team normally consists of cybersecurity professionals with specific expertise in incident response. In larger organizations, these may be full-time employees dedicated to incident response, whereas smaller organizations may call on cybersecurity experts who fill other roles for their "day jobs" to step into CSIRT roles in the aftermath of an incident.

The Role of Management

Management should have an active role in incident response efforts. The primary responsibility of IT managers and senior leadership is to provide the authority, resources, and time required to respond appropriately to a security incident. This includes ensuring that the CSIRT has the budget and staff required to plan for security incidents and access to subject matter experts during a response.

Management may also be called on during an incident response to make critical business decisions about the need to shut down critical servers, communicate with law enforcement or the general public, and assess the impact of an incident on key stakeholders.

In addition to the core team members, the CSIRT may include representation from the following:

- Technical subject matter experts whose knowledge may be required during a response. This includes system engineers, network administrators, database administrators, desktop experts, and application experts.
- IT support staff who may be needed to carry out actions directed by the CSIRT.
- Legal counsel responsible for ensuring that the team's actions comply with legal, policy, and regulatory requirements and can advise team leaders on compliance issues and communication with regulatory bodies.
- Human resources staff responsible for investigating potential employee malfeasance.
- Public relations and marketing staff who can coordinate communications with the media and general public.

The CSIRT should be run by a designated leader with the clear authority to direct incident response efforts and serve as a liaison to management. This leader should be a skilled incident responder who is either assigned to lead the CSIRT as a full-time responsibility or serves in a cybersecurity leadership position.

Incident Response Providers

In addition to including internal team members on the CSIRT, the organization may decide to outsource some or all of their actions to an incident response provider. Retaining an incident response provider gives the organization access to expertise that might not otherwise exist inside the firm. This may come at significant expense, so the organizations should decide what types of incidents may be handled internally and which justify the use of an outside provider. Additionally, the organization should understand the provider's guaranteed response time and ensure that it has a plan in place to respond to the early stages of an incident before the provider assumes control.

CSIRT Scope of Control

The organization's incident response policy should clearly outline the scope of the CSIRT. This includes answers to the following questions:

- What triggers the activation of the CSIRT? Who is authorized to activate the CSIRT?
- Does the CSIRT cover the entire organization or is it responsible only for certain business units, information categories, or other divisions of responsibility?
- Is the CSIRT authorized to communicate with law enforcement, regulatory bodies, or other external parties and, if so, which ones?
- Does the CSIRT have internal communication and/or escalation responsibilities? If so, what triggers those requirements?

Testing the Incident Response Plan

Testing cybersecurity incident response plans is a critical component of any organization's incident response strategy. Testing reassures the organization that the plan will function properly in the event of an actual incident and provides a critical training exercise for the team members who would respond to a real-world cybersecurity crisis.

If you are responsible for your organization's incident response plan, you should conduct regular simulation tests to walk team members through the processes they would follow when responding to a real cybersecurity incident.

Coordination and Information Sharing

During an incident response effort, CSIRT team members often need to communicate and share information with both internal and external partners. Smooth information sharing is essential to an effective and efficient incident response, but it must be done within the clearly established parameters of an incident communication plan. The organization's incident response policies should limit communication to trusted parties and put controls in place to prevent the inadvertent release of sensitive information outside of those trusted partners.

Internal Communications

Internal communications among the CSIRT and with other employees within the organization should take place over secure communications channels that are designated in advance and tested for security. This may include email, instant messaging, message boards, and other collaboration tools that pass security muster. The key is to evaluate and standardize those communications tools in advance so that responders are not left to their own devices to identify tools in the heat of an incident.

External Communications

CSIRT team members, business leaders, public relations teams, and legal counsel may all bring to the table requirements that may justify sharing limited or detailed information with external entities. The incident response plan should guide these efforts. Types of external communications may include the following:

- Law enforcement may wish to be involved when a cybersecurity incident appears to be criminal in nature. The organization may choose to cooperate or decline participation in an investigation but should always make this decision with the advice of legal counsel.
- Information sharing partners, such as the Information Sharing and Analysis Center (ISAC), provide community-based warnings of cybersecurity risks. The organization may choose to participate in one of these consortiums and, in some cases, share information about ongoing and past security incidents to partners in that consortium.
- Vendors may be able to provide information crucial to the response. The manufacturers of hardware and software used within the organization may be able to provide patches, troubleshooting advice, or other guidance crucial to the response effort.
- Other organizations may be actual or potential victims of the same attack. CSIRT members may wish to coordinate their incident response with other organizations.
- Communications with the media and the general public may be mandatory under regulatory or legislative reporting requirements, voluntary, or forced by media coverage of a security incident.

It is incumbent upon the CSIRT leader to control and coordinate external communications in a manner that meets regulatory requirements and best serves the response effort.

Classifying Incidents

Each time an incident occurs, the CSIRT should classify the incident by both the type of threat and the severity of the incident according to a standardized incident severity rating system. This classification aids other personnel in understanding the nature and severity of the incident and allows the comparison of the current incident to past and future incidents.

Threat Classification

In many cases, the incident will come from a known threat source that facilitates the rapid identification of the threat. NIST provides the following attack vectors that are useful for classifying threats:

External/Removable Media An attack executed from removable media or a peripheral device—for example, malicious code spreading onto a system from an infected USB flash drive.

Attrition An attack that employs brute-force methods to compromise, degrade, or destroy systems, networks, or services—for example, a DDoS attack intended to impair or deny access to a service or application or a brute-force attack against an authentication mechanism.

Web An attack executed from a website or web-based application—for example, a cross-site scripting attack used to steal credentials or redirect to a site that exploits a browser vulnerability and installs malware.

Email An attack executed via an email message or attachment—for example, exploit code disguised as an attached document or a link to a malicious website in the body of an email message.

Impersonation An attack involving replacement of something benign with something malicious—for example, spoofing, man-in-the-middle attacks, rogue wireless access points, and SQL injection attacks all involve impersonation.

Improper Usage Any incident resulting from violation of an organization's acceptable usage policies by an authorized user, excluding the previous categories; for example, a user installs file-sharing software, leading to the loss of sensitive data, or a user performs illegal activities on a system.

Loss or Theft of Equipment The loss or theft of a computing device or media used by the organization, such as a laptop, smartphone, or authentication token.

Unknown An attack of unknown origin.

Other An attack of known origin that does not fit into any of the previous categories.

In addition to understanding these attack vectors, cybersecurity analysts should be familiar with the concept of an *advanced persistent threat (APT)*. APT attackers are highly skilled and talented attackers focused on a specific objective. These attackers are often funded by nation-states, organized crime, and other sources with tremendous resources. APT attackers are known for taking advantage of *zero-day vulnerabilities*—vulnerabilities that are unknown to the security community and, as a result, are not included in security tests performed by vulnerability scanners and other tools and have no patches available to correct them.

Severity Classification

CSIRT members may investigate dozens, hundreds, or even thousands of security incidents each year, depending on the scope of their responsibilities and the size of the organization. Therefore, it is important to use a standardized process to communicate the severity of each incident to management and other stakeholders. Incident severity information assists in the prioritization and scope of incident response efforts.

Two key measures used to determine the incident severity are the scope of the impact and the types of data involved in the incident.

Scope of Impact

The scope of an incident's impact depends on the degree of impairment that it causes the organization as well as the effort required to recover from the incident.

Functional Impact

The functional impact of an incident is the degree of impairment that it causes to the organization. This may vary based on the criticality of the data, systems or processes affected by the incident, as well as the organization's ability to continue providing services to users as an incident unfolds and in the aftermath of the incident. NIST recommends using four categories to describe the functional impact of an incident, as shown in Table 11.1.

TABLE 11.1 NIST functional impact categories

Category	Definition
None	No effect to the organization's ability to provide all services to all users.
Low	Minimal effect; the organization can still provide all critical services to all users but has lost efficiency.
Medium	The organization has lost the ability to provide a critical service to a subset of system users.
High	The organization is no longer able to provide some critical services to any users.

Source: NIST SP 800-61

There is one major gap in the functional impact assessment criteria provided by NIST: it does not include any assessment of the economic impact of a security incident on the organization. This may be because the NIST guidelines are primarily intended to serve a government audience. Organizations may wish to modify the categories in Table 11.1 to incorporate economic impact or measure financial impact using a separate scale, such as the one shown in Table 11.2.

TABLE 11.2 Economic impact categories

Category	Definition
None	The organization does not expect to experience any financial impact or the financial impact is negligible.
Low	The organization expects to experience a financial impact of $10,000 or less.
Medium	The organization expects to experience a financial impact of more than $10,000 but less than $500,000.
High	The organization expects to experience a financial impact of $500,000 or more.

The financial thresholds included in Table 11.2 are intended as examples only and should be adjusted according to the size of the organization. For example, a security incident causing a $500,000 loss may be crippling for a small business, whereas a Fortune 500 company may easily absorb this loss.

Recoverability Effort

In addition to measuring the functional and economic impact of a security incident, organizations should measure the time that services will be unavailable. This may be expressed as a function of the amount of downtime experienced by the service or the time required to recover from the incident. Table 11.3 shows the recommendations suggested by NIST for assessing the recoverability impact of a security incident.

Datatypes

The nature of the data involved in a security incident also contributes to the incident severity. When a security incident affects the confidentiality or integrity of sensitive information, cybersecurity analysts should assign a data impact rating. The data impact rating scale recommended by NIST appears in Table 11.4.

TABLE 11.3 NIST recoverability effort categories

Category	Definition
Regular	Time to recovery is predictable with existing resources.
Supplemented	Time to recovery is predictable with additional resources.
Extended	Time to recovery is unpredictable; additional resources and outside help are needed.
Not Recoverable	Recovery from the incident is not possible (e.g., sensitive data exfiltrated and posted publicly); launch investigation.

Source: NIST SP 800-61

Although the impact scale presented in Table 11.4 is NIST's recommendation, it does have some significant shortcomings. Most notably, the definitions included in the table are skewed toward the types of information that might be possessed by a government agency and might not map well to information in the possession of a private organization. Some analysts might also object to the inclusion of "integrity loss" as a single category separate from the three classification-dependent breach categories.

TABLE 11.4 NIST information impact categories

Category	Definition
None	No information was exfiltrated, changed, deleted, or otherwise compromised.
Privacy breach	Sensitive personally identifiable information (PII) of taxpayers, employees, beneficiaries, and so on was accessed or exfiltrated.
Proprietary breach	Unclassified proprietary information, such as protected critical infrastructure information (PCII) was accessed or exfiltrated.
Integrity loss	Sensitive or proprietary information was changed or deleted.

Source: NIST SP 800-61

Table 11.5 presents an alternative classification scheme that private organizations might use as the basis for their own information impact categorization schemes.

TABLE 11.5 Private organization information impact categories

Category	Definition
None	No information was exfiltrated, changed, deleted, or otherwise compromised.
Regulated information breach	Information regulated by an external compliance obligation was accessed or exfiltrated. This may include personally identifiable information (PII) that triggers a data breach notification law, protected health information (PHI) under HIPAA, and/or payment card information protected under PCI DSS. For organizations subject to the European Union's General Data Protection Regulation (GDPR), it should also include sensitive personal information (SPI) as defined under GDPR. SPI includes information from special categories, such as genetic data, trade union membership, and sexual information.
Intellectual property breach	Sensitive intellectual property was accessed or exfiltrated. This may include product development plans, formulas, or other sensitive trade secrets.
Confidential information breach	Corporate confidential information was accessed or exfiltrated. This includes information that is sensitive or classified as a high-value asset but does not fit under the categories of regulated information or intellectual property. Examples might include corporate financial information or information about mergers and acquisitions.
Integrity loss	Sensitive or proprietary information was changed or deleted.

As with the financial impact scale, organizations will need to customize the information impact categories in Table 11.5 to meet the unique requirements of their business processes.

Exam Note

As you prepare for the CySA+ exam, be sure that you are familiar with all of the different categories of sensitive information that contribute to criticality ratings. These include personally identifiable information (PII), protected health information (PHI), sensitive personal information (SPI), high-value assets, financial information, intellectual property, and corporate information.

Summary

Incident response programs provide organizations with the ability to respond to security issues in a calm, repeatable manner. Security incidents occur when there is a known or suspected violation or imminent violation of an organization's security policies. When a security incident occurs, the organization should activate its computer security incident response team (CSIRT).

The CSIRT guides the organization through the four stages of incident response: preparation; detection and analysis; containment, eradication, and recovery; and postincident activities. During the preparation phase, the organization ensures that the CSIRT has the proper policy foundation, has operating procedures that will be effective in the organization's computing environment, receives appropriate training, and is prepared to respond to an incident.

During the detection and analysis phase, the organization watches for signs of security incidents. This includes monitoring alerts, logs, publicly available information, and reports from internal and external staff about security anomalies. When the organization suspects a security incident, it moves into the containment, eradication, and recovery phase, which is designed to limit the damage and restore normal operations as quickly as possible.

Restoration of normal activity doesn't signal the end of incident response efforts. At the conclusion of an incident, the postincident activities phase provides the organization with the opportunity to reflect upon the incident by conducting a lessons learned review. During this phase, the organization should also ensure that evidence is retained for future use according to policy.

Exam Essentials

Distinguish between security events and security incidents. An event is any observable occurrence in a system or network. A security event includes any observable occurrence that relates to a security function. A security incident is a violation or imminent threat of violation of computer security policies, acceptable use policies, or standard security practices. Every incident consists of one or more events, but every event is not an incident.

Name the four phases of the cybersecurity incident response process. The four phases of incident response are preparation; detection and analysis; containment, eradication, and recovery; and postincident activities. The process is not a simple progression of steps from start to finish. Instead, it includes loops that allow responders to return to prior phases as needed during the response.

Identify security event indicators. Alerts originate from intrusion detection and prevention systems, security information and event management systems, antivirus software, file integrity checking software, and third-party monitoring services. Logs are generated by operating systems, services, applications, network devices, and network flows. Publicly available information exists about new vulnerabilities and exploits detected "in the wild" or in a controlled laboratory environment. People from inside the organization or external sources report suspicious activity that may indicate that a security incident is in progress.

Explain how policies, procedures, and playbooks guide incident response efforts. The incident response policy serves as the cornerstone of an organization's incident response program. This policy should be written to guide efforts at a high level and provide the authority for incident response. Procedures provide the detailed, tactical information that CSIRT members need when responding to an incident. CSIRT teams often develop playbooks that describe the specific procedures that they will follow in the event of a specific type of cybersecurity incident.

Know that incident response teams should represent diverse stakeholders. The core incident response team normally consists of cybersecurity professionals with specific expertise in incident response. In addition to the core team members, the CSIRT may include representation from technical subject matter experts, IT support staff, legal counsel, human resources staff, and public relations and marketing teams. The team will also need to coordinate with internal and external stakeholders, including senior leadership, law enforcement, and regulatory bodies.

Explain how incidents can be classified according to the attack vector where they originate. Common attack vectors for security incidents include external/removable media, attrition, the web, email, impersonation, improper usage, loss or theft of equipment, and other/unknown sources.

Explain how response teams classify the severity of an incident. The functional impact of an incident is the degree of impairment that it causes to the organization. The economic impact is the amount of financial loss that the organization incurs. In addition to measuring the functional and economic impact of a security incident, organizations should measure the time that services will be unavailable and the recoverability effort. Finally, the nature of the data involved in an incident also contributes to the severity as the information impact.

Lab Exercises

Activity 11.1: Incident Severity Classification

You are the leader of cybersecurity incident response team for a large company that is experiencing a denial-of-service attack on its website. This attack is preventing the organization from selling products to its customers and is likely to cause lost revenue of at least $2 million per day until the incident is resolved.

The attack is coming from many different sources, and you have exhausted all of the response techniques at your disposal. You are currently looking to identify an external partner that can help with the response.

Classify this incident using the criteria described in this chapter. Assign categorical ratings for functional impact, economic impact, recoverability effort, and information impact. Justify each of your assignments.

Activity 11.2: Incident Response Phases

Identify the correct phase of the incident response process that corresponds to each of the following activities:

Activity	Phase
Conducting a lessons learned review session	
Receiving a report from a staff member about a malware infection	
Upgrading the organization's firewall to block a new type of attack	
Recovering normal operations after eradicating an incident	
Identifying the attackers and attacking systems	
Interpreting log entries using a SIEM to identify a potential incident	
Assembling the hardware and software required to conduct an incident investigation	

Activity 11.3: Develop an Incident Communications Plan

You are the CSIRT leader for a major e-commerce website, and you are currently responding to a security incident where you believe attackers used a SQL injection attack to steal transaction records from your backend database.

Currently, only the core CSIRT members are responding. Develop a communication plan that describes the nature, timing, and audiences for communications to the internal and external stakeholders that you believe need to be notified.

Review Questions

1. Which one of the following is an example of a computer security incident?
   - A. User accesses a secure file
   - B. Administrator changes a file's permission settings
   - C. Intruder breaks into a building
   - D. Former employee crashes a server
2. During what phase of the incident response process would an organization implement defenses designed to reduce the likelihood of a security incident?
   - A. Preparation
   - B. Detection and analysis
   - C. Containment, eradication, and recovery
   - D. Postincident activity
3. Alan is responsible for developing his organization's detection and analysis capabilities. He would like to purchase a system that can combine log records from multiple sources to detect potential security incidents. What type of system is best suited to meet Alan's security objective?
   - A. IPS
   - B. IDS
   - C. SIEM
   - D. Firewall
4. Ben is working to classify the functional impact of an incident. The incident has disabled email service for approximately 30 percent of his organization's staff. How should Ben classify the functional impact of this incident according to the NIST scale?
   - A. None
   - B. Low
   - C. Medium
   - D. High
5. What phase of the incident response process would include measures designed to limit the damage caused by an ongoing breach?
   - A. Preparation
   - B. Detection and analysis
   - C. Containment, eradication, and recovery
   - D. Postincident activity

6. Grace is the CSIRT team leader for a business unit within NASA, a federal agency. What is the minimum amount of time that Grace must retain incident handling records?
   A. Six months
   B. One year
   C. Two years
   D. Three years

7. Karen is responding to a security incident that resulted from an intruder stealing files from a government agency. Those files contained unencrypted information about protected critical infrastructure. How should Karen rate the information impact of this loss?
   A. None
   B. Privacy breach
   C. Proprietary breach
   D. Integrity loss

8. Matt is concerned about the fact that log records from his organization contain conflicting timestamps due to unsynchronized clocks. What protocol can he use to synchronize clocks throughout the enterprise?
   A. NTP
   B. FTP
   C. ARP
   D. SSH

9. Which one of the following document types would outline the authority of a CSIRT responding to a security incident?
   A. Policy
   B. Procedure
   C. Playbook
   D. Baseline

10. A cross-site scripting attack is an example of what type of threat vector?
    A. Impersonation
    B. Email
    C. Attrition
    D. Web

11. Which one of the following parties is not commonly the target of external communications during an incident?
    A. The perpetrator
    B. Law enforcement
    C. Vendors
    D. Information sharing partners

12. Robert is finishing a draft of a proposed incident response policy for his organization. Who would be the most appropriate person to sign the policy?
    A. CEO
    B. Director of security
    C. CIO
    D. CSIRT leader

13. Which one of the following is not an objective of the containment, eradication, and recovery phase of incident response?
    A. Detect an incident in progress
    B. Implement a containment strategy
    C. Identify the attackers
    D. Eradicate the effects of the incident

14. Renee is responding to a security incident that resulted in the unavailability of a website critical to her company's operations. She is unsure of the amount of time and effort that it will take to recover the website. How should Renee classify the recoverability effort?
    A. Regular
    B. Supplemented
    C. Extended
    D. Not recoverable

15. Which one of the following is an example of an attrition attack?
    A. SQL injection
    B. Theft of a laptop
    C. User installs file sharing software
    D. Brute-force password attack

16. Who is the best facilitator for a postincident lessons learned session?
    A. CEO
    B. CSIRT leader
    C. Independent facilitator
    D. First responder

17. Which one of the following elements is not normally found in an incident response policy?
    A. Performance measures for the CSIRT
    B. Definition of cybersecurity incidents
    C. Definition of roles, responsibilities, and levels of authority
    D. Procedures for rebuilding systems

18. A man-in-the-middle attack is an example of what type of threat vector?
    - A. Attrition
    - B. Impersonation
    - C. Web
    - D. Email

19. Tommy is the CSIRT team leader for his organization and is responding to a newly discovered security incident. What document is most likely to contain step-by-step instructions that he might follow in the early hours of the response effort?
    - A. Policy
    - B. Baseline
    - C. Playbook
    - D. Textbook

20. Hank is responding to a security event where the CEO of his company had her laptop stolen. The laptop was encrypted but contained sensitive information about the company's employees. How should Hank classify the information impact of this security event?
    - A. None
    - B. Privacy breach
    - C. Proprietary breach
    - D. Integrity loss

Analyzing Indicators of Compromise

THE COMPTIA CYBERSECURITY ANALYST (CYSA+) EXAM OBJECTIVES COVERED IN THIS CHAPTER INCLUDE:

✓ **Domain 4.0: Incident Response**

- 4.3 Given an incident, analyze potential indicators of compromise.

Responding to security incidents and network events is a common task for cybersecurity analysts, and to do so, you need to know how to recognize common indicators of compromise. Network problems such as excessive or suspicious bandwidth consumption, probes and scans, and rogue devices are all likely to be encountered by security professionals and can indicate problems. Host and application issues are also frequently part of response processes, including host performance problems, malware, and more focused attacks. That makes knowing what to look for, how to find it, and what your response options are an important part of cybersecurity operations.

In the first section of this chapter, you learn about common network events ranging from bandwidth use and data exfiltration to scans, probes, and denial-of-service attacks, as well as some of the tools that are frequently used to detect them and to perform that analysis. In the sections that follow, you learn about host and application problems, detection and analysis techniques to address them, and examples of handling methods for common issues related to these symptoms.

Analyzing Network Events

Many incidents start with the discovery of suspicious or unexpected network traffic. These events may take the form of bandwidth consumption, attack traffic, or unexpected devices showing up on the network. As a cybersecurity analyst, you need to be able to gather, correlate, and analyze the data from a multitude of systems and network devices to detect, or better, to prevent these incidents from becoming serious issues.

Many organizations differentiate between events and incidents (as we defined in the previous chapter). Events are typically defined as observable events like an email or a file download. Incidents are often classified as a violation of a security policy, unauthorized use or access, denial of service, or other malicious actions that may cause harm. Alerts are sent when events cause notification to occur. Make sure you know how your organization describes events, incidents, and alerts to help prevent confusion.

Capturing Network-Related Events

One of the first steps in gaining a high-level understanding of a network is getting visibility into how the available bandwidth for the network is being used. This is typically done through one of three common methods: router-based monitoring, active monitoring, or passive monitoring.

Router-Based Monitoring

Router-based monitoring relies on routers or switches with routing capabilities to provide information about the flow of traffic on the network and the status of the network device itself. Since routers are normally placed at network borders or other internal boundaries, router-based monitoring can provide a useful view of traffic at those points.

Most router-based monitoring relies on capturing data about the traffic that is passing through the device. This information about traffic flow is often referred to as *network flows*. A number of technologies exist to capture flows and other router information, including

- *NetFlow*, or similar technologies like *sFlow*, *J-Flow*, and others, are standards for monitoring *traffic flows*. They count information about traffic at network device interfaces and then send that information to flow collectors. Flows are often sampled due to the sheer quantity of data, meaning that one in a thousand or one in a hundred packets are sampled rather than every packet.
- *RMON* was developed to monitor local area networks and operates at layers 1–4 of the network stack. RMON typically operates in a client/server model and uses monitoring devices (probes) to gather data. It is implemented as a *management information base* (*MIB*), which provides monitoring groups with information about networks and focuses on flow-based information, including statistics, history, alarms, and events.
- In addition to flow-based reporting, the *Simple Network Management Protocol (SNMP)* is commonly used to collect information from routers and other network devices and provides more information about the devices themselves instead of the network traffic flow information provided by RMON or NetFlow or related flow-capture protocols.

Exam Note

The CS0-002 Exam Objectives ask about bandwidth consumption, beaconing, irregular peer-to-peer communication, rogue devices, scans and sweeps, unusual traffic spikes, and common protocols sent over non-standard ports. Each of these can be detected by capturing and analyzing network events, and that's why we start with this section—first, you need to know how to get the data and then you can analyze it.

In Figure 12.1, a simple example of a typical network shows how the central placement of routers can provide visibility into the overall traffic flow of a network. Traffic sent from the distribution switches to the other division's network, or to the Internet, will be sent through the division routers and possibly through the border router, allowing network flow information to be captured on a central flow collection system.

FIGURE 12.1 Routers provide a central view of network traffic flow by sending data to flow collectors.

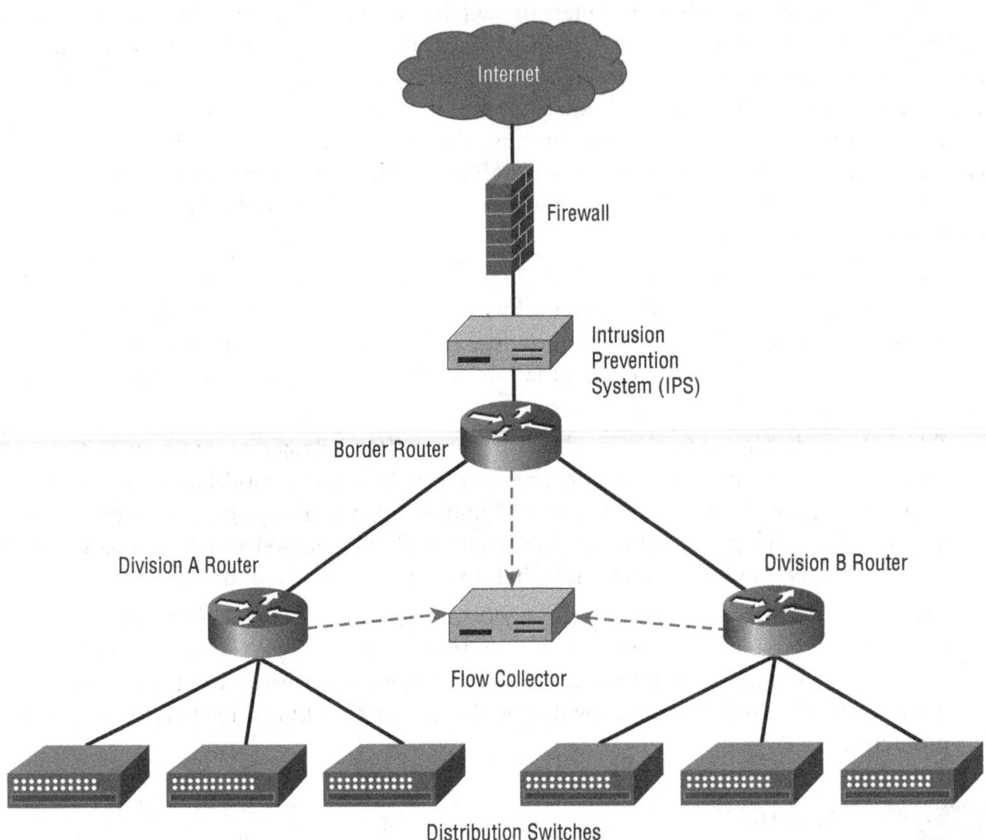

Flow information can look a lot like information from a typical phone bill—you can see who you called, what number they were at, and how long you talked. With flows, you can see the source, its IP address, the destination, its IP address, how many packets were sent, how much data was sent, and the port and protocol that was used, allowing a good guess about what application was in use. Figure 12.2 shows an example of PRTG's NetFlow tool, with this data listed in a way that allows data to be sorted and searched.

FIGURE 12.2 NetFlow data example

1 to 12 of 12

Pos	Source IP	Source Port	Destination IP	Destination Port	Protocol	Bytes	
1.	216.58.216.235	443	192.168.1.227	63287	6	197 Byte	14 %
2.	192.168.1.227	63287	216.58.216.235	443	6	196 Byte	14 %
3.	192.168.1.14	53250	198.41.215.68	443	6	190 Byte	13 %
4.	192.168.1.14	53273	157.240.2.35	443	6	190 Byte	13 %
5.	192.168.1.14	53276	157.240.2.25	443	6	190 Byte	13 %
6.	NP-13A185131948 (192.168.1.215)	38970	ec2-54-186-29-214.us-west-2.compute.amazonaws.com (54.186.29.214)	443	6	135 Byte	10 %
7.	198.41.215.68	443	192.168.1.14	53250	6	92 Byte	6 %
8.	android-cbf9ddc66a19c6ef (192.168.1.212)	42671	ord30s26-in-f228.1e100.net (216.58.192.228)	443	6	83 Byte	6 %
9.	157.240.2.25	443	192.168.1.14	53276	6	52 Byte	4 %
10.	157.240.2.35	443	192.168.1.14	53273	6	52 Byte	4 %
11.	ord30s26-in-f228.1e100.net (216.58.192.228)	443	android-cbf9ddc66a19c6ef (192.168.1.212)	42671	6	40 Byte	3 %
Other						0 Byte	< 1 %

1 to 12 of 12

This information can be very useful for both day-to-day monitoring and for investigations. In addition, feeding flow data to a security monitoring tool that uses behavior-based detection capabilities can identify issues like unexpected communications to remote command and control (C&C) systems. In Figure 12.2, you can see that local hosts are browsing remote sites—192.168.1.14 visits 157.240.2.35—a Facebook content delivery network host. If you saw traffic that was not expected when you reviewed traffic or if you were investigating suspicious traffic, flows can provide a useful way to quickly review what a given host is doing. Network flow data can be used both proactively, to monitor overall network health and traffic levels, and reactively, to monitor for unexpected traffic or for sudden changes in network bandwidth usage. This data is often combined with other network and system log and event data using a security information and event management (SIEM) device or log analysis tool to provide deeper analysis and response capabilities.

Active Monitoring

Active monitoring techniques reach out to remote systems and devices to gather data. Unlike flows and SNMP monitoring, where data is gathered by sending information to collectors, active monitors are typically the data gathering location (although they may then forward that information to a collector). Active monitoring typically gathers data about availability, routes, packet delay or loss, and bandwidth.

Two examples of active monitoring are

- *Pings*—Network data can also be acquired actively by using Internet Control Message Protocol (ICMP) to ping remote systems. This provides only basic up/down information, but for basic use, ICMP offers a simple solution.
- *iPerf*—A tool that measures the maximum bandwidth that an IP network can handle. Public iPerf servers allow remote testing of link bandwidth in addition to internal bandwidth testing. iPerf testing data can help establish a baseline for performance to help identify when a network will reach its useful limits.

Both active and router-based monitoring add traffic to the network, which means that the network monitoring systems may be competing with the traffic they are monitoring. When significant network bandwidth utilization issues appear, this type of network monitoring data may be lost or delayed as higher-priority traffic is likely to be prioritized over monitoring data.

Although it is possible to implement your own ping script for monitoring, tools like Nagios have available ping plug-ins that can use both ICMP and TCP pings with a variety of additional capabilities. Using a full-featured monitoring tool can allow active ping monitoring to be combined with other data easily, providing far more useful analysis capabilities than a ping script.

Passive Monitoring

Passive monitoring relies on capturing information about the network as traffic passes a location on a network link. In Figure 12.3, a network monitor uses a network tap to send a copy of all the traffic sent between endpoints A and B. This allows the monitoring system to capture the traffic that is sent, providing a detailed view of the traffic's rate, protocol, and content, as well as details of the performance of sending and receiving packets.

FIGURE 12.3 Passive monitoring between two systems

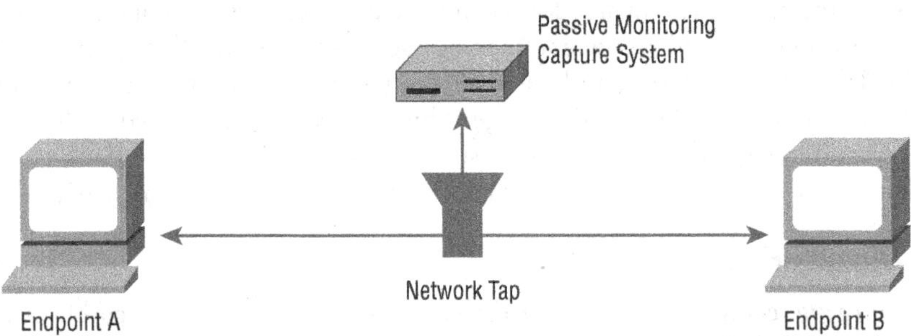

Unlike active and router-based monitoring, passive monitoring does not add additional traffic to the network. It also performs after-the-fact analysis, since packets must be captured and analyzed, rather than being recorded in real time as they are sent. This means that the trade-offs between each monitoring method should be considered when choosing a technique.

Network Monitoring Tools

Network monitoring involves much more than a view of just the routers or the traffic passing through interfaces. Gathering information from multiple network devices and combining that data into useful views for analysis and reporting is critical to ensuring that you have a good view of what is occurring on your network. Fortunately, tools are available that are specifically designed to provide this visibility.

PRTG

One common choice for monitoring bandwidth usage is PRTG (the Paessler Router Traffic Grapher). PRTG provides a variety of network monitoring capabilities, including server monitoring, network monitoring, and bandwidth monitoring. PRTG combines four types of monitoring to provide a more accurate picture of bandwidth utilization:

- Packet sniffing, which monitors only the headers of packets to determine what type of traffic is being sent. This can identify information from packets that the sensor can read, but an encrypted session may not reveal much.
- Flows, which can send either information about all connections, or a sampled dataset.
- SNMP (Simple Network Management Protocol), a protocol that allows network devices to send information about important events as *SNMP traps*.
- *WMI* (Windows Management Instrumentation), which provides an interface that allows script and application access for automation of administrative tasks, as well as a means of accessing management data for the operating system, and can provide reports to tools like System Center Operations Manager for Windows systems. A hybrid mode allows access to Windows performance counters using the remote registry service, with WMI as a fallback. This approach can make a Windows system's native monitoring capability useful for a central view.

Figure 12.4 shows PRTG's overview window. Traffic over time as well as flow information are shown in near real time. To investigate a problem, you can simply drill down by clicking the appropriate view.

Overview and dashboard screens in tools like PRTG are often used to provide a high-level overview of network performance. A sudden drop-off or increase in network usage can be quickly seen on the overview chart, and drilling down by clicking the chart can help to isolate or identify a system or interface that is affected or that may be causing the issue. More detailed searches and filters can also be accessed in tools like this to answer specific questions if you are working from existing knowledge like an IP address or interface that needs to be investigated.

FIGURE 12.4 PRTG network overview

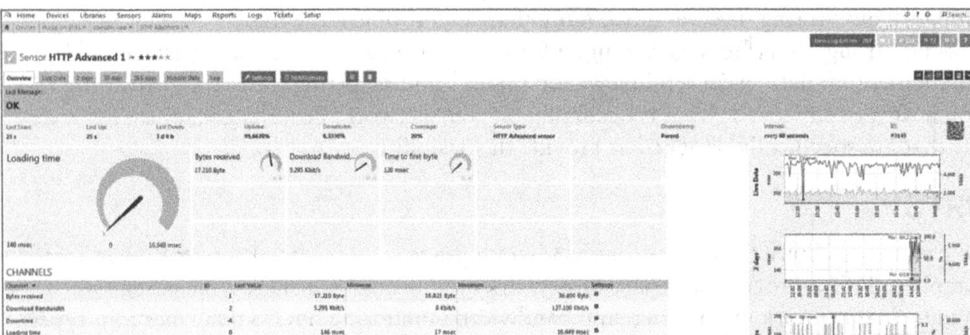

Capturing data from large networks or networks with a lot of bandwidth usage can result in so much traffic that network analysis tools can't handle the load. That's where sampling comes in handy. Often, traffic analysis is done using trend and anomaly analysis rather than looking for specific individual behaviors. With this in mind, a sample rate of 1 in 10, or even 1 in 1000, can still provide useful aggregate data. If your flow collector or analysis system is having problems keeping up, consider using sampling instead of complete capture.

SolarWinds

SolarWinds sells a variety of network monitoring tools that address multiple types of data gathering. Combining the ability to identify network issues and intelligence about network bandwidth and flows can provide a better view of what is occurring on a network, making a pairing of tools like this a good solution when trying to understand complex network issues.

SolarWinds provides a demo of their tools at `oriondemo.solarwinds.com/Orion/`. You can watch videos of each of the tools at `demo.solarwinds.com/sedemo/` for more detail on how to use them.

Nagios

Nagios is a popular network and system log monitoring tool. Nagios supports a broad range of plug-ins, including the ability to build and integrate your own plug-ins using Perl or executable applications. Nagios provides a broad range of monitoring capabilities beyond network monitoring, making it a useful tool if you want to have a central view of system and network data in one place.

There are two major versions of Nagios: Nagios Core, which is open source and free, and Nagios XI, which is a commercial tool. If you want to give Nagios Core a try, you can at `www.nagios.org/projects/nagios-core/`.

Cacti

Cacti is an open source tool that uses SNMP polling to poll network devices for status information and provides graphical views of network and device status. Additional data can be included by using scripts with data stored in a database, allowing Cacti to provide visibility into a range of devices and data types. Cacti leverages RRDTool, a graphing and analysis package to provide detailed graphical views of the data it gathers.

Detecting Common Network Issues

Once you have visibility into your network's bandwidth and device status, you can use that knowledge to track common network problems. These common problems include bandwidth consumption, link and connection failures, beaconing, and unexpected traffic. Although each of these problems is common, the causes of each type of issue can be quite varied!

We will cover unexpected traffic shortly, so keep it in mind as you read about bandwidth consumption and beaconing, and how they are related to it.

Bandwidth Consumption

Bandwidth consumption can cause service outages and disruptions of business functions, making it a serious concern for both security analysts and network managers. In a well-designed network, the network will be configured to use logging and monitoring methods that fit its design, security, and monitoring requirements, and that data will be sent to a central system that can provide bandwidth usage alarms. Techniques we have already discussed in this chapter can provide the information needed to detect bandwidth consumption issues:

- Tools like PRTG that use flow data can show trend and status information indicating that network bandwidth utilization has peaked.
- Monitoring tools can be used to check for high usage levels and can send alarms based on thresholds.
- Real-time or near-real-time graphs can be used to monitor bandwidth as usage occurs.
- SNMP data can be used to monitor for high load and other signs of bandwidth utilization at the router or network device level.

Real World Scenario

The Importance of Detecting Data Exfiltration

In 2015, Penn State University disclosed a breach of systems in their College of Engineering. The breach was reported to potentially include research that was being conducted for the U.S. Department of Defense—a critical concern for both the U.S. military and the university.

When attackers specifically target an organization, they're often looking for data. That means that once they find a way in and get to the data that they're interested in, they'll need to get the data out. *Data exfiltration*, or the process of attackers getting data out of their target systems and back to them, is a major worry for organizations that rely on the security of their data.

Monitoring for data exfiltration can be incredibly challenging. At a university like Penn State, massive amounts of data of all types move between systems on a daily basis, and the prevalence of encrypted communications can make it hard to determine whether the traffic sent to an external site is legitimate traffic or your sensitive data heading out the door.

Network monitoring can help to prevent exfiltration if a network is well controlled and well understood. Servers shouldn't reach out to external systems, and large data transfers to outside systems from sensitive file stores shouldn't be expected. That means that a combination of anomaly detection and behavior analysis as well as technologies like data loss prevention systems or software can help.

Unfortunately, determined attackers are likely to figure out a way to steal data, and proving that data didn't leave can be nearly impossible. That means that protecting data from being accessed is a much better solution than trying to stop bad guys as they take the data out of your network.

Beaconing

Beaconing activity (sometimes a heartbeat) is activity sent to a C&C system as part of a botnet or malware remote control system and is typically sent as either HTTP or HTTPS traffic. Beaconing can request commands, provide status, download additional malware, or perform other actions. Since beaconing is often encrypted and blends in with other web traffic, it can be difficult to identify, but detecting beaconing behavior is a critical part of detecting malware infections.

Detection of beaconing behavior is often handled by using an IDS or IPS with detection rules that identify known botnet controllers or botnet-specific behavior. In addition, using flow analysis or other traffic-monitoring tools to ensure that systems are not sending unexpected traffic that could be beaconing is also possible. This means that inspecting outbound traffic to ensure that infected systems are not resident in your network is as important as controls that handle inbound traffic.

Figure 12.5 shows simulated beaconing behavior, with a host reaching out to a remote site via HTTP every 10 seconds. This type of repeated behavior can be difficult to find when it is slow, but automated analysis can help to identify it. Using a tool like Wireshark to directly capture the traffic, as shown in the figure, can be useful for detailed analysis, but flows and IDSs and IPSs are more useful for a broader view of network traffic.

FIGURE 12.5 Beaconing in Wireshark

No.	Time	Source	Destination	Protoc
66	31.538876037	10.0.2.15	192.168.1.1	DNS
67	31.540080521	192.168.1.1	10.0.2.15	DNS
68	31.672776791	192.168.1.1	10.0.2.15	DNS
8	0.369157221	10.0.2.15	104.155.5.19	HTTP
15	0.483471214	104.155.5.19	10.0.2.15	HTTP
28	10.754906620	10.0.2.15	104.155.5.19	HTTP
35	10.886511298	104.155.5.19	10.0.2.15	HTTP
48	21.303051037	10.0.2.15	104.155.5.19	HTTP
59	21.531966939	104.155.5.19	10.0.2.15	HTTP
72	31.789818761	10.0.2.15	104.155.5.19	HTTP
83	32.017497173	104.155.5.19	10.0.2.15	HTTP
5	0.252749594	10.0.2.15	104.155.5.19	TCP
6	0.368868964	104.155.5.19	10.0.2.15	TCP
7	0.368930078	10.0.2.15	104.155.5.19	TCP
9	0.482285602	104.155.5.19	10.0.2.15	TCP

If you want to test your organization's defenses against beaconing, you can simulate a beacon with techniques discussed at `blog.opensecurity-research.com/2012/12/testing-your-defenses-beaconing.html`.

Unexpected Traffic

Unexpected traffic on a network can take many forms: scans and probes, irregular peer-to-peer traffic between systems that aren't expected to communicate directly, spikes in network traffic, or more direct attack traffic. Unexpected traffic can be detected by behavior-based detection capabilities built into IDSs and IPSs, by traffic-monitoring systems, or manually by observing traffic between systems. Understanding what traffic is expected and what traffic is unexpected relies on three major techniques:

- *Baselines*, or *anomaly-based detection*, which requires knowledge of what normal traffic is. Baselines are typically gathered during normal network operations. Once baseline data is gathered, monitoring systems can be set to alarm when the baselines are exceeded by a given threshold or when network behavior deviates from the baseline behaviors that were documented.
- *Heuristics*, or *behavior-based detection,* using network security devices and defined rules for scans, sweeps, attack traffic, and other network issues.
- *Protocol analysis*, which uses a protocol analyzer to capture packets and check for problems. Protocol analyzers can help find unexpected traffic, like VPN traffic in a network where no VPN traffic is expected, or IPv6 tunnels running from a production IPv4 network. They can also help identify when common protocols are being sent over an uncommon port, possibly indicating an attacker setting up an alternate service port.

Not all unexpected traffic is malicious, but it is important to ensure that you have appropriate systems and methods in place to detect anomalies and unexpected behaviors and that you can identify when unexpected traffic is occurring so that you can respond appropriately.

Figure 12.6 shows an IDS detection based on unexpected traffic between a local host (Iodine) and a system in Russia. This detection was flagged as a potential malware download based on its behavior.

FIGURE 12.6 Unexpected network traffic shown in flows

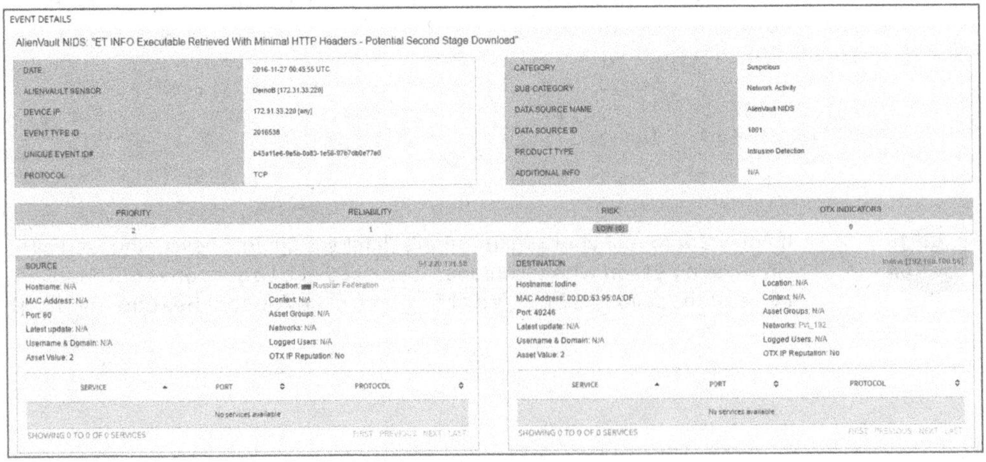

Exam Note

At this point in the chapter, you've read about a number of potential indicators of compromise (IOCs). Objective 4.3 covers a wide range of IOCs, including network IOCs such as bandwidth consumption, beaconing, traffic spikes, and host-related issues, memory and drive capacity consumption, and abnormal system and process behavior. Make sure you review the full list and consider how you could identify these behaviors or issues and how you might be able to tell them apart from every day, non-compromise-related issues. After all, not every full disk or sudden increase in network usage is due to an attack!

Detecting Scans and Probes

Scans, sweeps, and probes are typically not significant threats to infrastructure by themselves, but they are often a precursor to more focused attacks. Detecting scans and probes is often quite simple: network scans are often easily detectable due to the behaviors they include, such as sequential testing of service ports, connecting to many IP addresses in a network, and repeated requests to services that may not be active. More stealthy scans and probes can be harder to detect among the general noise of a network, and detecting stealthy scans from multiple remote systems on a system connected to the Internet can be quite challenging.

Fortunately, most IDSs and IPSs, as well as other network security devices like firewalls and network security appliances, have built-in scan detection capabilities. Enabling these can result in a lot of noise, and in many cases there is little you can do about a scan. Many organizations choose to feed their scan detection data to a security information management tool to combine with data from attacks and other events, rather than responding to the scans and probes directly.

To test your ability to detect scans, sweeps, and probes, use a scanning tool like nmap and verify that you can detect your own scans. Increase the difficulty by using more advanced features like stealth scans (using the `nmap -sS` flag) and nmap's timing flag, where `-T0` is the slowest scan and `-T5` is a full-speed aggressive scan.

Detecting Denial-of-Service and Distributed Denial-of-Service Attacks

Denial-of-service (DoS) attacks can take many forms, but the goal remains the same: preventing access to a system or service. They can be conducted from a single system, or from many systems as part of a distributed denial-of-service (DDoS) attack. Detecting and preventing DoS attacks is an increasingly important part of a cybersecurity analyst's skillset.

DoS Attacks

DoS attacks typically include one or more of the following patterns of attack:

- Attempts to overwhelm a network or service through the sheer volume of requests or traffic
- Attacks on a specific service or system vulnerability to cause the system or service to fail
- Attacks on an intermediary system or network to prevent traffic from making it between two locations

Each of these types of attacks requires slightly different methods of detection. This means that your network, system, and service monitoring capabilities need to be set up to monitor for multiple types of attacks depending on which might target your infrastructure.

A DoS attack from a single system or network can typically be stopped by blocking that system or network using a firewall or other network security device. IPSs can also block known attack traffic, preventing a DoS attack from occurring. Single-system DoS attacks are not as likely as DDoS attacks unless the target suffers from a specific service or application vulnerability, or the target can be easily overwhelmed by a single remote system due to limited bandwidth or other resources.

Distributed Denial-of-Service Attacks

Distributed denial-of-service (DDoS) attacks come from many systems or networks at the same time. They can be harder to detect due to the traffic coming from many places, and that also makes them much harder to stop. Many DDoS attacks are composed of compromised systems in botnets, allowing attackers to send traffic from hundreds or thousands of systems.

Tools like the Low Orbit Ion Cannon (LOIC) have also made participation in DDoS attacks a voluntary effort as part of hacktivist efforts from groups like Anonymous. Understanding why your organization might be targeted, and by whom, is an important part of planning for and responding to DoS and DDOS attacks.

Detecting DoS and DDoS Attacks

Since there are many flavors of DoS and DDoS attacks, building an effective DoS and DDoS detection capability usually involves multiple types of tools and monitoring systems. These often include the following:

- Performance monitoring using service performance monitoring tools
- Connection monitoring using local system or application logs
- Network bandwidth or system bandwidth monitoring
- Dedicated tools like IDS or IPSs with DoS and DDoS detection rules enabled

During incident response, the same command-line tools that you can use to analyze network traffic (like netstat) can help with troubleshooting on local servers, but a view from the network or service perspective will typically provide a broader view of the issue.

Real World Scenario

Surviving a Denial-of-Service Attack

If your organization has a public Internet presence, you're likely to have to deal with a DoS attack at some point, whether it's on purpose or accidental. Fortunately, services and tools now exist to help organizations weather these attacks.

Here are two common ways to survive a DDoS attack:

- Using a dedicated service designed to handle these attacks that uses a large distributed network of endpoints combined with DDoS mitigation tools to ensure that your service (typically a website) can be accessed even if one or more distribution locations is offline. In the following graphic, a DDoS mitigation system distributes copies of a website's content to globally distributed content distribution network (CDN) servers while blocking DDoS attacks using a centrally managed defense mechanism. This ensures that legitimate users receive a response from a CDN node that is close to them, avoiding potential issues with the main website or networks that serve it during a DDoS.

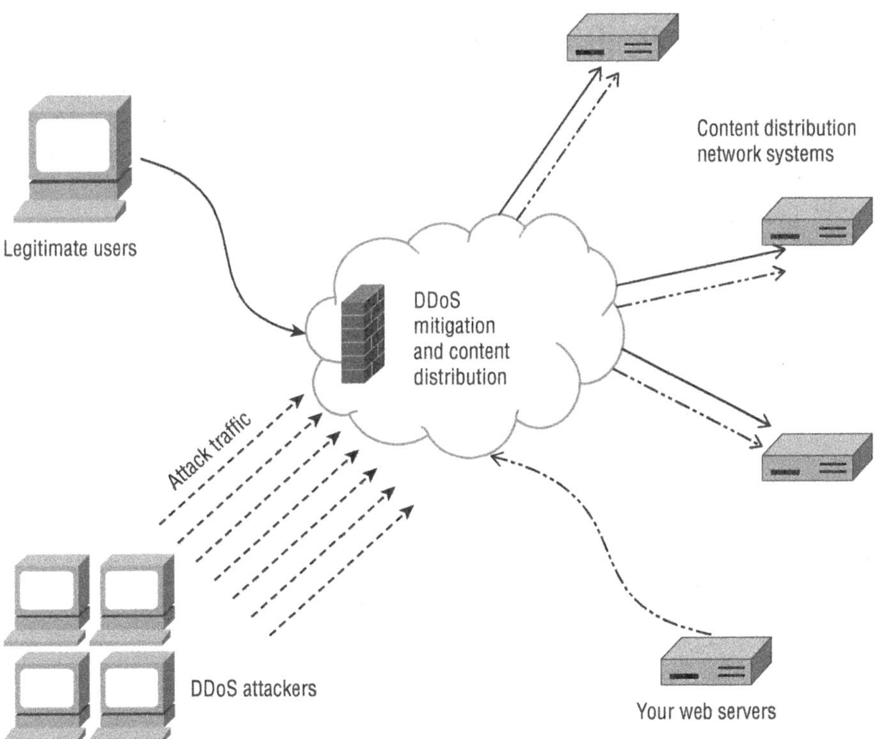

- Deploying a DDoS mitigation device or technology. These often analyze flows or sit in-line between the protected systems and the public Internet. They then gather data to provide a view of traffic to a network or service and redirect or drop bad traffic based on signatures or behavior analysis.

Detecting Other Network Attacks

Other network-based attacks can be detected using the same techniques outlined earlier:

- Use an IDS or IPS
- Monitor flows, SNMP, and other network information for suspect behaviors
- Feed logs from firewalls, routers, switches, and other network devices to a central log analysis and monitoring system
- Use a SIEM device to review and automatically alarm them about problem traffic

A subscription to a frequently updated and well-managed feed of IDS/IPS rules and subscribing to groups that monitor for trending attacks can help make sure that you stay ahead of the attacks you may find aimed at your network.

Detecting and Finding Rogue Devices

Rogue devices are devices that are connected to a network that should not be, either by policy or because they have been added by an attacker. Finding rogue devices can be challenging—many networks have hundreds or thousands of devices, and device management may not be consistent across the network.

There are a number of common methods for identifying rogue devices:

Valid MAC Address Checking Uses MAC address information provided to network devices to validate the hardware address presented by the device to a list of known devices.

MAC Address Vendor Information Checking Vendors of network equipment use a vendor prefix for their devices. This means that many devices can be identified based on their manufacturer.

Network Scanning Performed using a tool like nmap to identify new devices.

Site Surveys Involve physically reviewing the devices at a site either by manual verification or by checking wireless networks on-site.

Traffic Analysis Used to identify irregular or unexpected behavior.

You can look up hardware vendors from a MAC address at sites like `www.macvendors.com` or `www.macvendorlookup.com`. Remember that it is possible to change MAC addresses, so the address presented by a device isn't guaranteed to be correct!

Wired and wireless networks face slightly different threats from rogue devices, and you need to be aware of those differences when responding to potential incidents.

Wired Rogues

Most wired rogues rely on open or unauthenticated networks to connect. Open networks without access controls like *port security*, which checks for trusted MAC addresses, or *network access control* (NAC) technology are easy targets for wired rogue devices. A wired rogue device typically means that one of two likely scenarios has occurred:

- An employee or other trusted member of the organization has connected a device, either without permission or without following the process required to connect a device.
- An attacker has connected a device to the network.

The first scenario may be a simple mistake, but the second implies that an attacker has had physical access to your network! In either case, rogue devices connected to a wired network should be responded to quickly so that they can be removed or otherwise handled appropriately.

Preventing wired rogue devices can be accomplished by either restricting which devices can connect (via port security or a similar MAC address limiting technology) or via NAC and requiring authentication to the network. Unfortunately, MAC address filtering won't stop determined attackers—they only need to replace a legitimate device with their own with the MAC address set to match the trusted device—but it will stop casual attempts to connect.

Wireless Rogues

Wireless rogues can create additional challenges because they can't always easily be tracked to a specific physical location. That means that tracking down a rogue may involve using signal strength measures and mapping the area where the rogue is to attempt to locate it. Fortunately, if the wireless rogue is plugged into your network, using a port scan with operating system identification turned on can often help locate the device. In Figure 12.7, a common consumer router was scanned after it was connected to a network. In this example, nmap cannot immediately identify the device, but it is obvious that it is not a typical desktop system since it shows the router as potentially being a VoIP phone, firewall, or other embedded device.

FIGURE 12.7 nmap scan of a potential rogue system

```
Starting Nmap 7.01 ( https://nmap.org ) at 2016-09-04 11:55 EDT
Nmap scan report for demo.localnet.com (192.168.1.1)
Host is up (0.11s latency).
Not shown: 997 closed ports
PORT     STATE SERVICE
53/tcp   open  domain
80/tcp   open  http
1723/tcp open  pptp
Device type: VoIP phone|firewall|specialized
Running (JUST GUESSING): Grandstream embedded (90%), FireBrick embedded (87%), 2N embedded (87%)
OS CPE: cpe:/h:grandstream:gxp1105 cpe:/h:firebrick:fb2700 cpe:/h:2n:helios
Aggressive OS guesses: Grandstream GXP1105 VoIP phone (90%), FireBrick FB2700 firewall (87%), 2N Helios
IP VoIP doorbell (87%)
No exact OS matches for host (test conditions non-ideal).

OS detection performed. Please report any incorrect results at https://nmap.org/submit/ .
Nmap done: 1 IP address (1 host up) scanned in 130.45 seconds
```

Wireless rogues can also create issues by spoofing legitimate networks, persuading legitimate users that they're part of your organization's network. This normally involves overpowering legitimate access points, so using enterprise wireless controllers that can detect interference and report on it (or even automatically overpower it!) can help prevent the problem.

Investigating Host-Related Issues

Security issues for servers and workstations can be challenging to identify. Modern malware is extremely good at remaining hidden. Fortunately, system monitoring tools can help identify unexpected behaviors by checking for host-related issues. That means system monitoring is useful for both security and day-to-day system health purposes.

System Resources

The most basic monitoring for most servers and workstations is resource monitoring. Utilization information for system resources like CPU, memory, disk, and network can provide valuable details about the state of the system, its workloads, and whether a problem exists.

Processor Monitoring

Understanding what processes are consuming CPU time, how much CPU utilization is occurring, and when the processes are running can be useful for incident detection and response. Sudden spikes, or increased *processor consumption* in CPU usage on a system with otherwise consistent usage levels, may indicate new software or a process that was not previously active. Consistently high levels of CPU usage can also point to a DoS condition.

Used alone, CPU load information typically will not tell the whole story, but it should be part of your monitoring efforts.

Memory Monitoring

Most operating system level memory monitoring is focused on memory utilization or *memory consumption*, rather than what is being stored in memory. That means your visibility into memory usage is likely to focus on consumption and process identification. Most protective measures for memory-based attacks occur as part of an operating system's built-in memory management or when code is compiled.

Most organizations set memory monitoring levels for alarms and notification based on typical system memory usage and an "emergency" level when a system or application is approaching an out-of-memory condition. This can be identified by tracking memory usage during normal and peak usage and then setting *monitoring thresholds*, or levels where alarms or alerts will occur, based on that data.

If you're troubleshooting memory issues in Windows, you may encounter a result code titled `Buffer Overflow`—this doesn't mean you're under attack. Instead, it indicates that an application requested data but did not have sufficient memory space allocated. The Windows `Buffer Overflow` result tag simply indicates insufficient memory allocation.

Memory Leaks

Memory leaks are a frequent culprit in system crashes and outages. A memory leak occurs when a program doesn't release memory after it is no longer needed. Over time, an application with a memory leak will consume more and more memory until the application fails or the operating system runs out of available memory. This can cause an application or system crash.

Memory monitoring can help prevent memory leaks from resulting in a crash by sounding the alarm when memory utilization increases, but it can't stop a memory leak. If there is no patch for the issue, the only recourse for an application or service with a memory leak is to periodically restart the service or the system it runs on.

Drive Capacity Monitoring

Drive capacity monitoring typically focuses on specific capacity levels and is intended to prevent the drive or volume from filling up, causing an outage. Tools to monitor *drive capacity consumption* are available for all major operating systems, as well as centralized monitoring and management systems like *System Center Operations Manager (SCOM)* for Windows or Nagios for Linux. Microsoft Endpoint Configuration Manager can also provide information about disk usage, but it is not a real-time reporting mechanism. Disk monitoring in real time can help prevent outages and issues more easily than a daily report since disks can fill up quickly.

Filesystem Changes and Anomalies

Monitoring in real time for filesystem changes can help to catch attacks as they are occurring. Tools like the open source Wazuh security platform provide file integrity monitoring that keeps an eye on files, permissions, ownership, and file attributes and then sends alerts based on that monitoring.

If you want to check out Wazuh, you can find it at `wazuh.com`.

Open source tools like Tripwire (Tripwire is available as both a commercial and an open source tool) and Advanced Intrusion Detection Environment (AIDE) as well as a wide variety of commercial products offer this type of functionality. The trade-off for most products is noise level due to filesystem changes that are part of normal operations versus catching unexpected changes.

Manual verification of files using known good checksums is also part of many incident responders practice. Sites like the National Software Reference Library (NSRL) collect digital signatures to allow verification against known checksums: `www.nist.gov/itl/ssd/software-quality-group/national-software-reference-library-nsrl`.

System Resource Monitoring Tools

Windows provides built-in resource and performance monitoring tools. *Resource Monitor*, or *resmon*, is the Windows resource monitor and provides easy visibility into the CPU, memory, disk, and network utilization for a system. In addition to utilization, its network monitoring capability shows processes with network activity, which TCP connections are open, and what services are associated with open ports on the system. Figure 12.8 shows the Resource Monitor overview screen for a sample Windows 10 system.

Performance Monitor, or *perfmon*, provides much more detailed data, with counters ranging from energy usage to disk and network activity. It also supports collection from remote systems, allowing a broader view of system activity. For detailed data collection, perfmon is a better solution, whereas resmon is useful for checking the basic usage measures for a machine quickly. Figure 12.9 shows perfmon configured with a disk and processor monitor. This data can be combined into user- or system-defined reports.

The Sysinternals suite for Windows provides extensive monitoring capabilities beyond the built-in set of tools. You can download the Sysinternals tools at `technet.microsoft.com/en-us/sysinternals/`, or you can run them live at the Windows command prompt or from File Explorer by entering `https://live.sysinternals.com/toolname`, replacing ***toolname*** with the name of the tool you want to use.

To start resmon or perfmon (as well as other Windows Control Panel plug-ins), simply type their names into the Windows search or run menu.

FIGURE 12.8 The Windows Resource Monitor view of system resources

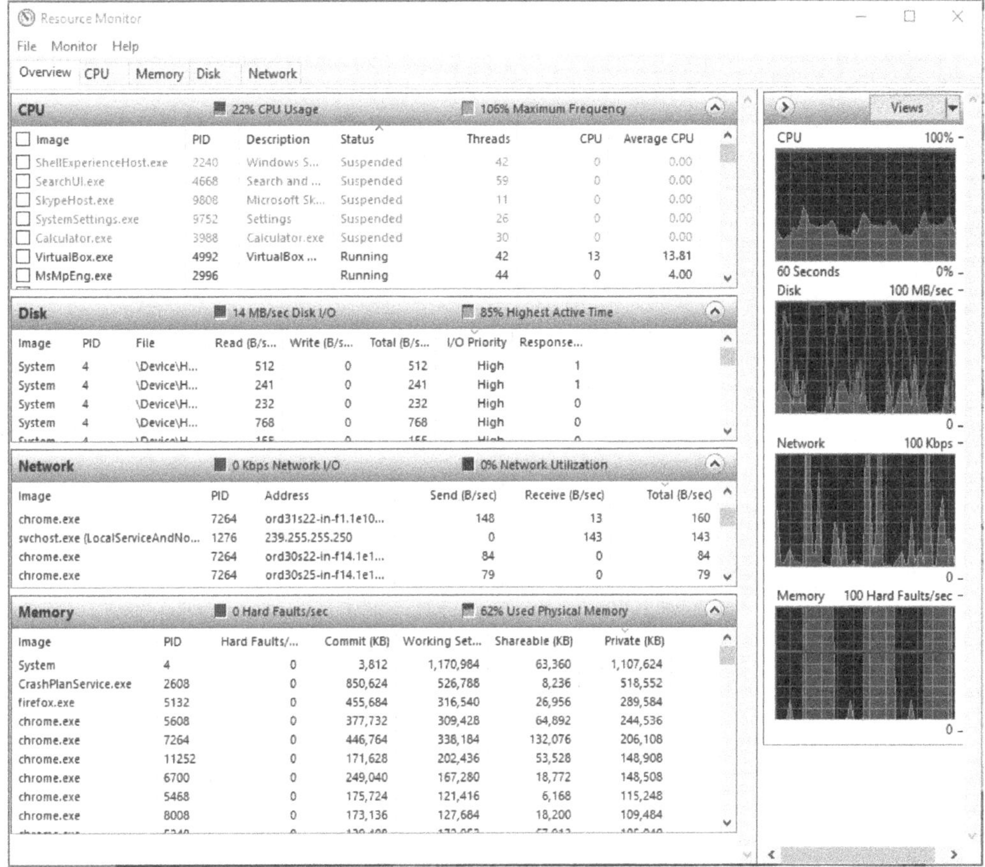

Linux has a number of built-in tools that can be used to check CPU, disk, and memory usage. They include the following:

- `ps` provides information about CPU and memory utilization, the time that a process was started, and how long it has run, as well as the command that started each process.
- `top` provides CPU utilization under CPU stats and also shows memory usage as well as other details about running processes. `top` also provides interaction via hotkeys, including allowing quick identification of `top` consumers by entering **A**.
- `df` displays a report of the system's disk usage, with various flags providing additional detail or formatting.
- `w` indicates which accounts are logged in. Although this isn't directly resource related, it can be useful when determining who may be running a process.

FIGURE 12.9 The Windows Performance Monitor view of system usage

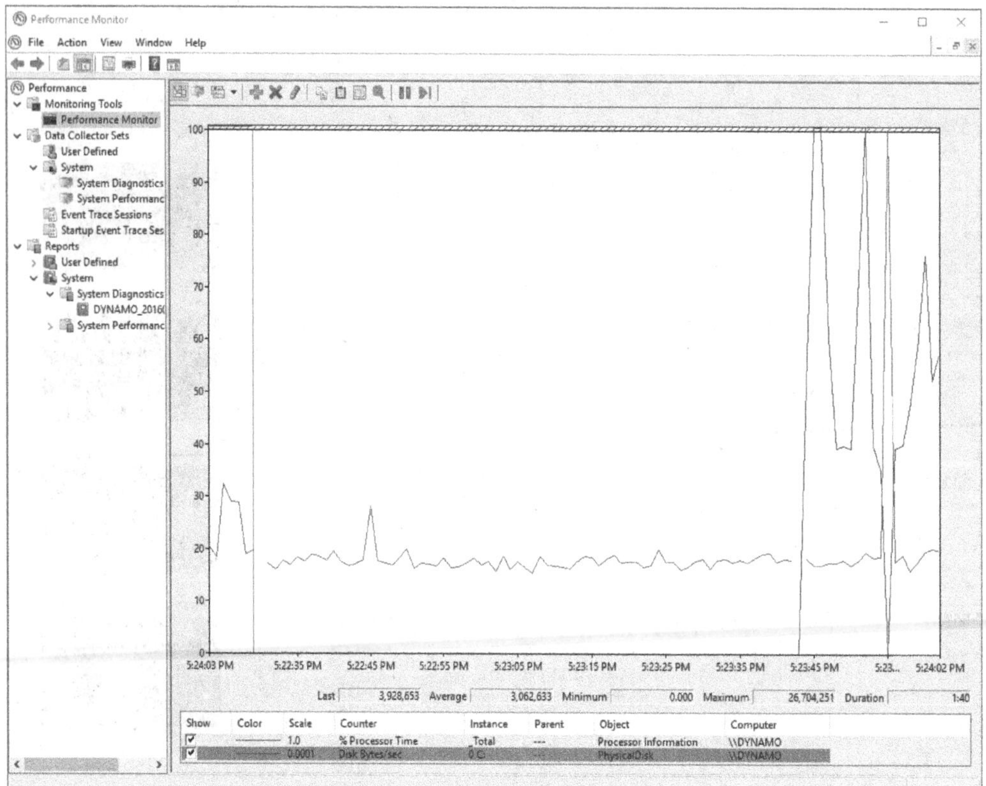

Many other Linux tools are available, including graphical tools; however, almost all Linux distributions will include `ps`, `top`, and `df`, making them a good starting point when checking the state of a system.

In Linux, use the `-h` flag for `df` to show filesystem usage in a human-readable format.

Malware, Malicious Processes, and Unauthorized Software

Unauthorized software and malware is a major cause of system issues. Software issues can range from application and driver incompatibilities to unauthorized software that sends network traffic, resulting in issues for other systems on the network.

Exam Note

The CySA+ exam objectives mention malicious processes and unauthorized software, but not malware in this section. When you prepare for the exam, you should remember the CySA+ terms, but bear in mind the fact that malware, viruses, and similar terms can all be used to describe the same types of things.

Detecting malware, *malicious processes*, and unauthorized software typically relies on one of four major methods:

- Central management tools like Microsoft Endpoint Configuration Manager, which can manage software installation and report on installed software.
- Antivirus and antimalware tools, which are designed to detect potentially harmful software and files.
- Software and file *blacklisting*, which uses a list of disallowed software and files and prohibits its installation. This differs from antivirus and antimalware by potentially providing a broader list of prohibited files than only malicious or similar files.
- *Application whitelisting*, which allows only permitted files and applications on a system. In a fully whitelisted environment, no files that are not previously permitted are allowed on a system.

Most managed environments will use more than one of these techniques to manage the software and applications that are present on workstations, servers, and mobile devices.

Real World Scenario

When Innocuous Tools Aren't

A common Linux command-line utility known as netcat, or its Windows equivalent `nc.exe`, is often associated with penetration testing and compromises. Netcat allows you to create UDP or TCP connections using simple commands like `nc -l -p 37337 -e cmd.exe` (which opens a remote shell on port 37337, which connects to `cmd.exe`). Due to this, it is often baked into exploits to provide easy connectivity. If you find netcat (or `nc.exe`) on a system where it shouldn't be, your system may have been owned!

Abnormal OS Process Behavior

Abnormal behavior observed in operating system processes can be an indicator of a rootkit or other malware that has exploited an operating system component. For Windows systems, a handful of built-in tools are most commonly associated with attacks like these, including `cmd.exe`, `at.exe` and `schtasks.exe`, `wmic.exe`, `powershell.exe`, `net.exe`, `reg.exe`, and `sc.exe`, and similar useful tools.

Tools like Metasploit have built-in capabilities to inject attack tools into running legitimate processes. Finding these processes requires tools that can observe the modified behavior or check the running process against known good process fingerprints.

Another common technique is to name rogue processes with similar names to legitimate operating system components or applications, or use DLL execution via `rundll32.exe` to run as services via `svchost`.

SANS provides an excellent poster called "Know Normal. . .Find Evil" with many more details than we can include here. You can find it at `digital-forensics.sans.org/media/dfir_poster_2014.pdf`.

Unauthorized Access, Changes, and Privileges

Unauthorized access to systems and devices, as well as use of privileges that result in unexpected changes, are a major cause for alarm. Unfortunately, the number and variety of systems, as well as the complexity of the user and permissions models in use in many organizations, can make monitoring for unauthorized activity challenging.

The good news is that monitoring for unauthorized access, changes, and privileges uses many of the same set of techniques and technologies we have already discussed. Table 12.1 lists some of the possible methods for detection for each of these types of unauthorized use.

TABLE 12.1 Unauthorized use and detection mechanisms

Unauthorized use type	Data logged	Location of data	Analysis tools
Unauthorized access	Authentication User creation	Authentication logs User creation logs	Central management suite SIM/SIEM
Unauthorized changes	File creation Settings changes	System logs Application logs Monitoring tools	Central management suite SIM/SIEM File and directory integrity checking tools (Tripwire)
Unauthorized privilege use	Privilege use attempts Privilege escalation	Security event logs Application logs	SIM/SIEM Log analysis tools

Each of these techniques requires a strong understanding of what access is expected on each system or devices so that exceptions can be detected. Change management, permission management, and identity management are all important administrative processes to apply in addition to the technical controls listed earlier.

Unauthorized privileges can be harder to track, particularly if they are not centrally managed and audited. Fortunately, tools like Sysinternals's AccessChk can help by validating the access that a specific user or group has to objects like files, registry keys, and services. On the other hand, while the audit system in Linux can help detect uses of privileges, checking for specific permissions will typically require you to write a script to check the specific privileges you are concerned about.

Registry Changes or Anomalies

The Windows registry is a favorite location for attackers who want to maintain access to Windows systems. Using run keys, the Windows Startup folder, and similar techniques is a common persistence technique.

Registry run keys can be found in

- `HKEY_LOCAL_MACHINE\Software\Microsoft\Windows\CurrentVersion\Run`
- `HKEY_CURRENT_USER\Software\Microsoft\Windows\CurrentVersion\Run`
- `HKEY_LOCAL_MACHINE\Software\Microsoft\Windows\CurrentVersion\RunOnce`
- `HKEY_CURRENT_USER\Software\Microsoft\Windows\CurrentVersion\RunOnce`

That means that monitoring the Windows registry for changes can be an important part of incident response. For systems with infrequent changes like servers, protecting the registry can be relatively easily done through the use of application whitelisting. In cases where registry monitoring tools are not an option, lockdown tools can be used that prohibit registry changes. When changes are required, the tools can be turned off or set into a mode that allows changes during patching windows, and then turned back on for daily operations. For workstations where changes may be made more frequently, more in-depth control choices like an agent-based tool may be required to prevent massive numbers of false positives.

Unauthorized Scheduled Tasks

Scheduled tasks, or cron jobs in Linux, are also a popular method for attackers to maintain persistent access to systems. Checking for unexpected scheduled tasks (or cron jobs) is a common part of incident response processes.

To check scheduled tasks in Windows, you can access the Task Scheduler via Start ➢ Windows Administrative Tools ➢ Task Scheduler. Figure 12.10 shows the detail you can access via the graphical Task Scheduler interface, including when the task ran, when it was created, and other information.

FIGURE 12.10 The Windows Task Scheduler showing scheduled tasks and creation times

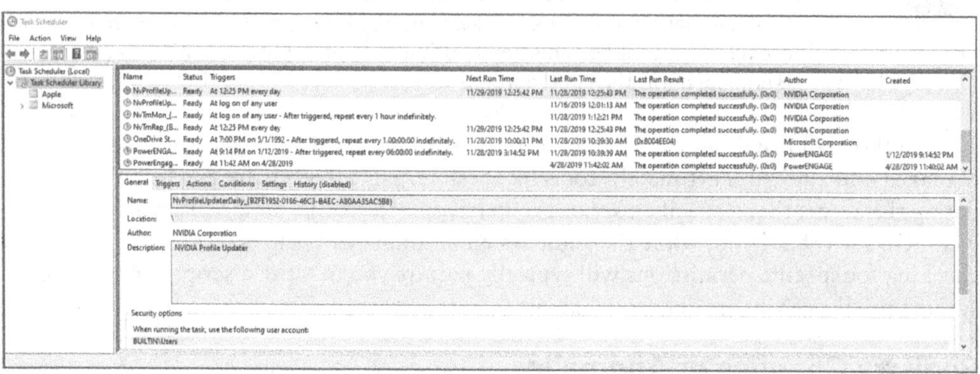

Checking scheduled tasks from the Windows command line is as easy as using the `schtasks` command. You'll probably want to pipe it to more using a command like `schtasks | more` so you don't have to scroll back through it.

You can detect unexpected scheduled tasks in Linux by checking cron. You can check crontab itself by using `cat /etc/crontab`, but you may also want to check `/etc/cron` for anything stashed there. Listing cron jobs is easy as well; use the `crontab -l` command to do so. You should pay particular attention to jobs running as root or equivalent users, and using the `-u` root flag in your crontab list command will do that.

Exam Note

The CySA+ Exam Objectives don't list cron jobs. Instead, they specifically mention scheduled tasks, which is the Windows term. Since you may encounter Unix, Linux, and macOS systems that use cron, we have included it here as well.

Investigating Service and Application-Related Issues

Investigating application and service issues requires information about what services and applications are running, how they are expected to behave, as well as self-reported and system-reported information about the services. In many organizations, active service monitoring will also be used to determine if the service is working properly.

Application- and service-related events like incorrect behavior, unexpected log messages or errors, new users or processes, and file changes are all common signs of a possibly compromised service. Fortunately, many of the tools you need to investigate these problems are already built into Windows and Linux systems.

Application and Service Monitoring

Monitoring applications and services is critical to an organization's operations and can also provide important security insight by showing where unexpected behavior is occurring or where applications and services are being abused.

In this section, we use the terms *application* and *service* interchangeably. Some organizations will separate them, with services characterized as specialized and often accessed by other programs, and applications more generalized and often accessed by humans. This distinction can get a bit fuzzy!

Application and service monitoring can be categorized into a few common monitoring areas:

- Up/down—is the service running?
- Performance—does it respond quickly and as expected?
- Transactional logging—information about the function of the service is captured, such as what actions users take or what actions are performed.
- Application or service logging—logs about the function or status of the service.

Each of these areas provides part of the puzzle for visibility into an application's or service's status, performance, and behavior. During an investigation, you will often need to identify behavior that does not match what the service typically logs.

Application Logs

Application logs can provide a treasure trove of information, but they also require knowledge of what the application's log format is and what those logs will contain. While many Linux logs end up in `/var/log`, Windows application logs can end up gathered by the Windows logging infrastructure or in an application specific directory or file.

Part of a security professional's work is to ensure that appropriate logging is set up before an incident occurs so that logs will be available and will be protected from modification or deletion by an attacker. Sending critical application logs to a central log collection and/or analysis service is a common part of that strategy.

Application and Service Anomaly Detection

Anomalous activity from services and applications can be relatively common. A variety of non-security-related problems can result in issues, such as

- Application or service-specific errors, including authentication errors, service dependency issues, and permissions issues
- Applications or services that don't start on boot, either because of a specific error or, in the case of services, because the service is disabled
- Service failures, which are often caused by updates, patches, or other changes

Service and application failure troubleshooting typically starts with an attempt to start, or restart, the service. If that is not successful, a review of the service's log message or error messages can provide the information needed to resolve the problem.

Anomalies in services and applications due to security issues may be able to be detected using the same monitoring techniques; however, additional tools can be useful to ensure that the service and its constituent files and applications are not compromised. In addition to common service and log monitoring tools, you might choose to deploy additional protection such as the following:

- Antimalware and antivirus tools
- File integrity checking tools
- Whitelisting tools

Windows provides WinDbg for debugging issues. Crash dump debugging is outside the scope of this book, but you can find details at `msdn.microsoft.com/en-us/library/windows/hardware/mt219729(v=vs.85).aspx`.

Windows Service Status

Windows service status can be checked either via the Services administrative tool (`services.msc`) or by using command-line tools like `sc`, the Service Controller application, which accepts command-line flags that set the start type for service, specify the error level it should set if it fails during boot, and provide details of the service. PowerShell also provides service interaction scriptlets like `Start-Service` to interact with services on local and remote Windows hosts.

Linux Service Status

Linux services can be checked on most systems by using the `service` command. `service [`*`servicename`*`] status` will return the status of many, but not all, Linux services. You can try the command to list the state of all services by running

```
service --status-all
```

Linux systems that use `init.d` can be checked by running a command like

```
/etc/init.d/servicename status
```

Linux service restart processes vary depending on the distribution. Check your distribution to verify how it expects services to be restarted.

Application Error Monitoring

Most Windows applications log to the Windows Application log (although some maintain their own dedicated log files as well). To check for application errors, you can view the Application log via the Windows Event Viewer. You can also centralize these logs using SCOM.

Many Linux applications provide useful details in the `/var/log` directory or in a specific application log location. Using the `tail` command, these logs can be monitored while the application is tested. Much like Windows, some Linux applications store their files in an application-specific location, so you may have to check the application's documentation to track down all the data the application provides.

Application Behavior Analysis

Applications that have been compromised or that have been successfully attacked can suddenly start to behave in ways that aren't typical: outbound communications may occur, the application may make database or other resource requests that are not typically part of its behavior, or new files or user accounts may be created. Understanding typical application behavior requires a combination of

- Documentation of the application's normal behavior, such as what systems it should connect to and how those connections should be made
- Logging, to provide a view of normal operations
- Heuristic (behavioral) analysis using antimalware tools and other security-monitoring systems to flag when behaviors deviate from the norm

Application and Service Issue Response and Restoration

There are many reasons that applications and services encounter issues, ranging from incorrect credentials or rights, bad patches, and component versions to software flaws and actual attacks. Detecting issues with applications relies on many of the same techniques used for network and system issues, with the addition of application-specific monitoring tools and service-monitoring software.

When an application or service encounters an issue, it will often report an error. That means it is possible to handle errors and exceptions automatically by creating scripts or automated service restarts when the error is thrown.

Application monitoring services can also be scripted to take action when a service or server is offline. This requires that the monitoring system have rights to restart the appropriate system or service, and if the monitoring system is not correct about the outage, it can disrupt service. Automated responses should be carefully tested to ensure that they do not cause disruption rather than fix it.

Detecting Attacks on Applications

Attacks on applications can take a number of forms, ranging from web application attacks to malware that targets executable files. Focusing on the behaviors that indicate attacks can be one of the most important tools in your arsenal. Detecting the behaviors listed here as they happen, or before they result from an attack, is preferable, but being able to perform an analysis of why they have happened is often necessary too.

Exam Note

Pay particular attention to this section: each of these items is one that you may be expected to recognize and identify on the exam!

- *Anomalous activity*, or activity that does not match the application's typical behavior, is often the first indicator of an attack or compromise. Log analysis, behavior baselines, and filesystem integrity checking can all help detect unexpected behavior. User and administrator awareness training can also help make sure you hear about applications that are behaving in abnormal ways.
- *Introduction of new accounts*, particularly those with administrative rights, are often a sign of compromise. Application account creation is not always logged in a central location, making it important to find ways to track both account creation and privileges granted to accounts. Administrative controls that match a change management workflow and approvals to administrative account creation, paired with technical controls, can provide a stronger line of defense.
- *Unexpected output* can take many forms, from improper output or garbled data to errors and other signs of an underlying application issue. Unexpected output can also be challenging to detect using centralized methods for user-level applications. Server-based applications that provide file- or API-level output are often easier to check for errors based on validity checkers (if they exist!). This is another type of application error where user and administrator training can help identify problems.
- *Unexpected outbound communication,* like beaconing, outbound file transfers, and attacks, are common types of application exploit indicators. Using network monitoring software as well as a capable and well-tuned intrusion detection or prevention system monitoring outbound traffic is critical to detecting these problems.
- *Service interruption* can indicate a simple application problem that requires a service or server restart but can also indicate a security issue like a DoS attack or a compromised application. Monitoring tools should monitor application or service status as well as user experience to capture both views of how a service is working.

- *Memory overflows* may result in operating system errors and crashes, making crash dump reporting important. Monitoring for memory overflow errors can be a challenge due to limitations in memory handling for operating systems and applications, so your first warning may be an application crash or system reboot. Logging reboots and service restarts can help but may not detect a properly executed attack.

Summary

Incident response requires visibility into networks, systems, services, and applications. Gathering and centralizing information from each component of your organization's infrastructure and systems can allow you to more easily detect, respond to, or even prevent incidents. The same information can also help you detect indicators of compromise early, potentially allowing you to stop intrusions before they become significant breaches.

Network monitoring is often done via router-based monitoring, which relies on network flows, SNMP, and RMON, all common means of gathering information. Flows provide summary data about traffic, protocols, and endpoints; SNMP is used to gather device information; and RMON uses probes to gather statistical, historical, and event-based data. In addition, organizations employ active monitoring using ping and performance monitoring tools like iPerf to gather data by sending traffic. Passive monitoring relies on capturing information about the network and its performance as traffic travels through network devices. Passive monitoring doesn't add traffic to the network and acts after the fact, rather than providing real-time information, making it more useful for analysis than prevention of issues.

Network monitoring tools like PRTG, SolarWinds, and Cacti centralize multiple types of network data and provide both central visibility and detailed drill-down analysis capabilities. They are important to incident response and event management because they allow both easy visibility and the ability to look at data from multiple data sources in a single place, potentially allowing you to detect problems like link failure, beaconing, and unexpected traffic identified more easily. Attacks and probes can be detected using monitoring tools and sometimes may be identified and then prevented by network security devices.

Monitoring hosts requires visibility into resources, applications, and logs. Host resource monitoring typically focuses on processor, memory, and disk utilization, whereas applications are often managed using central management tools like Microsoft Endpoint Configuration Manager. Log monitoring relies on an understanding of what is logged and which issues are important to review.

Service and application issues are often detected by monitoring for service anomalies like errors, failures, or changes in service behavior. Security professionals look for anomalous activity, new and unexpected account creation, unexpected outputs or outbound communication, service interruptions, and memory overflow issues.

Exam Essentials

Know how network incidents start. Understanding how network bandwidth is consumed is an important part of detecting and analyzing events. Flows, SNMP, active, and passive monitoring all provide a view of network health and usage. Network monitoring tools like PRTG, Nagios, Cacti, and SolarWinds help to make large volumes of data from diverse devices accessible and centrally visible. Common network issues include bandwidth consumption, link failure, beaconing, and unexpected traffic.

Explain why network attacks and probes require specific responses. Scans and probes can be difficult to detect but can indicate interest by attackers or security issues that allow them to succeed. Denial-of-service attacks can be detected and techniques exist to limit their impact, including network security devices and DDoS mitigation services. Rogue devices, or devices that are not expected to be on a network, can be either wired or wireless. Wired rogues can be limited by using network admission technology, whereas wireless rogues require a monitoring and detection plan.

Be able to describe some host issues and how to detect them. Monitoring system resource usage, including CPU, memory, and disk space, can help to identify host issues. Monitoring tools like resmon and perfmon for Windows and `ps`, `top`, `df`, and `w` for Linux provide insight into the current state of a system's resources. Unauthorized software and malware can be detected by purpose-designed tools or can be controlled using whitelists, blacklists, and central management tools like Microsoft Endpoint Configuration Manager. Unauthorized access, changes, and privilege use can indicate a compromise, intentional, or inadvertent misuse. System and application logs as well as file integrity monitoring applications can help to catch issues as they occur or with investigation after the fact.

Name some causes of service and application issues and how to detect them. Monitoring applications relies on active monitoring of the application or service status, logging, and behavior analysis. Service anomalies can be detected by checking for errors or active monitoring but may not provide a direct indication of security issues. Successful attacks on applications are often indicated by new accounts, unexpected communications or output, service interruptions, or other anomalous activity.

Lab Exercises

Activity 12.1: Identify a Network Scan

In this lab you will use Wireshark to identify a network scan of a Linux system.

Part 1: Boot a Kali Linux system and a target system and set up the exercise.

1. Start your Kali Linux virtual machine and the Metasploitable virtual machine; log into both.
2. Open a terminal window and Wireshark on the Kali Linux system (Wireshark can be found in the Applications menu under option 09 Sniffing & Spoofing).
3. Determine the IP address of the target system. From the command prompt on the Metasploitable system, enter **`ifconfig -a`** and record its IP address.
4. Start the Wireshark capture. Select the eth0 interface and then choose Capture ➢ Start.

Part 2: Perform a network scan and visit the web server.

1. From the terminal, execute the following command: **`nmap -p 1-65535`** **[*ip address of the Metasploitable machine*]**.
2. Record one of the ports listed as open.
3. Start the IceWeasel browser in Kali and navigate to the IP address of the Metasploitable system.

Part 3: Identify scan traffic.

1. Stop the Wireshark capture. Click the red square stop button at the top left of the Wireshark screen.
2. Review the traffic you captured. Search for the port you found by entering **`tcp.port==`**[*port you identified*] in the Filter box.
3. What traffic was sent? If you rerun this scan with other TCP connection options like **`-sS`** or **`-ST`**, does this change?
4. Review traffic for port 80. You should see both the scan and a visit from the Kali Linux web browser. How do these differ?

Activity 12.2: Write a Service Issue Response Plan

Write an identification and response plan for services that an organization you are familiar with relies on. Your response plan should presume that a service issue or outage has been reported but that the cause is not known. Ensure that you cover key elements discussed in this chapter, including

- How you would identify potential issues using the application and system logs
- How you would monitor the service for problems
- What types of issues you would look for
- What the organization's response should be

Once you have completed your plan, walk through it using an example issue. Ensure that your plan would address the issue and that you would be able to provide a complete report to your organization's management about the issue.

Activity 12.3: Security Tools

Match each of the following tools to the correct description.

Flows	A set of packets passing from a source system to a destination in a given time interval
Resmon	A Windows tool that monitors memory, CPU, and disk usage
iPerf	A tool for testing the maximum available bandwidth for a network
PRTG	SNMP A network management and monitoring tool that provides central visibility into flows and SNMP data for an entire network
Beaconing	SNMP A network management and monitoring tool that provides central visibility into flows and SNMP data for an entire network
SNMP	A protocol for collecting information like status and performance about devices on a network
Top	A Linux command that displays processes, memory utilization, and other details about running programs
Perfmon	A Windows tool that monitors a wide range of devices and services, including energy, USB, and disk usage

Review Questions

1. Which of the following Linux commands will show you how much disk space is in use?
   - **A.** `top`
   - **B.** `df`
   - **C.** `lsof`
   - **D.** `ps`
2. What Windows tool provides detailed information including information about USB host controllers, memory usage, and disk transfers?
   - **A.** statmon
   - **B.** resmon
   - **C.** perfmon
   - **D.** winmon
3. What type of network information should you capture to be able to provide a report about how much traffic systems in your network sent to remote systems?
   - **A.** Syslog data
   - **B.** WMI data
   - **C.** Resmon data
   - **D.** Flow data
4. Which of the following technologies is best suited to prevent wired rogue devices from connecting to a network?
   - **A.** NAC
   - **B.** PRTG
   - **C.** Port security
   - **D.** NTP
5. As part of her job, Danielle sets an alarm to notify her team via email if her Windows server uses 80 percent of its memory and to send a text message if it reaches 90 percent utilization. What is this setting called?
   - **A.** A monitoring threshold
   - **B.** A preset notification level
   - **C.** Page monitoring
   - **D.** Perfmon calibration

6. Chris wants to use an active monitoring approach to test his network. Which of the following techniques is appropriate?
   A. Collecting NetFlow data
   B. Using a protocol analyzer
   C. Pinging remote systems
   D. Enabling SNMP
7. What term describes a system sending heartbeat traffic to a botnet command and control server?
   A. Beaconing
   B. Zombie ping
   C. CNCstatus
   D. CNClog
8. Cameron wants to be able to detect a denial-of-service attack against his web server. Which of the following tools should he avoid?
   A. Log analysis
   B. Flow monitoring
   C. iPerf
   D. IPS
9. What can the MAC address of a rogue device tell you?
   A. Its operating system version
   B. The TTL of the device
   C. What type of rogue it is
   D. The manufacturer of the device
10. How can Jim most effectively locate a wireless rogue access point that is causing complaints from employees in his building?
    A. Nmap
    B. Signal strength and triangulation
    C. Connecting to the rogue AP
    D. NAC
11. Which of the following tools does not provide real-time drive capacity monitoring for Windows?
    A. Microsoft Endpoint Configuration Manager
    B. Resmon
    C. SCOM
    D. Perfmon

12. What three options are most likely to be used to handle a memory leak?
    - **A.** Memory management, patching, and buffer overflow prevention
    - **B.** Patching, service restarts, and system reboots
    - **C.** Service restarts, memory monitoring, and stack smashing prevention
    - **D.** System reboots, memory management, and logging

13. Sayed is planning to prohibit a variety of files, including games, from being installed on the Windows workstations he manages. What technology is his best option to prevent known, unwanted files from being installed or copied to machines?
    - **A.** Blacklisting
    - **B.** Microsoft Endpoint Configuration Manager
    - **C.** SCOM
    - **D.** Whitelisting

14. While Susan is monitoring a router via network flows, she sees a sudden drop in network traffic levels to zero, and the traffic chart shows a flat line. What has likely happened?
    - **A.** The sampling rate is set incorrectly.
    - **B.** The router is using SNMP.
    - **C.** The monitored link failed.
    - **D.** A DDoS attack is occurring.

15. What are SNMP alert messages called?
    - **A.** SNMP launches
    - **B.** SNMP traps
    - **C.** SNMP bolts
    - **D.** SNMP packets

16. Which of the following options is not a valid way to check the status of a service in Windows?
    - **A.** Use `sc` at the command line
    - **B.** Use `service --status` at the command line
    - **C.** Use `services.msc`
    - **D.** Query service status via PowerShell

17. Avik has been asked to identify unexpected traffic on her organization's network. Which of the following is not a technique she should use?
    - **A.** Protocol analysis
    - **B.** Heuristics
    - **C.** Baselining
    - **D.** Beaconing

18. Sofia suspects that a system in her datacenter may be sending beaconing traffic to a remote system. Which of the following is not a useful tool to help verify her suspicions?
    A. Flows
    B. A protocol analyzer
    C. SNMP
    D. An IDS or IPS
19. Alex wants to prohibit software that is not expressly allowed by his organization's desktop management team from being installed on workstations. What type of tool should he use?
    A. Whitelisting
    B. Heuristic
    C. Blacklisting
    D. Signature comparison
20. Juan wants to see a list of processes along with their CPU utilization in an interactive format. What built-in Linux tool should he use?
    A. `df`
    B. `top`
    C. `tail`
    D. `cpugrep`

Performing Forensic Analysis and Techniques

THE COMPTIA CYBERSECURITY ANALYST (CYSA+) EXAM OBJECTIVES COVERED IN THIS CHAPTER INCLUDE:

✓ **Domain 4.0: Incident Response**

- 4.4 Given a scenario, utilize basic digital forensic techniques.

Computer forensic investigations are used to determine what activities, changes, and other actions have occurred on a system, who or what performed them, and what data is stored there. This means that computer forensic techniques are used in a variety of scenarios, including police investigations, inquiries into system administrator misuse, compromise and malware analysis, and investigations related to internal policy violations.

In this chapter you will learn how to be prepared to conduct basic forensic investigations. You will learn about forensics kits, their contents, and the use of the devices and tools they contain. Then, you will explore forensic tools and processes needed to capture and preserve forensics data for network-based, endpoint-based, mobile, and cloud and virtual investigations.

Building a Forensics Capability

One of the first steps to being able to conduct a forensic investigation is to gather the right set of tools. Forensic tools come with a broad variety of capabilities, costs, and purposes. You should determine what types of investigations you are likely to conduct, what types of systems and devices you will need to analyze, and what evidentiary standards you will need to comply with before you build your toolkit.

Exam Note

The second edition of the CySA+ exam objectives no longer require you to know what goes into a forensic toolkit—but understanding how to conduct the disk, memory, and other forensic investigations that are in the objectives means you need to know about what a forensic kit typically contains and why. You won't see this on the exam directly, but we have included it for context in case you're not a forensic expert.

Building a Forensic Toolkit

A complete forensic toolkit is an important part of any forensic investigation. Not only can having the right tools and materials make the process easier, but it can also help ensure that your investigation has the right documentation and support materials in case you need to provide proof of your process—either in court, to management, or to auditors.

Over the next few pages you will learn about the major components of a forensic toolkit, including a forensic workstation, data capture tools and devices, and the administrative tools that help provide proper chain-of-custody tracking. Keep in mind how your organization is likely to conduct forensic investigations—not all of these components may be needed for your use cases.

Key Toolkit Components

The following components are common to most forensic toolkits. Forensic workstations may be a desktop, a laptop, or even a server, and the specific components should be tailored to your organization. But this basic set of items will allow you to perform forensic investigations under most circumstances.

- A digital forensics workstation. A good forensic workstation is designed to allow for data capture and analysis, and those tasks can benefit from a powerful, multicore CPU and plenty of RAM. Having lots of fast, reliable storage is also important, since large investigations can deal with terabytes of data.
- A forensic investigation suite or forensic software like FTK, EnCase, the SANS Investigate Forensic Kit (SIFT), or The Sleuth Kit (TSK) that provides the ability to capture and analyze forensic images as well as track forensic investigations.
- Write blockers, which ensure that drives connected to a forensic system or device cannot be written to. This helps to ensure the integrity of the forensic investigation; having file access times changed—or worse, having the system that is analyzing the data modify the content of the files on the drive—can prevent forensic evidence from being useful.
- Forensic drive duplicators, which are designed to copy drives for forensic investigation and then provide validation that the original drive and the content of the new drive match. Many forensic tools and suites also offer this capability, but a dedicated cloning device can be useful (and can sometimes make it easier to prove that the duplication process was completed in a forensically sound manner).
- Wiped drives and wiped removable media of sufficient capacity to handle any drive or system that you are likely to encounter. Fortunately, large SATA hard drives, portable NAS devices, and large SSDs make it a lot easier to capture and transport multiple forensic images. Removable media, in the form of large USB thumb drives, writable Blu-ray or DVD media, or flash media, can also be valuable for transporting forensic data or for sending it to other organizations when necessary.

Properly wiping the media to ensure that you don't have any remnant data is crucial—remnant data can call your entire forensic process into question! It is particularly important to understand how wear leveling on flash media and SSDs can impact data remanence.

- Cables and drive adapters of various types to ensure that you can connect to most types of devices you are likely to encounter. In a corporate environment, you are likely to know what types of machines and drives your organization deploys, allowing you to select the right adapters and cables to match what you have. In law enforcement, consulting, or other environment where you may not know what you will encounter, having a broad selection of cables and adapters can be incredibly helpful.
- A camera to document system configurations, drive labels, and other information. Cameras are a surprisingly important part of forensic capture because they can speed up data recording and can provide a visual record of the state of a system or device.
- Labeling and documentation tools, including a label maker or labels, indelible pens, and other tools to help with chain-of-custody and forensic process documentation.
- Notebooks and preprepared documentation forms and checklists to record forensic investigation processes and notes. Common types of forms include chain-of-custody forms that track who was in possession of evidence at any time, incident response forms for tracking a response process, incident response plans and incident forms, and escalation lists or call lists of people to contact during a response process. These are sometimes replaced by a forensic recording software package or another software tool that provides ways to validate log entries and that tracks changes. Figure 13.1 shows an example of a chain-of-custody form.

Forensic Workstations

If you are using commercial forensic software, the vendor is likely to provide minimum specifications for the software package. Both EnCase and FTK have system recommendation guidelines:

Guidance Software, makers of EnCase provides theirs at `www.guidancesoftware.com/document/whitepaper/encase-processor-hardware-and-configuration-recommendations`.

FTK's can be found at `support.accessdata.com/hc/en-us/articles/202905229-System-Specification-Guide-FTK`.

Both EnCase and FTK provide distributed processing capabilities that can help by spreading the load between multiple systems—a useful capability if you frequently do large-scale forensic data analysis.

Make sure that you have an ongoing budget to upgrade or refresh your forensic workstation and equipment on a periodic basis. Technology changes and increases in the volume of data acquired can make an older forensic workstation out of date surprisingly quickly.

FIGURE 13.1 Sample chain-of-custody form

Affix Case Number Tag Here

Example Organization

COMPUTER EVIDENCE CHAIN OF CUSTODY TRACKING FORM

Case Number: ____________________ Item Number: ____________________

Evidence Description: ____

____

____

Collection method: ____

____

Evidence storage method: _______________________________________

How is evidence secured? _______________________________________

Collected by: (Name/ID#) _______________________________________

Signature of collector: ____

Copy History		
Date	**Copied method**	**Disposition of original and all copies**

Chain of Custody				
Item #	**Date/Time**	**Released by** (Signature & ID#)	**Received by** (Signature & ID#)	**Comments/Location**

APD_Form_#PE003_v.1 (12/2012) Page 1 of 2 pages (See back)

Mobile Device Forensic Toolkit Components

Handling *mobile device forensics* can create additional challenges. The diversity of mobile device operating systems, connection types, security options, and software versions can make capturing data from devices difficult. Having the right tools plays a big role in successfully connecting to and capturing data from mobile devices. If you need to build a mobile forensic toolkit, you may need to add some or all of the following to your existing forensic kit:

- Tools for accessing SIM cards and flash memory cards. For some phones, this is simply a pin-style push device, whereas others may require small screwdrivers or other tools.
- A mobile device connection cable kit that includes the most common connector types for current and recent phones. This has become simpler in recent years, and having USB micro, Lightning, and USB-C connectors will cover most smartphones and tablets. Connecting to older phones and non-smartphones can still require additional proprietary cables. Fortunately, many vendors provide mobile device forensic cable kits, allowing you to buy many of the most common cables at once.
- Mobile device–specific forensic software and tools designed to target mobile device operating systems.

It might seem as if it is nearly impossible to break into a phone that has a passcode set but that doesn't have a known exploit or other method available to access the data stored on the phone. Fortunately, companies like Susteen Inc. have built robotic tools that can use a camera to identify the keypad on a phone and try thousands of passcodes in an automated fashion until the phone unlocks. This type of mobile device brute-force attack works only if the phone isn't set to wipe after a set number of attempts to access it, but it's a cleverly engineered way to break into "burner" phones that may not otherwise allow access to the data they contain. You can see it in action at `secureview.us/burner-breaker.html`.

Understanding Forensic Software

There are many types of forensic software, ranging from purpose-built forensic suites and tools like FTK, EnCase, CAINE, Autopsy, and SIFT to forensic utilities like DumpIt and Memoryze. Many common Linux and Windows utilities also have forensic applications, including utilities like dd and WinDbg.

Capabilities and Application

Forensic investigations can take many forms, which means that you'll need a broad software toolkit to handle situations, systems, and specific requirements you encounter. Key forensic tool capabilities to include in your forensic software toolkit are imaging, analysis, hashing and validation, process and memory dump analysis, password cracking, and log viewers.

Exam Note

The CySA+ exam objectives specifically call out endpoint disk and memory forensics including carving (more specifically called *file carving* in common use), hashing, and data acquisition. They also include legal holds and other procedures, all of which we cover in this section.

Imaging Media and Drives

The first step in many forensic investigations is to create copies of the media or disks that may contain data useful for the investigation. This is done using an imaging utility, which can create a forensic image of a complete disk, a disk partition, or a logical volume.

Forensic images exactly match the original source drive, volume, partition, or device, including slack space and unallocated space. Slack space is the space left when a file is written. This unused space can contain fragments of files previously written to the space or even files that have been intentionally hidden. Unallocated space is space that has not been partitioned. When used properly, imaging utilities ensure that you have captured all of this data.

Forensic copies and drive wiping programs may not properly handle spare sectors and bad sectors on traditional spinning disks or reserved space retained to help with wear leveling for SSDs. This means it is possible to miss potentially useful forensic data, and it's something you should be particularly aware of when wiping disks.

Analysis Utilities

Forensic analysis utilities provide a number of useful capabilities that can help offer insight into what occurred on a system. Examples include the following:

- Timelines of system changes
- Validation tools that check known-good versions of files against those found on a system
- Filesystem analysis capabilities that can look at filesystem metadata (like the Windows Master File Table for NTFS) to identify file changes, access, and deletions
- File carving tools that allow the recovery of files without the filesystem itself available
- Windows Registry analysis
- Log file parsing and review

These analysis tools can help identify information that is useful for a forensic investigation but using them well requires detailed forensic knowledge to avoid missing important data.

Some forensic investigators use open source utilities like SIFT, CAINE, and Autopsy since they are freely available. Although commercial forensic tools can be costly, they may be easier to defend in court, which means you'll sometimes see professional forensic investigators using commercial tools like FTK or EnCase rather than freely available open source tools. Make sure your organization is comfortable with the pros and cons of any tool that you choose to use.

Carving

When data is recovered as part of forensic analysis, the original filesystem may no longer be intact. In this, and other scenarios where the original filesystem cannot be used, file *carving* tools come in handy. File carving tools look at data on a block-by-block basis, looking for information like file headers and other indicators of file structure. When they find them, they attempt to recover complete or even partial files.

Three common types of file carving methods are as follows:

- Header- and footer-based carving, which focuses on headers like those found in JPEG files. For example, JPEGs can be found by looking for `\xFF\xD8` in the header and `\xFF\xD9` in the footer.
- Content-based carving techniques look for information about the content of a file such as character counts and text recognition.
- File structure-based carving techniques that use information about the structure of files.

Figure 13.2 shows a JPEG file opened in HxD, a free hex editor tool. At the top left of the image you can see the header information for the JPEG showing FF and D8 as the first pair of entries in the file.

Chain-of-Custody Tracking

Support for properly maintaining chain-of-custody documentation in an automated and logged manner is an important part of a forensic suite, and it is an important part of their documented forensic procedures for many organizations. Maintaining chain-of-custody documentation ensures that drive images and other data, as well as the actions taken using the suite, are properly validated and available for review, thus reducing the potential for legal challenges based on poor custodial practices.

Legal Holds

One common use of forensic tools is in support of legal holds. A *legal hold* (or litigation hold) is conducted when information must be retained for a legal case. In this scenario, forensic and backup tools are often leveraged to ensure that a current copy of the target system, drive, or network storage location is preserved and maintained as required by the hold. Although forensic tools are often leveraged as part of this process, a purpose-built eDiscovery tool is often the better choice if your organization deals with a reasonable volume of legal holds.

FIGURE 13.2 Carving a JPEG file using HxD

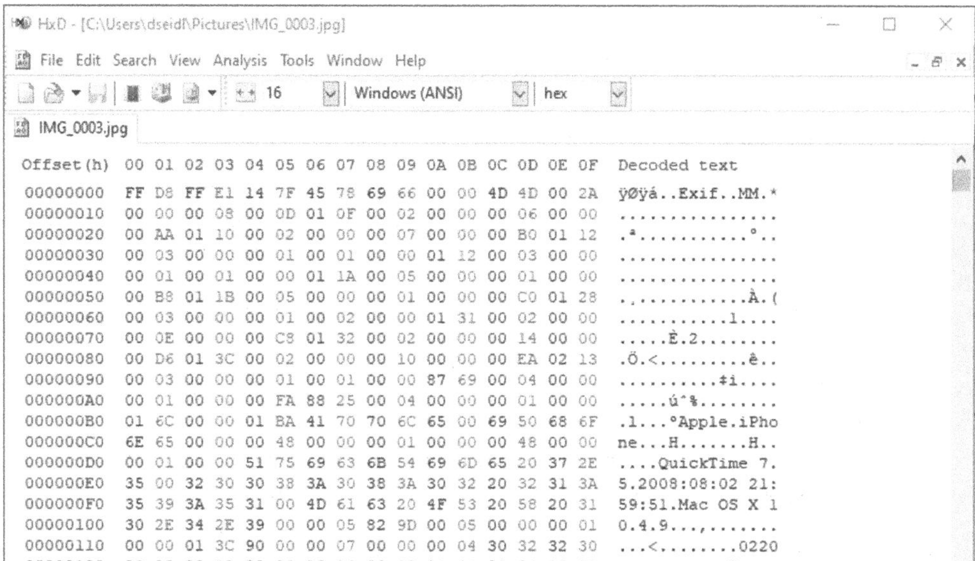

Hashing and Validation

Verification of the forensic integrity of an image is an important part of forensic imaging. Fortunately, this can be done using *hashing* utilities built into a forensics suite or run independently to get a hash of the drive to validate the contents of the copy. The goal of this process is to ensure that the copy exactly matches the source drive or device.

Forensic image formats like EnCase's EO1 format provide built-in hashing as part of the file. In cases where formats like these are not used, both MD5 and SHA1 hashes are frequently used for this purpose. Hashing large drives can take quite a bit of time even using a fast algorithm like MD5, but the process itself is quite simple as shown here. The following provides the MD5 hash of a volume mounted on a Linux system:

```
user@demo:~# md5sum /dev/sda1
9b98b637a132974e41e3c6ae1fc9fc96  /dev/sda1
```

To validate an image, a hash is generated for both the original and the copy. If the hashes match, the images are identical. Both hashes should be recorded as part of the forensic log for the investigation.

You may be wondering why MD5 is used for forensic imaging when most security practitioners recommend against using it. MD5 remains in use because it is fast and widely available, and the attacks against MD5 are primarily threats for reasons that don't apply to forensic images. As a practitioner, you are unlikely to encounter someone who can or would intentionally make two drives with different contents hash to the same value.

Hashing is also often used to validate binaries and other application related files to detect changes to the binaries. Manual checksums using MD5 or SHA1 utilities can be used to check if a file matches a known good version or one from a backup, or it can be checked against a provided checksum from a vendor or other source.

Exam Note

Hashing and changes to binaries show up in Exam Objective 4.4, so make sure you think about how you would respond to questions about them on the exam.

Fortunately for incident responders and forensic analysts, known file hash databases are maintained by a handful of organizations, including these:

- The OWASP File Hash Repository: `www.owasp.org/index.php/OWASP_File_Hash_Repository`
- The NIST National Software Reference Library, which includes the Reference Data Set with digital signatures for software: `www.nist.gov/itl/ssd/software-quality-group/national-software-reference-library-nsrl`

Many organizations also track known hashes of malware, allowing responders to upload suspected malicious code to have it checked.

What's a binary? The term is used to describe files that aren't text files, which typically means executable applications in common use but might mean a variety of other types of files as well. The key concept is that they are machine readable but not human readable. You may still be able to pull some human-readable text out using a utility like `strings` on a Linux system—a useful forensic trick used by many incident responders.

Conducting Endpoint Forensics

Traditionally, the great majority of forensic activity has taken place on endpoint systems: servers, desktops, laptops, and mobile devices of all types. As organizations increasingly move to the cloud, more forensic activity is taking place there, but a majority of forensic work is likely to continue to involve traditional endpoints for most practitioners.

Operating System, Process, and Memory Dump Analysis

Information about the state of the operating system (OS), including the data that is stored in memory by processes, can be important to both forensic investigations as well as investigations of malware infections or compromise. Often data that is otherwise kept encrypted is accessible in memory to processes, or the encryption keys that those processes use to access encrypted data are available. The ability to capture memory, process information and data, as well as operate specific analysis capabilities, is a useful forensic capability. OS analysis can provide key data about what was occurring on a system during the timeframe targeted by an investigation.

In addition to live memory capture and analysis, memory dump analysis can be particularly valuable when recovering decryption keys for full-disk encryption products like BitLocker. Hibernation files and crash dumps can both contain the data needed to decrypt the drive, which makes accessing an unlocked machine critically important for a forensic practitioner.

Disk Forensics

The most common forensic activity for endpoints is disk, or storage-based analysis. This can range from manual inspection of files to complete imaging and analysis of entire disks or volumes as mentioned earlier in the chapter.

We will walk you through a forensic scenario later in this chapter, including disk capture, so if you want to read more about disk forensics, skip ahead.

Memory Forensics

Conducting memory forensics requires either running live forensic analysis on a running machine or making a copy of live memory to point in time forensic memory analysis. Tools like Volatility, an open source memory forensics framework, can capture and analyze memory.

Volatility has a wide range of plug-in commands, including the ability to detect API hooks, read the keyboard buffer, grab the Windows clipboard, look for live TCP connections, scan for driver objects, and many more. If there is data accessible in live memory in an unencrypted form, you should assume it can be recovered—and if it is encrypted, the encrypted version can be accessed and potentially decrypted if the key is available.

Memory forensics can be particularly useful when attempting to recover security artifacts that are stored in memory when in use such as encryption keys and passwords. As a forensic practitioner, you should keep in mind that system crash dumps often contain a copy of live memory, making them an attractive target for both practitioners and knowledgeable attackers.

Mobile Device and Cell Phone Forensics

Mobile device forensic capabilities exist in many commercial forensic suites, as well as in the form of stand-alone tools. Due to the security features that many phone operating systems provide, they often have specialized decryption or brute-forcing capabilities to allow them to capture data from a locked and encrypted phone or phone volume.

Phone backup forensic capabilities are also a useful tool for mobile forensics. Backups may not have all current data, but they can contain older data that was deleted and may not have the same level of security that the phone itself does, thus making them an attractive target for forensic acquisition and review.

Password Crackers and Password Recovery

An increasing number of drives and devices are encrypted or use a password to protect the system or files. This makes password recovery tools (also called password crackers) very useful to a forensic examiner. Common places to discover password protection beyond the operating system or account level include Microsoft Office files, PDFs, as well as ZIP and RAR compressed files.

Recovering passwords for forensic investigations can be challenging, but tools like ElcomSoft's Advanced Office Password Recovery, shown in Figure 13.3, provide brute-force password breaking for a range of file types.

FIGURE 13.3 Advanced Office Password Recovery cracking a Word DOC file

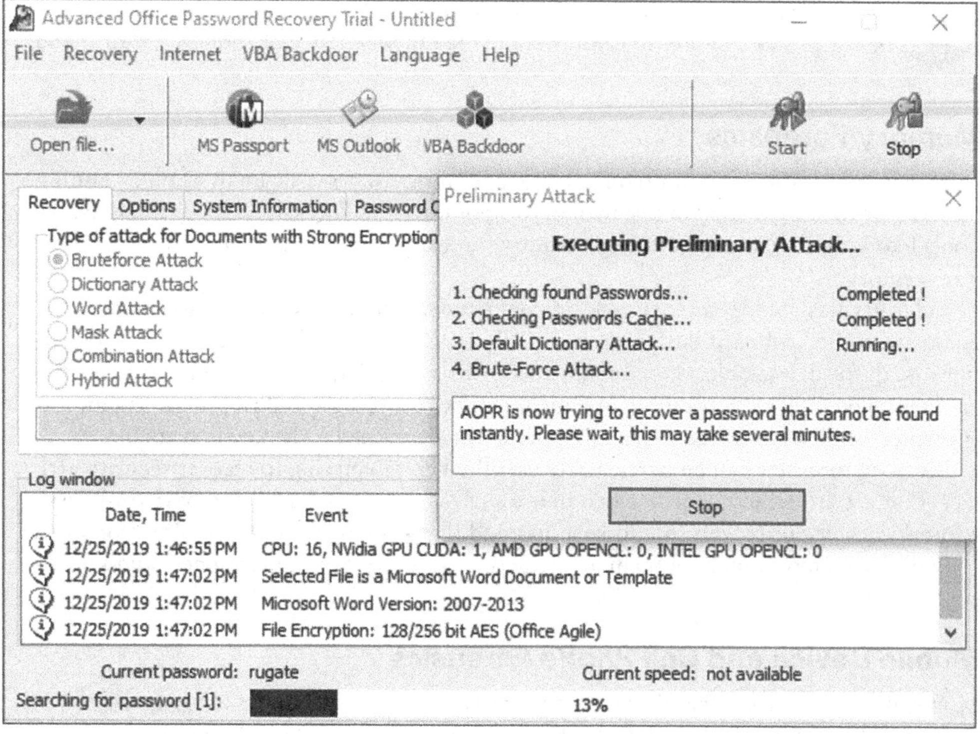

Some forensic workstations include powerful graphics cards. This is partially due to the ability of many password-cracking tools to use the graphics card or GPU to perform password cracking operations. Using a GPU can result in massive speed increases over traditional CPU-based cracking, making a powerful CPU a worthwhile investment if you ever need to perform a brute-force password cracking attack and your forensic tools support it.

Cryptography Tools

Cryptographic tools are common both to protect forensic data and to protect data and applications from forensics. Forensic tools often have encryption capabilities to ensure that sensitive data under forensic investigation is not breached as part of the investigation when drives or files are transferred, or if the forensic environment is compromised.

Encryption tools are also needed to handle encrypted drives and network protocols. These capabilities vary from tool to tool, but handling BitLocker, Microsoft Office, and other common encryption mechanisms are common tasks during forensic investigations.

When forensic techniques are used to investigate malware, encryption and other protection schemes are frequently encountered as a means of preventing code analysis of malware. Many malware packages use tools called "packers," intended to protect them from reverse engineering. Packers are intended to make direct analysis of the code difficult or impossible. Some forensic tools provide support for unpacking and decoding from packing techniques like Base64 encoding.

Log Viewers

Log files can provide information about the system state, actions taken on the system, and errors or problems, as well as a wide variety of other information. This makes log entries particularly useful when you are attempting to understand what occurred on a system or device. Forensic suites typically build in *log viewers* that can match log entries to other forensic information, but specialized logs may require additional tools.

Network Forensics

Network traffic forensics require capturing traffic on the network or reviewing artifacts of that traffic like security or network device logs, traffic monitoring data, or other information that can help forensic practitioners to reconstruct events and incidents.

Exam Note

The CySA+ exam objectives specifically call out two tools from a basic network forensics perspective: Wireshark and tcpdump. There are many more, but here we will focus on just those two. Learning how to use either of these tools well could take an entire book, so we suggest that you select a tutorial like those found at `hackertarget.com/wireshark-tutorial-and-cheat-sheet/`.

> Tutorials for tcpdump are also available, including `Opensource.com`'s introduction to tcpdump: `opensource.com/article/18/10/introduction-tcpdump` and Daniel Miessler's handy list of tcpdump techniques at `danielmiessler.com/study/tcpdump/`.

For the purposes of the CySA+ exam, you will need to know the basics of both Wireshark and tcpdump.

Wireshark Network Forensics

Wireshark is an open source network protocol analyzer (sometimes called a packet sniffer, or sniffer). It runs on many modern operating systems and can allow users to capture and view network data in a GUI. Captures can be saved, analyzed, and output in a number of formats.

Figure 13.4 shows a simple Wireshark capture of traffic to the CompTIA website. Note the DNS query that you can see that starts the connection. If you scrolled further you'd see the multitude of trackers and ad sites that also get hit along the way!

FIGURE 13.4 Wireshark view of network traffic

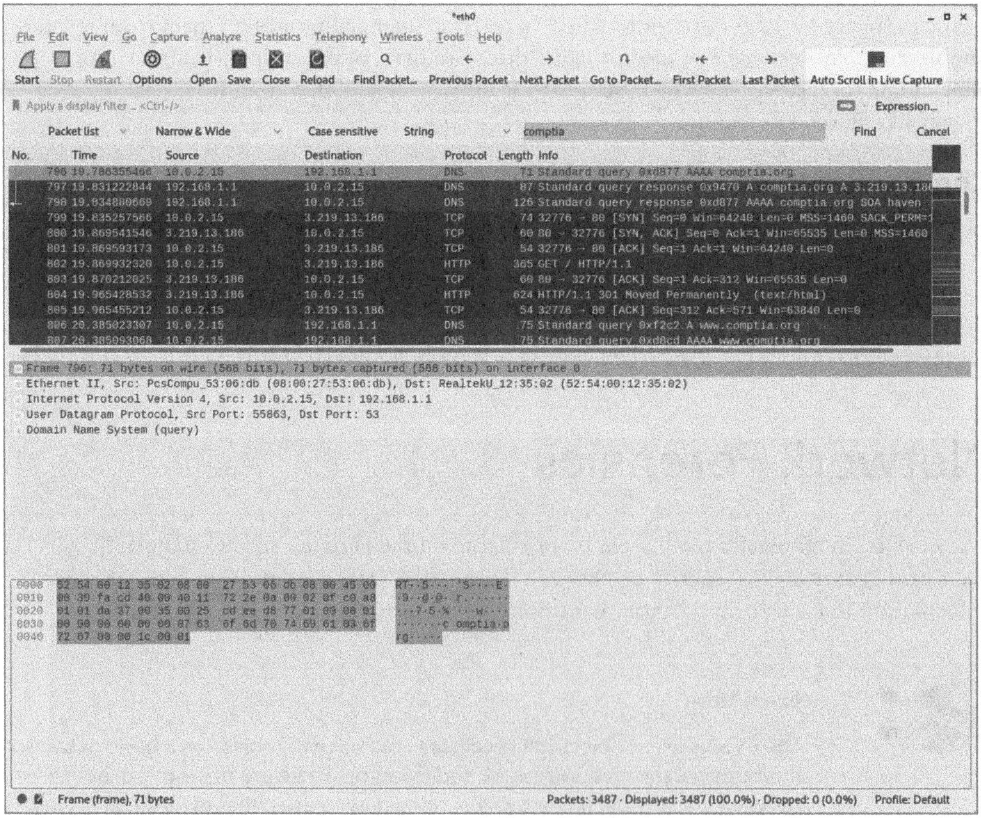

As you prepare for the CySA+ exam, you should spend a little time capturing traffic using Wireshark and tcpdump, and make sure you know the basics of how to find a packet by text strings and protocols. You should also be able to identify what common traffic like the start of a TCP connection looks like.

Tcpdump Network Forensics

Tcpdump is a command-line packet capture utility found on many Linux and Unix systems. Tcpdump is a powerful tool, particularly when combined with other tools like grep to sort and analyze the same packet data that you could capture with Wireshark. Although Wireshark typically has to be installed on systems, tcpdump is more likely to be installed by default.

In Figure 13.5, you can see a tcpdump watching network traffic for DNS traffic.

FIGURE 13.5 Tcpdump of network traffic

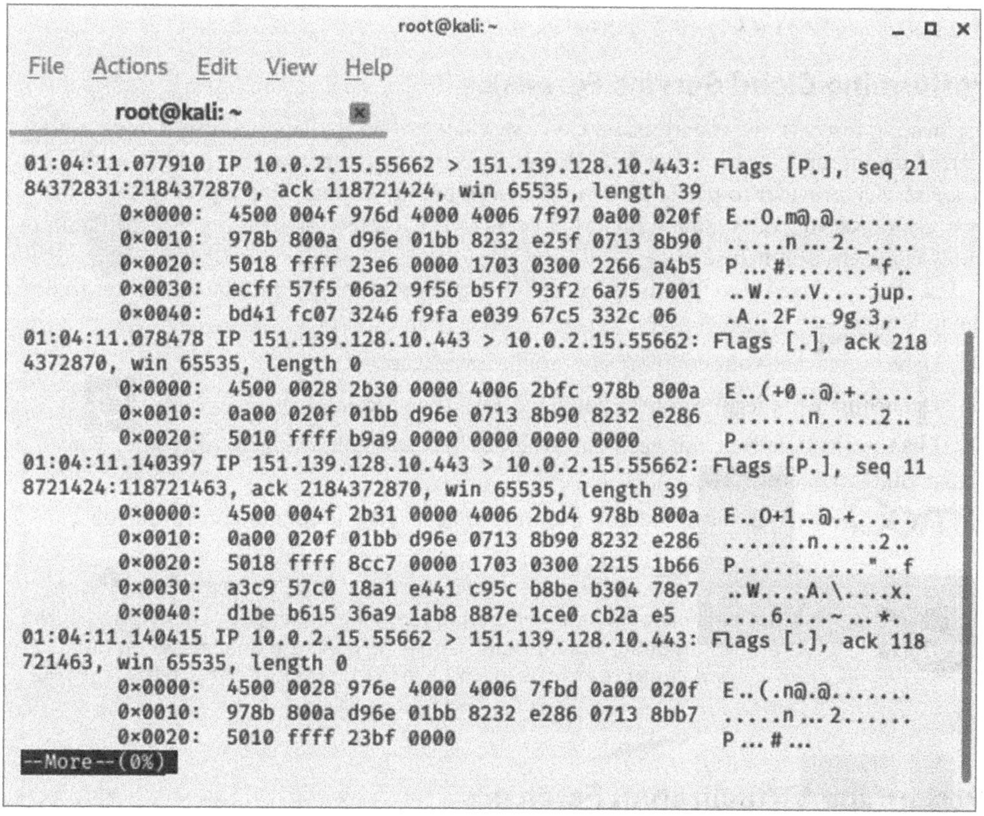

```
root@kali: ~
File  Actions  Edit  View  Help
root@kali: ~
01:04:11.077910 IP 10.0.2.15.55662 > 151.139.128.10.443: Flags [P.], seq 21
84372831:2184372870, ack 118721424, win 65535, length 39
        0x0000:  4500 004f 976d 4000 4006 7f97 0a00 020f  E..O.m@.@.......
        0x0010:  978b 800a d96e 01bb 8232 e25f 0713 8b90  .....n...2._....
        0x0020:  5018 ffff 23e6 0000 1703 0300 2266 a4b5  P...#......."f..
        0x0030:  ecff 57f5 06a2 9f56 b5f7 93f2 6a75 7001  ..W....V....jup.
        0x0040:  bd41 fc07 3246 f9fa e039 67c5 332c 06    .A..2F....9g.3,.
01:04:11.078478 IP 151.139.128.10.443 > 10.0.2.15.55662: Flags [.], ack 218
4372870, win 65535, length 0
        0x0000:  4500 0028 2b30 0000 4006 2bfc 978b 800a  E..(+0..@.+.....
        0x0010:  0a00 020f 01bb d96e 0713 8b90 8232 e286  .......n.....2..
        0x0020:  5010 ffff b9a9 0000 0000 0000 0000       P.............
01:04:11.140397 IP 151.139.128.10.443 > 10.0.2.15.55662: Flags [P.], seq 11
8721424:118721463, ack 2184372870, win 65535, length 39
        0x0000:  4500 004f 2b31 0000 4006 2bd4 978b 800a  E..O+1..@.+.....
        0x0010:  0a00 020f 01bb d96e 0713 8b90 8232 e286  .......n.....2..
        0x0020:  5018 ffff 8cc7 0000 1703 0300 2215 1b66  P..........."..f
        0x0030:  a3c9 57c0 18a1 e441 c95c b8be b304 78e7  ..W....A.\....x.
        0x0040:  d1be b615 36a9 1ab8 887e 1ce0 cb2a e5    ....6....~...*.
01:04:11.140415 IP 10.0.2.15.55662 > 151.139.128.10.443: Flags [.], ack 118
721463, win 65535, length 0
        0x0000:  4500 0028 976e 4000 4006 7fbd 0a00 020f  E..(.n@.@.......
        0x0010:  978b 800a d96e 01bb 8232 e286 0713 8bb7  .....n...2......
        0x0020:  5010 ffff 23bf 0000                      P...#...
--More--(0%)
```

As you can see, text representations of packets can be harder to sort through. In fact, when capturing this example the authors had to output the capture to a file rather than to the terminal buffer because loading the CompTIA website generated more traffic than the terminal's default buffer. Tcpdump is powerful and helpful, but you will need to learn how to filter the output and read through it.

Cloud, Virtual, and Container Forensics

Cloud computing, virtualization, and containerization have created a new set of challenges for forensic practitioners. Many of the artifacts that would have once been available are now part of ephemeral virtual machines or containers, or are hosted by third-party providers. Practitioners must plan in advance for how they will conduct forensic investigations, meaning you need to know what artifacts you can gather, what you will need to do to gather them, and what you may need to partner with a cloud provider to obtain, or if they will provide the access or data you need at all.

Performing Cloud Service Forensics

Performing forensic investigations on cloud services can be challenging, if not impossible. Shared tenant models mean that forensic data can be hard to get and often require the cloud service provider to participate in the investigation. Maintaining a proper chain of custody, preserving data, and many other parts of the forensic process are more difficult in many cloud environments.

If a cloud service is likely to be part of your forensic investigation, you may want to do the following:

- Determine what your contract says about investigations.
- Determine what legal recourse you have with the vendor.
- Identify the data that you need and whether it is available via methods you or your organization controls.
- Work with the vendor to identify a course of action if you do not control the data.

More detail about cloud computing forensic challenges can be found in NIST draft NISTIR 8006, NIST Cloud Computing Forensic Challenges, at `csrc.nist.gov/publications/drafts/nistir-8006/draft_nistir_8006.pdf`.

Performing Virtualization Forensics

Virtualization forensics can be somewhat less complex than attempting forensics on a hosted environment. Virtualized systems can be copied and moved to a secure environment for analysis, but as a forensic practitioner you will need to keep in mind your forensic goals. Incident response forensics may be easier since the evidentiary requirements are typically less than those found in a legal case, making how you handle the forensic copies of systems and how and when you capture them less critical.

Regardless of whether you're conducting an investigation for incident response, an internal investigation, or law enforcement, you will need to understand the limitations of what your capture and copying methods can do. Remember to also consider the underlying virtualization environment—and what you would do if the environment itself were the target of the forensic work!

Virtualization and containerization share many of the same goals and operate in somewhat similar ways. Figure 13.6 shows how the two concepts look at a high level. Note the separation of the virtual machines in the virtualized environment versus the applications running under the same containerization engine.

FIGURE 13.6 Virtualization vs. containerization

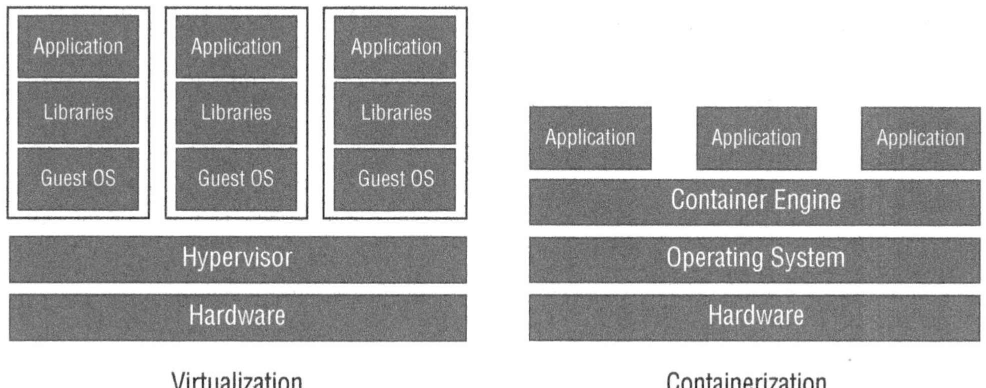

Container Forensics

Containers are increasingly common, and container forensics can create some unique issues. Perhaps the most important of them is that most containers are designed to be disposable, and thus if something goes wrong many organizations will have processes in place to shut down, destroy, and rebuild the container in an automated or semi-automated fashion. Even if there isn't a security issue, due to their ephemeral nature, containers may be destroyed or rescheduled to a different node. This means that forensic artifacts may be lost.

Containerization technology also creates other challenges: internal lots and filesystem artifacts are ephemeral; they communicate over software-defined networks that change frequently as containers are bought online, taken offline, or moved; and security contexts are dynamically modified by the containerization orchestration tool.

All of this means that if you anticipate the need to respond to incidents involving containerized applications, you need to preplan to capture the data you will need. That means identifying tooling and processes to audit activities, as well as methods to capture data that may be necessary for container forensics. Fortunately, containerization security tools are available that can help with this.

Exam Note

The CySA+ exam objectives in this version don't address container forensics as a distinct topic from virtualization forensics. With the speed that containerization is growing in use, you're likely to run into it outside of the exam environment. As you study for the exam, just remember that the objective lists virtualization, and spend your study time there.

Conducting a Forensic Investigation

Forensic investigations rely on more than just a forensic toolkit and a forensic suite. The process of conducting an investigation is often complex due to the number of systems, devices, individuals, and other material involved. Next, we will look at a typical forensic process.

Forensic Procedures

Forensic investigations can take many forms and there are many formal models for forensic investigations, but the basic process involved when conducting them remains the same. In almost all investigations you will take these steps:

1. Determine what you are trying to find out. You may be asked to investigate a compromised system, to analyze the actions taken by malware, or to find out if a system administrator made an unauthorized change to a system. This forms the problem statement that helps to define what forensic activities you will take.
2. Outline the locations and types of data that would help you answer the questions from step 1. Data may exist in many forms, and applications and systems can determine the format and accessibility of the data. Knowing where and how you need to collect data will also influence what your forensic process looks like. At this stage, you may not know the specific hardware or log locations, but you should be able to come up with the types of data and systems you will need to capture data from.
3. Document and review your plan.
4. Acquire and preserve evidence. The acquisition process may require cloning media, seizing systems or devices, or making live memory images to ensure that information is not lost when a system is powered off.

5. Perform initial analysis, carefully tracking your actions, the systems and data you work with, and your findings, as well as any questions you need to answer.
6. Use the initial analysis to guide further work, including deeper investigation, and review where the initial analysis pointed to additional data or where information is missing that is needed to answer the questions you originally asked.
7. Report on the findings of the investigation.

Acquisition processes need to take into account the *order of volatility*, which measures how easily data is to lose. This means that data stored in memory or caches is considered highly volatile, since it will be lost if the system is turned off, whereas data stored in printed form or as a backup is considered much less volatile. Figure 13.7 shows a view of the order of volatility of common storage locations that data is likely to be acquired from during a forensic investigation.

FIGURE 13.7 Order of volatility of common storage locations

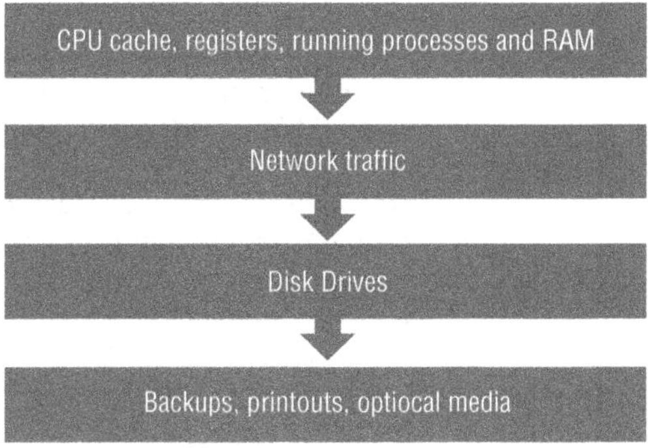

Unexpected Forensic Discoveries

Forensic investigations can result in finding data that you did not intend to uncover as part of the investigation. Knowing what you will do if you find signs of issues or problems outside of the scope of the investigation you are conducting is helpful to avoid problems. This can be as simple as finding evidence of an employee violating company policies while investigating a compromise, or as potentially complex as discovering evidence of illegal activities during an investigation. Make sure you know if you have a duty to report certain types of finding, under local, state, or federal law, or due to your own organization's policies.

Target Locations

Target locations differ based on operating system or device type, but Windows, macOS, and Linux systems are the most common targets of forensic acquisition. Table 13.1 lists common locations and examples of how they might be used for Windows forensics.

This isn't an exhaustive list, and the needs of each forensic investigation will vary, but knowing where to look and what files you may need can help guide your decisions when determining which systems and volumes to image. Unfortunately, each Linux distribution and macOS version tends to have slightly different locations, making it harder to provide a simple list of common locations. You can find a useful macOS listing at `forensicswiki.xyz/wiki/index.php?title=Mac_OS_X`. Linux forensics analysts will often target the contents of `/var`, `/home`, and `/etc` as excellent starting locations for system logs, user data, and configuration information.

TABLE 13.1 Forensic application of Windows system artifacts

Windows	Use
Windows Registry	Information about files and services, locations of deleted files, evidence of applications being run
Autorun keys	Programs set to run at startup (often associated with malware or compromise)
Master File Table (MFT)	Details of inactive/removed records
Event logs	Logins, service start/stop, evidence of applications being run
INDX files and change logs	Evidence of deleted files, MAC timestamps
Volume shadow copies	Point-in-time information from prior actions
User directories and files	Logged-in user artifacts
Recycle Bin contents	Files that were intended to be deleted but forgotten
Hibernation files and memory dumps	Memory artifacts of commands run
Temporary directories	Artifacts of software installation, user temporary file storage, or other limited lifespan data
Application logs	Application-specific data
Removable drives (including flash drives)	System logs may indicate drives were plugged in; data may be relevant to investigations

Acquiring and Validating Drive Images

Drive and media images must be captured in a forensically sound manner. They also require hashing and validation, and with the exception of live system forensics where it cannot be completely avoided, forensic duplication should not change the source drive or device. To do this, an exact bit-for-bit copy is made using an imaging utility, write blockers are employed to prevent the possibility of modifying the source drive, and multiple copies are made so that the original drive can be retained for evidence.

You may discover that your investigation touches systems, networks, or data that you or your organization does not own. Company Bring Your Own Device (BYOD) practices, cloud services, and employee use of third-party services for their private use on institutional systems can all complicate forensic examinations. Make sure you know your organization's policies about each of those areas, as well as privacy policies and related standards, before you begin a forensic investigation.

Forensic Copies

Forensic copies of media don't work the same way that simply copying the files from one drive to another would. Forensic copies retain the exact same layout and content for the entire device or drive, including the contents of "empty" space, unallocated space, and the slack space that remains when a file does not fill all the space in a cluster.

The need for a verifiable, forensically sound image means that you need to use an imaging tool to create forensic images rather than using the copy command or dragging and dropping files in a file manager. Fortunately, there are a number of commonly available tools like dd or FTK's Imager Lite built into major forensic suites that can create forensic images.

The Importance of Bit-by-Bit Copies

One reason that copies are not done using a copy command is to ensure that slack space and unallocated space are both copied as part of the image. This captures deleted files that have not yet been overwritten, fragments of older files in the space that was not written to by new files, and data that was stored on a drive before it was partitioned. Slack and unallocated space can provide rich detail about the history of a system, and simply copying files will not provide that visibility.

Imaging with dd

The Linux *dd* utility is often used to clone drives in RAW format, a bit-by-bit format. dd provides a number of useful operators that you should set to make sure your imaging is done quickly and correctly:

- Block size is set using the `bs` flag and is defined in bytes. By default, dd uses a 512-byte block size, but this is far smaller than the block size of most modern disks. Using a larger block size will typically be much faster, and if you know the block size for the device you are copying, using its native block size can provide huge speed increases. This is set using a flag like `bs = 64k`.
- The operator `if` sets the input file; for example, `if = /dev/disk/sda1`.
- The operator `of` sets the output file; for example, `of = /mnt/usb/`.

Avoiding Mistakes: dd Input and Output Locations

It is critical that you verify the input and output locations for a dd command. To list drives, you can use commands like `fdisk -l` or `lsblk`. You can ask `lsblk` for more detail by using additional flags: `lsblk --output NAME,FSTYPE,LABEL,UUID,MODE` will show the device name, filesystem type, the disk label, the UUID, and the mode it is mounted in, giving you a much better view. Take careful note of which drive is which, and review your command before pressing Enter. This is where a write blocker can save the day!

Figure 13.8 shows a sample dd copy of a mounted drive image to a USB device. The speed of copies can vary greatly based on block size, the relative speeds of the source and destination drive, and other variables like whether the system is virtual or physical.

FIGURE 13.8 dd of a volume

```
root@demo:/dev/disk/by-label# dd bs=64k if=/dev/disk/by-label/IR3_SSS_X64FREE_EN
-US_DV9 of=/dev/disk/by-label/Blank
69309+1 records in
69309+1 records out
4542291968 bytes (4.5 GB) copied, 949.99 s, 4.8 MB/s
```

A Complete Chain of Custody

Maintaining a fully documented chain of custody is critical for investigations performed by law enforcement or that may need to survive scrutiny in court. That means you need to document what is collected; who collected or analyzed the data; when each action occurred; and when devices and other evidence were transferred, handled, accessed, and securely stored. You have to track this information for each drive, device, machine, or other item you handle during an investigation. You may need a third party in the room to validate your statements for the entire process.

Handling Encrypted Drives

Drive and device encryption is increasingly common, making dealing with drive images more challenging. Of course, live system imaging will avoid many of the issues found with encrypted volumes, but it brings its own set of challenges. Fortunately, commercial forensic suites handle many of the common types of encryption that you are likely to encounter, as long as you have the password for the volume. They also provide distributed cracking methods that use multiple computers to attack encrypted files and volumes.

Avoiding Brute Force

Brute-force cracking of encryption keys can be very slow. Getting the encryption key from the user or an administrator, or by retrieving it from the memory of a live system, is preferable if at all possible.

In 2013, the FBI located Ross Ulbricht, the operator of the Silk Road, a darknet trading site. Ulbricht, also known as the Dread Pirate Roberts, was captured in a public library where he was logged into the Silk Road site and other accounts. Since he was known to use disk encryption, the FBI waited until his computer was open and logged in and then arrested him and got access to his laptop before he could lock or turn off the system. This gave the FBI the opportunity to image the system without defeating the strong encryption that Ulbricht was likely to use to secure it.

Using Write Blockers

Write blockers are an important tool for both forensic investigation and forensic drive image acquisition. During drive acquisition, using a write blocker can ensure that attaching the drive to a forensic copy device or workstation does not result in modifications being made to the drive, thus destroying the forensic integrity of the process. The same capability to prevent writes is useful during forensic analysis of drives and other media because it ensures that no modifications are made to the drive accidentally.

- Hardware write blockers prevent writes from occurring while a drive is connected through them. Hardware write blockers can be certified to a NIST standard, and testing information is available via the NIST Computer Forensics Tool Testing program at `www.cftt.nist.gov/hardware_write_block.htm`.
- Software write blockers are typically less popular than hardware write blockers, making them less common. Due to the possibility of problems, hardware write blockers are more frequently used when preventing writes from occurring is important.

Verifying Images

Image verification is critical to ensuring that your data is forensically sound. Commercial tools use built-in verification capabilities to make sure the entire image matches the original. When investigators use dd or other manual imaging tools, md5sum or sha1sum hashing utilities are frequently used to validate images. Each time you generate an image, you should record the hash or verification information for both the original and the cloned copy, and that information should be recorded in your forensic logbook or chain-of-custody form. FTK's Imager Lite will display the hash values in a report at the end of the process, as shown in Figure 13.9.

FIGURE 13.9 FTK image hashing and bad sector checking

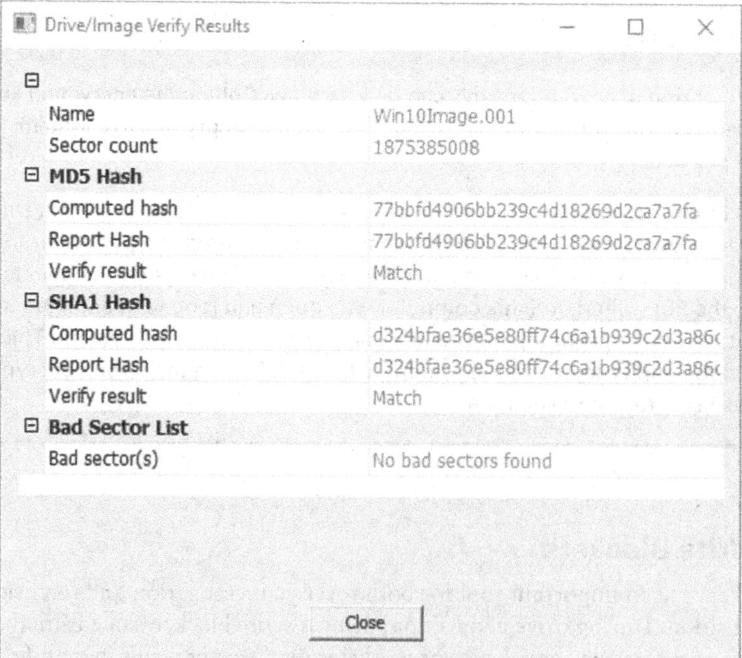

Imaging Live Systems

When systems are using full disk encryption, or when applications, malware, or other software may be memory resident without a copy on the disk, an image may need to be collected while the system is running.

Live imaging may not obtain some desirable data:

- Live imaging can leave remnants due to the imaging utility being mounted from a removable drive or installed.
- The contents of a drive or memory may change during the imaging process.
- Malware or other software may be able to detect the imaging tool and could take action to avoid it or disable it.
- Live images typically do not include unallocated space.

Both commercial and open source tools provide portable versions that can be loaded on a live system to provide live imaging capabilities.

Acquiring Other Data

There are many other types of specialized data beyond drive images that you may want to specifically target during acquisition. Fortunately, in most cases, forensic images of the host drives will also provide access to that data if it is resident on the systems. A few of the other areas you may want to specifically target include log data, USB device histories, application data, browser cache and history, email, and user-generated files.

Acquiring and Reviewing Log Data

Log data is often stored remotely and may not be accurate in the case of a compromised machine or if an administrator was taking actions they wanted to conceal. At other times an investigation may involve actions that are logged centrally or on network devices, but not on a single local system or device that you are likely to create a forensic image of. In those cases, preserving logs is important and will require additional work.

To preserve and analyze logs:

- Determine where the logs reside and what format they are stored in.
- Determine the time period that you need to preserve. Remember that you may want to obtain logs from a longer period in case you find out that an issue or compromise started before you initially suspected.
- Work with system or device administrators to obtain a copy of the logs and document how the logs were obtained. Checksums or other validation are often appropriate.
- Identify items of interest. This might include actions, user IDs, event IDs, timeframes, or other elements identified in your scope.
- Use log analysis tools like Splunk, Sawmill, Event Log Analyzer, or even a text editor to search and review the logs.

Viewing USB Device History

Windows tracks the history of USB devices connected to a system, providing a useful forensic record of thumb drives and other devices. USB Historian can be used to review this based on a mounted drive image. During a forensic examination, the information provided by USB Historian or similar tools can be used to match an inventory of drives to those used on a computer, or to verify whether specific devices were in use at a given time. USB Historian, shown in Figure 13.10, provides such data as the system name, the device name, its serial number, the time it was in use, the vendor ID of the device, what type of device it is, and various other potentially useful information.

FIGURE 13.10 USB Historian drive image

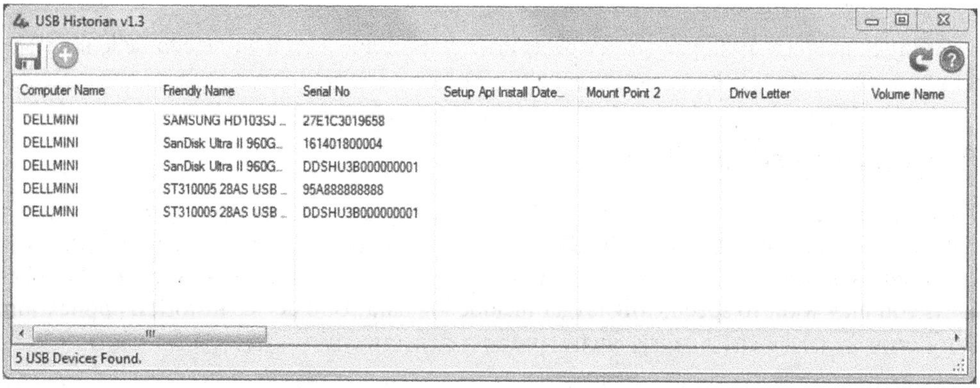

USB Historian v1.3

Computer Name	Friendly Name	Serial No	Setup Api Install Date...	Mount Point 2	Drive Letter	Volume Name
DELLMINI	SAMSUNG HD103SJ ...	27E1C3019658				
DELLMINI	SanDisk Ultra II 960G...	161401800004				
DELLMINI	SanDisk Ultra II 960G...	DDSHU3B000000001				
DELLMINI	ST310005 28AS USB ...	95A888888888				
DELLMINI	ST310005 28AS USB ...	DDSHU3B000000001				

5 USB Devices Found.

Capturing Memory-Resident Data

Shutting down a system typically results in the loss of the data stored in memory. That means that forensic data like information in a browser memory cache or program states will be lost. Although capture information in memory isn't always important in a forensic investigation, it is critical to be able to capture memory when needed.

There are a number of popular tools for memory captures, with a variety of capabilities, including the following:

- fmem and LiME, both Linux kernel modules that allow access to physical memory. fmem is designed to be used with dd or similar tools; LiME directly copies data to a designated path and file.
- DumpIt, a Windows memory capture tool that simply copies a system's physical memory to the folder where the DumpIt program is. This allows easy capture to a USB thumb drive and makes it a useful part of a forensic capture kit.

- The Volatility Framework supports a broad range of operating systems, including Windows, Linux, and macOS, and has a range of capabilities, including tools to extract encryption keys and passphrases, user activity analysis, and rootkit analysis.
- Both EnCase and FTK have built-in memory capture and analysis capabilities as well.

Using Core Dumps and Hibernation Files

In addition to memory images, core dumps and crash dump files can provide useful forensic information, both for criminal and malware investigations. Since they contain the contents of live memory, they can include data that might not otherwise be accessible on the drive of a system, such as memory-resident encryption keys, malware that runs only in memory, and other items not typically stored to the disk.

The Windows crash dump file can be found by checking the setting found under Control Panel ➢ System And Security ➢ System ➢ Advanced System Settings ➢ Startup And Recovery ➢ Settings. Typically, crash dump files will be located in the system root directory: `%SystemRoot%\MEMORY.DMP`. Windows memory dump files can be analyzed using WinDbg; however, you shouldn't need to analyze a Windows kernel dump for the CySA+ exam.

Many of the techniques involved in a forensic investigation are useful for incident response and internal investigations that may not have the same evidentiary requirements that a forensic investigation may require. This means it is often reasonable to bypass some of the strictest parts of chain-of-custody documentation and other procedural requirements—but only if you are absolutely certain that the investigation will not become a legal or police matter. When in doubt, it is safer to err on the side of over-documentation to avoid problems in court.

Acquisitions from Mobile Devices

Mobile device forensic acquisition typically starts with disabling the device's network connectivity and then ensuring that access to the device is possible by disabling passcodes and screen lock functionality. Once this is done, physical acquisition of the SIM card, media cards, and device backups occurs. Finally, the device is imaged, although many devices may be resistant to imaging if the passcode is not known or the device is locked.

There are four primary modes of data acquisition from mobile devices:

- Physical, by acquisition of the SIM card, memory cards, or backups
- Logical, which usually requires a forensic tool to create an image of the logical storage volumes
- Manual access, which involves reviewing the contents of the live, unlocked phone and taking pictures and notes about what is found
- Filesystem, which can provide details of deleted files as well as existing files and directories

Much like desktop and server operating system forensics, a key part of mobile forensics is knowing the key file locations for useful forensic data. Table 13.2 lists some of the key locations for iOS devices.

TABLE 13.2 Key iOS file locations

Location	Content
`com.apple.commcenter.plist`	Device identification data
`com.apple.Maps.plist`	Map search history and latitude/longitude data
`SystemConfiguration/com.apple.wifi.plist`	Wi-Fi network data
`Library/CallHistory/call_history.db`	Phone call logs
`Library/SMS/sms.db`	SMS messages
`Library/SMS/Attachments`	MMS files
`Library/Safari`	Safari web browser data
`Library/Caches/com.apple.WebAppCache/ApplicationCache.db`	Web browser cache
`Library/Accounts/Accounts3.sqlite`	Account information
`/private/var/mobile/Library/Caches/com.apple.routined/`	Frequent location data (binary plist)

Similar information exists on Android, Windows, and other devices, although different carriers and OS versions may place data in slightly different locations. As you can see from the partial list of important files in Table 13.2, mobile phones can provide a very detailed history of an individual's location, communications, and other data if all of their data can be acquired.

SANS provides a detailed smartphone acquisition guide in poster form at `digital-forensics.sans.org/media/DFIR-Smartphone-Forensics-Poster.pdf`, which breaks out iOS, Android, and other mobile operating system procedures.

Forensic Investigation: An Example

In the following section, you will learn the basics of a forensic analysis using FTK. Since we have already discussed imaging, we will start from a previously acquired forensic image and will perform analysis, including

- Import of the data into FTK, including indexing and case management
- Evidence of the data leakage
- Email communication with third parties about the files
- Web browser information pointing to antiforensic activities
- Evidence of application installs
- Evidence of filesystem changes, including renaming files

Remember that a full forensic examination of a system can involve more tasks than those listed here and that the scope and direction of the investigation will help to determine what those tasks are. You are also likely to encounter additional clues that will point you in new directions for forensic examination as you explore a system image.

Examples in this section were prepared using the Data Leakage Case found at `www.cfreds.nist.gov/data_leakage_case/data-leakage-case.html`, part of the NIST Computer Forensic Reference Data Sets (CFReDS). The case includes 60 different forensic tasks, including those listed in this chapter. If you want to practice forensic techniques in more depth, you can download the forensic dataset and a forensic toolkit like SIFT or CAINE to test your skills. The dd image file for just the Windows 7 workstation used in this case is 20 GB when extracted, so make sure you have plenty of available hard drive space. It is important to note that some companies may not want you to download tools like this and may have policies or even technology in place that will prevent it. Our technical editor from the first edition of this book had to get special permission to do so at her company!

Importing a Forensic Image

Once you have a forensic image in hand and have made a copy to use in your investigation, you will typically import it into your forensic tool. Figure 13.11 shows how information about the case is captured as an image is imported.

Once your image has been imported into a case and properly logged, the image is then indexed and analyzed. This includes identifying file types, searching slack and unallocated space, building an index of file timestamps, and other analysis items. This can take some time, especially with large drives. Figure 13.12 shows the forensic image used for this case partially through the indexing process.

FIGURE 13.11 Initial case information and tracking

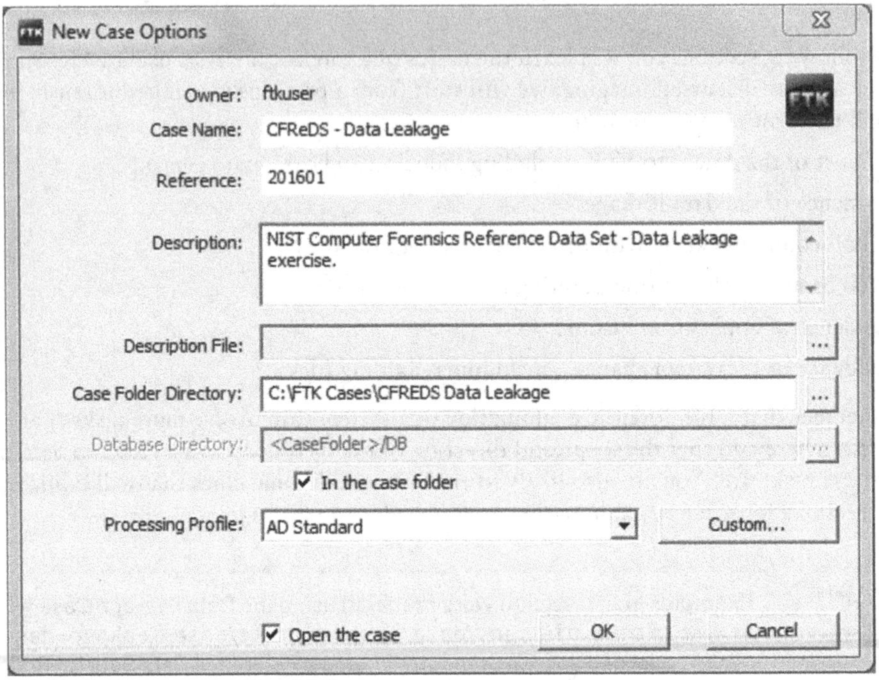

FIGURE 13.12 Case information and tracking partly through the indexing process

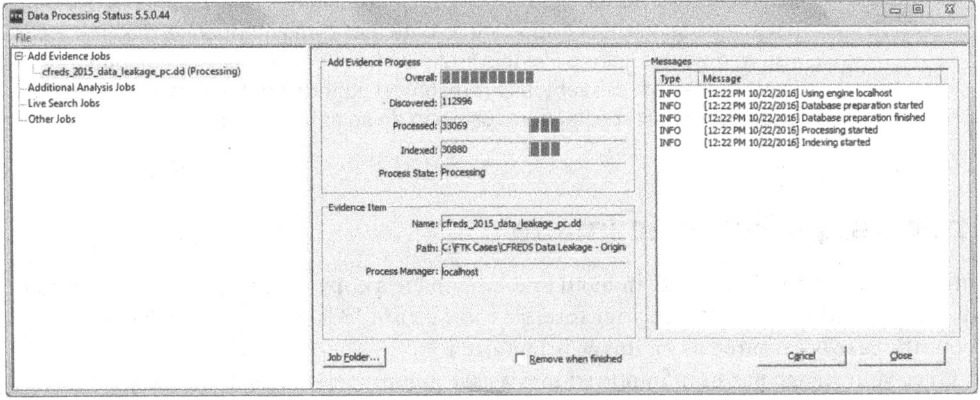

With indexing done, you can now begin to explore the forensic image. FTK provides a series of tabs with common evidence categories, including email, graphics, video, Internet/chat, bookmarks, and others. Most investigators will take some time to ensure that the operating system, time zone, and other computer information (such as which users have accounts on the system) are recorded at this stage.

Analyzing the Image

Since this is a data leakage case, Internet browser history and email are likely to be of particular interest. Figure 13.13 shows how email can be read via FTK's browser capability. We can see an email that was sent reading "successfully secured." Other emails also mention a USB device, and that spy would like it if the informant can deliver the storage devices directly. This provides another clue for further investigation.

FIGURE 13.13 Email extraction

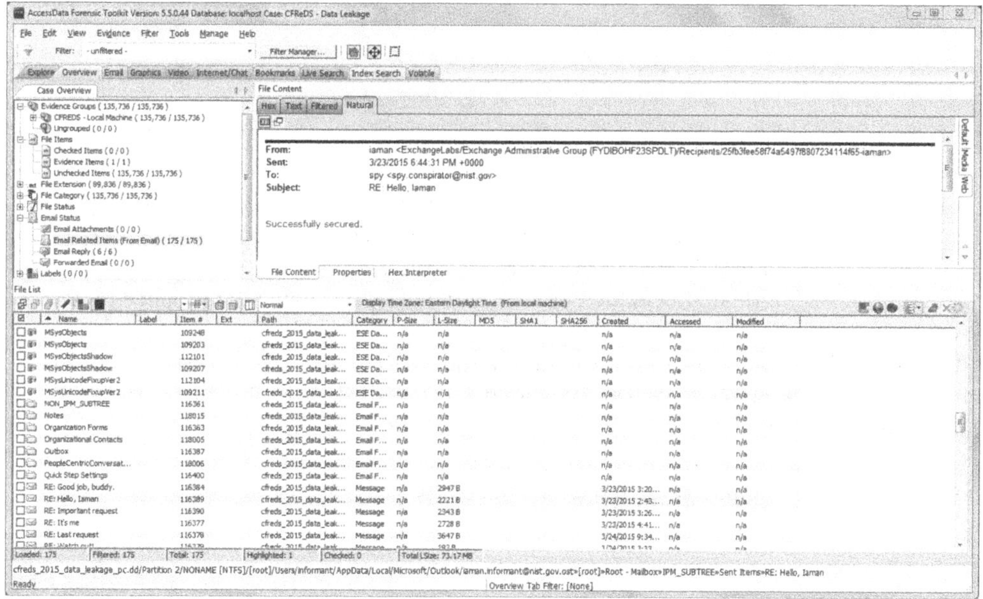

Searching the web browser history provides more information about the informant's likely behavior. The history file for Chrome includes searches for antiforensics techniques and a visit to the antiforensics techniques page of `forensicswiki.org`, as shown in Figure 13.14.

FIGURE 13.14 Web search history

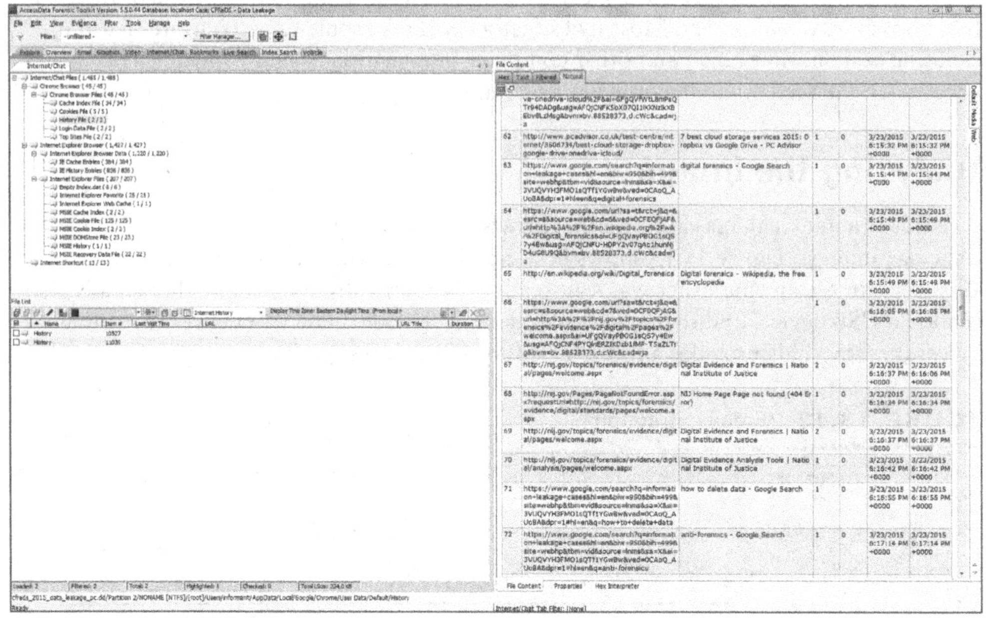

Since the informant searched for antiforensic techniques, it is likely that they applied them with some degree of success. A visit to the antiforensics techniques page, as well as searches for data that was deleted or otherwise hidden, is needed.

Some of this additional information can be gathered by reviewing data cached by Windows, including install information from the local user directories. Since the sample image is a Windows 7 machine, install information resides in `C:\Users\<username>\AppData\Local\Temp`. Checking there shows that iCloud was installed in the middle of the timeframe that email communications were occurring, as shown in Figure 13.15.

FIGURE 13.15 iCloud setup log with timestamp

File List

Normal | Display Time Zone: Eastern Daylight Time (From local machine)

Name	Label	Item #	Ext	Path	Category	P-Size	L-Size	MD5	SHA1	SHA256	Created	Accessed	Modified
TCD76D9.tmp		17026		cfreds_2015_data_leak...	Folder	48 B	48 B				3/23/2015 2:38...	3/23/2015 2:38...	3/23/2015 2:38...
TCD76FC.tmp		17018		cfreds_2015_data_leak...	Folder	48 B	48 B				3/23/2015 2:38...	3/23/2015 2:38...	3/23/2015 2:38...
TCD76FB.tmp		17738		cfreds_2015_data_leak...	Folder	48 B	48 B				3/23/2015 2:38...	3/23/2015 2:38...	3/23/2015 2:38...
TCD771D.tmp		17861		cfreds_2015_data_leak...	Folder	48 B	48 B				3/23/2015 2:38...	3/23/2015 2:38...	3/23/2015 2:38...
TCD7730.tmp		17009		cfreds_2015_data_leak...	Folder	48 B	48 B				3/23/2015 2:38...	3/23/2015 2:38...	3/23/2015 2:38...
TCD7733.tmp		16688		cfreds_2015_data_leak...	Folder	48 B	48 B				3/23/2015 2:38...	3/23/2015 2:38...	3/23/2015 2:38...
TCD7732.tmp		16690		cfreds_2015_data_leak...	Folder	48 B	48 B				3/23/2015 2:38...	3/23/2015 2:38...	3/23/2015 2:38...
TCD7784.tmp		16691		cfreds_2015_data_leak...	Folder	48 B	48 B				3/23/2015 2:38...	3/23/2015 2:38...	3/23/2015 2:38...
TCD7A63.tmp		17727		cfreds_2015_data_leak...	Folder	48 B	48 B				3/23/2015 2:38...	3/23/2015 2:38...	3/23/2015 2:38...
TCD7C0A.tmp		16682		cfreds_2015_data_leak...	Folder	48 B	48 B				3/23/2015 2:38...	3/23/2015 2:38...	3/23/2015 2:38...
TCD7D54.tmp		16680		cfreds_2015_data_leak...	Folder	48 B	48 B				3/23/2015 2:38...	3/23/2015 2:38...	3/23/2015 2:38...
TCD7E6F.tmp		16677		cfreds_2015_data_leak...	Folder	48 B	48 B				3/23/2015 2:38...	3/23/2015 2:38...	3/23/2015 2:38...
TCD8064.tmp		16674		cfreds_2015_data_leak...	Folder	48 B	48 B				3/23/2015 2:38...	3/23/2015 2:38...	3/23/2015 2:38...
CVRADAE.tmp.cvr		16671	cvr	cfreds_2015_data_leak...	Zero Le...	0 B	0 B				3/23/2015 3:27...	3/23/2015 3:27...	3/23/2015 3:27...
SetupAdmin394.log		16667	log	cfreds_2015_data_leak...	Text	1012 KB	1008 KB	a1bbb1...	5420d2...	0feb4e...	3/23/2015 4:00...	3/23/2015 4:00...	3/23/2015 4:01...
icloudsetupE88.log		16668	log	cfreds_2015_data_leak...	Text	4096 B	2481 B	0a3f78...	349bda...	26451c...	3/23/2015 4:00...	3/23/2015 4:00...	3/23/2015 4:02...
msohtmlclip1		17046		cfreds_2015_data_leak...	Folder	136 B	136 B				3/23/2015 5:02...	3/23/2015 5:02...	3/23/2015 5:02...
msohtmlclip		17403		cfreds_2015_data_leak...	Folder	48 B	48 B				3/23/2015 5:02...	3/23/2015 5:02...	3/23/2015 5:02...

Loaded: 129 | Filtered: 129 | Total: 154 | Highlighted: 1 | Checked: 0 | Total LSize: 12.78 MB

cfreds_2015_data_leakage_pc.dd/Partition 2/NONAME [NTFS]/[root]/Users/informant/AppData/Local/Temp/icloudsetupE88.log

Ready | Explore Tab Filter: [None]

FTK also indexes and displays deleted files, allowing you to see that CCleaner, a system cleanup program that removes browser history and cache and wipes other information useful for forensic investigations, was removed from the system in Figure 13.16, and that Eraser, a file wiping utility, appears to have been partially deleted but left a remnant directory in the Program Files folder. Both of these utilities are likely to be found as part of an antiforensics attempt, providing further evidence of the user's intention to delete evidence.

FIGURE 13.16 CCleaner remnant data via the Index Search function

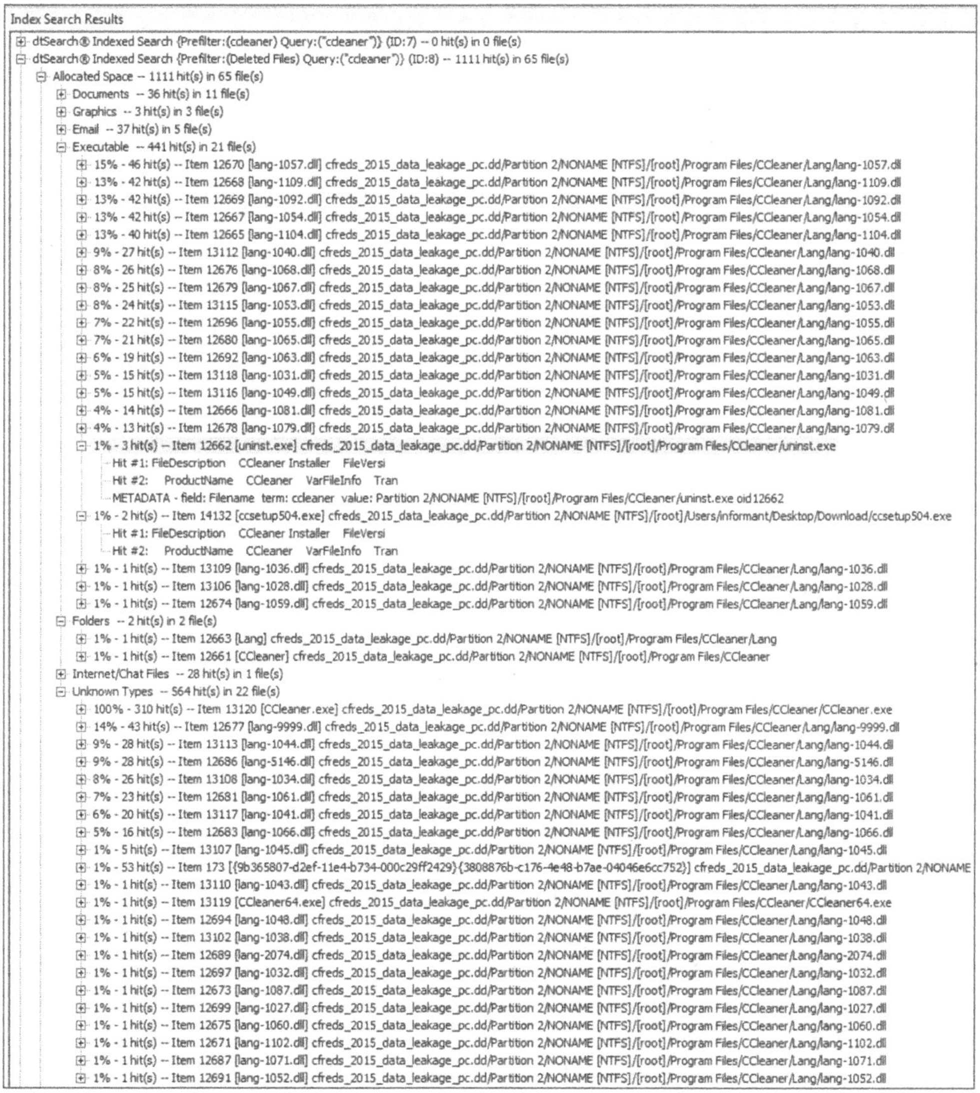

```
Index Search Results
dtSearch® Indexed Search {Prefilter:(ccleaner) Query:("ccleaner")} (ID:7) -- 0 hit(s) in 0 file(s)
dtSearch® Indexed Search {Prefilter:(Deleted Files) Query:("ccleaner")} (ID:8) -- 1111 hit(s) in 65 file(s)
  Allocated Space -- 1111 hit(s) in 65 file(s)
    Documents -- 36 hit(s) in 11 file(s)
    Graphics -- 3 hit(s) in 3 file(s)
    Email -- 37 hit(s) in 5 file(s)
    Executable -- 441 hit(s) in 21 file(s)
      15% - 46 hit(s) -- Item 12670 [lang-1057.dll] cfreds_2015_data_leakage_pc.dd/Partition 2/NONAME [NTFS]/[root]/Program Files/CCleaner/Lang/lang-1057.dll
      13% - 42 hit(s) -- Item 12668 [lang-1109.dll] cfreds_2015_data_leakage_pc.dd/Partition 2/NONAME [NTFS]/[root]/Program Files/CCleaner/Lang/lang-1109.dll
      13% - 42 hit(s) -- Item 12669 [lang-1092.dll] cfreds_2015_data_leakage_pc.dd/Partition 2/NONAME [NTFS]/[root]/Program Files/CCleaner/Lang/lang-1092.dll
      13% - 42 hit(s) -- Item 12667 [lang-1054.dll] cfreds_2015_data_leakage_pc.dd/Partition 2/NONAME [NTFS]/[root]/Program Files/CCleaner/Lang/lang-1054.dll
      13% - 40 hit(s) -- Item 12665 [lang-1104.dll] cfreds_2015_data_leakage_pc.dd/Partition 2/NONAME [NTFS]/[root]/Program Files/CCleaner/Lang/lang-1104.dll
      9% - 27 hit(s) -- Item 13112 [lang-1040.dll] cfreds_2015_data_leakage_pc.dd/Partition 2/NONAME [NTFS]/[root]/Program Files/CCleaner/Lang/lang-1040.dll
      8% - 26 hit(s) -- Item 12676 [lang-1068.dll] cfreds_2015_data_leakage_pc.dd/Partition 2/NONAME [NTFS]/[root]/Program Files/CCleaner/Lang/lang-1068.dll
      8% - 25 hit(s) -- Item 12679 [lang-1067.dll] cfreds_2015_data_leakage_pc.dd/Partition 2/NONAME [NTFS]/[root]/Program Files/CCleaner/Lang/lang-1067.dll
      8% - 24 hit(s) -- Item 13115 [lang-1053.dll] cfreds_2015_data_leakage_pc.dd/Partition 2/NONAME [NTFS]/[root]/Program Files/CCleaner/Lang/lang-1053.dll
      7% - 22 hit(s) -- Item 12696 [lang-1055.dll] cfreds_2015_data_leakage_pc.dd/Partition 2/NONAME [NTFS]/[root]/Program Files/CCleaner/Lang/lang-1055.dll
      7% - 21 hit(s) -- Item 12680 [lang-1065.dll] cfreds_2015_data_leakage_pc.dd/Partition 2/NONAME [NTFS]/[root]/Program Files/CCleaner/Lang/lang-1065.dll
      6% - 19 hit(s) -- Item 12692 [lang-1063.dll] cfreds_2015_data_leakage_pc.dd/Partition 2/NONAME [NTFS]/[root]/Program Files/CCleaner/Lang/lang-1063.dll
      5% - 15 hit(s) -- Item 13118 [lang-1031.dll] cfreds_2015_data_leakage_pc.dd/Partition 2/NONAME [NTFS]/[root]/Program Files/CCleaner/Lang/lang-1031.dll
      5% - 15 hit(s) -- Item 13116 [lang-1049.dll] cfreds_2015_data_leakage_pc.dd/Partition 2/NONAME [NTFS]/[root]/Program Files/CCleaner/Lang/lang-1049.dll
      4% - 14 hit(s) -- Item 12666 [lang-1081.dll] cfreds_2015_data_leakage_pc.dd/Partition 2/NONAME [NTFS]/[root]/Program Files/CCleaner/Lang/lang-1081.dll
      4% - 13 hit(s) -- Item 12678 [lang-1079.dll] cfreds_2015_data_leakage_pc.dd/Partition 2/NONAME [NTFS]/[root]/Program Files/CCleaner/Lang/lang-1079.dll
      1% - 3 hit(s) -- Item 12662 [uninst.exe] cfreds_2015_data_leakage_pc.dd/Partition 2/NONAME [NTFS]/[root]/Program Files/CCleaner/uninst.exe
        Hit #1: FileDescription   CCleaner Installer   FileVersi
        Hit #2:   ProductName   CCleaner   VarFileInfo   Tran
        METADATA - field: Filename  term: ccleaner  value: Partition 2/NONAME [NTFS]/[root]/Program Files/CCleaner/uninst.exe oid12662
      1% - 2 hit(s) -- Item 14132 [ccsetup504.exe] cfreds_2015_data_leakage_pc.dd/Partition 2/NONAME [NTFS]/[root]/Users/informant/Desktop/Download/ccsetup504.exe
        Hit #1: FileDescription   CCleaner Installer   FileVersi
        Hit #2:   ProductName   CCleaner   VarFileInfo   Tran
      1% - 1 hit(s) -- Item 13109 [lang-1036.dll] cfreds_2015_data_leakage_pc.dd/Partition 2/NONAME [NTFS]/[root]/Program Files/CCleaner/Lang/lang-1036.dll
      1% - 1 hit(s) -- Item 13106 [lang-1028.dll] cfreds_2015_data_leakage_pc.dd/Partition 2/NONAME [NTFS]/[root]/Program Files/CCleaner/Lang/lang-1028.dll
      1% - 1 hit(s) -- Item 12674 [lang-1059.dll] cfreds_2015_data_leakage_pc.dd/Partition 2/NONAME [NTFS]/[root]/Program Files/CCleaner/Lang/lang-1059.dll
    Folders -- 2 hit(s) in 2 file(s)
      1% - 1 hit(s) -- Item 12663 [Lang] cfreds_2015_data_leakage_pc.dd/Partition 2/NONAME [NTFS]/[root]/Program Files/CCleaner/Lang
      1% - 1 hit(s) -- Item 12661 [CCleaner] cfreds_2015_data_leakage_pc.dd/Partition 2/NONAME [NTFS]/[root]/Program Files/CCleaner
    Internet/Chat Files -- 28 hit(s) in 1 file(s)
    Unknown Types -- 564 hit(s) in 22 file(s)
      100% - 310 hit(s) -- Item 13120 [CCleaner.exe] cfreds_2015_data_leakage_pc.dd/Partition 2/NONAME [NTFS]/[root]/Program Files/CCleaner/CCleaner.exe
      14% - 43 hit(s) -- Item 12677 [lang-9999.dll] cfreds_2015_data_leakage_pc.dd/Partition 2/NONAME [NTFS]/[root]/Program Files/CCleaner/Lang/lang-9999.dll
      9% - 28 hit(s) -- Item 13113 [lang-1044.dll] cfreds_2015_data_leakage_pc.dd/Partition 2/NONAME [NTFS]/[root]/Program Files/CCleaner/Lang/lang-1044.dll
      9% - 28 hit(s) -- Item 12686 [lang-5146.dll] cfreds_2015_data_leakage_pc.dd/Partition 2/NONAME [NTFS]/[root]/Program Files/CCleaner/Lang/lang-5146.dll
      8% - 26 hit(s) -- Item 13108 [lang-1034.dll] cfreds_2015_data_leakage_pc.dd/Partition 2/NONAME [NTFS]/[root]/Program Files/CCleaner/Lang/lang-1034.dll
      7% - 23 hit(s) -- Item 12681 [lang-1061.dll] cfreds_2015_data_leakage_pc.dd/Partition 2/NONAME [NTFS]/[root]/Program Files/CCleaner/Lang/lang-1061.dll
      6% - 20 hit(s) -- Item 13117 [lang-1041.dll] cfreds_2015_data_leakage_pc.dd/Partition 2/NONAME [NTFS]/[root]/Program Files/CCleaner/Lang/lang-1041.dll
      5% - 16 hit(s) -- Item 12683 [lang-1066.dll] cfreds_2015_data_leakage_pc.dd/Partition 2/NONAME [NTFS]/[root]/Program Files/CCleaner/Lang/lang-1066.dll
      1% - 5 hit(s) -- Item 13107 [lang-1045.dll] cfreds_2015_data_leakage_pc.dd/Partition 2/NONAME [NTFS]/[root]/Program Files/CCleaner/Lang/lang-1045.dll
      1% - 53 hit(s) -- Item 173 [{9b365807-d2ef-11e4-b734-000c29ff2429}{3808876b-c176-4e48-b7ae-04046e6cc752}] cfreds_2015_data_leakage_pc.dd/Partition 2/NONAME
      1% - 1 hit(s) -- Item 13110 [lang-1043.dll] cfreds_2015_data_leakage_pc.dd/Partition 2/NONAME [NTFS]/[root]/Program Files/CCleaner/Lang/lang-1043.dll
      1% - 1 hit(s) -- Item 13119 [CCleaner64.exe] cfreds_2015_data_leakage_pc.dd/Partition 2/NONAME [NTFS]/[root]/Program Files/CCleaner/CCleaner64.exe
      1% - 1 hit(s) -- Item 12694 [lang-1048.dll] cfreds_2015_data_leakage_pc.dd/Partition 2/NONAME [NTFS]/[root]/Program Files/CCleaner/Lang/lang-1048.dll
      1% - 1 hit(s) -- Item 13102 [lang-1038.dll] cfreds_2015_data_leakage_pc.dd/Partition 2/NONAME [NTFS]/[root]/Program Files/CCleaner/Lang/lang-1038.dll
      1% - 1 hit(s) -- Item 12689 [lang-2074.dll] cfreds_2015_data_leakage_pc.dd/Partition 2/NONAME [NTFS]/[root]/Program Files/CCleaner/Lang/lang-2074.dll
      1% - 1 hit(s) -- Item 12697 [lang-1032.dll] cfreds_2015_data_leakage_pc.dd/Partition 2/NONAME [NTFS]/[root]/Program Files/CCleaner/Lang/lang-1032.dll
      1% - 1 hit(s) -- Item 12673 [lang-1087.dll] cfreds_2015_data_leakage_pc.dd/Partition 2/NONAME [NTFS]/[root]/Program Files/CCleaner/Lang/lang-1087.dll
      1% - 1 hit(s) -- Item 12699 [lang-1027.dll] cfreds_2015_data_leakage_pc.dd/Partition 2/NONAME [NTFS]/[root]/Program Files/CCleaner/Lang/lang-1027.dll
      1% - 1 hit(s) -- Item 12675 [lang-1060.dll] cfreds_2015_data_leakage_pc.dd/Partition 2/NONAME [NTFS]/[root]/Program Files/CCleaner/Lang/lang-1060.dll
      1% - 1 hit(s) -- Item 12671 [lang-1102.dll] cfreds_2015_data_leakage_pc.dd/Partition 2/NONAME [NTFS]/[root]/Program Files/CCleaner/Lang/lang-1102.dll
      1% - 1 hit(s) -- Item 12687 [lang-1071.dll] cfreds_2015_data_leakage_pc.dd/Partition 2/NONAME [NTFS]/[root]/Program Files/CCleaner/Lang/lang-1071.dll
      1% - 1 hit(s) -- Item 12691 [lang-1052.dll] cfreds_2015_data_leakage_pc.dd/Partition 2/NONAME [NTFS]/[root]/Program Files/CCleaner/Lang/lang-1052.dll
```

At the end of the timeline for the informant in our case, a resignation letter is created and printed. This can be found easily using a timeline of events on the system, or as part of a manual file review using the indexed list of files and searching for Microsoft Office documents, as shown in Figure 13.17.

FIGURE 13.17 Resignation letter found based on document type

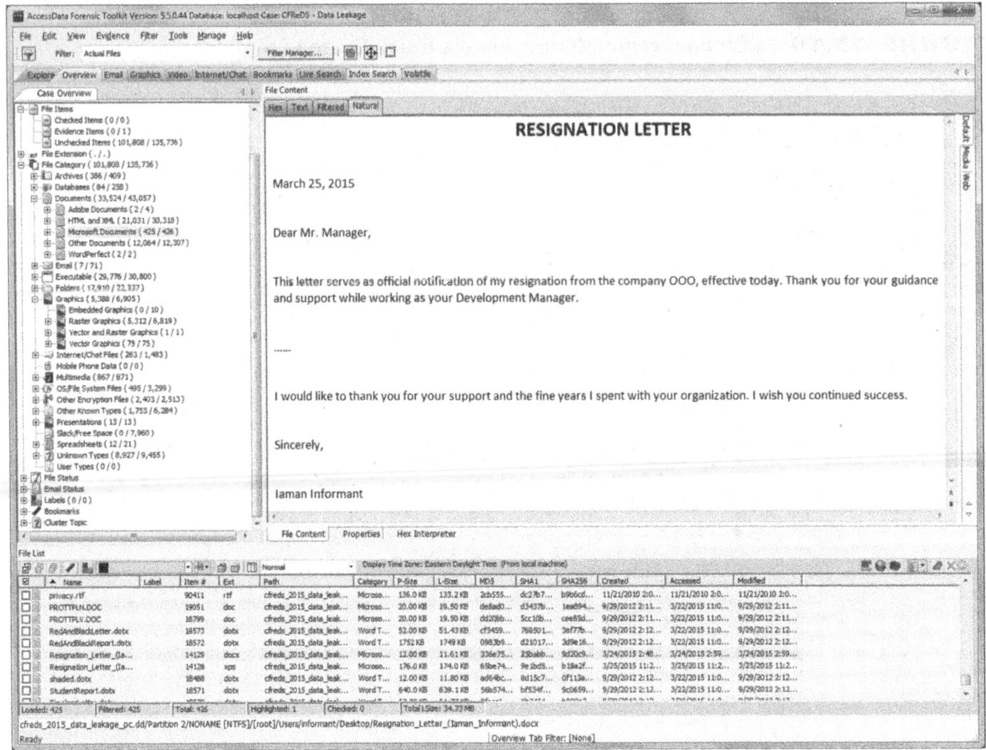

Reporting

The final stage of forensic investigation is preparing and presenting a report. Reports should include three major components: the goals and scope of the investigation; the target or targets of the forensic activities, including all systems, devices, and media; and a complete listing of the findings and results.

Goals of the Investigation

This section of your report should include the goals of the investigation, including the initial scope statement for the forensic activities. This section will also typically include information about the person or organization that asked for the investigation. An example of a statement of the goals of an investigation is "John Smith, the Director of Human Resources, requested that we review Alice Potter's workstation, email, and the systems she administers to ensure that the data that was recently leaked to a competitor was not sent from her email account or workstation."

Targets

The report you create should include a list of all the devices, systems, and media that was captured and analyzed. Targets should be all listed in your tracking notes and chain-of-custody forms if you are using them. The same level of detail used to record the system or device should be used in this listing. A sample entry might read:

> Alice Potter's workstation, internal inventory number 6108, Lenovo W540 laptop, with Samsung SSD serial number S12KMFBD644850, item number 344

If large numbers of devices or systems were inspected, the full listing of targets is often moved to an appendix, and the listing of what was reviewed will list a high-level overview of systems, applications, devices, and other media, with a reference to the appendix for full detail.

Findings and Analysis

Findings are the most critical part of the document and should list what was discovered, how it was discovered, and why it is important. The Stroz Friedberg forensic investigation conducted as part of a contract dispute about the ownership of Facebook provides an example of the detail needed in forensic findings, as shown in Figure 13.18. While the report is now dated, many of the same forensic artifacts and concepts still show up—although floppy disks have been replaced with flash media and cloud storage!

FIGURE 13.18 Sample forensic finding from Stroz Friedberg's Facebook contract investigation

Stroz Friedberg found seven entries related to this file on a floppy disk produced in Chicago, Illinois. One of the seven entries relates to an active file and the remaining six relate to deleted versions of the file. The active file purports to have been created, last modified, and last accessed on July 23, 2004. However, two of the records related to deleted copies indicate that the file was created, last modified, and last accessed on the earlier date of October 21, 2003, as follows:

File Name	State	File Created	Last Written	Last Accessed
Mark harvard emails up to Dec.doc	Active	07/23/2004 09:47:01 AM	07/23/2004 06:15:54 PM	7/23/2004
Mark harvard emails up to Dec.doc	Deleted	10/21/2003 11:54:12 AM	10/21/2003 11:54:14 AM	10/21/2003
Mark harvard emails up to Dec.doc	Deleted	10/21/2003 11:54:49 AM	10/21/2003 11:54:50 AM	10/21/2003

Again, a document that was last modified in October 2003 could not contain authentic emails from December 2003. It also is highly unlikely that this file would be named "Mark harvard emails up to Dec.doc" if it actually had been created and last modified in October 2003. This discrepancy likely resulted from the files having been saved with a computer whose system clock had been backdated to October 21, 2003, which is the same date as the deleted version of "Mark emails july04.doc" was saved.

Wired provided the full Stroz Friedberg forensic report from the public record for the case, and it can be found at `www.wired.com/images_blogs/threatlevel/2012/03/celiginvestigation.pdf`.

Summary

Cybersecurity analysts need to understand the tools, techniques, and processes required to conduct forensics. Forensics toolkits are typically built around powerful forensic workstations that may run a purpose-built forensic investigation suite or may provide individual forensic utilities and tools. Toolkits also often include write blockers, forensic duplicators, media, and documentation equipment and supplies. Specialized tools exist for mobile device forensics, law enforcement, and other types of specific forensic investigations.

Forensic software provides the ability to image and analyze systems, carve filesystems, and acquire data from various types of drives and devices. It also often supports important forensic functions, allowing analysts to maintain chain-of-custody documentation to provide who had access to an image and what was done with it. Hashing and validation are also critical to prove that forensic images match the original.

The forensic process includes identifying targets, conducting acquisition and validating that the images match, analysis, and reporting. A host of specific tools, techniques, file locations, and other elements come together as part of an investigation to create a complete forensic case. In the end, a forensic report must include the goals of the investigation, the targets, a listing of what was found, and careful analysis of what that data means.

Exam Essentials

Explain the purpose of forensic software and how it provides specialized capabilities for investigations. Forensic tools include analysis utilities that can provide timelines; file validation; filesystem analysis for changes, deletions, and other details; log file viewing; and other analysis. Key data acquisition capabilities include dead, or offline system, cloning and validation via hashing, the ability to identify changes to binaries and other files, filesystem carving, chain-of-custody and activity logging, and live system imaging. Password cracking and recovery, as well as the ability to decrypt common types of encrypted files, are necessary for many systems. Mobile forensic tools provide the ability to perform the same types of activities for iOS, Android, and other mobile platforms and their unique types of data.

Know where forensic activities take place and in what contexts and environments. Forensic activities occur on the network, endpoint systems and devices, on mobile devices, and in cloud, virtualization and containerized environments. Tools like Wireshark, tcpdump, and dd are used to conduct these investigations.

Be familiar with what's involved in a forensic investigation. This stage includes scoping, identifying locations of relevant data, planning, acquisition, analysis, and reporting. Targets include system information; file modification, access, and change detail; lots; user artifacts; and stored data like memory dumps, shadow copies, and Recycle Bin contents. Acquisition requires forensic validation and care to not modify the source data, typically including the use of write blockers.

Describe what tools are used in forensic investigations to review what occurred on a targeted system or device. Chain of custody and tracking of actions taken are critical to conducting a sound forensic investigation. Tools to capture and read network traffic, such as Wireshark, as well as endpoint tools that can read email, web history, deleted files, installed files, disk, memory, and other events make analysis simpler. Forensic discoveries will often result in further work to fully understand the timeline of events on a system.

Lab Exercises

Activity 13.1: Create a Disk Image

In this exercise you will use dd to create a disk image and then verify the checksum of the image.

Part 1: Boot a Kali Linux system and mount a drive

1. Start your Kali Linux virtual machine.
2. Select a USB thumb drive that is formatted as FAT32 to make an image of for this practice session. A smaller drive will be faster to image, and you should make sure you image a drive smaller than the space you have available for your Kali Linux system.
3. In the Devices menu for the running Kali virtual machine, select USB and then the drive you have inserted. The device should now show up on your Kali Linux desktop.
4. Verify that you can navigate to the drive from the command line. Open a terminal window, then navigate to `/dev/disk/by-label`, and make sure you see the name of the thumb drive you have mounted.

Part 2: Clone the drive

1. Create a temporary working directory for your volume by running the following in your terminal window:

```
mkdir ~/tmp
```

This will create a directory called `tmp` in your `home` directory.

2. Create an MD5 checksum of the volume you intend to clone in your home directory:

```
md5sum /dev/disk/by-label/[label of your drive] > ~/exercise7_1_original.md5
```

3. Clone the volume or disk:

```
dd if=/dev/disk/by-label/[label of your drive] of=~/tmp/exercise7_1_disk.img bs=64k
```

4. Once this completes, verify the integrity of the image using MD5:

```
md5sum ~/tmp/exercise7_1_disk.img > ~/exercise7_1_clone.md5
```

5. Now compare the MD5 files. You can do that by using the `more` command to view the files, or you can record the values here:

   ____

   ____

   The values should be the same if your clone was successful.

Activity 13.2: Conduct the NIST Rhino Hunt

The National Institute of Standards and Technology provides a set of practice forensic images that can be freely downloaded and used to hone your forensic skills. You can find the full set at `www.cfreds.nist.gov`. For this exercise we will use the Rhino hunt scenario as well as the SANS SIFT image available from `digital-forensics.sans.org/community/downloads`.

1. Run SIFT. If you prefer VMware, you can run it directly; otherwise, use the import tool to import it into VirtualBox. (If you import the VM into VirtualBox, you will need to run `sudo apt-get install virtualbox-guest-dkms` and then reboot to get a useful screen resolution.)
2. Log in using the default username with the password `forensics`.
3. Download the SANS Rhino hunt:

```
wget http://www.cfreds.nist.gov/dfrws/DFRWS2005-RODEO.zip
```

4. Unzip the Rhino hunt:

```
unzip DFRWS2005-RODEO.zip
```

5. Use SIFT to find the rhino pictures.
   - Mount the file:

   ```
   sudo mount -o loop, ro RHINOUSB.dd /mnt/usb
   ```

   - Review the contents of the mount:

   ```
   ls /mnt/usb
   ```

Note that you will see only two recipes for gumbo. Something was done to this drive that overwrote the original contents, and they need to be recovered!

Next we will recover deleted files using foremost, a utility that automatically recovers files based on file headers and other information.

6. Create a directory for the output:

```
mkdir output
```

7. Run foremost against the RHINOUSB image.

```
foremost -o output/ RHINOUSB.dd
```

8. Review the output.

To open the file you have recovered, click the filing cabinet icon at the top left of the screen, navigate to Home ➢ Output ➢ Doc, and then double-click on the DOC file you recovered. Read to the end of the file to determine what happened to the hard drive.

Once you know where the hard drive went, you are done with this exercise. The Rhino hunt has a lot more to it, so feel free to continue based on the NIST page's instructions.

Activity 13.3: Security Tools

Match each of the following tools to the correct description:

dd	A memory forensics and analysis suite
md5sum	A GUI network traffic sniffer
Volatility Framework	A device used to prevent forensic software from modifying a drive while accessing it
FTK	Used to validate whether a drive copy is forensically sound
Eraser	A Linux tool used to create disk images
Write blocker	A command-line network packet sniffer
WinDbg	A full-featured forensic suite
Forensic drive duplicator	A tool used to review Windows memory dumps
Wireshark	A drive and file wiping utility sometimes used for anti-forensic purposes
tcpdump	A device designed to create a complete forensic image and validate it without a PC

Review Questions

1. Which format does dd produce files in while disk imaging?
   A. ddf
   B. RAW
   C. EN01
   D. OVF

2. File carving is used to find file remnants found in clusters on disks that have been only partially rewritten by new files. What is the technical term for where these files are found?
   A. Outer
   B. Slack
   C. Unallocated space
   D. Non-Euclidean

3. Mike is looking for information about files that were changed on a Windows endpoint system. Which of the following is least likely to contain useful information for his investigation?
   A. The MFT
   B. INDX files
   C. Event logs
   D. Volume shadow copies

4. Alice wants to copy a drive without any chance of it being modified by the copying process. What type of device should she use to ensure that this does not happen during her data acquisition process?
   A. A read blocker
   B. A drive cloner
   C. A write blocker
   D. A hash validator

5. Frederick's organization has been informed that data must be preserved due to pending legal action. What is this type of requirement called?
   A. A retainer
   B. A legal hold
   C. A data freeze
   D. An extra-legal hold

6. What two files may contain encryption keys normally stored only in memory on a Window system?
   - A. The MFT and the hash file
   - B. The Registry and hibernation files
   - C. Core dumps and encryption logs
   - D. Core dumps and hibernation files

7. Jeff is investigating a system compromise and knows that the first event was reported on October 5th. What forensic tool capability should he use to map other events found in logs and files to this date?
   - A. A timeline
   - B. A log viewer
   - C. Registry analysis
   - D. Timestamp validator

8. During her forensic copy validation process, Danielle hashed the original, cloned the image files, and received the following MD5 sums. What is likely wrong?

```
b49794e007e909c00a51ae208cacb169  original.img
d9ff8a0cf6bc0ab066b6416e7e7abf35  clone.img
```

   - A. The original was modified.
   - B. The clone was modified.
   - C. dd failed.
   - D. An unknown change or problem occurred.

9. Jennifer wants to perform memory analysis and forensics for Windows, MacOS, and Linux systems. Which of the following is best suited to her needs?
   - A. LiME
   - B. DumpIt
   - C. fmem
   - D. The Volatility Framework

10. Alex is conducting a forensic examination of a Windows system and wants to determine if an application was installed. Where can he find the Windows installer log files for a user named Jim?
   - A. `C:\Windows\System 32\Installers`
   - B. `C:\Windows\Install.log`
   - C. `C:\Windows\Jim\Install.log`
   - D. `C:\Windows\Jim\AppData\Local\Temp`

11. Kathleen needs to find data contained in memory but only has an image of an offline Windows system. Where does she have the best chance of recovering the information she needs?
    - A. The Registry
    - B. `%SystemRoot%\MEMORY.DMP`
    - C. A System Restore point file
    - D. `%SystemRoot%/WinDbg`

12. Carl does not have the ability to capture data from a cell phone using mobile forensic or imaging software, and the phone does not have removable storage. Fortunately, the phone was not set up with a PIN or screen lock. What is his best option to ensure he can see email and other data stored there?
    - A. Physical acquisition
    - B. Logical access
    - C. Filesystem access
    - D. Manual access

13. What forensic issue might the presence of a program like CCleaner indicate?
    - A. Antiforensic activities
    - B. Full disk encryption
    - C. Malware packing
    - D. MAC time modifications

14. Which of the following is *not* a potential issue with live imaging of a system?
    - A. Remnant data from the imaging tool
    - B. Unallocated space will be captured
    - C. Memory or drive contents may change during the imaging process
    - D. Malware may detect the imaging tool and work to avoid it

15. During his investigation, Jeff, a certified forensic examiner, is provided with a drive image created by an IT staff member and is asked to add it to his forensic case. What is the most important issue that Jeff could encounter if the case goes to court and his procedures are questioned?
    - A. Bad checksums
    - B. Hash mismatch
    - C. Antiforensic activities
    - D. Inability to certify chain of custody

16. Jeff is investigating a system that is running malware that he believes encrypts its data on the drive. What process should he use to have the best chance of viewing that data in an unencrypted form?
    - A. Live imaging
    - B. Offline imaging

C. Brute-force encryption cracking

D. Cause a system crash and analyze the memory dump

17. Susan needs to capture network traffic from a Linux server that does not use a GUI. What packet capture utility is found on many Linux systems and works from the command line?

A. tcpdump

B. netdd

C. Wireshark

D. snifman

18. During a forensic investigation Ben asks Chris to sit with him and to sign off on the actions he has taken. What is he doing?

A. Maintaining chain of custody

B. Over-the-shoulder validation

C. Pair forensics

D. Separation of duties

19. Which tool is *not* commonly used to generate the hash of a forensic copy?

A. MD5

B. FTK

C. SHA1

D. AES

20. Which of the following issues makes both cloud and virtualized environments more difficult to perform forensics on?

A. Other organizations manage them.

B. Systems may be ephemeral.

C. No forensic tools work in both environments.

D. Drive images cannot be verified.

Containment, Eradication, and Recovery

THE COMPTIA CYBERSECURITY ANALYST (CYSA+) EXAM OBJECTIVES COVERED IN THIS CHAPTER INCLUDE:

✓ **Domain 4.0: Incident Response**

- 4.2: Given a scenario, apply the appropriate incident response procedure.

Chapter 11, "Building an Incident Response Program," provided an overview of the steps required to build and implement a cybersecurity incident response program according to the process advocated by the National Institute of Standards and Technology (NIST). In their *Computer Security Incident Handling Guide*, NIST outlines the four-phase incident response process shown in Figure 14.1.

FIGURE 14.1 Incident response process

Source: NIST SP 800-61: *Computer Security Incident Handling Guide*

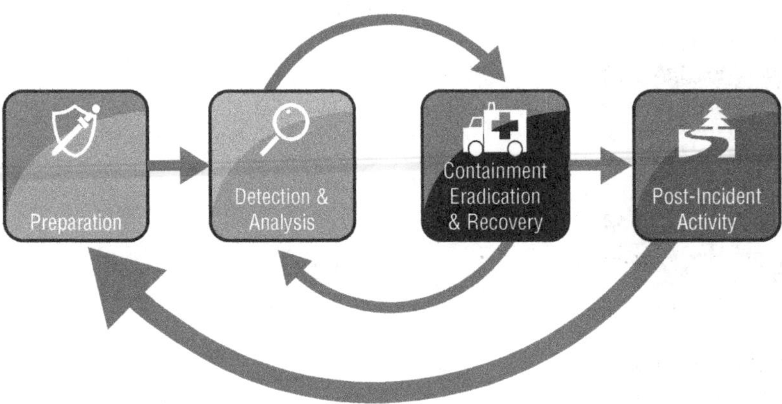

The remainder of Chapter 11 provided an overview of the Preparation phase of incident response. Chapter 12, "Analyzing Indicators of Compromise," and Chapter 13, "Performing Forensic Analysis and Techniques," covered the details behind the Detection and Analysis phase, including sources of cybersecurity information and forensic analysis. This chapter concludes the coverage of CySA+ Domain 4.0: Incident Response with a detailed look at the final two phases of incident response: Containment, Eradication, and Recovery, and Postincident Activity.

Containing the Damage

The Containment, Eradication, and Recovery phase of incident response moves the organization from the primarily passive incident response activities that take place during the Detection and Analysis phase to more active undertakings. Once the organization understands that a cybersecurity incident is underway, it takes actions designed to minimize the damage caused by the incident and restore normal operations as quickly as possible.

Containment is the first activity that takes place during this phase, and it should begin as quickly as possible after analysts determine that an incident is underway. Containment activities are designed to isolate the incident and prevent it from spreading further. If that phrase sounds somewhat vague, that's because containment means very different things in the context of different types of security incidents. For example, if the organization is experiencing active exfiltration of data from a credit card processing system, incident responders might contain the damage by disconnecting that system from the network, preventing the attackers from continuing to exfiltrate information. On the other hand, if the organization is experiencing a denial-of-service attack against its website, disconnecting the network connection would simply help the attacker achieve its objective. In that case, containment might include placing filters on an upstream Internet connection that blocks all inbound traffic from networks involved in the attack or blocks web requests that bear a certain signature.

Exam Note

When you take the exam, remember that containment is a critical priority. You want to stop the spread of any potential security threats before you worry about eradicating the damage or recovering data.

Containment activities typically aren't perfect and often cause some collateral damage that disrupts normal business activity. Consider the two examples described in the previous paragraph. Disconnecting a credit card processing system from the network may bring transactions to a halt, causing potentially significant losses of business. Similarly, blocking large swaths of inbound web traffic may render the site inaccessible to some legitimate users. Incident responders undertaking containment strategies must understand the potential side effects of their actions while weighing them against the greater benefit to the organization.

Containment Strategy Criteria

Selecting appropriate containment strategies is one of the most difficult tasks facing incident responders. Containment approaches that are too drastic may have an unacceptable impact on business operations. On the other hand, responders who select weak containment approaches may find that the incident escalates to cause even more damage.

In the *Computer Security Incident Handling Guide*, NIST recommends using the following criteria to develop an appropriate containment strategy and weigh it against business interests:

- Potential damage to and theft of resources
- Need for evidence preservation
- Service availability (e.g., network connectivity, services provided to external parties)
- Time and resources needed to implement the strategy
- Effectiveness of the strategy (e.g., partial containment, full containment)
- Duration of the solution (e.g., emergency workaround to be removed in four hours, temporary workaround to be removed in two weeks, permanent solution)

Unfortunately, there's no formula or decision tree that guarantees responders will make the "right" decision while responding to an incident. Incident responders should understand these criteria, the intent of management, and their technical and business operating environment. Armed with this information, responders will be well positioned to follow their best judgment and select an appropriate containment strategy.

Segmentation

Cybersecurity analysts often use *network segmentation* as a proactive strategy to prevent the spread of future security incidents. For example, the network shown in Figure 14.2 is designed to segment different types of users from each other and from critical systems. An attacker who is able to gain access to the guest network would not be able to interact with systems belonging to employees or in the datacenter without traversing the network firewall.

You learned how network segmentation is used as a proactive control in a defense-in-depth approach to information security in Chapter 7, "Infrastructure Security and Controls."

In addition to being used as a proactive control, network segmentation may play a crucial role in incident response. During the early stages of an incident, responders may realize that a portion of systems are compromised but wish to continue to observe the activity on those systems while they determine other appropriate responses. However, they certainly want to protect other systems on the network from those potentially compromised systems.

Figure 14.3 shows an example of how an organization might apply network segmentation during an incident response effort. Cybersecurity analysts suspect that several systems in the datacenter were compromised and built a separate virtual LAN (VLAN) to contain those systems. That VLAN, called the quarantine network, is segmented from the rest of the datacenter network and controlled by very strict firewall rules. Putting the systems on this network segment provides some degree of isolation, preventing them from damaging systems on other segments but allowing continued live analysis efforts.

FIGURE 14.2 Proactive network segmentation

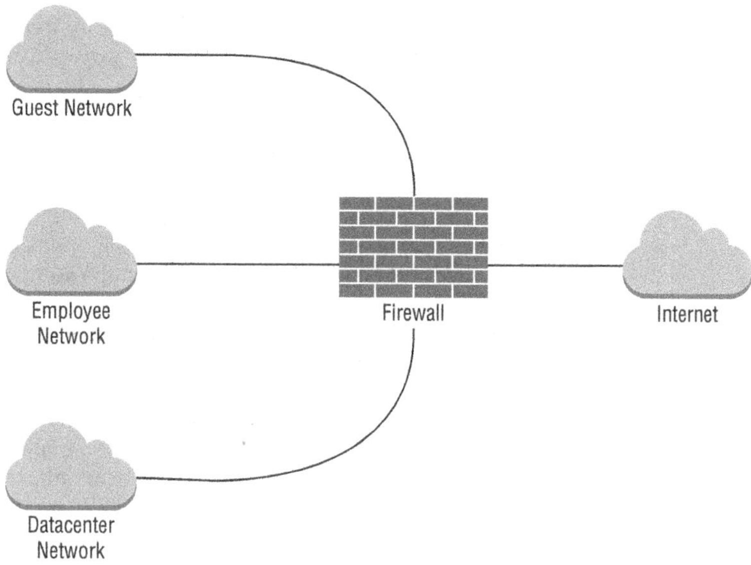

FIGURE 14.3 Network segmentation for incident response

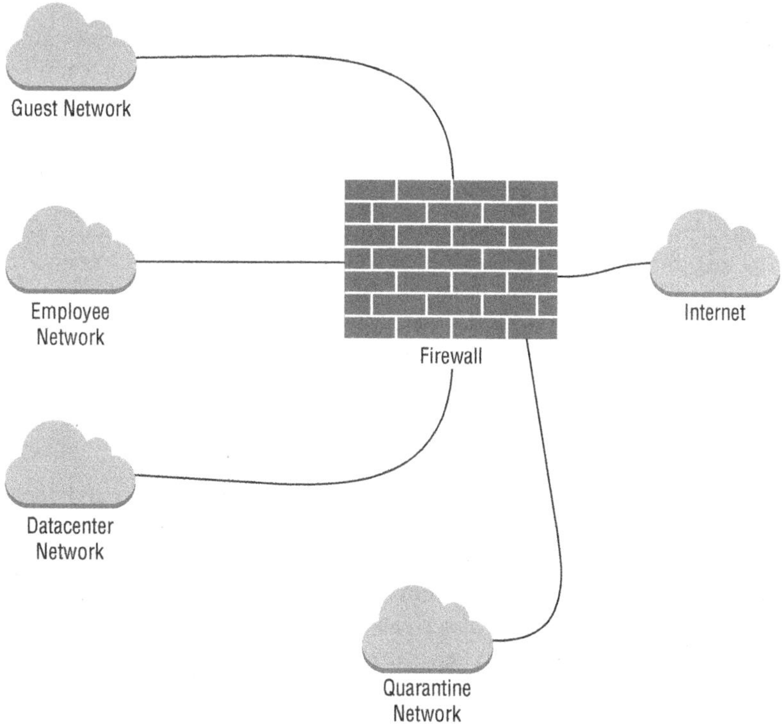

Isolation

Although segmentation does limit the access that attackers have to the remainder of the network, it sometimes doesn't go far enough to meet containment objectives. Cybersecurity analysts may instead decide that it is necessary to use stronger *isolation* practices to cut off an attack. Two primary isolation techniques may be used during a cybersecurity incident response effort: isolating affected systems and isolating the attacker.

Segmentation and isolation strategies carry with them significant risks to the organization. First, the attacker retains access to the compromised system, creating the potential for further expansion of the security incident. Second, the compromised system may be used to attack other systems on the Internet. In the best case, an attack launched from the organization's network against a third party may lead to some difficult conversations with cybersecurity colleagues at other firms. In the worst case, the courts may hold the organization liable for knowingly allowing the use of their network in an attack. Cybersecurity analysts considering a segmentation or isolation approach to containment should consult with both management and legal counsel.

Isolating Affected Systems

Isolating affected systems is, quite simply, taking segmentation to the next level. Affected systems are completely disconnected from the remainder of the network, although they may still be able to communicate with each other and the attacker over the Internet. Figure 14.4 shows an example of taking the quarantine VLAN from the segmentation strategy and converting it to an isolation approach.

Notice that the only difference between Figures 14.3 and 14.4 is where the quarantine network is connected. In the segmentation approach, the network is connected to the firewall and may have some limited access to other networked systems. In the isolation approach, the quarantine network connects directly to the Internet and has no access to other systems. In reality, this approach may be implemented by simply altering firewall rules rather than bypassing the firewall entirely. The objective is to continue to allow the attacker to access the isolated systems but restrict their ability to access other systems and cause further damage.

Isolating the Attacker

Isolating the attacker is an interesting variation on the isolation strategy and depends on the use of *sandbox* systems that are set up purely to monitor attacker activity and that do not contain any information or resources of value to the attacker. Placing attackers in a sandboxed environment allows continued observation in a fairly safe, contained environment. Some organizations use honeypot systems for this purpose. For more information on honeypots, see Chapter 1, "Today's Cybersecurity Analyst."

FIGURE 14.4 Network isolation for incident response

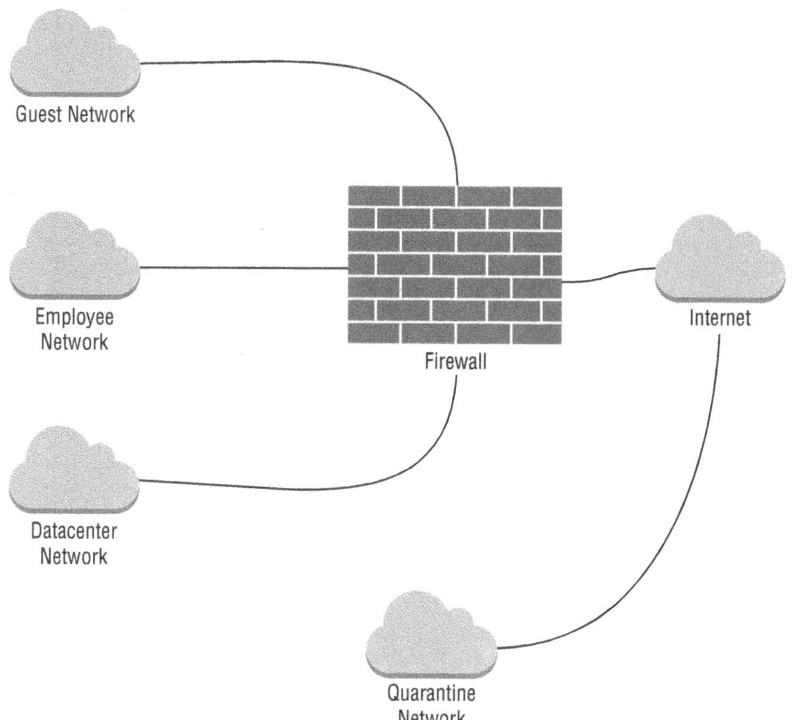

Removal

Removal of compromised systems from the network is the strongest containment technique in the cybersecurity analyst's incident response toolkit. As shown in Figure 14.5, removal differs from segmentation and isolation in that the affected systems are completely disconnected from other networks, although they may still be allowed to communicate with other compromised systems within the quarantine VLAN. In some cases, each suspect system may be physically disconnected from the network so that they are prevented from communicating even with each other. The exact details of removal will depend on the circumstances of the incident and the professional judgment of incident responders.

Study the differences between segmentation, isolation, and removal as you prepare for the exam. Be ready to answer questions that ask you to identify which approach is in use.

FIGURE 14.5 Network removal for incident response

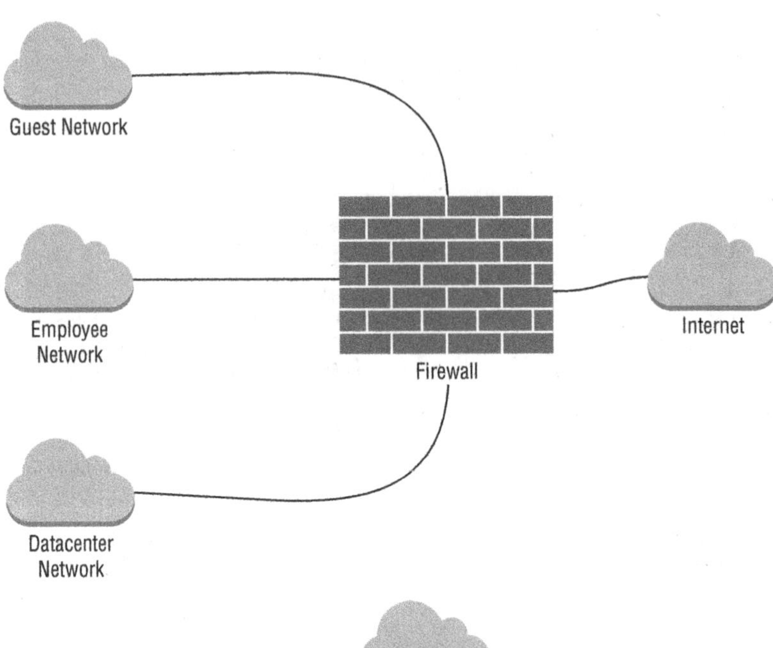

Real World Scenario

Removal Isn't Foolproof

Removing a system from the network is a common containment step designed to prevent further damage from taking place, but NIST points out in their *Computer Security Incident Handling Guide* that it isn't foolproof. They present a hypothetical example of an attacker using a simple ping as a sort of "dead man's switch" for a compromised system, designed to identify when the adversary detects the attack and removes the system from the network.

In this scenario, the attacker simply sets up a periodic ping request to a known external host, such as the Google public DNS server located at 8.8.8.8. This server is almost always accessible from any network, and the attacker can verify this connectivity after initially compromising a system.

The attacker can then write a simple script that monitors the results of those ping requests and, after detecting several consecutive failures, assumes that the attack was detected and the system was removed from the network. The script can then wipe out evidence of the attack or encrypt important information stored on the server.

The moral of the story is that although removal is a strong weapon in the containment toolkit, it isn't foolproof!

Evidence Gathering and Handling

The primary objective during the containment phase of incident response is to limit the damage to the organization and its resources. Although that objective may take precedence over other goals, responders may still be interested in gathering evidence during the containment process. This evidence can be crucial in the continuing analysis of the incident for internal purposes, or it can be used during legal proceedings against the attacker.

Chapter 7 provided a thorough review of the forensic strategies that might be used during an incident investigation. Chapter 1 also included information on reverse engineering practices that may be helpful during an incident investigation.

If incident handlers suspect that evidence gathered during an investigation may be used in court, they should take special care to preserve and document evidence during the course of their investigation. NIST recommends that investigators maintain a detailed evidence log that includes the following:

- Identifying information (for example, the location, serial number, model number, hostname, MAC addresses, and IP addresses of a computer)
- Name, title, and phone number of each individual who collected or handled the evidence during the investigation
- Time and date (including time zone) of each occurrence of evidence handling
- Locations where the evidence was stored

Failure to maintain accurate logs will bring the evidence chain-of-custody into question and may cause the evidence to be inadmissible in court.

Identifying Attackers

Identifying the perpetrators of a cybersecurity incident is a complex task that often leads investigators down a winding path of redirected hosts that crosses international borders. Although you might find IP address records stored in your logs, it is incredibly unlikely that they correspond to the actual IP address of the attacker. Any attacker other than the most rank of amateurs will relay their communications through a series of compromised systems, making it very difficult to trace their actual origin.

Before heading down this path of investigating an attack's origin, it's very important to ask yourself why you are pursuing it. Is there really business value in uncovering *who* attacked you, or would your time be better spent on containment, eradication, and recovery activities? The NIST *Computer Security Incident Handling Guide* addresses this issue head on, giving the opinion that "Identifying an attacking host can be a time-consuming and futile process that can prevent a team from achieving its primary goal—minimizing the business impact."

Law enforcement officials may approach this situation with objectives that differ from those of the attacked organization's cybersecurity analysts. After all, one of the core responsibilities of law enforcement organizations is to identify criminals, arrest them, and bring them to trial. That responsibility may conflict with the core cybersecurity objectives of containment, eradication, and recovery. Cybersecurity and business leaders should take this conflict into consideration when deciding whether to involve law enforcement agencies in an incident investigation and the degree of cooperation they will provide to an investigation that is already underway.

Law enforcement officers have tools at their disposal that aren't available to private cybersecurity analysts. If you do have a pressing need to identify an attacker, it may be wise to involve law enforcement. They have the ability to obtain search warrants that may prove invaluable during an investigation. Officers can serve search warrants on Internet service providers and other companies that may have log records that assist in untangling the winding trail of an attack. Additionally, law enforcement agencies may have access to sensitive government databases that contain information on known attackers and their methodologies.

Incident Eradication and Recovery

Once the cybersecurity team successfully contains an incident, it is time to move on to the *eradication* phase of the response. The primary purpose of eradication is to remove any of the artifacts of the incident that may remain on the organization's network. This could include the removal of any malicious code from the network, the sanitization of compromised media, and the securing of compromised user accounts.

The *recovery* phase of incident response focuses on restoring normal capabilities and services. It includes reconstituting resources and correcting security control deficiencies that may have led to the attack. This could include rebuilding and patching systems, reconfiguring firewalls, updating malware signatures, and similar activities. The goal of recovery is not just to rebuild the organization's network but also to do so in a manner that reduces the likelihood of a successful future attack.

During the eradication and recovery effort, cybersecurity analysts should develop a clear understanding of the incident's root cause. This is critical to implementing a secure recovery that corrects control deficiencies that led to the original attack. After all, if you don't understand how an attacker breached your security controls in the first place, it will be hard to correct those controls so that the attack doesn't reoccur! Understanding the root cause of an attack is a completely different activity than identifying the attacker. Root cause assessment is a critical component of incident recovery whereas, as mentioned earlier, identifying the attacker can be a costly distraction.

Root cause analysis also helps an organization identify other systems they operate that might share the same vulnerability. For example, if an attacker compromises a Cisco router and root cause analysis reveals an error in that device's configuration, administrators may correct the error on other routers they control to prevent a similar attack from compromising those devices.

Reconstruction and Reimaging

During an incident, attackers may compromise one or more systems through the use of malware, web application attacks, or other exploits. Once an attacker gains control of a system, security professionals should consider it completely compromised and untrustworthy. It is not safe to simply correct the security issue and move on because the attacker may still have an undetected foothold on the compromised system. Instead, the system should be rebuilt, either from scratch or by using an image or backup of the system from a known secure state.

Rebuilding and/or restoring systems should always be done with the incident root cause analysis in mind. If the system was compromised because it contained a security vulnerability, as opposed to through the use of a compromised user account, backups and images of that system likely have that same vulnerability. Even rebuilding the system from scratch may reintroduce the earlier vulnerability, rendering the system susceptible to the same attack. During the recovery phase, administrators should ensure that rebuilt or restored systems are remediated to address known security issues.

Patching Systems and Applications

During the incident recovery effort, cybersecurity analysts will patch operating systems and applications involved in the attack. This is also a good time to review the security patch status of all systems in the enterprise, addressing other security issues that may lurk behind the scenes.

Cybersecurity analysts should first focus their efforts on systems that were directly involved in the compromise and then work their way outward, addressing systems that were indirectly related to the compromise before touching systems that were not involved at all. Figure 14.6 shows the phased approach that cybersecurity analysts should take to patching systems and applications during the recovery phase.

FIGURE 14.6 Patching priorities

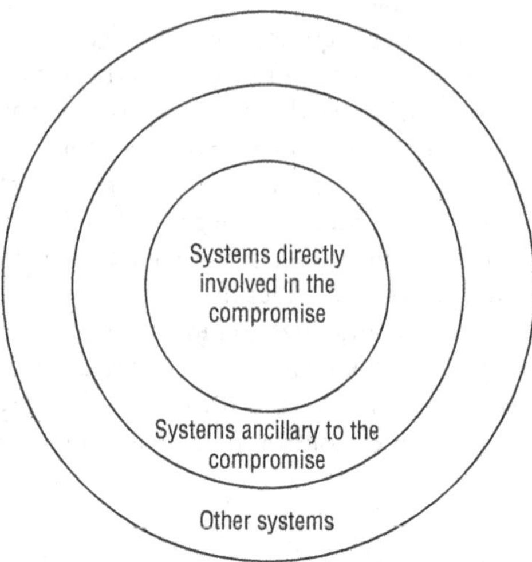

Sanitization and Secure Disposal

During the recovery effort, cybersecurity analysts may need to dispose of or repurpose media from systems that were compromised during the incident. In those cases, special care should be taken to ensure that sensitive information that was stored on that media is not compromised. Responders don't want the recovery effort from one incident to lead to a second incident!

Generally speaking, there are three options available for the secure disposition of media containing sensitive information: clear, purge, and destroy. NIST defines these three activities clearing in NIST SP 800-88: *Guidelines for Media Sanitization*:

- *Clear* applies logical techniques to sanitize data in all user-addressable storage locations for protection against simple noninvasive data recovery techniques; this is typically applied through the standard Read and Write commands to the storage device, such as by rewriting with a new value or using a menu option to reset the device to the factory state (where rewriting is not supported).
- *Purge* applies physical or logical techniques that render target data recovery infeasible using state-of-the-art laboratory techniques. Examples of purging activities include overwriting, block erase, and cryptographic erase activities when performed through the use of dedicated, standardized device commands. *Degaussing* is another form of purging that uses extremely strong magnetic fields to disrupt the data stored on a device.
- *Destroy* renders target data recovery infeasible using state-of-the-art laboratory techniques and results in the subsequent inability to use the media for storage of data. Destruction techniques include disintegration, pulverization, melting, and incinerating.

These three levels of data disposal are listed in increasing order of effectiveness as well as difficulty and cost. Physically incinerating a hard drive, for example, removes any possibility that data will be recovered but requires the use of an incinerator and renders the drive unusable for future purposes.

Figure 14.7 shows a flowchart designed to help security decision makers choose appropriate techniques for destroying information and can be used to guide incident recovery efforts. Notice that the flowchart includes a Validation phase after efforts to clear, purge, or destroy data. Validation ensures that the media sanitization was successful and that remnant data does not exist on the sanitized media.

FIGURE 14.7 Sanitization and disposition decision flow

Source: NIST SP 800-88: *Guidelines for Media Sanitization*

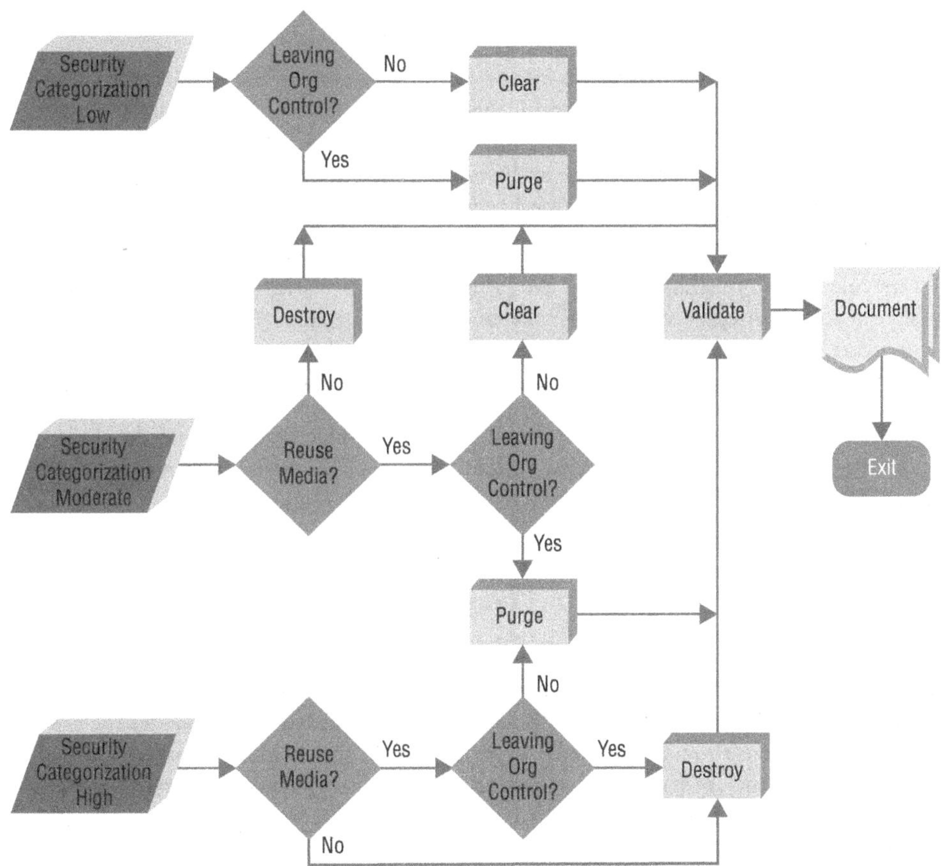

Validating the Recovery Effort

Before concluding the recovery effort, incident responders should take time to verify that the recovery measures put in place were successful. The exact nature of this verification will depend on the technical circumstances of the incident and the organization's infrastructure. Four activities that should always be included in these validation efforts follow:

Validate that only authorized user accounts exist on every system and application in the organization. In many cases, organizations already undertake periodic account reviews that verify the authorization for every account. This process should be used during the recovery validation effort.

Verify the proper restoration of permissions assigned to each account. During the account review, responders should also verify that accounts do not have extraneous permissions that violate the principle of least privilege. This is true for normal user accounts, administrator accounts, and service accounts.

Verify that all systems are logging properly. Every system and application should be configured to log security-related information to a level that is consistent with the organization's logging policy. Those log records should be sent to a centralized log repository that preserves them for archival use. The validation phase should include verification that these logs are properly configured and received by the repository.

Conduct vulnerability scans on all systems. Vulnerability scans play an important role in verifying that systems are safeguarded against future attacks. Analysts should run thorough scans against systems and initiate remediation workflows where necessary. For more information on this process, see Chapter 4, "Designing a Vulnerability Management Program," and Chapter 5, "Analyzing Vulnerability Scans."

These actions form the core of an incident recovery validation effort and should be complemented with other activities that validate the specific controls put in place during the Containment, Eradication, and Recovery phase of incident response.

Wrapping Up the Response

After the immediate, urgent actions of containment, eradication, and recovery are complete, it is very tempting for the CSIRT to take a deep breath and consider their work done. While the team should take a well-deserved break, the incident response process is not complete until the team completes postincident activities that include managing change control processes, conducting a lessons learned session, and creating a formal written incident report.

Managing Change Control Processes

During the containment, eradication, and recovery process, responders may have bypassed the organization's normal change control and configuration management processes in an effort to respond to the incident in an expedient manner. These processes provide important management controls and documentation of the organization's technical infrastructure. Once the urgency of response efforts pass, the responders should turn back to these processes and use them to document any emergency changes made during the incident response effort.

Conducting a Lessons Learned Session

At the conclusion of every cybersecurity incident, everyone involved in the response should participate in a formal lessons learned session that is designed to uncover critical information about the response. This session also highlights potential deficiencies in the incident response plan and procedures. For more information on conducting the post-incident lessons learned session, see the "Lessons Learned Review" section in Chapter 11.

During the lessons learned session, the organization may uncover potential changes to the incident response plan. In those cases, the leader should propose those changes and move them through the organization's formal change process to improve future incident response efforts.

During an incident investigation, the team may encounter new *indicators of compromise (IOCs)* based on the tools, techniques, and tactics used by attackers. As part of the lessons learned review, the team should clearly identify any new IOC and make recommendations for updating the organization's security monitoring program to include those IOCs. This will reduce the likelihood of a similar incident escaping attention in the future.

Developing a Final Report

Every incident that activates the CSIRT should conclude with a formal written report that documents the incident for posterity. This serves several important purposes. First, it creates an institutional memory of the incident that is useful when developing new security controls and training new security team members. Second, it may serve as an important record of the incident if there is legal action that results from the incident. Finally, the act of creating the written report can help identify previously undetected deficiencies in the incident response process that may feed back through the lessons learned process.

Important elements that the CSIRT should cover in a postincident report include the following:

- Chronology of events for the incident and response efforts
- Root cause of the incident

- Location and description of evidence collected during the incident response process
- Specific actions taken by responders to contain, eradicate, and recover from the incident, including the rationale for those decisions
- Estimates of the impact of the incident on the organization and its stakeholders
- Results of postrecovery validation efforts
- Documentation of issues identified during the lessons learned review

Incident summary reports should be classified in accordance with the organization's classification policy and stored in an appropriately secured manner. The organization should also have a defined retention period for incident reports and destroy old reports when they exceed that period.

Evidence Retention

At the conclusion of an incident, the team should make a formal determination about the disposition of evidence collected during the incident. If the evidence is no longer required, then it should be destroyed in accordance with the organization's data disposal procedures. If the evidence will be preserved for future use, it should be placed in a secure evidence repository with the chain of custody maintained.

The decision to retain evidence depends on several factors, including whether the incident is likely to result in criminal or civil action and the impact of the incident on the organization. This topic should be directly addressed in an organization's incident response procedures.

Summary

After identifying a security incident in progress, CSIRT members should move immediately into the containment, eradication, and recovery phase of incident response. The first priority of this phase is to contain the damage caused by a security incident to lower the impact on the organization. Once an incident is contained, responders should take actions to eradicate the effects of the incident and recovery normal operations. Once the immediate response efforts are complete, the CSIRT should move into the postincident phase, conduct a lessons learned session, and create a written report summarizing the incident response process.

Exam Essentials

Explain the purpose of containment activities. After identifying a potential incident in progress, responders should take immediate action to contain the damage. They should select appropriate containment strategies based on the nature of the incident and impact on the organization. Potential containment activities include network segmentation, isolation, and removal of affected systems.

Know the importance of collecting evidence during a response. Much of the evidence of a cybersecurity incident is volatile in nature and may not be available later if not collected during the response. CSIRT members must determine the priority that evidence collection will take during the containment, eradication, and recovery phase and then ensure that they properly handle any collected evidence that can later be used in legal proceedings.

Explain how identifying attackers can be a waste of valuable resources. Most efforts to identify the perpetrators of security incidents are futile, consuming significant resources before winding up at a dead end. The primary focus of incident responders should be on protecting the business interests of the organization. Law enforcement officials have different priorities, and responders should be aware of potentially conflicting objectives.

Explain the purpose of eradication and recovery. After containing the damage, responders should move on to eradication and recovery activities that seek to remove all traces of an incident from the organization's network and restore normal operations as quickly as possible. This should include validation efforts that verify security controls are properly implemented before closing the incident.

Define the purpose of postincident activities. At the conclusion of a cybersecurity incident response effort, CSIRT members should conduct a formal lessons learned session that reviews the entire incident response process and recommends changes to the organization's incident response plan, as needed. Any such changes should be made through the organization's change control process. The team should also complete a formal incident summary report that serves to document the incident for posterity. Other considerations during this process include evidence retention, indicator of compromise (IoC) generation, and ongoing monitoring.

Lab Exercises

Activity 14.1: Incident Containment Options

Label each one of the following figures with the type of incident containment activity pictured.

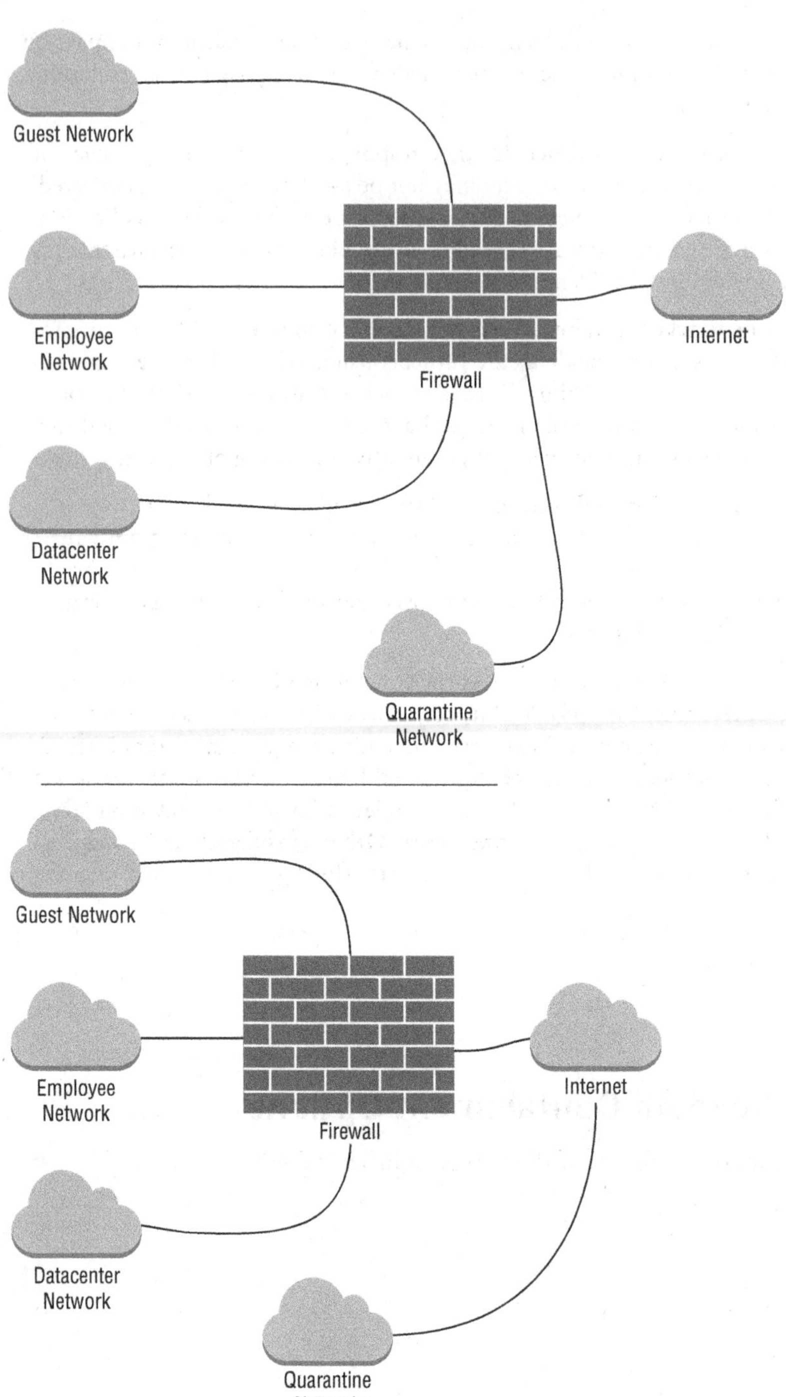
Guest Network
Employee Network
Firewall
Internet
Datacenter Network
Quarantine Network
Guest Network
Employee Network
Firewall
Internet
Datacenter Network
Quarantine Network

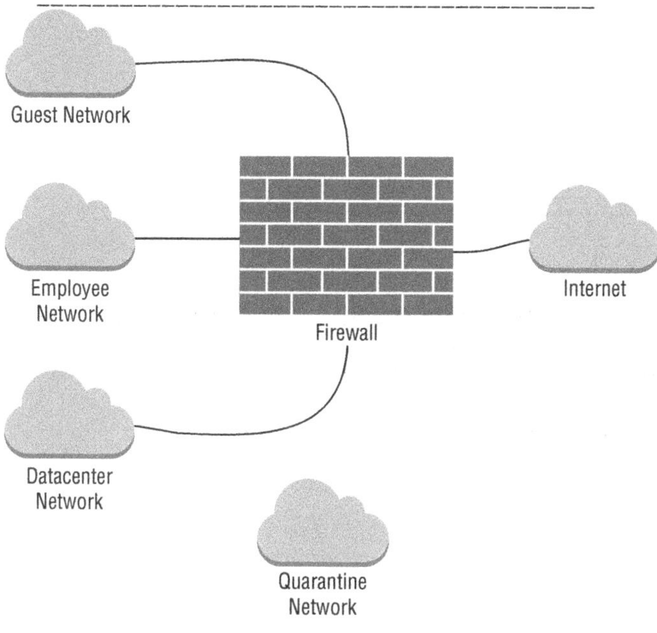

Activity 14.2: Incident Response Activities

For each of the following incident response activities, assign it to one of the following CompTIA categories:

- Containment
- Eradication
- Validation
- Postincident Activities

Remember that the categories assigned by CompTIA differ from those used by NIST and other incident handling standards.

Patching ________________

Sanitization ________________

Lessons learned ________________

Reimaging ________________

Secure disposal ________________

Isolation ________________

Scanning ________________

Removal ________________

Reconstruction ________________

Permission verification ________________

User account review ________________

Segmentation ________________

Activity 14.3: Sanitization and Disposal Techniques

Fill in the flowchart with the appropriate dispositions for information being destroyed following a security incident.

Each box should be completed using one of the following three words:

Clear

Purge

Destroy

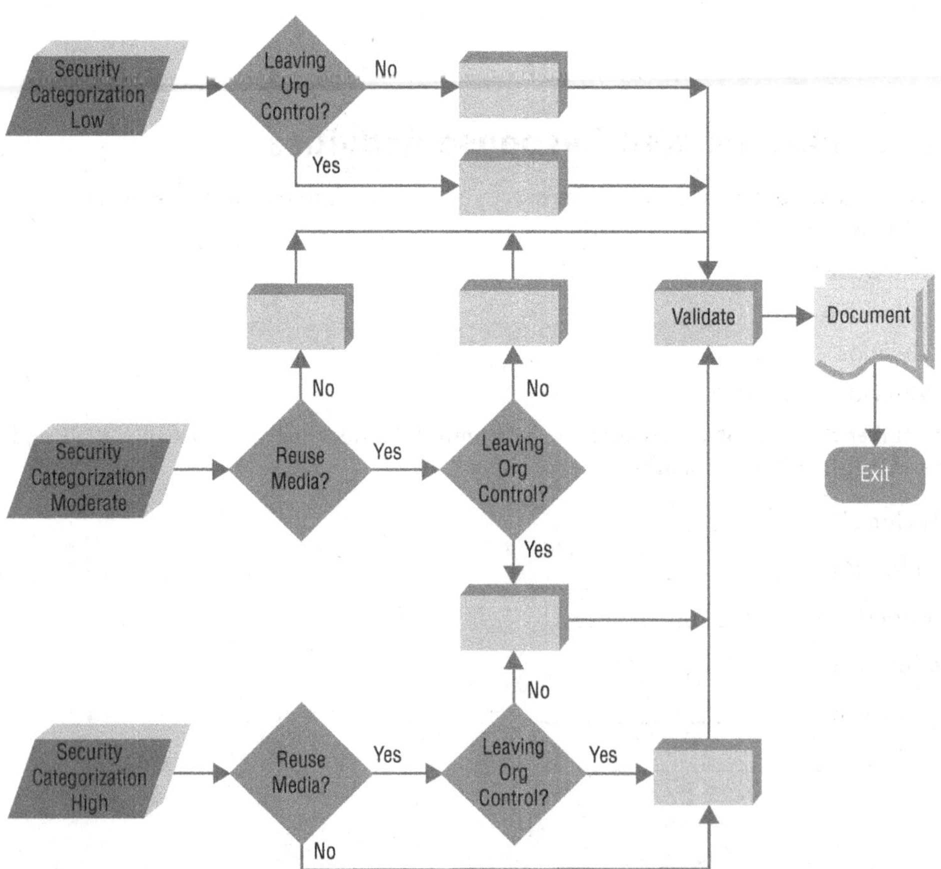

Review Questions

1. Which one of the phases of incident response involves primarily active undertakings designed to limit the damage that an attacker might cause?
   A. Containment, Eradication, and Recovery
   B. Preparation
   C. Postincident Activity
   D. Detection and Analysis
2. Which one of the following criteria is *not* normally used when evaluating the appropriateness of a cybersecurity incident containment strategy?
   A. Effectiveness of the strategy
   B. Evidence preservation requirements
   C. Log records generated by the strategy
   D. Cost of the strategy
3. Alice is responding to a cybersecurity incident and notices a system that she suspects is compromised. She places this system on a quarantine VLAN with limited access to other networked systems. What containment strategy is Alice pursuing?
   A. Eradication
   B. Isolation
   C. Segmentation
   D. Removal
4. Alice confers with other team members and decides that even allowing limited access to other systems is an unacceptable risk and decides instead to prevent the quarantine VLAN from accessing any other systems by putting firewall rules in place that limit access to other enterprise systems. The attacker can still control the system to allow Alice to continue monitoring the incident. What strategy is she now pursuing?
   A. Eradication
   B. Isolation
   C. Segmentation
   D. Removal
5. After observing the attacker, Alice decides to remove the Internet connection entirely, leaving the systems running but inaccessible from outside the quarantine VLAN. What strategy is she now pursuing?
   A. Eradication
   B. Isolation
   C. Segmentation
   D. Removal

6. Which one of the following tools may be used to isolate an attacker so that they may not cause damage to production systems but may still be observed by cybersecurity analysts?
   A. Sandbox
   B. Playpen
   C. IDS
   D. DLP
7. Tamara is a cybersecurity analyst for a private business that is suffering a security breach. She believes the attackers have compromised a database containing sensitive information. Which one of the following activities should be Tamara's first priority?
   A. Identifying the source of the attack
   B. Eradication
   C. Containment
   D. Recovery
8. Which one of the following activities does CompTIA classify as part of the recovery validation effort?
   A. Rebuilding systems
   B. Sanitization
   C. Secure disposal
   D. Scanning
9. Which one of the following pieces of information is most critical to conducting a solid incident recovery effort?
   A. Identity of the attacker
   B. Time of the attack
   C. Root cause of the attack
   D. Attacks on other organizations
10. Lynda is disposing of a drive containing sensitive information that was collected during the response to a cybersecurity incident. The information is categorized as a high security risk and she wishes to reuse the media during a future incident. What is the appropriate disposition for this information?
    A. Clear
    B. Erase
    C. Purge
    D. Destroy
11. Which one of the following activities is not normally conducted during the recovery validation phase?
    A. Verify the permissions assigned to each account
    B. Implement new firewall rules

C. Conduct vulnerability scans

D. Verify logging is functioning properly

12. What incident response activity focuses on removing any artifacts of the incident that may remain on the organization's network?

A. Containment

B. Recovery

C. Postincident Activities

D. Eradication

13. Which one of the following is not a common use of formal incident reports?

A. Training new team members

B. Sharing with other organizations

C. Developing new security controls

D. Assisting with legal action

14. Which one of the following data elements would not normally be included in an evidence log?

A. Serial number

B. Record of handling

C. Storage location

D. Malware signatures

15. Sondra determines that an attacker has gained access to a server containing critical business files and wishes to ensure that the attacker cannot delete those files. Which one of the following strategies would meet Sondra's goal?

A. Isolation

B. Segmentation

C. Removal

D. None of the above

16. Joe would like to determine the appropriate disposition of a flash drive used to gather highly sensitive evidence during an incident response effort. He does not need to reuse the drive but wants to return it to its owner, an outside contractor. What is the appropriate disposition?

A. Destroy

B. Clear

C. Erase

D. Purge

17. Which one of the following is not typically found in a cybersecurity incident report?
    A. Chronology of events
    B. Identity of the attacker
    C. Estimates of impact
    D. Documentation of lessons learned
18. What NIST publication contains guidance on cybersecurity incident handling?
    A. SP 800-53
    B. SP 800-88
    C. SP 800-18
    D. SP 800-61
19. Which one of the following is not a purging activity?
    A. Resetting to factory state
    B. Overwriting
    C. Block erase
    D. Cryptographic erase
20. Ben is responding to a security incident and determines that the attacker is using systems on Ben's network to attack a third party. Which one of the following containment approaches will prevent Ben's systems from being used in this manner?
    A. Removal
    B. Isolation
    C. Detection
    D. Segmentation

Risk Management

THE COMPTIA CYBERSECURITY ANALYST (CYSA+) EXAM OBJECTIVES COVERED IN THIS CHAPTER INCLUDE:

✓ **Domain 5.0: Compliance and Assessment**

- 5.1: Understand the importance of data privacy and protection.
- 5.2: Given a scenario, apply security concepts in support of organizational risk mitigation.

The first 14 chapters of this book dealt with the sort of deep-in-the-details technical work that fills the days of most cybersecurity analysts. These are the activities that we engage in regularly to identify and address threats and vulnerabilities, implement and maintain secure systems, monitor the status of our cybersecurity efforts, and respond to incidents when they occur. We now shift gears to look at the big picture of cybersecurity in a large organization. How do we evaluate and manage risks to ensure that we're spending our limited time and money on the controls that will have the greatest effect? That's where risk management comes into play.

Analyzing Risk

We operate in a world full of risks. If you left your home and drove to your office this morning, you encountered a large number of risks. You could have been involved in an automobile accident, encountered a train delay, been struck by a bicycle on the sidewalk, or even contracted a dangerous virus from another rider in an elevator. We're aware of these risks in the back of our minds, but we don't let them paralyze us. Instead, we take simple precautions to help manage the risks that we think have the greatest potential to disrupt our lives.

In an *enterprise risk management (ERM)* program, organizations take a formal approach to risk analysis that begins with identifying risks, continues with determining the severity of each risk, and then results in adopting one or more *risk management* strategies to address each risk.

Before we move too deeply into the risk assessment process, let's define a few important terms that we'll use during our discussion:

- *Threats* are any possible events that might have an adverse impact on the confidentiality, integrity, and/or availability of our information or information systems.
- *Vulnerabilities* are weaknesses in our systems or controls that could be exploited by a threat.
- *Risks* occur at the intersection of a vulnerability and a threat that might exploit that vulnerability. A threat without a corresponding vulnerability does not pose a risk, nor does a vulnerability without a corresponding threat.

Figure 15.1 illustrates this relationship between threats, vulnerabilities, and risks.

Consider the example from earlier of walking down the sidewalk on your way to work. The fact that you are on the sidewalk without any protection is a vulnerability. A bicycle speeding down that sidewalk is a threat. The result of this combination of factors is that you are at risk of being hit by the bicycle on the sidewalk. If you remove the vulnerability by parking in a garage beneath your building, you are no longer at risk for that particular threat. Similarly, if the city erects barriers that prevent bicycles from entering the sidewalk, you are also no longer at risk.

FIGURE 15.1 Risk exists at the intersection of a threat and a corresponding vulnerability.

Let's consider another example drawn from the cybersecurity domain. In Chapters 4 and 5, you learned about the vulnerability management process. Organizations regularly conduct vulnerability scans designed to identify potential vulnerabilities in their environment. One of these scans might identify a server that exposes TCP port 22 to the world, allowing brute-force SSH attempts by an attacker. Exposing port 22 presents a vulnerability to a brute-force attack. An attacker with a brute-force scanning tool presents a threat. The combination of the port exposure and the existence of attackers presents a risk.

In this case, you don't have any way to eliminate attackers, so you can't really address the threat, but you do have control over the services running on your systems. If you shut down the SSH service and close port 22, you eliminate the vulnerability and, therefore, also eliminate the risk.

Of course, we can't always completely eliminate a risk because it isn't always feasible to shut down services. We might decide instead to take actions that reduce the risk. We'll talk more about those options when we get to risk management strategies later in this chapter.

Risk Identification

The *risk identification process* requires identifying the threats and vulnerabilities that exist in your operating environment. We've already covered the many ways that you might conduct risk identification in this book; we just haven't put them together in the big picture frame of risk management.

Chapters 2 and 3 discussed the concepts of threat intelligence. You learned how you can leverage internal and external information sources to identify the many threats facing your organization.

Chapters 4 and 5 discussed the concepts of vulnerability management. You learned how you can create a vulnerability management program for your organization and how you can automate portions of that program through routine vulnerability scans. Chapters 7 through 9 covered the concept of software and systems security, providing you with the information you need to conduct *systems assessments* that supplement vulnerability scanning results.

There's not much more to the risk identification process. You may already be conducting all the technical activities that you need to identify risks. Now you just need to pull that information together and develop a comprehensive list of threats, vulnerabilities, and risks.

Risk Calculation

Not all risks are equal. Returning to the example of a pedestrian on the street, the risk of being hit by a bicycle is far more worrisome than the risk of being struck down by a meteor. That makes intuitive sense, but let's explore the underlying thought process that leads to that conclusion. It's a process called *risk calculation.*

When we evaluate any risk, we do so by using two different factors:

- The *probability*, or likelihood, that the risk will occur. We might express this as the percent chance that a threat will exploit a vulnerability over a specified period of time, such as within the next year.
- The *magnitude*, or impact, that the risk will have on the organization if it does occur. We might express this as the financial cost that we will incur as the result of a risk, although there are other possible measures.

Exam Note

The two factors that contribute to the degree of a risk are its probability and its magnitude (or impact). Keep this in the back of your mind as you approach any questions about risk on the CySA+ exam.

Using these two factors, we can assign each risk a conceptual score by combining the probability and the magnitude. This leads many risk analysts to express the severity of a risk using this formula:

Risk Severity = Probability * Magnitude

It's important to point out that this equation does not always have to be interpreted literally. Although you may wind up multiplying these values together in some risk assessment processes, it's best to think of this conceptually as combining the magnitude and impact to determine the severity of a risk.

When we assess the risks of being struck by a bicycle or a meteor on the street, we can use these factors to evaluate the risk severity. There might be a high probability that we will be struck by a bicycle. That type of accident might have a moderate magnitude, leaving us willing to consider taking steps to reduce our risk. Being struck by a meteor would clearly have a catastrophic magnitude of impact, but the probability of such an incident is incredibly unlikely, leading us to acknowledge the risk and move on without changing our behavior.

Business Impact Analysis

The *business impact analysis (BIA)* is a formalized approach to risk prioritization that allows organizations to conduct their reviews in a structured manner. BIAs follow two different analysis methodologies:

- *Quantitative risk assessments* use numeric data in the analysis, resulting in assessments that allow the very straightforward prioritization of risks.
- *Qualitative risk assessments* substitute subjective judgments and categories for strict numerical analysis, allowing the assessment of risks that are difficult to quantify.

As organizations seek to provide clear communication of risk factors to stakeholders, they often combine elements of quantitative and qualitative risk assessments. Let's review each of these approaches.

Quantitative Risk Assessment

Most quantitative risk assessment processes follow a similar methodology that includes the following steps:

1. Determine the asset value (AV) of the asset affected by the risk. This *asset value (AV)* is expressed in dollars, or other currency, and may be determined using the cost to acquire the asset, the cost to replace the asset, or the depreciated cost of the asset, depending on the organization's preferences.
2. Determine the likelihood that the risk will occur. Risk analysts consult subject matter experts and determine the likelihood that a risk will occur in a given year. This is expressed as the number of times the risk is expected each year, and is described as the *annualized rate of occurrence (ARO)*. A risk that is expected to occur twice a year has an ARO of 2.0, whereas a risk that is expected once every one hundred years has an ARO of 0.01.
3. Determine the amount of damage that will occur to the asset if the risk materializes. This is known as the *exposure factor (EF)* and is expressed as the percentage of the asset expected to be damaged. The exposure factor of a risk that would completely destroy an asset is 100 percent, whereas a risk that would damage half of an asset has an EF of 50 percent.
4. Calculate the single loss expectancy. The *single loss expectancy (SLE)* is the amount of financial damage expected each time a risk materializes. It is calculated by multiplying the AV by the EF.
5. Calculate the annualized loss expectancy. The *annualized loss expectancy (ALE)* is the amount of damage expected from a risk each year. It is calculated by multiplying the SLE and the ARO.

It's important to note that these steps assess the quantitative scale of a single risk—that is, one combination of a threat and a vulnerability. Organizations conducting quantitative risk assessments would repeat this process for each threat/vulnerability combination.

Let's walk through an example of a quantitative risk assessment. Imagine that you are concerned about the risk associated with a denial-of-service (DoS) attack against your email server. Your organization uses that server to send email messages to customers offering products for sale. It generates $1,000 in sales per hour that it is in operation. After consulting threat intelligence sources, you believe that a DoS attack is likely to occur three times a year and last for three hours before you are able to control it.

The asset in this case is not the server itself, because the server will not be physically damaged. The asset is the ability to send email and you have already determined that it is worth $1,000 per hour. The asset value for three hours of server operation is, therefore, $3,000.

Your threat intelligence estimates that the risk will occur three times per year, making your annualized rate of occurrence 3.0.

After consulting your email team, you believe that the server would operate at 10 percent capacity during a DoS attack, as some legitimate messages would get out. Therefore, your exposure factor is 90 percent, because 90 percent of the capacity would be consumed by the attack.

Your single loss expectancy is calculated by multiplying the asset value ($3,000) by the exposure factor (90 percent) to get the expected loss during each attack. This gives you an SLE of $2700.

Your annualized loss expectancy is the product of the SLE ($2700) and the ARO (3.0), or $8100.

Exam Note

Be prepared to explain the terminology of quantitative risk assessment and perform these calculations when you take the CySA+ exam.

Organizations can use the ALEs that result from a quantitative risk assessment to prioritize their remediation activities and determine the appropriate level of investment in controls that mitigate risks. For example, it would not normally make sense (at least in a strictly financial sense) to spend more than the ALE on an annual basis to protect against a risk. In the previous example, if a DoS prevention service would block all of those attacks, it would make financial sense to purchase it if the cost is less than $8100 per year.

Qualitative Risk Assessment

Quantitative techniques work very well for evaluating financial risks and other risks that can be clearly expressed in numeric terms. Many risks, however, do not easily lend themselves to quantitative analysis. For example, how would you describe reputational damage, public health and safety, or employee morale in quantitative terms? You might be able to draw some inferences that tie these issues back to financial data, but the bottom line is that quantitative techniques simply aren't well suited to evaluating these risks.

Qualitative risk assessment techniques seek to overcome the limitations of quantitative techniques by substituting subjective judgment for objective data. Qualitative techniques still use the same probability and magnitude factors to evaluate the severity of a risk, but do so using subjective categories. For example, Figure 15.2 shows a simple qualitative risk assessment that evaluates the probability and magnitude of several risks on a subjective "Low/Medium/High" scale. Risks are placed on this chart based on the judgments made by subject matter experts.

FIGURE 15.2 Qualitative risk assessments use subjective rating scales to evaluate probability and magnitude.

Magnitude \ **Probability**	Low	Medium	High
High	Data Center Intrusion	Website DDoS	Stolen Unencrypted Device Spear phishing
Medium		Malware on Endpoint	
Low	Guest User Retains Network Access		

Although it's not possible to directly calculate the financial impact of risks that are assessed using qualitative techniques, this risk assessment scale makes it possible to prioritize risks. For example, reviewing the risk assessment in Figure 15.2, we can determine that the greatest risks facing this organization are stolen unencrypted devices and spear phishing attacks. Both of these risks share a high probability and high magnitude of impact. If we're considering using funds to add better physical security to the datacenter, this risk assessment informs us that our time and money would likely be better spent on full-disk encryption for mobile devices and a secure email gateway.

Many organizations combine quantitative and qualitative techniques to get a well-rounded picture of both the tangible and the intangible risks they face.

Supply Chain Assessment

When evaluating the risks to your organization, don't forget about the risks that occur based on third-party relationships. You rely on many different vendors to protect the confidentiality, integrity, and availability of your data. Performing vendor due diligence is a crucial security responsibility.

For example, how many cloud service providers handle your organization's sensitive information? Those vendors become a crucial part of your supply chain from both operational and security perspectives. If they don't have adequate security controls in place, your data is at risk.

Similarly, the hardware that you use in your organization comes through a supply chain as well. How certain are you that it wasn't tampered with on the way to your organization? Documents leaked by former NSA contractor Edward Snowden revealed that the U.S. government intercepted hardware shipments to foreign countries and implanted malicious code deep within their hardware. Performing hardware source authenticity assessments validates that the hardware you received was not tampered with after leaving the vendor.

Managing Risk

With a completed risk assessment in hand, organizations can then turn their attention to addressing those risks. *Risk management* is the process of systematically addressing the risks facing an organization. The risk assessment serves two important roles in the risk management process:

- The risk assessment provides guidance in prioritizing risks so that the risks with the highest probability and magnitude are addressed first.
- Quantitative risk assessments help determine whether the potential impact of a risk justifies the costs incurred by adopting a risk management approach.

Risk managers should work their way through the risk assessment and identify an appropriate management strategy for each risk included in the assessment. They have four strategies to choose from: risk mitigation, risk avoidance, risk transference, and risk acceptance. In the next several sections, we discuss each of these strategies using two examples.

First, we discuss the financial risk associated with the theft of a laptop from an employee. In this example, we are assuming that the laptop does not contain any unencrypted sensitive information. The risk that we are managing is the financial impact of losing the actual hardware.

Second, we discuss the business risk associated with a distributed denial-of-service (DDoS) attack against an organization's website.

We use these two scenarios to help you understand the different options available when selecting a risk management strategy and the trade-offs involved in that selection process.

Risk Mitigation

Risk mitigation is the process of applying security controls to reduce the probability and/or magnitude of a risk. Risk mitigation is the most common risk management strategy, and the vast majority of the work of security professionals revolves around mitigating risks through the design, implementation, and management of security controls. Many of these controls involve engineering trade-offs between functionality, performance, and security. We'll discuss some examples of security controls later in this chapter and take a more in-depth look at the categories and types of controls in Chapter 16, "Policy and Compliance."

When you choose to mitigate a risk, you may apply one security control or a series of security controls. Each of those controls should reduce the probability that the risk will materialize, the magnitude of the risk should it materialize, or both the probability and magnitude.

In our first scenario, we are concerned about the theft of laptops from our organization. If we want to mitigate that risk, we could choose from a variety of security controls. For example, purchasing cable locks for laptops might reduce the probability that a theft will occur.

We could also choose to purchase a device registration service that provides tamper-proof registration tags for devices, such as the STOP tags shown in Figure 15.3. These tags provide a prominent warning to potential thieves when attached to a device, as shown in Figure 15.3(a). This serves as a deterrent to theft, reducing the probability that the laptop will be stolen in the first place. If a thief does steal the device and removes the tag, it leaves the permanent residue, shown in Figure 15.3(b). Anyone finding the device is instructed to contact the registration vendor for instructions, reducing the potential impact of the theft if the device is returned.

In our second scenario, a DDoS attack against an organization's website, we could choose among several mitigating controls. For example, we could simply purchase more bandwidth and server capacity, allowing us to absorb the bombardment of a DDoS attack, thus reducing the impact of an attack. We could also choose to purchase a third-party DDoS mitigation service that prevents the traffic from reaching our network in the first place, thus reducing the probability of an attack.

Risk Avoidance

Risk avoidance is a risk management strategy where we change our business practices to completely eliminate the potential that a risk will materialize. Risk avoidance may initially seem like a highly desirable approach. After all, who wouldn't want to eliminate the risks

FIGURE 15.3 (a) STOP tag attached to a device (b) Residue remaining on device after attempted removal of a STOP tag

(a)

(b)

facing their organization? There is, however, a major drawback. Risk avoidance strategies typically have a serious detrimental impact on the business.

For example, consider the laptop theft risk discussed earlier in this chapter. We could adopt a risk avoidance strategy and completely eliminate the risk by not allowing employees to purchase or use laptops. This approach is unwieldy and would likely be met with strong opposition from employees and managers due to the negative impact on employee productivity.

Similarly, we could avoid the risk of a DDoS attack against the organization's website by simply shutting down the website. If there is no website to attack, there's no risk that a DDoS attack can affect the site. But it's highly improbable that business leaders will accept shutting down the website as a viable approach. In fact, you might consider being driven to shut down your website to avoid DDoS attacks as the *ultimate* denial of service attack!

Risk Transference

Risk transference shifts some of the impact of a risk from the organization experiencing the risk to another entity. The most common example of risk transference is purchasing an insurance policy that covers a risk. When purchasing insurance, the customer pays a premium to the insurance carrier. In exchange, the insurance carrier agrees to cover losses from risks specified in the policy.

In the example of laptop theft, property insurance policies may cover the risk. If an employee's laptop is stolen, the insurance policy would provide funds to cover either the value of the stolen device or the cost to replace the device, depending on the type of coverage.

It's unlikely that a property insurance policy would cover a DDoS attack. In fact, many general business policies exclude all cybersecurity risks. An organization seeking insurance coverage against this type of attack should purchase cybersecurity insurance, either as a separate policy or as a rider on an existing business insurance policy. This coverage would repay some or all of the cost of recovering operations and may also cover lost revenue during an attack.

Risk Acceptance

Risk acceptance is the final risk management strategy and it boils down to deliberately choosing to take no other risk management strategy and to simply continue operations as normal in the face of the risk. A risk acceptance approach may be warranted if the cost of mitigating a risk is greater than the impact of the risk itself.

Risk acceptance is a deliberate decision that comes as the result of a thoughtful analysis. It should not be undertaken as a default strategy. Simply stating that "we accept this risk" without analysis is not an example of an accepted risk; it is an example of an unmanaged risk!

In our laptop theft example, we might decide that none of the other risk management strategies are appropriate. For example, we might feel that the use of cable locks is an unnecessary burden and that theft recovery tags are unlikely to work, leaving us without a viable risk mitigation strategy. Business leaders might require that employees have laptop devices, taking risk avoidance off the table. And the cost of a laptop insurance policy might be too high to justify. In that case, we might decide that we will simply accept the risk and cover the cost of stolen devices when thefts occur. That's risk acceptance.

In the case of the DDoS risk, we might go through a similar analysis and decide that risk mitigation and transference strategies are too costly. In the event we continue to operate the site, we might do so accepting the risk that a DDoS attack could take the site down.

Exam Note

Understand the four risk management strategies—risk mitigation, risk avoidance, risk acceptance, and risk transference—before you take the CySA+ exam. Be prepared to provide examples of these strategies and to identify which strategy is being used in a given scenario.

Security Controls

Security controls are designed to mitigate one or more risks facing an organization by reducing the probability and/or magnitude of that risk. Throughout this book, you've already read about a large number of security controls.

Exam Note

In this section, we recap some of the security controls that CompTIA specifically mentions in an exam objective covering the "importance of data privacy and protection." It's reasonable to assume that you might see questions about these specific controls on the CySA+ exam.

In this chapter, we're grouping security controls into the broad categories of technical and nontechnical controls. In Chapter 16, we present a more formal framework that groups security controls into three categories (managerial, operational, and technical) and six types (preventive, detective, corrective, deterrent, compensating, and physical).

Nontechnical Controls

Most of this book focused on technical controls, ranging from vulnerability management and threat assessment to software and systems security. Technical topics do make up the vast majority of the CySA+ exam objectives, but it's important to remember that there are also nontechnical controls that we can use to mitigate the risks facing our organizations.

Data Ownership

One of the most important things that we can do to protect our data is to create clear *data ownership* policies and procedures. Using this approach, the organization designates specific senior executives as the data owners for different data types. For example, the vice president of Human Resources might be the data owner for employment and payroll data, whereas the vice president for Sales might be the data owner for customer information.

Clear lines of data ownership place responsibility for data in the hands of executives who best understand the impact of decisions about that data on the business. They don't make all of these decisions in isolation, however. Data owners delegate some of their responsibilities to others in the organization and also rely on advice from subject matter experts, such as cybersecurity analysts and data protection specialists.

Information Classification

Information classification programs organize data into categories based on the sensitivity of the information and the impact on the organization should the information be inadvertently disclosed. For example, the U.S. government uses the following four major classification categories:

- *Top Secret* information requires the highest degree of protection. The unauthorized disclosure of Top Secret information could reasonably be expected to cause exceptionally grave damage to national security.
- *Secret* information requires a substantial degree of protection. The unauthorized disclosure of Secret information could reasonably be expected to cause serious damage to national security.
- *Confidential* information requires some protection. The unauthorized disclosure of Confidential information could reasonably be expected to cause identifiable damage to national security.
- *Unclassified* information is information that does not meet the standards for classification under the other categories. Information in this category is still not publicly releasable without authorization.

Businesses generally don't use the same terminology for their levels of classified information. Instead, they might use friendlier terms, such as Highly Sensitive, Sensitive, Internal, and Public.

Data classification allows organizations to clearly specify the security controls required to protect information with different levels of sensitivity. For example, the U.S. government requires the use of brightly colored cover sheets, such as those shown in Figure 15.4, to identify classified information in printed form.

FIGURE 15.4 Cover sheets used to identify classified U.S. government information

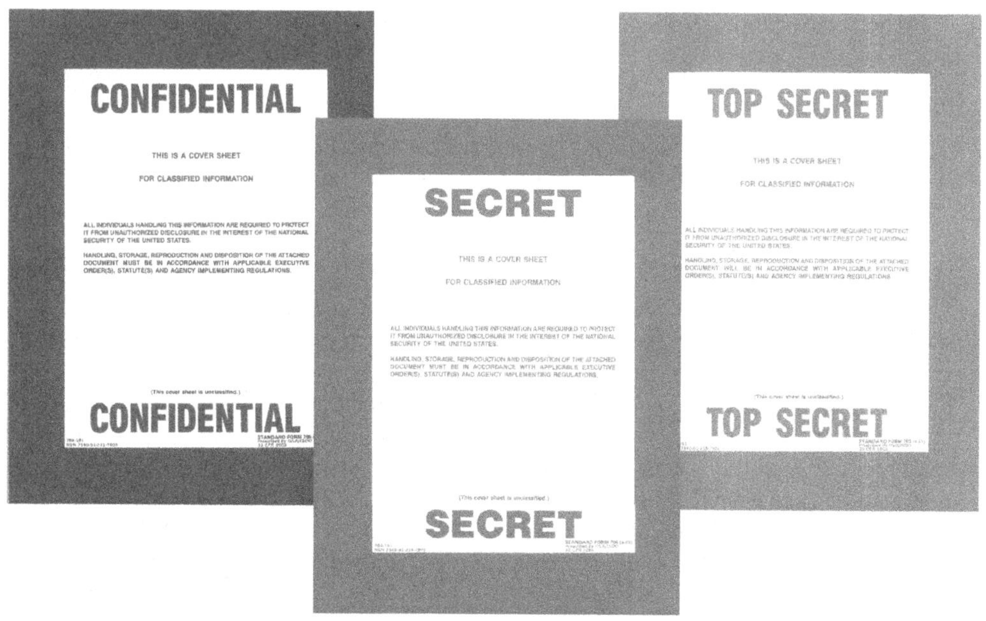

Data Life Cycle

Data protection should continue at all stages of the data life cycle, from the time the data is originally collected until the time it is eventually disposed.

At the early stages of the data life cycle, organizations should practice *data minimization*, where they collect the smallest possible amount of information necessary to meet their business requirements. Information that is not necessary should either be immediately discarded or, better yet, not collected in the first place.

While information remains within the care of the organization, the organization should practice *purpose limitation*. This means that information should only be used for the purpose that it was originally collected and that was consented to by the data subjects.

Finally, the organization should implement *data retention* standards that guide the end of the data life cycle. Data should only be kept for as long as it remains necessary to fulfill the purpose for which it was originally collected. At the conclusion of its life cycle, data should be securely destroyed.

Exam Note

Reducing the amount of data that you retain is a great way to minimize your security risk. Remember this as you answer exam questions that ask you to identify the best or most effective strategy for reducing risk.

Compliance Requirements

You may also implement nontechnical controls to satisfy *legal requirements* facing your organization. We'll discuss some of those specific requirements in Chapter 16, but there are two specific controls that CompTIA recommends in this category for data protection initiatives.

Data Sovereignty

Whether an organization builds their own infrastructure or relies on cloud service providers, they commonly distribute customer data across geographically distant data centers to mitigate the risk of an infrastructure failure. If one datacenter experiences a major operational issue, datacenters located in other regions automatically take over processing requirements.

This geographic distribution of data does introduce an important concern. The principle of *data sovereignty* says that data is subject to the legal restrictions of any jurisdiction where it is collected, stored, or processed.

Think about the impact here. If a company in the United States collects information from a U.S. citizen and stores it in a U.S. datacenter, that data is very clearly subject to U.S. law and immune from European Union (EU) law. If the EU tried to assert authority over that data under the General Data Protection Regulation (GDPR), the case would be thrown out of court because the EU regulators have no jurisdiction. However, if the U.S. company backs up their data to an alternate datacenter in Italy, suddenly the distinction is less clear. What laws now apply to the data?

Data sovereignty says that both EU and U.S. laws would apply and that could cause serious issues for the company. They were only attempting to protect the availability of their data in the event of a disaster, and they wound up subject to a whole new compliance regime.

Security professionals should pay careful attention to data sovereignty issues and take action to protect their organization against unwanted regulatory burdens:

- Before deploying any new service, determine where data will be stored and the regulatory implications of that storage.
- Ask cloud providers to specify the locations where data will be stored in writing and require that they provide advance notice before moving data into any new jurisdiction.
- Use encryption to protect data against prying eyes. If a foreign government demands that a cloud provider give them access to your data, they won't be able to read it if you hold the decryption key.

Nondisclosure Agreements

Nondisclosure agreements (NDAs) also play an important role in supporting compliance obligations. When an organization handles sensitive data, it should require that all employees working with that data sign NDAs that prohibit them from sharing that information with unauthorized individuals. NDAs contain language and penalties that survive the employment relationship, meaning that they continue to remain in force even after the employee leaves the organization.

Training and Exercises

Organizations conduct a wide variety of training programs designed to help employees understand their cybersecurity role. Cybersecurity analysts often participate in training programs that are set up as exercises using a competition-style format, pitting a team of attackers against a team of defenders.

Running exercises helps to identify vulnerabilities in the organization's systems, networks, and applications, similar to the results achieved from penetration testing. Exercises also provide employees with hands-on experience both attacking and defending systems. This helps boost cybersecurity skills and awareness among the technical staff.

When conducting an exercise, participants are often divided into three teams:

- *Red team* members are the attackers who attempt to gain access to systems.
- *Blue team* members are the defenders who must secure systems and networks from attack. The blue team also monitors the environment during the exercise, conducting active defense techniques. The blue team commonly gets a head start with some time to secure systems before the attack phase of the exercise begins.
- *White team* members are the observers and judges. They serve as referees to settle disputes over the rules and watch the exercise to document lessons learned from the test. The white team is able to observe the activities of both the red and blue teams and is also responsible for ensuring that the exercise does not cause production issues.

Capture the flag (CTF) exercises are a fun way to achieve training objectives. In a CTF exercise, the red team begins with set objectives, such as disrupting a website, stealing a file from a secured system, or causing other security failures. The exercise is scored based on how many objectives the red team was able to achieve compared to how many the blue team prevented them from executing.

Exercises don't need to take place using production systems. In many cases, an organization might set up a special environment solely for the purpose of the exercise. This provides a safe playground for the test and minimizes the probability that an attack will damage production systems. Other exercises may not even use real systems at all. *Tabletop exercises* simply gather participants in the same room to walk through their response to a fictitious exercise scenario.

Exam Note

Understand the different roles played by red, white, and blue teams in an exercise as you prepare for the exam.

Technical Controls

Throughout this book, you learned about many of the technical controls used to mitigate security risks. In this section, we recap some of the specific security controls that CompTIA advocates for using to protect data from prying eyes.

Encryption

Encryption technology uses mathematical algorithms to protect information from prying eyes, both while it is in transit over a network and while it resides on systems. Encrypted data is unintelligible to anyone who does not have access to the appropriate decryption key, making it safe to store and transmit encrypted data over otherwise insecure means.

Data Loss Prevention

Data loss prevention (DLP) systems help organizations enforce information handling policies and procedures to prevent data loss and theft. They search systems for stores of sensitive information that might be unsecured and monitor network traffic for potential attempts to remove sensitive information from the organization. They can act quickly to block the transmission before damage is done and alert administrators to the attempted breach.

DLP systems work in two different environments:

- Host-based DLP
- Network-based DLP

Host-based DLP uses software agents installed on systems that search those systems for the presence of sensitive information. These searches often turn up Social Security Numbers, credit card numbers, and other sensitive information in the most unlikely places!

Detecting the presence of stored sensitive information allows security professionals to take prompt action to either remove it or secure it with encryption. Taking the time to secure or remove information now may pay handsome rewards down the road if the device is lost, stolen, or compromised.

Host-based DLP can also monitor system configuration and user actions, blocking undesirable actions. For example, some organizations use host-based DLP to block users from accessing USB-based removable media devices that they might use to carry information out of the organization's secure environment.

Network-based DLP systems are dedicated devices that sit on the network and monitor outbound network traffic, watching for any transmissions that contain unencrypted sensitive information. They can then block those transmissions, preventing the unsecured loss of sensitive information.

DLP systems may simply block traffic that violates the organization's policy or, in some cases, they may automatically apply encryption to the content. This automatic encryption is commonly used with DLP systems that focus on email.

DLP systems also have two mechanisms of action:

- *Pattern matching*, where they watch for the telltale signs of sensitive information. For example, if they see a number that is formatted like a credit card or Social Security Number, they can automatically trigger on that. Similarly, they may contain a database of sensitive terms, such as "Top Secret" or "Business Confidential" and trigger when they see those terms in a transmission.
- *Watermarking*, where systems or administrators apply electronic tags to sensitive documents and then the DLP system can monitor systems and networks for unencrypted content containing those tags.

Watermarking technology is also commonly used in *digital rights management* (DRM) solutions that enforce copyright and data ownership restrictions.

Data Minimization

If we can't completely remove data from a dataset, we can often transform it into a format where the original sensitive information is deidentified. The *deidentification* process removes the ability to link data back to an individual, reducing its sensitivity.

An alternative to deidentifying data is transforming it into a format where the original information can't be retrieved. This is a process called *data obfuscation* and we have several tools at our disposal to assist with it:

- *Hashing* uses a hash function to transform a value in our dataset to a corresponding hash value. If we apply a strong hash function to a data element, we may replace the value in our file with the hashed value.

- *Tokenization* replaces sensitive values with a unique identifier using a lookup table. For example, we might replace a widely known value, such as a student ID, with a randomly generated 10-digit number. We'd then maintain a lookup table that allows us to convert those back to student IDs if we need to determine someone's identity. Of course, if you use this approach, you need to keep the lookup table secure!
- *Masking* partially redacts sensitive information by replacing some or all of sensitive fields with blank characters. For example, we might replace all but the last four digits of a credit card number with X's or *'s to render the card number unreadable.

Although it isn't possible to retrieve the original value directly from the hashed value, there is one major flaw to this approach. If someone has a list of possible values for a field, they can conduct something called a rainbow table attack. In this attack, the attacker computes the hashes of those candidate values and then checks to see if those hashes exist in our data file.

For example, imagine that we have a file listing all the students at our college who have failed courses but we hash their student IDs. If an attacker has a list of all students, they can compute the hash values of all student IDs and then check to see which hash values are on the list. For this reason, hashing should only be used with caution.

Access Controls

Organizations may also leverage their existing access control systems to provide enhanced protection for sensitive information, such as by implementing *geographic access requirements* that limit access by authorized user to certain locations, such as from within the office. You'll find more coverage of this topic in the "Context-Based Authentication" section of Chapter 8, "Identity and Access Management Security."

Exam Note

As you prepare for the exam, you should understand each of these technical controls and the types of scenarios where they might be appropriate risk mitigation controls.

Summary

Cybersecurity efforts are all about risk management. In this chapter, you learned about the techniques that cybersecurity analysts use to identify, assess, and manage a wide variety of risks. You learned about the differences between risk mitigation, risk avoidance, risk transference, and risk acceptance and when it is appropriate to use each. You also explored the different types of security controls that organizations can use to mitigate risks. In the next chapter, we continue this discussion and wrap up your preparation for the CySA+ exam with a look at policy and compliance issues.

Exam Essentials

Explain how risk identification and assessment helps organizations prioritize cybersecurity efforts. Cybersecurity analysts seek to identify all the risks facing their organization and then conduct a business impact analysis to assess the potential degree of risk based on the probability that it will occur and the magnitude of the potential effect on the organization. This work allows security professionals to prioritize risks and communicate risk factors to others in the organization.

Know that vendors are a source of external risk. Organizations should conduct their own systems assessments as part of their risk assessment practices, but they should conduct supply chain assessments as well. Performing vendor due diligence reduces the likelihood that a previously unidentified risk at a vendor will negatively impact the organization. Hardware source authenticity techniques verify that hardware was not tampered with after leaving the vendor's premises.

Describe a variety of risk management strategies. Risk avoidance strategies change business practices to eliminate a risk. Risk mitigation techniques seek to reduce the probability or magnitude of a risk. Risk transference approaches move some of the risk to a third party. Risk acceptance acknowledges the risk and continues normal business operations despite the presence of the risk.

Know that exercises play a crucial role in an organization's training program. Exercises may take place in a tabletop manner or may use real-world techniques. Live action exercises use blue teams to defend the network and red teams to attack those defenses. White teams serve as referees and neutral arbiters during the exercise.

Describe how security controls mitigate risks. Organizations implementing security controls often make engineering trade-offs as they seek to balance security and operational concerns. They may choose to implement nontechnical controls, including data ownership, classification, and retention policies. They may also adopt technical controls, including the use of encryption, data loss prevention, digital rights management, access controls, masking, deidentification, and tokenization.

Lab Exercises

Activity 15.1: Risk Management Strategies

On the next page, match the following risk management strategies with their descriptions.

Risk avoidance	Choosing to continue operations as normal despite the potential risk
Risk transference	Changing business activities to eliminate a risk
Risk mitigation	Shifting the impact of a risk to another organization
Risk acceptance	Implementing security controls that reduce the probability and/or magnitude of a risk

Activity 15.2: Risk Identification and Assessment

For this exercise, use your own organization. If you are not currently employed, you may use your school or another organization that you are familiar with.

Think of a business process that is critical to your organization's continued existence. Identify all the risks to the continued operation of that business process. Then choose one of those risks and conduct a quantitative or qualitative risk assessment of that risk.

Activity 15.3: Risk Management

Take the risk assessment that you developed in Activity 15.2. Identify at least one way that you could use each of the following risk management strategies to address that risk:

- Risk mitigation
- Risk avoidance
- Risk acceptance
- Risk transference

Which of these strategies do you feel is most appropriate for your scenario? Why? Feel free to choose more than one strategy if you believe it is the best way to manage the risk.

Review Questions

1. Jen identified a missing patch on a Windows server that might allow an attacker to gain remote control of the system. After consulting with her manager, she applied the patch. From a risk management perspective, what has she done?
   A. Removed the threat
   B. Reduced the threat
   C. Removed the vulnerability
   D. Reduced the vulnerability

2. You notice a high number of SQL injection attacks against a web application run by your organization, and you install a web application firewall to block many of these attacks before they reach the server. How have you altered the severity of this risk?
   A. Reduced the magnitude
   B. Eliminated the vulnerability
   C. Reduced the probability
   D. Eliminated the threat

Questions 3–7 refer to the following scenario:
Aziz is responsible for the administration of an e-commerce website that generates $100,000 per day in revenue for his firm. The website uses a database that contains sensitive information about the firm's customers. He expects that a compromise of that database would result in $500,000 in fines against his firm.
Aziz is assessing the risk of a SQL injection attack against the database where the attacker would steal all of the customer personally identifiable information (PII) from the database. After consulting threat intelligence, he believes that there is a 5 percent chance of a successful attack in any given year.

3. What is the asset value (AV)?
   A. $5,000
   B. $100,000
   C. $500,000
   D. $600,000

4. What is the exposure factor (EF)?
   A. 5 percent
   B. 20 percent
   C. 50 percent
   D. 100 percent

5. What is the single loss expectancy (SLE)?
   A. $5,000
   B. $100,000
   C. $500,000
   D. $600,000

6. What is the annualized rate of occurrence (ARO)?
   A. 0.05
   B. 0.20
   C. 2.00
   D. 5.00

7. What is the annualized loss expectancy (ALE)?
   A. $5,000
   B. $25,000
   C. $100,000
   D. $500,000

Questions 8–11 refer to the following scenario:
Grace recently completed a risk assessment of her organization's exposure to data breaches and determined that there is a high level of risk related to the loss of sensitive personal information. She is considering a variety of approaches to managing this risk.

8. Grace's first idea is to add a web application firewall to protect her organization against SQL injection attacks. What risk management strategy does this approach adopt?
   A. Risk acceptance
   B. Risk avoidance
   C. Risk mitigation
   D. Risk transference

9. Business leaders are considering dropping the customer activities that collect and store sensitive personal information. What risk management strategy would this approach use?
   A. Risk acceptance
   B. Risk avoidance
   C. Risk mitigation
   D. Risk transference

10. The business decided to install the web application firewall and continue doing business. They still were worried about other risks to the information that were not addressed by the firewall and considered purchasing an insurance policy to cover those risks. What strategy does this use?
   A. Risk acceptance
   B. Risk avoidance

C. Risk mitigation

D. Risk transference

11. In the end, risk managers found that the insurance policy was too expensive and opted not to purchase it. They are taking no additional action. What risk management strategy is being used in this situation?

    A. Risk acceptance

    B. Risk avoidance

    C. Risk mitigation

    D. Risk transference

12. Which one of the following U.S. government classification levels requires the highest degree of security control?

    A. Secret

    B. Confidential

    C. Top Secret

    D. Unclassified

13. Asa believes that her organization is taking data collected from customers for technical support and using it for marketing without their permission. What principle is most likely being violated?

    A. Data minimization

    B. Data retention

    C. Purpose limitation

    D. Data sovereignty

14. A U.S. company stores data in an EU data center and finds that it is now subject to the requirements of GDPR. This is an example of ________.

    A. Data minimization

    B. Data retention

    C. Purpose limitation

    D. Data sovereignty

Questions 15–17 refer to the following scenario:
Golden Dome Enterprises is conducting a cybersecurity exercise designed to test the effectiveness of its security controls. Participants have been divided into different teams to perform different functions. The team led by Ed is responsible for facilitating the exercise and arbitrating rules disputes. Barb's team is responsible for securing the systems in the exercise environment and defending them against attacks. Sofia's team is conducting offensive operations and attempting to break into the systems protected by Barb's team.

15. What term best describes the role that Sofia's team is playing in the exercise?

    A. Black team

    B. White team

C. Red team

D. Blue team

16. What term best describes the role that Ed's team is playing in the exercise?

A. Black team

B. White team

C. Red team

D. Blue team

17. What term best describes the role that Barb's team is playing in the exercise?

A. Black team

B. White team

C. Red team

D. Blue team

18. Which one of the following data protection techniques is reversible when conducted properly?

A. Tokenization

B. Masking

C. Hashing

D. Shredding

19. What security control can be used to clearly communicate to users the level of protection required for different data types?

A. Classification policies

B. Retention standards

C. Life cycle practices

D. Confidentiality controls

20. Alfonso is concerned that users might leave his organization and then share sensitive information that they retained with future employers. What security control would best protect against this risk?

A. IPS

B. DRM

C. DLP

D. NDA

Policy and Compliance

THE COMP TIA CYBERSECURITY ANALYST (CYSA+) EXAM OBJECTIVES COVERED IN THIS CHAPTER INCLUDE:

✓ **Domain 5.0: Compliance and Assessment**

- 5.3: Explain the importance of frameworks, policies, procedures, and controls.

Policy serves as the foundation for any cybersecurity program, setting out the principles and rules that guide the execution of security efforts throughout the enterprise. Often, organizations base these policies on best practice frameworks developed by industry groups, such as the National Institute of Standards and Technology (NIST) or the International Organization for Standardization (ISO). In many cases, organizational policies are also influenced and directed by external compliance obligations that regulators impose on the organization. In this chapter, you will learn about the important elements of the cybersecurity policy framework.

Understanding Policy Documents

An organization's *information security policy framework* contains a series of documents designed to describe the organization's cybersecurity program. The scope and complexity of these documents vary widely, depending on the nature of the organization and its information resources. These frameworks generally include four different types of document:

- Policies
- Standards
- Procedures
- Guidelines

In the remainder of this section, you'll learn the differences between each of these document types. However, keep in mind that the definitions of these categories vary significantly from organization to organization, and it is very common to find the lines between them blurred. Though at first glance that may seem "incorrect," it's a natural occurrence as security theory meets the real world. As long as the documents are achieving their desired purpose, there's no harm and no foul.

Policies

Policies are high-level statements of management intent. Compliance with policies is mandatory. An information security policy will generally contain broad statements about cybersecurity objectives, including:

- A statement of the importance of cybersecurity to the organization
- Requirements that all staff and contracts take measures to protect the confidentiality, integrity, and availability of information and information systems
- Statement on the ownership of information created and/or possessed by the organization
- Designation of the chief information security officer (CISO) or other individual as the executive responsible for cybersecurity issues
- Delegation of authority granting the CISO the ability to create standards, procedures, and guidelines that implement the policy

In many organizations, the process to create a policy is laborious and requires very high-level approval, often from the chief executive officer (CEO). Keeping policy statements at a high level provides the CISO with the flexibility to adapt and change specific security requirements with changes in the business and technology environments. For example, the five-page information security policy at the University of Notre Dame simply states that

> The Information Governance Committee will create handling standards for each Highly Sensitive data element. Data stewards may create standards for other data elements under their stewardship. These information handling standards will specify controls to manage risks to University information and related assets based on their classification. All individuals at the University are responsible for complying with these controls.

By way of contrast, the federal government's Centers for Medicare & Medicaid Services (CMS) has a 95-page information security policy. This mammoth document contains incredibly detailed requirements, such as

> A record of all requests for monitoring must be maintained by the CMS CIO along with any other summary results or documentation produced during the period of monitoring. The record must also reflect the scope of the monitoring by documenting search terms and techniques. All information collected from monitoring must be controlled and protected with distribution limited to the individuals identified in the request for monitoring and other individuals specifically designated by the CMS Administrator or CMS CIO as having a specific need to know such information.

The CMS document even goes so far as to include a complex chart describing the many cybersecurity roles held by individuals throughout the agency. An excerpt from that chart appears in Figure 16.1.

This approach may meet the needs of CMS, but it is hard to imagine the long-term maintenance of that document. Lengthy security policies often quickly become outdated as necessary changes to individual requirements accumulate and become neglected because staff are weary of continually publishing new versions of the policy.

FIGURE 16.1 Excerpt from CMS roles and responsibilities chart

Source: Centers for Medicare and Medicaid Services Information Systems Security and Privacy Policy, May 21, 2019. (`www.cms.gov/Research-Statistics-Data-and-Systems/CMS-Information-Technology/InformationSecurity/Downloads/CMS-IS2P2.pdf`)

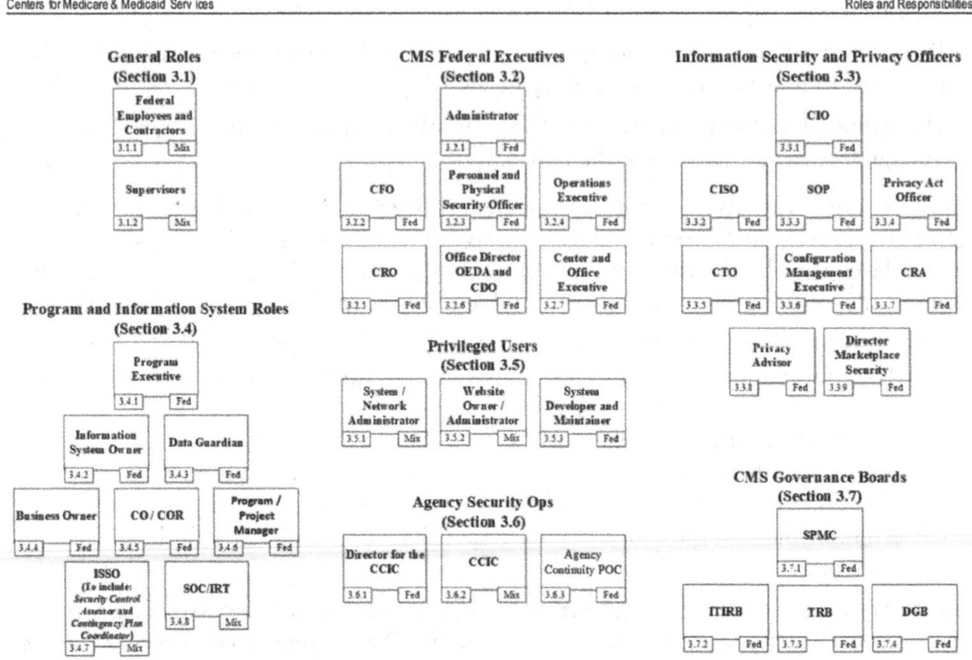

Organizations commonly include the following documents in their information security policy library:

- *Information security policy* that provides high-level authority and guidance for the security program
- *Acceptable use policy (AUP)* that provides network and system users with clear direction on permissible uses of information resources
- *Data ownership policy* that clearly states the ownership of information created or used by the organization
- *Data classification policy* that describes the classification structure used by the organization and the process used to properly assign classifications to data
- *Data retention policy* that outlines what information the organization will maintain and the length of time different categories of work product will be retained prior to destruction

- *Account management policy* that describes the account life cycle from provisioning through active use and decommissioning
- *Password policy* that sets forth requirements for password length, complexity, reuse, and similar issues
- *Continuous monitoring policy* that describes the organization's approach to monitoring and informs employees that their activity is subject to monitoring in the workplace
- *Code of conduct/ethics* that describes expected behavior of employees and affiliates and serves as a backstop for situations not specifically addressed in policy

As you read through the list, you may notice that some of the documents listed tend to conflict with our description of policies as high-level documents and seem to better fit the definition of a standard in the next section. That's a reasonable conclusion to draw. CompTIA specifically includes these items as elements of information security policy while many organizations would move some of them, such as password requirements, into standards documents.

Exam Note

As you prepare for the exam, be sure that you're familiar with the following examples of policies and procedures given by CompTIA in the exam objectives:

- Code of conduct/ethics
- Acceptable use policy (AUP)
- Password policy
- Data ownership policy
- Data retention policy
- Account management policy
- Continuous monitoring policy
- Work product retention

Standards

Standards provide mandatory requirements describing how an organization will carry out its information security policies. These may include the specific configuration settings used for a common operating system, the controls that must be put in place for highly sensitive information, or any other security objective. Standards are typically approved at a lower organizational level than policies and, therefore, may change more regularly.

For example, the University of California at Berkeley maintains a detailed document titled the Minimum Security Standards for Electronic Information, available online at `security.berkeley.edu/minimum-security-standards-electronic-information`. This document divides information into four different data protection levels (DPLs) and then describes what controls are required, optional, or not required for data at different levels using a detailed matrix. An excerpt from this matrix appears in Figure 16.2.

FIGURE 16.2 Excerpt from UC Berkeley Minimum Security Standards for Electronic Information

Source: University of California at Berkeley Minimum Security Standards for Electronic Information

MSSEI Controls	DPL 0 (TBD)	DPL 1 Individual	DPL 1 Privileged	DPL 1 Institutional	DPL 2 Individual	DPL 2 Privileged	DPL 2 Institutional	DPL 3 (TBD)	Guidelines
1.1 Removal of non-required covered data		o	√	√	√	√	√		see secure deletion guideline and UCOP disposition schedules database
1.2 Covered system inventory			√	√		√	√		1.2 guideline
1.3 Covered system registration			+	√		√	√		1.3 guideline
1.4 Annual registration renewal			√	√		√	√		1.4 guideline
2.1 Managed software inventory			+	√	o	√	√		2.1 guideline
3.1 Secure configurations		o	+	√	√	√	√		3.1 guideline
4.1 Continuous vulnerability assessment & remediation			+	√		√	√		4.1 guideline

The standard then provides detailed descriptions for each of these requirements with definitions of the terms used in the requirements. For example, requirement 3.1 in Figure 16.2 simply reads "Secure configurations." Later in the document, UC Berkeley expands this to read "Resource Custodians must utilize well-managed security configurations for hardware, software, and operating systems based on industry standards." It goes on to defined "well-managed" as

- Devices must have secure configurations in place prior to deployment.
- Any deviations from defined security configurations must be approved through a change management process and documented. A process must exist to annually review deviations from the defined security configurations for continued relevance.
- A process must exist to regularly check configurations of devices and alert the Resource Custodian of any changes.

This approach provides a document hierarchy that is easy to navigate for the reader and provides access to increasing levels of detail as needed. Notice also that many of the requirement lines in Figure 16.2 provide links to guidelines. Clicking on those links leads to advice to organizations subject to this policy that begins with this text:

> UC Berkeley security policy mandates compliance with Minimum Security Standards for Electronic Information for devices handling covered data. The recommendations below are provided as optional guidance.

This is a perfect example of three elements of the information security policy framework working together. Policy sets out the high-level objectives of the security program and requires compliance with standards, which includes details of required security controls. Guidelines provide advice to organizations seeking to comply with the policy and standards.

In some cases, organizations may operate in industries that have commonly accepted standards that the organization either must follow due to a regulatory requirement or choose to follow as a best practice. Failure to follow industry best practices may be seen as negligence and can cause legal liability for the organization. Many of these industry standards are expressed in the standard frameworks discussed later in this chapter.

Procedures

Procedures are detailed, step-by-step processes that individuals and organizations must follow in specific circumstances. Similar to checklists, procedures ensure a consistent process for achieving a security objective. Organizations may create procedures for building new systems, releasing code to production environments, responding to security incidents, and many other tasks. Compliance with procedures is mandatory.

For example, Visa publishes a document titled *What To Do If Compromised* (`usa.visa.com/dam/VCOM/download/merchants/cisp-what-to-do-if-compromised.pdf`) that lays out a mandatory process that merchants suspecting a credit card compromise must follow. Although the document doesn't contain the word *procedure* in the title, the introduction clearly states that the document "establishes procedures and timelines for reporting and responding to a suspected or confirmed Compromise Event." The document provides requirements covering the following areas of incident response:

- Notify Visa of the incident within three days
- Provide Visa with an initial investigation report
- Provide notice to other relevant parties
- Provide exposed payment account data to Visa
- Conduct PCI forensic investigation
- Conduct independent investigation
- Preserve evidence

Each of these sections provides detailed information on how Visa expects merchants to handle incident response activities. For example, the forensic investigation section describes the use of Payment Card Industry Forensic Investigators (PFI) and reads as follows:

> Upon discovery of an account data compromise, or receipt of an independent forensic investigation notification, an entity must:
>
> - Engage a PFI (or sign a contract) within five (5) business days.
> - Provide Visa with the initial forensic (i.e., preliminary) report within ten (10) business days from when the PFI is engaged (or the contract is signed).
> - Provide Visa with a final forensic report within ten (10) business days of the completion of the review.

There's not much room for interpretation in this type of language. Visa is laying out a clear and mandatory procedure describing what actions the merchant must take, the type of investigator they should hire, and the timeline for completing different milestones.

Organizations commonly include the following procedures in their policy frameworks:

- *Monitoring procedures* that describe how the organization will perform security monitoring activities, including the possible use of continuous monitoring technology
- *Evidence production procedures* that describe how the organization will respond to subpoenas, court orders, and other legitimate requests to produce digital evidence
- *Patching procedures* that describe the frequency and process of applying patches to applications and systems under the organization's care

Of course, cybersecurity teams may decide to include many other types of procedures in their frameworks, as dictated by the organization's operational needs.

Guidelines

Guidelines provide best practices and recommendations related to a given concept, technology, or task. Compliance with guidelines is not mandatory, and guidelines are offered in the spirit of providing helpful advice. That said, the "optionality" of guidelines may vary significantly depending on the organization's culture.

In April 2016, the chief information officer (CIO) of the state of Washington published a 25-page document providing guidelines on the use of electronic signatures by state agencies. The document is not designed to be obligatory but, rather, offers advice to agencies seeking to adopt electronic signature technology. The document begins with a purpose section that outlines three goals of the guideline:

1. Help agencies determine if, and to what extent, their agency will implement and rely on electronic records and electronic signatures.
2. Provide agencies with information they can use to establish policy or rule governing their use and acceptance of digital signatures.

3. Provide direction to agencies for sharing of their policies with the Office of the Chief Information Officer (OCIO) pursuant to state law.

The first two stated objectives line up completely with the function of a guideline. Phrases like "help agencies determine" and "provide agencies with information" are common in guideline documents. There is nothing mandatory about them and, in fact, the guidelines explicitly state that Washington state law "does not mandate that any state agency accept or require electronic signatures or records."

The third objective might seem a little strange to include in a guideline. Phrases like "provide direction" are more commonly found in policies and procedures. Browsing through the document, the text relating to this objective is only a single paragraph within a 25-page document, reading

> The Office of the Chief Information Officer maintains a page on the `OCIO.wa.gov` website listing links to individual agency electronic signature and record submission policies. As agencies publish their policies, the link and agency contact information should be emailed to the OCIO Policy Mailbox. The information will be added to the page within 5 working days. Agencies are responsible for notifying the OCIO if the information changes.

Reading this paragraph, the text does appear to clearly outline a mandatory procedure and would not be appropriate in a guideline document that fits within the strict definition of the term. However, it is likely that the committee drafting this document thought it would be much more convenient to the reader to include this explanatory text in the related guideline rather than drafting a separate procedure document for a fairly mundane and simple task.

The full Washington state document, Electronic Signature Guidelines, is available for download from the Washington State CIO's website at `ocio.wa.gov/policy/electronic-signature-guidelines`.

Exceptions and Compensating Controls

When adopting new security policies, standards, and procedures, organizations should also provide a mechanism for exceptions to those rules. Inevitably, unforeseen circumstances will arise that require a deviation from the requirements. The policy framework should lay out the specific requirements for receiving an exception and the individual or committee with the authority to approve exceptions.

The state of Washington uses an exception process that requires the requestor document the following information:

- Standard/requirement that requires an exception
- Reason for noncompliance with the requirement
- Business and/or technical justification for the exception
- Scope and duration of the exception
- Risks associated with the exception
- Description of any supplemental controls that mitigate the risks associated with the exception
- Plan for achieving compliance
- Identification of any unmitigated risks

Many exception processes require the use of *compensating controls* to mitigate the risk associated with exceptions to security standards. The Payment Card Industry Data Security Standard (PCI DSS) includes one of the most formal compensating control processes in use today. It sets out three criteria that must be met for a compensating control to be satisfactory:

1. The control must meet the intent and rigor of the original requirement.
2. The control must provide a similar level of defense as the original requirement, such that the compensating control sufficiently offsets the risk that the original PCI DSS requirement was designed to defend against.
3. The control must be "above and beyond" other PCI DSS requirements.

For example, an organization might find that it needs to run an outdated version of an operating system on a specific machine because software necessary to run the business will only function on that operating system version. Most security policies would prohibit using the outdated operating system because it might be susceptible to security vulnerabilities. The organization could choose to run this system on an isolated network with either very little or no access to other systems as a compensating control.

The general idea is that a compensating control finds alternative means to achieve an objective when the organization cannot meet the original control requirement. While PCI DSS offers a very formal process for compensating controls, the use of compensating controls is a common strategy in many different organizations, even those not subject to PCI DSS. Compensating controls balance the fact that it simply isn't possible to implement every required security control in every circumstance with the desire to manage risk to the greatest feasible degree.

In many cases, organizations adopt compensating controls to address a temporary exception to a security requirement. In those cases, the organization should also develop remediation plans designed to bring the organization back into compliance with the letter and intent of the original control.

Complying with Laws and Regulations

Legislators and regulators around the world take an interest in cybersecurity due to the potential impact of cybersecurity shortcomings on individuals, government, and society. While the European Union (EU) has a broad-ranging data protection regulation, cybersecurity analysts in the United States are forced to deal with a patchwork of security regulations covering different industries and information categories.

Some of the major information security regulations facing U.S. organizations include the following:

- The *Health Insurance Portability and Accountability Act (HIPAA)* includes security and privacy rules that affect healthcare providers, health insurers, and health information clearinghouses.
- The *Payment Card Industry Data Security Standard (PCI DSS)* provides detailed rules about the storage, processing, and transmission of credit and debit card information. PCI DSS is not a law but rather a contractual obligation that applies to credit card merchants and service providers.
- The *Gramm–Leach–Bliley Act (GLBA)* covers financial institutions, broadly defined. It requires that those institutions have a formal security program and designate an individual as having overall responsibility for that program.
- The *Sarbanes–Oxley (SOX) Act* applies to the financial records of publicly traded companies and requires that those companies have a strong degree of assurance around the IT systems that store and process those records.
- The *Family Educational Rights and Privacy Act (FERPA)* requires that educational institutions implement security and privacy controls for student educational records.
- Various *data breach notification laws* describe the requirements that individual states place on organizations that suffer data breaches regarding notification of individuals affected by the breach.

Remember that this is only a brief listing of security regulations. There are many other laws and obligations that apply to specific industries and data types. You should always consult your organization's legal counsel and subject matter experts when designing a compliance strategy for your organization. The advice of a well-versed attorney is crucial when interpreting and applying cybersecurity regulations to your specific business and technical environment.

Exam Note

The CySA+ exam objectives only mention compliance in a generic sense, with a single bullet reading "compliance" as one of the topics that cybersecurity analysts should be able to explain. Rather than diving into the details of specific regulations, you should have a good working knowledge of what regulations might apply to a specific industry and how to integrate an understanding of compliance issues into a cybersecurity program.

Adopting a Standard Framework

Developing a cybersecurity program from scratch is a formidable undertaking. Organizations will have a wide variety of control objectives and tools at their disposal to meet those objectives. Teams facing the task of developing a new security program or evaluating an existing program may find it challenging to cover a large amount of ground without a roadmap. Fortunately, there are several standard security frameworks available to assist with this task and provide a standardized approach to developing cybersecurity programs.

Exam Note

Frameworks may be prescriptive or risk-based. This concept is specifically listed in the CySA+ exam objectives and you should be familiar with it when taking the exam. Prescriptive frameworks mandate the controls that an organization must implement with little flexibility for interpretation. Risk-based frameworks provide high-level control objectives and then allow the organization to design situation-appropriate controls based on their own assessment of the risk environment.

NIST Cybersecurity Framework

The National Institute for Standards and Technology (NIST) is responsible for developing cybersecurity standards across the U.S. federal government. The guidance and standard documents they produce in this process often have wide applicability across the private sector and are commonly referred to by nongovernmental security analysts due to the fact that they are available in the public domain and are typically of very high quality.

In 2014, NIST released a Cybersecurity Framework designed to assist organizations attempting to meet one or more of the following five objectives:

- Describe their current cybersecurity posture.
- Describe their target state for cybersecurity.
- Identify and prioritize opportunities for improvement within the context of a continuous and repeatable process.
- Assess progress toward the target state.
- Communicate among internal and external stakeholders about cybersecurity risk.

The NIST framework includes three components:

- The Framework Core, shown in Figure 16.3, is a set of five security functions that apply across all industries and sectors: identify, protect, detect, respond, and recover. The framework then divides these functions into categories, subcategories, and informative references. Figure 16.4 shows a small excerpt of this matrix in completed form, looking specifically at the Identify (ID) function and the Asset Management category. If you would like to view a fully completed matrix, see NIST's document Framework for Improving Critical Infrastructure Cybersecurity.

- The framework implementation tiers assess how an organization is positioned to meet cybersecurity objectives. Table 16.1 shows the framework implementation tiers and their criteria. This approach is an example of a *maturity model* that describes the current and desired positioning of an organization along a continuum of progress. In the case of the NIST maturity model, organizations are assigned to one of four maturity model tiers.
- Framework profiles describe how a specific organization might approach the security functions covered by the framework core. An organization might use a framework profile to describe its current state and then a separate profile to describe its desired future state.

FIGURE 16.3 NIST Cybersecurity Framework Core Structure

Source: Framework for Improving Critical Infrastructure Cybersecurity, National Institute of Standards and Technology (`nvlpubs.nist.gov/nistpubs/CSWP/NIST.CSWP.04162018.pdf`)

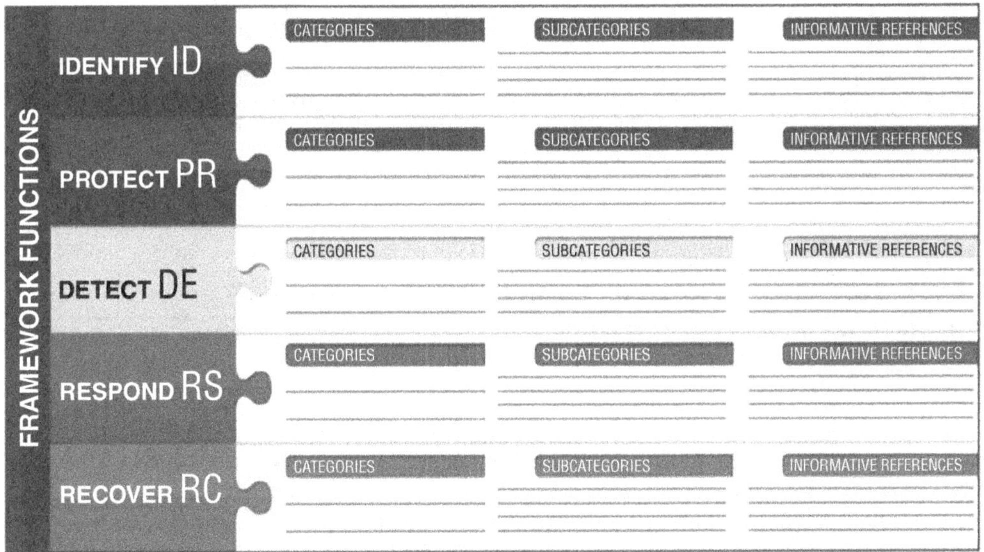

The NIST Cybersecurity Framework provides organizations with a sound approach to developing and evaluating the state of their cybersecurity programs.

FIGURE 16.4 Asset Management Cybersecurity Framework

Source: Framework for Improving Critical Infrastructure Cybersecurity, National Institute of Standards and Technology (`nvlpubs.nist.gov/nistpubs/CSWP/NIST.CSWP.04162018.pdf`)

Function	Category	Subcategory	Informative References
IDENTIFY (ID)	**Asset Management (ID.AM):** The data, personnel, devices, systems, and facilities that enable the organization to achieve business purposes are identified and managed consistent with their relative importance to business objectives and the organization's risk strategy.	**ID.AM-1:** Physical devices and systems within the organization are inventoried	• **CCS CSC** 1 • **COBIT 5** BAI09.01, BAI09.02 • **ISA 62443-2-1:2009** 4.2.3.4 • **ISA 62443-3-3:2013** SR 7.8 • **ISO/IEC 27001:2013** A.8.1.1, A.8.1.2 • **NIST SP 800-53 Rev. 4** CM-8
		ID.AM-2: Software platforms and applications within the organization are inventoried	• **CCS CSC** 2 • **COBIT 5** BAI09.01, BAI09.02, BAI09.05 • **ISA 62443-2-1:2009** 4.2.3.4 • **ISA 62443-3-3:2013** SR 7.8 • **ISO/IEC 27001:2013** A.8.1.1, A.8.1.2 • **NIST SP 800-53 Rev. 4** CM-8
		ID.AM-3: Organizational communication and data flows are mapped	• **CCS CSC** 1 • **COBIT 5** DSS05.02 • **ISA 62443-2-1:2009** 4.2.3.4 • **ISO/IEC 27001:2013** A.13.2.1 • **NIST SP 800-53 Rev. 4** AC-4, CA-3, CA-9, PL-8
		ID.AM-4: External information systems are catalogued	• **COBIT 5** APO02.02 • **ISO/IEC 27001:2013** A.11.2.6 • **NIST SP 800-53 Rev. 4** AC-20, SA-9
		ID.AM-5: Resources (e.g., hardware, devices, data, time, and software) are prioritized based on their classification, criticality, and business value	• **COBIT 5** APO03.03, APO03.04, BAI09.02 • **ISA 62443-2-1:2009** 4.2.3.6 • **ISO/IEC 27001:2013** A.8.2.1 • **NIST SP 800-53 Rev. 4** CP-2, RA-2, SA-14
		ID.AM-6: Cybersecurity roles and responsibilities for the entire workforce and third-party stakeholders (e.g., suppliers, customers, partners) are established	• **COBIT 5** APO01.02, DSS06.03 • **ISA 62443-2-1:2009** 4.3.2.3.3 • **ISO/IEC 27001:2013** A.6.1.1

TABLE 16.1 NIST Cybersecurity framework implementation tiers

Source: Framework for Improving Critical Infrastructure Cybersecurity, National Institute of Standards and Technology

Tier	Risk management process	Integrated risk management program	External participation
Tier 1: Partial	Organizational cybersecurity risk management practices are not formalized, and risk is managed in an ad hoc and sometimes reactive manner.	There is limited awareness of cybersecurity risk at the organizational level. The organization implements cybersecurity risk management on an irregular, case-by-case basis due to varied experience or information gained from outside sources.	The organization does not understand its role in the larger ecosystem with respect to either its dependencies or dependents.

Tier	Risk management process	Integrated risk management program	External participation
Tier 2: Risk Informed	Risk management practices are approved by management but may not be established as organizationwide policy.	There is an awareness of cybersecurity risk at the organizational level, but an organizationwide approach to managing cybersecurity risk has not been established.	Generally, the organization understands its role in the larger ecosystem with respect to either its own dependencies or dependents, but not both.
Tier 3: Repeatable	The organization's risk management practices are formally approved and expressed as policy.	There is an organizationwide approach to manage cybersecurity risk.	The organization understands its role, dependencies, and dependents in the larger ecosystem and may contribute to the community's broader understanding of risks.
Tier 4: Adaptive	The organization adapts its cybersecurity practices based on previous and current cybersecurity activities, including lessons learned and predictive indicators.	There is an organizationwide approach to managing cybersecurity risk that uses risk-informed policies, processes, and procedures to address potential cybersecurity events.	The organization understands its role, dependencies, and dependents in the larger ecosystem and contributes to the community's broader understanding of risks.

ISO 27001

The International Organization for Standardization (ISO) publishes *ISO 27001*, a standard document titled "Information technology—Security techniques—Information security management systems—Requirements." This standard includes control objectives covering 14 categories:

1. Information security policies
2. Organization of information security
3. Human resource security
4. Asset management
5. Access control

6. Cryptography
7. Physical and environmental security
8. Operations security
9. Communications security
10. System acquisition, development, and maintenance
11. Supplier relationships
12. Information security incident management
13. Information security aspects of business continuity management
14. Compliance with internal requirements, such as policies, and with external requirements, such as laws

The ISO 27001 standard was once the most commonly used information security standards, but it is declining in popularity outside of highly regulated industries that require ISO compliance. Organizations in those industries may choose to formally adopt ISO 27001 and pursue *certification* programs where an external assessor validates their compliance with the standard and certifies them as operating in accordance with ISO 27001.

Control Objectives for Information and Related Technologies (COBIT)

The *Control Objectives for Information and Related Technologies (COBIT)* is a set of best practices for IT governance developed by the Information Systems Audit and Control Association (ISACA). COBIT divides information technology activities into four domains:

- Plan and Organize
- Acquire and Implement
- Deliver and Support
- Monitor and Evaluate

COBIT addresses each of these four domains of technology by providing five COBIT framework components:

1. COBIT framework
2. Process descriptions
3. Control objectives
4. Management guidelines
5. Maturity models

Information Technology Infrastructure Library (ITIL)

The *Information Technology Infrastructure Library (ITIL)* is a framework that offers a comprehensive approach to IT service management (ITSM) within the modern enterprise. ITIL covers five core activities:

- Service Strategy
- Service Design
- Service Transition
- Service Operation
- Continual Service Improvement

Figure 16.5 shows how these activities fit together in the ITIL service life cycle. Although it is not widely used as a cybersecurity framework, many organizations choose to adopt ITIL ITSM practices and then include cybersecurity functions within their ITIL implementation.

FIGURE 16.5 ITIL service life cycle

Implementing Policy-Based Controls

Security policy frameworks and the specific security policies adopted by organizations lay out *control objectives* that an organization wishes to achieve. These control objectives are statements of a desired security state, but they do not, by themselves, actually carry out security activities. *Security controls* are specific measures that fulfill the security objectives of an organization.

Security Control Categories

Security controls are categorized based on their mechanism of action—the way that they achieve their objectives. There are three different categories of security control:

- *Technical controls* enforce confidentiality, integrity, and availability in the digital space. Examples of technical security controls include firewall rules, access control lists, intrusion prevention systems, and encryption.
- *Operational controls* include the processes that we put in place to manage technology in a secure manner. These include user access reviews, log monitoring, and vulnerability management.
- *Managerial controls* are procedural mechanisms that focus on the mechanics of the risk management process. Examples of administrative controls include periodic risk assessments, security planning exercises, and the incorporation of security into the organization's change management, service acquisition, and project management practices.

Organizations should select a set of security controls that meets their control objectives based on the criteria and parameters that they either select for their environment or have imposed on them by outside regulators. For example, an organization that handles sensitive information might decide that confidentiality concerns surrounding that information require the highest level of control. At the same time, they might conclude that the availability of their website is not of critical importance. Given these considerations, they would dedicate significant resources to the confidentiality of sensitive information while perhaps investing little, if any, time and money protecting their website against a denial-of-service attack.

Many control objectives require a combination of technical, operational, and management controls. For example, an organization might have the control objective of preventing unauthorized access to a datacenter. They might achieve this goal by implementing biometric access control (technical control), performing regular reviews of authorized access (operational control), and conducting routine risk assessments (managerial control).

Security Control Types

CompTIA also divides security into types, based on their desired effect. The types of security control include

- *Preventive controls* intend to stop a security issue before it occurs. Firewalls and encryption are examples of preventive controls.
- *Detective controls* identify security events that have already occurred. Intrusion detection systems are detective controls.
- *Corrective controls* remediate security issues that have already occurred. Restoring backups after a ransomware attack is an example of a corrective control.
- *Deterrent controls* seek to prevent an attacker from attempting to violate security policies. Vicious guard dogs and barbed wire fences are examples of deterrent controls.
- *Physical controls* are security controls that impact the physical world. Examples of physical security controls include fences, perimeter lighting, locks, fire suppression systems, and burglar alarms.
- *Compensating controls*, discussed earlier in this chapter, are designed to mitigate the risk associated with exceptions made to a security policy.

Exam Note

These control categories and types are unique to CompTIA. If you've already studied similar categories as part of your preparation for another security certification program, be sure to study these carefully and use them when answering exam questions.

Security Control Verification and Quality Control

Quality control procedures verify that an organization has sufficient security controls in place and that those security controls are functioning properly. Every security program should include procedures for conducting regular internal tests of security controls and supplement those informal tests with formal evaluations of the organization's security program. Those evaluations may come in two different forms: audits and assessments.

Audits are formal reviews of an organization's security program or specific compliance issues conducted on behalf of a third party. Audits require rigorous, formal testing of controls and result in a formal statement from the auditor regarding the entity's compliance.

Audits may be conducted by internal audit groups at the request of management or by external audit firms, typically at the request of an organization's governing body or a regulator.

Assessments are less formal reviews of security controls that are typically requested by the security organization itself in an effort to engage in process improvement. During an assessment, the assessor typically gathers information by interviewing employees and taking them at their word, rather than preforming the rigorous independent testing associated with an audit.

Summary

Policies form the basis of every strong information security program. A solid policy framework consists of policies, standards, procedures, and guidelines that work together to describe the security control environment of an organization. In addition to complying with internally developed policies, organizations often must comply with externally imposed compliance obligations. Security frameworks, such as the NIST Cybersecurity Framework and ISO 27001, provide a common structure for security programs based on accepted industry best practices. Organizations should implement and test security controls to achieve security control objectives that are developed based on the business and technical environment of the organization.

Exam Essentials

Describe policy frameworks and what they consist of. Policies are high-level statements of management intent for the information security program. Standards describe the detailed implementation requirements for policy. Procedures offer step-by-step instructions for carrying out security activities. Compliance with policies, standards, and procedures is mandatory. Guidelines offer optional advice that complements other elements of the policy framework. Frameworks used to set security approaches may be either prescriptive or risk-based.

Describe how organizations often adopt a set of security policies covering different areas of their security programs. Common policies used in security programs include an information security policy, an acceptable use policy, a data ownership policy, a data retention policy, an account management policy, and a password policy. The specific policies adopted by any organization will depend on that organization's culture and business needs.

Know that policy documents should include exception processes. Exception processes should outline the information required to receive an exception to security policy and the approval authority for each exception. The process should also describe the requirements for compensating controls that mitigate risks associated with approved security policy exceptions.

Understand the variety of security compliance requirements that organizations face. Healthcare providers must comply with the Health Insurance Portability and Accountability Act (HIPAA). Merchants and credit card service providers must comply with the Payment Card Industry Data Security Standard (PCI DSS). Financial institutions are subject to the Gramm–Leach–Bliley Act (GLBA), whereas public companies must comply with the Sarbanes–Oxley Act (SOX). Educational institutions must follow the Family Educational Rights and Privacy Act (FERPA).

Define the purpose of standards frameworks. Organizations may choose to base their security programs on a framework, such as the NIST Cybersecurity Framework, ISO 27001, or the IT Infrastructure Library (ITIL). These frameworks sometimes include maturity models that allow an organization to assess its progress. Some frameworks also offer certification programs that provide independent assessments of an organization's progress toward adopting a framework.

Know that controls may be categorized based on their mechanism of action and their intent. Controls are grouped into the categories of managerial, operational, and technical based on the way that they achieve their objectives. They are divided into the types of preventive, detective, corrective, deterrent, compensating, and physical based on their intended purpose.

Explain how audits and assessments are used to monitor compliance with requirements. Audits are externally commissioned, formal reviews of the capability of an organization to achieve its control objectives. Assessments are less rigorous reviews of security issues, often performed or commissioned by IT staff.

Lab Exercises

Activity 16.1: Policy Documents

Match the following policy documents with their descriptions.

Policy	Outlines a step-by-step process for carrying out a cybersecurity activity
Standard	Includes advice based on best practices for achieving security goals that are not mandatory
Guideline	Provides high-level requirements for a cybersecurity program
Procedure	Offers detailed requirements for achieving security control objectives

Activity 16.2: Using a Cybersecurity Framework

Download and read the current version of the NIST Framework for Improving Critical Infrastructure Cybersecurity (`nvlpubs.nist.gov/nistpubs/CSWP/NIST.CSWP.04162018.pdf`).

Choose a specific category from the framework core that appears in Table 2 at the end of the document. If you are currently employed, describe how your organization addresses each of the subcategories for that function and category. If you are not currently employed, perform the same analysis for an organization with which you are familiar to the best of your ability.

Activity 16.3: Compliance Auditing Tools

The Payment Card Industry Data Security Standard (PCI DSS) includes detailed testing procedures for each one of the standard's requirements.

Download a copy of the current PCI DSS standard from the PCI Security Standards Council website (`www.pcisecuritystandards.org/document_library?category=pcidss&document=pci_dss`). Find the section of the standard that includes requirements for password construction (section 8.2.3 in PCI DSS version 3.2.1).

Describe the testing procedures that an auditor would follow to determine whether an organization is in compliance with this requirement.

Review Questions

1. Joe is authoring a document that explains to system administrators one way that they might comply with the organization's requirement to encrypt all laptops. What type of document is Joe writing?
   A. Policy
   B. Guideline
   C. Procedure
   D. Standard
2. Which one of the following statements is not true about compensating controls under PCI DSS?
   A. Controls used to fulfill one PCI DSS requirement may be used to compensate for the absence of a control needed to meet another requirement.
   B. Controls must meet the intent of the original requirement.
   C. Controls must meet the rigor of the original requirement.
   D. Compensating controls must provide a similar level of defense as the original requirement.
3. What law creates cybersecurity obligations for healthcare providers and others in the health industry?
   A. HIPAA
   B. FERPA
   C. GLBA
   D. PCI DSS
4. Which one of the following is *not* one of the five core security functions defined by the NIST Cybersecurity Framework?
   A. Identify
   B. Contain
   C. Respond
   D. Recover
5. What ISO standard applies to information security management controls?
   A. 9001
   B. 27001
   C. 14032
   D. 57033

6. Which one of the following documents must normally be approved by the CEO or similarly high-level executive?
   A. Standard
   B. Procedure
   C. Guideline
   D. Policy
7. Greg recently conducted an assessment of his organization's security controls and discovered a potential gap: the organization does not use full-disk encryption on laptops. What type of control gap exists in this case?
   A. Detective
   B. Corrective
   C. Deterrent
   D. Preventive
8. What law governs the financial records of publicly traded companies?
   A. GLBA
   B. SOX
   C. FERPA
   D. PCI DSS
9. What type of security policy often serves as a backstop for issues not addressed in other policies?
   A. Account management
   B. Data ownership
   C. Code of conduct
   D. Continuous monitoring
10. Which one of the following would *not* normally be found in an organization's information security policy?
    A. Statement of the importance of cybersecurity
    B. Requirement to use AES-256 encryption
    C. Delegation of authority
    D. Designation of responsible executive
11. Darren is updating the organization's risk management process. What type of control is Darren creating?
    A. Operational
    B. Technical
    C. Corrective
    D. Managerial

12. Which one of the following control models describes the five core activities associated with IT service management as service strategy, service design, service transition, service operation, and continual service improvement?
    A. COBIT
    B. TOGAF
    C. ISO 27001
    D. ITIL
13. What compliance obligation applies to merchants and service providers who work with credit card information?
    A. FERPA
    B. SOX
    C. HIPAA
    D. PCI DSS
14. Which one of the following policies would typically answer questions about when an organization should destroy records?
    A. Data ownership policy
    B. Account management policy
    C. Password policy
    D. Data retention policy
15. While studying an organization's risk management process under the NIST Cybersecurity Framework, Rob determines that the organization adapts its cybersecurity practices based on lessons learned and predictive indicators derived from previous and current cybersecurity activities. What tier should he assign based on this measure?
    A. Tier 1
    B. Tier 2
    C. Tier 3
    D. Tier 4
16. Which one of the following security policy framework components does not contain mandatory guidance for individuals in the organization?
    A. Policy
    B. Standard
    C. Procedure
    D. Guideline

17. Tina is creating a set of firewall rules designed to block denial-of-service attacks from entering her organization's network. What type of control is Tina designing?
    - A. Technical control
    - B. Physical control
    - C. Managerial control
    - D. Operational control
18. Allan is developing a document that lists the acceptable mechanisms for securely obtaining remote administrative access to servers in his organization. What type of document is Allan writing?
    - A. Policy
    - B. Standard
    - C. Guideline
    - D. Procedure
19. Which one of the following is not a common use of the NIST Cybersecurity Framework?
    - A. Describe the current cybersecurity posture of an organization.
    - B. Describe the target future cybersecurity posture of an organization.
    - C. Communicate with stakeholders about cybersecurity risk.
    - D. Create specific technology requirements for an organization.
20. Shelly is writing a document that describes the steps that incident response teams will follow upon first notice of a potential incident. What type of document is she creating?
    - A. Policy
    - B. Standard
    - C. Guideline
    - D. Procedure

Practice Exam

This appendix contains a full-length practice exam designed to be similar to the CompTIA Cybersecurity Analyst (CySA+) exam. The questions are balanced among the CySA+ domains, and the question content is similar to what you will find on the exam.

Our recommendation is that you save this exam until you have completed your first round of studying and then attempt the exam in a single sitting to simulate the real exam experience.

After grading your exam, you may use it to highlight areas of study that you should revisit before taking the real exam. You will find the answers and explanations to this exam listed in Appendix B.

Good luck with the practice test and best wishes for success on the CySA+ exam!

Exam Questions

1. Tom is preparing to build a credit card processing system. As he creates his design, he realizes that the operating environment will not allow him to include one of the PCI DSS required elements. What type of control should Tom discuss implementing?

   A. Technical control

   B. Operational control

   C. Administrative control

   D. Compensating control

2. Shane administers a Linux server running Apache. During the middle of his workday, tweets start to appear in his Twitter feed about compromises of Apache servers due to a flaw that had not been previously reported. What type of threat is this?

   A. A local exploit

   B. Advanced persistent threat

   C. A zero-day exploit

   D. A zero-knowledge threat

3. Juan is analyzing systems on his network for known indicators of compromise. What term best describes the work he is performing?

   A. Threat hunting

   B. Vulnerability scanning

   C. Intrusion prevention

   D. Data mining

4. Which one of the following controls may be used to attract the attention of intruders who gain access to a network segment so that they are distracted from high-value targets and may be monitored?

   A. MAC

   B. Honeypot

   C. Intrusion prevention system

   D. Rogue AP

5. While engaging in an attack, the attacker sends an email message to the targeted victim that contains malicious software as an attachment. What phase of the Cyber Kill Chain is occurring?

   A. Weaponization

   B. Delivery

   C. Action on Objectives

   D. Reconnaissance

6. Betsy receives many requests from IT staff members for remote access to internal systems through the DMZ. What type of system might Betsy place in the DMZ to accommodate these requests?

   A. Jump box

   B. Virtual machine

   C. Honeypot

   D. Firewall

7. Karen is configuring the host firewall on a web server that allows both encrypted and unencrypted web connections. It also must allow SSH access for users to securely drop off files. Which one of the following ports should *not* be open on the host firewall?

   A. 22

   B. 80

   C. 443

   D. 1433

8. Jacob has been tasked with using NetFlow to monitor network traffic flows in his organization, but the systems he is using are unable to keep up with the volume of data. What is his best option to deal with the traffic without adding new hardware while retaining visibility into the entire network?

   A. Switch to RMON monitoring

   B. Use flow sampling

   C. Decrease the number of flows allowed for each user

   D. Use packet shaping to reduce traffic rates to one that the flow collector can keep up with

9. Brooke is helping her organization implement a new cloud service. She is configuring the operating system on a server built in the cloud provider's environment. What cloud service model is in use?

   A. PaaS

   B. FaaS

   C. SaaS

   D. IaaS

10. Barry joins a hotel wireless network and opens a web browser. No matter which page he visits, he is redirected to a web page requesting him to provide his name and room number. What type of network access control is the hotel using?

   A. In-band

   B. Out-of-band

   C. 802.1x

   D. Agent-based

11. Charles has been asked to secure the wired network that is normally a suite of offices that will be temporarily used by a visiting team from another company. If he wants to continue to allow members of his team to use the jacks, what technical means can he use to do this while also verifying the security posture of the systems that connect?

    A. NAC
    B. MAC filtering
    C. Port security
    D. HIPS

12. Which one of the following components is built into most modern computer systems and is used to store disk encryption keys?

    A. HSM
    B. Trusted foundry
    C. Root of trust
    D. TPM

13. Which media disposition is typically the most expensive option from NIST's options in NIST SP 800-88?

    A. Clearing
    B. Purging
    C. Destruction
    D. Obliteration

14. What type of firewall is able to incorporate contextual information about the user and application when making permit/deny decisions?

    A. NGFW
    B. Perimeter firewall
    C. Stateful inspection
    D. Packet filter

15. During a network attack simulation exercise, which team is responsible for securing the targeted environment?

    A. Red
    B. White
    C. Blue
    D. Black

16. Laura is investigating a potential security breach within her organization. She believes that an attacker stole a file containing employee information. Which information security tenet would this attack violate?

    A. Confidentiality
    B. Integrity

C. Availability
D. Nonrepudiation

17. Which of the following incident response activities should *not* happen during the eradication phase of incident response?
   A. Sanitization
   B. Reconstruction/re-imaging
   C. Secure disposal
   D. Segmentation

18. Karen is conducting a risk analysis for her organization and identifies that one potential threat is a widespread power outage that disrupts service to her organization's datacenters. How should Karen classify this threat?
   A. Accidental
   B. Adversarial
   C. Structural
   D. Environmental

19. Which of the following is *not* a law?
   A. HIPAA
   B. PCI DSS
   C. FERPA
   D. SOX

20. Which of the following is *not* typically involved in the initial phases of a CSIRT activation?
   A. Technical staff
   B. CSIRT leader
   C. Law enforcement
   D. First responder

21. Which one of the following activities would *not* normally occur during the attack phase of a penetration test?
   A. System browsing
   B. Network reconnaissance
   C. Escalating privileges
   D. Gaining access

22. Bob is evaluating the risk to his organization from advanced persistent threat (APT) attackers. He assesses the likelihood of this risk occurring to be medium and the impact high. How would this risk be categorized under most organizations' risk evaluation matrices?
   A. Low risk
   B. Moderate risk

C. Semi-moderate risk

D. High risk

23. Which of the following is *not* a common network issue?

A. Bandwidth consumption

B. Beaconing

C. Link aggregation

D. Unexpected traffic

24. Richard wants to build DDoS detection capability into his network. Which of the following tools is *not* appropriate for that task?

A. Network bandwidth monitoring tools

B. IPS

C. Active performance monitoring tools

D. Network fuzzers

25. Which one of the following technologies is commonly used to integrate software as a service (SaaS) productivity platforms?

A. API

B. SOAR

C. SCAP

D. CI/CD

26. What concern may make active monitoring less attractive in some heavily used networks?

A. Active monitoring can't monitor busy networks.

B. Active monitoring bypasses IPSs.

C. Active monitoring consumes additional bandwidth.

D. Active monitoring requires SNMP to be enabled.

27. What security tool generated the output shown here?

```
Host is up (0.00020s latency).
Not shown: 996 closed ports
PORT     STATE SERVICE
22/tcp   open  ssh
25/tcp   open  smtp
80/tcp   open  http
3306/tcp open  mysql
```

A. Nessus

B. Traceroute

C. Nmap

D. Syslog

28. Which one of the following analysis techniques requires samples of known malicious activity to identify future instances of the same activity?
   A. Signature analysis
   B. Trend analysis
   C. Behavioral analysis
   D. Anomaly analysis

29. Fiona is investigating the misuse of her company's network and needs to capture network traffic for analysis. She wants to use a dedicated open source tool that is designed for packet capture and analysis. Which one of the following tools best meets her needs?
   A. Nessus
   B. Nmap
   C. Wireshark
   D. Nikto

30. Bill is analyzing a system that is experiencing strange symptoms. He would like a list of the open network connections on that system. Which one of the following tools would be helpful in this scenario?
   A. Traceroute
   B. Netstat
   C. Tcpdump
   D. Wireshark

31. Which of the following is *not* a reason to avoid imaging live systems?
   A. The drive may be modified by the forensic tool.
   B. The drive contents may change during the imaging process.
   C. Unallocated space will not be included.
   D. Capturing memory contents is more difficult.

32. Which incident response phase includes filing catch-up change requests in the organization's change control process?
   A. Eradication
   B. Containment
   C. Recovery
   D. Postincident activities

33. Brian is a new hire to his company as a threat hunter and he is beginning by developing scenarios of potential attacks. What threat hunting activity is Brian performing?
    A. Reducing the attack surface area
    B. Establishing the hypothesis
    C. Profiling threat actors
    D. Gathering evidence
34. Rodney's company wants to prevent phishing attacks from resulting in account compromise. Which of the following solutions will provide the most effective solution?
    A. Implement context-aware authentication.
    B. Use enhanced password requirements.
    C. Add token-based authentication.
    D. Set a shorter password lifespan.
35. The group of developers that Cynthia is part of tests each software component or function before integrating it into larger software modules. What is this process called?
    A. Code segmentation
    B. Unit testing
    C. UAT
    D. Fagan inspection
36. At what stage in the incident response process does a CSIRT move from primarily passive to primarily active work?
    A. Preparation
    B. Detection and Analysis
    C. Containment, Eradication, and Recovery
    D. Postincident Activity
37. Howard is analyzing the logs from his firewall and sees that the same IP address attempted blocked connections to the same server many different times. What is the most likely explanation for this activity?
    A. Denial-of-service attack
    B. Port scan
    C. SQL injection
    D. Cross-site scripting
38. Ron is reviewing Cisco router logs from his organization and would like an easy way to filter the logs down to those that are most critical. What Cisco log level represents an emergency situation?
    A. 0
    B. 1
    C. 6
    D. 7

39. Angela wants to search for rogue devices on her network. Which of the following techniques will best help her identify systems if she has a complete hardware and systems inventory?

 A. MAC address vendor checking
 B. Site surveys
 C. Traffic analysis for unexpected behavior
 D. MAC address verification

40. What type of control can be put in place and documented if an existing security measure is too difficult to implement or does not fully meet security requirements?

 A. Cost limiting
 B. Administrative
 C. Compensating
 D. Break-fix

41. What security tool generated the output shown here?

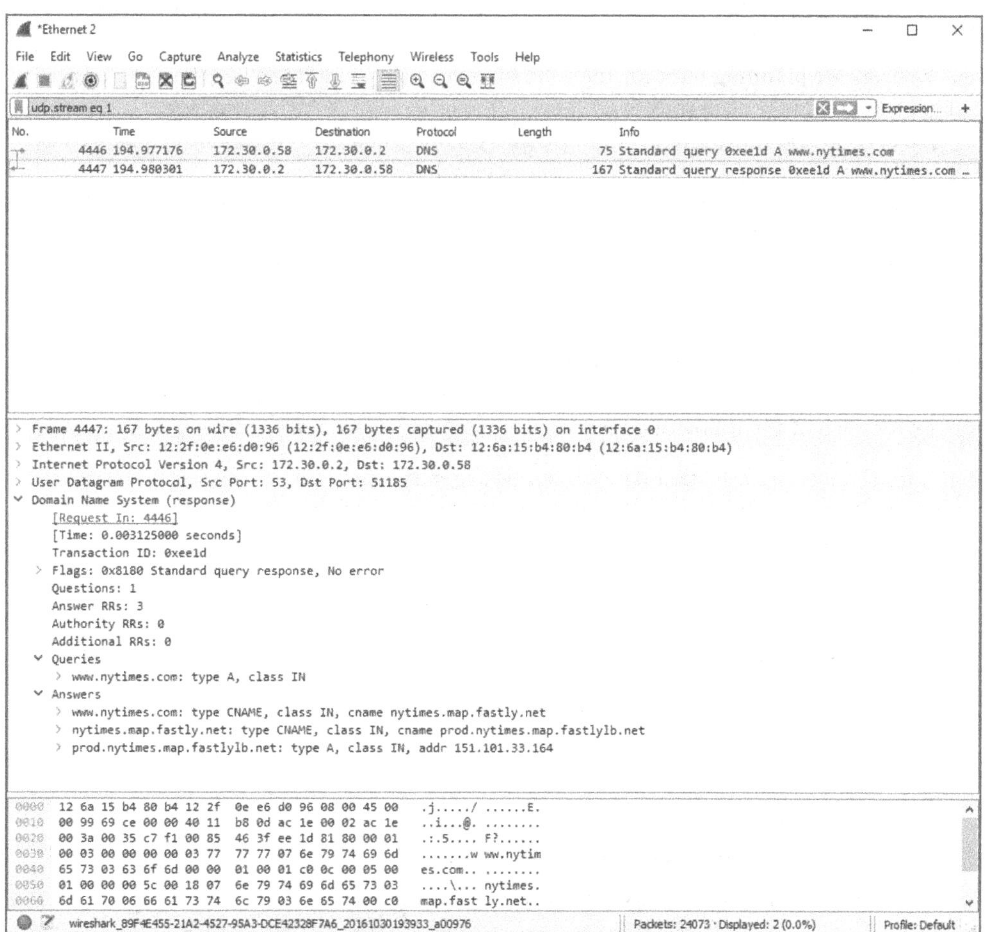

A. Wireshark

B. Nessus

C. Nmap

D. Nexpose

42. Tom would like to use nmap to perform service fingerprinting and wants to request banner information from scanned services. What flag should he use?

A. `-oG`

B. `-sS`

C. `-b`

D. `-sV`

Use the following scenario for questions 43–45.

Insecure, Inc. has experienced multiple data breaches over the past 6 months and has recently hired Cynthia, a new information security officer. Cynthia's first task is to review Insecure, Inc.'s defenses with the goal of identifying appropriate defenses to put in place.

Cynthia knows that her new employers had two major breaches. Breach A occurred when an employee took home a USB external drive with sensitive customer information as well as corporate planning data for the following year. The employee left the drive in their car, and the car was broken into overnight. In the morning, the drive was gone. Insecure, Inc. is uncertain about the fate of the drive and is concerned that customer data as well as their top-secret plans to best their competitors may have been exposed.

Breach B was caused when Insecure, Inc.'s new web application was attacked by unknown attackers who used a SQL injection attack to insert new data into their e-commerce application. Insecure, Inc.'s website was quickly deluged with deal seekers, who put in hundreds of orders for Insecure's newly inexpensive products—the attackers had managed to change the price for almost every product they sold. Insecure, Inc. managed to cancel most of the orders before they shipped, but they have had to deal with angry customers since the event.

Using this information, your task is to help Cynthia recommend the best defensive strategy for each of the following questions.

43. Cynthia wants to ensure that data cannot be lost in the same way as the loss that occurred during Breach A. Which of the following would make a lost drive not a major concern?

A. Encrypt the drive with SHA1.

B. Encrypt the drive with AES256.

C. Encrypt the drive with DES.

D. Encrypt the drive with MD5.

44. If Cynthia wants to address the human side of the issues she has discovered, what solution would best help prevent future issues?

A. Policy and awareness training

B. Dual control and cross training

C. Cross training and an awareness program

D. Implementing a continuous improvement program

45. What technical solution can Cynthia use to detect and possibly stop both SQL injection attacks and denial-of-service attacks against her web applications?

A. An IDS

B. A PRNG

C. DLP

D. An IPS

46. Kevin ran a port scan on a system and determined that it is listening on port 1433. What type of server is Kevin most likely scanning?

A. Web server

B. Database server

C. AAA server

D. Email server

47. Phil ran a port scan on a server and discovered the following results:

```
Starting Nmap 6.40 ( http://nmap.org ) at 2017-01-17 18:36 EST
Nmap scan report for localhost (127.0.0.1)
Host is up (0.00017s latency).
Not shown: 996 closed ports
PORT      STATE SERVICE
22/tcp    open  ssh
25/tcp    open  smtp
80/tcp    open  http
3306/tcp open  mysql

Nmap done: 1 IP address (1 host up) scanned in 0.04 seconds
```

Which one of the services running on this server can Phil be confident is using encryption?

A. SSH

B. HTTP

C. MySQL

D. SMTP

48. What requirement of shared authentication is a key differentiator from SSO?

A. It requires authentication for each site.

B. It uses the same authentication key for each site.

C. Shared authentication provides end-to-end encryption.

D. The shared authentication standard is an open standard.

49. NIST's data impact rating scale describes what category of data impact as "Sensitive personally identifiable information (PII) of taxpayers, employees, beneficiaries, etc., was accessed or exfiltrated"?

A. Confidentiality breach

B. Privacy breach

C. Proprietary breach

D. Integrity loss

50. Tara ran an nmap scan against a server and received the following results:

```
Host is up (0.026s latency).
Not shown: 987 filtered ports
PORT     STATE  SERVICE
53/tcp   closed domain
80/tcp   open   http
443/tcp  open   https
8080/tcp closed http-proxy
8081/tcp closed blackice-icecap
8082/tcp closed blackice-alerts
8083/tcp closed us-srv
8084/tcp closed unknown
8085/tcp closed unknown
8086/tcp closed d-s-n
8087/tcp closed simplifymedia
8088/tcp closed radan-http
8089/tcp closed unknown
```

Of the services listed, which port is most unusual to find on a web server?

A. 53

B. 80

C. 443

D. 8080

51. What Windows tool provides detailed data, including counters, that can measure information about a system like energy consumption, disk usage, and network activity?

A. Winmon

B. Perfmon

C. Sysctl

D. Resmon

52. Kyle used nslookup to determine the IP address for `nytimes.com` and received the following results:

```
> nytimes.com
Server:         172.30.0.2
Address:        172.30.0.2#53

Non-authoritative answer:
Name:   nytimes.com
Address: 151.101.1.164
Name:   nytimes.com
Address: 151.101.65.164
Name:   nytimes.com
Address: 151.101.129.164
Name:   nytimes.com
Address: 151.101.193.164
```

What is the IP address of the server that answered Kyle's request?

A. 172.30.0.2

B. 151.101.1.164

C. 151.101.65.164

D. 151.101.193.164

53. A part of his forensic investigation, Alex signs and notes in his log when the drive copy he prepared is transferred to legal counsel. What is this process known as?

A. Handoff documentation

B. Chain-of-custody tracking

C. Asset tracking

D. Forensic certification

54. Ryan uses the following command as part of his forensic image preparation:

```
root@demo:~# md5sum image1.raw
441fb68910e08fd0ed2db3bdb4e49233  image1.raw
```

What task has he performed?

A. Encryption

B. Image creation

C. Hashing

D. Secure wipe

55. Ryan uses the following command later in his forensic investigation and receives the response shown. What has occurred?

```
root@demo:~# md5sum -c image1.md5 image1v2.md5
image1.raw: FAILED
md5sum: WARNING: 1 computed checksum did NOT match
image1.raw: OK
```

A. The hash was miscalculated.

B. No hash was created.

C. The files are the same.

D. The files are different.

56. Ed is preparing an incident response report, and he discovers that some systems were not properly configured to use NTP. What critical element of incident reports may suffer based on this?

A. The root cause analysis

B. The chronology of events

C. The postrecovery validation report

D. The documentation of specific actions taken to remediate issues

57. Which one of the following criteria would normally be considered least important when making decisions about the scope of vulnerability scanning programs?
    A. Regulatory requirements
    B. Data classification
    C. Operating system type
    D. Corporate policy

58. Bernie is designing a PCI DSS–compliant vulnerability management program for his business. Who may conduct the internal scans required by the standard?
    A. Scans must be conducted by an approved scanning vendor (ASV).
    B. Scans must be conducted by an internal audit group or an ASV.
    C. Scans must be conducted by a PCI DSS–certified individual.
    D. Scans may be conducted by any qualified individual.

59. Which one of the following elements of the Security Content Automation Protocol (SCAP) provides a standard nomenclature for describing security-related software flaws?
    A. CVSS
    B. CPE
    C. CVE
    D. OVAL

60. Which of the following is *not* a Linux memory forensic tool?
    A. fmem
    B. LiME
    C. The Volatility Framework
    D. DumpIt

61. What step is missing from the vulnerability management life cycle shown here?

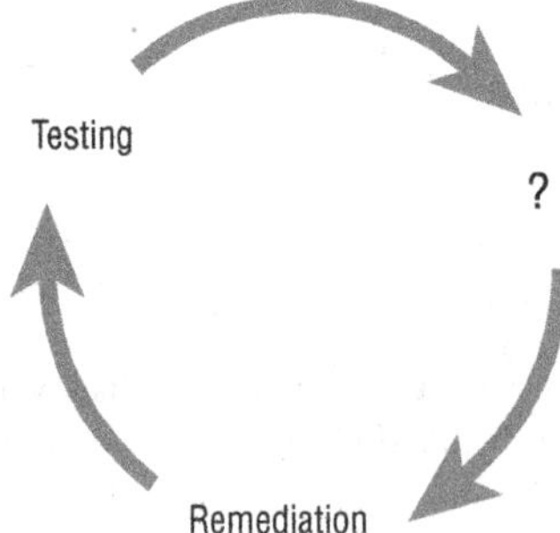

    A. Assessment
    B. Detection
    C. Patching
    D. Scanning

62. The NIST Cybersecurity framework includes three major measures. Which three major measures are included in the measures that allow an organization to evaluate which tier they are at?

 A. Risk management process, integrated risk management program, external participation

 B. Risk management program, risk tolerance, controls structure

 C. Risk management process, incident response program, external data sources

 D. Risk management program, vulnerability management program, external data sources

63. Bryan is preparing to conduct a vulnerability scan and wishes to use credentialed scanning for maximum effectiveness. What type of account should Bryan use to perform this scanning in a secure manner?

 A. Domain administrator

 B. Root user

 C. Local administrator

 D. Read-only user

64. Gary is the cybersecurity manager for a federal government agency subject to FISMA. He is evaluating the potential confidentiality impact of a system and decides that the unauthorized disclosure of information stored on the system could have a serious adverse impact on citizens served by his agency. How should Gary rate the confidentiality impact?

 A. Low

 B. Moderate

 C. High

 D. Critical

65. What major Kerberos-centric concern faces administrators of an Active Directory forest or domain if the AD server itself is compromised?

 A. All Kerberos tickets will be invalidated.

 B. Attackers can create a "golden ticket."

 C. There is no way to notify users of the issue.

 D. Previously issued user tickets will be exposed.

66. Which of the following is *not* a common attack against LDAP servers?

 A. Exploiting of insecure binding

 B. Directory harvesting

 C. LDAP injection

 D. Silver ticket attacks

67. Oliver is developing a prioritization scheme for vulnerability remediation. Which one of the following is *not* generally accepted as an important criterion for prioritizing remediation?

 A. Vulnerability severity

 B. Age of vulnerability

C. Criticality of system

D. Difficulty of remediation

68. What regulatory schemes specifically require the use of vulnerability scanning?

A. FISMA and PCI DSS

B. PCI DSS and HIPAA

C. HIPAA and GLBA

D. GLBA and FISMA

69. What type of term describes review of code by running it?

A. The Run/Test method

B. Runtime inspection

C. Static code analysis

D. Dynamic code analysis

70. After completing a vulnerability scan, Bob received a report of a blind SQL injection vulnerability. Bob worked with the application developer to inspect the vulnerability and determined that the attack was not possible. What type of error occurred?

A. True positive

B. True negative

C. False positive

D. False negative

71. Which of the following types of staff are *not* frequently part of a CSIRT?

A. Technical subject matter experts

B. IT support staff

C. Legal counsel

D. Comptrollers

72. Which of the following is *not* well suited to identifying network scans and probes?

A. IPS

B. SNMP traps

C. Firewall

D. SIEM

73. Olivia has requested that her development team run their web application security testing tools against their web applications, despite the fact that they just installed the most recent patches. What is this type of testing called?

A. Regression testing

B. Patch state validation

C. WAV testing

D. HTTP checking

74. What type of testing directly targets error handing paths, particularly those that are rarely used or might otherwise be missed during normal testing?

A. Fuzzing

B. Mutation testing

C. Fault injection

D. Fagan inspection

75. Which of the following pieces of information does Windows *not* capture by default about USB devices when they are plugged in?

A. The capacity of the device

B. The device name

C. The device serial number

D. The unit's vendor ID

76. What type of process is shown here?

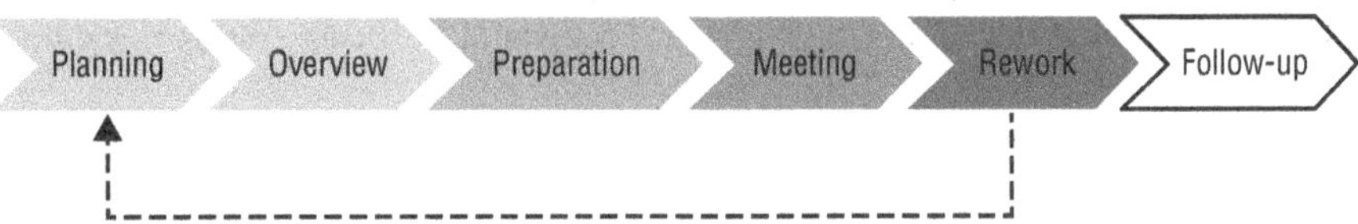

A. A Waterfall SDLC

B. Mutation testing

C. Dynamic code analysis

D. Fagan inspection

77. When searching a Windows system for forensic data, where can point-in-time details of prior actions taken on the machine sometimes be found?

A. The Windows Registry

B. Autorun keys

C. Hibernation files

D. Volume shadow copies

78. Harry identified the following vulnerability in one of his systems:

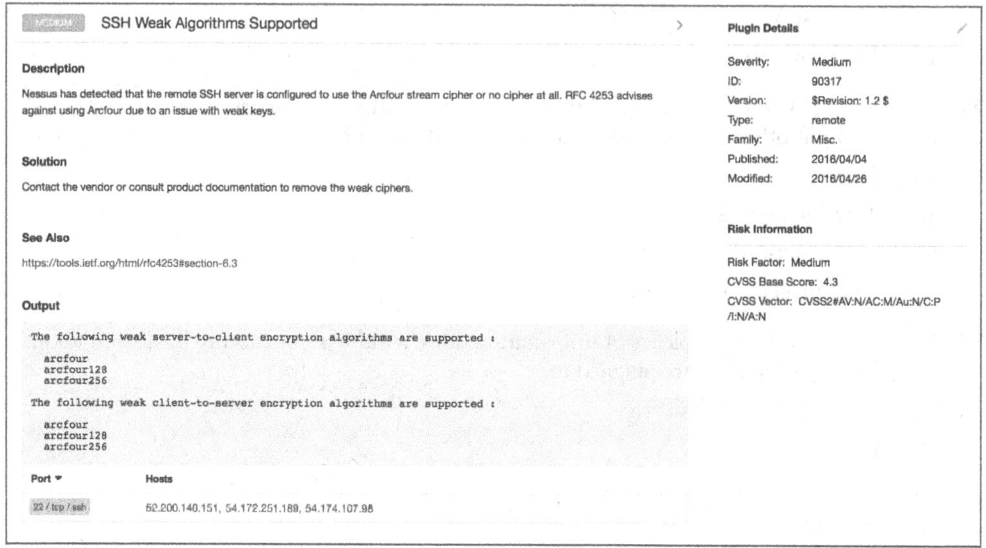

MEDIUM SSH Weak Algorithms Supported

Description

Nessus has detected that the remote SSH server is configured to use the Arcfour stream cipher or no cipher at all. RFC 4253 advises against using Arcfour due to an issue with weak keys.

Solution

Contact the vendor or consult product documentation to remove the weak ciphers.

See Also

https://tools.ietf.org/html/rfc4253#section-6.3

Output

```
The following weak server-to-client encryption algorithms are supported :

  arcfour
  arcfour128
  arcfour256

The following weak client-to-server encryption algorithms are supported :

  arcfour
  arcfour128
  arcfour256
```

Port	Hosts
22 / tcp / ssh	52.200.140.151, 54.172.251.189, 54.174.107.98

Plugin Details

Severity:	Medium
ID:	90317
Version:	$Revision: 1.2 $
Type:	remote
Family:	Misc.
Published:	2016/04/04
Modified:	2016/04/26

Risk Information

Risk Factor: Medium
CVSS Base Score: 4.3
CVSS Vector: CVSS2#AV:N/AC:M/Au:N/C:P/I:N/A:N

He would like to search network traffic to identify connection attempts that might have attempted to exploit this vulnerability. What port would traffic exploiting this vulnerability most likely use?

A. 22

B. 80

C. 443

D. 1521

79. Erik identified the following vulnerability in one of his systems:

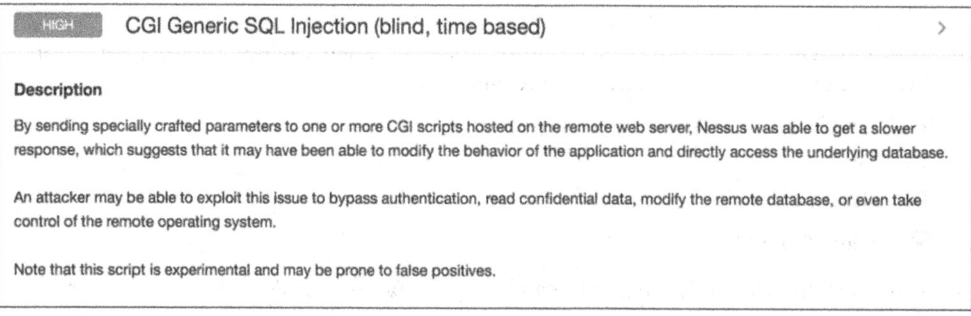

HIGH CGI Generic SQL Injection (blind, time based)

Description

By sending specially crafted parameters to one or more CGI scripts hosted on the remote web server, Nessus was able to get a slower response, which suggests that it may have been able to modify the behavior of the application and directly access the underlying database.

An attacker may be able to exploit this issue to bypass authentication, read confidential data, modify the remote database, or even take control of the remote operating system.

Note that this script is experimental and may be prone to false positives.

What technique would be the most effective way to combat this vulnerability?

A. Firewall rule

B. Input validation

C. Honeypot

D. Patching

80. Bonnie ran a vulnerability scan against one of her servers and received a report that the server contains buffer overflow vulnerabilities in the operating system. Which one of the following would be the most effective defense?

A. Input validation

B. Firewall

C. Operating system patching

D. Intrusion prevention system

81. Which one of the following protocols would *not* generate a network vulnerability report if run on a production system?

A. SSLv2

B. SSLv3

C. TLS 1.1

D. All three would generate a vulnerability.

82. Ben identified the following vulnerability in one of his systems:

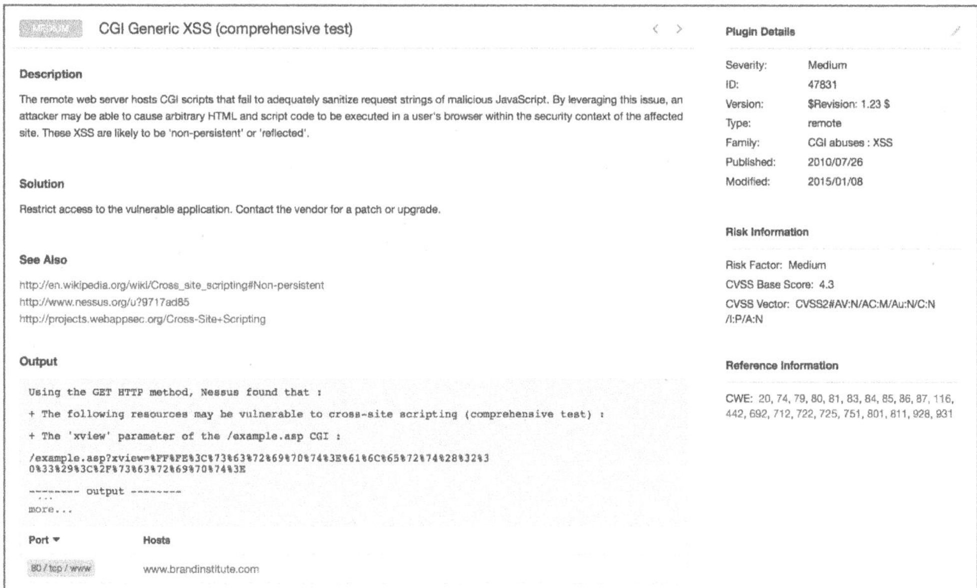

What technique would be the most effective way to combat this vulnerability?

A. Firewall rule

B. Input validation

C. Honeypot

D. Patching the operating system

83. Chelsea's company runs an industrial control system (ICS) from a vendor that no longer provides support. The system has a newly discovered vulnerability to buffer overflow attacks. What would be the best way to defend this system?

A. Apply a patch

B. Rewrite the code

C. Place it on a segmented network

D. Use encryption

84. What component of a virtualized infrastructure is responsible for ensuring that software running on one virtualized system does not receive access to areas of memory that are reserved for use by another virtualized system?

A. Hypervisor

B. Virtual guest

C. Virtual host

D. Physical hardware

85. Frank received a phone call from a user who is traveling and accessing the Wi-Fi network at a hotel. The user tried to access a corporate website and received an error message that the certificate was invalid. No other users are receiving this error. What is the most likely explanation for this error message?

A. The company's website is using an expired certificate.

B. The company's website has an incorrect certificate installed.

C. The hotel uses a captive portal.

D. Another user on the hotel network is attempting to eavesdrop on the connection.

Answers to Review Questions and Practice Exam

Chapter 1: Today's Cybersecurity Analyst

1. B. The three primary objectives of cybersecurity professionals are confidentiality, integrity, and availability.

2. B. In this scenario, Tommy identified a deficiency in the security of his web server that renders it vulnerable to attack. This is a security vulnerability. Tommy has not yet identified a specific risk because he has not identified a threat (such as a hacker) that might exploit this vulnerability.

3. C. The NIST risk assessment process says that organizations should identify threats before identifying vulnerabilities or determining the likelihood and impact of risks.

4. D. Widespread infrastructure failures, such as those affecting the power grid or telecommunications circuits, are considered man-made disasters and fall under the category of environmental threats.

5. A. Adversarial threat analysis requires examining the capability of the threat source, the intent of the threat source, and the likelihood that the threat will target the organization.

6. D. In an availability attack, the attacker disrupts access to information or a service by legitimate users. In this attack, the attacker disrupted access to the organization's website, violating the principle of availability.

7. D. Penetration tests are an example of an operational security control. Encryption software, network firewalls, and antivirus software are all examples of technical security controls.

8. A. Any action that an organization takes to reduce the likelihood or impact of a risk is an example of risk mitigation. In this case, Paul chose to implement a technical control—a network firewall—to mitigate the likelihood of a successful attack.

9. B. Network access control (NAC) solutions are able to verify the security status of devices before granting them access to the organization's network. Devices not meeting minimum security standards may be placed on a quarantine network until they are remediated.

10. D. The Remote Access Dial-In User Service (RADIUS) is an authentication protocol used for communications between authenticators and the authentication server during the 802.1x authentication process.

11. A. Any device that wishes to join an 802.1x network must be running an 802.1x supplicant that can communicate with the authenticator before joining the network.

12. D. The Secure HTTP (HTTPS) protocol uses TCP port 443 for communications between web browsers and the web server.

13. A. Next-generation firewalls (NGFWs) incorporate contextual information about users, applications, and business processes in their decision-making process.

14. B. Port 23, used by the Telnet protocol, is unencrypted and insecure. Connections should not be permitted to the jump box on unencrypted ports. The services running on ports 22 (SSH), 443 (HTTPS), and 3389 (RDP) all use encryption.

15. A. Administrators may use Group Policy Objects (GPOs) to control a wide variety of Windows settings and create different policies that apply to different classes of system.

16. A. During the planning phase of a penetration test, the testers should confirm the timing, scope, and authorization for the test in writing.

17. A. After the completion of the discovery phase, penetration testers first seek to gain access to a system on the targeted network and then may use that system as the launching point for additional attacks.

18. A. The red team plays the role of the attacker and uses reconnaissance and exploitation tools to attempt to gain access to the protected network.

19. D. Sandboxing is an approach used to detect malicious software based on its behavior rather than its signatures. Sandboxing systems watch systems and the network for unknown pieces of code and, when they detect an application that has not been seen before, immediately isolate that code in a special environment known as a sandbox where it does not have access to any other systems or applications.

20. B. Web application firewalls (WAFs) are specialized firewalls designed to protect against web application attacks, such as SQL injection and cross-site scripting.

Chapter 2: Using Threat Intelligence

1. B. While higher levels of detail can be useful, it isn't a common measure used to assess threat intelligence. Instead, the timeliness, accuracy, and relevance of the information are considered critical to determining whether you should use the threat information.

2. C. STIX is an XML-based language, allowing it to be easily extended and modified while also using standard XML-based editors, readers, and other tools.

3. D. Threat intelligence dissemination or sharing typically follows threat data analysis. The goal is to get the threat data into the hands of the organizations and individuals who need it.

4. A. Understanding what your organization needs is important for the requirements gathering phase of the intelligence cycle. Reviewing recent breaches and compromises can help to define what threats you are currently facing. Current vulnerability scans can identify where you may be vulnerable but are less useful for threat identification. Data handling standards do not provide threat information, and intelligence feed reviews list new threats, but those are useful only if you know what type of threats you're likely to face so that you can determine which ones you should target.

5. D. The U.S. government created the information sharing and analysis centers (ISACs). ISACs help infrastructure owners and operators share threat information, as well as provide tools and assistance to their members.

6. A. Nation-state actors are government sponsored and typically have the greatest access to resources, including tools, money, and talent.

7. A. Hacktivists execute attacks for political reasons, including those against governments and businesses. The key element in this question is the political reasons behind the attack.

8. B. Attack vectors, or the means by which an attacker can gain access to their target, can include things like USB key drops. You may be tempted to answer this question with adversary capability, but remember the definition: the resources, intent, or ability of the likely threat actor. Capability here doesn't mean what they can do, but their ability to do so. The attack surface might include the organization's parking lot in this example, but this is not an example of an attack surface, and there was no probability assessment included in this problem.

9. A. Behavioral assessments are very useful when you are attempting to identify insider threats. Since insider threats are often hard to distinguish from normal behavior context of the actions performed such as after-hours logins, misuse of credentials, logins from abnormal locations or in abnormal patterns, other behavioral indicators are often used.

10. D. TAXII, the Trusted Automated Exchange of Indicator Information protocol, is specifically designed to communicate cyber threat information at the application layer. OpenIOC is a compromise indicator framework, and STIX is a threat description language.

11. C. The installation phase of the Cyber Kill Chain focuses on providing persistent backdoor access for attackers. Delivery occurs when the tool is put into action either directly or indirectly, whereas exploitation occurs when a vulnerability is exploited. Command and control (C2) uses two-way communications to provide continued remote control.

12. C. The Kill Chain includes actions outside the defended network which many defenders cannot take action on, resulting in one of the common criticisms of the model. Other criticisms include the focus on a traditional perimeter and on antimalware-based techniques, as well as a lack of focus on insider threats.

13. B. Patching against zero-day attacks won't stop a command and control capability, although it might stop the initial exploit that results in the installation of C2 tools. Network hardening, deploying additional capabilities to detect C2 traffic, and staying ahead of the latest in C2 methods and technology so that detections and hardening match them are all common techniques.

14. C. The confidence level of your threat information is how certain you are of the information. A high confidence threat assessment will typically be confirmed either by multiple independent and reliable sources or via direct verification.

15. A. ISACs were introduced in 1998 as part of a presidential directive, and they focus on threat information sharing and analysis for critical infrastructure owners.

16. D. STRIDE, PASTA, and LINDDUN are all examples of threat classification tools. LINDDUN focuses on threats to privacy, STRIDE is a Microsoft tool, and PASTA is an attacker-centric threat modeling tool.

17. A. The threat indicators built into OpenIOC are based on Mandiant's indicator list. You can extend and include additional indicators of compromise beyond the 500 built-in definitions.

18. B. Advanced persistent threats (APTs) are most commonly associated with nation-state actors. The complexity of their operations and the advanced tools that they bring typically require significant resources to leverage fully.

19. B. The ATT&CK framework specifically defines threat actor tactics in standardized ways. The Diamond Model is useful for guiding thought processes about threats, and the Cyber Kill Chain is most useful for assessing threats based on a set of defined stages. The Universal Threat Model was made up for this question!

20. C. Forensic data is very helpful when defining indicators of compromise (IOCs). Behavioral threat assessments can also be partially defined by forensic data, but the key here is where the data is most frequently used.

Chapter 3: Reconnaissance and Intelligence Gathering

1. D. DNS zone transfers provide a method to replicate DNS information between DNS servers, but they are also a tempting target for attackers due to the amount of information that they contain. A properly secured DNS server will only allow zone transfers to specific, permitted peer DNS servers. DNSSEC is a suite of DNS security specifications, AXR is a made-up term (AXFR is the zone transfer command), and DNS registration is how you register a domain name.

2. C. Nmap's operating system identification flag is `-O` and it enables OS detection. `-A` also enables OS identification and other features. `-osscan` with modifiers like `-limit` and `-guess` set specific OS identification features. `-os` and `-id` are not nmap flags.

3. B. Traceroute (or tracert on Windows systems) is a command-line tool that uses ICMP to trace the route that a packet takes to a host. Whois and nslookup are domain tools, and routeview is not a command-line tool.

4. B. Exif (Exchangeable Image Format) data often includes location and camera data, allowing the images to be mapped and identified to a specific device or type of camera.

5. A. Log level 0 is used for emergencies in Cisco's logging level scheme. Log level 7 is for debugging information and is at the bottom of the scale.

6. C. UDP connections are not shown by netstat because UDP is a connectionless protocol. Active TCP connections, executables that are associated with them, and route table information are all available via netstat.

7. D. Although it is possible that a system named "db1" with a hostname "sqldb1" is not a Microsoft SQL Server, the most likely answer is that it is a Microsoft SQL Server.

8. B. Microsoft Windows security logs can contain information about files being opened, created, or deleted if configured to do so. Configuration and httpd logs are not a type of Windows logs, and system logs contain information about events logged by Windows components.

9. D. The Internet Assigned Numbers Authority manages the global IP address space. ARIN is the American Registry for Internet Numbers, WorldNIC is not an IP authority, and NASA tackles problems in outer space, not global IP space.

10. C. Metadata scrubbing removes hidden information about a file such as the creator, creation time, system used to create the file, and a host of other information. The other answers are made up.

11. C. Heuristic analysis focuses on behaviors, allowing a tool using it to identify malware behaviors instead of looking for a specific package. Trend analysis is typically used to identify large-scale changes from the norm, and it is more likely to be useful for a network than for a single PC. Regression analysis is used in statistical modeling.

12. B. Registering manually won't prevent DNS harvesting, but privacy services are often used to prevent personal or corporate information from being visible via domain registrars. CAPTCHAs, rate limiting, and blacklisting systems or networks that are gathering data are all common anti-DNS harvesting techniques.

13. D. The `axfr` flag indicates a zone transfer in both the dig and host utilities.

14. C. A packet capture can't provide plausible deniability, as it provides evidence of action. Packet capture is often used to document work, including the time that a given scan or process occurred, and it can also be used to provide additional data for further analysis.

15. D. Operating system detection often uses TCP options support, IP ID sampling, and window size checks, as well as other indicators that create unique fingerprints for various operating systems. Service identification often leverages banners since TCP capabilities are not unique to a given service. Fuzzing is a code testing method, and application scanning is usually related to web application security.

16. B. Netflow is a Cisco network protocol that collects IP traffic information that allows analysis of traffic flow and volume. Netstat provides information about local connections, which applications have made them, and other useful local system information. Libpcap is the Linux packet capture library and would not be used alone. Pflow is a made-up term.

17. B. Zone transfers are intended to allow DNS database replication, but an improperly secured DNS server can also allow third parties to request a zone transfer, exposing all of their DNS information. Traceroute is used to determine the path and latency to a remote host, whereas dig is a useful DNS query tool. DNS sync is a made-up technical term.

18. A. The Internet Archive maintains copies of sites from across the Internet, and it can be used to review the historical content of a site. WikiLeaks distributes leaked information, whereas the Internet Rewinder and TimeTurner are both made-up names.

19. B. Social media can be a treasure trove of personal information. Company websites and forums are usually limited in the information they provide, and Creepy is a geolocation tool that gathers data from social media and geotagging.

20. C. Whois provides information that can include the organization's physical address, registrar, contact information, and other details. Nslookup will provide IP address or hostname information, whereas host provides IPv4 and IPv6 addresses as well as email service information. Traceroute attempts to identify the path to a remote host as well as the systems along the route.

Chapter 4: Designing a Vulnerability Management Program

1. C. The Federal Information Security Management Act (FISMA) requires that federal agencies implement vulnerability management programs for federal information systems.

2. D. The Federal Information Security Management Act (FISMA) requires vulnerability management programs for all federal information systems, regardless of their assigned impact rating.

3. A. An asset inventory supplements automated tools with other information to detect systems present on a network. The asset inventory provides critical information for vulnerability scans.

4. D. PCI DSS requires that organizations conduct vulnerability scans on at least a quarterly basis, although many organizations choose to conduct scans on a much more frequent basis.

5. B. Qualys, Nessus, and OpenVAS are all examples of vulnerability scanning tools. Snort is an intrusion detection system.

6. A. PCI DSS requires that organizations conduct vulnerability scans quarterly, which would have Bethany's next regularly scheduled scan scheduled for June. However, the standard also requires scanning after any significant change in the payment card environment. This would include an upgrade to the point-of-sale system, so Bethany must complete a new compliance scan immediately.

7. D. Credentialed scans only require read-only access to target servers. Renee should follow the principle of least privilege and limit the access available to the scanner.

8. C. Common Platform Enumeration (CPE) is an SCAP component that provides standardized nomenclature for product names and versions.

9. D. Internal scans completed for PCI DSS compliance purposes may be conducted by any qualified individual.

10. C. The Federal Information Security Management Act (FISMA) requires that government agencies conduct vulnerability scans. HIPAA, which governs hospitals and doctors' offices, does not include a vulnerability scanning requirement, nor does GLBA, which covers financial institutions. Banks may be required to conduct scans under PCI DSS, but this is a contractual obligation and not a statutory requirement.

11. C. Control enhancement number 4 requires that an organization determine what information about the system is discoverable by adversaries. This enhancement only applies to FISMA high systems.

12. B. The organization's risk appetite is its willingness to tolerate risk within the environment. If an organization is extremely risk averse, it may choose to conduct scans more frequently to minimize the amount of time between when a vulnerability comes into existence and when it is detected by a scan.

13. D. Scan schedules are most often determined by the organization's risk appetite, regulatory requirements, technical constraints, business constraints, and licensing limitations. Most scans are automated and do not require staff availability.

14. B. If Barry is able to limit the scope of his PCI DSS compliance efforts to the isolated network, then that is the only network that must be scanned for PCI DSS compliance purposes.

15. C. Ryan should first run his scan against a test environment to identify likely vulnerabilities and assess whether the scan itself might disrupt business activities.

16. C. Although reporting and communication are an important part of vulnerability management, they are not included in the life cycle. The three life-cycle phases are detection, remediation, and testing.

17. A. Continuous monitoring incorporates data from agent-based approaches to vulnerability detection and reports security-related configuration changes to the vulnerability management platform as soon as they occur, providing the ability to analyze those changes for potential vulnerabilities.

18. B. Systems have a moderate impact from a confidentiality perspective if the unauthorized disclosure of information could be expected to have a serious adverse effect on organizational operations, organizational assets, or individuals.

19. A. The Common Vulnerability Scoring System (CVSS) provides a standardized approach for measuring and describing the severity of security vulnerabilities. Jessica could use this scoring system to prioritize issues raised by different source systems.

20. B. While any qualified individual may conduct internal compliance scans, PCI DSS requires the use of a scanning vendor approved by the PCI SSC for external compliance scans.

Chapter 5: Analyzing Vulnerability Scans

1. B. Although the network can support any of these protocols, internal IP disclosure vulnerabilities occur when a network uses Network Address Translation (NAT) to map public and private IP addresses but a server inadvertently discloses its private IP address to remote systems.

2. C. The privileges required (PR) metric indicates the type of account access the attacker must have.

3. C. An attack complexity of "low" indicates that exploiting the vulnerability does not require any specialized conditions.

4. D. A value of High (H) for an impact metric indicates the potential for complete loss of confidentiality, integrity, and/or availability.

5. D. Version 3.1 of CVSS is currently available but is not as widely used as the more common CVSS version 2.0.

6. B. The CVSS exploitability score is computed using the attack vector, attack complexity, privileges required, and user interaction metrics.

7. B. Vulnerabilities with CVSS base scores between 4.0 and 6.9 fit into the medium risk category.

8. A. A false positive error occurs when the vulnerability scanner reports a vulnerability that does not actually exist.

9. B. It is unlikely that a database table would contain information relevant to assessing a vulnerability scan report. Logs, SIEM reports, and configuration management systems are much more likely to contain relevant information.

10. A. Microsoft discontinued support for Windows Server 2003, and it is likely that the operating system contains unpatchable vulnerabilities.

11. D. Buffer overflow attacks occur when an attacker manipulates a program into placing more data into an area of memory than is allocated for that program's use. The goal is to overwrite other information in memory with instructions that may be executed by a different process running on the system.

12. B. In October 2016, security researchers announced the discovery of a Linux kernel vulnerability dubbed Dirty COW. This vulnerability, present in the Linux kernel for nine years, was extremely easy to exploit and provided successful attackers with administrative control of affected systems.

13. D. Telnet is an insecure protocol that does not make use of encryption. The other protocols mentioned are all considered secure.

14. D. TLS 1.1 is a secure transport protocol that supports web traffic. The other protocols listed all have flaws that render them insecure and unsuitable for use.

15. B. Digital certificates are intended to provide public encryption keys, and this would not cause an error. The other circumstances are all causes for concern and would trigger an alert during a vulnerability scan.

16. D. In a virtualized datacenter, the virtual host hardware runs a special operating system known as a *hypervisor* that mediates access to the underlying hardware resources.

17. A. VM escape vulnerabilities are the most serious issue that can exist in a virtualized environment, particularly when a virtual host runs systems of differing security levels. In an escape attack, the attacker has access to a single virtual host and then manages to leverage that access to intrude on the resources assigned to a different virtual machine.

18. B. Intrusion detection systems (IDSs) are a security control used to detect network or host attacks. The Internet of Things (IoT), supervisory control and data acquisition (SCADA) systems, and industrial control systems (ICSs) are all associated with connecting physical world objects to a network.

19. D. In a cross-site scripting (XSS) attack, an attacker embeds scripting commands on a website that will later be executed by an unsuspecting visitor accessing the site. The idea is to trick a user visiting a trusted site into executing malicious code placed there by an untrusted third party.

20. A. In a SQL injection attack, the attacker seeks to use a web application to gain access to an underlying database. Semicolons and apostrophes are characteristic of these attacks.

Chapter 6: Cloud Security

1. C. One of the key characteristics of cloud computing is that customers can access resources on-demand with minimal service provider interaction. Cloud customers do not need to contact a sales representative each time they wish to provision a resource but can normally do so on a self-service basis.

2. A. Under the shared responsibility model, the customer only bears responsibility for operating system security in IaaS environments. In all other environments, the service provider is responsible for securing the operating system.

3. B. Helen is using IaaS services to create her payroll product. She is then offering that payroll service to her customers as an SaaS solution.

4. A. This is an example of public cloud computing because Tony is using a public cloud provider, Microsoft Azure. The fact that Tony is limiting access to virtual machines to his own organization is not relevant because the determining factor for the cloud model is whether the underlying infrastructure is shared, not whether virtualized resources are shared.

5. B. ScoutSuite is the only cloud assessment tool listed here that performs security scans of Azure environments. Inspector and Prowler are AWS-specific tools. Pacu is an exploitation framework used in penetration testing.

6. C. This is an example of function as a service (FaaS) computing, a subset of platform as a service (PaaS). Although both terms may be used to describe the service Kevin uses, the best answer is FaaS, because it is more specific.

7. D. In the shared responsibility model, the customer always retains either full or partial responsibility for data security. Responsibility for hardware and physical datacenters is the cloud provider's responsibility under all models. Responsibility for applications is the customer's responsibility under IaaS, the provider's responsibility under SaaS, and a shared responsibility under PaaS.

8. B. AWS Lambda, Google Cloud Functions, and Microsoft Azure Functions are all examples of function as a service (FaaS) computing. AWS DeepLens is an AI-enabled camera.

9. D. Hybrid cloud environments blend elements of public, private, and/or community cloud solutions. A hybrid cloud requires the use of technology that unifies the different cloud offerings into a single, coherent platform.

10. A. Customer relationship management (CRM) packages offered in the cloud would be classified as software as a service (SaaS), since they are not infrastructure components. Storage, networking, and computing resources are all common IaaS offerings.

11. C. DevOps approaches to software development and technology operations increase the frequency of releases by automating software testing and release processes. The other options are characteristic of legacy approaches to technology.

12. C. Infrastructure as code is any approach that automates the provisioning, management, and deprovisioning of cloud resources. Defining resources through JSON or YAML is IaC, as is writing code that interacts with an API. Provisioning resources through a web interface is manual, not automated, and therefore does not qualify as IaC.

13. D. All of these issues are security vulnerabilities that should be addressed. Cloud assessment tools would be able to identify most of these issues, but they would have no way of knowing that two or more developers are sharing an API key.

14. D. API-based CASB solutions interact directly with the cloud provider through the provider's API. Inline CASB solutions intercept requests between the user and the provider. Outsider and comprehensive are not categories of CASB solutions.

15. C. Community cloud deployments may offer IaaS, PaaS, and/or SaaS solutions. Their defining characteristic is that access is limited to members of a specific community.

16. D. Cloud service providers bear sole responsibility for datacenter security in all cloud service models.

17. C. Inline CASB solutions require either network reconfiguration or the use of a software agent. They intercept requests from users to cloud providers and, by doing so, are able to both monitor activity and enforce policy.

18. B. API keys are used to identify and authenticate the user, system, or application that is connecting to an API.

19. D. Pacu is an AWS-specific exploitation framework. It is particularly well suited to identifying the permissions available to an account during a penetration test. ScoutSuite, Inspector, and Prowler are all assessment tools that would not directly provide the information that Gina seeks.

20. C. Customers are typically charged for server instances in both IaaS environments, where they directly provision those instances, and PaaS environments, where they request the number of servers needed to support their applications. In an SaaS environment, the customer typically has no knowledge of the number of server instances supporting their use.

Chapter 7: Infrastructure Security and Controls

1. D. Jump boxes are used to access and manage devices that are in another security zone from where the user is. This means they have connectivity into both zones, either via a VPN or similar technology. Option A may be tempting, but jump boxes aren't only used for DMZs. Remember this when you're studying—often questions will have a likely looking answer that isn't fully correct.

2. C. Ben has set up a honeypot, a system intended to be attractive to attackers, allowing defenders to observe their behavior while gathering information and potentially capturing copies of their tools. Sinkholes are systems or devices that are used as a destination for redirected traffic. Often, this is used defensively to redirect traffic via DNS. Blackholes and beehives are not common terms.

3. A. Polymorphic techniques change malware each time it infects a system, making simple hashing unable to be used to check if the malware matches. More advanced techniques include behavior monitoring–based techniques as well as other more in-depth analytical techniques that identify components of the malware package.

4. B. Ric's best option is to implement backup Internet connectivity using a different make and model of router. This reduces the chance of the same exploit being able to take down both types of device while removing the single point of failure for connectivity. Adding a second identical router in either active/active or active/passive mode does not work around the flaw since an attacker could immediately repeat the attack to take down the matching router. A firewall might help, but in many cases attacks against routers take place on a channel that is required for the router to perform its function.

5. C. Whitelisting technologies can be used to only allow programs that have been preapproved to run on systems that use it. Blacklisting prevents specific programs from running. An antivirus uses a number of techniques to identify malicious software and might even include blacklisting and whitelisting capabilities, but we cannot assume that is the case. VDI provides virtualized desktops and can be useful for controlling systems but does not specifically provide this capability.

6. B. A multitier firewall is least likely to be an effective security control when Susan's organization deals with compromised credentials. Multifactor authentication would require the attacker to have the second factor in addition to the password, an awareness program may help Susan's employees avoid future scams, and a SIEM monitoring for logins that are out of the ordinary may spot the attacker logging in remotely or otherwise abusing the credentials they obtained.

7. D. Retirement is the last step at the end of the life cycle for a standard or process. Of course, this means that if the process is retired, a final update to it is not needed! The standards for other, currently maintained operating systems should undergo regular scheduled review, and staff who support them may participate in a continuous improvement process to keep the standards up to date.

8. A. Example Corporation is using network segmentation to split their network up into security zones based on their functional requirements. They may use multiple-interface firewalls for this, and they may try to avoid single points of failure, but the question does not provide enough information to know if that is the case. Finally, zoned routing is a made-up term—zone routing is an actual technical term, but it is used for wireless networks.

9. B. Firewalls are commonly used to create network protection zones, to protect network borders, and at the host level to help armor the host against attacks. Encryption at rest is most frequently used at the host layer, whereas DMZs are typically used at the edge of a network for publicly accessible services. Antivirus is sometimes used at each layer but is most commonly found at the host layer.

10. C. Data loss prevention (DLP) tools attempt to identify sensitive or controlled data and to prevent it from being removed from systems or the local network. In this case, Jason's answer should be to use a DLP and to tag sensitive data to help ensure that another sensitive database is not stolen. He should also make sure that management is aware that a DLP cannot always detect all data that might leave, and that encrypted or otherwise obscured data may still be at risk.

11. A. This diagram shows two potential single points of failure, but only one that meets Michelle's goals: the single connection to the Internet from the ISP is an immediate concern at Point A. Point D shows single connections to each edge switch, which would result in the devices connected to that switch failing, but that would not result in the impact to the core network that Michelle is concerned about. Points B and C both have fully redundant network devices with heartbeat connections.

12. C. Sending logs to a remote log server or bastion host is an appropriate compensating control. This ensures that copies of the logs exist in a secure location, allowing them to be reviewed if a similar compromise occurred. Full-disk encryption leaves files decrypted while in use and would not secure the log files from a compromise, whereas log rotation simply means that logs get changed out when they hit a specific size or timeframe. TLS encryption for data (including logs) in transit can keep it private and prevent modification but wouldn't protect the logs from being deleted.

13. B. While each of the items listed can help as part of a comprehensive security architecture, using centralized patch management software will typically have the largest impact in an organization's handling of vulnerabilities related to software updates. Vulnerability scanning can help detect issues, and an IPS with the appropriate detections enabled may help prevent exploits, but both are less important than patching itself. Similarly, standards for patching help guide what is done but don't ensure that the patching occurs.

14. B. Since Ben must assume that data that leaves may be exposed, his best option is to enforce encryption of files that leave the organization. Mandatory data tagging and DLP monitoring can help catch data that is accidentally sent, and network segmentation can help reduce the number of points he has to monitor, but encryption is the only control that can have a significant impact on data that does leave.

15. B. Trend analysis using historical data will show James what his network traffic's behavior has been. James may notice an increase since a new storage server with cloud replication was put in, or he may notice that a DMZ host has steadily been increasing its outbound traffic. Automated reporting might send an alarm if it has appropriate thresholds set, and log aggregation is the foundation of how a SIEM gathers information, but neither will individually give James the view he needs. BGP is a routing protocol, and graphing it won't give James the right information either.

16. C. File integrity checking tools like Tripwire can notify an administrator when changes are made to a file or directory. Angela can implement file integrity monitoring for her critical system files, thus ensuring she is warned if they change without her knowledge. Antimalware tools only detect behaviors like those of malware and may not detect manual changes or behaviors that don't match the profile they expect. Configuration management tools can control configuration files but may not note changes that are made, and logging utilities often don't track changes to files.

17. A. A web application firewall (WAF) can provide protection against unknown threats and zero-day exploits by restricting attacks based on behavior or by implementing custom protection based on known exploit behavior. A patch from the vendor is often not immediately available, an IDS cannot stop an attack—at best it will report the attack—and least privilege for accounts may limit the impact of an attack but won't stop it.

18. A. Mike reduced the organization's attack surface. This occurs when the number of potential targets is reduced. Since the question describes only one security activity, we don't know that defense-in-depth has been implemented. The firewall may be a corrective control, but the question does not specify whether it's there as part of a response or to deal with a specific problem, and firewalls are technical controls rather than administrative controls.

19. A. Port security is a switch layer 2 security option that will allow only specific MAC addresses to access the port.

20. C. Tony is using a sinkholing technique by causing traffic that would normally go to a malicious site to go to another host. One common option is to send traffic like this to an internally controlled site that lets users know they would have gone somewhere dangerous.

Chapter 8: Identity and Access Management Security

1. B. While it may seem like Gabby has implemented three different factors, both a PIN and a passphrase are knowledge-based factors and cannot be considered distinct factors. She has implemented two distinct factors with her design. If she wanted to add a third factor, she could replace either the password or the PIN with a fingerprint scan or other biometric factor.

2. B. An individual's job title is an attribute, which means that attribute-based access control is the appropriate answer. Titles may be used to help identify a role, but they do not necessarily match roles directly, meaning that role-based access control is not the right choice. Discretionary access control empowers users to make decisions about rights, and mandatory access control enforces access control at the system level.

3. B. The nightmare scenario of having a compromised Kerberos server that allows attackers to issue their own ticket-granting tickets (TGTs), known as golden tickets, would result in attackers being able to create new tickets, perform account changes, and even to create new accounts and services. A KDC is a Kerberos key distribution center; MGT and master tickets were both made up for this question.

4. B. The NT LAN Manager (NTLM) security protocols are associated with Active Directory. SAML, OAuth, and RADIUS do not use NTLM.

5. D. Privilege creep occurs as staff members change roles but their rights and permissions are not updated to match their new responsibilities. This violates the concept of least privilege. Rights mismanagement and permission misalignment are both terms made up for this question.

6. A. OAuth redirect exploits are a form of impersonation attack, allowing attackers to pretend to be a legitimate user. Session hijacking would take advantage of existing sessions, whereas man-in-the-middle (MitM) attacks take advantage of being in the path of communications. Protocol analysis is a networking term used when reviewing packet contents.

7. C. Breaches of passwords stored in easily recoverable or reversible formats paired with user IDs or other identifying information create significant threats if users reuse passwords. Attackers can easily test the passwords they recover against other sites and services. Poor password reset questions are a threat even without a breach, and unencrypted password storage is an issue during breaches, but this type of breach is enabled by poor storage, rather than a result of the breach. Use of federated credentials are not a critical concern in cases like this.

8. B. Context-based authentication allows authentication decisions to be made based on information about the user, the system they are using, or other data like their geographic location, behavior, or even the time of day. Token-based authentication uses a security token to generate a onetime password or value, and NAC (network access control) is a means of validating systems and users that connect to a network. System-data contextual is a made-up answer for this question.

9. C. Common attacks against Kerberos include attacks aimed at administrative accounts, particularly those that attempt to create a ticket-granting ticket (TGT). Ticket reuse attacks are also common. Open redirect-based attacks are associated with OAuth rather than Kerberos.

10. B. LDAP is sometimes used for single sign-on (SSO) but is not a shared authentication technology. OpenID Connect, OAuth, and Facebook Connect are all examples of shared authentication technologies.

11. B. LDAP access control lists (ACLs) can limit which accounts or users can access objects in the directory. LDAP replication may help with load issues or denial-of-service attacks, TLS helps to protect data in transit, but MD5 storage for secrets like passwords is a bad idea!

12. D. TACACS+ should be run on an isolated management network to protect it from attackers. It does not provide built-in encryption, TACACS++ does not exist, and while enabling auditing features is a good idea, it won't stop attacks from occurring.

13. A. Jason's exploit is a form of privilege escalation, which uses a flaw to gain elevated privileges. Local users have a far greater ability to attempt these attacks in most organizations, since flaws that are only exploitable locally often get less attention from administrators than those that can be exploited remotely. A zero-day attack would use previously unknown flaws to exploit a system, rootkits are aimed at acquiring and maintaining long term access to systems, and session hijacking focuses on taking over existing sessions.

14. C. Chris has identified a problem with the maintenance and modification processes his organization uses. He should review how employee accounts are reviewed and how changes are requested when employees change positions in the organization.

15. B. CAPTCHAs, login throttling, and locking out accounts after a set number of failed logins are all useful techniques to stop or delay brute-force password guessing attacks. Some sites also use unique URLs, or limit the IP ranges that systems can authenticate from. Returning an HTTP error actually works in the attacker's favor, as they can key off of that error to try their next login attempt!

16. C. Identity providers (IDPs) make assertions about identities to relying parties and service providers in a federation. CDUs and APs are not terms used in federated identity designs.

17. C. NIST SP 800 63-3 recommends that SMS be deprecated due to issues with VoIP, including password reuse and the ability to redirect SMS sent via VoIP calls. In addition, SMS itself is relatively insecure, allowing attackers with the right equipment to potentially intercept it. The good news is that SMS can send unique tokens, they're just text!

18. C. Ben successfully conducted a session hijacking attack by copying session information and using the existing session. If he had impersonated a legitimate user, it would have been an impersonation attack, whereas an MitM attack would require being in the flow of traffic between two systems or services. Privilege escalation attacks focus on acquiring higher levels of privilege.

19. D. Gabby is attempting a privilege escalation attack. After acquiring the web server's privileges, she is now attempting to gain root (administrative) privileges.

20. B. Michelle's security token is an example of a possession factor, or "something you have." A password or PIN would be a knowledge factor or "something you know," and a fingerprint or retina scan would be a biometric, or inherence, factor.

Chapter 9: Software and Hardware Development Security

1. B. A Trusted Platform Module (TPM) stores encryption keys to be used for hardware authentication. Hardware security models (HSMs) are used to create, manage, and store encryption keys and to offload cryptographic processing. SED stands for self-encrypting drive, and a trusted foundry is a trusted validated secure microelectronics supplier or manufacturer.

2. D. During the rework stage of Fagan inspection, issues may be identified that require the process to return to the planning stage and then proceed back through the remaining stages to re-review the code.

3. B. Adam is conducting static code analysis by reviewing the source code. Dynamic code analysis requires running the program, and both mutation testing and fuzzing are types of dynamic analysis.

4. B. Sam is conducting a regression test, which verifies that changes have not introduced new issues to his application. Code review focuses on the application code, whereas stress testing verifies that the application will perform under load or other stress conditions. Whiffing isn't a term used in this type of review.

5. C. Tiffany is stress testing the application. Stress testing intentionally goes beyond the application's normal limits to see how it responds to extreme loads or other abnormal conditions beyond its normal capacity. Unit testing tests individual components of an application, and regression testing is done to ensure that new versions don't introduce old bugs. Fagan testing is a formal method of code inspection.

6. C. Charles should perform user input validation to strip out any SQL code or other unwanted input. Secure session management can help prevent session hijacking, logging may provide useful information for incident investigation, and implementing TLS can help protect network traffic, but only input validation helps with the issue described.

7. D. A source control management tool like Subversion or Git can help prevent old code from being added to current versions of an application. Developer practices still matter, but knowing what version of the code you are checking in and out helps! Stress testing would help determine whether the application can handle load, a WAF or web application firewall can protect against attacks, but neither would resolve this issue. Pair programing might detect the problem, but the question specifically asks for a tool, not a process.

8. A. A parameterized query (sometimes called a prepared statement) uses a prebuilt SQL statement to prevent SQL-based attacks. Variables from the application are fed to the query, rather than building a custom query when the application needs data. Encoding data helps to prevent cross-site scripting attacks, as does input validation. Appropriate access controls can prevent access to data that the account or application should not have access to, but they don't use precompiled SQL statements.

9. C. User acceptance testing (UAT) is the process of testing to ensure that the users of the software are satisfied with its functionality. Stress testing verifies that the application will perform when under high load or other stress, and unit testing validates individual components of the application. CNA is not a term associated with application development.

10. A. Bus encryption protects data in transit between the processor and other devices. An HSM is used to create, store, and manage cryptographic keys as well as to offload cryptographic processing, and a TPM chip is used to store cryptographic keys. LAMP encryption is made up for this question.

11. D. TLS satisfies the "protect data" best practice by ensuring that network traffic is secure. Parameterizing queries uses prebuilt SQL, while encoding data removes control characters that could be used for cross-site scripting attacks and other exploits. Validating all inputs requires treating all user input as untrusted.

12. B. Pass-around reviews normally rely on email to move code between developers. In Kristen's case, a pass-around review will exactly meet her needs. Pair programming and over-the-shoulder review both require developers to work together, whereas tool-assisted reviews require implementation of a tool to specifically support the review.

13. D. `strcpy` does not include size information for the data it accepts, making it a popular target for buffer overflow attacks.

14. A. RESTful designs are the most common and popular for modern web services because of their flexibility. SOAP remains in use, but is not broadly used for public APIs. SAML is a security assertion markup language and would be useful for making security assertions, not for building a general use SOA. RAD is an application development model.

15. A. Improper error handling often exposes data to users and possibly attackers that should not be exposed. In this case, knowing what SQL code is used inside the application can provide an attacker with details they can use to conduct further attacks. Code exposure is not one of the vulnerabilities we discuss in this book, and SQL code being exposed does not necessarily mean that SQL injection is possible. Although this could be caused by a default configuration issue, there is nothing in the question to point to that problem.

16. D. Load testing is used to validate the performance of an application under heavy loads like high numbers of concurrent user sessions. Fuzzing, fault injection, and mutation testing are all types of code review and testing.

17. A. Interception proxies are designed to allow testers to intercept, view, and modify traffic sent from web browsers and are often used for penetration testing and web application security testing. Fuzzers are used for application testing by sending invalid data to the application, a WAF is a web application firewall, and a sniffer is useful for monitoring traffic, but not for modifying web traffic in a live, easy-to-use manner.

18. D. Fault injection directly inserts faults into the error handling paths for an application to verify how it will handle the problem. Stress testing focuses on application load, dynamic code analysis describes any type of live application testing, and fuzzing sends invalid data to applications to ensure that they can deal with it properly.

19. B. The application has a race condition that occurs when multiple operations cause undesirable results due to their order of completion. Dereferencing would occur if a memory location was incorrect, an insecure function would have security issues in the function itself, and improper error handling would involve an error and how it was displayed or what data it provided.

20. B. While this example includes continuous integration, the key thing to notice is that the code is then delivered/deployed into production. This means that Susan is operating in a continuous delivery/deployment environment, where code is both continually integrated and deployed. Agile is a development methodology, and often uses CI/CD, but we cannot determine if Susan is using an Agile.

Chapter 10: Security Operations and Monitoring

1. A. DMARC (Domain-based Message Authentication, Reporting, and Conformance) is a protocol that combines SPF and DKIM to prove that a sender is who they claim to be. DKIM validates that a domain is associated with a message, whereas SPF lists the servers that are authorized to send from your domain. POP3 is an email protocol but does not perform the function described.

2. D. A disassembler can translate binary machine code into assembly code, allowing it to be far more human readable. Once he has run a disassembler against the binary, Ben can perform further analysis of the program and its functions.

3. B. The syslog file is found in `/var/log` on most Linux hosts.

4. C. Charles is performing trend analysis. He has noticed a consistent change in pattern and has checked it over a period of time. His next step will likely be to look at the source and destination of the traffic, as well as details like the port and protocol associated with the traffic. With that information, he can determine if there is any security concern.

5. A. Piping output to `more` will break it up into pages, allowing Ian to page through the output from the top one at a time. `grep` would be useful for searching if he provided search terms. Neither of the flags shown will paginate `top`'s output.

6. C. Ben's best option is a workflow orchestration system that can define and manage the logical flow of his business processes. A continuous deployment (CD) pipeline can ensure that rules are deployed, but there is no mention of continuous integration, which is important for testing in addition to implementation. Finally, a SIEM is a security information and event management tool, and a fuzzer is used to test software by inserting random data. Neither will help Ben with this issue.

7. A. NetFlow does not capture the packet payload, and Chris will not be able to see this.

8. B. A user and entity behavior analytics (UEBA) tool will be her best bet. UEBA tools monitor end-user behavior using agents and focus on detection of anomalous behavior paired with analytics and correlation capabilities. A network analyzer would be useful for reviewing packets, antimalware with heuristics can detect malware but aren't focused on user behavior in most cases, and a DMARC tool would help with email security configuration.

9. B. Chris can block many known malicious links by implementing a DNS blackhole that is fed by a DNS reputation service. Blocking all links in email is likely to cause significant business impact, SPF and DKIM will not have an impact on links in email, and a proxy can filter web traffic. However, determining which URLs are from email links and which may have been browsed for or manually entered isn't likely to be able to be implemented in any reasonable way.

10. D. The analyst is performing data enrichment, the process of enhancing or improving data. In this case, the threat feeds and syslog input review will improve the overall quality of both the SIEM's threat feed and the data it is used to analyze.

11. B. The key entry here is the note inside the file that says, "This program cannot be run in DOS mode." This indicates that the file is actually an executable, and that it is not actually a TIFF file. Michelle will need to do more investigation!

12. B. Elaine should check `/var/log/auth.log`, which is the default collection point for authentication logs for Linux systems. Red Hat and Centos logs for authentication go to `/var/log/secure`, but since that isn't listed, `auth.log` is the best and only correct answer among those listed.

13. A. Joseph hasn't taken into account the impact to the organization that the server being down may have, and he likely needs to assess whether the files were also uploaded or otherwise exposed. This means that he has looked at the localized impact to just the system and the immediate impact by noting what the impact is at the moment instead of what longer-term issues may arise.

14. B. While IP reputation tools can be useful, much like any automated blacklisting tool, they can also result in desired sites and services being blocked. Attacks that rely on popular services like Google Forms can result in services being blocked until they are manually whitelisted or fall out of the blacklist.

15. A. Tripwire and OSSEC are both open source options that provide host intrusion detection capabilities, including filesystem monitoring. The other answers were made up for this question.

16. C. The `-v` flag for `grep` returns any line that doesn't match the string. In this case, it will search for all logs in `/var/log/boot.log` without the string `"error"` in them. Charlene likely needs a better search string, since most of the `boot.log` file won't include the string error!

17. D. DMARC relies on both SPF and DKIM being set up properly, so Megan may need to walk their email administrator through all three steps to be able to use DMARC with them.

18. C. User agent information can include useful information about the originating device. In this case we can clearly see that the user agent lists Android 9 on a Samsung SM-N950U device. If you were to search for that term, you'd find out that the user was using a Galaxy Note 8. There is additional extraneous data about WebKit browsers, but the key element here is the clearly identified Samsung Android device.

19. C. The `/var/log/faillog` log file contains failed login attempts on Linux systems.

20. C. All Tony needs to verify that an email is from Mal is Mal's public key. The email will be signed with Mal's private key. If the public key works, then Mal signed it.

Chapter 11: Building an Incident Response Program

1. D. A former employee crashing a server is an example of a computer security incident because it is an actual violation of the availability of that system. An intruder breaking into a building may be a security event, but it is not necessarily a computer security event unless they perform some action affecting a computer system. A user accessing a secure file and an administrator changing file permission settings are examples of security events but are not security incidents.

2. A. Organizations should build solid, defense-in-depth approaches to cybersecurity during the preparation phase of the incident response process. The controls built during this phase serve to reduce the likelihood and impact of future incidents.

3. C. A security information and event management (SIEM) system correlates log entries from multiple sources and attempts to identify potential security incidents.

4. C. The definition of a medium functional impact is that the organization has lost the ability to provide a critical service to a subset of system users. That accurately describes the situation that Ben finds himself in. Assigning a low functional impact is only done when the organization can provide all critical services to all users at diminished efficiency. Assigning a high functional impact is only done if a critical service is not available to all users.

5. C. The containment protocols contained in the containment, eradication, and recovery phases are designed to limit the damage caused by an ongoing security incident.

6. D. The National Archives General Records Schedule requires that all federal agencies retain incident handling records for at least three years.

7. C. In a proprietary breach, unclassified proprietary information is accessed or exfiltrated. Protected critical infrastructure information (PCII) is an example of unclassified proprietary information.

8. A. The Network Time Protocol (NTP) provides a common source of time information that allows the synchronizing of clocks throughout an enterprise.

9. A. An organization's incident response policy should contain a clear description of the authority assigned to the CSIRT while responding to an active security incident.

10. D. A web attack is an attack executed from a website or web-based application—for example, a cross-site scripting attack used to steal credentials or redirect to a site that exploits a browser vulnerability and installs malware.

11. A. CSIRT members do not normally communicate directly with the perpetrator of a cybersecurity incident.

12. A. The incident response policy provides the CSIRT with the authority needed to do their job. Therefore, it should be approved by the highest possible level of authority within the organization, preferably the CEO.

13. A. Detection of a potential incident occurs during the detection and analysis phase of incident response. The other activities listed are all objectives of the containment, eradication, and recovery phase.

14. C. Extended recoverability effort occurs when the time to recovery is unpredictable. In those cases, additional resources and outside help are typically needed.

15. D. An attrition attack employs brute-force methods to compromise, degrade, or destroy systems, networks, or services—for example, a DDoS attack intended to impair or deny access to a service or application or a brute-force attack against an authentication mechanism.

16. C. Lessons learned sessions are most effective when facilitated by an independent party who was not involved in the incident response effort.

17. D. Procedures for rebuilding systems are highly technical and would normally be included in a playbook or procedure document rather than an incident response policy.

18. B. An impersonation attack involves the replacement of something benign with something malicious—for example, spoofing, man-in-the-middle attacks, rogue wireless access points, and SQL injection attacks all involve impersonation.

19. C. Incident response playbooks contain detailed, step-by-step instructions that guide the early response to a cybersecurity incident. Organizations typically have playbooks prepared for high-severity and frequently occurring incident types.

20. A. The event described in this scenario would not qualify as a security incident with measurable information impact. Although the laptop did contain information that might cause a privacy breach, that breach was avoided by the use of encryption to protect the contents of the laptop.

Chapter 12: Analyzing Indicators of Compromise

1. B. The `df` command will show you a system's current disk utilization. Both the `top` command and the `ps` command will show you information about processes, CPU, and memory utilization, whereas `lsof` is a multifunction tool for listing open files.

2. C. Perfmon, or Performance Monitor, provides the ability to gather detailed usage statistics for many items in Windows. Resmon, or Resource Monitor, monitors CPU, memory, and disk usage, but does not provide information about things like USB host controllers and other detailed instrumentation. Statmon and winmon are not Windows built-in tools.

3. D. Flow data provides information about the source and destination IP address, protocol, and total data sent and would provide the detail needed. Syslog, WMI, and resmon data is all system log information and would not provide this information.

4. A. Network access control (NAC) can be set up to require authentication. Port security is limited to recognizing MAC addresses, making it less suited to preventing rogue devices. PRTG is a monitoring tool, and NTP is the network time protocol.

5. A. A monitoring threshold is set to determine when an alarm or report action is taken. Thresholds are often set to specific values or percentages of capacity.

6. C. Active monitoring is focused on reaching out to gather data using tools like ping and iPerf. Passive monitoring using protocol analyzers collects network traffic and router-based monitoring using SNMP, and flows gather data by receiving or collecting logged information.

7. A. Beaconing activity (sometimes called heartbeat traffic) occurs when traffic is sent to a botnet command and control system. The other terms are made up.

8. C. Log analysis, flow monitoring, and deploying an IPS are all appropriate solutions to help detect denial-of-service attacks. iPerf is a performance testing tool used to establish the maximum bandwidth available on a network connection.

9. D. Hardware vendor ID codes are part of MAC addresses and can be checked for devices that have not had their MAC address changed. It is possible to change MAC addresses, so relying on only the MAC address is not recommended.

10. B. Locating a rogue AP is often best done by performing a physical survey and triangulating the likely location of the device by checking its signal strength. If the AP is plugged into the organization's network, nmap may be able to find it, but connecting to it is unlikely to provide its location (or be safe!). NAC would help prevent the rogue device from connecting to an organizational network but won't help locate it.

11. A. Microsoft Endpoint Configuration Manager provides non-real-time reporting for disk space. Resmon, perfmon, and SCOM can all provide real-time reporting, which can help to identify problems before they take a system down.

12. B. The best way to deal with memory leaks is to patch the application or service. If a patch is not available, restarting the service or the underlying operating system is often the only solution. Buffer overflow and stack smashing prevention both help deal with memory-based attacks rather than memory leaks, and monitoring can help identify out-of-memory conditions but don't directly help deal with a memory leak.

13. A. A blacklisting application or tool can allow Sayed to specifically prevent specific files or applications from being installed. Microsoft Endpoint Configuration Manager could be used to uninstall files, and SCOM could be used to monitor machines for files, but neither is as well suited. Whitelisting works in the opposite manner by listing allowed files.

14. C. The most likely answer is that the link has failed. Incorrectly set sampling rates will not provide a good view of traffic, and a DDoS attack is more likely to show large amounts of traffic. SNMP is a monitoring tool and would not result in flow data changing.

15. B. SNMP alerts are called SNMP traps, and they are sent from endpoints to a central management system or collector where they are typically stored and analyzed. The rest of the answers were made up for this question.

16. B. The `service --status` command is a Linux command. Windows service status can be queried using `sc`, the Services snap-in for the Microsoft Management Console, or via a PowerShell query.

17. D. Protocol analysis, using heuristic (behavior)-based detection capabilities, and building a network traffic baseline are all common techniques used to identify unexpected network traffic. Beaconing occurs when a system contacts a botnet command and control system, and it is likely to be a source of unexpected traffic.

18. C. SNMP will not typically provide specific information about a system's network traffic that would allow you to identify outbound connections. Flows, sniffers (protocol analyzers), and an IDS or IPS can all provide a view that would allow the suspect traffic to be captured.

19. A. Whitelisting software prevents software that is not on a preapproved list from being installed. Blacklists prevent specific software from being installed, whereas heuristic and signature-based detection systems focus on behavior and specific recognizable signatures, respectively.

20. B. The `top` command in Linux provides an interactive interface to view CPU utilization, memory usage, and other details for running processes. `df` shows disk usage, `tail` displays the end of a file, and `cpugrep` is a made-up command.

Chapter 13: Performing Forensic Analysis and Techniques

1. B. dd creates files in RAW, bit-by-bit format. EN01 is the EnCase forensic file format, OVF is virtualization file format, and ddf is a made-up answer.

2. B. Slack space is the space that remains when only a portion of a cluster is used by a file. Data from previous files may remain in the slack space since it is typically not wiped or overwritten. Unallocated space is space on a drive that has not been made into part of a partition. Outer space and non-Euclidean space are not terms used for filesystems or forensics.

3. C. Event logs do not typically contain significant amounts of information about file changes. The Master File Table and file indexes (INDX files) both have specific information about files, whereas volume shadow copies can help show differences between files and locations at a point in time.

4. C. Write blockers ensure that no changes are made to a source drive when creating a forensic copy. Preventing reads would stop you from copying the drive, drive cloners may or may not have write blocking capabilities built in, and hash validation is useful to ensure contents match but don't stop changes to the source drive from occurring.

5. B. A legal hold is a process used to preserve all data related to pending legal action, or when legal action may be expected. A retainer is paid to a lawyer to keep them available for work. The other two terms were made up for this question.

6. D. Core dumps and hibernation files both contain an image of the live memory of a system, potentially allowing encryption keys to be retrieved from the stored file. The MFT provides information about file layout, and the Registry contains system information but shouldn't have encryption keys stored in it. There is no hash file or encryption log stored as a Windows default file.

7. A. Timelines are one of the most useful tools when conducting an investigation of a compromise or other event. Forensic tools provide built-in timeline capabilities to allow this type of analysis.

8. D. Since Danielle did not hash her source drive prior to cloning, you cannot determine where the problem occurred. If she had run MD5sum prior to the cloning process as well as after, she could verify that the original disk had not changed.

9. D. The Volatility Framework is designed to work with Windows, macOS, and Linux, and it provides in-depth memory forensics and analysis capabilities. LiME and fmem are Linux tools, whereas DumpIt is a Windows-only tool.

10. D. Windows installer logs are typically kept in the user's temporary app data folder. Windows does not keep install log files, and System32 does not contain an Installers directory.

11. B. Windows crash dumps are stored in %SystemRoot%\MEMORY.DMP and contain the memory state of the system when the system crash occurred. This is her best bet for gathering the information she needs without access to a live image. The Registry and System Restore point do not contain this information, and WinDbg is a Windows debugger, not an image of live memory.

12. D. Manual access is used when phones cannot be forensically imaged or accessed as a volume or filesystem. Manual access requires that the phone be reviewed by hand, with pictures and notes preserved to document the contents of the phone.

13. A. CCleaner is a PC cleanup utility that wipes Internet history, destroys cookies and other cached data, and can impede forensic investigations. CCleaner may be an indication of intentional antiforensic activities on a system. It is not a full disk encryption tool or malware packer, nor will it modify MAC times.

14. B. Unallocated space is typically not captured during a live image, potentially resulting in data being missed. Remnant data from the tool, memory and drive contents changing while the image is occurring, and malware detecting the tool are all possible issues.

15. D. Jeff did not create the image and cannot validate chain of custody for the drive. This also means he cannot prove that the drive is a copy of the original. Since we do not know the checksum for the original drive, we do not have a bad checksum or a hash mismatch—there isn't an original to compare it to. Anti-forensics activities may have occurred, but that is not able to be determined from the question.

16. A. Imaging the system while the program is live has the best probability of allowing Jeff to capture the encryption keys or decrypted data from memory. An offline image after the system is shut down will likely result in having to deal with the encrypted file. Brute-force attacks are typically slow and may not succeed, and causing a system crash may result in corrupted or nonexistent data.

17. A. The tcpdump utility is a command-line packet capture tool that is found on many Linux systems. Wireshark is a GUI tool available for most operating systems. Netdd and snifman were made up for this question.

18. A. Ben is maintaining chain-of-custody documentation. Chris is acting as the validator for the actions that Ben takes, and acts as a witness to the process.

19. D. While AES does have a hashing mode, MD5, SHA1, and built-in hashing tools in FTK and other commercial tools are more commonly used for forensic hashes.

20. B. Both cloud and virtualized environments are often temporary (ephemeral) and thus can be difficult to perform forensics on. If you have a cloud, virtualized, or containerized environment, make sure you have considered how you would perform forensics, and what data preservation techniques you may need to use.

Chapter 14: Containment, Eradication, and Recovery

1. A. The containment, eradication, and recovery phase of incident response includes active undertakings designed to minimize the damage caused by the incident and restore normal operations as quickly as possible.
2. C. NIST recommends using six criteria to evaluate a containment strategy: the potential damage to resources, the need for evidence preservation, service availability, time and resources required (including cost), effectiveness of the strategy, and duration of the solution.
3. C. In a segmentation approach, the suspect system is placed on a separate network, where it has very limited access to other networked resources.
4. B. In the isolation strategy, the quarantine network is directly connected to the Internet or restricted severely by firewall rules so that the attacker may continue to control it but not gain access to any other networked resources.
5. D. In the removal approach, Alice keeps the systems running for forensic purposes but completely cuts off their access to or from other networks, including the Internet.
6. A. Sandboxes are isolation tools used to contain attackers within an environment where they believe they are conducting an attack but, in reality, are operating in a benign environment.
7. C. Tamara's first priority should be containing the attack. This will prevent it from spreading to other systems and also potentially stop the exfiltration of sensitive information. Only after containing the attack should Tamara move on to eradication and recovery activities. Identifying the source of the attack should be a low priority.
8. D. CompTIA includes patching, permissions, security scanning, and verifying logging/communication to monitoring in the set of validation activities that cybersecurity analysts should undertake in the aftermath of a security incident.
9. C. Understanding the root cause of an attack is critical to the incident recovery effort. Analysts should examine all available information to help reconstruct the attacker's actions. This information is crucial to remediating security controls and preventing future similar attacks.
10. C. Lynda should consult the disposal flowchart. Following that chart, the appropriate disposition for media that contains high security risk information and will be reused within the organization is to purge it.
11. B. New firewall rules, if required, would be implemented during the eradication and recovery phase. The validation phase includes verifying accounts and permissions, verifying that logging is working properly, and conducting vulnerability scans.

12. D. The primary purpose of eradication is to remove any of the artifacts of the incident that may remain on the organization's network. This may include the removal of any malicious code from the network, the sanitization of compromised media, and the securing of compromised user accounts.

13. B. There are many potential uses for written incident reports. First, it creates an institutional memory of the incident that is useful when developing new security controls and training new security team members. Second, it may serve as an important record of the incident if there is legal action that results from the incident. These reports should be classified and not disclosed to external parties.

14. D. Malware signatures would not normally be included in an evidence log. The log would typically contain identifying information (e.g., the location, serial number, model number, hostname, MAC addresses and IP addresses of a computer), the name, title and phone number of each individual who collected or handled the evidence during the investigation, the time and date (including time zone) of each occurrence of evidence handling, and the locations where the evidence was stored.

15. D. Even removing a system from the network doesn't guarantee that the attack will not continue. In the example given in this chapter, an attacker can run a script on the server that detects when it has been removed from the network and then proceeds to destroy data stored on the server.

16. A. The data disposition flowchart directs that any media containing highly sensitive information that will leave the control of the organization must be destroyed. Joe should purchase a new replacement device to provide to the contractor.

17. B. Incident reports should include a chronology of events, estimates of the impact, and documentation of lessons learned, in addition to other information. Incident response efforts should not normally focus on uncovering the identity of the attacker, so this information would not be found in an incident report.

18. D. NIST SP 800-61 is the Computer Security Incident Handling Guide. NIST SP 800-53 is Security and Privacy Controls for Federal Information Systems and Organizations. NIST SP 800-88 is Guidelines for Media Sanitization. NIST SP 800-18 is the Guide for Developing Security Plans for Federal Information Systems.

19. A. Resetting a device to factory state is an example of a data clearing activity. Data purging activities include overwriting, block erase, and cryptographic erase activities when performed through the use of dedicated, standardized device commands.

20. A. Only removal of the compromised system from the network will stop the attack against other systems. Isolated and/or segmented systems are still permitted access to the Internet and could continue their attack. Detection is a purely passive activity that does not disrupt the attacker at all.

Chapter 15: Risk Management

1. C. By applying the patch, Jen has removed the vulnerability from her server. This also has the effect of eliminating this particular risk. Jen cannot control the external threat of an attacker attempting to gain access to her server.

2. C. Installing a web application firewall reduces the probability that an attack will reach the web server. Vulnerabilities may still exist in the web application, and the threat of an external attack is unchanged. The impact of a successful SQL injection attack is also unchanged by a web application firewall.

3. C. The asset at risk in this case is the customer database. Losing control of the database would result in a $500,000 fine, so the asset value (AV) is $500,000.

4. D. The attack would result in the total loss of customer data stored in the database, making the exposure factor (EF) 100 percent.

5. C. We compute the single loss expectancy (SLE) by multiplying the asset value (AV) ($500,000) and the exposure factor (EF) (100 percent) to get an SLE of $500,000.

6. A. Aziz's threat intelligence research determined that the threat has a 5 percent likelihood of occurrence each year. This is an ARO of 0.05.

7. B. We compute the annualized loss expectancy (ALE) by multiplying the SLE ($500,000) and the ARO (0.05) to get an ALE of $25,000.

8. C. Installing new controls or upgrading existing controls is an effort to reduce the probability or magnitude of a risk. This is an example of a risk mitigation activity.

9. B. Changing business processes or activities to eliminate a risk is an example of risk avoidance.

10. D. Insurance policies use a risk transference strategy by shifting some or all of the financial risk from the organization to an insurance company.

11. A. When an organization decides to take no further action to address remaining risk, they are choosing a strategy of risk acceptance.

12. C. Top Secret is the highest level of classification under the U.S. system and, therefore, requires the highest level of security control.

13. C. Organizations should only use data for the purposes disclosed during the collection of that data. In this case, the organization collected data for technical support purposes and is now using it for marketing purposes. That violates the principle of purpose limitation.

14. D. The principle of data sovereignty says that data is subject to the legal restrictions of any jurisdiction where it is collected, stored, or processed.

15. C. Red team members are the attackers who attempt to gain access to systems. Sofia's team is fulfilling this role.

16. B. White team members are the observers and judges. They serve as referees to settle disputes over the rules and watch the exercise to document lessons learned from the test.

17. D. Blue team members are the defenders who must secure systems and networks from attack. The blue team also monitors the environment during the exercise, conducting active defense techniques.

18. A. Tokenization techniques use a lookup table and are designed to be reversible. Masking and hashing techniques replace the data with values that can't be reversed back to the original data if performed properly. Shredding, when conducted properly, physically destroys data so that it may not be recovered.

19. A. Classification policies create different categories of data used within an organization and then specify the level of security control required for each classification level. Using classifications helps users understand the type of protection necessary for each data type they encounter.

20. D. Once an employee leaves the organization, they would no longer be subject to any of the technical controls that Alfonso might implement. These include intrusion prevention systems (IPSs), data loss prevention (DLP) systems, and digital rights management (DRM) systems. The best way to protect against unauthorized sharing of information by former employees is through the use of nondisclosure agreements (NDAs).

Chapter 16: Policy and Compliance

1. B. The key word in this scenario is "one way." This indicates that compliance with the document is not mandatory, so Joe must be authoring a guideline. Policies, standards, and procedures are all mandatory.

2. A. PCI DSS compensating controls must be "above and beyond" other PCI DSS requirements. This specifically bans the use of a control used to meet one requirement as a compensating control for another requirement.

3. A. The Health Insurance Portability and Accountability Act (HIPAA) includes security and privacy rules that affect healthcare providers, health insurers, and health information clearinghouses.

4. B. The five security functions described in the NIST Cybersecurity Framework are identify, protect, detect, respond, and recover.

5. B. The International Organization for Standardization (ISO) publishes ISO 27001, a standard document titled "Information technology—Security techniques—Information security management systems—Requirements."

6. D. Policies require approval from the highest level of management, usually the CEO. Other documents may often be approved by other managers, such as the CISO.

7. D. The use of full-disk encryption is intended to prevent a security incident from occurring if a device is lost or stolen. Therefore, this is a preventive control gap.

8. B. The Sarbanes–Oxley (SOX) Act applies to the financial records of publicly traded companies and requires that those companies have a strong degree of assurance around the IT systems that store and process those records.

9. C. The code of conduct is often used as a backstop for employee behavior issues that are not addressed directly by another policy.

10. B. Security policies do not normally contain prescriptive technical guidance, such as a requirement to use a specific encryption algorithm. This type of detail would normally be found in a security standard.

11. D. Managerial controls are procedural mechanisms that focus on the mechanics of the risk management process. Examples of managerial controls include periodic risk assessments, security planning exercises, and the incorporation of security into the organization's change management, service acquisition, and project management practices.

12. D. The Information Technology Infrastructure Library (ITIL) is a framework that offers a comprehensive approach to IT service management (ITSM) within the modern enterprise. ITIL covers five core activities: Service Strategy, Service Design, Service Transition, Service Operation, and Continual Service Improvement.

13. D. The Payment Card Industry Data Security Standard (PCI DSS) provides detailed rules about the storage, processing, and transmission of credit and debit card information. PCI DSS is not a law but rather a contractual obligation that applies to credit card merchants and service providers.

14. D. The data retention policy outlines what information the organization will maintain and the length of time different categories of information will be retained prior to destruction.

15. D. The description provided matches the definition of a Tier 4 (Adaptive) organization's risk management practices under the NIST Cybersecurity Framework.

16. D. Guidelines are the only element of the security policy framework that is optional. Compliance with policies, standards, and procedures is mandatory.

17. A. Technical controls enforce confidentiality, integrity, and availability in the digital space. Examples of technical security controls include firewall rules, access control lists, intrusion prevention systems, and encryption.

18. B. Standards describe specific security controls that must be in place for an organization. Allan would not include acceptable mechanisms in a high-level policy document, and this information is too general to be useful as a procedure. Guidelines are not mandatory, so they would not be applicable in this scenario.

19. D. The NIST Cybersecurity Framework is designed to help organizations describe their current cybersecurity posture, describe their target state for cybersecurity, identify and prioritize opportunities for improvement, assess progress, and communicate with stakeholders about risk. It does not create specific technology requirements.

20. D. Procedures provide checklist-style sets of step-by-step instructions guiding how employees should react in a given circumstance. Procedures commonly guide the early stages of incident response.

Practice Exam Answers

1. D. Compensating controls are used to fulfill the same control objective as a required control when it is not feasible to implement that required control. The scenario describes a need for a compensating control. This control may be technical, operational, and/or administrative in nature.

2. C. Zero-day exploits take advantage of a security vulnerability that is not known until the exploit has been used—there is no time (zero days) between the discovery and the attack.

3. A. Threat hunting activities presume that a compromise has already taken place and search for indicators of that compromise. Vulnerability scanning activities probe systems for known vulnerabilities. Juan's activity could be described as intrusion detection, but not as intrusion prevention because he is not taking any action to block future attacks. Data mining is a generic term used in machine learning activities and Juan is not leveraging data mining in this work.

4. B. Honeypots are decoy systems used to attract the attention of intruders so that they may be monitored in a controlled environment. Mandatory access controls (MACs) are used to enforce system security policies. Intrusion prevention systems are designed to detect and block malicious activity. Rogue access points provide an unauthorized means of wireless access.

5. B. This is an example of delivering the payload to the victim, so it is from the Delivery stage of the Cyber Kill Chain.

6. A. A jump box is a system designed to accept remote connection requests and act as an intermediary between those remote systems and local hosts. Virtual machines, honeypots, and firewalls may all exist in the DMZ but do not have the express purpose of providing remote administrative access.

7. D. Port 1433 is used for Microsoft SQL Server and should not be exposed on a web server. Ports 22, 80, and 443 are required for SSH, HTTP, and HTTPS connectivity, respectively.

8. B. Sampling is often used to retain flow visibility while reducing the overall flow rates to a reasonable level. Rates of 1:10, 1:100, or 1:1000 can significantly decrease the load that flows create while providing useful visibility. RMON does not provide visibility into flow data. Decreasing the number of flows per user would require reducing users' ability to use the network, much like using packet shaping to reduce traffic rates would cause the network to be less usable—not a desirable option in almost any network!

9. D. Infrastructure as a service (IaaS) is the only cloud service model where customers would configure operating systems themselves. In platform as a service (PaaS), function as a service (FaaS), and software as a service (SaaS) models, the cloud service provider is responsible for operating system configuration.

10. A. This is an example of a captive portal network access control (NAC) solution, which is an in-band NAC because it inserts a device between Barry and the Internet. Out-of-band solutions, such as 802.1x, require that Barry's system communicate with the network switch to support NAC. Agent-based solutions would require the installation of software on Barry's computer.

11. A. A network access control (NAC) system can allow Charles to require network authentication while performing security posture assessments on the systems that connect. This will allow his team to authenticate and use the network if they have secure systems.

12. D. The Trusted Platform Module (TPM) is a hardware chip found inside most modern computers that is used to store disk encryption keys. Hardware security modules (HSMs) also store encryption keys, but they are dedicated, costly devices. Trusted foundries are trusted sources for hardware, and the root of trust is a concept used to describe how trust flows through the components of a secure system.

13. C. Destruction is both the most effective and the costliest option identified in the NIST Guidelines for Media Sanitization. Clearing by using logical methods to clear addressable storage locations and using overwriting and cryptographic erase techniques for purging are both cheaper and easier to perform. Obliteration is not an option in the NIST listing.

14. A. Next-generation firewalls (NGFWs) are able to incorporate contextual information about a connection attempt when making access control decisions. This capability is not available in packet filters or stateful inspection firewalls. While an NGFW may be a perimeter firewall, not all perimeter firewalls have next-generation capabilities.

15. C. During a network attack simulation, the blue team is responsible for securing the targeted environment and keeping the attacking (red) team out. The white team serves as referees. There is no black team during a network attack simulation.

16. A. The three pillars of information security are confidentiality, integrity, and availability. Attacks against confidentiality seek to disclose sensitive information. Attacks against integrity seek to alter information in an unauthorized manner. Attacks against availability seek to prevent legitimate use of information or systems.

17. D. Segmentation occurs in the containment phase in the CompTIA incident response process. Bear in mind that CompTIA's incident response process differs from the NIST standard, and places sanitization, reconstruction/re-imaging, and secure disposal in the eradication and recovery phase.

18. D. Environmental threats are natural or man-made disasters outside the control of the organization. Accidental threats occur when an inadvertent action jeopardizes security. Adversarial threats occur when someone is actively seeking to attack the organization. Structural threats occur when there is an exhaustion of available resources.

19. B. PCI DSS is an information security standard required by major payment card brands for organizations that use their cards. HIPAA, SOX, and FERPA are all U.S. laws.

20. C. For most organizations, CSIRT activities initially involve internal resources. Law enforcement is involved only when it is believed that a crime has been committed, requiring participation of law enforcement officers.

21. B. Network reconnaissance normally takes place during the discovery phase of a penetration test. The attack phase consists of gaining access, escalating privileges, system browsing, and installing additional tools.

22. D. Under the risk management matrix used by most organizations, a risk with a medium likelihood and high impact would be considered a high risk.

23. C. Bandwidth consumption, beaconing, and unexpected traffic are all common network issues that you should monitor for. Link aggregation refers to combining links to create a higher throughput link.

24. D. Distributed denial-of-service (DDoS) attacks can be detected in many ways, including use of SIEM devices, IDSs and IPSs, network bandwidth and connection monitoring tools, and performance monitoring utilities. Fuzzers are used to send unexpected data to applications and won't help detect a DDoS.

25. A. Application programming interfaces (APIs) are used to programmatically integrate systems, including SaaS platforms. Security orchestration, automation, and response (SOAR) does integrate systems but specifically in the security, not productivity, space. The Security Content Automation Protocol (SCAP) also is used to integrate security, not productivity, systems. Continuous integration/continuous delivery (CI/CD) is an operational philosophy and not a specific technology.

26. C. Although the bandwidth used for active monitoring is typically relatively low, it does add to the total network traffic load. If the monitoring traffic is not prioritized, information is available less quickly than desired, and if it is prioritized, it may compete with other important traffic.

27. C. Nmap is a network port scanner and generated the output shown in the question: a list of network ports. Nessus is a vulnerability scanner and would produce a detailed report of vulnerabilities. Traceroute determines the path between two points on a network. Syslog is a logging facility on Linux systems.

28. A. Signature analysis uses a fingerprint or signature to detect threats or other events. This means that a signature has to exist before it can be detected, but if the signature is well designed, it can reliably detect the specific threat or event.

29. C. Wireshark is a protocol analyzer and can be used to capture network traffic in a standard format. Nessus and Nmap are vulnerability scanners. Nikto is a web application security scanner.

30. B. The Netstat tool shows all open connections on a system. Tcpdump and Wireshark are capable of capturing traffic from open connections but will not display connections that are silent during the capture period. Traceroute shows the path between two systems.

31. D. There are many reasons to avoid imaging live machines if it is not absolutely necessary, but one advantage that imaging a live machine has is the ability to directly capture the contents of memory. Risks of capturing images from live machines include inadvertent modification of the systems, changes that may occur on the machine during imaging, the potential for malware to attack the imaging system or to detect and avoid it, and the fact that most live images don't capture unallocated space.

32. D. Organizational change management processes are often bypassed during an incident response process due to the urgency of the need to make quick changes. Once the incident response has been completed, changes are often filed as catch-up documentation as part of the postincident activities.

33. B. Brian is developing potential scenarios that might result in a successful attack. This is an example of establishing a threat-hunting hypothesis. Next, Brian should look for evidence of such an attack in an attempt to confirm or refute his hypothesis.

34. C. Multifactor authentication like token-based authentication can help prevent phishing attacks that result in stolen credentials resulting in attackers accessing systems. As long as attackers do not also acquire the token (often an app on a smartphone or a physical device kept in the user's pocket), the attacker will not have all the factors they need to authenticate. Context-aware authentication might help if attackers log in from places that legitimate users don't, but enhanced password requirements and shorter password lifespans have a relatively small impact, if any.

35. B. Unit testing tests the smallest testable parts of an application or program, ensuring that each component works properly before they are put together. UAT is user acceptance testing, Fagan inspection is a form of formal code review, and code segmentation is not a term used in software engineering or development.

36. C. Once a security incident has been detected and analyzed, CSIRTs move into an active phase of containment, eradication, and recovery. Active measures seek to limit the damage, gather evidence, identify the attackers and systems they are using, and eradicate the effects of the incident.

37. B. This is most likely a port scan being used to conduct reconnaissance and determine what ports are open on the server. A DoS attack would more likely use requests to a service allowed through the firewall. SQL injection and cross-site scripting would be successful only against a web server that was allowed to receive connections through the firewall.

38. A. Cisco uses log level 0 for emergency situations. Log level 1 is for alerts. Log level 6 is for information, and log level 7 is for debugging.

39. D. Since Angela already knows the MAC addresses of all the devices due to her systems inventory, she can simply search for associated MAC addresses that do not match the list.

40. C. When existing controls are insufficient, do not resolve the issue, or are too difficult to implement, a compensating control is often put in place. It is important to document compensating controls, because they differ from the expected or typical control that would normally be in place.

41. A. The image shows a screenshot of network traffic captured using the Wireshark protocol analyzer.

42. D. The -sV flag reports banner and version information. The -oG flag generates greppable output. The -sS flag requests a TCP SYN scan. The -b flag is used to detect servers supporting FTP bounce.

43. B. Encrypting a drive with strong encryption like AES256 will make the loss of a drive less of an issue. In general, strong encryption with a key that has not also been exposed can make confidentiality risks like this negligible. Both MD5 and SHA1 are not encryption methods—they are hashes. DES is an older, weaker encryption method, and it would not provide strong protection for the drive.

44. A. It can be easy to forget how important policies and the standards and practices that derive from them are, but policies make up the foundation of an organization's security practices. When combined with awareness training, it is far more likely that the employees that Cynthia works with will avoid bad practices like taking unencrypted drives home or neglecting to use web application security development best practices.

45. D. Cynthia's design should include an intrusion prevention system (IPS). An in-line IPS with the right signatures installed can detect and stop attacks, including SQL injection, cross-site scripting, and even denial-of-service (DoS) attacks. An intrusion detection system (IDS) could detect the attacks but can't stop them, whereas data loss prevention (DLP) systems are designed to prevent data from exiting an organization. A PRNG, or pseudo-random number generator, is not a security technology.

46. B. Port 1433 is used by Microsoft SQL Server, so Kevin is most likely scanning a database server.

47. A. The Secure Shell (SSH) protocol uses encryption by default. HTTP, MySQL, and SMTP do not use encryption unless configured to do so.

48. A. The key difference between a shared authentication model and a single sign-on (SSO) model is that shared authentication systems require users to enter credentials when authenticating to each site. Single sign-on only requires a single sign-on—exactly as the name says!

49. B. In NIST's classification scheme, this is a privacy breach, involving personally identifiable information. NIST defines four ratings: none, privacy breaches, proprietary information breaches, and integrity loss. Proprietary information breaches involve unclassified proprietary information, such as protected critical infrastructure information. Integrity losses occur when sensitive or proprietary information is changed or deleted. NIST does not use the broad term *confidentiality breaches*, instead preferring more specific definitions.

50. A. Port 53 is reserved for the Domain Name Service (DNS), which does not normally run on web servers. Ports 80 and 443 are used for HTTP and HTTPS, respectively. Ports in the range of 80xx are commonly used for web services running on nonstandard ports.

51. B. Perfmon (Performance Monitor) provides the ability to perform detailed data collection, unlike resmon's (Resource Monitor) high-level view, which does not include the use of counters. Winmon is a name typically associated with malware, and sysctl is a Linux tool used for changing kernel parameters at runtime.

52. A. The DNS server that answered Kyle's request is identified in the first line of the response. The IP addresses that appear at the bottom are the server's response to Kyle's query.

53. B. Chain-of-custody tracking indicates who has access to and authority over drives, devices, and forensic data throughout their life cycle. This is a critical element in investigations that may end up in court or that will involve law enforcement.

54. C. Ryan has created an MD5 hash of his image file. This can be compared to the original, or if it is the original, it can be compared to figure copies to validate their integrity.

55. D. Hashes are compared to verify that the files are the same. Since MD5 returns a warning that the checksum did not match, we know that the files are different.

56. B. NTP (Network Time Protocol) is used to ensure that events that are logged and other actions taken that use system time line up properly. Without NTP enabled, it may be significantly more difficult to determine when events occurred, making the chronological view of events harder, or even impossible, to build.

57. C. The most important criteria when making decisions about the scope of vulnerability management programs are regulatory requirements, corporate policy, asset classification, and data classification.

58. D. PCI DSS only requires that internal scans be conducted by a qualified individual. External scans must be conducted by an approved scanning vendor (ASV).

59. C. Common Vulnerabilities and Exposures (CVE) provides a standard nomenclature for describing security-related software flaws. Common Vulnerability Scoring System (CVSS) provides a standardized approach for measuring and describing the severity of security-related software flaws. Common Platform Enumeration (CPE) provides a standard nomenclature for describing product names and versions. Open Vulnerability and Assessment Language (OVAL) is a language for specifying low-level testing procedures used by checklists.

60. D. DumpIt is a Windows-only memory forensics tool. LiME and fmem are both Linux kernel modules that allow access to physical memory, and the Volatility Framework is a multiplatform tool with support for a broad range of memory forensics activities.

61. B. The three steps in the vulnerability management life cycle are detection, remediation, and testing.

62. A. NIST uses three critical measures to determine an organization's tier in the framework: how mature their risk management process is, whether there is an integrated risk management program, and if the organization is effectively participating with external partners.

63. D. Credentialed scanning should always be performed with a read-only account to limit the potential impact on the system should the scanner malfunction or the account become compromised.

64. B. The system should be rated as moderate impact for confidentiality if "the unauthorized disclosure of information stored on the system could have a serious adverse impact on organizational operations, organizational assets, or individuals," according to FIPS 199.

65. B. Kerberos generating tickets, also known as golden tickets, can be created if attackers are able to gain domain administrator or local administrator access to the AD controller. This would allow attackers to set arbitrary ticket lifespans and to act as any user in the domain or forest.

66. D. LDAP attacks often focus on insecure binding methods, harvesting directory information by taking advantage of improper ACLs, LDAP injection, or denial-of-service attacks. Silver ticket attacks are associated with Kerberos, where the term is used to describe compromised service account credentials.

67. B. The most commonly accepted criteria for vulnerability prioritization include criticality of the systems and information affected by the vulnerability, difficulty of remediating the vulnerability, severity of the vulnerability, and exposure of the vulnerability.

68. A. The Federal Information Security Management Act (FISMA) and the Payment Card Industry Data Security Standard (PCI DSS) both require the use of vulnerability scanning. The Gramm–Leach–Bliley Act (GLBA) and Health Insurance Portability and Accountability Act (HIPAA) have no such requirement.

69. D. Testing code by running it is known as dynamic code analysis. Static code analysis looks at the source code for an application. Runtime is when a program is running, but runtime inspection is not a common term used in software engineering. There is no Run/Test method.

70. C. This scenario describes a false positive error—the condition where a scanner reports a vulnerability but that vulnerability does not actually exist.

71. D. Technical subject matter experts, IT support staff, legal counsel, human resources staff members, and public relations and marking staff are all frequently part of the CSIRT. Comptrollers are rarely part of the response process.

72. B. IPS and firewall devices can detect scans and probes, and may have built-in detection methods. A SIEM can pull data from multiple sources, identifying scans and probes against a variety of devices. SNMP traps provide information about the state of a device but are not useful when attempting to detect network scans or probes.

73. A. Regression testing focuses on ensuring that changes have not reintroduced problems or created new issues. Olivia has asked her team to do regression testing to make sure that the patches have not created new problems or brought an old problem back.

74. C. Fault injection directly injects faults into the error handling paths of an application and focuses on areas that might otherwise be missed. Fuzzing sends unexpected data, whereas mutation testing modifies the program itself to see how it handles unexpected behaviors. Fagan inspection is a formal inspection process.

75. A. Windows captures quite a bit of useful data about USB devices when they are connected, but it does not capture the device's capacity. The device name, serial number, vendor, brand, and even the user ID of the currently logged-in user when it was plugged in are captured.

76. D. This process shows a Fagan inspection, which consists of six phases: Planning, Overview, Preparation, Meeting, Rework and Follow-Up.

77. D. Windows workstations can be a treasure trove of forensic information. Volume shadow copies are manual or automatic copies of files or volumes kept by Windows systems for backup.

78. A. This vulnerability is in the SSH protocol, which uses TCP port 22, as shown in the bottom portion of the graphic.

79. B. The most effective defense against SQL injection is the use of input validation. Firewall rules would not likely be effective because the web server likely requires access from the outside world. Honeypots and patching would not serve as a defense against a SQL injection attack.

80. C. Buffer overflow vulnerabilities in an operating system require a vendor-supplied patch to correct. Input validation would not be an effective defense. While firewalls and intrusion prevention systems may block an attack, they would not resolve the underlying problem.

81. D. None of these protocols should be used on a secure network. All versions of SSL contain unfixable vulnerabilities, as do TLS versions earlier than 1.2.

82. B. The most effective defense against cross-site scripting is the use of input validation. Firewall rules would not likely be effective because the web server likely requires access from the outside world. Honeypots and operating system patching would not serve as a defense against a SQL injection attack.

83. C. Network segmentation is a strong security control for ICS networks. Chelsea does not have access to the source code so she cannot rewrite it. No patch is available because the vendor no longer provides support. Encryption would not provide a defense against a buffer overflow attack.

84. A. In a virtualized datacenter, the virtual host hardware runs a special operating system known as a hypervisor that mediates access to the underlying hardware resources.

85. C. The most likely scenario is that the hotel is running a captive portal and the user must authenticate before trying to access other websites. While the other scenarios are possible, they are not as likely. If the error was with the company's certificate, other users would be reporting the same problem. It is possible that another hotel guest is attempting to trick the user into accepting a false certificate, but this is unlikely.

Appendix C

Answers to Lab Exercises

Chapter 1: Today's Cybersecurity Analyst

Solution to Activity 1.4: Recognize Security Tools

Firewall	Filters network connections based on source, destination, and port
Decompiler	Attempts to recover source code from binary code
Antivirus	Scans a system for malicious software
NAC	Determines what clients may access a wired or wireless network
GPO	Deploys configuration settings to multiple Windows systems
Hash	Creates a unique fingerprint of a file
Honeypot	System intentionally created to appear vulnerable
WAF	Protects against SQL injection attacks

Chapter 2: Using Threat Intelligence

Solution to Activity 2.3: Intelligence Gathering Techniques

Requirements gathering	Assess missing controls from a recent breach
Threat data collection	Download data via STIX
Threat data analysis	Convert manually gathered threat data to STIX format
Threat intelligence dissemination	Provide information about a threat to an IPS administrator
Gathering feedback	Update requirements for your intelligence gathering program

Chapter 3: Reconnaissance and Intelligence Gathering

Solution to Activity 3.3: Intelligence Gathering Tools

Route to a system	traceroute
Open services via a network	Nmap
IP traffic flow and volume	netflow
Organizational contact information associated with domain registration	Whois
Connections listed by protocol	netstat
Zone transfer	Dig
Packet capture	Wireshark
Social media geotagging	Creepy

Chapter 5: Analyzing Vulnerability Scans

Solution to Activity 5.2: Analyze a CVSS Vector

The CVSS vector for the IKE vulnerability shown in Figure 5.23 is CVSS:3.0/AV:N/AC:L/PR:N/UI:N/S:U/C:L/I:N/A:N. Breaking this down piece by piece gives us the following:

- **AV:N** indicates that an attacker may exploit the vulnerability remotely over a network. This is the most serious value for this metric.
- **AC:L** indicates that exploiting the vulnerability does not require any specialized conditions. This is the most serious value for this metric.
- **PR:N** indicates that attackers do not need any authenticated privileges. This is the most serious value for this metric.
- **UI:N** indicates that no user interaction is necessary to exploit the vulnerability.
- **S:U** indicates that the access gained by exploiting this vulnerability is limited to the scope of control of the compromised component.

- C:L indicates that a successful exploitation of this vulnerability would yield partial access to information. This is the middle value for this metric.
- I:N indicates that a successful exploitation of this vulnerability would not allow the unauthorized modification of information. This is the least serious value for this metric.
- A:N indicates that a successful exploitation of this vulnerability would have no availability impact. This is the least serious value for this metric.

Based on this CVSS analysis, the first vulnerability in Figure 5.22 is more serious. They have identical CVSS vectors except for the integrity metric, which is higher for the SSL vulnerability.

Chapter 7: Infrastructure Security and Controls

Solution to Activity 7.3: Security Architecture Terminology

Air gap	A physical separation between devices or networks to prevent access.
Containerization	A technology that bundles together an application and the files, libraries, and other dependencies it needs to run, allowing the application to be deployed to multiple platforms or systems.
VPC	A logically isolated segment of a cloud that provides you with control of your own environment.
Cloud access security broker	Software or service that enforces security for cloud applications.
Blacklisting	An access control mechanism that permits all things to pass through except those that are specifically blocked.
Asset tagging	Labeling or otherwise identifying systems, devices, or other items.
NAC	A system that validates systems and sometimes users before they connect to a network.
Data loss prevention	A system that scans outbound traffic and prevents it from being transmitted if it contains specific content types.

Chapter 8: Identity and Access Management Security

Solution to Activity 8.1: Federated Security Scenario

Part 1: You should identify two major problems: use of HTTP, rather than HTTPS, and the development team's creation of their own OAuth libraries.

Part 2: Answers may vary but should include detail similar to:

1. What recommendations and advice would you provide to the implementation team?

   The implementation team should use open source or Facebook-provided libraries and code and should follow recommended best practices for implementation. Secure connections should be required for all authentication and authorization traffic.

   A strong answer might also reference the OWASP Facebook development guide at `www.owasp.org/index.php/Facebook`.

2. What should Example Corp.'s incident response plan include to handle issues involving Facebook Login?

   Responses will vary but should take into account the fact that Example Corp. will now be relying on a third party and will need to know how to contact Facebook, what they will do if Facebook is compromised, and how individual account issues will be handled.

3. Does using Facebook Login create more or less risk for Example Corp.? Why?

   Responses will vary but should take into account use of a third-party authentication service and lack of control of accounts versus the utility of a third-party service provider.

Solution to Activity 8.2: On-site Identity Issues Scenario

Part 1: You should suggest solutions involving local authentication with appropriate monitoring, logging, and management to ensure that local accounts are secure.

Part 2: You should suggest a central identity and access management system to centrally manage credentials and rights, and administrative policies and controls that ensure that roles and rights are updated when users change positions or roles.

Part 3: Answers are left to your own analysis of your work.

Solution to Activity 8.3: Identity and Access Management Terminology

TACACS+	A Cisco-designed authentication protocol.
Identity	The set of claims made about an account holder.
ADFS	Microsoft's identity federation service.
Privilege creep	This issue occurs when accounts gain more rights over time due to role changes.
Directory service	LDAP is deployed in this role.
OAuth 2.0	An open standard for authorization used for websites and applications.
SAML	An XML-based protocol used to exchange authentication and authorization data.
RADIUS	A common AAA system for network devices.
Privilege management	The practice of managing and controlling identities and rights.
Multifactor authentication (MFA)	The combination of multiple means of proving an identity to authenticate.
Single sign-on (SSO)	A technical system that allows access to many different systems or services with a single authentication event.
Federation	The linking of an individual's identity across multiple identity management systems.
Role-based	An access control scheme based on an individual's job duties or other position in an organization.
Attribute-based	Access control based on elements like things that describe the user (role, title), what action is being attempted, or other similar data
Mandatory	An access control scheme where the operating system constrains the ability of the user or subject to take action.
Manual review	Checking rights without an automated system.

Chapter 9: Software and Hardware Development Security

Solution to Activity 9.3: Security Tools

Subversion	A source control management tool
Agile	An SDLC model that relies on sprints to accomplish tasks based on user stories
Dynamic code analysis	A code analysis that is done using a running application
Fuzzing	A code analysis done using a running application that relies on sending unexpected data to see if the application fails
Fagan inspection	A formal code review process that relies on specified entry and exit criteria for each phase
Over-the-shoulder	A code review process that requires one developer to explain their code to another developer
Waterfall	The first SDLC model, replaced in many organizations but still used for very complex systems
Backlog	An Agile term that describes the list of features needed to complete a project

Chapter 10: Security Operations and Monitoring

Solution to Activity 10.3: Security Architecture Terminology

Heuristics	A technique used to find previously unknown malware by observing behaviors common to malicious software
DMARC	An email authentication, policy, and reporting protocol

Reverse engineering	The process of disassembling or decompiling a malware package to understand what it does
Digital signature	A means of providing assurance that an email has not been modified and that it was sent by the correct sender that relies on a certificate and public key cryptography
UEBA	A technology designed to monitor end user behavior to prevent targeted attacks and insider threats
DKIM	An email authentication method designed to detect forged sender addresses
SOAR	A technique used to find previously unknown malware by observing behaviors common to malicious software
SPF	An email authentication technique that detects forged sender addresses

Chapter 11: Building an Incident Response Program

Solution to Activity 11.1: Incident Severity Classification

The functional impact of this incident is high because the organization has lost the ability to sell products to customers. This fits the definition of the "organization is no longer able to provide some critical services to any users."

The economic impact of this incident is high. The organization expects to lose $2 million per day. This fits the definition of the high category: "The organization expects to experience a financial impact of $500,000 or more."

The recoverability effort of this incident is extended. The organization has exhausted all internal resources and is seeking a consultant to assist. This fits the extended category definition of "Time to recovery is unpredictable; additional resources and outside help are needed."

The information impact of this incident is none. The attack described in this scenario is a denial-of-service attack, and there is no indication of the compromise of sensitive information. This fits the none category definition of "No information was exfiltrated, changed, deleted or otherwise compromised."

Solution to Activity 11.2: Incident Response Phases

Activity	Phase
Conducting a lessons learned review session	Postincident Activity
Receiving a report from a staff member about a malware infection	Detection and Analysis
Upgrading the organization's firewall to block a new type of attack	Preparation
Recovering normal operations after eradicating an incident	Containment, Eradication, and Recovery
Identifying the attacker(s) and attacking system(s)	Containment, Eradication, and Recovery
Interpreting log entries using a SIEM to identify a potential incident	Detection and Analysis
Assembling the hardware and software required to conduct an incident investigation	Preparation

Chapter 12: Analyzing Indicators of Compromise

Solution to Activity 12.3: Security Tools

Flows	A set of packets passing from a source system to a destination in a given time interval
Resmon	A Windows tool that monitors memory, CPU, and disk usage
iPerf	A tool for testing the maximum available bandwidth for a network
PRTG	SNMP A network management and monitoring tool that provides central visibility into flows and SNMP data for an entire network
Beaconing	Traffic sent to a command and control system by a PC that is part of a botnet

SNMP	A protocol for collecting information like status and performance about devices on a network
`top`	A Linux command that displays processes, memory utilization, and other details about running programs
Perfmon	A Windows tool that monitors a wide range of devices and services, including energy, USB, and disk usage

Chapter 13: Performing Forensic Analysis and Techniques

Solution to Activity 13.2: Conduct the NIST Rhino Hunt

You can find a complete answer to the NIST Rhino hunt from Activity 13.2 at `www.cfreds.nist.gov/dfrws/DFRWS2005-answers.pdf`.

Solution to Activity 13.3: Security Tools

dd	A Linux tool used to create disk images
md5sum	Used to determine whether a drive is forensically sound
Volatility Framework	A memory forensics and analysis suite
FTK	A full-featured forensic suite
Eraser	A drive and file wiping utility sometimes used for anti-forensic purposes
Write blocker	A device used to prevent forensic software from modifying a drive while accessing it
WinDbg	A tool used to review Windows memory dumps
Forensic drive duplicator	A device used to create a complete forensic image and validate it without a PC
Wireshark	A GUI network traffic sniffer
tcpdump	A command-line network packet sniffer

Chapter 14: Containment, Eradication, and Recovery

Solution to Activity 14.1: Incident Containment Options

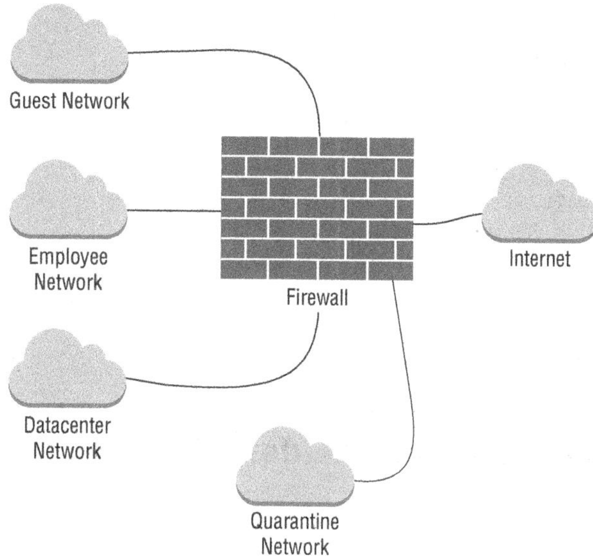

Network segmentation

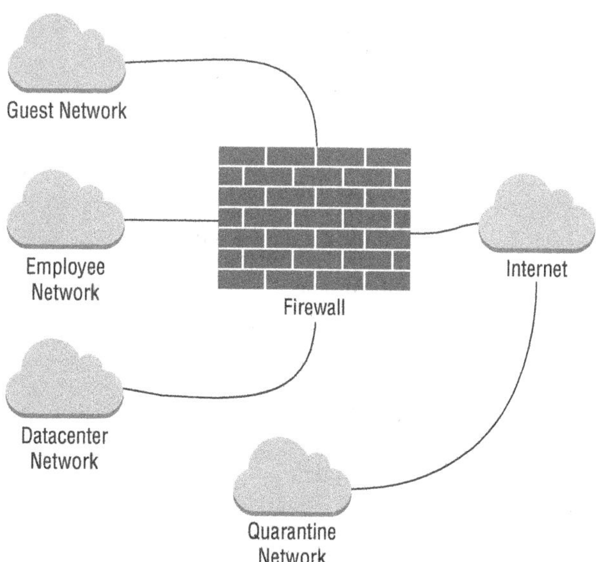

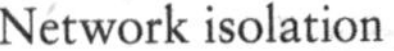

Network isolation

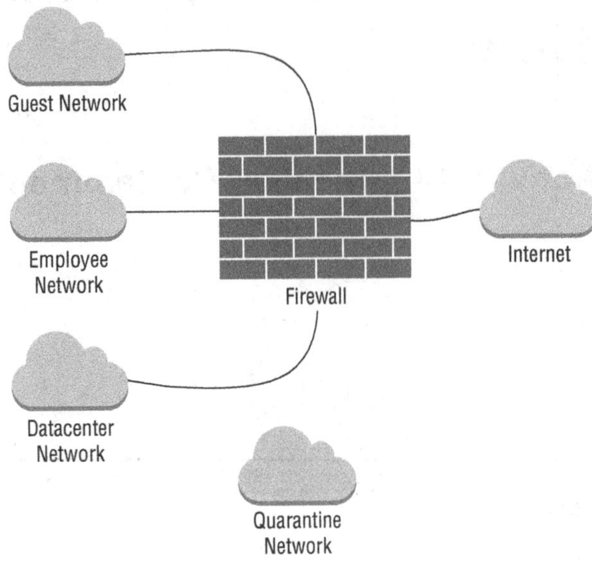

Network removal

Solution to Activity 14.2: Incident Response Activities

Response activity	CompTIA category
Patching	Validation
Sanitization	Eradication
Lessons learned	Postincident Activities
Reimaging	Eradication
Secure disposal	Eradication
Isolation	Containment
Scanning	Validation
Removal	Containment
Reconstruction	Eradication
Permission verification	Validation
User account review	Validation
Segmentation	Containment

Solution to Activity 14.3: Sanitization and Disposal Techniques

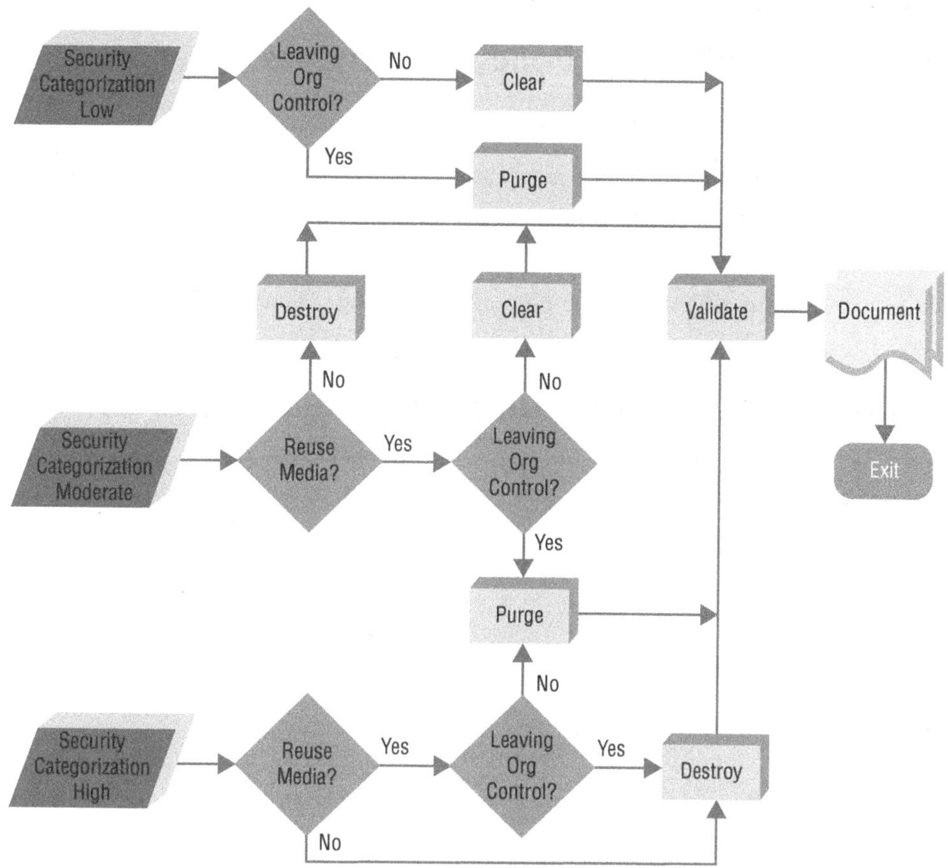

Chapter 15: Risk Management

Solution to Activity 15.1: Risk Management Strategies

Risk avoidance	Changing business activities to eliminate a risk
Risk transference	Shifting the impact of a risk to another organization
Risk mitigation	Implementing security controls that reduce the probability and/or magnitude of a risk
Risk acceptance	Choosing to continue operations as normal despite the potential risk

Chapter 16: Policy and Compliance

Solution to Activity 16.1: Policy Documents

Policy	Provides high-level requirements for a cybersecurity program
Standard	Offers detailed requirements for achieving security control objectives
Guideline	Includes advice based on best practices for achieving security goals that are not mandatory
Procedure	Outlines a step-by-step process for carrying out a cybersecurity activity

Solution to Activity 16.3: Compliance Auditing Tools

The testing procedures for PCI DSS requirement 8.2.3 instruct auditors to inspect system configuration settings and verify that the user password/passphrase requirements are set to require a minimum length of at least seven characters and to require that passwords contain both alphabetic and numeric characters.

Index

A

B

C

D

E

F

G

H

I

J

K

L

M

N

O

P

Q

R

S

T

U

V

W

Y

Z